Safe GRE

*Safe Twinwall material – No glass to shatter

*Adjustable ventilation

*Efficient heat retention

*Good light penetration

*Easy to assemble

*Sturdy aluminium frame in choice of finishes

SPECIFICALLY DESIGNED FOR SAFETY GLAZING

SolarGro PRODUCTS LIMITED

For details of your nearest Showsite please contact: **Solargro Products Ltd.,** 102 Brunel Road, Earlstrees Industrial Estate, Corby, Northants NN17 4LS
Tel: 01536 206900   Fax: 01536 264800

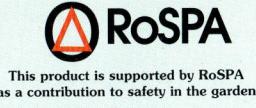

RoSPA This product is supported by RoSPA as a contribution to safety in the garden

---

COMPOSTING HAS NEVER BEEN SO EASY

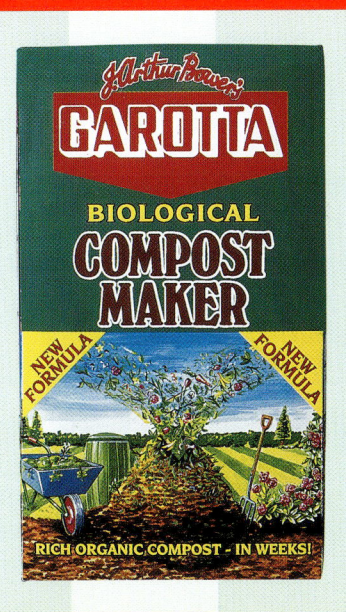

Market leaders Biotal and New Biological Garotta compost makers now make it easier than ever to turn your garden and household waste into rich organic compost - biologically. This means no more trips to the tip, saving you time and effort, and less money spent on mulches, peats and potting composts.

Simply add either Biotal or Garotta to your compost heap and see the results for yourself - in weeks!

The only decision for you is whether you prefer a liquid or a powder.

So for everyone's benefit, compost it - **NOW**.

For more information contact your local garden centre.

BIOTAL & GAROTTA
The Biological way to compost - today.

GARDEN FURNITURE · BARBECUES · PARASOLS · CUSHIONS

Make sure you have Fun in the Sun!

If you want to make the most of your garden, patio or conservatory it's important to choose the products that best suit your lifestyle and your budget. We can help.

LOFA, The Leisure and Outdoor Furniture Association represents the major manufacturers and suppliers of Garden Furniture, Barbecues, Barbecue Accessories, Cushions and Parasols in the UK.

LOFA members supply garden furniture in all types of wood, cane, cast, lightweight tubular and wrought metal, resin and plastic together with upholstery, cushions and parasols.

In the Barbecue Sector members offer a broad product range including portables, open brazier grills, wagons, kettle grills, built-in, gas fired, electric and barbecue fuels and accessories.

**We can help with information on all these products.
Expert advice is only a phone call away. Call LOFA on 01376 518861.**

LOFA
The Leisure and Outdoor Furniture Association
Promoting the industry for the benefit of everyone.

GARDEN FURNITURE · BARBECUES · PARASOLS · CUSHIONS

Put the cut and thrust back in your mowing!

Superb engineering • Outstanding value • Unrivalled choice

HAYTER 50 YEARS

No wonder there's a lively demand for the Hayter range – now more than ever before!
For a start, we've just launched our highly affordable new Jubilee range.

HAYTER
Makers of the finest mowers

Then there's our revolutionary new cordless electric mower. And, of course, there's our best-selling Harrier 48 – now with advanced new safety features. **For selected dealers see Address Book**

Hayter Limited Spellbrook, Bishop's Stortford, Herts CM23 4BU, England. Tel: 01279 723444 Fax: 01279 600338

Bolens
Garden Tractors
Top quality performance and outstanding value for money

The new UK range of Bolens Tractors offers a wider choice of models and accessories to suit every need. The entire range is designed for durability and long life.

Manufactured using a unique ladder chassis rail together with top quality fittings and engines throughout the range

Inner strength inside
Bolens use a tough channelled steel frame, thick front axle and protective bumpers for extra strength, durability and long working life. All frames are welded into rigid steel channels and braced with steel lateral supports.

Standard features include:
- Comfortable coiled spring seat
- Large capacity fuel tank
- Precisely geared steering
- Briggs & Stratton engines
- Foot pedal hydrostatic drive
- Wide tread tyres
- Reverse air flow cooling

For further information on Bolens Tractors contact Helen Sinfield at Claymore or visit your local dealer

CLAYMORE GRASS MACHINERY
Waterloo Industrial Estate, Bidford-on-Avon
Warwickshire B50 4JH
Telephone: 01789 490177 Fax: 01789 490170

FREE 3 YEAR LIMITED NO FEAR WARRANTY

Every Bolens Garden Tractor is covered by Bolens FREE 3 year No Fear Domestic Warranty

---

The Daily Telegraph
GREEN FINGERS
The Gardener's Sourcebook

Should your company be listed in the next edition of Green Fingers?

If your business makes or supplies products or services useful to gardeners - amateur or professional - then you should be listed in Green Fingers.

If you want your company to be listed - or if you know of another business which should be included, please apply to The Gardening Editor, Windrow & Greene Limited, 5 Gerrard Street, London W1V 7LJ

Whilst we make every effort to ensure that the information in Green Fingers is correct, it is inevitable that changes will occur after the book has gone to press. A voucher giving 20% discount off the next edition of the directory will be sent to anyone supplying information which will make the next edition even more useful.

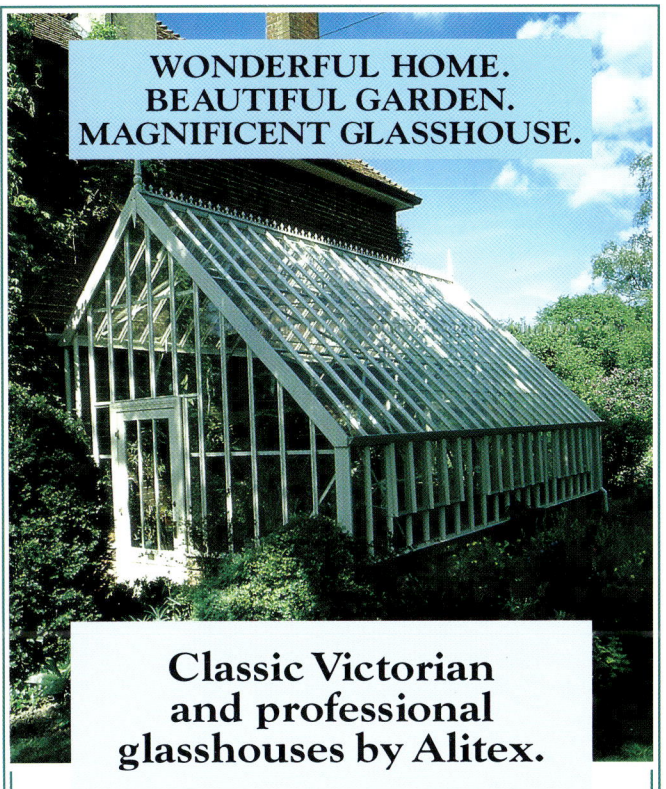

WONDERFUL HOME. BEAUTIFUL GARDEN. MAGNIFICENT GLASSHOUSE.

Classic Victorian and professional glasshouses by Alitex.

For over 40 years, Alitex have designed and built glasshouses and greenhouses of all shapes and sizes for some of the most beautiful gardens in the country.

Made and embellished with high-quality aluminium, our structures are elegant, workable and maintenance-free.

And because every garden is unique, every Alitex glasshouse is designed and built to individual requirements.

From Lands End to John O'Groats, people have found the results, like our service, beyond compare.

For a colour brochure and more details, please call **01420 82860**. Or write to Alitex Ltd, Ref DTS, Station Road, Alton, Hampshire GU34 2PZ.

Represented in Belgium, Germany, Holland and USA.

ALITEX

IV

Weeds

on your patio?

Kill them off fast with the AgrEvo Patio Weed Killer.

- Easy-to-use spray pack.
- Controls even the most stubborn of weeds without damage to the roots of nearby plants.
- Biodegradable - so leaves no harmful residues in the soil.
- Children and pets need not be excluded from treated areas.

For fast, effective control of even the most stubborn of weeds

AgrEvo gardencare products are available from most good garden centres and garden shops.

AgrEvo Patio Weed Killer contains Glufosinate-ammonium. Read the label before you buy. Use pesticides safely.

AgrEvo
Your powerful new friend in the garden

Ashworth
L E I S U R E

Ashworth Leisure Limited,
Sycamore Avenue, Burnley,
Lancashire BB12 6QR
United Kingdom

Ashworth furniture is imaginatively designed and skilfully manufactured.
The combination of traditional designs and modern materials result in products of everlasting beauty and appeal. Available in a range of colours. Finished in a chip resistant powder coating.
Unlike cast iron, aluminium is light and easy to manage, yet strong enough to withstand and amount of wear and tear.

Tel: 01282 425901   Fax: 01282 416465 for brochure

Royal table, carver chairs and dining chairs

THE ROYAL HORTICULTURAL SOCIETY

Save £5

A year of gardening inspiration for only £27

As a special introductory offer to the readers of *Green Fingers*, we are delighted to offer membership for just £20 (plus £7 enrolment fee). For this, you can benefit from a year's membership of the world's premier gardening organisation, the Royal Horticultural Society. From inspirational shows and gardens to a fascinating monthly magazine and a free advisory service, no other organisation pulls together Britain's top gardening brains specially for you.

Membership Privileges include:

Free gardening magazine – A year's subscription to one of the most fascinating gardening magazines – *The Garden*.

Privileged tickets to the world's top flower shows including the Chelsea Flower Show, the Hampton Court Palace Flower Show, BBC Gardeners' World Live and Scotland's National Gardening Show.

Free unlimited visits to twenty four of the most beautiful gardens across Britain.

Free unlimited gardening advice from Britain's top gardening experts.

As a registered charity, we rely entirely on the money we raise ourselves and subscriptions are a vital contribution. Please accept our invitation to join today.

To apply, complete and return the form with a cheque for £27 (normal price £32), payable to The Royal Horticultural Society, to The Membership Department, The Royal Horticultural Society, PO Box 313, London SW1P 2PE.

**Green Fingers readers
– special RHS membership offer**

❏ I would like to join the RHS.
❏ Please send me further information on joining the RHS.

Please complete in block capitals. If you do not wish to cut out the coupon, please send your name and address on a separate sheet and quote code 894 with your cheque. Code 894

Title	Surname	Initials
Address		
Postcode	Daytime Tel. No.	

© 1997 Windrow & Greene Ltd

This edition published in Great Britain 1997 by
Windrow & Greene Ltd
5 Gerrard Street
London W1V 7LJ

All rights reserved.
No part of this publication may be reproduced or
transmitted in any form or by any means, electronic or
mechanical, including photocopy, recording, or in any information storage or retrieval system, without the prior written
consent of the publishers.

A CIP record for this book is available from the
British Library

ISBN 1 85915 096 9

Printed and bound in Great Britain by Hillman Printers
through Amon-Re Ltd

Advertising agents for this book:
KP Partners in Publishing
57a Hatton Garden
London EC1N 8HE
Tel: 0171 831 1131

Designed and produced by
Hodgson Williams Associates
71 Bridge Street
Cambridge CB2 1UR
Tel: 01223 460786

The Daily Telegraph
GREEN FINGERS
The Gardener's Sourcebook

GREEN FINGERS has been compiled from a variety of sources; the descriptive entries, facilities and opening times have been supplied by the companies listed. The selection of entries for inclusion has been made on the basis of their interest and use to the amateur and professional gardener. Suggestions and applications for inclusion in future editions of Green Fingers will be very welcome.

Using the index system

Companies are listed alphabetically within the section which describes their main service or product. Within these sections you will find full company details and, in many cases, a description of the service offered.

In Chapter 14 Garden Centres and Chapter 15 Gardens to Visit companies are listed alphabetically by country and district, to help you select gardens and suppliers within the area in which you are living or touring.

Indexes

Company Index
All entries are listed by company name and page number.

Specialities Index
Some of the major plant groups and gardening concerns are listed with reference to the companies which specialise in these areas.

Geographical Index
To find a company by geographical area use the Geographical Index on page 136.

CONTENTS

SECTION 1   GARDEN SUPPLIES
Indexed alphabetically by company name

Chapter 1	Arboricultural Services	6
Chapter 2	Conservatories & Summerhouses	7
Chapter 3	Design & Landscaping	10
Chapter 4	Fencing, Trelliswork, Gates & Pergolas	17
Chapter 5	Furniture	18
Chapter 6	Greenhouses, Sheds & Accessories	21
Chapter 7	Horticultural Sundries	24
Chapter 8	Machinery	32
Chapter 9	Ornaments, Containers & Stonework	35
Chapter 10	Paving	38
Chapter 11	Rockery Specialists	39
Chapter 12	Seedsmen & Seed Exchange Schemes	40
Chapter 13	Water Garden & Pond Specialists	42

SECTION 2   PLANTS & INSPIRATION
Indexed alphabetically by country, district & company name

| Chapter 14 | Garden Centres & Nurseries | 48 |
| Chapter 15 | Gardens to Visit | 82 |

SECTION 3   INFORMATION & EDUCATION
Indexed alphabetically by company name

Chapter 16	Booksellers Specialising in Gardening Books	106
Chapter 17	Colleges & Horticultural Education	107
Chapter 18	Gardeners' Holidays	112
Chapter 19	Magazines & Journals	113
Chapter 20	Shows & Events	114
Chapter 21	Societies & Organisations	116

INDEXES

Company name Index	125
Specialities Index	133
Geographical Index	136
Advertisers	147

GARDEN SUPPLIES

Creating a garden is not just a matter of buying the right plants. As a serious gardener you need a wide range of equipment and machinery; garden furniture and other structures; weapons in the battle against pests and disease; and experts to call on for a second opinion, a professional service or an extra pair of hands.

In this section we cover many of these services, listed alphabetically by company name. Some of the companies listed are also specialist suppliers of plants and seeds.

ARBORICULTURAL SERVICES

Boward Tree Surgery Ltd
St Leonards Farm, New Years Green Lane, Harefield, Uxbridge, Middlesex UB9 6LX
Tel: 01895 633226
Fax: 01895 633342

Arboricultural Association approved contractors operating throughout West London and adjoining areas. All treework to BS 3998.

Brian G Crane & Associates
483 Green Lanes, London N13 4BS
Tel/fax: 0181 886 0812

C & C Trees
The Old School, High Rd, Wortwell, Harleston, Norfolk IP20 0HH
Contact: Carl Ansell
Tel/fax: 01379 852455

East Anglian based specialist in comprehensive woodland and estate management, including all aspects of tree surgery, felling, hedging, planting, design, scrub clearance. Conservation/ advisory service.

Complete Tree Services
Wayside, Kingston Stert, Chinnor, Oxfordshire OX9 4NL
Tel/fax: 01844 351488

Planting, pruning, felling, clearance and consultancy. Professional work carried out by fully insured people who care.

Connick Tree Care
New Pond Farm, Woodmatch Road, Reigate, Surrey RH2 7QHY
Tel: 01737 779191
Fax: 01737 765775

Specialist in the preservation and maintenance of trees. Tree surgery, felling, planting, stump grinding. Professional advice & free estimates. Working area London & South East.

Douglas Lewis Tree Surgeons
11 The Nashes, Clifford Chambers, Stratford upon Avon, Warwickshire CV37 8JB
Tel: 01789 295825
Fax: 01789 261496

For all aspects of tree surgery & arboriculture. Felling, crown thinning, deadwooding, cable bracing, planting, hedge work, tree reports, stump grinding, wood chips. Free quotations.

Euro Tree Service
Caxton Lodge Farm, Lodge Lane, Cronton, Widnes, Cheshire WA8 9QA
Tel: 0151 424 0333
Fax: 0151 430 7836

Keith Banyard Tree Surgeons
Nettletree Farm, Horton Heath, Wimborne, Dorset BH21 7JN
Tel: 01202 828800
Fax: 01202 820128

We offer a complete tree and landscape service, both interior and exterior. We are AA approved contractors having achieved ISO 9000 and members of BALI.

Landford Trees
Landford Lodge, Landford, Salisbury, Wiltshire SP5 2EH
Contact: C D Pilkington
Tel: 01794 390808
Fax: 01794 390037

Landford Trees is growing 600 varieties of quality trees, ornamental fruit and forestry. Specialities include acer, malus, prunus, sorbus. Delivery at cost. Free catalogue.

P G Biddle
Willowmead, Ickleton rd, Wantage, Oxfordshire OX12 9JA
Tel: 01235 762478
Fax: 01235 768034

Peter Wynn Arboricultural Consultant
Barclays Bank Chambers, Town Hall Street, Sowerby Bridge, Yorkshire (W.) HX6 2DY
Tel: 01422 834587
Fax: 01422 831141

Professional advice on all aspects of tree surgery, felling, planting and aftercare. Expert advice on tree preservation orders, other council constraints, insurance claims and litigation.

Raven Tree Services
Florida Close, Hot Lane Industrial Estate, Burslem, Stoke on Trent, Staffordshire ST6 2DJ
Tel/fax: 01782 837755

Arboricultural Association approved contractor offering: tree surgery (inc. bracing), felling, planting, stump removal, surveys and advisory service, brushwood chipper available, courses in arboriculture and forestry.

Robert Southern BA Hons NCH(Arb)
Stafford, 68 Chertsey Rd, Chobham, Woking, Surrey GU24 8PJ
Tel/fax: 01276 856115

Treework contractors and tree consultants.

Roy Finch Tree Care
Welland Way, Gloucester Rd, Welland, Malvern, Hereford & Worcester WR13 6LD
Tel: 01684 310700
Fax: 01684 310867

All aspects of tree care. Stump grinder and branchwood chipper also available with operator.

Ruskins Arboricultural Group
The Arboretum, St Marys Lane, Uppminster, Essex RM14 3HP
Contact: R Wilkins
Tel: 01708 64114
Fax: 01708 641155

We specialise in the supply and transplanting of large trees.

Southern Tree Surgeons
Turners Hill Rd, Crawley Down, Sussex (W.) RH10 4HL
Tel: 01342 717171
Fax: 01342 717662

Topiarist
26 Bramshaw Rise, New Malden, Surrey KT3 5JU
Contact: Simon Rose
Tel: 0181 942 1502
Fax: 0181 330 0464

Topiarist, Simon Rose, will supply, plant and maintain hedges, parterres and specimens. Restoration and pruning of established plants. General landscaping to highest standard.

Tree Group
10 Maple Way, Kensworth, Bedfordshire LU6 3RT
Tel/fax: 01582 872178

Wolverhampton Tree Service
89 Common Road, Wombourn, Wolverhampton, Staffordshire WV5 0LW
Contact: Bob Smith
Tel/fax: 01902 892652

Fully insured professional tree surgeons - approved by eight local authorities and The Arboricultural Association. Covering Shropshire - Staffordshire and the West Midlands. For emergencies we are open 24hrs 7 days a week.

The Daily Telegraph *Green Fingers*   Conservatories & Summerhouses

CONSERVATORIES & SUMMERHOUSES

Aanco Conservatories
Lustrum Avenue, Portrack Lane,
Stockton on Tees, Cleveland
TS18 2RB
Tel: 01642 612204
Fax: 01642 615854
Catalogue

Abbey Conservatories
268-270 Lavender Hill,
Battersea, London SW11 1LJ
Tel: 0171 924 5881
Fax: 0171 924 7069

Acorn Windows & Conservatories
Unit 4, 94 Royston Rd, Byfleet,
Surrey
Tel/fax: 0181 547 3637

Amdega Ltd
Faverdale Ind. Estate, Darlington,
Co Durham DL3 0PW
Tel: 01325 468522
Fax: 01325 849209

Manufacturer of traditional timber conservatories and summerhouses. For a copy of our catalogue and details of our exclusive 'air miles' offers contact Amdega Marketing on Freephone 0800 591523. (See our full colour advertisement on page 150).
Catalogue

Anglian Conservatory Co
PO Box 65, Norwich, Norfolk
NR6 6EJ
Tel: 01603 787000
Fax: 01603 487102

Ardep Ltd
Greenforge Way, Cwmbran,
Gwent NP44 3UZ
Tel: 01633 872134
Fax: 01633 876466

The UK's largest manufacturer of conservatories designed specially for enclosing swimming pools. Contact us now for a full colour brochure.
Catalogue

Ashcroft Conservatories
Freepost LOL2318, Tebworth,
Bedfordshire LU7 9BR
Tel/fax: 0800 317081
Catalogue

B A C Conservatories Ltd
Freepost, Romford, Essex
RM7 1BR
Tel/fax: 0800 666 444
Catalogue

Banbury Cross Conservatories
Station Parade, Ickenham Rd,
West Ruislip, Middlesex HA4 7DL
Tel: 01895 675370
Fax: 01895 678112

Bartholomew Conservatories
5 Haslemere Industrial Estate,
Haslemere, Surrey GU27 1DW
Tel: 01428 658771
Fax: 01428 656370

Canadian Cedarworks UK
18 Harnall Close, Shirley, Solihull,
Midlands (W.) B90 4QR
Tel/fax: 0121 744 5621

Cascade Blinds
The Building Centre, Woolners
Way, Stevenage, Hertfordshire
SG1 3AF
Tel/fax: 01438 361671
Catalogue

Chalfont Conservatory Company
Fulling Mill Lane, Welwyn,
Hertfordshire AL6 9NP
Tel/fax: 01438 840777

Conservatory Association
2nd Floor, Godwin House,
George Street, Huntingdon,
Cambridgeshire PE18 6BU
Contact: Bunny Lane
Tel: 01480 458278
Fax: 01480 411326

The Conservatory Association exists to regulate the industry. Members must satisfy standards of design, manufacture, trading practices and are strictly vetted prior to Association membership.
Catalogue; Mail order

Conservatory Factory
Teesway, North Tees Industrial
Estate, Portrack Lane, Stockton
on Tees, Cleveland TS18 2RS
Tel: 01642 670774
Fax: 01642 601990
Catalogue; Mail order

Conservatory Gardens
17 Hartington Rd, Chiswick,
London W4 3TL
Contact: Joan Phelan
Tel/fax: 0181 994 6109

Advice on all aspects of conservatories. Pre-building advice. Guidance on suitable plants, pots and accessories. Planting plans. Plants obtained and planted. Maintenance and on-going advice. Brochure and price list available.

Cope Conservatories
20A Hanworth Rd, Hounslow,
Middlesex TW3 1UA
Tel/fax: 0181 741 2200

Cornhill Conservatories
Grove House, 9 Pyrcroft Rd,
Chertsey, Surrey
Tel/fax: 01932 569255

Courtyard Designs
Suckley, Worcester, Hereford &
Worcester WR6 5EH
Contact: Ursula Mason
Tel: 01886 884640
Fax: 01886 884444

Cedar summerhouses built to today's highest quality and specifications in a period style. Traditional clay tile roofs, lead flashing and glazing styles of your choice.
Catalogue

Being exclusive has its price.
However, it is all-inclusive.

There's nothing common or garden about a Courtyard Designs' summerhouse or gazebo. With re-claimed clay tiles and lead capping, interchangeable panels and wide range of period glazing styles, you can tailor your own exclusive design that blends in with your individual house and garden beautifully.

Summerhouse prices start at £5,900 for a hexagonal including delivery, foundations, construction and VAT.

So when you order your elegant hideaway, you know there will be no hidden costs.

Courtyard Designs
SUMMER HOUSES

For a free brochure: Tel 01886 884640 or fax 01886 884444 any time.
Courtyard Designs, (GF/S), Suckley, Worcester, WR6 5EH.

7

The Daily Telegraph *Green Fingers* — Conservatories & Summerhouses

Crowther of Syon Lodge
Busch Corner, London Rd, Isleworth, Middlesex TW7 5BH
Tel: 0181 560 7978
Fax: 0181 568 7572

The oldest architectural antiques business in Britain. Stock includes chimney-pieces in pine, marble and stone, classical statuary, garden temples, vases, wellheads and fountains, plus period panelled rooms and period designed summerhouses.

Deans Blinds & Awnings Ltd
4 Haslemere Industrial Estate, Ravensbury Terrace, Earlsfield, London SW18
Tel/fax: 0181 947 8931

Durabuild Conservatories Ltd
Freepost CV22 36, Coventry, Midlands (W.) CV3 4BR
Tel/fax: 0800 243484

English Oak Buildings
High Street, Wadhurst, Sussex (E.) TN5 6AJ
Tel/fax: 01892 784135
Catalogue

Everglade Windows Ltd
Unit 41 & 45, Silicon Business Centre, 28 Wadsworth Rd, Perivale, Middlesex UB6 7JZ
Tel: 0181 998 8775
Fax: 0181 997 0300

Fairmitre Thames Valley
Henson House, Farm Rd, Henley-on-Thames, Oxfordshire RG9 1EJ
Tel: 01491 574220
Fax: 01491 410246

Fiesta Blinds Ltd
72-76 Yarm Lane, Stockton on Tees, Cleveland TS18 1EW
Tel: 01642 611130
Fax: 01642 617846

Coolscreen quality conservatory roof blinds. The most advanced roof blind system for all types of conservatories - free survey and installation nationwide. Freephone 0800 591539.

Finch Conservatories Ltd
Freepost, Eastleigh, Hampshire SO50 4AW
Tel/fax: 0800 378168
Catalogue

Fleur de Lys Conservatory Plants
The Lodge, Upperton Farm, Petworth, Sussex (W.) GU28 9BE
Contact: Lisa Rawley
Tel/fax: 01798 343742

Fleur de Lys grows, sells, advises upon and maintains collections of conservatory plants. Contact Lisa Rawley for the best advice before you plant. Visits by appointment only.
Catalogue

Frances Traylen Martin Dip ISGD
Saint's Hill House, Penshurst, Tonbridge, Kent TN11 8EN
Contact: Frances Traylen Martin
Tel: 01892 870331
Fax: 01892 870332

Parterre design competition winner. Professional, imaginative and practical design for period or modern gardens from planting plans for individual borders to full design and contract supervision. Interior design for conservatories and garden rooms.

Frost & Co
The Old Forge, Tempsford, Sandy, Bedfordshire SG19 2AG
Tel: 01767 40808
Fax: 01767 40561

Custom design and manufacture of double and treble glazed automatically ventilated hardwood conservatories.
Catalogue

Glass Houses
63 Islington Park Street, London N1 1QB
Tel: 0171 607 6071
Fax: 0171 609 6050
Catalogue

Glazed Additions
18 Oakfields Avenue, Knebworth, Hertfordshire SG3 6NP
Tel: 0143 8812255
Fax: 01438 815035

Goldcrest Conservatories
Woolners Way, Stevenage, Hertfordshire SG1 3AF
Tel: 01438 361671
Fax: 01438 743258

Grovewood Marketing Ltd
2 Shipley Court, Manners Industrial Estate, Ilkeston, Derbyshire DE7 8EF
Tel/fax: 0115 9445890

Headen Ltd
218 High Street, Potters Bar, Hertfordshire EN6 5BJ
Tel: 01707 660540
Fax: 01707 645372

Full range of quality aluminium greenhouses and accessories, including free-standing, lean-to and conservatory styles. Also steel framed sheds, workshops. Nationwide delivery service.
Mail order

Image Creations
67/68 Ipswich Rd, Yaxley, Eye, Suffolk IP23 8BZ
Tel/fax: 01379 783687
Catalogue

Inside Out
68 Upper Richmond Rd, London SW15 2RP
Tel: 0181 875 1611
Fax: 0181 875 1440

Just Blinds
Manor Farm, Farndish, Wellingborough, Northamptonshire NN9 7HJ
Tel/fax: 01933 411465

Lewes Road Sawmills
Standlake, Witney, Oxfordshire OX8 7PR
Tel: 01865 300444
Fax: 01865 300284
Catalogue

Lloyd Christie
1 New Kings Rd, London SW6 4SB
Contact: Tony Christie
Tel: 0171 731 3484
Fax: 0171 371 9952

Lloyd Christie designs, manufactures and installs trellis, decking, planters, arbours, rose arches, pergolas and conservatories. Please call for an appointment or brochure.
Catalogue

Malbrook Conservatories Ltd
London House, 68 Upper Richmond Rd, London SW15 2RP
Tel/fax: 0181 875 1441

Oak Leaf Conservatories Ltd
Clifton Common Industrial Pk, Kettlestring Lane, York, Yorkshire (N.) YO3 8XF
Tel: 01904 690401
Fax: 01904 690945
Catalogue

Oakleigh Conservatories
Freepost (BR1065), Findon Valley, Worthing, Sussex (W.) B14 0BR
Tel/fax: 01903 692256

Offshore Conservatory Interiors
Longwood House, Love Lane, Cirencester, Gloucestershire GL7 1YG
Contact: Malcolm Shaw
Tel/fax: 01285 641118

For all your conservatory interior requirements. Specialist suppliers of cane and wicker furniture, dining sets, plant stands, planters and numerous conservatory accessories.
Catalogue

Owen Brown Tents
Station Rd, Castle Donington, Derby, Derbyshire DE7 2NX
Tel: 01332 850000
Fax: 01332 850005

Portland Conservatories
Portland House, Ouse Street, Salford, Manchester, Gt M5 2EW
Tel: 0161 745 7920
Fax: 0161 745 8935

Raffles - Thatched Garden Buildings
Laundry Cottage, Prestwold Hall, Prestwold, Loughborough, Leicestershire LE12 5SQ
Contact: A V Raffle
Tel/fax: 01509 881426

We are specialists in design, consultancy, commissions, construction and restoration of all types of thatched garden buildings. For a fixed price quotation contact Raffles.

Realwood Conservatories
Unit 2, 93a Church Lane, Sarratt, Hertfordshire
Tel/fax: 01727 873716
Catalogue

Redfields Leisure Buildings
Redfields Garden Centre, Ewshot Lane, Church Crookham, Fleet, Hampshire GU13 0UB

Roger Platts Garden Design
Faircombe, Maresfield, Sussex (E.) TN22 2EH
Contact: Roger Platts
Tel/fax: 01825 764077

A garden design and plants service including construction and planting. Handcrafted English oak pergolas and garden buildings in a traditional style. Chelsea Flower Show exhibitor.
Mail order

Room Outside
Goodwood Gardens, Goodwood, Chichester, Sussex (W.) PO18 0QB
Contact: Mr Jim Gemmill
Tel: 01243 776563
Fax: 01243 776313

For over 25 years, Room Outside Conservatories have designed and built some of the finest bespoke timber conservatories and summer houses throughout the United Kingdom.
Catalogue

The Daily Telegraph *Green Fingers* — **Conservatories & Summerhouses**

Rutland County
'Snowshill', Preston, Oakham, Rutland, Leicestershire LE15 9NJ

Contact: Mike or Veronica Bowden
Tel: 01572 737502 (24hrs)
Fax: 01572 737602

Tailor made conservatories with an exceptional ventilation system. Nationwide design, planning and building service. Phone for information or site visit.

Samuel Wernick Garden Buildings
Russell Gardens, Wickford, Essex Ss11 8BL

Tel: 01268 561199
Fax: 01268 560026

Catalogue

Secret Garden Company of Ware Ltd
Ware, Hertfordshire SG12 0YJ

Contact: Susan King
Tel/fax: 01920 462081

Cedar and iroko summerhouses and gazebos with cedar-shingled roofs. Substantial construction and high quality finish. The quality of the interiors is particularly remarkable. Visits by appointment.
Catalogue

Smart Systems Ltd
North End Rd, Yatton, Avon BS19 4AW

Tel/fax: 01934 876 100
Catalogue

Solaris Laminates Ltd
Freepost, Bournemouth, Dorset BH22 8BR

Contact: Sarah Clarke
Tel: 01202 870067
Fax: 01202 870068

Conservatory too hot in summer? Cut summer temperatures by up to 40F, reduce glare, insulate in winter. Economical to install, guaranteed performance, free information/quotation.

Stuart Garden Architecture
Burrow Hill Farm, Wiveliscombe, Somerset TA4 2RN

Tel: 01984 667458
Fax: 01984 667455

Gazebos, summerhouses and garden buildings manufactured in hardwood to individual specification. Catalogue available.

Sun Building Developments Ltd
Hollies Way, Off High Street, Potters Bar, Hertfordshire EN6 5BH

Tel: 01707 663209
Fax: 01707 645372

Full range of quality aluminium greenhouses and accessories, including free-standing and lean-to styles. Also conservatory-style lean-to. Nationwide delivery service.
Mail order

Thai House Company
11 The Paddock, Maidenhead, Berkshire SL6 6SD

Tel/fax: 01628 75091

Vale Garden Houses
Melton Rd, Harlaxton, Grantham, Lincolnshire NG32 1HQ

Tel: 01476 64433
Fax: 01476 78555

Catalogue

Victoriana Conservatories Ltd
4 Mortlake Terrace, Kew, Richmond, Surrey TW9 3DT

Contact: J C Hunting
Tel: 0181 332 2989
Fax: 0181 948 2511

Manufacturer of bespoke high quality timber conservatories, also doors and windows. Design and erection service available. Very competitive prices and prompt delivery.
Catalogue

Walton Conservatories
15 Wheatsheaf Lane, Staines, Middlesex TW18 2PD

Tel/fax: 01784 450491

Catalogue

Westbury Conservatories
Martels, High Easter Rd, Barnston, Great Dunmow, Essex CM6 1NA

Tel/fax: 01371 876576

Catalogue

Wiltshire Summerhouses
137 High Street, Littleton Panell, Devizes, Wiltshire SN10 4EU

Contact: Sally Peake
Tel/fax: 01380 818967

Bespoke timber buildings. Edwardian style rotating summerhouse available complete including erection or as a kit delivered. Please phone for current literature and further information.
Catalogue

Woodworks Workshop
11 Belwell Lane, Four Oaks, Sutton Coldfield, Midlands (W.) B74 4AA

Tel/fax: 0121 323 3326

"RUTLAND COUNTY"
Offer a wide range of tailor made conservatories

Nationwide Design, Planning and Building Service by a reliable competitive company

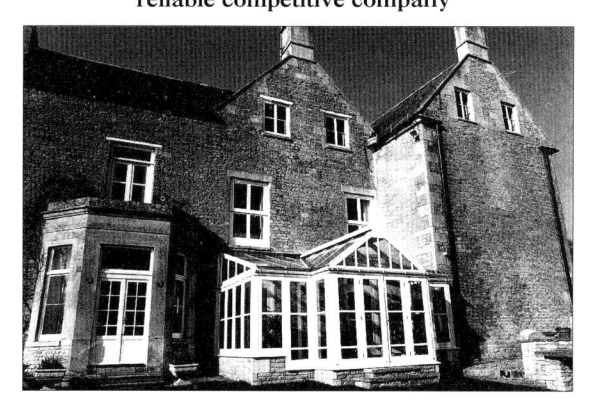

Many conservatories are poorly ventilated hothouses. However, our superb ventilation system avoids the "Sauna Bath Syndrome".
If you would like more information or a site visit to discuss size, design and price please contact –
Mike or Veronica Bowden Tel: 01572 737502 (24hrs).
Fax: 01572 737602
or London 0181 541 1161 Birmingham 0121 643 3223

"Snowshill", Preston, Oakham, Rutland, Leics LE15 9NJ for free advice without obligation. We offer an efficient service and a quality product at a fair price – not a hard sell. Come and see what we're capable of

DESIGN & LANDSCAPING

Acorn Landscapes
Oak Tree Nursery, Mill Lane, Barlow, Selby, Yorkshire (N.) YO8 8EY
Contact: C J Plowes
Tel/fax: 01757 618409

Full garden design and implementation service available for both domestic and industrial clients. Garden plans and schemes drawn up. Free local estimates.

Acres Wild (Landscape & Garden Design)
45a High Street, Billingshurst, Sussex (W.) RH14 9PP
Contact: Ian Smith & Debbie Roberts
Tel/fax: 01403 785385

Designers of bold structural gardens, softened with full and naturalistic planting to reflect the character of the client, their home and the wider landscape setting.

Alexander Armstrong
The Garden Studio, 2a Pond Rd, Blackheath, London SE3 9JL
Tel: 0181 318 7416
Fax: 0181 318 7417

Alexander Armstrong is a garden designer who has combined an architectural training with his extensive gardening knowledge to provide all aspects of exterior domestic design.

Alison Brett Garden Design
Wimbleweather, Hammer Vale, Haslemere, Surrey GU27 1QG
Contact: Alison Brett
Tel/fax: 01428 651704

Realise the potential of your garden with the help of imaginative, fully qualified garden designer. Creative, contemporary designs for almost anything from single border to large country garden. Surrey / Sussex / Hampshire.

Allan Hart Associates
Orchard House, 61 Christchurch Rd, East Sheen, London SW14 7AN
Contact: Allan Hart
Tel: 0181 878 2017
Fax: 0181 878 1638

The practice has been established since 1968. Private, commercial and government projects of varying size, complexity and value throughout the UK, Middle and Far East.

Allseasons Landscapes
Spinners, High Street, Upper Beeding, Steyning, Sussex (W.)
Tel: 01903 815079
Fax: 01903 813225

We specialise in all forms of landscape design, construction and planting. Please phone for free advice or quotation.

Andrew Evans - Landscape Designer
5 Nadder Terrace, Churchfields Rd, Salisbury, Wiltshire SP2 7NN
Tel/fax: 01722 328998

Annabel Allhusen
Capstitch House, Compton Abbas, Shaftesbury, Dorset SP7 0NB
Tel/fax: 01747 811622

Dorset, Hampshire, Wiltshire and Somerset areas. Professional garden design including site survey, soil test, detailed design drawings, full planting plans, plant schedules and site supervision.

Anthea Sokell Cert.GD
Rickledon, Maddox Lane, Bookham, Leatherhead, Surrey KT23 3BS
Tel/fax: 01372 452052

Garden design. Professionally qualified. Consultations, from outline to full design service. Informal, formal, cottage or gardens with flair. Personal, imaginative, practical designs. Reputable contractors recommended.

Anthony George & Associates
The Old Brick House, Village Rd, Dorney, Windsor, Berkshire SL4 6QJ
Tel: 01628 604224
Fax: 01628 604401

Anthony Short & Partners
34 Church Street, Ashbourne, Derbyshire DE6 1AE
Tel: 01335 342345
Fax: 01335 300624

Anthos Design
47 Bennerley Rd, London SW11 6DR
Tel: 0171 228 2288
Fax: 0171 978 4148

Antony Young
Ridleys Cheer, Mountain Bower, Chippenham, Wiltshire SN14 7AJ
Tel: 01225 891204
Fax: 01225 891139

Comprehensive design and landscaping service. Concepts, consultancy, planning, sourcing, planting. All types of project undertaken from the smallest potager to gardens exceeding five acres.

Architectural Landscape Design Ltd
3-5 Kelsey Park Rd, Beckenham, Kent BR3 3LH
Tel: 0181 658 4455
Fax: 0181 658 2785

An award winning design and build landscape company, with a highly skilled, friendly team of designers, builders and horticulturists.

Arena Landscapes
50 Grove Hill, Caversham, Reading, Berkshire RG4 8PR
Tel/fax: 01734 475315

Artscapes & Theseus Maze Designs
Silk Mill House, 24 Winchester Street, Whitchurch, Hampshire RG28 7DD
Tel/fax: 01256 892837

Ash Consulting Group
21 Carlton Court, Glasgow, Strathclyde G5 9JP
Tel/fax: 0141 420 3131

Avenue Fisheries
46 Rookery Road, Wyboston, Bedfordshire MK44 3AX
Tel/fax: 01480 215408

Full pond design, landscaping and construction service, specializing in high specification koi ponds as can be viewed at our premises.

Barnsdale Plants & Gardens
The Avenue, Exton, Oakham, Leicestershire LE15 8AH
Tel: 01572 813200
Fax: 01572 813346

Our innovative garden designer is now offering individual, practical and creative designs, consultancy and a full building service. Commissions undertaken anywhere in the country.

Barton Grange Landscapes
Garstang Road, Barton, Preston, Lancashire PR3 5AA
Contact: Mr C R Greenhill
Tel: 01772 866226
Fax: 01772 862219

A complete and professional quality landscape gardening service in design and construction for both domestic and commercial sectors from back garden rockeries to major parkland.

Baylis Landscape Design & Construction
236 Rochester Rd, Gravesend, Kent DA12 4TZ
Tel: 01474 569576
Fax: 01474 564334

Drives, patios, water features, timber structures, automatic irrigation systems, golf greens, tees, croquet lawns, fine lawns, tarmac and artificial grass tennis courts.

Beau Jardin
PO Box 49, Rochdale, Lancashire OL12 6WW
Tel/fax: 01706 525188

Belmont Gardens by Design
10 Belmont Drive, Trull Rd, Taunton, Somerset TA1 4QB
Contact: Sonia Stearn
Tel/fax: 01823 331267

Complete personal design service. Specialist in design for flower arrangers.

Berrys Garden Company Ltd
6 Hodford Rd, London NW11 8NP
Contact: Brian Berry
Tel: 0181 209 0194
Fax: 0181 458 6442

Landscaping, garden design, patios, planting, turfing, irrigation systems, garden lighting, fencing, paving, garden maintenance. BALI member.

Bonita Bulaitis Landscape & Garden Design
6 Watton Rd, Ware, Hertfordshire SG12 0AA
Tel: 01920 466466
Fax: 01920 462816

Award winning designer of unique gardens, alive with atmosphere and enchantment. Bonita's natural planting style enhances seasonal change, to create contrasts in time and mood.

Brent Surveys & Designs
158a Edenvale Rd, Westbury, Wiltshire BA13 3QG
Tel: 01373 827331
Fax: 01373 777148

Brodie & Hickin Landscapes
134 Walton Rd, East Molesey, Surrey KT8 0HP
Tel: 0181 941 5865
Fax: 0181 783 1576

Bunny Guinness Landscape Design
Sibberton Lodge, Thornhaugh, Peterborough, Cambridgeshire PE8 6NH
Contact: Bunny Guiness
Tel/fax: 01780 782518

Bunny Guinness BSc(Hons) Hort.DipLA ALI designs schemes for gardens large and small, private and commercial, at home and abroad. Has won 3 Gold Medals at Chelsea Flower Show.

Cabbages & Kings
Wilderness Farm, Wilderness Lane, Hadlow Down, Sussex (E.) TN22 4HU
Contact: Ryl Nowell
Tel: 01825 830552
Fax: 01825 830736

Imaginative garden developed by designer Ryl Nowell to help people realise the full potential of their own gardens. Adults £2.50, senior citizens & children £2. Plants for sale. Teas.

Capital Garden Landscapes
1 Townsend Yard, Highgate High Street, London N6 5JF
Tel: 0181 342 8977
Fax: 0181 341 5032

London's award-winning gardeners specialise in creating and maintaining sophisticated town gardens with particular emphasis on utilisation of space for outdoor living. Free estimates.

Carol Messham
41 Feversham Drive, Kirbymoorside, York, Yorkshire (N.) YO6 6DH
Tel/fax: 01751 432071

Carol Messham Garden Design - covering North Humberside, Yorkshire and Cheshire. Plans prepared ready for construction by client or contractor. Telephone 01751 432071 or 01244 818513.

Cecily Hazell Garden Design
14 Brudenell Rd, London SW17 8DA
Tel/fax: 0181 767 2380

Charles Hogarth Garden Landscapes
Wissellii House, 19 Dunsley Place, London Road, Tring, Hertfordshire HP23 6JL
Contact: Charles Hogarth
Tel: 01442 890985
Fax: 01442 823817

We create an image. From artist's impression to reality, professionally constructed by qualified personnel; your concept of a complete garden carried through with detailed consultation.

Chenies Landscapes Ltd
Bramble Lane, London Rd East, Amersham, Buckinghamshire HP7 9DH
Tel: 01494 728004
Fax: 01494 721403

Chris Burnett Associates
New Russia Hall, Tattenhall, Chester, Cheshire CH3 9AH
Tel: 01829 71241
Fax: 01829 71152

Christopher Bradley-Hole
20 Fitzgerald Avenue, London SW14 8SZ
Tel/fax: 0181 241 8056

Garden designer, architect and gardener - designer of the "Gardens Illustrated" garden at Chelsea Flower Show 1994, his work has been featured on BBC Television and extensively in the press, including a series of designs for readers' gardens in The Daily Telegraph during 1996. Current projects include London town gardens, a large secret garden in Gloucestershire, a walled kitchen garden in Sussex, the restoration of a distinguished historic garden in Suffolk, and The Daily Telegraph garden for Chelsea Flower Show 1997. He likes to work closely with clients to develop designs which reflect their special interests and the context of the site.

Colvin & Moggridge
Filkins, Lechlade, Gloucestershire GL7 3JQ
Contact: David McQuitty
Tel: 01367 860225
Fax: 01367 860564

Landscape design of every type. Specialists in restoration of historic parks and gardens. Imaginative designs for new gardens. Advice from outline design to full implementation.

Cotswold Range of Garden Ornamental Ironwork
Stonebank, Ablington, Bibury, Cirencester, Gloucestershire GL7 5NU
Tel/fax: 01285 740412

Top quality garden ornamental ironwork. Arches, bowers, centre-pieces, obelisks. Full pergola service from design to installation. Solid construction, rust proofed, finished Cotswold green/black. Free colour brochure.

Courtyard Garden Design
26 Algar Rd, Old Isleworth, Middlesex TW7 7AG
Contact: Ms Sally Court ISD
Tel/fax: 0181 568 5263

Professional design service with a personal approach for domestic, commercial, town and country projects by award winning designer Sally Court.

Crowther Landscapes
Ongar Rd, Abridge, Essex RM4 1AA
Tel: 01708 688581
Fax: 01708 688677

D Wells Landscaping
The Cottage, 15 Park Avenue, Eastbourne, Sussex (E.) BN21 2XG
Tel/fax: 01323 502073

Dagenham Landscapes Ltd
Redcrofts Farm, Ockendon Rd, Upminster, Essex RM14 2DJ
Tel: 01708 222379
Fax: 01708 221050

Design and build specialist working in Essex, North London, through to the city. Maintenance contacts undertaken. Members of the British Association of Landscape Industries.

Daniel Pearson
50 Bonnington Square, Vauxhall, London SW8 1TQ
Tel/fax: 0171 582 8371

David Brown Landscape Design
10 College Rd, Impington, Cambridge, Cambridgeshire CB4 4PD
Tel: 01223 232366
Fax: 01223 235293

Landscape architecture, garden historical research and arboricultural consultancy. Projects from town gardens to two thousand acre estates have been undertaken by the practice.

David Ireland Landscape Architect
Thames Sailing Barge Scone, City Harbour, Off East Ferry Rd, Isle of Dogs, London E14 9TF
Tel/fax: 0171 515 8826

David Stevens International Ltd
Stowe Castle Business Park, Stowe, Buckinghamshire MK18 5AB
Tel: 01280 821097
Fax: 01280 821150

Debbie Jolley Garden Design
Maycotts, Matfield, Tonbridge, Kent TN12 7JU
Contact: Debbie Jolley
Tel: 01892 722203
Fax: 01892 723222

Individual and distinctive garden design and consultancy service for gardens large or small. An affiliate member of the Society of Garden Designers.

Diana Eldon - Garden Designer
27 Parsons Lane, Bierton, Aylesbury, Buckinghamshire HP22 5DF
Tel/fax: 01296 24138

Professional garden design service responsive to clients' needs. Advisory visits, detailed plans, garden design and planting plans. Teaches at adult education class, gives talks.

Dream Gardens
Ings Gate, Flaxman Croft, Copmanthorpe, York, Yorkshire (N.) YO2 3TU
Contact: Keith James, Dip GD LA
Tel: 01904 703833
Fax: 01904 709815

Experienced garden designer and landscape architect practice operating throughout the UK and Europe. Service also offers design and build, horticultural consultancy, specialising in individual projects both large and small in period listed and country house gardens, restoration. New sites, self build. Nature conservation and environment. Exclusive smaller commercial projects including atria, hotels, leisure complexes, marinas, golf courses. Britain, Ireland, Europe. Produces gardens of great flair at leading national and international shows.

Duncan Heather
Heathers of Henley, 34 Kings Rd, Henley-on-Thames, Oxfordshire Rg9 2DG
Tel: 01491 573577
Fax: 01491 411161

Elaine Horne
Newfield Cottage, Firbank, Sedbergh, Cumbria LA10 5EN
Tel/fax: 015396 20621

Specialist in unusual plantings and low maintenance schemes for small private gardens.

Elizabeth Banks Associates
13 Abercorn Place, London NW8 9EA
Tel: 0171 624 5740
Fax: 0171 372 0964

Elizabeth Whateley Garden Design
48 Glossop Rd, Sanderstead, South Croydon, Surrey CR2 0PU
Tel/fax: 0181 651 0226

Professional, practical design for any size of garden. Services include original layout plans, contract inspection and imaginative planting schemes. Member of Society of Garden Designers.

F F C Landscape Architects/The Garden Design Studio
Woodcote, Nelson Crescent, Cotesheath, Eccleshall, Staffordshire ST21 6ST
Contact: Mr F Colella
Tel/fax: 01782 791506

Fully professional garden and landscape design services across Midlands and North West. Inspired and cost-effective design solutions to all types of gardens.

F M G Garden Designs
21 Crescent Gardens, London SW19 8AJ
Contact: Nilla Gallanzi
Tel/fax: 0181 879 3168

F M G Designs is a company that works in everything your garden needs, from cleaning and pruning to elaborate plans made by our qualified designer, Mrs Nilla Gallanzi.

Fiona Harrison
23 Course Side, Ascot, Berkshire SL5 7HH
Tel: 01344 24543
Fax: 01344 873505

Frances Traylen Martin Dip ISGD
Saint's Hill House, Penshurst, Tonbridge, Kent TN11 8EN
Contact: Frances Traylen Martin
Tel: 01892 870331
Fax: 01892 870332

Parterre design competition winner. Professional, imaginative and practical design for period or modern gardens from planting plans for individual borders to full design and contract supervision. Interior design for conservatories and garden rooms.

G D Landscapes
31 Brinsley Rd, Harrow Weald, Middlesex HA3 5HY
Tel: 0181 863 8335
Fax: 0181 424 2131

G Miles & Son Ltd
School House, Great Ashfield, Bury St Edmunds, Suffolk IP31 3HJ
Tel: 01359 242356
Fax: 01359 241781

Miles specialises in all works involved in consultancy, design, renovation and construction of major existing and new water areas and features. National and international enquiries welcome.

Garden & Security Lighting
67 George Row, London SE16 4UH
Contact: Roger Beckett
Tel: 0171 231 5323
Fax: 0171 237 4342

Design, supply and installation of garden and landscape lighting equipment. Site demonstrations available. Garden lighting advisors in various locations.

Garden Solutions by Design
43 Park Drive North, Mirfield, Yorkshire (W.) WF14 9NJ
Tel/fax: 01924 495584

Gardens by Graham Evans
20 Grandfield Avenue, Radcliffe on Trent, Nottinghamshire NG12 1AL
Contact: Graham or Alison Evans
Tel/fax: 0115 9335737

Cottage garden, formal, Japanese, low maintenance, whatever your taste. We specialise in all styles and blends of landscaping to private gardens. Members of BALI.

Gardens of Distinction
The Old Canal Building, East Challow, Wantage, Oxfordshire OX12 9SY
Tel: 01235 769532
Fax: 01235 770040

Gardenscape
Fairview, Smelthouses, Summerbridge, Harrogate, Yorkshire (N.) HG3 4DH
Contact: Michael D Myers
Tel/fax: 01423 780291

Horticultural advisory and design service. Hard and soft landscaping - free quotes. Small nursery specialising in rare and unusual woodland plants. Hand-carved stone ornaments.

Gary Edwards Garden Designs
54 Durham Rd, Southend-on-Sea, Essex SS2 4LU
Tel/fax: 01702 611777

Offering a professional and personal consultation, design and project supervision service, tailored to your individual requirements - from concept to completion.

Geoffrey Coombs
47 Larcombe Rd, Petersfield, Hampshire GU32 3LS
Tel/fax: 01730 267417

Gillian Temple Associates
15 Woodside Avenue, Weston Green, Esher, Surrey KT10 8JQ
Contact: Gillian Temple
Tel: 0181 339 0323
Fax: 0181 339 0335

Garden designs, planting plans and horticultural consultancy for private and commercial properties. Large, small, urban and rural sites all individually designed to suit specific requirements.

Glenda Biggs BA Dip ISD
Berrylands Farm, Pookbourne Lane, Sayers Common, Sussex (W.) BN6 9HD
Tel/fax: 01444 881437

Grace Landscapes Ltd
Knowl Rd, Mirfield, Yorkshire (W.) WF19 9UU
Tel: 01924 492645
Fax: 01924 480518

Graham A Pavey & Associates
11 Princes Rd, Bromham, Bedfordshire MK43 8QD
Contact: Graham or Chris Pavey
Tel/fax: 01243 823860

Garden design and consultancy. From a single consultation in your garden to full design commissions, our knowledge, experience and professionalism make all the difference.

Green Stock
Church Hill, Pinhoe, Exeter, Devon EX4 9JG
Tel: 01392 462988
Fax: 01392 462977

Green Way
42 Lynwood Road, Redhill, Surrey RH1 1JS
Contact: David E Greenway
Tel/fax: 01737 212144

Fulfilling your gardening desires. Hard and soft landscaping. Patio, drive and pond construction. All types of walling and fencing undertaken.

Greenstone Gardens
14 William Dromey Court, Dyne Rd, London NW6 7XD
Tel/fax: 0171 625 5347

Ground Control Ltd
Ardmore House, London Rd, Billericay, Essex CM12 9HS
Contact: Mr S Harrod
Tel: 01277 650697
Fax: 01277 630746
Email:101540.1265@compuserve.com

BALI National Award winners 4 times. ISO 9002 quality assured. Clients include Royal Parks, Tesco and H.M. Tower of London.

H D R A Consultants
Ryton Organic Gardens, Ryton-on-Dunsmore, Coventry, Warwickshire CV8 3LG
Tel: 01203 308202
Fax: 01203 639229

Garden and landscape design and management service combining the expertise of Britain's premier organic organisation and leading garden designers to bring beautiful yet environmentally friendly solutions.

Hambrook Landscapes Ltd
Wangfield Lane, Curdridge, Southampton, Hampshire SO3 2DA
Tel: 01489 780505
Fax: 01489 785396

Heath Garden
Heath Hill, Sheriffhales, Shifnal, Shropshire TF11 8RR
Tel/fax: 01952 691341

Heather Goldsmark Partnership
Swallowfield, Eastgate Lane, Eastgate, Chichester, Sussex (W.) PO20 6SJ
Tel: 01243 543834
Fax: 01243 543708

Helen Cahill
15 Richmond Bridge Mansions, Willoughby Rd, East Twickenham, London TW1 2QJ
Tel/fax: 0181 892 2652

Hillier Landscapes
Ampfield House, Ampfield, Romsey, Hampshire SO51 9PA
Contact: Richard Barnard
Tel: 01794 368733
Fax: 01794 368813

Landscape and garden design practice, horticultural advisory service. Comprehensive hard and soft national landscape construction service. Brochure on request.

Hurtwood Landscapes
Garden Close, Gadbridge Lane, Ewhurst, Surrey GU6 7RW
Tel: 01483 277541
Fax: 01483 276856

Ian Roscoe
St Marys House, 40 St Marys Grove, Richmond, Surrey TW9 1UY
Tel/fax: 0181 940 3579

Jacqui Stubbs Associates
24 Duncan Rd, Richmond, Surrey
TW9 2JD
Tel: 0181 948 0744
Fax: 0181 255 6803

Garden design for South East England and the Republic of Ireland.

Jakobsen Landscape Architects
Mount Sorrel, West Approach Drive, Pittville, Cheltenham, Gloucestershire GL52 3AD
Contact: Preben Jakobsen ALI, RA Dip, Dip.HortKEW, FSGD
Tel: 01242 241501
Fax: 01242 520693

Leading landscape architecture and garden design practice. Holder of Landscape Institute medal and numerous awards. Esoteric, eccentric, sublime, futuristic, modern landscape/garden design our metier.

James Bolton Garden Design
Clapton Manor,
Clapton-on-the-Hill,
Bourton-on-the-Water,
Gloucestershire GL54 2LG
Contact: James Bolton
Tel/fax: 01451 810202

Designs for large or small gardens undertaken by plantsman/designer. From individual planting plans to long term involvement giving continuous planting/design/maintenance advice.

Janet Bacon Garden Design
36 Park Avenue West,
Stoneleigh, Epsom, Surrey
KT17 2NU
Tel/fax: 0181 393 7970

Jean Goldberry Garden Design
Garden Cottage, Vicarage Road, Blackawton, Totnes, Devon
TQ9 7AY
Contact: Jean Goldberry
Tel/fax: 01803 712611

Of 'More Front Gardens' and 'Gardening from Scratch' fame! Jean is a designer who can work for you either by post or by site visit.

Jeanne Paisley
Jacaranda, Wembury Park,
Lingfield, Surrey RH7 6HH
Tel/fax: 01342 832561

Jill Billington Garden Design
100 Fox Lane, London N13 4AX
Tel/fax: 0181 886 0898

Gardens thoughtfully and creatively designed by Jill Billington BA MSGD, who lectures and writes on the art of garden design.

Joanna Stay Garden Design
67 Dalton Street, St Albans, Hertfordshire AL3 5QH
Contact: Joanna Stay
Tel/fax: 01727 869765

Professionally qualified - offering advisory visits, layouts, planting plans, full working drawings, contract inspection. Reputable contractors recommended. Personal, comprehensive space designing for gardens great and small.

John A Davies Landscape Consultants
Fernhill Lodge, Llechryd, Cardigan, Dyfed SA43 2QL
Tel: 01239 87861
Fax: 01239 621004

John A Ford Landscape Architects
8 Church Rd, Trull, Taunton, Somerset TA3 7LG
Contact: Mr Ford
Tel/fax: 01823 279817

We offer specialist attention to corporate and private clients for leisure, community and commercial development, site planning, garden design, countryside improvement and environmental impact assessment.

John B Rickell
12 College Lane, Apley Park, Wellington, Telford, Shropshire
TF1 3DH
Tel/fax: 01952 249935

John Brookes - Landscape Designer
Clock House, Denmans, Fontwell, Arundel, Sussex (W.)
BN18 0SU
Tel: 01243 542808
Fax: 01243 544064

Landscape and garden design undertaken from the very tiny to the very large to suit all budgets and situations. Don't be afraid to telephone to discuss your requirements.

John H Lucas
Lansdowne House, 320 Chessington Rd, West Ewell, Surrey KT19 9XG
Contact: John Lucas
Tel/fax: 0181 393 9946

John H Lucas is an RHS award winning garden designer, lecturer and author of the book "Low Water Gardening". He writes for various well known national journals, is guest garden expert for Radio Mercury Extra and appeared in the Channel Four programme "Plantlife". John is a keen gardener and his garden is open to the public for private viewing, by appointment, during June and July. John offers realistically priced, creative and individual designs for the gardens of private and commercial properties.

John Medhurst Landscape Consultant
77 Harold Rd, Upper Norwood, London SE19 3SP
Contact: John Medhurst
Tel/fax: 0181 653 0921

An international and award winning designer providing landscape services for public and private parks and gardens in the United Kingdom and abroad.

John Moreland
Higher Trevarthen, Sancreed, Penzance, Cornwall TR20 8QY
Tel/fax: 01736 788993

Josephine Hindle - Designer & Gardener
11 Beechfield, Newton Tony, Salisbury, Wiltshire SP4 0HQ
Tel/fax: 01980 64323

Joy Jardine Garden Designer
Heath House, Alldens Lane, Munstead, Godalming, Surrey
GU8 4AP
Tel/fax: 01483 416961

Joy Jardine undertakes private commissions throughout the country, offering involvement from the initial brief to the completion of the project to the client's satisfaction.

Judith Woodget Garden Design
Rickyard House, Fyfield, Marlborough, Wiltshire SN8 1PQ
Tel: 01672 861314
Fax: 01672 861536

Imaginative but practical designs for gardens of all shapes and sizes, whether in town or the depths of the country. Free initial visit.

Julia Fogg & Susan Santer
Lee Common, Great Missenden, Buckinghamshire
Tel: 01494 837620
Fax: 01296 392825

Julia Mizen BA Dip ISD
56 Overstone Rd, London
W6 0AB
Tel/fax: 0181 741 0702

Julian Dowle Partnership
The Old Malt House, High St, Newent, Gloucestershire
GL18 1AY
Contact: Julian Dowle & Jacquie Gordon
Tel: 01531 820512
Fax: 01531 822421

With a record of eight Chelsea Gold Medals, the partnership offers a nationwide landscape design and garden consultancy service for rural and urban properties.

Julian Treyer-Evans
Magnolia House, 26 Cuckfield Rd, Hurstpierpoint, Sussex (W.)
BN6 9SA
Tel/fax: 01273 834833

Karen Saynor
42 Raleigh Rd, Richmond, Surrey
TW9 2DX
Tel/fax: 0181 940 2402

Katerina Georgi Landscapes
187 Ashmore Rd, London W9
3DB
Tel/fax: 0181 969 2924

Keith Pullan Garden Design
1 Amotherby Close, Amotherby, Malton, Yorkshire (N.)
YO17 0TG
Contact: Keith Pullan
Tel/fax: 01653 693885

A fully professional design service for any size garden, from consultation to complete plans and planting schemes, ready for implementation by the client or contractor.

Ken Higginbotham Garden Landscaping
31 Elmfield, Chapel-en-le-Frith, Stockport, Cheshire SK12 6TZ
Tel/fax: 01298 813051

Free leaflet on application. Free estimates. Design and drawings by arrangement. Qualified and experienced in all areas of garden construction, both horticultural and arboricultural.

Kexby Design
7 Lindfield Drive, Wellington, Shropshire TF1 1SF
Contact: John B Rickell MIHort, Dip Hort (Wisley)
Tel/fax: 01952 249935

Garden design and horticultural consultancy. Designs for contract or for DIY advice on plant selection, alpine garden designs top and soft fruit.

The Daily Telegraph *Green Fingers*   **Design & Landscaping**

Landmark Designs
47 Southbrook Rd, London SE12 8LJ

Contact: Sabina Marland
Tel/fax: 0181 318 4028

Good ideas for gardens, large and small. Landmark designs offers a professional design service from single consultation to full design, construction and planting.

Landscape Design Studio
3 Hatton Mains Cottages, Dalmahoy, Kirknewton, Midlothian, Lothian EH27 8EB

Tel/fax: 0131 333 1262

Garden design by qualified landscape architect. UK postal service. Phone or write for information pack. Site visits can be arranged in Scotland.

Landscapes by Tim Brayford
Hillside, Appleford Road, Godshill, Ventnor, Isle of Wight PO38 3LE

Contact: Tim Brayford
Tel/fax: 01983 551412

Design and construction of high quality gardens. BALI Award winners.

Landskip & Prospect
Talley, Llandeilo, Dyfed SA19 7YH

Contact: Andrew Sclater
Tel: 01558 685567
Fax: 01558 685745

Operational throughout UK. Repair/restoration of neglected gardens of historic interest. Detailed design capability. Cost-effective management plans for parts or whole gardens and estates.

Lennox-Boyd Landscape Design
45 Moreton Street, London SW1V 2NY

Tel: 0171 931 9995
Fax: 0171 821 6585

Lingard & Styles Landscape
Ladywell House, Park Street, Newtown, Powys SY16 1JB

Contact: Peter Styles
Tel: 01686 627600
Fax: 01686 622795

Professionally qualified garden designers and landscape architects offering personal service throughout the UK. Award winning designers with over 25 years' experience including Chelsea Show gardens.

Lotus Landscapes
9 Beresford Close, Frimley Green, Camberley, Surrey GU16 6LB

Tel/fax: 01252 838665

Louis Vincent Garden Design
2 Ford Cottage, Mamhead Rd, Kenton, Exeter, Devon EX6 8LY

Contact: Louis Vincent or Anita de Visser
Tel/fax: 01626 890926

Louis, MSGD, has a strong sense of harmony between home and surroundings resulting in comfortable gardens. Good assessment of problem areas, creative but practical solutions, making full use of your garden's potential. Professional and fully illustrated plans with working details for own construction or contractor. Mainly private town and country gardens, all sizes. An individual and enthusiastic approach guaranteed.

Marianne Ford Garden Design
Manor Farm House, Hulcott, Aylesbury, Buckinghamshire HP22 5AX

Tel: 01296 394364
Fax: 01296 399007

Marianne Ford offers an individual and comprehensive design service from single consultations to full design implementation for private gardens and nursing homes.

Marina Adams Landscape Architects
3 Pembroke Studios, Pembroke Gardens, London W8 6HX

Tel/fax: 0171 602 5790

Mark Ross Landscape Architects
Royal Arcade, Broad Street, Pershore, Hereford & Worcester WR10 1AG

Tel/fax: 01386 561961

Mark Westcott Landscape Architects
77 Cowcross Street, London EC1M 6BP

Tel: 0171 490 2984
Fax: 0171 490 2989

Architecture, landscape design, restoration, refurbishment and contemporary design.

Martin Berkley Landscape Architects
40 Berkeley Street, Glasgow, Strathclyde G3 7DW

Contact: Martin Berkley
Tel: 0141 204 1855
Fax: 0141 204 1813

Landscape architects, design & supervision of retail and leisure parks, corporate headquarters, sports facilities, motorway planting, reclamation and private gardens.

Mary Ann Lovegrove
Boarden House, Hawkenbury, Staplehurst, Kent TN12 0EB

Tel/fax: 01580 893018

Master Gardeners
8 Murray Street, Camden Square, London NW1 9RE

Tel: 0171 284 0483
Fax: 0171 267 7603

Design consultants and landscape contractors. Garden maintenance and improvements. Provided by skilled gardeners and expert horticulturalists.

Michael Ballam Design
66 Marchmont Rd, Edinburgh, Lothian EH19 1HS

Tel/fax: 0131 447 5089

Michael Littlewood Landscape Designer
Troutwells, Higher Hayne, Roadwater, Watchet, Somerset TA23 0RN

Tel/fax: 01984 41330

Mickfield Fish & Watergarden Centre
Debenham Rd, Mickfield, Stowmarket, Suffolk IP14 5LP

Contact: Mick C Burch
Tel: 01449 711336
Fax: 01449 711018

Two acres ornamental watergardens and nursery. Specialists in established water and pondside plants. Pond and water feature design and construction and maintenance. Large retail section. Catalogue 50p.

Moongate Designs
35 Balmoral Rd, Pilgrims Hatch, Brentwood, Essex CM15 9PW

Contact: P A Ellis
Tel: 01277 215721
Fax: 01277 260677

Specialising in the consultation, planning, design and specification of your personal environment. Try our postal design service for national coverage.

Mulberry Landscapes
Brook House Farm, Church Lane, Tetford, Lincolnshire LN9 6QL

Contact: Adrian Stockdale
Tel/fax: 01507 533591

Garden design and build service. Leaflet available on request.

Nicholas Roeber Landscapes
38 Wyatt Rd, London N5 2JU

Tel: 0171 354 3762
Fax: 0171 359 1996

Nigel Jeffries Landscapes
30 Yaverland Drive, Bagshot, Surrey GU19 5DX

Tel/fax: 01276 476365

We offer a full garden design service complemented by skilled construction and maintenance teams able to carry out a full range of garden services.

Nigel L Philips Landscape & Garden Design
18a Cliffe High Street, Lewes, Sussex (E.) BN7 2AH

Tel/fax: 01273 474948

Noel Kingsbury
18 Wellington Avenue, Montpelier, Bristol, Avon BS56 5HP

Tel/fax: 0117 9245602

Innovative design/consultancy for gardens large or small. Author of 'The New Perennial Garden' and 'Ultimate Planting Planner'.

North Surrey Landscapes
137 Upper Halliford Rd, Shepperton, Middlesex TW17 8SN

Contact: E D Bamforth
Tel: 01932 782863
Fax: 01932 785573

We provide a comprehensive landscaping service, including paving, planting, turfing, tree surgery and fencing, operating in West London, Surrey and Middlesex.

Original Terracotta Shop
8 Moorfield Road, Duxford Village, Cambridgeshire CB2 4PS

Tel/fax: 01223 832700

Experienced designer with creative ideas to solve your problems. Water features and unusual plants a speciality.

Otters Court Heathers
Back Street, West Camel, Yeovil, Somerset BA22 7QF

Contact: Mrs D H Jones
Tel/fax: 01935 850285

We specialise in a wide range of species for all soils and offer a design service. Send 3 x 1st class stamps for catalogue.

Oxford Garden Design Associates
The Corner House, Foxcombe Lane, Boars Hill, Oxfordshire OX1 5DH

Tel: 01865 735179
Fax: 01865 736604

A group of independent designers and landscapers who would be delighted to create a beautiful and individual garden for you.

P W Milne Atkinson
Landscape Architects, Hemington House, Hemington, Derby, Derbyshire DE74 2RB

Contact: Mrs P W Milne Atkinson FLI Dip Hort
Tel/fax: 01332 810295

Landscape architects giving a personal professional design and planning service for large/small projects, including business parks, estates, hospitals and industry. Also organising maintenance contracts.

Pathfinder Gardening
The Island, Wraysbury, Berkshire TW19 5AS

Tel: 01784 482677
Fax: 01784 482511

Contractors of Gold Medal gardens at Chelsea Flower Show. BALI members. Beautiful gardens expertly designed, created and maintained.

Patrick Butler
2 Whitehouse Cottage, The Street, Wickhambreaux, Canterbury, Kent CT3 1RJ

Tel/fax: 01227 721051

Paul Miles
43 Finlay Street, London SW6 6HE

Tel: 0171 371 7731
Fax: 0171 490 4417

Landscape and garden design, advice and garden restoration. Also available at 23 Seckford Street, Woodbridge, Suffolk IP12 4LY Phone 01394 383771.

Paul Norton Associates
6 Bayard Rd, Weymouth, Dorset DT3 6AJ

Tel/fax: 01305 832511

Landscape design with native plants and based on Feng Shui principles for a harmonious and beautiful environment.

Paul Temple Associates
24 Waldegrave Park, Twickenham, Middlesex TW1 4TQ

Contact: Paul Temple OBE, Fl Hort, F.SGD
Tel: 0181 744 0100
Fax: 0181 744 0104

Garden designer and advisor on construction and planting with many year's experience. Top awards Chelsea Show. Wide horticultural knowledge. Large and small gardens throughout UK.

Pelham Landscapes
27 Sun Street, Lewes, Sussex (E.) BN7 2QB

Contact: Sue Richards
Tel/fax: 01273 472408

Experienced, qualified garden/landscape design: plans fully measured/surveyed: detailed planting & construction advice: three hour sessions £75: average sized garden plan £500 minimum.

Penny Bennett Landscape Architects
8 High Peak, Blackstone Edge Old Rd, Littleborough, Lancashire OL15 0LQ

Contact: Penny Bennett
Tel: 01706 379378
Fax: 01706 371103

Garden design from £175. Practical & sensitive designs created to suit your consitions & requirementsa. Sketch layouts through to planting plan/construction details provided.

Petal Designs Ltd
76 Addison Rd, London W14 8EB

Tel: 0171 602 2599
Fax: 0171 602 7078

Peter Rogers Associates
Northdowns, Titsey Rd, Limpsfield, Surrey RH8 0DF

Tel/fax: 01883 715818

Practicality Brown Ltd
Iver Stud, Iver, Buckinghamshire SL0 9LA

Tel: 01753 652022
Fax: 01753 653007

PBL offers bulk supplies of bark and wood based mulches, the supply and planting of semi mature trees and relocating of existing semi mature trees.

Quartet Design
The Village School, Lillingstone Dayrell, Buckingham, Buckinghamshire MK18 5AP

Tel: 01280 860500
Fax: 01280 860468

Quartet Design places emphasis on high quality landscape and garden design. An imaginative design approach, personal service and practical experience create individual solutions.

Raw Talent Consultancy
56 Fordwater Rd, Chertsey, Surrey KT16 8HL

Tel: 01932 563613
Fax: 0171 976 5979

Ray Pitt Landscape Design
The Rest, Bradden Rd, Greens Norton, Towcester, Northamptonshire NN12 8BS

Tel/fax: 01327 350520

Robin Williams & Associates
Kennet House, 19 High Street, Hungerford, Berkshire RG17 0NL

Tel: 01488 686150
Fax: 01488 686124

Gold medal awards at Chelsea, Hampton Court and National Garden Festival. A bespoke design service is offered UK, Europe, USA suiting individual needs and budgets.

Robinson Penn Partnership
4th Floor, Cathedral Buildings, Dean Street, Newcastle upon Tyne, Tyne & Wear NE1 1PG

Tel: 0191 230 4339
Fax: 0191 230 5509

Roger Platts Garden Design
Faircombe, Maresfield, Sussex (E.) TN22 2EH

Contact: Roger Platts
Tel/fax: 01825 764077

A garden design and plants service including construction and planting. Handcrafted English oak pergolas and garden buildings in a traditional style. Chelsea Flower Show exhibitor.

Roof Garden Company Ltd
48 Carlingford Rd, Lower Morden, Surrey SM4 4NY

Tel/fax: 0181 330 1851

Rupert Golby
South View, Cross Hill Rd, Adderbury West, Banbury, Oxfordshire OX17 3EG

Tel/fax: 01295 810320

Sarah Massey - Landscape Designer
27 Chalgrove Road, Thame, Oxfordshire OX9 3TF

Tel/fax: 01844 215901

Tiny yards or rolling acres, transformed with an artist's eye. Consultancy and design service, UK and abroad. Alternative phone (London) 0181 458 1510.

Sarah Rycroft Landscape Architects
634 Wilmslow Rd, Didsbury, Manchester, Gt M20 3QX

Contact: Sarah Rycroft
Tel/fax: 0161 445 6375

The practice has considerable expertise, covering all aspects of landscape design, from the detailing of prestigious private gardens, through to high profile commercial developments.

Scottlandscape
78 Bousley Rise, Ottershaw, Surrey KT16 0LB

Contact: Robert Scott
Tel/fax: 01932 872667

Winners of Tudor Rose Award for best garden at Hampton Court Show 1992/1993/1994. Also RHS Gold Medal winners. All aspects of landscaping undertaken.

Secret Garden Designs
Fovant Hut, Fovant, Salisbury, Wiltshire SP3 5LN

Tel/fax: 01722 714756

Seven Counties Garden Design
143 Manor Green Rd, Epsom, Surrey KT19 8LL

Tel/fax: 01372 724660

Seymours Landscape Centre
Stoke Road, Stoke d'Abernon, Cobham, Surrey KT11 3PU

Contact: Chris Saunders
Tel: 01932 862530
Fax: 01932 862855

Gardens designed, constructed and planted to high standards. Founder BALI members. Hampton Court and RHS Chelsea Gold Awards for gardens. Also sales centre for all landscape materials to trade and retail customers.

Simon Richards & Associates
17 St Peters Rd, Cirencester, Gloucestershire GL7 1RE

Tel/fax: 01285 650828

Simpsons Nursery/ Landscaping & Tree Surgery
The Plant Nursery, High Street, Marsham, Norwich, Norfolk NR10 5QA

Contact: Gillian Simpson
Tel/fax: 01263 733432

A qualified horticultural family business growing unusual, interesting, good quality, reasonably priced plants. Sympathetic garden designs and landscaping service to suit customers' requirements. Professional advice.

Smeeden Foreman Partnership
14-15 Regent Parade, Harrogate, Yorkshire (N.) HD1 5AJ

Contact: Mark Smeeden ALI MI Hort
Tel: 01423 520222
Fax: 01423 525543

Landscape design, planning and management.

The Daily Telegraph *Green Fingers*   Design & Landscaping

Society of Garden Designers
6 Borough Rd,
Kingston-upon-Thames, Surrey
KT2 6BD

Contact: Sue Moller
Tel/fax: 0181 974 9483

The Society promotes high standards in garden design, recommending SGD-approved designers, courses and offering nationwide workshops and seminars. Send DL S.A.E. to Society Secretary.

Sol Jordens
Stocksbridge House, Coombe Bissett, Salisbury, Wiltshire SP5 4LZ

Tel/fax: 01722 77573

Song of the Earth
218 West Malvern Road, West Malvern, Hereford & Worcester WR14 4BA

Contact: Fiona Hopes
Tel/fax: 01684 892533

Individual and special gardens, created by a qualified and experienced designer, working with the subtle energies of the land to create sustainable landscapes that are ecologically sound, practical, productive and beautiful.

Sonya Millman Garden Design
53 Maidenhead Rd, Stratford upon Avon, Warwickshire CV37 6XU

Contact: Sonya Millman
Tel/fax: 01789 414237

Distinctive, practical designs and planting schemes created for town or country, domestic or commercial sites, for DIY or professional implementation. A comprehensive, professional service.

Stella Caws Associates
Stratheden, 4 Hardwick Hill, Chepstow, Gwent NP6 5PN

Contact: Stella Caws
Tel/fax: 01291 626645

Elegant designs for contemporary gardens and landscapes. Practical, economic, environmental and easy care. Gold and silver-gilt medal winners. Fifteen years experience. Consultations or full design service.

Sue de Bock Rowles Garden Design
15 Ruden Way, Epsom Downs, Surrey KT17 3LL

Contact: Sue de Bock Rowles
Tel: 01737 353898
Fax: 01737 371887

Design and landscaping gardens of all shapes and sizes in the Southern Home Counties.

Sue Hedger-Brown Landscape Architect
14 St Peters Close, Charsfield, Woodbridge, Suffolk IP13 7RG

Tel/fax: 01505 470762

Sue Pack Garden Design
9 Rudchesters, Bancroft, Milton Keynes, Buckinghamshire MK13 0PH

Contact: Sue Pack
Tel/fax: 01908 317029

Sue Pack provides innovative yet practical design solutions for projects of any size. The comprehensive design package includes survey, design, construction details and planting plan.

Susan Buckley
124 Ashton Lane, Sale, Cheshire M33 5QJ

Tel/fax: 0161 905 2327

Lanscape architect providing personal service to variety of clients in North West. Wide range of projects undertaken in all aspects of landscape planning, design and implementation.

Sutton Griffin & Morgan
Albion House, Oxford Street, Newbury, Berkshire RG13 1JE

Tel: 01635 521100
Fax: 01635 44188

Teamwork Landscaping
Myrtle Cottage, Knellers Lane, Totton, Southampton, Hampshire SO4 2EB

Contact: John & Linden Kuyser
Tel/fax: 01703 871919

Garden designers and contractors. A family-based, efficient business offering a comprehensive personal but professional horticultural service.

Tony Benger Landscaping
Burrow Farm Gardens, Dalwood, Axminster, Devon EX13 7ET

Contact: Tony Benger
Tel/fax: 01404 831844

Established family business, specialist in high quality private and commercial landscaping. Design, construction and maintenance. We are small enough to care, large enough to cope.

Topiarist
26 Bramshaw Rise, New Malden, Surrey KT3 5JU

Contact: Simon Rose
Tel: 0181 942 1502
Fax: 0181 330 0464

Topiarist, Simon Rose, will supply, plant and maintain hedges, parterres and specimens. Restoration and pruning of established plants. General landscaping to highest standard.

Town & Country Gardens
1 Hilltop Cottage, Southwell Road, Thurgarton, Nottinghamshire NG14 7GP

Tel/fax: 01636 830756

Full landscaping and design service. General maintenance and clearance. Small or large jobs. Competitive quote. Nottinghamshire area.

Tricia McPherson
Sunny Bank Cottage, Stock Green, Hereford & Worcester B96 6TA

Tel/fax: 01386 793208

Veronica Adams Garden Design
Lower Hopton Farm, Stoke Lacy, Bromyard, Hereford & Worcester HR7 4HX

Tel/fax: 01885 490294

Garden design - English country gardens for English country houses.

Veronica Ross Landscape Design
Bearfold, Ordie, Dinnet, Aberdeenshire, Grampian AB34 5LS

Contact: Veronica Ross BA DipLD ALI
Tel/fax: 013398 81651

The practice offers a personal service in the consultation with owners: survey, assessment, design and supervision on site for garden landscapes.

Victor A Shanley
6 Eastry Avenue, Hayes, Bromley, Kent BR2 7PF

Tel: 0181 462 1864
Fax: 0181 462 0988

Water Meadow Design & Landscape
Water Meadow Nursery, Cheriton, Alresford, Hampshire SO24 0QB

Contact: Roy Worth
Tel/fax: 01962 771895

From city courtyards to country estates, distinctive designs to suit individual tastes. Competitive rates for consultation only, design, planting plans, or complete landscape.

Waterers Landscape Ltd
Nursery Court, London Rd, Windlesham, Surrey GU20 6LQ

Tel/fax: 01344 28081

Wendy Wright Landscape & Garden Design
29 Lurline Gardens, London SW11 4DB

Wilkinsons
East Brocks Farm, Eaglescliffe, Stockton on Tees, Cleveland TS16 0QH

Tel: 01642 790409
Fax: 01642 780372

Wreford Landscapes
Pucknall Farm, Dores Lane, Braishfield, Romsey, Hampshire SO51 0QJ

Contact: Simon Wreford
Tel: 01794 368155
Fax: 01794 368218

Landscape design and construction for town houses to country manors. Commercial and business developments throughout southern England.

FENCING, TRELLISWORK, GATES & PERGOLAS

Agriframes
Charlwoods Rd, East Grinstead, Sussex (E.) RH19 2HG
Tel: 01342 328644
Fax: 01342 327233

Mail order company specialising in pergolas, arches, obelisks etc and plant protection. Servicing the general public, garden centres and export.
Catalogue; Mail order

Allan Calder
14 Regents Street, Leek, Staffordshire ST13 6LU
Tel/fax: 01538 387738

Catalogue; Mail order

Bridges Decorative Metalwork
Ditchford Farm,
Moreton-in-Marsh,
Gloucestershire GL56 9RD
Tel: 01608 662348
Fax: 01608 663512

Cannock Gates Ltd
Martindale, Hawks Green, Cannock, Staffordshire WS11 2XT
Tel/fax: 0800 462500

UK's leading manufacturer of wrought iron and timber gates and garden products. For your free catalogue Freephone 0800 462500.
Catalogue

Ceramica UK
Unit 17A Hillend Rd, Delph, Oldham, Lancashire OL3 5JA
Tel/fax: 01457 876583

Fence protector clamp. Reduces wind damage/rattling and corrects loosely fitting panels. Prolongs fence life and allows wood to contract/expand - easy to fit.
Catalogue; Mail order

Chilstone
Victoria Park, Fordcombe Road, Langton Green, Tunbridge Wells, Kent TN3 0RE
Tel: 01892 740866
Fax: 01892 740867

Handmade reconstituted stone - birdbaths, sundials, fountains, urns, statues, balustrading, seats, temples - all in classical style. Show gardens 1 hour from London. Catalogue available.
Catalogue; Mail order

Classic Gates
2 Holman Rd, Oaklands Farm Industrial Est, Liskeard, Cornwall PL14 3UR
Tel/fax: 01579 344388

Manufacturers of gates, railings and ornamental ironwork. Handbuilt in Cornwall. Direct from factory prices. Please send for free brochure and price list.
Catalogue; Mail order

D W Woodward & Son
Kiama, Windy Ridge Farm, Kirby Bellars, Melton Mowbray, Leicestershire LE14 2TH
Tel/fax: 01664 840700

Dextroplast Ltd
Old Great North Rd,
Sutton-on-Trent, Newark, Nottinghamshire NG23 6QL
Contact: W G Baker
Tel: 01636 821226
Fax: 01636 822101

We supply a range of PVC fencing and gates in three different styles. Ranch, picket and post & chain. Sizes 18in to 6ft high.
Mail order

English Hurdle Centre
Curload, Stoke St Gregory, Taunton, Somerset TA3 6JD
Tel: 01823 698418
Fax: 01823 698859

Woven willow hurdles and garden products.
Catalogue; Mail order

Forest Fencing Ltd
Stanford Court, Stanford Bridge, Worcester, Hereford & Worcester WR6 6SR
Tel/fax: 01886 812451
Catalogue

Frolics of Winchester
82 Cannon St, Winchester, Hampshire SO23 9JQ
Contact: Robert Dick-Read
Tel: 01962 856384
Fax: 01962 844896

Furniture made from hardwood and Medex painted any colour. Ornamental trelliswork cut from solid sheets. Infinite design range. Custom work undertaken. Many stock trompe-l'oeil designs.
Catalogue

Gate-A-Mation Ltd
Unit 8, Boundary Business Centre, Boundary Way, Woking, Surrey GU21 5DH
Tel: 01483 747373
Fax: 01483 776688

Quality intsallations and service associated with the design, supply and installation of automatic gate, door and barrier systems. Full literature pack is available on request.
Catalogue

Greenoak Gates
Furse Cottage East, Crowhurst Lane, Crowhurst, Nr Oxted, Surrey RH8 9NU
Contact: Mr P Devismes
Tel/fax: 01342 893553

Bespoke outdoor timber manufacturers, specialising in the design of timber gates of all sizes to suit customers' specific requirements.
Catalogue; Mail order

Jacksons Fine Fencing
8 Stowting Common, Ashford, Kent TN25 6BN
Tel/fax: 0800 414343
Catalogue

Jungle Giants Bamboo Growers
Plough Farm, Wigmore, Leominster, Hereford & Worcester HR6 9UW
Tel: 01568 86708
Fax: 01568 86383

Bamboo specialists. Growers of 150 hardy species. Also large diameter construction cane, bamboo screens, fences and gates. Wholesale and retail. Bamboo information pack send £5.75.
Catalogue; Mail order

Lemar Wrought Iron
Harrowbrook Industrial Estate, Hinckley, Leicestershire LE10 3DJ
Tel/fax: 01455 637077 (24hrs)
Catalogue

Lloyd Christie
1 New Kings Rd, London SW6 4SB
Contact: Tony Christie
Tel: 0171 731 3484
Fax: 0171 371 9952

Lloyd Christie designs, manufactures and installs trellis, decking, planters, arbours, rose arches, pergolas and conservatories. Please call for an appointment or brochure.
Catalogue

M C Products
Home Farm Cliffe, Piercebridge, Darlington, Co Durham DL2 3SS
Tel/fax: 01325 374676
Catalogue

Metpost Ltd
Mardy Rd, Cardiff, Glamorgan (S.) CF3 8EX
Tel: 01222 777877
Fax: 01222 779295

Manufacturers of metal/timber post supports for garden fencing. Also produce a range of trellis products made from 80% recycled polystyrene which requires no maintenance.
Catalogue

Podington Garden Centre
High Street, Podington, Wellingborough, Northamptonshire NN29 7HS
Contact: Colin Read
Tel: 01933 53656
Fax: 01933 410332

A plant person's paradise with thousands of plants all year round. Also a wide range of garden sundries, furniture, aquatics, garden ornaments, fencing and paving.

Rob Turner
Unit 16, Moores Yard, High Street, Statham, Norfolk NR12 9AN
Tel/fax: 01692 580091
Catalogue

Roger Platts Garden Design
Faircombe, Maresfield, Sussex
(E.) TN22 2EH
Contact: Roger Platts
Tel/fax: 01825 764077

A garden design and plants service including construction and planting. Handcrafted English oak pergolas and garden buildings in a traditional style. Chelsea Flower Show exhibitor.
Mail order

Samsons
Edwin Avenue, Hoo Farm Industrial Estate, Kidderminster, Hereford & Worcester DY1 7RA
Tel: 01562 825252
Fax: 01562 820380
Catalogue; Mail order

Sentinel Garden Products
PO Box 119, Shepcote Lane, Tinsley, Sheffield, Yorkshire (S.) S9 1TY
Tel: 0114 2562020
Fax: 0114 2610157

Seymours Garden & Leisure Group
The Pit House, Ewell By-Pass, Surrey KT17 1PS
Contact: James Seymour
Tel: 0181 393 0111
Fax: 0181 393 0237

Landscape and leisure centre with aquatics, landscape supplies, garden leisure departments and coffee shop under same ownership as Peters Plants and Garden Centre at Cobham (01932 862530).

Sparkford Sawmills Ltd
Sparkford, Nr Yeovil, Somerset BA22 7LH
Tel: 01963 440414
Fax: 01963 440982

We manufacture a wide range of quality timber gates, fencing and buildings to suit customers' requirements, complete with a full design, build and nationwide installation service.

Stuart Garden Architecture
Burrow Hill Farm, Wiveliscombe, Somerset TA4 2RN
Tel: 01984 667458
Fax: 01984 667455

Architectural garden features manufactured in hardwood using traditional mortice and tenon construction. Products are individually designed or created from the Modular systems. Catalogue available.
Catalogue; Mail order

Trelliscope
Oak View, Chard Street, Axminster, Devon EX13 5EB
Tel/fax: 01297 35735

West Country Ironcraft
6 Beechwood, Bridgwater, Somerset TA6 6JQ
Tel/fax: 01278 453782

Quality wrought ironwork. Mail order from free brochure or view at our workshop. Local fitting service. Topcoat painting available. Specialist commission work undertaken.
Catalogue; Mail order

FURNITURE

Acorn
The Manor, Hinton in the Hedges, Brackley, Northamptonshire NN13 5WE
Tel/fax: 01280 706813

Allibert Garden Furniture
Berry Hill Industrial Estate, Droitwich, Hereford & Worcester WR9 9AB
Tel: 01905 795796
Fax: 01905 794454

Alton Garden Centre
Arterial Rd, Wickford, Essex SS12 9JG
Tel: 01268 726421
Fax: 01268 590825

Andrew Crace Designs
21 Bourne Lane, Much Hadham, Hertfordshire SG10 6ER
Tel: 01279 842685
Fax: 01279 843646

Apcon Garden Products
Unit 5b, Gerston Farm, Greyfriars Lane, Storrington, Sussex (W.) RH20 4HE
Tel/fax: 01903 850196
Catalogue; Mail order

Ashley-Morris Garden Furniture
The Old Ice Cream Works, Bowness-on-Windermere, Cumbria LA23 3AU
Tel: 015394 47919
Fax: 015394 47918

Ashworth Leisure Ltd
Sycamore Avenue, Burnley, Lancashire BB12 6QR
Tel: 01282 425901
Fax: 01282 416465

Imaginatively designed and skilfully manufactured furniture, using traditional designs and the best modern materials. Available in a range of colours. Phone for brochure. (See page vi).
Catalogue

Attwoolls Tents Ltd
Whitminster, Gloucestershire GL2 7LX
Tel/fax: 01452 740278

Barlow Tyrie Ltd
Braintree, Essex CM7 2RN
Tel: 01376 003251
Fax: 01376 347052

Comprehensive range of fine teak outdoor furniture. Made in England with care, craftsmanship and over 75 years of experience. Barlow Tyrie, The English Garden Tradition. (See our full colour advertisement on page i).

Barnsley House Garden Furniture
Barnsley House, Cirencester, Gloucestershire GL7 5EE
Contact: Charles Verey
Tel: 01285 740561
Fax: 01285 740628

Charles Verey's classic teak furniture and Regency wrought iron. Catalogue free by post. Showroom at Rosemary Verey's Barnsley House Garden open Mon/Wed/Thurs/Sat.

Bolingbroke
Rectory Lodge, The Fairland, Higham, Norfolk NR9 4HU
Tel/fax: 01953 850197

Bramley Ltd
Crittall Drive, Braintree, Essex CM7 7RT
Tel: 01376 320210
Fax: 01376 327811

Capital Gardens - Four Garden Centres in London
1 Townsend Yard, Highgate High Street, London N6 5JF
Contact: Nicola Gray
Tel: 0181 348 5054
Fax: 0181 342 8578

A mail order service offering full range of garden products including furniture available at Capital Garden Centres. All major credit cards accepted. Please telephone for assistance.
Mail order

Chatsworth Carpenters
Estate Office, Edensor, Bakewell, Derbyshire DE45 1PJ
Tel: 01246 582242
Fax: 01246 583464

Chilstone
Victoria Park, Fordcombe Road, Langton Green, Tunbridge Wells, Kent TN3 0RE
Tel: 01892 740866
Fax: 01892 740867

Handmade reconstituted stone - birdbaths, sundials, fountains, urns, statues, balustrading, seats, temples - all in classical style. Show gardens 1 hour from London. Catalogue available.
Catalogue; Mail order

Country Style
Units 2 & 3, Second Avenue, Millwey Rise, Axminster, Devon EX13 5HH
Tel: 01297 35735
Fax: 01297 33550

David Craig
Units 10-11, Langley Moor Industrial Estate, Langley Moor, Co Durham DH7 8JE
Tel/fax: 0191 386 0384

We manufacture and design beautiful garden furniture. Tables, benches, chairs, loungers, planters and parasols.
Catalogue

English Classics
Teak House, Harbour Road, Rye, Sussex (E.) TN31 7TE
Tel: 01797 225101
Fax: 01797 226171

Our hand made teak garden and conservatory furniture is constructed from the most generous sections of timber available and will not be found elsewhere.
Catalogue

Frolics of Winchester
82 Cannon St, Winchester, Hampshire SO23 9JQ
Contact: Robert Dick-Read
Tel: 01962 856384
Fax: 01962 844896

Furniture made from hardwood and Medex painted any colour. Ornamental trelliswork cut from solid sheets. Infinite design range. Custom work undertaken. Many stock trompe-l'oeil designs.
Catalogue

GardenGlow
Clay Lane, South Nutfield, Redhill, Surrey RH1 4EG
Contact: Philip Abraham
Tel: 01737 822562
Fax: 01737 822472
Email: pac@gardengl.demon.co.uk

Hand crafted hardwood furniture from managed reserves. Competitively priced. Range of Versailles and rustic planters available.
Catalogue; Mail order

Gaze Burvill Ltd
Plain Farm, Old Dairy, East Tisted, Hampshire GU34 3RT
Contact: Simon Burvill
Tel: 01420 587467
Fax: 01420 587354

Manufacturers of a unique collection of oak garden furniture distinguished by its comfort, simplicity and strength. Deliveries worldwide. Colour brochure on request. Visits by appointment.
Catalogue; Mail order

Gloster Leisure Furniture
D-Scan (UK) Ltd, Concorde Rd, Patchway, Bristol, Avon BS12 5TB
Tel: 0117 315355
Fax: 0117 315334
Catalogue

Grandad's Garden
Broyle Mill Farm, The Broyle, Ringmer, Sussex (E.) BN8 5AR
Tel/fax: 01273 813429
Catalogue

Greenes Garden Furniture
Lower Farm House, Preston Crowmarsh, Wallingford, Oxfordshire OX10 6SL
Tel/fax: 01491 825519
Catalogue

Hall Farm Products
Harpswell, Gainsborough, Lincolnshire DN21 5UU
Contact: Pam Tatam
Tel/fax: 01427 668412

We offer a range of Victorian-style, wrought iron and wood garden furniture. We also make gates, arches, gazebos etc. to order.
Catalogue; Mail order

Hamptons Leisure
Freepost (GL56), Wotton under Edge, Gloucestershire GL12 8ES
Contact: Roger Emery
Tel: 01453 842889
Fax: 01453 843938

Hamptons offer a complete collection of quality garden furniture in teak hardwood and cast aluminium as well as a large range of hammocks and umbrellas.
Catalogue; Mail order

Heritage Woodcraft
Unit 5, Shelley Farm, Ower, Romsey, Hampshire SO51 6AS
Contact: David Smith
Tel/fax: 01703 814145

Handmade hardwood garden furniture, traditional wooden wheelbarrows, gazebos. All products made on premises. Commissions for furniture, garden features accepted. Mail order and catalogue available.
Catalogue; Mail order

Heveningham Collection
Weston Down, Weston Colley, Micheldever, Winchester, Hampshire SO21 2AQ
Contact: Annie Eadie
Tel: 01962 774990
Fax: 01962 774790

A collection of elegant iron furniture for both interior and exterior use. Designs range from luxury chaise longues, dining tables and chairs to Versailles tubs.
Catalogue; Mail order

High Cross Joinery
Sutes Farm, High Cross, Ware, Hertfordshire SG11 1BE
Contact: Mr Russell Parkins
Tel: 01920 466522
Fax: 01920 463480

Manufacturers of teak and iroko garden furniture of the highest quality at affordable prices. Full colour brochure available. Mail order specialist.
Catalogue; Mail order

Indian Ocean Trading Company
155-163 Balham Hill, London SW12 9DJ
Contact: Roger A Harlow
Tel: 0181 675 4808
Fax: 0181 675 4652

Over 200 classic and contemporary designs of high quality teak garden furniture. Visit our London or Chester showrooms, or call for a free colour brochure.
Catalogue; Mail order

Ironart of Bath
61 Walcot Street, Bath, Avon BA1 5BN
Tel/fax: 01225 446107
Catalogue

Jardine International Ltd
Rosemount Tower, Wallington Square, Wallington, Surrey SM6 8RR
Contact: P R B Slater
Tel: 0181 647 5108
Fax: 0181 669 8281

Cast aluminium garden tables, chairs, benches. Corrosive free, powder coated green/white, virtually indestructible. Range of hardwood furniture. All flat-packed, assembly quick and simple.
Mail order

Jardiniere
26A Priory Road, Hampton, Middlesex TW12 2NT
Contact: Brian Bird
Tel/fax: 0181 979 1880

Supply and hire of urns, pots & containers, olive oil jars, furniture, garden implements - antique, period or just plain intriguing. For exterior or interior decoration.

Jopasco Shade Umbrellas
Unit 1, Trident Industrial Estate, Blackthorne Road, Colnbrook, Berkshire SL3 0AX
Tel: 01753 680858
Fax: 01753 680223

Julian Chichester Designs
27 Parsons Green Lane, London SW6 4HH
Tel: 0171 371 9055
Fax: 0171 371 9066
Catalogue

Kiddie Wise
PO Box 433, Leek, Staffordshire ST13 7TZ
Tel: 01538 304235
Fax: 01538 304575

Children's timber play equipment for the larger garden. 20 page catalogue of swings, climbers, playhouses and sandpits in treated Norwegian deal.
Catalogue; Mail order

King Easton Ltd
The Green, Station Rd, Winchmore Hill, London N21 3NB
Tel: 0181 886 8783
Fax: 0181 882 2685
Catalogue

ENGLISH CLASSICS
Teak House, Harbour Road, Rye, East Sussex TN31 7TE
Telephone: (01797) 225101 Fax: (01797) 226171

English Classics are one of the few manufacturers of teak garden and conservatory furniture still handcrafting our furniture in our own work shops in England.

All our furniture is made to the same exacting standards of craftsmanship as found in the Victorian and Edwardian era. All our joints are morticed and tenoned and teak dowels are used for extra strength. All our fittings are brass and each piece is finished to the highest standard.

Choose from our standard collection or we can design your furniture to your own specifications.

For more details, contact our office for our **free** brochure or visit our showroom in picturesque Rye.

The William and Mary Folding Seat

Lister Teak Garden Furniture
South Rd, Hailsham, Sussex (E.)
BN27 3DT
Tel: 01323 840771
Fax: 01323 440109

Matthew Eden
Pickwick End, Corsham,
Wiltshire SN13 0JB
Tel: 01249 713335
Fax: 01249 713644
Catalogue; Mail order

Michael Hill Garden Furniture
Cressy Hall, Cawood Lane,
Gosberton, Spalding, Lincolnshire
PE11 4JD
Contact: Michael Hill
Tel: 01775 840925
Fax: 01775 840008

Cast iron garden furniture. Exact copies of the very best antique designs cast in sand and hand finished in the traditional way.
Catalogue

Montezumas
9 Oak Rd, Ealing, London W5 3SS
Tel: 0181 579 6293
Fax: 0181 566 2758
Catalogue

New England Gardens Ltd
22 Middle Street, Ashcott,
Somerset TA7 9QB
Tel/fax: 01458 210821
Catalogue; Mail order

Ollerton Engineering
Goosefoot Lane, Samlesbury
Bottoms, Preston, Lancashire
PR5 0RN
Tel: 01254 852127
Fax: 01254 854383

Oryx Trading Ltd
20 Roseneath Rd, London
SW11 6AH
Tel: 0171 938 2045
Fax: 0171 937 9087
Catalogue

Oxleys Garden Furniture
Lapstone Barn, Westington Hill,
Chipping Campden,
Gloucestershire GL55 6UR
Tel/fax: 01386 840466

Manufacturers of the finest solid cast aluminium furniture. Handmade in a variety of beautiful weatherproof finshes. Visitors are welcome at our lovely Cotswold premises.
Catalogue; Mail order

P J Bridgman & Company Ltd
Barnbridge Works, Lockfield
Ave, Brimsdown, Enfield,
Middlesex EN3 7PX
Tel: 0181 804 7474
Fax: 0181 805 0873
Catalogue

Pamal
The Cottage, Sproxton, Melton
Mowbray, Leicestershire LE14 4QS
Contact: M Graham
Tel: 01476 860266
Fax: 01476 860523

Manufacturers of timber outdoor furniture, planters, standard size or made to order, painted or natural wood. Catalogue available.
Catalogue; Mail order

Patterson Products
Unit 1, Frogs Leap Farm, Philpot
Lane, Chobham, Surrey GU24 8HE
Tel: 01276 855821
Fax: 01276 855796

Pepe Garden Furniture
Burhill, Buckland, Broadway,
Hereford & Worcester
WR12 7LY
Tel: 01386 858842
Fax: 01386 852883

Range of garden furniture made of pressure treated Baltic pine. Most popular are 2 and 3 seater swings. New lines include tree seats and folding table and chairs.
Catalogue; Mail order

Podington Garden Centre
High Street, Podington,
Wellingborough,
Northamptonshire NN29 7HS
Contact: Colin Read
Tel: 01933 53656
Fax: 01933 410332

A plant person's paradise with thousands of plants all year round. Also a wide range of garden sundries, furniture, aquatics, garden ornaments, fencing and paving.

Rayment Wirework
The Forge, Durlock, Minster,
Thanet, Kent CT12 4HE
Tel/fax: 01843 821628
Catalogue; Mail order

Rovergarden
152 Ewell Rd, Surbiton, Surrey
KT6 6HE
Tel: 0181 399 3699
Fax: 0181 390 3524

Rovergarden offer a range of quality furniture in resin, iroko wood and weatherproof wicker, also a wide selection of upholstery. Free retail catalogue available.
Catalogue

Rusco
Little Faringdon Mill, Lechlade,
Gloucestershire GL7 3QQ
Tel: 01367 252754
Fax: 01367 253406

The Garden Gate Collection from Rusco includes large Italian umbrellas, American hammocks and stands and both teak and wrought iron furniture. Catalogue free on request.
Catalogue

Sarah Burgoyne Revivals
Whyly, East Hoathly, Sussex (E.)
BN8 6EL
Tel/fax: 01825 840738

Seymours Garden & Leisure Group
The Pit House, Ewell By-Pass,
Surrey KT17 1PS
Contact: James Seymour
Tel: 0181 393 0111
Fax: 0181 393 0237

Landscape and leisure centre with aquatics, landscape supplies, garden leisure departments and coffee shop under same ownership as Peters Plants and Garden Centre at Cobham (01932 862530).

Skyshades
59 St Mars Street, Wallingford,
Oxfordshire OX10 0EL
Tel: 01491 834003
Fax: 01491 825452
Catalogue; Mail order

Stangwrach Leisure Products
Stangwrach, Llanfynydd,
Camarthen, Dyfed SA32 7TG
Tel/fax: 01558 668287

Stephenson Blake
199 Upper Allen Street,
Sheffield, Yorkshire (S.) S3 7GW
Tel: 0114 2728325
Fax: 0114 2720065
Catalogue; Mail order

Stuart Garden Architecture
Burrow Hill Farm, Wiveliscombe,
Somerset TA4 2RN
Tel: 01984 667458
Fax: 01984 667455

Folding and classical garden furniture manufactured in hardwood. Very individual designs and extremely high quality finish. Catalogue available.

Studio Forge
London Rd, Offham, Lewes,
Sussex (E.) BN7 3QD
Tel/fax: 01273 474173

Teak Tiger Trading Company
Sudbury, Suffolk CO10 8YZ
Tel: 01787 880900
Fax: 01787 880906

Teak garden furniture for outdoor and conservatory use. The collection includes benches, chairs, tables and loungers. Delivered to your home. Colour brochure available.
Mail order

Trading Bonsai
81 Bruntsfield Place, Edinburgh,
Lothian EH10 4HG
Contact: Alison Currie
Tel/fax: 0131 229 0539

Trading Bonsai Ltd offers a unique range of hand-crafted oriental furniture and collectable wooden artefacts.

Witbourne Ltd
Upperton Farmhouse, 2 Enys Rd,
Eastbourne, Sussex (E.) BN21 2DE
Tel: 01323 720288
Fax: 01323 730144

GREENHOUSES, SHEDS & ACCESSORIES

Access Garden Products
17 Yelvertoft Rd, Crick,
Northampton,
Northamptonshire NN6 7XS
Tel: 01788 822301
Fax: 01788 824256

Access Garden Products is the country's leading manufacturer of quality garden frames and mini greenhouses for sale by mail order. Extensively used by professional and leading gardeners throughout the country, all products are available with a wide range of accessories.
Catalogue; Mail order

Alibench
Wimbish, Saffron Walden, Essex
CB10 2XL
Tel/fax: 01799 599230

Alispeed
Unit B4, Horton Wood 10,
Telford, Shropshire TF1 4ES
Contact: J A Ford
Tel: 01952 677775
Fax: 01952 676919

Beautiful aluminium-framed greenhouses in two-tone colour finishes. Frames guaranteed 20 years. Also staging, shelving and other equipment.
Catalogue; Mail order

Alite Metals
Baynton Rd, Ashton, Bristol,
Avon BS3 2EB
Tel/fax: 0117 639872
Catalogue

Alitex - The Glasshouse Company
Station Rd, Alton, Hampshire
GU34 2PZ
Contact: Mike Wallis
Tel: 01420 82860
Fax: 01420 541097

Manufacturers of elegant made-to-measure glasshouses. Our product flexibility ranges from cold frames to large kitchen garden glasshouses. All structures are constructed to order on site and are supported by a practical range of horticultural accessories such as external shading, Victorian style benching, heaters and internal reservoirs. For a brochure and further details please phone or fax. (See our full colour advertisement on page iv).
Catalogue

Alton Greenhouses
Station Works, Fenny Compton,
Leamington Spa, Warwickshire
CV33 0XB
Contact: Grahame Lester
Tel: 01295 770795
Fax: 01295 770819

Alton is the acknowledged leading range of cedarwood greenhouses. Call our FREEPHONE 0800 269850 for a free colour brochure, price list and list of our 150 retailers throughout the country.
Catalogue; Mail order

Andmore Designs Ltd
10 Brunel Gate, West Portway,
Andover, Hampshire SP10 3SL
Tel/fax: 01264 356464
Catalogue

Archwood Greenhouses
Robinswood, Goodrich,
Hereford & Worcester HR9 6HT
Tel/fax: 01600 890125

Compost systems. Robust pressure preserved timber to BS4072 (Type 1), 2ft., 3ft. or 4ft. square bins. Removable front boards. Felt covered lids.
Catalogue; Mail order

Arunfabs Ltd
3 Hazelwood Trading Estate,
Worthing, Sussex (W.)
Tel: 01903 212306
Fax: 01903 212307

Backwoodsman Horticultural Products
Barcaldine, Oban, Argyll,
Strathclyde PA37 1SL
Contact: Andrew McIntyre
Tel/fax: 01631 720539

Manufacturer of Growmate - an innovative pyramid greenhouse that can raise up to 2,000 bedding plants in a space just 5' in diameter. Free brochure on request.
Catalogue; Mail order

Baxters Ltd
201-203 Cleethorpe Rd,
Grimsby, Humberside DN31 3BE
Tel/fax: 01472 343989

Leading supplier by mail order of soil warming, mist propagation, heating, ventilating and watering equipment. Phone or write for free catalogue. Established over 100 years.
Catalogue; Mail order

Bayliss Precision Components Ltd
Lysander Works, Blenheim Rd,
Ashbourne, Derbyshire DE6 1HA
Contact: Andrew Garside
Tel: 01335 342981
Fax: 01335 343860

Manufacturers and suppliers of automatic non-electric window openers for greenhouses and conservatories. Free illustrated brochure available on request.
Catalogue; Mail order

Bernilight
Wansbeck House, 295 Elswick
Rd, Newcastle upon Tyne, Tyne
& Wear NE4 8DL
Tel: 0191 273 0750
Fax: 0191 272 3199

Manufacturers of growlights, supplying retail and trade outlets. Catalogue of standard products available direct to the public.
Catalogue; Mail order

Cambridge Glasshouse Company Ltd
Barton Rd, Comberton,
Cambridge, Cambridgeshire CB3 7BY
Tel: 01223 262395
Fax: 01223 262713

Robust aluminium greenhouses, complete with accessories. Vast range of sizes. Choice of colours. Send now for a free catalogue and price list.
Catalogue; Mail order

Cheshire Aluminium
Unit 2 Beech Court, Taylor
Business Park, Risley, Derbyshire
WA3 6BL
Tel/fax: 01925 762888
Mail order

Citadel Products
10 Castle Rd, Kineton, Warwick,
Warwickshire CV35 0HY
Tel/fax: 01926 640196

Manufacturers of polytunnel greenhouses for over 20 years. Quality frames, variety of covers. Easy assembly. Free brochure. (Factory visits by appointment only please).
Catalogue; Mail order

Easilok
Valley Rd Industrial Estate,
Porters Wood, St Albans,
Hertfordshire AL3 6PQ
Tel/fax: 01727 847055

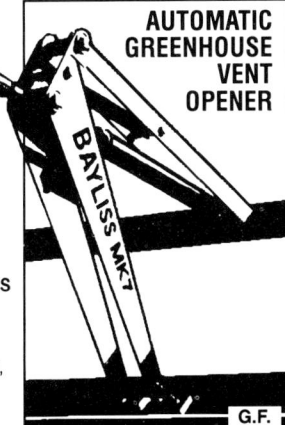

AUTOMATIC GREENHOUSE VENT OPENER

The Bayliss range of Autovents opens and closes greenhouse vents automatically without the need for electricity.
- EASY TO FIT
- EASY TO SET
- LOSES NO HEADROOM
- BRITISH MADE
- TEMPERATURE CONTROLLED
- GIVES VENTILATION WHEN YOU NEED IT
- GUARANTEED FOR TWO YEARS

Bayliss Precision Components Ltd
Lysander Works, Blenheim Road,
Airfield Ind. Est. Ashbourne,
Derbyshire DE6 1HA.
Telephone: 01335 342981

Easy Pot Staging
1 Edward Garden, Wickford, Essex SS11 7EH
Tel/fax: 01268 762272
Catalogue; Mail order

Eden Greenhouses
Carr Gate, Wakefield, Yorkshire (W.)
Tel/fax: 01924 829754

Edward Owen Engineering Ltd
C House, Stanhope Rd, Camberley, Surrey GU15 3BW
Contact: N Dangerfield
Tel: 01276 62262
Fax: 01276 692368

Manufacturers of high quality greenhouses and accessories. The greenhouses have extra large vents and a sealed glazing system. More light, more air, less heat loss.
Catalogue; Mail order

Essentials
13 Starling Close, Longfield, Kent DA3 7NP
Tel/fax: 01474 708693

The original bubble greenhouse insulation kit complete with clips. 8ft x 6ft greenhouse £15.99. Other sizes available.
Mail order

Excalibur (UK) Ltd
PO Box 37, Newtown, Powys SY17 5ZZ
Tel/fax: 01686 623174

Polytunnel greenhouses and replacement polythene covers available at low cost. Free brochure.

Ferryman Polytunnels
Bridge Road, Lapford, Crediton, Devon EX17 6AE
Contact: H L Briant-Evans
Tel: 01363 83444
Fax: 01363 83050

Manufacturers of polytunnel greenhouses and portable crop covers suitable for gardeners and professional growers. Despatch in easy-to-build kits. Free colour brochure available.
Catalogue; Mail order

First Tunnels
Mill Street, Barrowford, Lancashire B89 6EU
Tel/fax: 01282 601253

Specialists in domestic and commercial poly greenhouses plus a wide range of garden sundries. Contact us for a free, no obligation brochure.
Catalogue; Mail order

Fletcher-Green Horticulture
PO Box 605, Harrow, Middlesex HA2 9LZ
Tel: 0181 864 2138
Fax: 0181 864 2552

Garden Relax Ltd
PO Box 4, Henlow, Bedfordshire SG16 6LT
Tel/fax: 04162 814244
Catalogue

Garden Rewards
104 Branbridges Rd, East Peckham, Kent TN12 5HH
Tel/fax: 01622 871359
Catalogue

Greenhouses Direct
PO Box 290, Sawston, Cambridgeshire CB2 4TL
Tel: 01763 263358
Fax: 01763 261588

UK's leading mail order supplier. Huge range including octagonals, lean-to's and safety glazing. Guaranteed lowest prices. Write or telephone for free colour brochure/price list.
Catalogue; Mail order

Hartley Botanic Ltd
Clear Span, Greenfield, Oldham, Lancashire OL3 7AG
Contact: George Horton
Tel: 01457 873244
Fax: 01457 870151

Manufacturers of glasshouses for over 50 years. For our comprehensive free information pack call free on 0500 382077.
Catalogue

Haws Watering Cans
120 Beakes Rd, Smethwick, Midlands (W.) B67 5RN
Contact: John Massey
Tel: 0121 420 2494
Fax: 0121 429 1668

The famous 'genuine Haws' range of plastic and metal watering cans available through garden centres & stores. Free catalogue, spares and accessories direct from Haws.
Catalogue; Mail order

Highfield Packaging
Walstead Rd West, Walsall, Midlands (W.) WS5 4PE
Tel/fax: 01922 723700
Mail order

J & C R Wood
303 Hull Rd, Anlaby Common, Hull, Humberside HU4 7RZ
Tel: 01482 351915
Fax: 01482 502155

Offering Speed Shelf - the versatile and easy-to-fit shelving system for garden and leisure buildings. Available from selected garden centres and greenhouse suppliers.
Mail order

Jemp Engineering
Canal Estate, Station Rd, Langley, Berkshire SL3 6EG
Tel: 01753 548327
Fax: 01753 580137
Catalogue; Mail order

Lynkon Aquatic
Freepost, Lincoln, Lincolnshire LN2 4BR
Contact: S Armstrong
Tel: 01522 521768
Fax: 01522 514426

Lynkon Polycovers. Telephone or write to the above address for your free catalogue on replacement covers for garden polyhouses.
Catalogue; Mail order

Mastermind Products Ltd
Porter's Lodge, Bowerwood Rd, Fordingbridge, Hampshire SP6 2BS
Tel/fax: 01425 656942

Watermate - automatic waterer for greenhouses, and allied applications, using rainwater direct from the water butt. Please write/phone for further information.
Catalogue; Mail order

Mayflower Greenhouses (A E Headen Ltd)
Unit 2, Marshmoor Works, Great North Rd North Mymms, Hatfield, Hertfordshire AL9 5SD
Tel: 01707 652688(24hrs)
Fax: 01707 645372

Excellent range of quality aluminium greenhouses from reputable, long established firm. Delivery throughout UK mainland. Free colour catalogue. Small factory display site, manned office hours.
Catalogue; Mail order

Neptune Supplies & Services
Unit 3, Neptune Business Estate, Medway City Estate, Rochester, Kent ME2 4LT
Tel: 01634 290448
Fax: 01634 710206

Suppliers of polythene tunnels and Juliana greenhouses. Staging, propagators, heaters, irrigation systems and gardening equipment. Display showroom. Free brochure.
Catalogue; Mail order

Norfolk Greenhouses Ltd
PO Box 22, Watton, Norfolk IP25 6PA
Tel/fax: 01638 510568(orders)
Mail order

Nugent Gardens
484 Penistone Rd, Sheffield, Yorkshire (S.) S6 2FU
Catalogue

P L C Products
Westhall, Halesworth, Suffolk IP19 8RH
Contact: Peter Clifton
Tel/fax: 01502 575265

Glazing clips, aluminium nuts & bolts, glazing seals, Norplex glass substitute/insulation panels etc. All for immediate despatch (mail order). S.A.E. for full list.
Catalogue; Mail order

Parallax
17 Mapperley Street, Sherwood, Nottingham, Nottinghamshire NG5 4DE
Tel: 0115 9606086
Fax: 0115 9626716
Catalogue; Mail order

Parklines (Buildings) Ltd
Gala House, 3 Raglan Rd, Edgbaston, Birmingham, Midlands (W.) B5 7RA
Tel: 0121 446 6030 (24hr)
Fax: 0121 446 5991

A large range of garden buildings by mail order - 2-in-1 shed/greenhouse, cedar/aluminium greenhouses, chalets, sheds, garden room, workshops, garages, playhouse. Free catalogue.
Catalogue; Mail order

Parwin Power Heaters
Holme Rd, Yaxley, Peterborough, Cambridgeshire PE7 3NA
Tel/fax: 01733 240699 (24hrs)
Catalogue; Mail order

Podington Garden Centre
High Street, Podington, Wellingborough, Northamptonshire NN29 7HS
Contact: Colin Read
Tel: 01933 53656
Fax: 01933 410332

A plant person's paradise with thousands of plants all year round. Also a wide range of garden sundries, furniture, aquatics, garden ornaments, fencing and paving.

Pounds of Bewdley
Pound Garden Buildings, Coppice Gate, Lye Head, Bewdley, Hereford & Worcester DY12 2UX
Tel: 01299 266337
Fax: 01299 266644

Manufacturers of quality timber sheds, greenhouses, summerhouses and children's playhouses in softwood and cedar.
Catalogue; Mail order

The Daily Telegraph *Green Fingers* — Greenhouses, Sheds & Accessories

---

THERMOFORCE

Thermoforce, manufacturers for over 40 years, of quality ancillary garden and greenhouse equipment, for the hobby gardener.

For the full range of value for money Thermofor Ventcare and Camplex Plantcare products, write, phone or fax for your free full colour brochure.

- Electric Heating • Measuring Equipment • Ventilation & Environmental Control Systems • Soil Sterilisation Units • Soil Warming Cables and Thermostats • Plant Lighting Systems.

Thermoforce Ltd, Wakefield Road, Cockermouth, Cumbria CA13 0HS
Tel: 01900 823231 Fax: 01900 825965

Primus Ltd
Stephenson Way, Formby, Merseyside L37 8EQ
Tel/fax: 01704 878614

For details of Primus Gas Weed Burners, ACE greenhouse heaters and other products phone Howard, Shelagh or Marilyn in our sales office.

Regal
Cromford Works, Cromford Rd, Langley Mill, Nottinghamshire NG16 4EB
Tel: 01773 712128
Fax: 01773 530883

Cedarwood and PVC specialists. Family business for 48 years. Full installation and base laying service. 50 garden buildings on display.
Catalogue; Mail order

Robinsons of Winchester Ltd
Chilcomb Lane, Chilcomb, Winchester, Hampshire SO21 1HU
Tel: 01962 861917
Fax: 01962 841438

Rosemann Greenhouses
Holly Street, Leamington Spa, Warwickshire CV32 4TN
Tel/fax: 01926 428460

British manufacturers of quality greenhouses and accessories for the domesic market. (UK distribution and export)
Catalogue; Mail order

Seymours Garden & Leisure Group
The Pit House, Ewell By-Pass, Surrey KT17 1PS
Contact: James Seymour
Tel: 0181 393 0111
Fax: 0181 393 0237

Landscape and leisure centre with aquatics, landscape supplies, garden leisure departments and coffee shop under same ownership as Peters Plants and Garden Centre at Cobham (01932 862530).

Solar Tunnels
2 Melrose Place, Ashington, Sussex (W.) RH20 3HH
Tel/fax: 01903 742615

Solar tunnels in reinforced PVC: spacious, robust, relocatable, the attractive alternative to glass greenhouses. Many real advantages and plenty of room to grow.
Catalogue; Mail order

Solardome
Rosedale Engineers Ltd, 9 Bridlington Street, Hunmanby, Filey, Yorkshire (N.) YO14 0BR
Tel/fax: 01723 890303
Catalogue; Mail order

Solargro Products Ltd
102 Brunel Road, Earlstrees Industrial Estate, Corby, Northamptonshire NN17 4LS
Tel: 01536 206900
Fax: 01536 264800

Safety greenhouses in Twinwall material - no glass to shatter - with adjustable ventilation, efficient heat retention, good light penetration. Easy to assemble, sturdy aluminium frame in choice of finishes. Write or phone for details of your nearest showsite. (See our full colour advertisement on page ii).

Store More Garden Buildings
Store More House, Latham Close, Bredbury Industrial Park, Stockport, Cheshire SK6 2SD
Contact: Mr C E Downes
Tel: 0161 430 3347
Fax: 0161 406 6054

Maintenance-free steel garden storage buildings / boxes in either plain aluminium or green coated finish.
Catalogue; Mail order

Thermoforce Ltd
Wakefield Rd, Cockermouth, Cumbria CA13 0HS
Contact: Mr Laurie Kitchen
Tel: 01900 823231
Fax: 01900 825965

Free catalogue. Automatic window openers, instruments, sterilisers, heaters, soil warming cables, thermostats, mist propagation, supplementary lighting mercury and sodium, for amateur and professional growers.
Catalogue; Mail order

Tibshelf Garden Products
Freepost, Tibshelf, Derbyshire DE55 9BR
Tel/fax: 01773 873642
Catalogue

Traditional Garden Supply Company Ltd
PO Box 801, Chippenham, Wiltshire SN14 6TB
Tel: 01249 447000
Fax: 01249 448137

Beautiful cedar greenhouses, cold frames, tool sheds and benches made in our own workshops plus full range of tools and garden accessories. Free catalogue.
Catalogue; Mail order

Two Wests & Elliott Ltd
4 Carrwood Road, Sheepbridge Industrial Estate, Chesterfield, Derbyshire S41 9RH
Tel: 01246 451077
Fax: 01246 260115

Everything for the greenhouse - staging, benching, shelving, propagation and watering equipment, heating, lighting, shading, ventilation and more. Fruit cages, cold frames, mini-greenhouses. Free colour catalogue.
Catalogue; Mail order

Warrick Warming Cables Ltd
101 Sedlescombe Rd North, St Leonards-on-Sea, Sussex (E.)
Tel/fax: 01424 442485
Catalogue

HORTICULTURAL SUNDRIES

A Edwards
Strontian, Acharacle, Argyll, Highland PH36 4HY
Contact: Aidan Edwards
Tel/fax: 01967 402194

The new electric slug fence - a totally safe and effective way to banish slugs from your garden. £24 per 30m. Send for free leaflet.
Catalogue; Mail order

A Wright & Son Ltd
Garden Tool Manufacturers, Midland Works, 16-18 Sidney Street, Sheffield, Yorkshire (S.) S1 4RH
Tel/fax: 0114 2722677

Manufacturers of long reach weedpuller, long reach cut and hold flower gatherer, pruning and gardening knives, florists' and vine scissors.

Agralan Ltd
The Old Brick Yard, Ashton Keynes, Swindon, Wiltshire SN6 6QR
Tel: 01285 860015
Fax: 01285 860056

Yellow sticky traps, phoromone traps and Enviromesh for pest control. Eurofleece for frost protection. Agralan Soaker Hose for efficient watering. Permealay for weed suppression.
Catalogue; Mail order

Algoflash UK Ltd
Church Farm, Northgate Way, Terrington St Clement, Kings Lynn, Norfolk PE34 4LD
Tel: 01553 828882
Fax: 01553 827244
Mail order

Alitags
Unit 5, 35 Bourne Lane, Much Hadham, Hertfordshire SG10 6ER
Tel/fax: 01279 842685
Catalogue; Mail order

Anderson Ceramics
125 George Street, Romford, Essex RM1 2EB
Tel/fax: 01708 757568
Catalogue

Archwood Greenhouses
Robinswood, Goodrich, Hereford & Worcester HR9 6HT
Tel/fax: 01600 890125

Compost systems. Robust pressure preserved timber to BS4072 (Type 1), 2ft., 3ft. or 4ft. square bins. Removable front boards. Felt covered lids.
Catalogue; Mail order

Armillatox Ltd
121 Main Rd, Morton, Derbyshire DE55 6HL
Tel: 01773 590566
Fax: 01733 590681

Armillatox sterilises soil-borne fungi such as clubroot and honey fungus. It clears moss and algae from lawns, greenhouses and asphalt.

Aston Agricultural Research
57 Station Approach, South Ruislip, Middlesex HA4 6SL
Tel/fax: 01924 865048

B J Crafts
17 Coopers Wood, Crowborough, Sussex (E.) TN6 1SW
Contact: B R Welbury
Tel/fax: 01892 655899

Original watercolour flower paintings. From miniatures to the size and flower of your choice.
Catalogue; Mail order

Basic Bonsai Supplies
56 Quarry Lane, Halesowen, Midlands (W.) B63 4PD
Tel/fax: 0850 396930
Catalogue

Biotal Industrial Products Ltd
5 Chiltern Close, Cardiff, Glamorgan (S.) CF4 5DL
Tel/fax: 01222 747414

Composting specialists - see our full colour advertisement on page ii.

Blackwall Products
Unit 1-4, Riverside Industrial Estate, 150 River Way, London SE10 0BH
Tel: 0181 305 1431
Fax: 0181 305 1418
Catalogue; Mail order

Boughton Loam Ltd
Telford Way, Telford Way Industrial Estate, Kettering, Northamptonshire NN16 8UN
Tel: 01536 510515
Fax: 01536 510691

Suppliers of Kettering loam - bagged or bulk. Special horticultural mixes. Grass seed. Tree and shrub planting composts and soft landscaping materials.
Catalogue

Boulder Barrows
99 Westfield Rd, Woking, Surrey GU22 9QR
Tel/fax: 01483 730 658
Catalogue

Bulldog Tools Ltd
Clarington Forge, Wigan, Lancashire WN1 3DD
Tel: 01942 244281
Fax: 01942 824316

Manufacturers of horticultural hand tools. Trade names: Premier, Evergreen, Gardencare, Springbok.
Catalogue; Mail order

Burnt Earth Pottery
122 Rowan Rd, Havant, Hampshire PO9 2UU
Tel/fax: 01705 473100

Burton McCall Group
163 Parker Drive, Leicester, Leicestershire LE4 0JP
Tel/fax: 0116 340800
Catalogue; Mail order

Butterflies Galore
5 Westall Centre, Holberrow Green, Redditch, Hereford & Worcester B96 6JY
Tel/fax: 01386 793240
Catalogue; Mail order

C D A/Micron Sprayers
Three Mills, Bromyard, Hereford & Worcester HR7 4HU
Tel: 01885 482397
Fax: 01885 483043

C F Hanson Ltd
32 Blackburn Rd, Rishton, Blackburn, Lancashire BB1 4BS
Contact: C J Huddleston
Tel/fax: 01254 884302

Manufacturers of garden netting, green or white, for shading, windbreak, insulation, crop protection. Rot-proof, knitted polyethylene, fine mesh. SAE for samples.
Mail order

Cambrian Controls
PO Box 35, Woodchurch, Ashford, Kent TN26 3YW
Tel: 01233 861218
Fax: 01233 860029
Catalogue

Capstan Software
Freepost (KT 4335), Epsom, Surrey KT18 7BR
Tel/fax: 01372 727446
Mail order

Chase Organics
Coombelands House, Addlestone, Surrey KT15 1HY
Tel: 01932 820958
Fax: 01932 829322

Free mail order catalogue of untreated seeds and organic gardening supplies. Goods can be collected from our shop.
Catalogue; Mail order

ENGLISH WOODLANDS BIOCONTROL

BIOLOGICAL CONTROL
for greenhouse and garden, as used by the professionals.

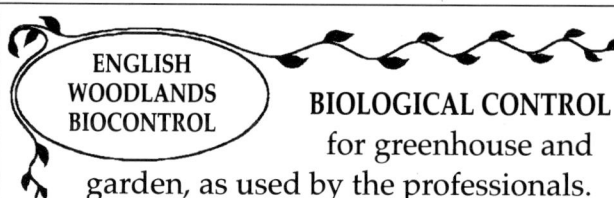

For your FREE guidebook, please ring
ENGLISH WOODLANDS BIOCONTROL
01798 867574

We combine up-to-date methods with old-fashioned personal service.

Chempak Products
Geddings Rd, Hoddesdon,
Hertfordshire EN11 0LR

Tel: 01992 441888
Fax: 01992 467908

Specialist supplier of fertilisers, organic and natural products. Hanging basket requirements, trace elements, lawn and green products, sundries. Over 200 items supplied.
Catalogue; Mail order

Concept Research
Forge House, Therfield, Herts
SG8 9QA

Tel: 01763 287684
Fax: 01763 287685

Catwatch - the ultimate cat deterrent. Product test best buys in Garden Answers, Your Garden, Practical Fishkeeping magazines. Phone for brochure and local stockist.
Mail order

Consumer Direct Ltd
Lower Street, Quainton,
Aylesbury, Buckinghamshire
HP22 4BL

Tel: 01296 75217
Fax: 01296 75371

Catalogue; Mail order

Continental Awnings (UK)
Unit 4 Streamside Court, Aspen Way, Yalberton Industrial Estate, Paignton, Devon TQ4 7QR

Tel: 01803 665221
Fax: 01803 665017

Plastic Rieid Panes for security & double glazing. Multiwall conservatory roofing and new sun shade vinyl. Synthetic rubber DIY flat roof cover. Free catalogue on request.
Catalogue; Mail order

Darlac Products
PO Box 996, Slough, Berkshire
SL3 9JF

Tel: 01753 547790
Fax: 01753 580524

New, innovative and traditional tools and sundries including pruners, loppers, shears, knives, watering accessories etc. Colour catalogue available free on request.
Catalogue; Mail order

Davies Systems (C)
Brandsby Lodge, Brandsby, York, Yorkshire (N.) YO6 4SJ

Contact: D P Davies
Tel: 01347 888224
Fax: 01347 888337

Y-Stakes. Easy unobtrusive plant supports made of strong brown pointed aluminium tube with pliable green non-rusting wire fork in the top. Sizes 1-5ft.
Catalogue; Mail order

Defenders Ltd
PO Box 131, Wye, Ashford, Kent
TN25 5TQ

Contact: Geoff Siddons
Tel: 01233 813121
Fax: 01233 813633

For free price list and information on biological control of slugs, vine weevil, whitefly, red spider mite (please specify) write to the above address.
Catalogue; Mail order

Cookson Plantpak Ltd
Burnham Rd, Mundon, Maldon,
Essex CM9 6NT

Tel: 01621 740140
Fax: 01296 75371

Cottage Garden Ceramics
7 Haslemere Rd, Southsea,
Hampshire PO4 8BB

Tel/fax: 01243 826102
Catalogue

Crest Garden Products
102-104 Church Rd, Teddington,
Middlesex TW11 8PY

Tel/fax: 0181 339 0312
Mail order

Croxden Horticultural Products Ltd
Cheadle, Stoke on Trent,
Staffordshire ST10 1HR

Tel: 01538 723641
Fax: 01538 723041

D I Y Plastics (UK) Ltd
Regal Way, Faringdon,
Oxfordshire SN7 7XD

Tel: 01367 242932
Fax: 01367 242200

Dibco Garden Sundries
Unit D5 Chaucer Business Park, Watery Lane, Kemsing, Sevenoaks, Kent TN15 6NR

Tel: 01732 763536
Fax: 01732 763538

Dickensons Compost
Eswip Edmonton, Angel Rd,
Edmonton, London N18 3AG

Tel: 0181 803 1322
Fax: 0181 884 0537
Catalogue

Diplex Ltd
PO Box 172, Watford,
Hertfordshire WD1 1BX

Tel: 01923 231784
Fax: 01923 243791
Catalogue; Mail order

Domestic Paraphernalia Co
Dept H G, Unit 15 Marine Business Ctr, Dock Rd, Lytham, Lancashire FY8 5AJ

Tel: 01253 736334 (24hrs)
Fax: 01253 795191
Mail order

Forsham Cottage Arks
Goreside Farm, Great Chart, Ashford, Kent TN26 1JU

AS SEEN AT CHELSEA & HAMPTON COURT

DOVECOTES • AVAIRIES • KENNELS • HUTCHES

POULTRY & WATERFOWL HOUSING

FREE Colour Brochure - 01233 820702 (24hrs)
or fax request: 01233 820157 Sales Tel: 01233 820229

Please send me a Colour Brochure
Name................
Address................
Postcode................
T.G.F

Dovecote Joinery
58B Station Rd, Upper Poppleton, York, Yorkshire (N.) YO2 6PQ

Tel/fax: 01904 789734
Catalogue

Dromana Irrigation (UK)
Fairwinds, Church Lane, Sunninghill, Ascot, Berkshire SL5 7DD

Catalogue

Dupre Vermiculite
Tamworth Rd, Hertford,
Hertfordshire SG13 7DL

Tel: 01992 582541
Fax: 01992 553436
Catalogue

Durston Peat Products
Avalon Farm, Sharpham, Nr Street, Somerset BA16 9SE

Tel: 01458 442688
Fax: 01458 448327

Manufacturers and producers of peat and peat free growing media including peat, multi-purpose composts, growbags, peat walling blocks, coconut composts, composted and ornamental bark.

E H Thorne (Beehives) Ltd
Beehive Works, Wragby, Lincoln,
Lincolnshire LN3 5LA

Tel: 01673 858555
Fax: 01673 857004

Comprehensive range of beekeeping equipment. Walkaround 'superstore' the only one of its type in the UK. 40 page colour catalogue available on request. Southern branch near Windsor.
Catalogue; Mail order

E J Godwin (Peat Industries) Ltd
Batch Farm, Meare, Glastonbury,
Somerset BA6 9SP

Tel: 01458 860644
Fax: 01458 860587

Catalogue

Edington Sporting Co
8-10 White Hays North, Quartermaster Rd, West Wilts Trading Estate, Westbury, Wiltshire BA13 4JT

Tel/fax: 01373 825469

Catalogue

Horticultural Sundries

English Woodlands Biocontrol
Hoyle, Graffham, Petworth,
Sussex (W.) GU28 0LR
Tel/fax: 01798 867574

Biological controls for greenhouse and garden pests sold by mail order to amateur gardeners and professional growers. Free guidebook available on request.
Catalogue; Mail order

Ferrum Dried Flowers
Love Hill Farm, Trotton,
Petersfield, Sussex (W.) GU31 5ER
Tel/fax: 01730 817277
Mail order

Fertile Fibre
Tenbury Wells, Hereford & Worcester WR15 8LT
Contact: Rob Hurst
Tel: 01584 781575
Fax: 01584 781483

Coir - from blocks to ready-to-use composts. Mail order throughout Britain. Also garden fertilisers. Soil Association symbol holder. Write for free sample.

Flora & Fauna Europe Ltd
Orchard House, Patmore End,
Ugley, Bishops Stortford,
Hertfordshire CM22 6JA
Tel: 01799 88289
Fax: 01799 88586
Catalogue; Mail order

Flower Arrangers Show Shop
PO Box 38, Stratford upon Avon,
Warwickshire CV37 6WJ
Catalogue; Mail order

Forsham Cottage Arks
Goreside Farm, Great Chart,
Ashford, Kent TN26 1JU
Tel: 01233 820229
Fax: 01233 820157

Dovecotes to America; rabbit hutches to Tokyo; chicken houses to the Falkland Islands; aviaries to Germany; dog kennels to Belgium. If the rest of the world think we are the best, then we must be. Twenty years of specialising has made us specialists in the design and making of fowl and pet houses. Door to door delivery or via authorised stockists. We can be seen at numerous flower shows. Colour brochure.

Franklin Mint Limited
138 Bromley Rd, Catford,
London SE6 2XG
Tel: 0181 697 8121
Fax: 0181 698 4476

Gardena UK Ltd
Dunhams Lane, Letchworth,
Hertfordshire SG6 1BD
Tel: 01462 686688
Fax: 01462 686789
Catalogue

Gardeners' Choice
Stadroyd Mill, Cottontree,
Colne, Lancashire BB8 7BW
Tel: 01282 873100
Fax: 01282 870779

We offer a wide selection of products for home and garden, available by mail order from our free catalogue.
Catalogue; Mail order

Gardeners' Pal
Oadby House, Hinckley Rd,
Burbage, Hinckley, Leicestershire LE10 2AQ
Tel: 01455 633414
Fax: 01455 251388

GardenGlow Direct (TGP1)
Clay Lane, South Nutfield,
Redhill, Surrey RH1 4EG
Tel/fax: 01737 822562

GardenGlow Cocoa Shell - mulch, fertilizer and soil conditioner. Free brochure on request.
Catalogue; Mail order

Geebro Ltd
Soulch Road, Hailsham, Sussex (E.) BN27 3DT
Tel: 01323 840771
Fax: 01323 440109

Established in 1830 in the village of Hailsham, Rainbow offer the very best in traditional quality English garden products from plant labels to ornamental arches.

Globe Organic Services
163A Warwick Road, Solihull,
Midlands (W.) B92 7AR
Contact: Tom Raitt
Tel: 0121 707 4120
Fax: 0121 707 4934

Equipment and machinery for the rapid recycling of green organic waste: shredders, chippers, compost makers and smart carts.

Glowcroft Ltd
PO Box 137, Gloucester,
Gloucestershire GL4 7YB
Tel: 01452 372385
Fax: 01452 372381
Catalogue; Mail order

Green Gardener for Bio-Control
41 Strumpshaw Rd, Brundall,
Norfolk NR13 5PG
Tel/fax: 01603 715096

Friendly advice service. Suppliers of biological control of greenhouse and conservatory pests (whitefly, red spider etc). Bio-control for vine weevil and slugs, anywhere. Send 2 x 1st class stamps for information-filled catalogue.
Catalogue; Mail order

Greenacres Horticultural Supplies
PO Box 1228, Iver,
Buckinghamshire SL0 0EH
Contact: Ivor Ludford
Tel: 01895 835235
Fax: 01753 672906

Professional products for amateur gardeners and commercial users. Pre-germinated grass seed, controlled release fertilisers, water storing polymers, sulphur products. Small gardens to large estates supplied.
Catalogue; Mail order

Greenspan Designs Ltd
8 Mentmore Close, Kenton,
Harrow, Middlesex HA3 0EA

Manufacturers of Supergrow Dice, Grorock, Cocogro, Cocoliners for hanging baskets, Cocopoles. With robust accessories, transform the dice into unique hanging gardens, floral mushrooms and columns.
Catalogue; Mail order

GROWING SUCCESS

GROWING SUCCESS ORGANICS LTD
South Newton, Salisbury, Wilts SP2 0QW
Tel (01722) 742500   Fax (01722) 742571

<u>MANUFACTURERS AND SUPPLIERS
TO THE TRADE ONLY, WITH:</u>

Safer and Effective Pest Control Products.
Children and Pets need not be excluded
from the treated areas:

Slug & Snail Killer   Cat Repellent
Ant Killer
Deep Root Tree Stump Killer

<u>**Also – for lining Hanging Baskets:**</u>
Cocobasket Liners®   Coco-Moss®
made from 100% coconut fibre

GardenGlow Cocoa Shell

Mulch, Fertilizer & Soil Conditioner
♦ It looks superb ♦ Control weeds
♦ Deters slugs, snails and many cats.

FREE UK DELIVERY

GardenGlow will nourish & condition the structure of all soils making them easier to cultivate & more fertile! Also, with a total nutrient value far greater than farmyard manure GardenGlow will get your plants off to a great start!

FREE COMPREHENSIVE BROCHURE ON REQUEST

BEST BUY
1 x 100 lt. sack £7.95
2 sacks £14.30   4 sacks £27.80
10 sacks £65.00   20 + sacks £5.99

To order, call the number below or send a cheque, P/O or credit card details, made payable to:
GardenGlow Direct (TGP1)
Clay Lane, South Nutfield, REDHILL RH1 4EG

PHONE NOW!   01737 822562

Horticultural Sundries

Greenvale Farm Ltd
Clapham Lodge, Leeming,
Northallerton, Yorkshire (N.)
DL7 9LY
Tel: 01677 422953
Fax: 01677 425358

Growell Hydroponics & Plant Lighting
Jardinerie Garden Centre,
Kenilworth Rd,
Hampton-in-Arden, Midlands
(W.) B92 0LP
Tel: 01675 443950
Fax: 01675 443951
Email: 101476.216
@compuserve.com

Retail and mail order of hydroponic systems, growlights, nutrients, rockwool, books, magazines and associated equipment.
Catalogue; Mail order

Growing Success Organics Ltd
South Newton, Salisbury,
Wiltshire SP2 0QW
Tel: 01722 742500
Fax: 01722 742571

Manufacturers and suppliers to the trade only - safe and effective pest control products. Also Cocobasket Liners and Coco-Moss for lining hanging baskets.

Growth Technology Ltd
Fremantle House, 21-25 Priory Avenue, Taunton, Somerset TA1 1XX
Tel: 01823 325291
Fax: 01823 325487
Catalogue

H 2 O
The Stables, Winwick Warren,
West Haddon, Northampton,
Northamptonshire NN6 7NS
Tel: 01788 510529
Fax: 01788 510728
Catalogue

Hanging Garden Pot Holders
Grangewood, High Shincliffe,
Durham, Co Durham DH1 2PP
Tel: 0191 384 7726
Fax: 0191 386 7726
Mail order

Haselden Enterprise UK
Dept GF, PO Box 44, Cranleigh,
Surrey GU6 7YH
Tel/fax: 01483 273664
Email: hasel@interads.co.uk

HASEL through-feed garden hose reel. Wall mounted yet easily removable. Aluminium / stainless steel construction. 5 year leak-free guarantee. Up to 200ft / 60m capacity. Quality accessories from hose to metal spray nozzles supplied.
Catalogue; Mail order

Haws Watering Cans
120 Beakes Rd, Smethwick,
Midlands (W.) B67 5RN
Contact: John Massey
Tel: 0121 420 2494
Fax: 0121 429 1668

The famous 'genuine Haws' range of plastic and metal watering cans available through garden centres & stores. Free catalogue, spares and accessories direct from Haws.
Catalogue; Mail order

Hayne-West
Units 1 & 2, Stoneyhill Industrial Estate, Whitchurch,
Ross-on-Wye, Hereford & Worcester HR9 6BX
Contact: Sheila M Howarth
Tel: 01600 890119
Fax: 01600 890133

Personalised cast aluminium house signs, numbers and post boxes made to order. Send SAE for coloured brochure.
Catalogue; Mail order

Homecare Products
118 Bellhouse Rd, Eastwood,
Essex SS9 5NG
Mail order

Hop Shop
Castle Farm, Shoreham,
Sevenoaks, Kent TN14 7UB
Contact: Caroline Alexander
Tel: 01959 523219
Fax: 01959 524220

Producers of over 70 varieties of dried flowers, herbs and grasses, plus seasonal hop bines. RHS gold medal winners - Chelsea '93 and '94. Mail order service (send 4 x 1st class stamps for colour brochure). Farm shop in scenic valley near M20/M25.
Catalogue; Mail order

Hotbox Heaters Ltd
7 Gordleton Industrial Park,
Sway Rd, Lymington, Hampshire SO41 8JD
Tel: 01590 683788
Fax: 01590 683511
Mail order

Hotterotter Group
The Old Rectory, Bryn,
Abergavenny, Gwent NP7 9AP
Tel/fax: 01873 840328

Top quality insulated composters, made from 86% recycled material. 500 litre and 200 litre from £49.95 and £29.95 plus mail order, or from garden centres.
Mail order

Hozelock Ltd
Haddenham, Aylesbury,
Buckinghamshire HP17 8JD
Tel: 01844 291881
Fax: 01844 290344
Catalogue

Humus Wyse Ltd
Gallants Bower, Dartmouth,
Devon TQ6 0JN
Contact: Bill Hunt
Tel/fax: 01803 834687

Worm composting. Worm inoculation. Domestic to industrial application. Home of Willy Worm's Compost Box (includes educational version). Suppliers of worms. Telephone for details.
Catalogue; Mail order

Hydrocut Ltd
Sudbury, Suffolk CO10 6HB
Tel/fax: 01787 371171
Mail order

I C I Garden Products
Fernhurst, Haslemere, Surrey GU27 3JE
Tel: 01428 645454
Fax: 01428 657222

Ingram Topiary Frames Ltd
15 Freke Rd, London SW11 5PU
Tel/fax: 0171 350 1842
Catalogue; Mail order

Insublind
Freepost, Colne, Lancashire BB8 7BR
Tel/fax: 01282 443348
Catalogue

J H May Ltd (Reproductions)
15-20 The Oval, Hackney Rd,
Bethnal Green, London E2 9DX
Tel: 0171 739 7923
Fax: 0171 739 8764

Jiffy Products Ltd
14-16 Commercial Rd, March,
Cambridgeshire PE15 8QP
Tel: 01354 52565
Fax: 01354 51891
Catalogue

John McLauchlan Horticulture
50a Market Place, Thirsk,
Yorkshire (N.) YO7 1LH
Contact: John McLauchlan
Tel: 01845 525585
Fax: 01845 523133

Please send SAE for mail order catalogue. Products include Humate growth enhancers and Viresco micro-organism products which suppress disease and banish certain leaf pests.
Mail order

Kemp Compos Tumbler
Dept GW694, Freepost BM 2930, Solihull, Midlands (W.) B92 7BR
Tel/fax: 0121 707 4120
Catalogue; Mail order

Kemps Coconut Products
Kemps Mushrooms, Chapel Rd,
Ford, Aylesbury,
Buckinghamshire HP17 8XG
Tel/fax: 01296 748932
Catalogue

Kontsmide UK Ltd
Hardwick View Rd, Holmewood Industrial Estate, Holmewood,
Chesterfield, Derbyshire S42 5SA
Tel: 01246 852140
Fax: 01246 854297

Europe's largest manufacturer/distributor of electrical Christmas decorations including the popular Swedish candlestick. The company also makes/sells outdoor lighting of great quality.
Catalogue; Mail order

Kootensaw Dovecotes
Waterleat Cottage, Tuckenhay,
Totnes, Devon TQ9 7EH
Tel/fax: 01803 732003

Kut & Dried
PO Box 50, Penrith, Cumbria CA11 8RY
Tel/fax: 01768 892275
Catalogue; Mail order

L & P Peat Ltd
Tollund House, 8 Abbey Street,
Carlisle, Cumbria CA3 8TX
Tel: 01228 22181
Fax: 01228 41460

L B S Horticulture
Cottontree, Nr Colne,
Lancashire BB8 7BW
Tel: 01282 871777
Fax: 01282 869850

Suppliers of all horticultural sundries including polythene. pots, netting, irrigation, polythene tunnels, vacuum formed trays, labels, heaters, cloches and everything for the gardener.
Catalogue; Mail order

Labelplant
Unit F2, Duck Farm,
Bockhampton, Dorchester,
Dorset DT2 8QL
Tel: 01305 849089
Fax: 01305 849042

Horticultural labelling systems, 150 types, 20 colours including black, outdoor markers, specialist sundries.
Catalogue; Mail order

Labels Unlimited
Unit 12, 33c Bourne Lane, Much Hadham, Hertfordshire SG10 6ER

The Daily Telegraph *Green Fingers* — Horticultural Sundries

NEW SUPADRIPPA (Pat.)
FOR DRIP IRRIGATION

Don't throw away your household soft plastic bottles. They are the FREE water reservoirs for the Supadrippa.
- Easily mounted – re-fillable – re-usable
- Save your house, garden and greenhouse plants during holidays and absences
- 3 litres = circa 3 weeks

DRIBBLEDY-DRIP – THE GARDENERS' TIP

Supadrippas – 2 £2.99; 4 £4.99; 10 £9.99
Inc. VAT & delivery   Trade discounts available
LANGDON (LONDON) LTD., Ickford, Aylesbury, Bucks. HP18 9JJ
Tel: 01844 339337   Fax: 01844 339666

Lady Muck
Marshwood House, Whitegate
Forton, Chard, Somerset
TA20 4HL
Contact: Jane Down
Tel: 01460 220822
Fax: 01460 67768

Lady Muck is a traditional, superior, rich, organic cow manure-based compost, packed with nutrients. Use for excellent soil conditioner, planting medium and top dressing.
Mail order

Landscape Irrigation Systems
River View, Salisbury Rd,
Ringwood, Hampshire BH24 1AS
Tel: 01425 473790
Fax: 01425 471157

Langdon (London)
Ickford, Aylesbury,
Buckinghamshire HP18 9JJ
Tel: 01844 339337
Fax: 01844 339666

Supadrippa - re-cycle household plastic bottles for drip irrigation - save your plants whilst away. 10 £9.99. Kanelock cane supports - makes 2 wigwam/ridge frames £3.50. VAT/delivery included.

Leaky Pipe Systems Ltd
Frith Farm, Dean Street, East
Farleigh, Maidstone, Kent
ME15 0PR
Tel: 01622 746495
Fax: 01622 745118

Supply and/or installation of sub-surface irrigation systems using porous rubber hose. Do-it-yourself kits available for the amateur gardener.
Catalogue; Mail order

Leisuredeck Ltd
Maylands House, Maylands
Avenue, Hemel Hempstead,
Hertfordshire HP2 7DE
Tel: 01442 242700
Fax: 01442 212599
Catalogue

Levington Horticulture
Paper Mill Lane, Bramford,
Ipswich, Suffolk IP8 4BZ
Tel: 01473 830492
Fax: 01473 830386/046

Manufacturers of Levington composts, Evergreen lawn fertilizers, Murphy chemicals and Liquinure. Enquiries for advice welcome, but all sales are through garden retailers.

Lindum Seeded Turf
West Grange, Thorganby, York,
Yorkshire (N.) YO4 6DJ
Contact: Stephen Fell
Tel: 01904 448675
Fax: 01904 448713
Email: lindum@legend.co.uk

Growers of a range of speciality turf for top quality lawns and landscaping. Send for brochures or view www.lindumturf.yorks.com/turf/
Catalogue

Link-Stakes Ltd
30 Warwick Rd, Upper
Boddington, Daventry,
Northamptonshire NN11 6DH
Tel: 01327 260329 (24hrs)
Fax: 01327 262428

Make and sell plant support and protection products. Ask for free leaflets on Link-Stakes, Loop-Stakes, Cloister Cloches and Micro-cages.
Catalogue; Mail order

Lord Roberts Workshops
Freepost, 6 Western Corner,
Edinburgh, Lothian EH12 5PY
Tel/fax: 0131 337 6951

M W Horticultural Supplies
PO Box 15, Edenbridge, Kent
TN8 6SD
Tel/fax: 01732 864967
Catalogue; Mail order

Macalda Electronics Ltd
Macalda House, Manaton Court,
Manaton Close, Exeter, Devon
EX2 8PF
Tel/fax: 01392 823806

MacPenny Products
Bransgore, Nr Christchurch,
Dorset BH23 8DB

Long-life plant labels available from MacPenny Nurseries.

Mailbox UK
5 Railway Cottages, Heath Rd,
Holmewood, Chesterfield,
Derbyshire S42 5RQ
Catalogue; Mail order

Maxicrop International Ltd
Weldon Rd, Corby,
Northamptonshire NN17 5US
Tel: 01536 402182
Fax: 01536 204254

Melcourt

MULCHES, SOIL CONDITIONERS and PLAY SURFACES

Available in small quantities from our national network of Melcourt Small-Load Stockists

For your nearest Stockist contact:–
Melcourt Industries Limited
Eight Bells House,
Tetbury, Glos GL8 8JG
Tel: 01666 503919   Fax: 01666 504398

LBS Horticulture
The U.K.'s leading supplier of horticulture products

*Thousands of Growers Sundries
Polythene & Plastic
Pots & Trays
Trucks & Trolleys
Polytunnels
Irrigation Design, Supply & Installation*

Call now for your free 192 page catalogue – **01282 873333**
LBS Horticulture, Standroyd Mill, Cottontree, Nr Colne BB8 7BW

The Daily Telegraph *Green Fingers* — Horticultural Sundries

Maxicrop is the unique range of plant growth stimulants and fertilisers based on seaweed extract. Leaflet available with advice on how to get the best results.
Catalogue; Mail order

Meadow Herbs
Unit 11, Headlands Business Park, Salisbury Rd, Ringwood, Hampshire BH24 3PB
Tel: 01425 470009
Fax: 01425 480405

Melcourt Industries Ltd
Eight Bells House, Tetbury, Gloucestershire GL8 8JG
Tel: 01666 503919
Fax: 01666 504398

Mulches, soil conditioners and play surfaces available in small quantities from our national network of Melcourt Small-Load stockists. Call for details of nearest stockist.

Miracle Garden Care Ltd
Salisbury House, Weyside Park, Catteshall Lane, Godalming, Surrey GU7 1XE
Contact: Paul Patton
Tel: 01483 410210
Fax: 01483 410220

Garden fertilisers and chemicals: Miraclegro, Grasshopper, Scotts, Weedol, Patticlear, Verdonne, Bug Guns, Sybol, Minrod, Rapid, No Clog Feeders.
Catalogue

Molecatcher
PO Box 3186, Wokingham, Berkshire RG11 5FJ
Mail order

Monsanto Garden Care
Thames Tower, Burleys Way, Leicester, Leicestershire LE1 3TP
Tel: 0116 2620864
Fax: 0116 2530320
Catalogue

Multimesh Products
PO Box 24, Callington, Cornwall PL18 9YZ
Contact: C W Dean
Tel: 01822 833036
Fax: 01822 834132

Suppliers of polytunnels, extruded and woven nets (windbreak, shade, bird & insect protection), fruit cages, permeable ground cover, fleece, garden sundries. No catalogue charge.
Catalogue; Mail order

Natural Organic Supplies
Old Meadows Farm, Dog Pits Lane, Broadclough, Bacup, Lancashire OL13 8PU
Contact: Garry Lomas IEng MI Mech IE
Tel/fax: 01706 873224

Working with nature - breeders of turbo tiger worms and suppliers, to the public and local authorities, of worm bins, DIY kits and associated products.
Catalogue; Mail order

Natural Pest Control Ltd
Yapton Rd, Barnham, Bognor Regis, Sussex (W.) PO22 0BQ
Tel: 01243 553250
Fax: 01243 552879
Catalogue; Mail order

Netlon Ltd
Kelly Street, Blackburn, Lancashire BB2 4PJ
Contact: Michael J Carr
Tel: 01254 262431
Fax: 01251 661624

Manufacturers of plastic nets and mesh providing support and protection. Also available are windbreaks and shading along with a range of timber and wire products.

Noma Lites Ltd
Brooklands, Weybridge, Surrey KT3 0YU

Moonrays garden lights - fully automatic, totally DIY low voltage garden lighting system in a variety of styles. Write for further details. (See our full colour advertisement on page ii)
Catalogue

Norbark (Northern Bark Ltd)
6 Northern Rd, Belfast, Co Antrim
Tel: 01232 754936
Fax: 01232 754937
Catalogue

Norfolk Farm Composts Ltd
Docking Farm, Oulton, Norwich, Norfolk NR11 6BR
Tel: 01603 872096
Fax: 01603 872952
Mail order

Nutriculture Ltd
Ormskirk, Lancashire L40 2QB
Tel/fax: 01704 822536
Catalogue

Organic Concentrates Ltd
3 Broadway Court, Chesham, Buckinghamshire HP5 1EN
Tel: 01494 792229
Fax: 01494 792199
Catalogue; Mail order

Original Organics Ltd
Units 4/5, Farthing Lodge Business Centre, Plymtree, Devon EX15 2JY
Tel: 01884 277681
Fax: 01884 277642

Makers of the original wormery, a high quality composting bin complete with tiger worms. Green gardens catalogue of mail order composting and garden products available.
Catalogue; Mail order

P A C Organic Products
79 Loudon Rd, London NW8 0DQ
Tel/fax: 0171 624 5599
Mail order

Pan Brittanica Industries Ltd
Brittanica House, Waltham Cross, Hertfordshire EN8 7DY
Tel: 01992 623691
Fax: 01992 626452

Papronet
Direct Wire Ties Ltd, Wyke Works, Hedon Rd, Hull, Humberside HU9 5HL
Tel/fax: 01482 712630
Catalogue

Park Forge
23 Court Hey Avenue, Bowring Park, Liverpool, Merseyside L36 4JB
Tel/fax: 0151 480 0606
Catalogue

Phostrogen
Corwen, Clwyd LL21 0EE
Tel: 01490 412662
Fax: 01490 412177
Catalogue

Pinks & Carnations
22 Chetwyn Avenue, Bromley Cross, Bolton, Lancashire BL7 9BN
Tel/fax: 01204 306273

Perpetual flowering carnations. Garden pinks. Tri-port plant support system. PVC canes. Galvanised wire support rings. Dianthus fertilizer. Seed. Write, phone or fax for catalogue.
Catalogue; Mail order

Plastics-by-Post Ltd
Freepost, Ventnor, Isle of Wight PO38 1BR
Tel/fax: 01983 853114
Mail order

Plysu Housewares Ltd
Wolseley Rd, Kempston, Bedfordshire MK42 7UD
Contact: Peter Fraser
Tel: 01234 841771
Fax: 01234 841037

Manufacturer of watering cans, water butts and stands, dustbins and refuse sack bins and garden accessories including pots and planters.
Catalogue

Podington Garden Centre
High Street, Podington, Wellingborough, Northamptonshire NN29 7HS
Contact: Colin Read
Tel: 01933 53656
Fax: 01933 410332

A plant person's paradise with thousands of plants all year round. Also a wide range of garden sundries, furniture, aquatics, garden ornaments, fencing and paving.

Porous Pipe
PO Box 2, Colne, Lancashire
Tel/fax: 01282 871778
Catalogue; Mail order

Power Garden Products
7 Bonneville Close, Allesley, Coventry, Midlands (W.) CV5 9QG
Contact: Mrs J Fallon
Tel/fax: 01676 522257

Mail order plant supports and barn cloches. Catalogue 1 x 1st class stamp.
Catalogue; Mail order

Practicality Brown Ltd
Iver Stud, Iver, Buckinghamshire SL0 9LA
Tel: 01753 652022
Fax: 01753 653007

PBL offers bulk supplies of bark and wood based mulches, the supply and planting of semi mature trees and relocating of existing semi mature trees.

Precise Irrigation (UK) Ltd
78 Grove Street, Wantage, Oxfordshire OX12 7BG
Tel: 01235 763760
Fax: 01235 765467
Catalogue; Mail order

Raindrain Ltd
Albert Mills, Mill Street West, Dewsbury, Yorkshire (W.) WF12 9AE
Tel/fax: 01924 468564

Redashe Ltd
Unit 11, Hewitts Industrial Estate, Elmbridge Rd, Cranleigh, Surrey GU6 8LW
Tel: 01483 275774
Fax: 01483 277947
Mail order

Rolawn (Turf Growers Ltd)
Elvington, York, Yorkshire (N.) YO4 5AR
Tel: 01904 608661
Fax: 01904 608272

Insist on Britain's finest turf - grown from the world's top cultivars to give a classic British lawn. Don't compromise. Buy genuine Rolawn turf.

The Daily Telegraph *Green Fingers* **Horticultural Sundries**

Sandvik Saws & Tools
Manor Way, Halesowen, Midlands (W.) B62 8QZ
Tel: 0121 550 4700
Fax: 0121 501 3667

Scarletts Plantcare
Nayland Rd, West Bergholt, Colchester, Essex CO6 3DH
Tel: 01206 240466
Fax: 01206 242530
Catalogue; Mail order

Shamrock Horticulture Ltd
The Crescent Centre, Temple Back, Bristol, Avon BS1 6EZ
Tel: 0117 9211666
Fax: 0117 9225501

Shamrock manufacture a wide range of growing media for the garden market including many peat free composts. Please telephone for your nearest stockist.

Sheen Developments Ltd
11 Earl Rd, East Sheen, London SW14 7JH
Contact: John Hockley
Tel/fax: 0181 878 8842

Botanic garden style, engraved plant labels and black aluminium stems as supplied to the Royal Botanic Gardens, Kew.
Catalogue; Mail order

Sherston Earl Vineyards Ltd
Bennerley Rd, Hullavington, Chippenham, Wiltshire SN1 6ET
Tel/fax: 01666 837979

Simply Control
Picket Piece, Andover, Hampshire SP11 6RU
Tel/fax: 01264 334805 (24hrs)
Catalogue

Simply Garlands
51 Albion Rd, Pitstone, Bedfordshire LU7 9AY
Tel/fax: 01296 661425
Catalogue; Mail order

Skyview Systems Ltd
Skyview House, Alresford, Essex CO7 8BZ
Tel: 01206 823185
Fax: 01206 825328
Catalogue; Mail order

Somerset Postal Flowers
Carew Cottage, Crowcombe, Taunton, Somerset TA4 4AD
Tel/fax: 01984 8314
Catalogue; Mail order

Spear & Jackson Garden Products
Handsworth Rd, Sheffield, Yorkshire (S.) S13 9BR
Tel/fax: 0114 2449911
Catalogue

Sportsmark Group Ltd
Sportsmark House, Ealing Rd, Brentford, Middlesex TW8 0LH
Contact: D J Lloyd
Tel: 0181 560 2010/12
Fax: 0181 568 2177

Artificial grass, patio entrance halls, swimming pool surrounds, balconies, sports equipment for over 42 sports, goal-posts, nets & netting, line markers and material, court marking service.
Catalogue; Mail order

Starkie & Starkie Ltd
39 The Heathers Ind Park, Freemen's Common, Leicester, Leicestershire LE2 7SQ
Contact: Richard Starkie
Tel: 0116 2854772
Fax: 0116 2854884

Dmt diamond sharpening systems, whetstones, cones, files and steels will sharpen all garden tools. Secateurs, shears, loppers, scythes and many more household tools.
Catalogue; Mail order

Suffolk Smallholders
Ashfield Road, Elmswell, Suffolk
Tel/fax: 01359 242834

Sunlight Systems
Unit 3, St Marys Works, Burnmoor Street, Leicester, Leicestershire LE2 7JJ
Tel: 0116 2470490
Fax: 0116 2470485
Catalogue; Mail order

Sunshine of Africa (UK) Ltd
Cocoa Shell, Afton Manor, Freshwater, Isle of Wight PO40 9TW
Tel: 01983 754575
Fax: 01983 755388

Sunshine of Africa supply their own brand of cocoa shell garden mulch for all types of garden application. N.P.K. 3:1:3 and excellent weed suppression.

Super Natural Ltd
Bore Place Farm, Chiddingstone, Edenbridge, Kent TN8 7AR
Contact: Caroline Dunmall
Tel: 01732 463255
Fax: 01732 740264

Organic garden compost, houseplant compost, mulch and soil conditioner (peat free), liquid plant food. Made from cow manure from the company's own dairy herd.
Catalogue

Tamar Organics
Unit 10, West Devon Business Park, Brook Lane, Tavistock, Devon PL19 9DP
Tel/fax: 01822 618765

Free mail order catalogue for untreated seeds, organic seed potatoes, organic peat free composts, fertilisers, wormeries, compost bins and mulch.
Catalogue; Mail order

Tank Exchange
Lewden House, Barnsley Rd, Dodworth, Barnsley, Yorkshire (S.) S75 3JU
Tel/fax: 01226 203852/206157
Catalogue; Mail order

Telford Garden Supplies
Unit 3, Hadley Park Industrial Estate, Hadley, Telford, Shropshire TF1 4PY
Tel/fax: 01952 248955/243904
Catalogue; Mail order

Tensor Ltd
Yarm Rd Industrial Estate, Darlington, Co Durham DL1 4XX
Tel: 01325 469181
Fax: 01325 381386

Tensor marketing is a mail order company specialising in pest control and other products, ultrasonic pest repellers, molechasers and moulds for walkways.
Mail order

Thames Valley Wirework Co
792 Weston Rd, Slough Trading Estate, Slough, Berkshire SL1 4HR
Tel: 01753 521992
Fax: 01753 574160

The makers of Gro.Thru plant supports. Call or write for a brochure and details of your nearest Gro.Thru stockist.
Catalogue; Mail order

Thermoforce Ltd
Wakefield Rd, Cockermouth, Cumbria CA13 0HS
Contact: Mr Laurie Kitchen
Tel: 01900 823231
Fax: 01900 825965

Free catalogue. Automatic window openers, instruments, sterilisers, heaters, soil warming cables, thermostats, mist propagation, supplementary lighting mercury and sodium, for amateur and professional growers.
Catalogue; Mail order

Tiger Developments Ltd
Milwards, Laughton, Lewes, Sussex (E.) BN8 6BN
Tel: 01323 811683
Fax: 01323 881294

Tokonoma Bonsai
14 London Rd, Shenley, Radlett, Hertfordshire WD7 9EN
Tel: 01923 857587
Fax: 01923 852596

Town & Country Products
State House, Morledge Street, Leicester, Leicestershire LE1 1TA
Tel: 0116 2536001
Fax: 0116 2513337
Catalogue; Mail order

Trade & DIY Products Ltd
The Pump House, Hazelwood Rd, Duffield, Belper, Derbyshire DE56 4AA
Contact: Mr R Barlow
Tel: 01332 842685
Fax: 01332 842806

Suppliers of brand leading Plantex weed control, garden fleece, Hydromat capillary matting and cloches. Free information pack on request.
Catalogue; Mail order

Trading Bonsai
81 Bruntsfield Place, Edinburgh, Lothian EH10 4HG
Contact: Alison Currie
Tel/fax: 0131 229 0539

Trading Bonsai Ltd offers an impressive collection of indoor and outdoor bonsai trees and is Scotland's largest supplier to both the retail and trade markets.

Trailer Barrow Co
Bellbrook Park, Uckfield, Sussex (E.) TN22 1QF
Tel: 01825 748200
Fax: 01825 761212

Trailerbarrows are single handled load movers which effortlessly carry heavy or bulky loads over two wheels. Larger models can even be adapted for tractor towing.

Truggery
Coopers Croft, Herstmonceaux, Hailsham, Sussex (E.) BN27 1QL
Contact: Sarah Page
Tel/fax: 01323 832314

Sussex trug baskets entirely hand crafted in willow and sweet chestnut. Strongly built for harvesting vegetables, carrying logs, displaying flowers, fruit, eggs.
Catalogue; Mail order

Trugrind
32 Brooklands Gardens, Hornchurch, Essex RM11 2AE
Tel/fax: 01708 444348
Mail order

Tyrite - Brighton Manufacturing Co
PO Box 61, Alton, Hampshire GU34 3YU
Tel/fax: 01420 588546

Tyrite plant support - The Wire with Loops - easy to assemble on walls, posts or fences. Tie plants to the loops to train and secure.
Catalogue; Mail order

The Daily Telegraph *Green Fingers*   **Horticultural Sundries**

Wartnaby Garden Labels
Melton Mowbray, Leicestershire
LE14 3HY
Tel: 01664 822549
Fax: 01664 822231

Zinc metal labels in five different shapes to hang or push into the ground. Can be marked with pencil, pen, permanent marking ink, adhesive tape or engraved.
Catalogue; Mail order

Warwick Warming Cables Ltd
101 Sedlescombe Rd North, St Leonards-on-Sea, Sussex (E.) TN37 7EJ
Tel/fax: 01424 442485

Water Diverter Ltd
63 Gloucester Road, Croydon, Surrey CR0 2DL
Tel/fax: 0181 778 2650

Water Works
91A Wareham Rd, Corfe Mullen, Wimborne, Dorset BH21 3JY
Tel/fax: 01202 600004
Mail order

Watermill Company
Pottery Lane, Ferrybridge, Knottingley, Yorkshire (W.) WF11 8JX
Tel/fax: 01977 678112
Mail order

Waters Green Direct
Waters Green House, Macclesfield, Cheshire SK11 6LF
Mail order

Weather Signs
Unit 4, Broadwindsor Craft Centre, Broadwindsor, Beaminster, Dorset DT8 3PX
Tel/fax: 01308 867650
Catalogue

Wells & Winter
Mere House Barn, Mereworth, Maidstone, Kent ME18 5NB
Tel/fax: 01622 813627

Labels, botannical cards, Y-stake plant supports, herb and wildflower seeds, small edging hurdles.
Catalogue; Mail order

Wessex Horticultural Products Ltd
South Newton, Salisbury, Wiltshire SP2 0QW
Tel: 01722 742500
Fax: 01722 742571

Manufacturers and suppliers to the trade only - soil-based, peat-based and peat-free growing media; horticultural sands and grits; decorative stones; turf dressings; soil improvers; mulches.

West Meters Ltd
Western Bank Industrial Estate, Wigton, Cumbria CA7 9SJ
Tel: 01697 344288
Fax: 01697 344616

Free colour brochure available containing details of gardening thermometers, pool thermometers, soil meters, rainfall measures, humidity meters, barometers, digital instruments and gadgets.
Catalogue; Mail order

Westland Horticulture
97 Moy Rd, Dungannon, Co Tyrone
Contact: Seamus McGrone
Tel: 01868 784007
Fax: 01868 784077
Catalogue

Wiggly Wigglers
Lower Blakemere, Hereford & Worcester HR2 9PX
Tel/fax: 01981 500391
Catalogue; Mail order

William Sinclair Horticulture
Firth Rd, Lincoln, Lincolnshire LN6 7AH
Tel: 01522 537561
Fax: 01522 513609

Wolf Garden
Alton Road, Ross on Wye, Hereford & Worcester HR9 5NE
Contact: Alan Calverley
Tel: 01989 767600
Fax: 01989 765589

Write or call for a free catalogue of Wolf's comprehensive range of garden tools and powered products including lawn mowers, barbecues and garden lighting. Stockists nationwide.
Catalogue

Woodgrow Horticulture Ltd
Burton Rd, Findern, Derby, Derbyshire DE6 6BE
Contact: Arnold or Philip Woodhouse
Tel: 01332 516 392
Fax: 01332 511481

Suppliers to the landscape industry of bark, topsoils, composts, timber, tree stakes, ties and shelters, Plantex geotextile membrane, hardy nursery stock and specialist grass seed.
Catalogue

20" Wire Support for Tie-on Label.

WARTNABY GARDEN LABELS

Tie-on Label 3½" x 2½"
Pure Zinc Stem Label 2¼" x 4½" and 4" x 7"

Tie Label & Small Stem Label:
£11.00 for 20 (p&p £2.00)
Large Stem Label:
£11.00 for 10 (p&p £2.00)
Marking Pen: £1.20 (p&p inc.)
Marking Tape: 35p per label
20"Galvanised Wire Support:
50p each (p&p £2.00 for 10)
Electric Engraver & Stencil:
Price on application.
Marking Solution: £2.80 (p&p £1.00)
Engraving Service: £1.50 per label

Collections in London can be arranged

Wartnaby Gardens (TG)
MELTON MOWBRAY, LEICESTERSHIRE LE14 3HY
TEL: 01664 822549 • FAX: 01664 822231

Wessex Horticultural Products Ltd

South Newton, Salisbury, Wilts SP2 0QW
Tel (01722) 742500   Fax (01722) 742571

MANUFACTURERS AND SUPPLIERS
TO THE TRADE ONLY, WITH:

Soil-based Growing Media
Peat-based Growing Media
Peat-free Growing Media

Horticultural Sands and Grits

Decorative Stones

Turf Dressings

Soil Improvers   Mulches

WESSEX – COMMITTED TO QUALITY

MACHINERY

Ariens (UK) Ltd
PO Box 34, Huntingdon,
Cambridgeshire PE18 8EN
Tel: 01244 671166
Fax: 01480 459580

Lawn tractors and mowing systems, made in America to the highest standards since 1933 - see advertisement.

Atco-Qualcast Ltd
Suffolk Works, Stowmarket,
Suffolk IP14 1EY
Tel: 01449 742000
Fax: 01449 674243

Atco and Qualcast and Suffolk Punch lawnmowers and powered garden products. Range includes cylinder, rotary and hover mowers in all power sources, plus electric hedgecutters, lawn rakes, shredder and garden vacuum.
Catalogue; Mail order

Autocar Equipment Ltd
77-85 Newington Causeway,
London SE1 6BJ
Tel: 0171 403 5959
Fax: 0171 378 1270

Axminster Power Tool Centre
Chard Street, Axminster, Devon
EX13 5DZ
Tel: 01297 33656
Fax: 01297 35242
Catalogue; Mail order

B C S Tracmaster Ltd
Teknol House, Victoria Rd,
Burgess Hill, Sussex (W.)
RH15 9QF
Tel: 01444 247689
Fax: 01444 871612
Catalogue; Mail order

Black & Decker Ltd
Westpoint, The Grove, Slough,
Berkshire SL1 1QQ
Tel/fax: 01753 511234

Bob Andrews Ltd
1 Bilton Industrial Estate,
Bracknell, Berkshire RG12 8YT
Contact: Ken Salt or Roy Mason
Tel: 01344 862111
Fax: 01344 861345

Distributors of mechanised garden labour-savers via a network of garden machinery dealers countrywide, including outdoor vacuums, fertiliser spreaders, lawn scarifyers and lawn edgers.
Catalogue

Bosch Ltd
Power Tools Division, PO Box 98, Broadwater Park Denham,
Uxbridge, Middlesex UB9 5HJ
Tel/fax: 01895 838383

Claymore Grass Machinery
Waterloo Industrial Estate,
Bidford-on-Avon, Warwickshire
B50 4JH
Contact: Helen Sinfield
Tel: 01789 490177
Fax: 01789 490170

The new UK range of Bolens garden tractors offers a wide choice of models and accessories to suit every need. The entire range is designed for durability and long life. Contact Claymore for further information or visit your local dealer. (See our full colour advertisement on page iv).

Countax
Countax House, Haseley
Industrial Estate, Great Haseley,
Oxford, Oxfordshire OX44 7PF
Tel: 0500 279927
Fax: 01844 278792

Britain's best selling garden tractor. Send for free brochure. See our full colour advertisement and feature on pages 148–149.

Ariens Lawn Tractors Are Sheer MOW-tivation.

Sierra™ 1440G

5YR LIMITED WARRANTY

- Converts to mulch, dethatch, bag or remove snow with optional attachments
- Automotive-style seat adjustment and plenty of leg room for a comfortable ride
- Foot-controlled hydrostatic transmission
- Electric PTO and electric start are standard
- Spring-assisted fender deck lift for easy deck height adjustment
- 40 inch deck with rolled-under lip for superior cutting performance
- 5-Year limited consumer warranty
- Made in America since 1933

Ariens®
The best from start to finish.™

The Ariens 4-in-1 Mowing System

LM12SP

5YR LIMITED WARRANTY

- Ariens' 4-in-1 Mowing System that mows, mulches, bags, and vacuums
- Self-propelled with variable speed control
- 2.5 Bushel Rear Bagger
- 21 inch Cutting Width
- Powerful 5.5 HP Engine with Easy Pull Start
- 6 cutting heights
- Rolled-under deck design creates better air flow for bagging
- 5-Year Limited Warranty
- Made In America Since 1933

Ariens®
Engineered For The Extremes™

Ariens (UK) Ltd, PO Box 34, Huntingdon, Cambs PE18 8EN   Admin & Parts: Tel: 01480 450909   Fax: 01480 459580   Sales: Tel: 01244 671166   Fax: 01244 674499

RECYCLE ALL YOUR GARDEN AND KITCHEN WASTE – *FAST*

Make weed-free compost in only 14 days and all the woodchips and mulch you need, limited only by your supply of "waste". Our tried and tested machines really do make it easy!

- **Award-winning electric shredders**
For the smaller garden. 1600, 1800 and 2200 watts. Chip up to 1½ inches (4cm) diameter. Awarded "Best Buy" recommendation in independent tests.
- **Petrol-engined and PTO-driven shredder/chippers**
For the larger garden. 5, 8 and 11-hp. Your choice of engine. Recoil or battery start. PTO model fits any tractor with 3-point hitch. Chip up to 3 inches (7.5cm) diameter. Produce 1 to 2 cubic metres an hour. Rugged, robust and British made!
- **ComposTumblers**
Two sizes: 12 and 23 cu. ft. (340 and 650 litres). Fill with shredded garden waste, turn for one minute once a day. Make weed-free compost in only 14 days! You don't believe it? Then take advantage of our no-risk 30-day FREE home trial.
- **Smart Carts**
The finest garden wheel-barrow ever! Two sizes: 7 and 12 cu. ft. (200 and 340 litres). Aircraft-quality aluminium frame and linear polyethylene pans. Will not rust, rot, warp, splinter or crack in any weather. Weigh less than 40lb, carry up to 600 lb. LIFETIME WARRANTY.

For brochures and further information contact:–
Globe Organic Services Limited,
Dept DTGF, FREEPOST BM 2930, Solihull, West Midlands B92 7BR or call FREEPHONE 0800 018 4120.

Dennis
Ashbourne Rd, Kirk Langley, Derby, Derbyshire DE6 4NJ

Tel: 01332 824777
Fax: 01332 824525

DENNIS manufacture a range of grasscare equipment from the heavy duty 36" Premier cylinder mowers to the 20" FT510 that can cut, scarify, verti-cut, brush etc.

E P Barrus Ltd
Launton Rd, Bicester, Oxfordshire OX6 0UR

Contact: Martin Wasley
Tel: 01869 363636
Fax: 01869 363600

High performance garden machinery recognised as the best buy around, our lawn and garden machinery products range from £99-£10,000 providing affordable quality solutions.

Echo GB
The Broadway, Didcot, Oxfordshire OX11 8ES

Tel: 01235 813936
Fax: 01235 811491

G W Thornton & Sons Ltd
Grether House, Crown Royal Industrial Park, Stockport, Manchester, Gt SK1 3HB

Tel: 0161 474 1525
Fax: 0161 477 9144

Suppliers of world famous Mantis lightweight cultivator system which digs, weeds, provides complete lawn care package and hedge trimmer conversion from just over £300.
Catalogue; Mail order

Garden Machinery Direct
4 Newtown Rd, Worcester, Hereford & Worcester WR5 1HF

Tel: 01905 619522
Fax: 01905 726241
Catalogue; Mail order

Garden Store
PO Box 68, Crowborough, Sussex (E.) TN6 1YH

Tel: 01892 664646
Fax: 01892 655773

Suppliers of garden machinery, equipment and power tools.

Gayways Lawn Mower Centre
213-217 Watford Rd, Harrow, Middlesex HA1 9PP

Tel: 0181 908 4744
Fax: 0181 904 6520

Sales of new and used garden machinery. Sales of spare parts and the repair of most makes of garden machinery. London's largest independent dealership.
Mail order

Globe Organic Services
163A Warwick Road, Solihull, Midlands (W.) B92 7AR

Contact: Tom Raitt
Tel: 0121 707 4120
Fax: 0121 707 4934

Equipment and machinery for the rapid recycling of green organic waste: shredders, chippers, compost makers and smart carts.

Haselden Enterprise UK
Dept GF, PO Box 44, Cranleigh, Surrey GU6 7YH

Tel/fax: 01483 273664
Email: hasel@interads.co.uk

HASEL through-feed garden hose reel. Wall mounted yet easily removable. Aluminium / stainless steel construction. 5 year leak-free guarantee. Up to 200ft / 60m capacity. Quality accessories from hose to metal spray nozzles supplied.
Catalogue; Mail order

Haygate Engineering Co Ltd
Manor Farm, Hannington, Basingstoke, Hampshire RG26 5TZ

Contact: Mike Kitching
Tel: 01635 299847
Fax: 01635 299024

Cut high hedges safely and quickly on Henchman wheeled platforms. Easy to manoeuvre, stays level on sloping ground, converts to cart/trailer. Free illustrated brochure.

Hayters plc
Spellbrook, Bishops Stortford, Hertfordshire CM23 4BU

Tel: 01279 723444
Fax: 01279 600338

Put the cut and thrust back in your mowing! Hayter offer a range of mowers, including the new, highly affordable Jubilee range; the revolutionary new cordless electric mower; the best-selling Harrier 48, now with advanced new safety features. Write or phone for details of selected dealers. (See full colour advertisement on page iii).
Catalogue

CUT HIGH HEDGES QUICKLY AND SAFELY ON THE HENCHMAN

- An adjustable and stable platform gives you the height and reach to cut tall hedges safely. • **Platform height now up to 8'**, length 5' or 7'. • Strong, light & easy to push. • Stays level on sloping ground. • Converts to trailer or cart. • Prices start from around £375 + VAT

FOR DETAILS RING (01635) 299847 QUOTE REF: 723

Haygate Engineering Co Ltd, Manor Farm, Hannington, Tadley, Hampshire RG26 5TZ

Honda UK
4 Power Rd, Chiswick, London W4 5YT

Tel: 0181 747 1400
Fax: 0181 746 9104

Honda mowers range from 13"-21" cut, electric and petrol. Ride-ons from 30-48" cut. Tillers up to 8hp. Most machines carry 5 year warranty.
Catalogue

Husqvarna Forest & Garden
Oldends Lane, Stonehouse, Gloucestershire GL10 3SY

Tel: 01453 822382
Fax: 01453 826936

Husqvarna offer a wide range of garden machinery from chainsaws to cultivators and lawntractors to brushcutters. Available from a network of servicing dealers.
Catalogue

Interploy Trading Co
Bovis House, Townmead Road, London SW6 2QH

Tel/fax: 0171 371 5377

John Deere Ltd
Harby Rd, Langar, Nottingham, Nottinghamshire NG13 9HT

Tel: 01949 860491
Fax: 01949 860490

Suppliers of quality walk-behind lawn mowers, ride-on mowers, lawn tractors and lawn edgers to the appointed servicing dealer.

K G Aerators
28 Southend Rd, Rochford, Essex SS4 1HQ

Tel/fax: 01702 545774
Mail order

Kubota (UK) Ltd
Dormer Rd, Thame, Oxfordshire OX9 3UN

Tel: 01844 214500
Fax: 01844 216685

A leading name in garden machinery Kubota (UK) Ltd offers a wide range of ride-on mowers together with power products including walk-behind mowers, brush cutters, hedge trimmers, pumps and generators.

Leaky Pipe Systems Ltd
Frith Farm, Dean Street, East Farleigh, Maidstone, Kent ME15 0PR

Tel: 01622 746495
Fax: 01622 745118

Supply and/or installation of sub-surface irrigation systems using porous rubber hose. Do-it-yourself kits available for the amateur gardener.
Catalogue; Mail order

Machine Mart Ltd
211 Lower Parliament Street, Nottingham, Nottinghamshire NG1 1GN

Contact: Mark Reade
Tel: 0115 9587666
Fax: 0115 9483117

Retailers of garden machinery. Nationwide service through 39 branches, providing high quality service, a wide selection of top brand goods at competitive prices.
Catalogue; Mail order

Michael Banks/Ascender
Yew Tree House, 144 Lower Green Rd, Esher, Surrey KT10 8HA

Contact: Michael Banks
Tel: 01372 467922
Fax: 01372 470160

Unique Ascender lift barrows enable gardeners to ground load items up to 5cwt and lift them to barrowing position quickly and easily. Free brochure.
Catalogue; Mail order

Noma Lites Ltd
Brooklands, Weybridge, Surrey KT3 0YU

Moonrays garden lights - fully automatic, totally DIY low voltage garden lighting system in a variety of styles. Write for further details. (See our full colour advertisement on page ii)
Catalogue

Outdoor Power Products Ltd
Dolmar House, Clare Street, Denton, Manchester, Gt M34 3LQ

Tel: 0161 320 8100
Fax: 0161 335 0114

The Trade Counter offers garden and forestry equipment and accessories at direct mail prices, with first class after sales care from a national dealer network.
Catalogue; Mail order

P L M Power Products
Units 5 & 6, The Shires Industrial Estate, Essington Close Birmingham Rd, Lichfield, Staffordshire WS14 9AZ

Tel: 01543 414477
Fax: 01543 414514

Pick Products
Elliot Rd, March, Cambridge, Cambridgeshire PE15 8QU

Tel/fax: 01354 660077
Mail order

Primus Ltd
Stephenson Way, Formby, Merseyside L37 8EQ

Tel/fax: 01704 878614

For details of Primus Gas Weed Burners, ACE greenhouse heaters and other products phone Howard, Shelagh or Marilyn in our sales office.

Ryobi Lawn & Garden (UK)
Cotteswold Rd, Tewkesbury, Gloucestershire GL20 5DJ

Tel: 01684 294606
Fax: 01684 294909

A complete range of powered garden tools including petrol, electric and battery powered trimmers, hedgecutters, sweeper vacs, chain saws, cultivators and lawn mowers.
Catalogue

Snapper Lawn Equipment (UK) Ltd
Hamble Court, Verdon Avenue, Hamble, Hampshire SO3 5HX

Tel: 01703 456504
Fax: 01703 456463

Solo Sprayers
4 Brunel Rd, Leigh-on-Sea, Essex SS9 5JN

Contact: R J Vale
Tel: 01702 525740
Fax: 01702 522752

Full range of brass double action sprayers and syringes, knapsack sprayers and pressure sprayers for every spraying job in the garden.
Catalogue; Mail order

Stihl Ltd
Stihl House, Stanhope Rd, Camberley, Surrey GU15 3YY

Tel: 01276 20202
Fax: 01276 670510

Manufacturers of chainsaws, brushcutters, lawn edgers, blowers, blower/vacuum units, hedge trimmers, pressure washers, brand-Stihl Vikings shredders, lawn mowers, electric hedge trimmers, tillers, sicklebar mowers, ride-on mowers.
Catalogue

Tool-Craft
PO Box 158, Bristol, Avon BS99 1SE

Tel/fax: 0800 581746

Toro Wheel Horse UK
154 Christchurch Rd, Ringwood, Hampshire BH24 3AP

Contact: Colin Gale
Tel: 01425 478424
Fax: 01425 476972

Manufacturer of revolutionary recycler mowers, which reduce mowing time by up to 38% and lead to a greener, healthier lawn. Pedestrian and ride-on models available.

'ZAP' those weeds! with the Primus Gas Weed Burner – only £29.95!

No more back-breaking work to get rid of those weeds! For further details of these products and our range of 'ACE' Greenhouse Heaters –

Please telephone Howard, Shelagh or Marilyn in the sales office or write to:

PRIMUS LIMITED
Stephenson Way, Formby, Merseyside, L37 8EQ
Telephone: 01704 878614

ORNAMENTS, CONTAINERS & STONEWORK

Trailer Barrow Co
Bellbrook Park, Uckfield, Sussex
(E.) TN22 1QF
Tel: 01825 748200
Fax: 01825 761212

Trailerbarrows are single handled load movers which effortlessly carry heavy or bulky loads over two wheels. Larger models can even be adapted for tractor towing.

Turk Scythes & Trimflex (UK)
18 Spiers Way, Horley, Surrey
RH6 7NY
Tel/fax: 01293 785069
Mail order

Vigo Vineyard Supplies
Bollhayes, Clayidon, Cullompton,
Devon EX15 3PN
Tel: 01823 680844
Fax: 01823 680347

Fruit presses. A range of traditional machines suitable for fruit juice, wine and cider making. Turn windfall and surplus fruit into pure fresh juice.
Catalogue; Mail order

Yamaha Motor (UK) Ltd
Sopwith Drive, Brooklands,
Weybridge, Surrey KT13 0UZ
Tel: 01932 358000
Fax: 01932 358090

A select range of self-propelled rear-roller lawn mowers that are extremely easy to use and give superb results. Avaliable only through specialist dealers.

Andrew Crace Designs
21 Bourne Lane, Much Hadham,
Hertfordshire SG10 6ER
Tel: 01279 842685
Fax: 01279 843646

Archer Designs
73 Westgate, Rotherham,
Yorkshire (S.) S60 1BQ
Catalogue

Architectural Heritage
Taddington Manor, Taddington,
Cutsdean, Nr Cheltenham,
Gloucestershire GL54 5RY
Tel: 01386 584414
Fax: 01386 584236
Hours: 9.30am–5.30pm Mon–Fri, 10.30am–4.30pm Sat

Vendors of high quality garden statuary, antique and reproduction, to include fountains, gazebos, seats, urns, statues in stone, lead, bronze, composition stone and terracotta. (See our full colour advertisement on page 147).
Catalogue

Barbary Pots
45 Fernshaw Road, London
SW10 0TN
Tel/fax: 0171 352 1053

Black Forge Art
Owley Farm, Wittersham,
Isle-of-Oxney, Kent TN30 7HJ
Tel/fax: 01797 270073

Bonhams Chelsea
65-69 Lots Rd, London SW10 0RN
Tel/fax: 0171 351 7111

British Museum Replicas
46 Bloomsbury Street, London
WC1B 3QQ
Contact: Carey Wells
Tel: 0171 323 1234
Fax: 0171 636 7186

Statues, reliefs and busts from the spectacular classical collection of the British Museum, cast in reconstituted marble using moulds of the original sculpture. Free catalogue.
Catalogue; Mail order

Bronze Collection
21b Bourne Lane, Much
Hadham, Hertfordshire SG10 6ER
Tel: 01279 812685
Fax: 01279 843646

Bulbeck Foundry
Reach Rd, Burwell,
Cambridgeshire CB5 0AH
Contact: Hugo Smith
Tel: 01638 743153
Fax: 01638 743374
Hours: 8.30am–5.30pm Mon–Fri. Please phone first

The Bulbeck Foundry makes top quality lead garden ornaments including statues, urns, plant containers, fountains, birdbaths and water tanks. Good colour brochure available.
Catalogue

Chilstone
Victoria Park, Fordcombe Road,
Langton Green, Tunbridge Wells,
Kent TN3 0RE
Tel: 01892 740866
Fax: 01892 740867
Hours: Mon–Fri & Sun Apr–Sept. Mon–Fri Oct–Mar

Handmade reconstituted stone - birdbaths, sundials, fountains, urns, statues, balustrading, seats, temples - all in classical style. Show gardens 1 hour from London. Catalogue available.
Catalogue; Mail order

Classic Garden
Lower Puncheston,
Haverfordwest, Pembrokeshire,
Dyfed SA62 5TG
Contact: Jan Warden
Tel/fax: 01348 881451

Versailles planters, tubs, troughs, window boxes - handmade in Welsh oak. Obelisks and plant supports. Europe-wide mail order service. Callers to workshop by appointment.
Mail order

Compton Acres Garden Centre
164 Canford Cliffs Rd, Poole,
Dorset BH13 7ES
Contact: John P B Heron
Tel/fax: 01202 701416
Email: north_and_south@msn.com
Hours: 9am–6pm daily Mar–Oct. 10am–4pm Tues–Fri Nov–Feb

Stoneware a speciality, terracotta, self contained water features, Japanese ornaments, wide range of plants expecially heathers, alpines and herbaceous. Landscape service available.

Connoisseur Sun Dials
Lane's End, Strefford, Craven
Arms, Shropshire SY7 8DE
Contact: Silas Higgon
Tel/fax: 01588 672126

Accurate working dials finely etched in solid bronze or brass. Armillary spheres, wall dials, equatorial, horizontal and polar dials. Simple setting instructions given.
Catalogue; Mail order

Cotswold Range of Garden Ornamental Ironwork
Stonebank, Ablington, Bibury,
Cirencester, Gloucestershire
GL7 5NU
Tel/fax: 01285 740412
Hours: Variable – please phone

Top quality garden ornamental ironwork. Arches, bowers, centre-pieces, obelisks. Full pergola service from design to installation. Solid construction, rust proofed, finished Cotswold green/black. Free colour brochure.
Catalogue; Mail order

Ornaments, Containers & Stonework

Country Collections
Unit 9, Ditton Priors Trading Estate, Bridgnorth, Shropshire WV16 6SS

Contact: Raymond Foster
Tel/fax: 01746 861330
Hours: By appointment only

Our free catalogue lists dozens of sundials in brass and bronze, including the best selling butterfly design. We also supply plant troughs in genuine weathered stone, hanging pot holders and alpine planters in clay and hypertufa.
Catalogue; Mail order

Courtyard Pottery
Groundwell Farm, Cricklade Rd, Swindon, Wiltshire SN2 5AU

Contact: John Huggins
Tel/fax: 01793 727466
Hours: 9am–5.30pm Mon–Sat, 1–5pm Sun April–Sept

Specialist makers of a wide range of hand-thrown terracotta flower pots and garden ornaments, especially dragons. Also large green glazed stoneware planters.
Catalogue; Mail order

Crowther of Syon Lodge
Busch Corner, London Rd, Isleworth, Middlesex TW7 5BH

Tel: 0181 560 7978
Fax: 0181 568 7572
Hours: 9am–5pm Mon–Fri, 11am–4pm Sat & Sun

The oldest architectural antiques business in Britain. Stock includes chimney-pieces in pine, marble and stone, classical statuary, garden temples, vases, wellheads and fountains, plus period panelled rooms and period designed summerhouses.

David Sharp Studio
201A Nottingham Rd, Somercotes, Derbyshire

Tel: 01773 606066
Fax: 01773 540737

Catalogue

Devonshire Statuary
Common Farm, Aylesbeare, Exeter, Devon EX5 2DG

Tel: 01395 233288
Fax: 01395 232380

Doyles Dovecotes
87 Maescader, Pencader, Dyfed SA39 9HH

Tel/fax: 01559 389169

Traditional full size garden dovecotes manufactured by craftsmen in a range of designs. Write or phone for free brochure.
Catalogue

Drummonds of Bramley Architectural Antiques
Birtley Farm, Horsham Rd, Bramley, Guildford, Surrey GU5 0LA

Tel: 01483 898766
Fax: 01483 894393

Farm & Garden Bygones
St Issey, Wadebridge, Cornwall PL27 7QA

Tel/fax: 01841 540744

Four Seasons Pottery
Culver Nurseries, Cattlegate Rd, Crews Hill, Enfield, Middlesex EN2 9DW

Hours: 9am–5pm Tues–Fri, 10am–2pm Sat/Sun

Manufacturers of frost-proof hand thrown and press moulded terracotta garden pots, water features, glazed gardenware and wall plaques. Retail and garden designers welcome.
Catalogue

Gardens in Wood
26 Staplers Heath, Great Totham, Maldon, Essex CM9 8PG

Tel/fax: 01621 893359

Gardenscape
Fairview, Smelthouses, Summerbridge, Harrogate, Yorkshire (N.) HG3 4DH

Contact: Michael D Myers
Tel/fax: 01423 780291
Hours: By appointment only

Horticultural advisory and design service. Hard and soft landscaping - free quotes. Small nursery specialising in rare and unusual woodland plants. Hand-carved stone ornaments.
Catalogue; Mail order

Glen Pottery
East Stour, Gillingham, Dorset SP8 5ND

Tel/fax: 01747 838697

Haddonstone Ltd
The Forge House, East Haddon, Northampton, Northamptonshire NN6 8DB

Tel: 01604 770711
Fax: 01604 770027
Hours: 9am–5.30pm Mon–Fri (except Bank & Xmas Hols)

Manufacturers of fine garden ornaments, including urns, statuary, sundials, bird baths, fountains, balustrading, temples and pavilions. 120 page full colour brochure £5. Beautiful show garden. Delivery worldwide.
Catalogue; Mail order

Hare Lane Pottery
Cranborne, Wimborne, Dorset BH21 5QT

Contact: Jonathan Garratt
Tel/fax: 01725 517700

Hours: Phone to check

Distinctive hand made terracotta pots, guaranteed frost-proof and fired exclusively with wood to produce subtle colours. The pottery is well known for unusual and innovative design.

Haresclough Pottery
Haresclough, Whitegate, Northwich, Cheshire CW8 2BP

Contact: Janet Durden Hay
Tel/fax: 01606 883681
Hours: By appointment

Specialists in hand-built stoneware pottery, both sculptural and functional. Including self-contained fountains for patio and conservatory, birdbaths, bird feeders and plant containers of original design.
Catalogue

Holloways
Lower Court, Suckley, Worcester, Hereford & Worcester WR6 5DE

Tel/fax: 01886 884665
Hours: 9.30am–5pm Mon–Sat

Large selection of antique and contemporary garden furniture, statuary and ornaments, conservatory furniture and accessories, conservatory plants. Send for free catalogue.
Catalogue; Mail order

J G S Weathervanes
High Street, Edlesborough, Dunstable, Bedfordshire LU6 2HS

Contact: John Sayer
Tel: 01525 220360
Fax: 01525 222786
Hours: 8am–4.30pm Mon–Fri, Sat by appt

Quality weathervanes of our own design and manufacture. Over 180 designs or commissions. Visitors welcome at workshops. Brochure free - stamp appreciated. Customers worldwide. Internet http://www.activeweb.co.uk/jgsweath.html
Catalogue; Mail order

Jardiniere
26A Priory Road, Hampton, Middlesex TW12 2NT

Contact: Brian Bird
Tel/fax: 0181 979 1880

Supply and hire of urns, pots & containers, olive oil jars, furniture, garden implements - antique, period or just plain intriguing. For exterior or interior decoration.

Jardinique
Kemps Place, Selborne Rd, Greatham, Liss, Hampshire GU33 6HG

Contact: Edward & Sarah Neish
Tel: 01420 538000
Fax: 01420 5387000
Hours: 10am–5pm Tues–Sat

Offers one of the most comprehensive ranges of decorative garden items comprising a unique mixture of garden antiques dating as far back as the 18th century and quality contemporary garden items handmade by skilled craftsmen. Set in attractive surroundings, the range of stock includes: urns, planters, plant stands, ornaments, statuary, figures, animals, staddle stones, furniture, pergolas, fountains, weather vanes, birdbaths, fencing panels, hand tools and gardenalia.
Catalogue

Kitchen Garden
14 George Street, Oban, Strathclyde TA34 5SB

Tel/fax: 01631 66332

Knight Terrace Pots
West Orchard, Shaftesbury, Dorset SP7 0LJ

Tel/fax: 01258 472685

Quality cast stone for gardens and buildings - ornaments, urns, seats, birdbaths, pedestals, balustrades, copings. Classic and modern designs. Copies and originals to order. Deliveries.
Catalogue; Mail order

Lannock Pottery
Weston, Hitchin, Hertfordshire SG4 7AX

Tel: 01462 790356
Fax: 01462 790704
Mail order

Melaleuca Pottery
Ian Watson, 52 Worple Way, Richmond, Surrey TW10 6DF

Tel/fax: 0181 332 7161
Catalogue

Mellors Garden Ceramics
Rosemead, Marshwood, Bridport, Dorset DT6 5QB

Tel/fax: 01297 678217
Hours: By appointment only

Individually hand-made glazed stoneware for the garden or conservatory, including lanterns, bird-baths, self contained fountains, planters and urns. Send large SAE for catalogue.
Catalogue; Mail order

Metalarts
Park Forge, Coryton, Okehampton, Devon EX20 4PG

Tel/fax: 01566 83454
Catalogue; Mail order

Nonington Pottery
Old Court Hill, Nonington, Dover, Kent CT15 4LQ

Tel/fax: 01304 840174
Catalogue; Mail order

Norfolk Garden Supplies
54B Yarmouth Rd, Thorpe,
Norwich, Norfolk NR7 0HE
Tel: 01603 38000
Fax: 01603 700003
Catalogue

Numbers & Names
PO Box 111, Wetherby,
Yorkshire (N.) LS22 5XB
Tel/fax: 01423 358415

Housename and number plaques of the highest quality traditionally crafted in wood or cast metal. Wide range of standard designs or bespoke service available.
Catalogue; Mail order

Olive Tree Trading Company Ltd
London Rd, Hook, Hampshire
RG27 9DJ
Tel: 01256 766666
Fax: 01256 765001

Original Terracotta Shop
8 Moorfield Rd, Duxford Village,
Cambridgeshire CB2 4PS
Tel/fax: 01223 832700
Hours: Summer 9am–5.30pm 7 days/Winter (Jan–1 Mar) weekends 10am–5pm, APT during week

A world of terracotta awaits you in Duxford Village. Open 7 days - ever changing displays for interior or exterior use; showrooms and gardens; ideas for all.
Catalogue

Ornamental Leadwork
Culag, Green Lane, Nafferton,
Driffield, Yorkshire (E.)
YO25 0LF
Contact: D Marston

Ornamental leadwork, completely handmade to the highest standards. All manner of unusual and entertaining items available, including containers, fountains, gargoyles etc. Send SAE for leaflet.

Ornate Products
Limecroft Rd, Knaphill, Surrey
GU23 7EF
Tel: 01483 486566
Fax: 01483 797809
Catalogue; Mail order

Pamal
The Cottage, Sproxton, Melton
Mowbray, Leicestershire
LE14 4QS
Contact: M Graham
Tel: 01476 860266
Fax: 01476 860523

Manufacturers of timber outdoor furniture, planters, standard size or made to order, painted or natural wood. Catalogue available.
Catalogue; Mail order

Plowman Trading
Broad Oak Farm, Sutton on
Forest, York, Yorkshire (N.)
YO6 1ER
Contact: Mrs P M Plowman
Tel: 01904 768230
Fax: 01904 765946
Hours: 9am–5pm daily

Browse or buy from a large selection of terracotta, glazed pots, statues and basketware for garden and home. Situated B1363 5 miles north of York.

Podington Garden Centre
High Street, Podington,
Wellingborough,
Northamptonshire NN29 7HS
Contact: Colin Read
Tel: 01933 53656
Fax: 01933 410332
Hours: 9am–6.30pm Summer, 9am–5.30pm Winter, 10.30am–4.30pm Sun

A plant person's paradise with thousands of plants all year round. Also a wide range of garden sundries, furniture, aquatics, garden ornaments, fencing and paving.

Posh Pots
Elkstone Manor, Elkstone,
Cheltenham, Gloucestershire
GL53 9PB
Tel: 01242 870525
Fax: 01242 870530

Plain terracotta pots and saucers, hand painted in eight glorious colours and finished in strong glossy varnish. Five sizes. Wholesale, retail and mail order.
Catalogue; Mail order

Pot Village
116 Watling Street, Radlett,
Hertfordshire WD7 7AB
Tel/fax: 01923 854746
Hours: 10am–6pm Mon–Sat

Pots & Pithoi
The Barns, East Street, Turners
Hill, Sussex (W.) RH10 4QQ
Tel/fax: 01342 714793
Hours: 10am–5pm daily, 4pm Winter

Handmade in Crete: beautiful terracotta garden, conservatory and patio pots. From 5" to over 4'. Select from over 10,000 pots, all frost-resistant. Free leaflet. (See our full colour advertisement on page i).
Catalogue

Real Stone Company
The Forge, Penthouse Hill, Bath,
Avon BA1 7EL
Tel/fax: 01225 858620

Redwood Stone Ltd
46 North Rd, Wells, Somerset
BA5 2TL
Tel: 01749 673601
Fax: 01749 675701

Manufacturers of cast stone garden ornaments and distributors of The China Dream range of bamboo, terracotta and granite oriental garden ornaments and water features.

Renaissance Bronzes
79 Pimlico Rd, London
SW1W 8PH
Contact: Simon Jacques
Tel: 0171 823 5149
Fax: 0171 730 4598
Catalogue

Renaissance Casting
19 Cranford Rd, Coventry,
Midlands (W.) CV5 8JF
Tel/fax: 01926 885567
Catalogue

Robus Pottery & Tiles
Evington Park, Hastingleigh,
Ashford, Kent TN25 5JH
Tel/fax: 01233 750330
Hours: 9am–5pm Mon–Sat

Manufacturers of ornamental terracotta garden pots, gazebos, follies, fountains, and floor tiles. Commissions undertaken.
Catalogue; Mail order

Roche Court
East Winterslow, Salisbury,
Wiltshire SP5 1BG
Tel: 01980 862204
Fax: 01980 862447
Hours: 11am–5pm Sat/Sun May–Oct

Ruardean Garden Pottery
West End, Ruardean,
Gloucestershire GL17 9TP
Tel: 01594 543577
Fax: 01594 544536
Hours: 9am–5.30pm Mon–Sat. Sun Apr–Sept 1–5pm

Specialist makers of hand-thrown, frost-proof terracotta - from tiny pots to huge feature planters. Also dragons, cats, lizards and large glazed stoneware pots.
Catalogue; Mail order

Scarcity of Scarecrows
Oakland Cottage, Greenway
Lane, Charlton Kings,
Cheltenham, Gloucestershire
GL52 6LA
Tel/fax: 01242 239071

Looking for an unusual gift? Designer scarecrows, hand made in rustic coloured hessian, 5' tall with cheeky crow and mouse. Phone 01242 239071. Price £85.
Catalogue

Seago
22 Pimlico Rd, London SW1W 8LJ
Tel: 0171 730 7502
Fax: 0171 730 9179
Hours: 9.30am–5.30pm Mon–Fri

Specialist suppliers of fine antique garden ornaments and sculpture.

Seymours Garden & Leisure Group
The Pit House, Ewell By-Pass,
Surrey KT17 1PS
Contact: James Seymour
Tel: 0181 393 0111
Fax: 0181 393 0237
Hours: Open daily. Sun 10am–4pm

Landscape and leisure centre with aquatics, landscape supplies, garden leisure departments and coffee shop under same ownership as Peters Plants and Garden Centre at Cobham (01932 862530).

Sothebys
Summers Place, Billingshurst,
Sussex (W.) RH14 9AD
Contact: Jackie Rees
Tel: 01403 783933
Fax: 01403 785153
Hours: 9.30am–4.30pm Mon–Fri

Twice yearly auctions of garden statuary, ornaments and architectural items at Sotheby's Country House saleroom. Illustrated catalogues with printed estimates. Free valuations and advice.
Catalogue; Mail order

Stephen C Markham
22X High Street, Caterham,
Surrey CR3 5UA
Tel: 01833 343407
Fax: 01883 344522

An exciting range of lead flower planters, fountains and plaques, all individually hand cast by one of the country's top craftsmen.
Catalogue; Mail order

Stiffkey Lampshop
Stiffkey, Wells-next-the-Sea,
Norfolk NR23 1AJ
Tel: 01328 830460
Fax: 01328 830005

Susan Symmonds Sculptures
Silver Hill Cottage, Pateley
Bridge, Harrogate, Yorkshire
(N.) HG3 5PG
Tel/fax: 01423 711360

Sweerts de Landas
Dunsborough Park, Ripley,
Woking, Surrey GU23 6AL
Tel: 01483 225366
Fax: 01483 224525
Hours: By appointment only

Dealer in fine quality 17th-19th century antique garden ornaments.
Catalogue

The Daily Telegraph *Green Fingers* Paving

PAVING

T I C Products Ltd
29 Brook Holloway, Stourbridge, Midlands (W.) DY9 8XL
Tel: 01384 896789
Fax: 01384 423661

Unusual and beautiful Victorian style scrollwork hanging basket bracket with sculptured hook. Manufactured in cast alloy to give strength and durability.
Mail order

Terrace & Garden
Orchard House, Patmore End, Ugley, Bishops Stortford, Hertfordshire CM22 6JA
Tel: 01799 543289
Fax: 01799 543586

TimberKits
Unit 20, Applins Farm, Farrington, Blandford Forum, Dorset DT11 8RA
Tel/fax: 01747 811497
Mail order

Webbs Distribution Ltd
Unit 2, 15 Station Rd, Knebworth, Stevenage, Hertfordshire SG3 6AP
Tel: 01438 814620
Fax: 01438 815047
Hours: *By appointment*

Supplier of many unique and innovative products and planters for both the garden and home, including an extensive range of craftsmen-made weathervanes. Free brochure.
Mail order

Westwood Dials
White House Farm, New Hall Lane, Mundon, Essex CM9 6PJ
Tel/fax: 01277 227665
Catalogue

Wetheriggs Pottery
Clifton Dykes, Penrith, Cumbria CA10 2DH
Tel: 01768 892733
Fax: 01768 892722
Catalogue; Mail order

Whichford Pottery
Whichford, Shipton on Stour, Warwickshire CV36 5PG
Tel: 01608 684416
Fax: 01608 684833

We handmake a large variety of frostproof terracotta flowerpots including special commissions for the National Trust. Visitors very welcome at the pottery.
Catalogue; Mail order

Willow Pottery
Crossleaze Farm, Woolley, Bath, Avon BA1 8AU
Tel: 01225 859902
Fax: 01225 859088

Dales Stone Company Ltd
Escrick Grange, Escrick, York, Yorkshire (N.) YO4 6EB
Tel: 01904 728748
Fax: 01904 728768
Hours: *By appointment*

Natural stone landscape materials. Paving, boulders, cobbles etc. Self contained water features. Nationwide delivery. Visitors please telephone for appointment and directions.
Catalogue; Mail order

English Heritage Driveways
Whitehall, School Lane, Hartford, Northwich, Cheshire CW8 1PF
Tel/fax: 0345 125466

Fired Earth
Twyford Mill, Adderbury, Oxfordshire OX17 3HP
Tel/fax: 01295 812088

Gardenscape
Fairview, Smelthouses, Summerbridge, Harrogate, Yorkshire (N.) HG3 4DH
Contact: Michael D Myers
Tel/fax: 01423 780291
Hours: *By appointment only*

Horticultural advisory and design service. Hard and soft landscaping - free quotes. Small nursery specialising in rare and unusual woodland plants. Hand-carved stone ornaments.
Catalogue; Mail order

Melcourt Industries Ltd
Eight Bells House, Tetbury, Gloucestershire GL8 8JG
Tel: 01666 503919
Fax: 01666 504398

Mulches, soil conditioners and play surfaces available in small quantities from our national network of Melcourt Small-Load stockists. Call for details of nearest stockist.

Northwold Rockery Stone & Crazy Paving
The Poplars, Thetford Rd, Northwold, Thetford, Norfolk TP26 5LW
Tel/fax: 01366 728342

Paris Ceramics
583 Kings Rd, London SW6 2EH
Tel/fax: 0171 371 7778

Podington Garden Centre
High Street, Podington, Wellingborough, Northamptonshire NN29 7HS
Contact: Colin Read
Tel: 01933 53656
Fax: 01933 410332
Hours: *9am–6.30pm Summer, 9am–5.30pm Winter, 10.30am–4.30pm Sun*

A plant person's paradise with thousands of plants all year round. Also a wide range of garden sundries, furniture, aquatics, garden ornaments, fencing and paving.
Toilets; Refreshments; Disabled access

Regency Driveways Ltd
Maritime House, The Quays, Salford Quays, Manchester, Manchester, Gt M5 2XN
Tel/fax: 0800 616170
Catalogue

Seymours Garden & Leisure Group
The Pit House, Ewell By-Pass, Surrey KT17 1PS
Contact: James Seymour
Tel: 0181 393 0111
Fax: 0181 393 0237
Hours: *Open daily. Sun 10am–4pm*

Landscape and leisure centre with aquatics, landscape supplies, garden leisure departments and coffee shop under same ownership as Peters Plants and Garden Centre at Cobham (01932 862530).
Toilets; Refreshments

Seymours Landscape Centre
Stoke Road, Stoke d'Abernon, Cobham, Surrey KT11 3PU
Contact: Chris Saunders
Tel: 01932 862530
Fax: 01932 862855
Hours: *Open daily. Sun 11am–5pm*

Gardens designed, constructed and planted to high standards. Founder BALI members. Hampton Court and RHS Chelsea Gold Awards for gardens. Also sales centre for all landscape materials to trade and retail customers.

Town & Country Paving Ltd
Unit 10, Shrubland Nurseries, Roundstone Lane, Angmering, Sussex (W.) BN16 4AT
Tel: 01903 776297
Fax: 01903 787637
Catalogue

Wreford Landscapes
Pucknall Farm, Dores Lane, Braishfield, Romsey, Hampshire SO51 0QJ
Contact: Simon Wreford
Tel: 01794 368155
Fax: 01794 368218
Hours: *7.30am–6pm Mon–Fri*

Landscape design and construction for town houses to country manors. Commercial and business developments throughout southern England.

ROCKERY SPECIALISTS

Brambling House Alpines
119 Sheffield Rd, Warmsworth, Doncaster, Yorkshire (S.) DN4 9QX
Contact: Jane McDonagh
Tel/fax: 01302 850730
Hours: 10am–6pm Closed Mon except Bank Hols

Large collection of sempervivums, auriculas, pubescent primulas, diascias, kabschia saxifragas, lewisias and other unusual plants. Phone before travelling to ensure attention. Catalogue: large SAE.
Catalogue; Mail order; Toilets

D H E Plants
Rose Lea, Darley House Estate, Matlock, Derbyshire DE4 2QH
Contact: Peter M Smith
Tel/fax: 01629 732512

Alpine and rock garden plants especially erodium, helianthemum, saxifraga, sisyrinchium. Nursery is at Robert Young Garden Centre, Bakewell Rd, Matlock.
Catalogue; Mail order

Greenslacks Nurseries
Ocot Lane, Scammonden, Huddersfield, Yorkshire (W.) HD3 3FR
Tel/fax: 01484 842584
Hours: 10am–4pm Mar–Oct. Closed Mon & Tues

A huge range of alpine and rockery plants from the very rare to the common-place. Mail order our forte. Catalogue £1 in stamps please.
Catalogue; Mail order; Toilets

Kexby Design
7 Lindfield Drive, Wellington, Shropshire TF1 1SF
Contact: John B Rickell MIHort, Dip Hort (Wisley)
Tel/fax: 01952 249935

Garden design and horticultural consultancy. Designs for contract or for DIY advice on plant selection, alpine garden designs top and soft fruit.

Mendle Nursery
Holme, Scunthorpe, Humberside DN16 3RF
Contact: Mrs A Earnshaw
Tel/fax: 01724 850864
Hours: 10am–4pm Tues–Sun

Specialist nursery listing over 800 varieties of alpines (primulas, sempervivums & saxifragas). Mail order available - no minimum order. Send 2 x 1st class stamps for catalogue.
Catalogue; Mail order; Toilets

Nicky's Rock Garden Nursery
Hillcrest, Broadhayes, Stockland, Honiton, Devon EX14 9EH
Contact: Bob & Diana Dark
Tel/fax: 01404 881213
Hours: 9am–dusk

Small family nursery specialising in plants for rockeries, scree, raised beds etc. Please ring first for directions and to check if open (most days).
Catalogue; Toilets

Northwold Rockery Stone & Crazy Paving
The Poplars, Thetford Rd, Northwold, Thetford, Norfolk TP26 5LW
Tel/fax: 01366 728342

Podington Garden Centre
High Street, Podington, Wellingborough, Northamptonshire NN29 7HS
Contact: Colin Read
Tel: 01933 53656
Fax: 01933 410332
Hours: 9am–6.30pm Summer, 9am–5.30pm Winter, 10.30am–4.30pm Sun

A plant person's paradise with thousands of plants all year round. Also a wide range of garden sundries, furniture, aquatics, garden ornaments, fencing and paving.
Toilets; Refreshments; Disabled access

Potterton & Martin
The Cottage Nursery, Moortown Rd, Nettleton, Nr Caistor, Lincolnshire LN7 6HX
Contact: Mr or Mrs Potterton
Tel: 01472 815792
Fax: 01472 851792
Hours: 9am–5pm daily

Alpines and dwarf bulbs. Mail order or at nursery. Seven Chelsea Golds and eight consecutive RHS Farrer Trophy awards 1988 to 1995. Catalogue 50p.
Catalogue; Mail order; Toilets

Ray Cheeseborough
The Cottage, Henrietta Mews, Handel Street, London WC1N 1PH
Tel/fax: 0171 837 2553

Seymours Garden & Leisure Group
The Pit House, Ewell By-Pass, Surrey KT17 1PS
Contact: James Seymour
Tel: 0181 393 0111
Fax: 0181 393 0237
Hours: Open daily. Sun 10am–4pm

Landscape and leisure centre with aquatics, landscape supplies, garden leisure departments and coffee shop under same ownership as Peters Plants and Garden Centre at Cobham (01932 862530).
Toilets; Refreshments

Slack Top Alpines
Slack Top, Hebden Bridge, Yorkshire (W.) HX7 7HA
Tel/fax: 01422 845348
Hours: 10am–6pm Mar–Oct. Closed Mons & Tues except Bank Hols

Visit our attractive alpine gardens and browse among our huge range of plants for sale, all grown here. Helpful and friendly advice. SAE for list.
Catalogue

Tough Alpine Nursery
Westhaybogs, Tough, Alford, Grampian AB33 8DU
Contact: Fred or Monika Carrie
Tel: 019755 62783
Fax: 019755 63561
Hours: 10am–4pm Mon–Fri Feb–Oct

Alpine plant specialists offering a wide range of quality plants including many rare and unusual varieties. Send 3 x 2nd class stamps for descriptive catalogue.
Catalogue; Mail order

Town Farm Nursery
Whitton Village, Stockton on Tees, Cleveland TS21 1LQ
Contact: David Baker
Tel/fax: 01740 631079
Hours: 10am–6pm Fri–Mon. Closed in Winter

Specialist nursery within easy reach of A1(M). Sheltered 3/4 acre garden with many unusual alpines, perennials and shrubs. Catalogue 3 x 1st class stamps. Open Friday to Monday. Closed mid-week except by previous appointment.
Catalogue; Mail order; Toilets

Very Interesting Rock Co
PO Box 27, Leamington Spa, Midlands (W.) CV32 5GR
Tel/fax: 01926 313465

White Cottage Alpines
Sunnyside Nurseries, Hornsea Road, Sigglesthorne, Yorkshire (E.) HU11 5QL
Contact: Mrs Sally Cummins
Tel/fax: 01964 542692
Hours: 10am–5pm Thurs–Sun. Closed Dec/Jan

Specialist nursery offering alpines and rockery plants for beginners or enthusiasts. Mail order by next day carrier. Send 4 x 1st class stamps for descriptive catalogue.
Catalogue; Mail order

Wreford Landscapes
Pucknall Farm, Dores Lane, Braishfield, Romsey, Hampshire SO51 0QJ
Contact: Simon Wreford
Tel: 01794 368155
Fax: 01794 368218
Hours: 7.30am–6pm Mon–Fri

Landscape design and construction for town houses to country manors. Commercial and business developments throughout southern England.

SEEDSMEN & SEED EXCHANGE SCHEMES

Andrew Norfield Seeds
Lower Meend, St Briavels,
Gloucestershire GL15 6RW
Tel: 01594 530134
Fax: 01594 530113

Pregerminated seed of those difficult to germinate species, including hardy trees, shrubs, climbers and house plants. Seed sent already growing. Maples, magnolia, palms, cycads and many other species.
Catalogue; Mail order

B & T World Seeds
Whitnell House, Whitnell,
Nether Stowey, Bridgwater,
Somerset TA5 1JE
Tel/fax: 01278 733209
Email: 10060.2351@compuserve.com

International seed distributor with world's largest trade seed list. Main list £10 in Europe, £14 elsewhere. Over 180 sub-lists. SAE for list index and order form.
Catalogue; Mail order

Bakker Holland
PO Box 111, Spalding,
Lincolnshire PE12 6EL
Tel/fax: 01775 711411
Hours: Mail order only
Catalogue; Mail order

British Seed Houses
Camp Road, Swinderby,
Lincolnshire LN6 9QJ
Tel: 01522 868714
Fax: 01522 868095

Complete range of quality seed for all types of lawn, including Family, Luxury, Lazy, Shaded and Meadow, plus Lawn Restorer Kit for overseeding damaged areas.
Mail order

C N Seeds
Denmark House, Pymoor, Ely,
Cambridgeshire CB6 2EG
Tel: 01353 699413
Fax: 01353 698806
Catalogue; Mail order

CTDA
174 Cambridge Street, London
SW1V 4QE
Contact: Dr B Smith
Tel/fax: 0171 976 5115
Hours: Mail order only

Specialist mail order supplier of plants, including hardy garden cyclamen, Ballard strain hellebores, aquilegia species, dierama; specialist seed supplier for hardy cyclamen and hellebores.
Catalogue; Mail order

Chadwell Himalayan Plant Seed
81 Parlaunt Rd, Slough, Berkshire
SL3 8DE
Contact: Chris Chadwell
Tel/fax: 01753 542823

Send 3 x 1st class stamps for seed catalogue offering unusual species from the Himalayas and world-wide.
Catalogue; Mail order

Chiltern Seeds
Bortree Stile, Ulverston,
Cumbria LA12 7PB
Tel: 01229 581137
Fax: 01229 584549
Hours: Mail order only
Catalogue; Mail order

Cottage Herbery
Mill House, Boraston, Tenbury Wells, Hereford & Worcester
WR15 8LZ
Tel: 01584 7821575
Fax: 01584 781483
Hours: Suns only May to July. Weekdays by appt

Beautiful tranquil setting, a true cottage garden with herbs, scented plants, old roses and vegetables. Totally organic. Good range of plants for sale. 4 x 1st class stamps for informative catalogue and seed list.
Catalogue; Mail order

D T Brown & Co Ltd
Station Rd, Poulton le Fylde,
Lancashire FY6 7HX
Tel: 01253 882371
Fax: 01253 890923
Hours: Mail order only
Catalogue; Mail order

David Bell Ltd
Eastfield Drive, Penicuik, Lothian
EH26 8BA
Tel: 01968 678480
Fax: 01968 678878
Hours: 8am–5.30pm Mon–Fri

Scotland's leading wholesale seed merchant, David Bell Ltd, offers agricultural and amenity seeds as well as a comprehensive range of bird feeds including wildbird food.
Catalogue

E W King & Co Ltd
Monks Farm, Pantlings Lane,
Coggeshall Road, Kelvedon,
Colchester, Essex CO5 9PG
Tel: 01376 570000
Fax: 01376 571189
Hours: 8.30am–5pm Mon–Fri

Suppliers of a very extensive range of traditional and unusual vegetable, flower and herb seeds for the conventional and organic garden and allotment holder.

Edwin Tucker & Sons
Brewery Meadow, Stonepark,
Ashburton, Devon TQ13 7DG
Contact: Geoff Penton
Tel: 01364 652403
Fax: 01364 654300
Hours: 8am–5pm Mon–Fri

Free mail order catalogue containing wide range of competitively priced vegetable and flower seed packets plus over 60 varieties of seed potatoes.
Catalogue; Mail order

Emorsgate Seeds
Terrington Court, Popes Lane,
Terrington St Clement, Kings
Lynn, Norfolk PE34 4NT
Tel/fax: 01553 829028
Hours: Mail order only

Wild flower and wild grass seeds for gardens, landscaping and farmland. Please write or telephone for a free colour catalogue. Large SAE appreciated.
Catalogue; Mail order

Gardeners' Seed Exchange
56 Red Willow, Harlow, Essex
CM19 5PD

The Gardeners' Seed Exchange. Helping gardeners to help each other. For introductory copy send 3 x 2nd class stamps to TGSE at above address.

Harefield Herbs
131 Harefield Rd, Coventry,
Midlands (W.) CV2 4BT
Tel/fax: 01203 450172

400 varieties of herbs and wild flowers. Seeds and plants available. Lavender hedging and chamomile lawns are specialities. Send 50p stamp for catalogue. Mail order and trade only.
Catalogue; Mail order

Henry Doubleday Research Association (HDRA)
Ryton Organic Gardens,
Ryton-on-Dunsmore, Coventry,
Midlands (W.) CV8 3LG
Tel: 01203 303517
Fax: 01203 639229

Britain's premier organic gardening organisation, with demonstration gardens at Coventry and Maidstone. Members get free advice, quarterly magazines, discounts from extensive mail order catalogue plus free entry to RHS and other gardens. Runs Heritage Seed Library for endangered vegetables. SAE for details.
Catalogue; Mail order

J E Martin
4 Church Street, Market
Harborough, Leicestershire LE16
7AA
Tel: 01858 462751
Fax: 01858 434544
Hours: Mail order only
Catalogue; Mail order

J W Boyce (Seedsmen)
Bush Pasture, Fordham, Ely,
Cambridgeshire CB7 5JU
Contact: Mr Roger Morley
Tel/fax: 01638 721158
Hours: 9am–1pm/2pm–5pm Mon–Fri. 9am–12noon Sat. Closed Sun

Catalogue free. 1,000 varieties of vegetables, flower seeds by packet or weight supplied by mail order or shop at Fordham. Family owned since turn of century.
Catalogue; Mail order

James Henderson & Sons
Kingholm Quay, Dumfries,
Dumfries & Galloway DG1 4SU
Tel: 01387 52234
Fax: 01387 62302
Hours: Mail order only
Catalogue; Mail order

Jim & Jenny Archibald
Bryn Collen, Ffostrasol, Llandysul, Dyfed SA44 5SB

Hours: Mail order only
Catalogue; Mail order

John Chambers Wild Flower Seeds
15 Westleigh Rd, Barton Seagrave, Kettering, Northamptonshire NN15 5AJ

Tel: 01933 652562
Fax: 01933 652576
Hours: Mail order only
Catalogue; Mail order

John Drake Aquilegias
Hardwicke House, Fen Ditton, Cambridge, Cambridgeshire CB5 8TF

Tel/fax: 01223 292246

Seed catalogue available August. Please send 1st class stamp & 50p.
Catalogue; Mail order

Johnsons Seeds
W W Johnson & Sons Ltd, London Rd, Boston, Lincolnshire PE21 8AD

Contact: Richard W Johnson
Tel: 01205 365051
Fax: 01205 310148
Hours: 8.30am–5.30pm Mon–Fri

Britain's leading supplier of lawn seed, flower and vegetable seed and bulbs. Catalogues available on request Freephone number 0800 614323.
Catalogue; Mail order

Landlife Wildflowers Ltd
The Old Police Station, Lark Lane, Liverpool, Merseyside L17 8UU

Contact: Gillian Watson
Tel: 0151 728 7011
Fax: 0151 728 8413
Hours: By appointment

Over 150 species of native wildflower seeds, plants and bulbs. Send SAE for catalogue. All proceeds covenanted to environmental charity Landlife.
Catalogue; Mail order

Marshalls
S E Marshall & Co Ltd, Wisbech, Cambridgeshire PE13 2RF

Tel: 01945 583407
Fax: 01945 588235

Kitchen garden specialists - vegetable seeds and soft fruit. Renowned range of potatoes and onion sets, plus vegetable plants. Catalogue free.
Catalogue; Mail order

Mr Fothergills Seeds Ltd
Gazeley Rd, Kentford, Newmarket, Suffolk CB8 7QB

Tel/fax: 01638 751887
Hours: Mail order only
Catalogue; Mail order

Native Australian Seeds
14 Launcelot Crescent, Thornhill, Cardiff, Glamorgan (S.) CF4 9AQ

Mail order sales of Australian tree, shrub and wildflower seeds. Hardy, half hardy and tender specimens from the land downunder. S.A.E. for list appreciated.
Catalogue; Mail order

Northside Seeds
323 Norwood Rd, London SE24 9AQ

Tel/fax: 0181 671 2654
Hours: Mail order only
Mail order

Peter Grayson - Sweet Pea Seedsman
34 Glenthorne Close, Brampton, Chesterfield, Derbyshire S40 3AR

Contact: Peter Grayson
Tel: 01246 278503
Fax: 01246 566918
Hours: Mail order only

We have the world's largest collection of old fashioned sweet peas and lathyrus species currently available to the public.
Catalogue; Mail order

Pinks & Carnations
22 Chetwyn Avenue, Bromley Cross, Bolton, Lancashire BL7 9BN

Tel/fax: 01204 306273
Hours: Mail order only

Perpetual flowering carnations. Garden pinks. Tri-port plant support system. PVC canes. Galvanised wire support rings. Dianthus fertilizer. Seed. Write, phone or fax for catalogue.
Catalogue; Mail order

Plant World Seeds
St Marychurch Road, Newton Abbot, Devon TQ12 4SE

Tel/fax: 01803 872939

Choice rare seeds. Possibly the world's biggest selection of aquilegias (40+), hardy geraniums (30+), campanulas, euphorbias and hundreds more. Exciting, comprehensively illustrated colour catalogue - 3 x 1st class stamps.
Catalogue; Mail order

Richard Stockwell - Rare Plants (GF)
64 Weardale Rd, Sherwood, Nottingham, Nottinghamshire NG5 1DD

Contact: Richard Stockwell
Tel/fax: 0115 9691063
Hours: Mail order only

Rarest climbers and dwarf species, many unavailable elsewhere. Seed exported world wide. Send 4 x 2nd class stamps or two International Reply Coupons for latest seed catalogue.
Catalogue; Mail order

Roy Young Seeds
23 Westland Chase, West Winch, Kings Lynn, Norfolk PE33 0QH

Tel/fax: 01553 840867
Hours: Mail order only

Cactus and succulent seed specialists. Wholesale, retail. UK - send 1 x 1st class stamp for catalogue (not illustrated) and wholesale list. Overseas - please send 3 x International Reply Coupons.
Catalogue; Mail order

S & N Brackley
117 Winslow Rd, Wingrave, Aylesbury, Buckinghamshire HP22 4QB

Tel/fax: 01296 681384
Hours: For collection in April only

Sweet pea specialists. We offer a wide selection of sweet peas from our internationally renowned seeds. SAE for lists of sweet peas and exhibition vegetables.
Catalogue; Mail order

S M McArd
39 West Rd, Pointon, Sleaford, Lincolnshire NG34 0NA

Contact: Susan McArd
Tel/fax: 01529 240765
Hours: Mail order only

Vegetable, herb and flower seeds. Unusual vegetable and herb plants, fruit etc. Catalogue 2 x 2nd class stamps.
Catalogue; Mail order

Salley Gardens
32 Lansdowne Drive, West Bridgford, Nottingham, Nottinghamshire NG2 7FJ

Contact: Richard Lewin
Tel/fax: 0115 9233878
Hours: Not open to the public

Medicinal plants and wildflowers, herbs and seeds by mail order only. List free.
Catalogue; Mail order

Samuel Dobie & Son Ltd
Broomhill Way, Torquay, Devon TQ2 7QW

Tel/fax: 01803 616281
Hours: Mail order only
Catalogue; Mail order

Sawyers Seeds
Sawyers Farm Ltd, Little Cornard, Sudbury, Suffolk CO10 0NY

Tel: 01787 228498
Fax: 01787 227258

Seed House
9a Widley Rd, Cosham, Portsmouth, Hampshire PO6 2DS

Contact: Richard Spearing
Tel/fax: 01705 325639

Specialising in Australian seeds for the European climate. Catalogue 4 x 1st class stamps or 4 International Postal coupons. Minimum order £5.
Catalogue; Mail order

Seeds-by-Size
45 Crouchfield, Boxmoor, Hemel Hempstead, Hertfordshire HP1 1PA

Contact: John Robert Size
Tel/fax: 01442 251458
Hours: Mail order only

1,400 vegetable varieties, 80 herb varieties and 4,100 flower varieties are offered for sale in any quantity required. Lists are free, S.A.E. appreciated.
Catalogue; Mail order

Stewarts (Nottm) Ltd
3 George Street, Nottingham, Nottinghamshire NG1 3BH

Tel/fax: 0115 9476338
Hours: 9am–5.30pm
Catalogue; Mail order

Suffolk Herbs
Monks Farm, Pantlings Lane, Coggeshall Road, Kelvedon, Colchester, Essex CO5 9PG

Tel: 01376 572456
Fax: 01376 571189
Hours: 8.30am–5pm Mon–Fri

A vast seed range of herbs, wild flowers, unusual and oriental vegetables, plus a large selection of books and other products for the organic grower.
Catalogue; Mail order

Suttons Seeds
Hele Rd, Torquay, Devon TQ2 7QJ

Tel/fax: 01803 612011

Suppliers of seeds, plants, bulbs, fertilisers and garden sundries. Free catalogue available on request. Products available in all good garden centres.
Catalogue; Mail order

Thompson & Morgan UK Ltd
Poplar Lane, Ipswich, Suffolk IP8 3BU

Tel: 01473 601090
Fax: 01473 680199

Free! The world's largest illustrated seed catalogue. 2,500+ varieties of flowers and vegetables, from acacia to zinnia, artichokes to zucchini, many new and exclusive.
Catalogue; Mail order

The Daily Telegraph *Green Fingers*   **Water Garden & Pond Specialists**

WATER GARDEN & POND SPECIALISTS

Unwins Seeds Ltd
Histon, Cambridge,
Cambridgeshire CB4 4LE
Tel: 01223 236236
Fax: 01223 237437

Suppliers of seeds and bulbs through mail order and through retailers nationwide. Trial grounds occasionally open under National Gardens Scheme.
Catalogue; Mail order

W Robinson & Sons Ltd
Sunny Bank, Forton, Preston, Lancashire PR3 0BN
Tel/fax: 01524 79121033
Hours: *Phone first*
Catalogue; Mail order

Wallis Seeds & Co
Broads Green, Great Waltham, Chelmsford, Essex CM3 1DS
Tel/fax: 01245 360413

Wild Seeds
25 Aran Street, Bala, Gwynedd LL23 7SP
Contact: D Lee
Hours: *Mail order only*

A free catalogue containing wildflower seeds, plants and bulbs, including bluebells, wild daffodils, snowdrops and wood anenomes.
Catalogue; Mail order

Addlestone Aquaria Pond & Aquatic Centre
Bourne Valley Nurseries,
Woodam Park Rd, Woodam,
Addlestone, Surrey
Tel/fax: 01932 349520
Hours: *Daily*

AllClear Water Purifiers
59 Hartswood Rd, Brentwood, Essex CM14 5AG
Tel: 01277 214911
Fax: 01277 201740

Specialists in purifying UK tapwater for fish. For information send large SAE or telephone for advice. Purifiers for large or small ponds and aquaria.
Mail order

Allpets (Stanmore) Ltd
The Kiln Nursery, Common Rd, Stanmore, Middlesex HA7 3JF
Tel: 0181 954 0008
Fax: 0181 954 0009
Hours: *9am–5.30pm Mon–Sat, 10.30am–4.30pm Suns*

One of the best selections of pond fish, potted plants, fountains, waterfalls, cascades and ornaments. Tropical and marine fish and large pet department.
Toilets; Refreshments; Disabled access

Alvenor Aquatics & Water Gardens
Murrow, Wisbech,
Cambridgeshire PE13 4HB
Tel/fax: 01945 700449
Hours: *9.30am–5pm Tues–Sun or by appt*

Aqua Company Ltd
Abbott House, 14a Hale Rd, Farnham, Surrey GU9 9QH
Contact: Mrs C H Stewart
Tel: 01252 712307
Fax: 01252 712308

For ponds. Sole distributor of O'Clear - eliminates algae/green water immediately. Safe for all fish and plants. Consultancy and algae treatment for large ponds.
Mail order

Aqua-Soil Products Ltd
Blue Waters Estate, Bovey Tracey, Devon TQ13 9YF
Tel/fax: 01626 835135

The complete range of Aqua-Soil products is available for the water gardener from over 600 aquatic retailers.

Aquaplancton
Clavering Cottage, Little London, Stowmarket, Suffolk IP14 2ES
Tel/fax: 01449 774532
Hours: *By arrangement*

Aquaplancton for crystal clear ponds the natural way. For free brochure and price list phone or send the approximate surface area of your pond.
Catalogue; Mail order

Aquapost
PO Box 1216, Littlehampton, Sussex (W.) BN17 6TB
Tel: 01903 733137
Fax: 01903 770237
Catalogue; Mail order

Aquatic Habit
Shurdington Rd, Brockworth, Gloucestershire GL3 4PU
Tel/fax: 01452 862791
Hours: *Daily except Wed*

Aquavita Centre
1 Lane End, Old Uxbridge Rd, Rickmansworth, Hertfordshire WD3 2XU
Contact: A J Benson
Tel: 01895 824556
Fax: 01895 823663
Hours: *9am–5pm*
Catalogue; Mail order

Aquazoo
202 Waterloo Rd, Burton on Trent, Staffordshire
Tel/fax: 01283 564174

The complete water garden specialists for first ponds, pumps, filters etc.

Astra Aquatics
35 Seaford Rd, Enfield, Middlesex EN1 1NS
Tel: 0181 366 1925
Fax: 0181 366 1904

Avenue Fisheries
46 Rookery Rd, Wyboston, Bedfordshire MK44 3AX
Tel/fax: 01480 215408
Hours: *9am–5.30pm Mar–Oct Weds*

Japanese koi specialists, also full range of pond equipment - filters, pumps, food, ultraviolets, books etc. Free price list. Pond design, maintenance and construction service.
Catalogue; Mail order; Toilets

Avon Aquatics
Sweet Knowle Farm, Ilmington Rd, Wimpstone, Stratford upon Avon, Warwickshire
Tel: 01789 450638
Fax: 01789 450967
Hours: *10am–6pm daily*
Refreshments

Bel Mondo Garden Features
11 Tatnell Rd, London SE23 1JX
Contact: Jamie Ripman
Tel/fax: 0181 291 1920
Hours: *By appointment*

Cast iron wall-mounted and free standing fountains. Continuous flow (pump supplied) or for tap use. Brass taps and spouts. Free brochure.
Catalogue; Mail order

Bennetts Water Gardens
Putton Lane, Chickerell, Weymouth, Dorset DT3 4AF
Tel: 01305 785150
Fax: 01305 781619
Hours: *Tues–Sun Apr–Aug. Tues–Sat 10am–5pm Sept*

Specialist growers of aquatic plants. Pond liners, pumps, fountain ornaments etc. 6 acres of lakes displaying NCCPG collection of water lilies. Admission to lakes £3.75.
Mail order; Toilets; Refreshments; Disabled access

Blagdon Water Garden Products plc
Bristol Rd, Bridgwater, Somerset TA6 4AW
Tel/fax: 01278 446464

Blue Lagoon Aquatics
157 Broad street, Dagenham, Essex
Tel/fax: 0181 595 9635

The Daily Telegraph *Green Fingers*   **Water Garden & Pond Specialists**

Bradshaws
Nicolson Link, Clifton Moor, York, Yorkshire (N.) YO1 1SS

Tel: 01904 691169
Fax: 01904 691133

Hours: 8.30am–5.30pm Mon–Fri, 8.30am–5pm Sat

Everything for garden ponds: liners, underlays, pumps, filters, lighting and pond treatments. Full assistance from trained telephone sales advisers. Speedy delivery. Free catalogue and samples.
Catalogue; Mail order

Butyl Products Ltd
11 Radford Crescent, Billericay, Essex CM12 0DW

Tel: 01277 653281
Fax: 01277 657921

Suppliers and installers of waterproof materials for lining ponds, lakes and reservoirs.
Mail order

C J Skilton Aquarist
Great Gibcracks Chase, Butts Green, Sandon, Chelmsford, Essex CM6 3TE

Tel: 01245 400535
Fax: 01245 400585

If you wish to install an aquatic feature then consult the experts. Consultants to RHS prize winners at Chelsea and Hampton Court shows in 1994.

Chilstone
Victoria Park, Fordcombe Road, Langton Green, Tunbridge Wells, Kent TN3 0RE

Tel: 01892 740866
Fax: 01892 740867

Hours: Mon–Fri & Sun Apr–Sept. Mon–Fri Oct–Mar

Handmade reconstituted stone - birdbaths, sundials, fountains, urns, statues, balustrading, seats, temples - all in classical style. Show gardens 1 hour from London. Catalogue available.
Catalogue; Mail order; Toilets

Crews Hill Aquarium & Water Garden Centre
c/o Browns Water Garden Centre, Crews Hill, Enfield, Middlesex EN2 9DG

Tel: 0181 366 1811
Fax: 0181 897 6550

Hours: 9am–6pm daily

Cumbrian Koi Co Ltd
Stank House, Stank Village, Barrow-in-Furness, Cumbria

Tel/fax: 01229 835420

Hours: Daily except Mon & Tues. Open Bank Hols

Cyprio Ltd
Hards Road, Frognall, Peterborough, Cambridgeshire PE6 8RR

Tel: 01778 344502
Fax: 01778 348093

The world leaders in pond filtration.
Mail order

Deanswood Plants
Deanswood, Potteries Lane, Littlethorpe, Ripon, Yorkshire (N.) HG4 3LS

Contact: Jacky Barber
Tel/fax: 01765 60344

Hours: 10am–5pm Apr–Sept. Closed Mon

A small nursery in garden setting (2 acres). Natural stream and three ponds. Nursery specialises in marginal, bog & pond plants. Groups welcome by appointment. Open for NGS.
Catalogue

Denmead Aquatic Nursery
Soake Rd, Denmead, Hampshire PO7 6HY

Tel/fax: 01705 252671

Hours: Daily

East Neuk Water Garden Centre
St Andrews Rd, Crail, Anstruther, Fife KY10 3UL

Tel: 01333 450530
Fax: 01333 450177

Hours: 9am–5pm daily

Everything for the water garden including a full range of aquatic plants and cold water fish. Catalogues, videos, mail order, delivery available. Definitely worth a visit.
Catalogue; Mail order

Egmont Water Garden Centre
132 Tolworth Rise South, Surbiton, Surrey

Tel/fax: 0181 337 9605

Hours: 10am–6pm Tues–Fri. 10am–5pm Sat/Sun Mons Mar–Aug

Fawcetts Liners
Longton, Lancashire PR4 5JA

Tel: 01772 612125
Fax: 01772 615360

Filterplas
Units 10 & 24, Phoenix Close Ind Estate, Green Lane, Heywood, Lancashire OL10 2JG

Tel/fax: 01706 621699

Freshfields Water Gardens & Aquarium
Moss Side, Formby, Liverpool, Merseyside L37 0AE

Tel/fax: 01704 877964

Hours: 10am–6pm daily

G Miles & Son Ltd
School House, Great Ashfield, Bury St Edmunds, Suffolk IP31 3HJ

Tel: 01359 242356
Fax: 01359 241781

Hours: 8.30am–5pm Mon–Fri

Miles specialises in all works involved in consultancy, design, renovation and construction of major existing and new water areas and features. National and international enquiries welcome.
Catalogue; Mail order

Goulds Pumps Ltd
Millwey Rise Industrial Estate, Axminster, Devon EX13 5HU

Contact: Mark Stevens
Tel: 01297 33374
Fax: 01297 35238

Pumps for fountains, waterfalls, cascades and for use with pond filters, also large water landscapes and high lift fountains.

Harrow Koi Company
269 Watford Rd, Harrow, Middlesex HA1 3TS

Tel/fax: 0181 423 0208

Hours: 9.30am–5.30pm. Closed Mons

Hewthorn Herbs & Wild Flowers
82 Julian Road, West Bridgford, Nottinghamshire NG2 5AN

Contact: Julie Scott
Tel/fax: 0115 9812861

Hours: Strictly by appointment

Medicinal herbs, wild flowers and native pond plants by mail order. All organically grown. Please send 4 x 2nd class stamps for list.
Mail order

Hill Farm Koi
Middleton St George, Darlington, Co Durham

Tel/fax: 01325 332838

Hours: Closed Mons except Bank Hols

Hobby-Fish Farm
Towchester Rd, Old Stratford, Milton Keynes, Buckinghamshire MK19 6BD

Tel: 01908 8543330
Fax: 01908 542149

Hours: 10am–5.30pm daily

Honeysome Aquatic Nursery
The Row, Sutton, Nr Ely, Cambridgeshire CB6 2PF

Contact: Mr D B Littlefield
Tel/fax: 01353 778889

Hours: By appointment only. Please phone.

Wide range of pond, moisture and shade loving plants - organically grown. Very informative mail order catalogue 2 x 1st class stamps.
Catalogue; Mail order

International Water Lily Society
c/o Hooper, Mill Lane, Bradfield, Manningtree, Essex CO11 2QP

Contact: Mr Harry Hooper

Join other enthusiastic amateur, professional and academic water gardeners. Quarterly journal, symposium and garden tours, reference library, research projects. Over 950 members worldwide dedicated to the furtherance of all aspects of water gardening.

Interpet Ltd
Interpet House, Vincent Lane, Dorking, Surrey RH4 3YX

Tel: 01306 881033
Fax: 01306 885009

Catalogue

Jardino Pumps
7 Commerce Way, Lawford, Manningtree, Essex CO11 1UT

Tel/fax: 01206 391291

Catalogue

Karobar Koi
62 Bucknalls Drive, Bricket Wood, St Albans, Hertfordshire

Tel: 01923 677734
Fax: 01923 681807

Catalogue

Koi Kraft
Mount Pleasant Farm, Brishing Rd, Chart Sutton, Maidstone, Kent ME17 3SP

Tel: 01622 743413
Fax: 01622 743307

Lotus Water Garden Products Ltd
PO Box 36, Junction Street, Burnley, Lancashire BB12 0NA

Tel: 01282 420771
Fax: 01282 412719

Number One in water gardening for over 30 years. Pumps, liners, filters, treatments, fountains, accessories. Contact the Lotus Helpline (01282 420771) for advice on your project.

Marks Water Garden
156 High Street, Teddington, Middlesex

Tel/fax: 0181 943 9799

Hours: Daily

Midland Butyl Liners
Freepost, 288 Ripley, Derbyshire DE5 9BR

Tel/fax: 01773 748169

Catalogue; Mail order

The Daily Telegraph *Green Fingers*   **Water Garden & Pond Specialists**

The driving force . . .

of water displays is more and more often an OASE fountain pump.

The reasons are crystal-clear. Quality. Long-term reliability. Up to 60% savings in power requirements. (Completely cost-free running in the case of solar-powered models.) Plus novel points like extra-large strainer baskets, neatly and completely enclosing the pumps and keeping cleaning frequency to a minimum. Turnover rates span 4-290 l/min (53-3828 gph), with a full supporting range of nozzles, lights, pond filters, pool liners and other accessories.

Call us for further information – and the name of your nearest OASE specialist stockist.

OASE (U.K.) Ltd.
West Portway Ind. Est.
Andover SP10 3SF
Tel: (01264) 333225
Fax: (01264) 333226

Mossatburn Watergardens
Kilrummy, Alford, Grampian
Tel/fax: 019755 712235
Hours: Daily

Nature's Corners
11 Bunyan Close, Pirton, Hitchin, Hertfordshire SG5 3RE
Contact: Douglas Crawley
Tel/fax: 01462 712519
Hours: Weekdays flexible – phone first. Weekends 10am–5pm.
Aquatic marginal plants, oxygenating aquatic, water lillies, aquatic planting soil, containers, pondside perennial plants, mail order aquatic price lists (free). Callers phone first.
Catalogue; Mail order

Nautilus Aquatics
Spring Green Nurseries, Pontefract Rd, Crofton, Wakefield, Yorkshire (W.) WF4 1LW
Tel: 01924 864779
Fax: 01924 865272
Hours: Daily

Neptune Aquatics
Sefton Meadows Garden Centre, Sefton Lane, Maghull, Liverpool, Merseyside
Tel/fax: 0151 526 0200

New Technology
N T Laboratories, 13 Branbridges Ind Estate, East Peckham, Tonbridge, Kent TN12 5HF
Tel: 01622 871387
Fax: 01622 872331
Manufacturers of pond treatments and water test kits including Barley Straw Pouches, Koi-care chemicals, New Wave pond products and Health Check test kit.
Catalogue; Mail order

Nitritech
119 Bristol Rd, Frampton Cotterell, Bristol, Avon BS17 2AU
Tel: 01454 776927
Fax: 01454 250753

Northampton Water Garden Centre
66-70 Kingsthorpe Rd, Kingsthorpe Hollow, Northampton, Northamptonshire
Tel/fax: 01604 716222
Hours: 8.30am–5.30pm Mon–Sat, 10am–5pm Suns (Apr–Aug)

Oase (UK) Ltd
West Portway Industrial Estate, Andover, Hampshire SP10 3SF
Tel: 01264 333225
Fax: 01264 333226
Oase fountain pumps for quality, reliability and economy. Solar-powered models available. Full range of nozzles, lights, pond filters, pool liners and other accessories. Call for details of local stockists.

Paul Bromfield Aquatics
Gosmore Hitchin, Hitchin, Hertfordshire SG4 7QD
Tel: 01462 457399
Fax: 01462 422652
Hours: By appointment
Mail order aquatic plants, moisture plants, grasses. Established over 25 years. Catalogue 3 x 2nd class stamps. Prices still at '93.
Catalogue; Mail order; Toilets

Pentangle Watergardens
Knaphill Garden Centre, Barrs Lane, Knaphill, Woking, Surrey
Tel/fax: 01483 489 757

Peters Plants & Garden Centre
Stoke Road, Stoke d'Abernon, Cobham, Surrey KT11 3PU
Tel: 01932 862530
Fax: 01932 866865
Hours: Daily. Sun 11am–5pm
High quality garden company providing comprehensive retail and contracting services. Excellent plants, aquatics, garden and conservatory furniture, gifts and coffee shop. Well worth a visit.
Toilets; Refreshments; Disabled access

Podington Garden Centre
High Street, Podington, Wellingborough, Northamptonshire NN29 7HS
Contact: Colin Read
Tel: 01933 53656
Fax: 01933 410332
Hours: 9am–6.30pm Summer, 9am–5.30pm Winter, 10.30am–4.30pm Sun
A plant person's paradise with thousands of plants all year round. Also a wide range of garden sundries, furniture, aquatics, garden ornaments, fencing and paving.
Toilets; Refreshments; Disabled access

Porton Aquatic Centre
Old Railway Station, Porton, Salisbury, Wiltshire
Tel/fax: 01980 611113
Hours: 9.15am–5pm Mon–Sat, 12–5pm Sun, 10am–5pm Bank Hols

Pumps 'n' Tubs
Holly Farm Business Park, Honiley, Kenilworth, Warwickshire CV8 1NP
Tel/fax: 01926 484244

Pumps 'n' Tubs are major suppliers of cast iron pumps, self contained oak water features, barrels and tubs. For your free brochure telephone 01926 484244.

Reef Aquatics
Floralands, G C Freepost, Nottingham, Nottinghamshire NG4 1BR
Tel: 0115 9676100
Fax: 0115 9262545
Catalogue; Mail order

Remanoid Ltd
Unit 44, Number One Industrial Estate, Medomsley Rd, Consett, Co Durham DH8 6SZ
Tel: 01207 591089
Fax: 01207 502512
Hours: 9am–5pm
Manufacturers of plastic garden ponds. Suppliers of pumps, treatments, indoor water features, stoneware and all related accessories, filters etc.
Catalogue; Mail order

Romilt Landscape Design & Construction Ltd
North Wyke Farm, Guildford Rd, Normandy, Surrey GU3 2AN
Contact: R J Milton
Tel/fax: 01483 811933
Construction and renovation of garden ponds, lakes, heritage and other water features. Design and construction of English gardens. BALI members. Chelsea medal winners.

Rowden Gardens
Brentor, Tavistock, Devon PL19 0NG
Contact: John Carter
Tel/fax: 01822 810275
Hours: 10am–5pm Sat/Sun & Bank Hol Mon Apr 1–Sept 30 or by appt
One of the leading specialists in aquatic and damp-loving plants. Also famous for its many rare and unusual varieties. Gardens admission £1. Catalogue £1.50.
Catalogue; Mail order; Toilets

Seymours Garden & Leisure Group
The Pit House, Ewell By-Pass, Surrey KT17 1PS
Contact: James Seymour
Tel: 0181 393 0111
Fax: 0181 393 0237
Hours: Open daily. Sun 10am–4pm
Landscape and leisure centre with aquatics, landscape supplies, garden leisure departments and coffee shop under same ownership as Peters Plants and Garden Centre at Cobham (01932 862530).
Toilets; Refreshments

South East Water Gardens
Bellers Bush, Sandwich, Kent
Tel/fax: 01304 614963

Stapeley Water Gardens Ltd
London Rd, Stapeley, Nantwich, Cheshire CW5 7LH
Tel: 01270 623868
Fax: 01270 624919
Hours: From 10am daily except Xmas Day
The world's largest water garden centre - for all your water garden needs, with The Palms Tropical Oasis, a huge tropical house and Yesteryear Museum.
Catalogue; Mail order; Toilets; Refreshments; Disabled access

Surbiton Aquaria
27-29 Brighton Rd, Surbiton, Surrey
Tel/fax: 0181 399 6783

Symbionics
The Old Post House, Church Lench, Evesham, Hereford & Worcester WR11 4UB
Tel/fax: 01386 870387
Catalogue

Technical Aquatic Products
Bristol, Avon
Tel/fax: 0117 9585588
T.A.P. professional for all pond products, including The Pond Doctor and Aqua Blocks.

Torbay Water Gardens
St Mary Church Rd, Newton Abbot, Devon
Tel/fax: 01803 873663

Trees in Miniature
21 Harrowes Meade, Edgware, Middlesex HA8 8RR
Contact: Bert Coleman
Tel: 0181 958 3574
Fax: 0181 958 7707
Hours: By appointment – please phone
Indoor water gardens (DIY) set up and working within 1 hour. Conservatories, reception areas, hotels, lounges etc. Incorporating unique dwarf trees which have the authentic sounds of nature built in. Bird songs during the day give way to crickets and tree frogs at dusk. Has the effect of bringing the great outdoors-indoors.

Trident Water Garden Products
Carlton Rd, Foleshill, Coventry, Midlands (W.) CV6 7FL
Catalogue

Ullesthorpe Garden & Aquatic Centre
Lutterworth Rd, Ullesthorpe, Leicestershire LE17 5DR
Tel: 01455 202144
Fax: 01455 202585
Hours: 9am–6pm Mon–Sat, 10.30am–4.30pm Sun
One of the finest centres for all gardening and aquatic needs, with pet centre and tea room. Well worth a visit. Open 7 days.
Toilets; Refreshments; Disabled access

Valley Aquatics
Plantation House, Flip Rd, Haslingden, Lancashire BB4 5EJ
Tel/fax: 01706 228960
Hours: Open 5 days 10am–6pm. Closed Tues & Wed

Washington Aquatic & Garden Supplies Ltd
London Rd, Washington, Sussex (W.) RH20 3BL
Tel/fax: 01903 892006
Hours: 9am–5.30pm daily
Catalogue; Mail order

Water Features Ltd
Flowers Farm, Redbourn, Hertfordshire AL3 7AE
Tel: 01582 793555
Fax: 01582 793288

Water Garden Nursery
Wembworthy, Chulmleigh, Devon EX18 7SG
Tel/fax: 01837 83566
Hours: 9.30am–12.30pm/1.30–5pm daily except Mon/Tues Apr–Sept
Plants for ponds, margins, bogs, watermeadows, moist woodland, dry surrounds. Waterlilies, "oxygenators", ferns, grasses. Over 250 varieties. Mail order list 3 x 1st class stamps.
Catalogue; Mail order

Water Meadow Nursery & Herb Farm
Cheriton, Alresford, Hampshire SO24 0JT
Contact: Mrs Sandy Worth
Tel/fax: 01962 771895
Hours: 9am–5pm Fri/Sat & Bank Hols, 2–5pm Sun Mar–Nov
Extensive collection of water garden plants, hardy shrubs, fragrant climbers, herbs, 500+ herbaceous perennials, many unusual. All in a garden setting. Mail order catalogue 75p. Landscape and design service available.
Catalogue; Mail order; Toilets

Waterlife Centre
476 Bath Rd, Longford, West Drayton, Middlesex UB7 0ED
Tel: 01753 685696
Fax: 01753 685437
Hours: 10am–6pm daily
Massive selection of aquatic equipment. Huge variety of aquatic livestock from all over the world. 100,000 gallon public aquarium. 95p adult, 50p children/OAPs.
Catalogue; Toilets; Refreshments; Disabled access

Waterlock Studios
Stourmouth, Kent CT3 1HZ
Tel/fax: 01227 722324

Watermeadows
35 Ashcroft Rd, Ipswich, Suffolk IP1 6AD
Tel/fax: 01473 464006

Watershed Systems Ltd
Pond Dept, Edinburgh TCC, Kings Buildings Mayfield Rd, Edinburgh, Lothian EH9 3JL
Tel/fax: 01243 555999

Waveney Fish Farm
Park Rd, Diss, Norfolk IP22 3AS
Tel: 01379 642697
Fax: 01379 651315
Hours: 9.30am–5.30pm daily
Water garden, aquarium and small pet centre. Specialists in water lilies and aquatic plants, ornamental fish, aquariums and tropical fish. Display gardens open daily.
Catalogue; Mail order; Toilets

Professional Aquarists use pond products from T.A.P.

TECHNICAL AQUATIC PRODUCTS LTD, BRISTOL, AVON.
Helpline: 0117-9692345. Enquiries: 0117-9585588
THE Pond Doctor   AQUA BLOCKS

West Country Water Gardens
Bow, Crediton, Devon EX17 6LB
Tel/fax: 01363 82438
Hours: 10am–5pm daily. Closed Winter

The West Country's largest range of pond plants, potted, pond ready, specimen. Water lilies, bog/herbaceous plants, ferns, pond fish. Ponds and all equipment. Callers only.

Westcountry Water Garden Centre
Bow, Crediton, Devon
Tel/fax: 01363 824388
Hours: Daily. Closed Thurs from Nov–Feb

Wharf Aquatics
95 Wharf Rd, Pinxton, Nottinghamshire
Tel/fax: 01773 861255
Hours: Daily except Wed

Wight Butyl Liners
Freepost, Market Square, St Neots, Cambridgeshire PE18 2BG
Tel/fax: 01480 403477

Specialists in pond lining materials. Butyl, Aqualast, PVC and Geotextile underlay.

Wildlife Services Ltd
74 Lythwood Rd, Bayston Hill, Shrewsbury, Shropshire SY3 0HT
Tel/fax: 01743 873705

Wildwoods Water Garden Centre
Theobalds Park Rd, Crews Hill, Enfield, Middlesex EN2 9BP
Tel/fax: 0181 366 0243
Hours: 9am–5pm daily

Woodside Water Gardens
Walesby Rd, Market Rasen, Lincolnshire LN8 3EY
Contact: Geoff Dixon
Tel/fax: 01673 843083
Hours: 10am–6pm Thurs/Fri/Sat/Sun Mar–Oct

Small nursery with big reputation for healthy fish (Including Koi carp) and plants. Full range of equipment at very competetive prices. Collection only. Access/Visa.

World of Water
93 Greatbridge Road, Romsey, Hampshire SO51 0HB
Tel: 01794 515923
Fax: 01794 830846
Hours: 9am–5.30pm Mon–Sat, 10.30am–4.30pm Sun

Specialists in the supply of water garden equipment. Huge stocks of ponds, liners, pumps, filters, statues, pond plants, coldwater and tropical fish.
Toilets; Refreshments

World of Water
Hastings Rd, Rolvenden, Cranbrook, Kent TN17 4PL
Tel/fax: 01580 241771
Hours: Daily

World of Water
Ersham Rd, Hailsham, Sussex (E.) BN27 2RH
Tel/fax: 01323 4424200
Hours: Daily

World of Water
Kennedys Garden Centre, Waddon Way, Purley Way, Croydon, Surrey CR0 4HY
Tel/fax: 0181 681 3132
Hours: Daily

World of Water
Silverlands, Holloway Hill, Chertsey, Surrey KT16 0AE
Tel: 01932 569690
Fax: 01932 569694
Hours: 9am–6pm daily Feb–Nov. 9am–5pm Nov–Feb closed Suns

Largest selection of pond equipment in Surrey - pumps, pool liners, lights, filter systems, treatments, books, self contained water features, fountains and much more.

World of Water
Bicester garden Centre, Oxford Rd, Bicester, Oxfordshire OX6 8MY
Tel/fax: 01869 322489
Hours: Daily

World of Water
166 Hyde End Rd, Shinfield, Reading, Berkshire RG2 9ER
Tel/fax: 01734 885492
Hours: Daily

World of Water
Turners Hill Rd, Worth, Crawley, Sussex (W.) RH10 4DS
Tel/fax: 01293 88323
Hours: Daily

Wreford Landscapes
Pucknall Farm, Dores Lane, Braishfield, Romsey, Hampshire SO51 0QJ
Contact: Simon Wreford
Tel: 01794 368155
Fax: 01794 368218
Hours: 7.30am–6pm Mon–Fri

Landscape design and construction for town houses to country manors. Commercial and business developments throughout southern England.

Wychwood Waterlilies
Farnham Rd (A287), Odiham, Basingstoke, Hampshire RG25 1HS
Contact: Ann or Clair Henley
Tel: 01256 702800
Fax: 01256 701001
Email: 101536.576 @compuserve.com
Hours: 10am–6pm daily.

Waterlilies, marginal plants etc, all naturally and organically grown. Plus the Odiham Waterlily Collection as seen on BBC Gardener's World. Catalogue 1st class stamp.
Catalogue; Mail order; Toilets; Refreshments; Disabled access

PLANTS AND INSPIRATION

> In this section you will find your local suppliers of plants and seeds, listed by country (Channel Islands, England, Northern Ireland, Scotland and Wales) and by district within each country. Changes in recent years have made the definition of a 'county' a contentious issue – we have tried to keep it to the best known counties or administrative areas, but please forgive us if the official name of your locality is wrongly listed.
>
> In Chapter 15 *Gardens to Visit* we list some of the major attractions, where you can gain inspiration from other gardeners, past and present, and sometimes have the opportunity to buy plants seen in the gardens.

GARDEN CENTRES & NURSERIES

Channel Islands

Guernsey

Martels Garden World
Route des Blicqs, St Andrews,
Guernsey GY6 8YD

Tel: 01481 36888
Fax: 01481 35542

Hours: 9am–6pm daily
Refreshments

Jersey

Ransoms Garden Centre
St Martin, Jersey JE3 6UD

Tel: 01534 856699
Fax: 01534 853779

Hours: 8.30am–6pm Mon–Sat.
Closed Sun

A large family run garden centre with excellent tea room/restaurant and gift shops. Lovely setting, ample parking, wheelchair friendly.
Toilets; Refreshments; Disabled access

St Peters Garden Centre
Airport Rd, St Peter, Jersey JE3 7BP

Tel: 01534 45903
Fax: 01534 46774

Hours: 8.30am–6pm Summer,
8.30am–5.30pm Winter

England

Avon

Alan Phipps Cacti
62 Samuel White Road, Hanham,
Bristol, Avon BS15 3LX

Contact: Alan Phipps
Tel/fax: 0117 9607591

Hours: Daily – phone first

Specialising in cacti: mammillaria, rebutia, astrophytum, from seedlings to mature plants. Send SAE for mail order catalogue.
Catalogue; Mail order

Arne Herbs
Limeburn Nurseries, Chew
Magna, Bristol, Avon BS18 8QW

Contact: Anthony Lyman-Dixon
Tel/fax: 01275 333399

Hours: Most days – phone first

Arne Herbs grow 600 culinary, aromatic and medicinal herbs. Wholesale and retail to public at door and by courier. Specialists in re-creation of historic gardens, lecture service available. Catalogues £1.50.
Catalogue; Mail order

Blackmore & Langdon
Stanton Nurseries, Pensford,
Bristol, Avon BS18 4JL

Tel/fax: 01275 332300

Hours: 9am–5pm daily
Catalogue; Mail order

Brackenwood Garden Centre
131 Nore Rd, Portishead, Bristol,
Avon BS20 8DU

Tel/fax: 01275 843484

Hours: 9am–5.30pm daily

Garden centre, woodland garden (8 acres), restaurant and tea room (seating 90+), rare and unusual plants grown at our plant centre.
Toilets; Refreshments; Disabled access

Brackenwood Plant Centre
Leigh Court Estate, Pill Rd,
Abbots Leigh, Nr Bristol, Avon

Tel/fax: 01275 375292

Hours: 9am–5.30pm,
9am–4.30pm Winter

12 acre nursery site producing large range of trees, shrubs, conifers, climbers and herbaceous plants. One mile from Clifton suspension bridge, Bristol.
Toilets

C S Lockyer
70 Henfield Rd, Coalpit Heath,
Bristol, Avon BS17 2UZ

Tel/fax: 01454 772219

Hours: Most days – phone First
Catalogue; Mail order

Hannays of Bath
Sydney Wharf Nursery,
Bathwick, Bath, Avon BA2 4ES

Contact: Spencer Hannay
Tel/fax: 01225 462230

Hours: 10am–5pm daily. Closed Tues

A working nursery in the heart of Bath with an exceptional range of rare and uncommon plants many from our own collections abroad. All grown in the nursery. Descriptive catalogue £1.40. Access from Sydney Mews at bottom of Bathwick Hill. Parking in nursery.
Catalogue

Hillier Garden Centre
Whiteway Rd, Bath, Avon
BA2 2RG

Tel/fax: 01225 421162

Hours: 9am–5.30pm Mon–Sat.
10.30am–4.30pm Sun

Good plant oriented garden centre.
Toilets; Refreshments

Jekkas Herb Farm
Rose Cottage, Shellards Lane,
Alveston, Bristol, Avon BS12 2SY

Tel/fax: 01454 418878
Catalogue; Mail order

John Sanday (Roses) Ltd
Over Lane, Almondsbury,
Bristol, Avon BS12 4DA

Tel/fax: 01454 612195

Hours: 9am–5pm Mon–Sat,
10am–5pm Sun
Catalogue; Mail order

Little Creek Nursey
39 Moor Rd, Banwell, Weston
super Mare, Avon BS24 6EF

Contact: Rhys & Julie Adams
Tel/fax: 01934 823739

Hours: By appointment

Specialist nursery supplying our own hellebores, hardy cyclamen and unusual perennials. Mail order catalogue 3 x 1st class stamps.
Catalogue; Mail order

Misses I Allen & M J Huish
Quarry Farm, Wraxall, Bristol,
Avon BS19 1LE

Hours: By appointment
Catalogue; Mail order

Monocot Nursery
Jacklands, Jacklands Bridge,
Tickenham, Clevedon, Avon
BS21 6SG

Hours: 10am–6pm by appt
Catalogue; Mail order

Park Garden Centre
Over Lane, Almondsbury,
Bristol, Avon BS12 4BP

Tel: 01454 612247
Fax: 01454 617559

Hours: 9am–6pm Summer,
9am–5pm Winter
Refreshments

Wyevale Garden Centre
Hicks Gate, Keynsham, Bristol,
Avon BS18 2AD

Tel: 0117 9778945
Fax: 0117 9776436

Wyevale offers a huge selection of plants, shrubs, gift ideas, furniture, BBQs and tools. Most centres have pet and aquatic departments and a restaurant. 0800 413213 for nearest stockist. See above.

Bedfordshire

Bickerdikes Garden Centre
London Rd, Sandy, Bedfordshire
SG19 1DW

Contact: Mark Bickerdike
Tel: 01767 680559
Fax: 01767 680356

Hours: 9am–5.30pm Mon–Sat.
10.30am–4.30pm Sun

Well run and stocked garden centre specialising in top quality plants and service.

Walter Blom & Sons Ltd
Coombelands Nurseries,
Thurleigh Rd, Milton Ernest,
Bedfordshire MK44 1RQ

Tel: 01234 782424
Fax: 01234 782495

Hours: 9am–5pm Mon–Fri,
9am–12pm Sat Sept only
Catalogue; Mail order

Wyevale Garden Centre
Dunstable Rd, Caddington,
Luton, Bedfordshire LU1 4AN

Tel: 01582 457313
Fax: 01582 480716

Wyevale offers a huge selection of plants, shrubs, gift ideas, furniture, BBQs and tools. Most centres have pet and aquatic departments and a restaurant. 0800 413213 for nearest stockist. See above.

Berkshire

Bressingham Plant Centre
Dorney Court, Dorney,
Windsor, Berkshire SL4 6QP
Tel: 01628 669999
Fax: 01628 669693
Hours: 9am–5.30pm daily. Closed Xmas/Boxing Day

Thousands of hardy plants, including the new, classic and unusual, from traditional Norfolk nurserymen, Blooms of Bressingham, plus the friendly advice of skilled plantsmen.
Toilets; Refreshments; Disabled access

Carliles Hardy Plants
Carliles Corner, Twyford,
Reading, Berkshire RG10 9PU
Tel/fax: 01734 340031

Foxgrove Plants
Foxgrove Farm, Enborne,
Newbury, Berkshire RG14 6RE
Tel/fax: 01635 40554
Hours: 10am–5pm Wed–Sun & Bank Hols. Closed Aug
Catalogue; Mail order

Gatehampton Fuchsias
Goring on Thames, Reading,
Berkshire RG8 9LU
Tel/fax: 01491 872894
Catalogue; Mail order

Hare Hatch Nursery
London Rd, Hare Hatch,
Twyford, Reading, Berkshire
RG10 9HW
Tel/fax: 01734 401600
Hours: 9am–5pm Sat & Sun only
Catalogue

Henry Street
Swallowfield Road, Arborfield,
Reading, Berkshire RG2 9JY
Tel: 0118 9761223
Fax: 0118 9761417
Hours: 9am–5.30pm Mon–Sat

Family run garden centre and nursery specialising in roses and bedding plants. Wide range of sundries, trees, shrubs, herbaceous and alpines stocked.
Catalogue; Mail order; Toilets; Refreshments; Disabled access

Hillier Garden Centre
Priors Court Rd, Hermitage,
Newbury, Berkshire RG16 9TG
Tel/fax: 01635 200442
Hours: 9am–5.30pm Mon–Sat. 10.30am–4.30pm Sun

Good plant oriented garden centre.
Toilets; Refreshments

Kingfisher Nurseries
Wyvols Court, Swallow Field,
Reading, Berkshire RG7 1PY
Tel/fax: 01734 756595
Hours: By appointment only
Catalogue; Mail order

M V Fletcher
70 South St, Reading, Berkshire
RG1 4RA
Tel/fax: 01734 571814
Hours: Mail order only
Catalogue; Mail order

Offshoots - Englefield Garden Centre
The Street, Englefield, Theale,
Reading, Berkshire RG7 5EL
Contact: Ron Hobbs
Tel/fax: 01734 304898
Hours: 9am–5pm Mon–Sat

Shurbs, herbaceous plants, bedding, herbs, alpines, fruit, roses, vegetable plants, hedging, trees, bulbs, compost and sundries - all in a country setting.
Toilets; Disabled access

Wyevale Garden Centre
Forest Rd, Binfield, Bracknell,
Berkshire RG12 5ND
Tel: 01344 869456
Fax: 01344 869541

Wyevale offers a huge selection of plants, shrubs, gift ideas, furniture, BBQs and tools. Most centres have pet and aquatic departments and a restaurant. 0800 413213 for nearest stockist. See above.

Wyevale Garden Centre
Heathlands Rd, Wokingham,
Berkshire RG11 3BG
Tel: 01734 773055
Fax: 01344 772949

See Bracknell centre above.

Wyld Court Rainforest
Conservation Centre of the,
World Land Trust, Hampstead
Norreys, Nr Newbury, Berkshire
RG16 0TN
Tel: 01635 200221
Fax: 01635 202440
Hours: 10am–5.30pm March–Oct. 10am–4.30pm Nov–Feb

Experience the sheer beauty of this unique conservation project. A collection of dramatic and endangered rare plant species and rainforest creatures thrive in tropical temperatures under 20,000 feet of glass. Visit the Vinery full of plants for sale, and the crafts and book shop. All profits go to the World Land Trust, a registered charity helping to preserve rainforests and other biologically important habitats from destruction. Every visitor to Wyld Court is helping to save a rainforest!
Toilets; Refreshments; Disabled access

For Quality & Value
Bressingham Plant Centres

Thousands of hardy plants, including many rare and unusual varieties raised by Blooms of Bressingham, Norfolk's famous traditional nurserymen. Friendly advice from skilled plantsmen plus the choice, quality, service and value which have made Bressingham best since 1946.

Bressingham, Diss, Norfolk. Tel: (01379) 687464/688133
3 miles west of Diss on the A1066.

Dorney Court, Dorney, Windsor. Tel: (01628) 669999
Exit 7 from M4 to A4, follow tourist signs to Dorney Court 2 miles along B3026.

Elton Hall, Elton, Peterborough. Tel: (01832) 280058
8 miles west of Peterborough on A605.

All 3 Centres open 9am to 5.30pm daily

Buckinghamshire

A J Palmer & Son
Denham Court Nursery,
Denham Court Drive, Denham,
Nr Uxbridge, Buckinghamshire
UB9 5PG
Contact: Sheila or John Palmer
Tel/fax: 01895 832035
Hours: Seasonal times. Ring to confirm

Family business offering personal service. Situated in middle of Buckinghamshire golf course. Main showfield A40 Denham roundabout. Nurseries open for viewing July-October. Free list available.
Catalogue; Mail order

Bernwode Plants
Kingswood Lane, Ludgershall,
Buckinghamshire HP18 9RB
Contact: Mr & Mrs D A Tolman
Tel/fax: 01844 237415
Hours: 10am–6pm Tues–Sun Mar–Oct

Nursery selling huge range of rare plants, shrubs and fruit trees, including 100 traditional apple varieties. Courier service. Detailed catalogue available for £1.50.
Catalogue; Mail order; Toilets

Buckingham Nurseries & Garden Centre
Tingewick Rd, Buckingham,
Buckinghamshire MK18 4AE
Tel: 01280 813556
Fax: 01280 815491
Hours: 8.30am–5.30pm Mon–Fri, 9.30am–5.30pm Sun. Summer closing 6pm

Mail order specialist in hedging plants and young trees. Free catalogue available. Wide range of container grown shrubs, trees, perennials and grasses. Many unusual varieties.
Catalogue; Mail order; Toilets

Burnwode Plants
Wotton Rd, Ludgershall,
Aylesbury, Buckinghamshire
HP18 9NZ
Tel/fax: 01844 237415
Catalogue; Mail order

Butterfields Nursery
Harvest Hill, Bourne End,
Buckinghamshire SL8 5JJ
Tel/fax: 01628 525455
Catalogue; Mail order

Conifer Garden
Hare Lane Nursery, Little
Kingshill, Great Missenden,
Buckinghamshire HP16 0EF
Contact: Mark Powell
Tel: 01494 890624/862086
Fax: 01494 862086
Hours: 11am–4pm Tues–Sat

Specialist conifer retail nursery. Over 500 varieties listed in stock or available. Enquiries for others welcome. For list and directions send 2 x 1st class stamps & SAE.
Catalogue; Mail order; Toilets

East Midlands Cactus Nursery
Manor Close, Broughton, Milton
Keynes, Buckinghamshire MK10 9AA
Tel/fax: 01908 665584
Catalogue; Mail order

Fulmer Plant Park
Cherry Tree Lane, Fulmer
Common Rd, Fulmer,
Buckinghamshire
Tel/fax: 01753 662604

Marlow Garden & Leisure Centre
Great Gardens of England Ltd,
Pump Lane South, Little Marlow,
Buckinghamshire SL7 3RB
Tel: 01628 482716
Fax: 01628 898135
Hours: 9am–5.30pm

49

The Daily Telegraph *Green Fingers*   Garden Centres & Nurseries

Morehavens
28 Denham Lane, Gerrards Cross, Buckinghamshire SL9 0EX
Contact: Brigid Farmer
Tel/fax: 01494 871563
Hours: Mail order only

We supply clones of Treneague camomile for lawns, patios, seats etc by mail order. Please send SAE for details. Cost £10 for 50 plants.
Catalogue; Mail order

Tamarisk Nurseries
Wing Rd, Stewkley, Leighton Buzzard, Buckinghamshire LU7 0JB
Tel/fax: 01525 240747
Hours: 12–5pm Mon–Fri, 10am–6pm Sat Sun & Bank Hols
Mail order

Waddesdon Nursery
Queen Street, Waddesdon, Aylesbury, Buckinghamshire HP18 0JW
Tel: 01296 658586
Fax: 01296 658852
Hours: 10am–5pm daily

Woodstock Orchids & Automations
Woodstock House, 50 Pound Hill, Great Brickhill, Milton Keynes, Buckinghamshire MK17 9AS
Contact: Bill or Joan Gaskell
Tel: 01525 261352
Fax: 01525 261724
Hours: By appointment only

We are suppliers of high quality orchids to retail, wholesale and hobbyists. IN.TN glasshouses and a wide range of equipment nationwide.

Wyevale Garden Centre
Junction Avebury Boulevard/, Secklow Gate, Milton Keynes, Buckinghamshire MK9 3BY
Tel: 01908 604011
Fax: 01908 664678

Wyevale offers a huge selection of plants, shrubs, gift ideas, furniture, BBQs and tools. Most centres have pet and aquatic departments and a restaurant. 0800 413213 for nearest stockist. See above.

Wyevale Garden Centre
Newport Rd, Woburn Sands, Milton Keynes, Buckinghamshire MK17 8UF
Tel: 01908 281161
Fax: 01908 281142

See Milton Keynes centre above.

Cambridgeshire

Anglesey Abbey & Gardens
Lode, Cambridge, Cambridgeshire CB5 9EJ
Tel/fax: 01223 811200
Hours: 11am–5.30pm Wed–Sun Apr–Oct

National Trust. Historic garden and house with plant centre. Featuring the Fairhaven Collection of statuary within the 40 hectare landscape garden.
Toilets; Refreshments; Disabled access

Anglia Bulbs
80 Sutton Rd, Wisbech, Cambridgeshire PE13 5DR
Mail order

Arbor Exotica
The Estate Office, Hall Farm, Weston Colville, Cambridgeshire CB1 5PE
Tel: 01223 290328
Fax: 01223 290650
Hours: By appointment only

Small private nursery stocking container-grown exotic trees. Catalogue £1.50 refundable on first order.
Catalogue; Mail order

Ballerina Trees Ltd
Maris Lane, Trumpington, Cambridgeshire CB2 2LQ
Tel: 01223 840411
Fax: 01223 842934

Supplier of Ballerina apple trees. Six varieties available - four dessert: Bolero, Polka, Waltz and Flamenco - one cooker: Charlotte - and one ornamental crab: Maypole.
Catalogue

Brampton Garden Centre
Buckden Rd, Brampton, Cambridgeshire PE18 8NF
Contact: Peter Bates
Tel: 01480 453048
Fax: 01480 414994
Hours: 9am–5.30pm Mon–Sat, 10am–4.30pm Sun

Well run and stocked garden centre specialising in top quality plants and service.
Toilets; Refreshments; Disabled access

Bressingham Plant Centre
Elton Hall, Elton, Peterborough, Cambridgeshire PE8 6SH
Tel: 01832 280058
Fax: 01832 280081
Hours: 9am–5.30pm daily except Xmas & Boxing Day

Thousands of hardy plants, including the new, classic and unusual from traditional Norfolk nurserymen Blooms of Bressingham, plus the friendly advice of skilled plantsmen.
Toilets; Refreshments; Disabled access

Countryside Wildflowers
Chatteris Road, Somersham, Cambridgeshire PE17 3DN
Contact: Nick Meakin or Judy Usher
Tel: 01487 841322
Fax: 01487 740206
Hours: By appointment

The biggest dedicated producer of wildflowers, supplying plants, bulbs and seeds. We also undertake conservatory and habitat restoration projects for both organisations and private clients.
Catalogue; Mail order

Diane Sewell
Overdene, 81 Willingham Rd, Over, Cambridge, Cambridgeshire CB4 5PF
Tel/fax: 01954 260614

Elsworth Herbs
31 Smith St, Elsworth, Cambridge, Cambridgeshire CB3 8HY
Contact: Dr J Twibell
Tel/fax: 01954 267414
Hours: By appointment

Silver, scented and unusual plants and herbs. Artemisias insectivorous (Cephalotus, Darlingtonia, Sarracenia), mandrake, conservatory plants (nerium oleander). Catalogue 2 x 1st class stamps.
Catalogue; Mail order

Fenland Bulbs
Asholt Corner, March Rd, Coldham, Wisbech, Cambridgeshire PE14 0LP
Tel: 01945 861116
Fax: 01945 860894
Catalogue; Mail order

Meadowcroft Fuchsias & Pelargonium
Church Street Nurseries, Woodhurst, Huntingdon, Cambridgeshire PE17 3BN
Contact: D N Pickard & R C Polhill
Tel/fax: 01487 823333
Hours: 9am–6pm Mar–Sept inc Bank Hols

Fuchsia nursery established over 25 years. Specialising in American hybrids. Good range of pelargonium. Wholesale and retail.
Catalogue; Mail order

Monksilver Nursery
Oakington Rd, Cottenham, Cambridgeshire CB4 4TW
Tel: 01954 251555
Fax: 01954 202666
Hours: 10am–4pm Fri–Sat Mar–Jun

Catalogue 6 x 1st class stamps. Specialities anthemis, arum, bulbs, euphorbia, pulmonaria, sedum, snowdrops, solidago, vinca, variegated plants, unusual perennials, labels.
Catalogue; Mail order

Notcutts Garden Centre
Oundle Rd, Orton Waterville, Peterborough, Cambridgeshire PE2 0UU
Tel/fax: 01733 234600
Hours: 9.30am–5.30pm Mon–Sat, 10am–5.30pm Sun (5pm Winter)
Catalogue; Refreshments

Scotsdale Nursery & Garden Centre
120 Cambridge Rd, Great Shelford, Cambridge, Cambridgeshire CB2 5JT
Tel: 01223 842777
Fax: 01223 844340
Hours: 9am–5.30pm Mon–Sat, 10.30am–4.30pm Sun

Scotsdales is a well laid out and spacious complex offering all you would expect from a modern garden centre and a lot more besides.
Toilets; Refreshments; Disabled access

Simply Plants
17 Duloe Brook, Eaton Socon, Cambridgeshire PE19 3DW
Contact: Christine Dakin
Tel/fax: 01480 475312
Hours: Appt only

Specialities are ornamental grasses and bamboos. Also hardy and unusual perennials and shrubs. 2 x 1st class stamps for catalogue.
Catalogue; Mail order

Cheshire

Astbury Meadow Garden Centre
Newcastle Road (A34), Astbury, Congleton, Cheshire CW12 4RL
Tel/fax: 01260 276466
Hours: Open daily

Garden Centres of Cheshire are five family run businesses, specialising in trees, shrubs, herbaceous, houseplants, funrture, fencing, paving, pets and aquatics, garden machinery and Christmas décor.
Toilets; Refreshments; Disabled access

Barton Grange Garden Centre
Chester Road, Woodford, Stockport, Cheshire SK7 1QS
Tel: 0161 439 0745
Fax: 0161 439 0840
Hours: 9am–5.30pm Mon–Sat, 10.30am–4.30pm Sun

A large garden centre offering top quality plants for the home and garden. The landscaped gardens and restaurant are outstanding at this superb garden centre.
Toilets; Refreshments; Disabled access

Bents Garden Centre & Nurseries
Warrington Rd, Glazebury, Leigh, Cheshire WA3 5NT
Tel: 01942 262066
Fax: 01942 261960
Hours: 9am–8pm Mon–Fri, 9.30am–5pm Sat–Sun
Refreshments

Bridgemere Nurseries
Bridgemere, Nantwich, Cheshire CW5 7QB
Tel/fax: 01936 5381
Hours: 9am–8pm Mon–Sat 10am–8pm Sun (Closes 5pm in Winter)
Refreshments

Caddicks Clematis Nursey
Lymm Rd, Thelwall, Warrington, Cheshire WA13 0UF
Contact: Mrs D Caddick
Tel/fax: 01925 757196
Hours: 10am–5pm Tues–Sun Feb–Oct. 10am–4pm Tues–Sat Nov.

Clematis specialist with a collection of over 300 varieties. Visitors and mail order welcome. Colour illustrated catalogue available. Please send £1 cheque/PO.
Catalogue; Mail order; Toilets

Cantilever Garden Centre
Station Road, Latchford, Warrington, Cheshire WA4 2AB
Tel: 01925 635799
Fax: 01925 417084
Hours: Open daily

Garden Centres of Cheshire are five family run businesses specialising in trees, shrubs, herbaceous, houseplants, furniture, fencing, paving, pets and aquatics, garden machinery and Christmas décor.
Toilets; Refreshments; Disabled access

Cheshire Herbs
Fourfields, Forest Rd, Little Budworth, Tarporley, Cheshire CW6 9ES
Tel: 01892 760578
Fax: 01892 760354
Catalogue; Mail order

Collinwood Nurseries
Mottram St Andrew, Macclesfield, Cheshire SK10 4QR
Contact: A Wright
Tel/fax: 01625 582272

Specialist mail order chrysanthemum growers listing early flowering disbuds and sprays. Garden Poms, Koreans, rubellums and Mums late flowering disbuds, sprays and singles. Catalogue of over 200 varieties 1 x 1st class stamp. Despatch dates for plants March/April/May.
Catalogue; Mail order

F Morrey & Son
Forest Nursery, Kelsall, Cheshire CW6 0SW
Tel: 01829 751342
Fax: 01829 752449
Hours: 9am–5pm Mon–Sat

An established family firm, with over 85 years experience. A 90 acre site produces good quality stock, specialising in rhododendrons, azaleas, shrubs, trees, conifers, roses.
Catalogue; Toilets

Fairy Lane Nurseries
Fairy Lane, Sale, Cheshire M33 2JT
Tel/fax: 0161 905 1137
Hours: 10am–5.30pm Mon–Sat, 10am–5pm Sun. Closes at dusk in Winter

Friendly and helpful "Plant Finder" listed nursery growing extensive range of perennials, hebes and grasses. Also shrubs, climbers, heathers and alpines. Herb and display gardens.
Catalogue; Toilets

Firs Nursery
Chelford Rd, Henbury, Macclesfield, Cheshire SK10 3LH
Contact: Fay Bowling
Tel/fax: 01625 426422
Hours: 9.30am–5pm April–Sept. Closed Wed & Sun

A small nursery specialising in a wide range of herbaceous perennials and alpines, many are growing in the garden. Catalogue 2 x 1st class stamps.
Catalogue

Fryer's Nurseries Ltd
Manchester Rd, Knutsford, Cheshire WA16 0SX
Tel: 01565 755455
Fax: 01565 653755
Hours: 9am–5.30pm Mon–Sat, 10.30am–4.30pm Sun & Bank Hols

North England's leading rose specialist. Fully stocked garden centre and extensive rose nursery with roses available throughout the year. Free colour catalogue available on request.
Catalogue; Mail order; Toilets; Refreshments; Disabled access

Goldenfield Nursery
C & K Jones, Barrow Lane, Tarvin, Cheshire CH3 8JF
Tel: 01829 740663
Fax: 01829 741877
Hours: 8.30am–5pm daily
Catalogue; Mail order

Gordale Nurseries Garden Centre
Chester High Rd, Burton, South Wirral, Cheshire L64 8TF
Contact: Mrs J Nicholson
Tel: 0151 336 2116
Fax: 0151 336 8152
Hours: 9am–5pm Winter, 9am–6pm Summer. Late night Thurs

Easy to find - 7 miles from Chester on the A540. Coffee shop with home made cakes. Landscaped gardens. Friendly, helpful, trained staff ready to assist.
Toilets; Refreshments; Disabled access

Harold Walker
Oakfield Nurseries, Huntingdon, Chester, Cheshire CH3 6EA
Tel: 01244 320731
Fax: 01244 342372
Hours: 9am–5pm daily Feb–Jun

Comprehensive mail order catalogue for chrysanthemums, fuchsias, basket plants and, for collection from nursery, annual bedding seedlings and young basket, bedding plants.
Catalogue; Mail order

Okells Nurseries
Duddon Heath, Tarporley, Cheshire CW6 0EP
Tel: 01829 741512
Fax: 01244 342372
Hours: 9am–5.30pm daily. Closes 7pm Sat & Sun May–Jun only
Catalogue

Phedar Nursery
Bunkers Hill, Romiley, Stockport, Cheshire SK6 3DS
Contact: Will McLewin
Tel/fax: 0161 430 3772
Hours: By appointment only

The widest range of hybrid and authentic, accurate species hellebores in the world. Herbaceous hybrid and species peonies, Chinese tree peonies. Hellebore and peony seed.
Catalogue; Mail order

Pilkington Garden Centre
Bold Heath (on A57), Widnes, Cheshire WA8 3UU
Tel/fax: 0151 424 6264
Hours: Open 7 days until 6pm Summer, 5pm Winter

Garden centre offers a comprehensive range of goods and plants: houseplants, gifts, floristry, aquatics and pets, café, sheds, greenhouses and conservatories. Christmas decorations a speciality.
Toilets; Refreshments; Disabled access

Robinsons of Whaley Bridge
20 Vaughan Rd, Whaley Bridge, Stockport, Cheshire SK12 7JT
Tel/fax: 01663 732991
Hours: By appointment only
Catalogue; Mail order

Stapeley Water Gardens Ltd
London Rd, Stapeley, Nantwich, Cheshire CW5 7LH
Tel: 01270 623868
Fax: 01270 624919
Hours: From 10am daily except Xmas Day

The world's largest water garden centre - for all your water garden needs, with The Palms Tropical Oasis, a huge tropical house and Yesteryear Museum.
Catalogue; Mail order; Toilets; Refreshments; Disabled access

Sycamore Park Garden Centre
Chester Road (A41), Great Sutton, South Wirral, Cheshire L66 2LX
Tel: 0151 339 1289
Fax: 0151 339 3313
Hours: Open daily

Garden Centres of Cheshire are five family run businesses specialising in trees, shrubs, herbaceous, houseplants, furniture, fencing, paving, pets and aquatics, garden machinery and Christmas décor.
Toilets; Refreshments; Disabled access

Weaver Vale Garden Centre
Winnington Lane (A533), Winnington, Northwich, Cheshire CW8 4EE
Tel: 01606 79965
Fax: 01606 784480
Hours: Open 7 days

Garden Centres of Cheshire are 5 family run businesses specialising in trees, shrubs, herbaceous plants, furniture, fencing, paving, pets and aquatics, garden machinery and Christmas décor.
Toilets; Refreshments; Disabled access

The Daily Telegraph *Green Fingers*   **Garden Centres & Nurseries**

Wilmslow Garden Centre
Manchester Rd (A34), Wilmslow, Cheshire SK9 2JN
Tel: 01625 525700
Fax: 01625 539800
Hours: *Open 7 days*

Garden Centres of Cheshire are 5 family run businesses specialising in trees, shrubs, herbaceous, houseplants, furniture, fencing, paving, pets and aquatics, garden machinery and Christmas décor.
Toilets; Refreshments; Disabled access

Wyevale Garden Centre
Otterspool, Dooley Lane, Marple, Stockport, Cheshire SK6 7HE
Tel: 0161 427 7211
Fax: 0161 449 7636

See above.

Cleveland

Arcadia Nurseries
Brasscastle Lane, Nunthorpe, Middlesbrough, Cleveland TS8 9EB
Tel/fax: 01642 310782
Hours: *Any day throughout Summer*
Catalogue; Mail order

Peter Barratt's Garden Centres
Yarm Rd, Stockton on Tees, Cleveland TS18 3SQ
Tel: 01642 613433
Fax: 01642 618185
Hours: *9am–5.30pm Mon–Sat (7pm Thurs), 10.30am–4.30pm Sun*

Excellent range of quality plants, gardening sundries, gifts and garden furniture; large pet and aquatic centre; conservatory show site plus 70 seater restaurant.
Toilets; Refreshments; Disabled access

Plantarama
30 Adcott Rd, Middlesbrough, Cleveland TS5 7ES
Mail order

Strikes Garden Centre
Urlay Nook Rd, Eaglescliffe, Cleveland TS16 0PE
Tel/fax: 01642 780481
Hours: *9am–6pm Mon–Sat, 10am–5pm Sun*

Town Farm Nursery
Whitton Village, Stockton on Tees, Cleveland TS21 1LQ
Contact: David Baker
Tel/fax: 01740 631079
Hours: *10am–6pm Fri–Mon. Closed in Winter*

Specialist nursery within easy reach of A1(M). Sheltered 3/4 acre garden with many unusual alpines, perennials and shrubs. Catalogue 3 x 1st class stamps. Open Friday to Monday. Closed mid-week except by previous appointment.
Catalogue; Mail order; Toilets

Westwinds Perennial Plants
Westwinds, Filpoke Lane, High Hesleden, Hartlepool, Cleveland TS27 4BT
Contact: Harry Blackwood
Tel/fax: 0191 518 0225
Hours: *Sat/Sun/Mon*

Hardy perennials, clematis, shrubs. Catalogue 2 x 1st class stamps.
Catalogue

Co Durham

Beamish Clematis Nursery
Stoney Lane, Beamish, Co Durham DH9 0SJ
Tel/fax: 0191 370 0202
Hours: *9am–5pm daily. Closed Dec & Jan*

We offer an outstanding selection of hardy ornamental trees, shrubs, climbers and conifers. Personal callers only.

Eggleston Hall Gardens
Eggleston Hall, Barnard Castle, Co Durham DL12 0AG
Tel: 01833 650403
Fax: 01833 650378
Hours: *10am–5pm daily*

An interesting walled garden with nurseries, specialising in the unusual. A stream and winding paths add interest. Organic produce in season.
Catalogue; Toilets; Disabled access

Elly Hill Herbs
Elly Hill house, Barmpton, Darlington, Co Durham DL1 3JF
Contact: Mrs Nina Pagan
Tel/fax: 01325 464682
Hours: *9.30am–12.30pm 4–5.30pm daily Mar–Oct. Phone first*

Elly Hill Herbs has a herb display garden. Herb parties with talk or tour. Individuals welcome too. Herb products and plants for sale. Brochure available.
Catalogue

Equatorial Plant Co
7 Gray Lane, Barnard Castle, Co Durham DL12 8PD
Tel/fax: 01833 690519
Catalogue; Mail order

Rookhope Nurseries
Rookhope, Weardale, Co Durham DL13 2DD
Tel/fax: 01388 517272
Hours: *9am–4pm daily mid Mar–end Sept*

The highest nursery in Northumbria (1100ft). Spectacular scenery. Mature garden with wide use of coloured foliage (free). We specialise in growing only the very best quality alpines and perennials, with many unusual varieties. Catalogue 3 x 1st class stamps.
Catalogue; Mail order

Strikes Garden Centre
Woodlands Rd, Cockerton, Darlington, Co Durham DL3 9AA
Tel/fax: 01325 468474
Hours: *9am–7pm Mon–Sat (6pm Sun) Summer 1 hr earlier Winter*

Cornwall

Bosvigo Plants
Bosvigo House, Bosvigo Lane, Truro, Cornwall TR1 3NH
Tel/fax: 01872 275774
Hours: *11am–6pm Wed–Sat Mar–Sept*

Small nursery specialising in unusual and hard-to-find herbaceous plants. 3 acre display gardens adjacent. No mail order. Catalogue 4 x 2nd class stamps.
Catalogue; Toilets

Bregover Plants
Middlewood, North Hill, Launceston, Cornwall PL15 7NN
Contact: Jennifer Bousfield
Tel/fax: 01566 782661
Hours: *11am–5pm Wed–Fri mid Mar–mid Oct*

An interesting range of hardy perennials grown in our cottage garden nursery situated between Liskeard and Launceston on the B3254. Please phone to confirm opening times, especially at weekends. Catalogue 2 x 1st class stamps.
Catalogue; Mail order

Brockings Exotics
North Petherwin, Launceston, Cornwall PL15 8LW
Contact: Ian & Joy Cooke
Tel/fax: 01566 785533
Hours: *By appointment only*

Specialists in tender perennials, cannas, named coleus and conservatory plants. Catalogue 3 x 1st class stamps.
Catalogue; Mail order

Burncoose & South Down Nurseries
Gwennap, Redruth, Cornwall TR16 6BJ
Tel: 01209 861112
Fax: 01209 860228
Hours: *9am–5pm Mon–Sat, 11am–5pm Sun*
Catalogue; Mail order

Carnon Downs Garden Centre
Quenchwell Rd, Carnon Downs, Truro, Cornwall TR3 4LN
Tel: 01872 863058
Fax: 01872 862162
Hours: *9am–5pm Mon–Sat. 10.30am–4.30pm Sun*

For all your garden needs.
Mail order; Toilets; Refreshments; Disabled access

Cornish Garden Nurseries
Perran-ar-Worthal, Truro, Cornwall TR3 7PE
Tel/fax: 01872 864380
Hours: *9am–5pm daily*

Hardy garden plants, trees, shrubs, perennials, conifers, herbs. 100 varieties of apple. 200 varieties camellias. Rhododendrons, fruits, heathers, hedging. Retail & wholesale. Landscaping - planning to planting.

Duchy of Cornwall Nursery
Cott Rd, Lostwithiel, Cornwall PL22 0BW
Tel: 01208 872668
Fax: 01208 872835
Hours: *9am–5pm Mon–Sat, 10am–5pm Sun. Closed Bank Hols*

A mouthwatering range of garden plants with many unusual varieties. Set in wooded valley with beautiful walks. Catalogue £2 appreciated. Sorry, no dogs in nursery.
Catalogue; Toilets; Refreshments

Little Treasures Nursery
Wheal Treasure, Horsedowns, Praze, Cornwall TR14 0NL
Contact: Mrs B Jackson
Tel/fax: 01209 831978
Hours: *10am–5pm Wed–Sat Mar–end Sept*

Cottage garden plants: herbaceous perennials, shrubs, climbers and tender perennials for containers and conservatories.
Catalogue; Mail order

Merlin Rooted Cuttings
Jackson, Little Drym, Praze, Camborne, Cornwall TR14 0NU
Hours: *9am–5pm Wed–Fri, 9am–1pm Sat Mar–Oct*
Catalogue; Mail order

Parkinson Herbs
Barras Moor Farm, Perran Ar Worthal, Truro, Cornwall TR3 7PE
Contact: Elizabeth Parkinson
Tel/fax: 01872 864380
Hours: *9am–5pm daily*

Wide range of herbs, scented leaf geraniums, named sweet violets. Free catalogue. Herb talks/demonstrations in Cornwall only.
Catalogue; Mail order

Tomperrow Farm Nurseries
Threemilestone, Truro, Cornwall
TR3 6BE
Tel/fax: 01872 560344
Hours: 10am–5pm Usually – phone first
Catalogue; Mail order

Trevena Cross Nurseries
Breage, Helston, Cornwall TR13 9PS
Tel: 01736 763880
Fax: 01736 762828
Hours: 9am–5pm Mon–Sat, 10.30am–4.30pm Sun

Nursery and garden centre, rare exotic plant specialists. Pet shop, coldwater aquatic centre. All plants grown on site.
Catalogue; Mail order; Toilets; Refreshments

Trewidden Estate Nursery
Trewidden, Penzance, Cornwall TR20 8TT
Tel: 01736 62087
Fax: 01736 331470
Hours: 8am–1pm, 2–5pm Mon–Sat. Closes 4pm Fri
Catalogue; Mail order

Trewithen Nurseries
Grampound Rd, Truro, Cornwall TR2 4DD
Tel: 01726 882764
Fax: 01726 882301
Hours: Mon–Sat all year

Nursery attached to Trewithen Gardens. Plants for sale all year.
Catalogue

Wall Cottage Nursery
Lockengate, Bugle, St Austell, Cornwall PL26 8RU
Contact: Mrs Jenny Clark
Tel/fax: 01208 831259
Hours: By appointment

Specialist rhododendron and azalea grower. Mail order. Min value £15. Catalogue cost 60p.
Catalogue; Mail order

Wyevale Garden Centre
Nut Lane, Hayle, Cornwall TR27 6LG
Tel: 01736 753731
Fax: 01736 757331

Wyevale offers a huge selection of plants, shrubs, gift ideas, furniture, BBQs and tools. Most centres have pet and aquatic departments and a restaurant. 0800 413213 for nearest stockist.

Cumbria

Beechcroft Nurseries
Bongate, Appleby, Cumbria CA16 6UE
Contact: Roger Brown
Tel: 017683 51201
Fax: 017683 52546
Hours: 9am–6pm daily

A small nursery specialising in field-grown trees (more than 100 varieties) and many interesting shrubs and herbaceous perennials. Landscape ideas and garden design service.
Catalogue; Mail order

Boonwood Garden Centre
Gosforth, Seascale, Cumbria CA20 1BP
Tel/fax: 01946 725330
Hours: 9am–5pm daily
Catalogue; Mail order

Halecat Garden Nurseries
Witherslack, Grange over Sands, Cumbria LA11 6RU
Contact: Mrs M C Stanley
Tel/fax: 015395 52229
Hours: 9am–4.30pm Mon–Fri all year, 2–4pm Sun Easter–Sept. Closed Sat

Garden with view. Free. Many plants in garden for sale in adjoining nursery. Over 80 varieties and species of hydrangea available. Catalogue 45p plus postage.
Catalogue

Hartside Nursery Garden
Alston, Cumbria CA9 3BL
Contact: Mrs S Huntley
Tel/fax: 01434 381372
Hours: 9am–4.30pm Mon–Fri, 12.30–4pm Sat/Sun Mar–Oct

Specialist nursery growing rare and unusual hardy plants. Alpines, hardy ferns, dwarf shrubs and plants for peat and rock garden. Visitors and mail order welcome.
Catalogue; Mail order

Hayes Garden World Ltd
Lake Road, Ambleside, Cumbria LA22 0DW
Contact: Richard Hayes
Tel: 015394 33434
Fax: 015394 34153
Hours: 9am–6pm Mon–Sat, 11am–5pm Sun

Stockists of one of the widest ranges of both indoor and outdoor plants, furniture, ceramics, chemicals and tools. Virtually everything you could ever want.
Toilets; Refreshments

Muncaster Plants
Muncaster Castle, Ravenglass, Cumbria CA18 1RJ
Tel: 01229 717614/203
Fax: 01229 717010
Hours: By appointment

Wide range of rhododendrons and azaleas to suit all gardens. Send 2 x 1st class stamps for availability list. Mail order and export service.
Catalogue; Mail order; Toilets; Refreshments; Disabled access

T H Barker & Son
Baines Paddock Nursery, Haverthwaite, Ulverston, Cumbria LA12 8PF
Tel/fax: 015395 58236
Hours: 9.30am–5.30pm Mar–Oct. Closed Tues. Nov–Feb by appt
Catalogue; Mail order

Weasdale Nurseries
Newbiggin on Lune, Kirkby Stephen, Cumbria CA17 4LX
Contact: Andrew Forsyth
Tel: 015396 23246
Fax: 015396 23277
Hours: 9am–5pm Mon–Fri

Located at an elevation of 850' on the Howgill Fells in East Cumbria, Weasdale Nurseries have specialised in the mail-ordering of hardy trees and shrubs since 1950. Their catalogue (£2.50 post paid) lists over 300 species and varieties of open-ground grown forest trees, hedging, native and ornamental trees and shrubs (both coniferous and broadleaved) which can be dispatched to any EC address.
Catalogue; Mail order

Webbs Garden Centre
Burneside Rd, Kendal, Cumbria LA9 4RT
Tel: 01539 720068
Fax: 01539 727328
Hours: 9am–6pm Mon–Sat, 10.30am–4.30pm Sun

Established 1810, this wonderful old garden centre boasts acres to wander around with a huge array of plants, sundries, in fact everything for the garden.
Toilets; Refreshments; Disabled access

Derbyshire

Bluebell Nursery
Blackfordby, Swadlincote, Derbyshire DE11 8AJ
Tel/fax: 01283 222091
Hours: Daily. Closed Xmas Eve–2 Jan
Catalogue; Mail order

Burrows Roses
Meadowcroft, Spondon Rd, Dale Abbey, Derby, Derbyshire DE7 4PQ
Tel/fax: 01332 668289
Hours: Mail order only

Roses. Small family firm specialising in old and new fragrant varieties. Free comprehensive colour catalogue available on request. 2 x 1st class stamps appreciated.
Catalogue; Mail order

Chatsworth Garden Centre
Calton Lees, Beeley, Matlock, Derbyshire DE4 2NX
Contact: John Tarbatt
Tel: 01692 734004
Fax: 01629 580503
Hours: 9am–5pm Mon–Sat, 9am–4.30pm Sun

Everything for the garden. Indoor plants. Floral sundries. Giftware. Clothing. Garden buildings. Furniture. Stoneware. Qualified staff. Local delivery service. Coffee shop. Access/Visa.
Toilets; Refreshments; Disabled access

Greenleaves Garden Centre
Birkin Lane, Wingerworth, Chesterfield, Derbyshire S42 6RD
Tel: 01246 204214
Fax: 016129 580503
Hours: 9am–5pm daily Oct–Feb/9am–5.30pm Mar–Sept

Highgates Nursery
166a Crich Lane, Belper, Derbyshire DE56 1EP
Tel/fax: 01773 822153
Hours: 10am–4.30pm Mon–Sat Mar 1–Sept 30

Wide range of alpines, dwarf rhododendrons. Catalogue 2 x 1st class stamps. Large display area.
Catalogue; Toilets; Disabled access

Matlock Garden Centre
Nottingham Rd, Tansley, Matlock, Derbyshire DE4 5FR
Contact: John Tarbatt
Tel: 01629 580500
Fax: 01629 580503
Hours: 9am–5pm Mon–Sat, 9.30am–4.30pm Sun

Everything for the garden. Indoor plants. Conservatories and garden buildings. Pet and aquatic department. Qualified staff. Local delivery service. Coffee shop and restaurant. Access/Visa.
Toilets; Refreshments; Disabled access

Riley's Chrysanthemums
Alfreton Nurseries, Ashover Rd, Woolley Moor, Alfreton, Derbyshire DE55 6FF
Tel/fax: 01246 590320
Hours: 10am–4pm daily except Sat Feb–June

Renowned raisers and retailers of all types of chrysanthemums by mail order. Two acres of outdoor blooms and sprays to view, Sundays in September.
Catalogue; Mail order

Devon

Altoona Nurseries
The Windmill, Tigley, Dartington, Totnes, Devon TQ9 6DW

Contact: Paul Harber
Tel/fax: 01803 868147

Hours: 9am–5pm by appt

Nursery specialising in Japanese maples wholesale & retail. Price list available for stamped addressed envelope.

Ann & Roger Bowden (Hostas)
Sticklepath, Okehampton, Devon EX20 2NN

Tel: 01837 840481
Fax: 01837 840482

Hours: By phoned arrangement & under NGS

Gardens of about one acre incorporating National Collection of Hostas and nursery. Admission £1. Mail order catalogue of 184 varieties 4 x 2nd class stamps.
Catalogue; Mail order; Toilets

Burnham Nurseries
Forches Cross, Newton Abbot, Devon TQ12 6PZ

Tel: 01626 52233
Fax: 01626 62167

Hours: 10am–4pm daily
Catalogue; Mail order

Decorative Foliage
Higher Badworthy, South Brent, Devon TQ10 9EG

Tel/fax: 01364 72768

Hours: Phone first
Catalogue; Mail order

Endsleigh Garden Centre
Ivybridge, Devon PL21 9JL

Tel: 01752 892254
Fax: 01752 690284

Hours: 9am–5pm Mon–Fri, 10am–5pm Suns

One of the west country's largest garden centres. Huge covered sales areas. Specialist departments for garden design, water gardening, swimming pools, pets, garden furniture, garden buildings and machinery.
Toilets; Refreshments; Disabled access

Feebers Hardy Plants
1 Feebers, Westwood, Broadclyst, Devon EX5 3DQ

Contact: Edna Squires
Tel/fax: 01404 822118

Hours: Thurs 10am–5pm, Sat 2–6pm Mar/Jul & Sept/Oct

Nursery specialising in unusual plants, especially those that will tolerate heavy clay and winter wet: many can be seen in the garden.
Catalogue

Fillan's Plants
Pound House Nursery, Buckland Monachorum, Yelverton, Devon PL20 7LJ

Tel/fax: 01822 855050
Catalogue; Mail order

Glebe Cottage Plants
Pixie Lane, Warkleigh, Umberleigh, Devon EX37 9DH

Tel/fax: 01769 540554

Hours: 10am–5pm Wed–Sun
Catalogue; Mail order

Greenway Gardens
Churston Ferrers, Brixham, Devon TQ5 0ES

Tel/fax: 01803 842382

Hours: 2–5pm Mon–Fri, 10am–12pm Sat

Huge range of very unusual trees and shrubs, two walled gardens packed with plants for sale. Phone for directions.
Catalogue; Mail order

H & S Wills
2 St Brannocks Park Rd, Ilfracombe, Devon EX34 8HU

Tel/fax: 01271 863949

Hours: Mail order only

Small, part time nursery specialising in houseleeks - sempervivum, jovibarba and rosularia species and cultivars. Over 300 varieties available. Mail order only. Send SAE for lists.
Catalogue; Mail order

High Garden
Courtwood, Newton Ferrers, Devon PL8 1BW

Contact: F Bennett
Tel/fax: 01752 872528

Hours: By appointment

Specialises in rhododendrons, pieris and Japanese azaleas.
Catalogue; Mail order

Hill House Nursery & Gardens
Landscove, Nr Ashburton, Newton Abbot, Devon TQ13 7LY

Contact: R Hubbard
Tel/fax: 01803 762273

We have a great nursery and marvellous tea room. Geoff Hamilton introduced us in March 1996 as "That fabulous garden in Devon" and finished by saying "The owner is a man after my own heart". And that's good enough by me.
Toilets; Refreshments

Jack's Patch Garden Centre
Newton Rd, Bishopsteignton, Teignmouth, Devon TQ14 9PN

Tel/fax: 01626 776996

Hours: 9am–5.30pm Mon–Sat, 10.30am–4.30pm Sun

Plant specialists with own 6-acre nursery and friendly, knowledgeable staff. Located on shore of beautiful Teign estuary with café, gift shop and large pet department.
Toilets; Refreshments; Disabled access

K & C Cacti
Fern Cottage, West Buckland, Barnstaple, Devon EX32 0SF

Contact: Keith & Jane Comer
Tel/fax: 01987 60393

Hours: Most days – phone first

Specialist growers of cacti and succulents especially haworthia, echeveria, crassula, adromischus, euphorbia, conophytum, sulcorebutia and dwarf opuntia. Please send SAE for catalogue and prices.
Catalogue; Mail order

Kenwith Nursery
The Old Rectory, Littleham, Bideford, Devon EX39 5HW

Tel/fax: 01237 473752

Hours: 10am–12pm 2–5pm Wed–Sat. Other times by appt
Catalogue; Mail order

Knightshayes Garden Trust
The Garden Office, Knightshayes, Tiverton, Devon EX16 7RG

Hours: 10.30am–5.30pm daily Apr–Oct
Catalogue; Refreshments

Lewdon Farm Alpine Nursery
Medland Lane, Cheriton Bishop, Exeter, Devon EX6 6HF

Tel/fax: 01647 24283

Hours: 9am–5.30pm daily Apr–Oct
Catalogue; Mail order

Nicky's Rock Garden Nursery
Hillcrest, Broadhayes, Stockland, Honiton, Devon EX14 9EH

Contact: Bob & Diana Dark
Tel/fax: 01404 881213

Hours: 9am–dusk

Small family nursery specialising in plants for rockeries, scree, raised beds etc. Please ring first for directions and to check if open (most days).
Catalogue; Toilets

North Devon Garden Centre
Ashford, Barnstaple, Devon EX31 4BW

Tel: 01271 42880
Fax: 01271 23972

Hours: 9am–5pm Mon–Sat, 10am–6pm Sun
Refreshments

Otter Nurseries (Torbay)
250 Babbacombe Road, Torquay, Devon TQ1 3TA

Contact: Keith Powell
Tel: 01803 214294
Fax: 01803 291481

Hours: 9am–5.30pm Mon–Sat, 10am–5pm Sun

Compact garden centre with plants and garden requisites. Ample car parking.
Catalogue

Otter Nurseries Ltd
Gosford Rd, Ottery St Mary, Devon EX11 1LZ

Tel: 01404 815815
Fax: 01404 815816

Hours: 9am–5.30pm Mon–Sat, 10.30–4.30pm Sun

One of the largest garden centres in the county. Large display of garden furniture. Superb coffee shop. Car parking for 400 cars.
Catalogue; Toilets; Refreshments; Disabled access

Otter Nurseries of Plymouth
Chittleburn Hill, Brixton, Plymouth, Devon PL8 2BH

Contact: Tony Solman
Tel: 01752 405422
Fax: 01752 484181

Hours: 9am–5.30pm Mon–Sat, 10.30am–4.30pm Sun

Garden centre plants and requisites including large display of garden furniture. Car parking. Coffee shop. Aquatics.
Catalogue; Toilets; Refreshments

Perrie Hale Forest Nursery
Northcote Hill, Honiton, Devon EX14 8TH

Tel: 01404 43344
Fax: 01404 47163

Hours: Mid Nov–early Apr
Catalogue; Mail order

Peveril Clematis Nursery
Christow, Exeter, Devon EX6 7NG

Contact: Barry Fretwell
Tel/fax: 01647 252937

Hours: 10am–1pm 2–5.30pm Mar–Dec. Closed Thurs & Sun morning.

Specialist clematis growers, leading raisers of new clematis. Catalogue 2 x 1st class stamps.
Catalogue

Plant World Botanic Gardens & Plant Centre
St Marychurch Rd, Newton Abbot, Devon TQ12 4SE

Contact: Ray Brown
Tel: 01803 87239
Fax: 01803 872939

Hours: 9am–5pm 6 days (closed Wed). Open Mar–Sept incl

Beautifully landscaped plantsman's gardens of the world on a Devon hillside. Fabulous Dartmoor views. Shown on BBC and ITV. Extensive nursery crammed with choice rarities.
Toilets

Pleasant View Nursery
Two Mile Oak, Newton Abbot,
Devon TQ12 6DG
Contact: Mrs C Yeo
Tel/fax: 01803 813388
Hours: 10am–5pm Wed–Sat mid Mar–end Oct

Plantsman's nursery with large selection of rare and choice shrubs and salvias, all propagated from plants in the garden. Mail order catalogue £1 stamps.
Catalogue; Mail order

Pounsley Plants
Pounsley Combe, Spriddlestone, Brixton, Plymouth, Devon PL9 0DW
Contact: Mrs Jane Hollow
Tel/fax: 01752 402873
Hours: 10am–5pm Mon–Sat but please phone first

Unusual herbaceous perennials and cottage plants. Selection of clematis and old fashioned roses.
Catalogue; Mail order

R D Plants
Homelea Farm, Tytherleigh, Axminster, Devon EX13 7BG
Hours: 9am–1pm 2–5.30pm almost daily Mar–Sept

Hellebores in flower, anemone sylvestris fully double, anemone hupensis Crispa, anemonella thalictroides semi-double white and single pink, decorative origanums, plants for retentive shade, good garden-worthy perennials, many choice and rare - 1,000 varieties. Grown in home-mixed compost containing loam, aiding establishment in garden soil. Mail order, conscientious service. Plants despatched next day by carrier. By using open-topped boxes most plants can be sent in full growth, ordinarily herbaceous in 2 litre pots. We do not grow specifically for mail order in small pots. Plant list 4 x 2nd class stamps. A358 - first property over county border.
Catalogue; Mail order

R H S Garden Rosemoor Plant Centre
Great Torrington, Devon EX38 8PH
Tel/fax: 01805 624067
Hours: 10am–6pm, 5pm Oct–Mar, 4pm Nov–Feb

The well stocked plant centre offers a selection of unusual hardy plants, bulbs, trees and shrubs, reflecting those displayed in the garden.
Toilets; Refreshments; Disabled access

Sampford Shrubs
Sampford Peverell, Tiverton, Devon EX16 7EW
Tel/fax: 01884 821164
Hours: 9am–5pm/dusk Thur–Sun

Retail nursery growing a comprehensive range of herbaceous and shrubby plants. Medium SAE for stocklist. Mail order November to February.
Catalogue; Mail order

Scotts Clematis
Lee, Ilfracombe, Devon EX34 8LW
Tel/fax: 01271 863366
Hours: 10am–5pm Tues–Sun

Small specialist nursery with over 250 varieties of standard and more unusual clematis. All plants produced by us. See us at all the major flower shows.
Catalogue; Mail order

Southwick Country Herbs
Southwick Farm, Nomansland, Tiverton, Devon EX16 8NW
Tel/fax: 01884 861099
Hours: 10am–5.30pm Mon–Sat, 11am–5.30pm Sun
Catalogue; Mail order; Refreshments

Stone Lane Gardens
Stone Farm, Chagford, Devon TQ13 8JU
Contact: Kenneth & June Ashburner
Tel/fax: 01647 231311
Hours: 2pm–6pm May–Sept or phone for appt

Birch and alder specialists - catalogue £2. Five acre landscaped arboretum and water garden in Dartmoor National Park. Summer sculpture exhibitions.
Catalogue; Mail order; Toilets

Thornhayes Nursery
St Andrews Wood, Dulford, Cullompton, Devon EX15 2DF
Contact: Kevin Croucher
Tel: 01884 266746
Fax: 01884 266739
Hours: By appointment

Specialist growers of an extensive range of ornamental and amenity trees plus traditional fruit tree varieties, including cider apples, perry pears, cobnuts, walnuts and chestnuts.
Catalogue; Mail order

Tropicana Nursery
Westhill Avenue, Torquay, Devon TQ1 4LH
Tel/fax: 01803 312618
Hours: By appointment only
Catalogue; Mail order

Veryans Plants
Glebe, Coryton, Okehampton, Devon EX20 4PB
Contact: Rebecca Millar
Tel/fax: 01822 860302
Hours: By appointment only

Specialist herbaceous nursery, specialities include primroses, grasses, hardy geraniums, pulmonarias, asters, plus many others. Mail order catalogue 3 x 1st class stamps.
Catalogue; Mail order

Westfield Cacti
Kennford, Exeter, Devon EX6 7XD
Contact: Ralph Northcott
Tel/fax: 01392 832921
Hours: 10am–5pm Wed–Sun

Large selection of cacti and succulents. Send 1st class stamp for mail order catalogue.
Catalogue; Mail order; Toilets

Withleigh Nurseries
Withleigh, Tiverton, Devon EX16 8JG
Contact: Chris Britton
Tel/fax: 01884 253351
Hours: 9am–5.30pm Tues–Sat. Also Mons Mar–June

Family nursery growing and selling a wide range of shrubs, perennials and bedding. Prices and quality to please.

Dorset

Abbey Plants
Chaffeymoor, Bourton, Gillingham, Dorset SP8 5BY
Contact: Mr K R Potts
Tel/fax: 01747 840841
Hours: 10am–1pm 2–5pm Tues–Sat. Closed Dec–Feb

A very wide selection of trees, shrubs, herbaceous and alpines including many unusual varieties which may be seen growing in our garden at Chiffchaffs.

Abbotsbury Sub-Tropical Gardens
Abbotsbury, Weymouth, Dorset DT3 4LA
Tel/fax: 01305 871344/412
Hours: 10am–5pm daily. Closed Mon Nov–Feb
Catalogue; Mail order; Toilets; Refreshments

C W Groves & Son
Nursery & Garden Centre, West Bay Rd, Bridport, Dorset DT6 4BA
Contact: Clive Groves
Tel: 01308 422654
Fax: 01308 420888

General garden centre selling plants, furniture, sundries. Good landscaped area, ponds, rose beds etc. Nursery specialises in sweet violets, mail order only. SAE for list.
Catalogue; Mail order; Toilets; Refreshments; Disabled access

Canford Magna Nurseries
Magna Rd, Wimborne, Dorset
Tel/fax: 01202 573728
Hours: Daily

Compton Acres Garden Centre
164 Canford Cliffs Rd, Poole, Dorset BH13 7ES
Contact: John P B Heron
Tel/fax: 01202 701416
Email: north_and_south@msn.com
Hours: 9am–6pm daily Mar–Oct. 10am–4pm Tues–Fri Nov–Feb

Stoneware a speciality, terracotta, self contained water features, Japanese ornaments, wide range of plants expecially heathers, alpines and herbaceous. Landscape service available.
Toilets; Disabled access

Cottage Garden Plants
Cox Cottage, Lower Street, East Morden, Wareham, Dorset BH20 7DL
Contact: Alex Brenton
Tel/fax: 01929 459496
Hours: 9am–3.30pm Mons or by appt

Small mail order nursery selling old and unusual primroses, violets, pinks, cheiranthus etc. Planting plans to order. Catalogue cost 2 x 1st class stamps. Phone for opening times and directions.
Catalogue; Mail order

Cranbourne Manor Garden Centre
Cranbourne, Wimborne, Dorset BH21 5PP
Tel/fax: 01725 517248
Hours: 9am–5pm Tues–Sat, 10am–5pm Sun & Bank Hols
Catalogue; Mail order

Global Orange Groves UK
PO Box 644, Poole, Dorset BH17 9AY
Tel/fax: 01202 691699
Hours: Most weekends – telephone for opening times

32 varieties of citrus trees; specialist citrus fertilizers; 254 page book "Success with Citrus". Send SAE for details.
Catalogue; Mail order; Toilets; Disabled access

Hardy Orchids Ltd
Newgate Farm, Scotchey Lane, Stour Provost, Gillingham, Dorset SP8 5LT
Contact: N J Heywood
Tel/fax: 01747 838308
Hours: 9am–5pm by appt

We grow hardy terrestrial orchids from seed (a laboratory process) through to flowering size. Cypripediums (Lady Slipper orchids) to Dactylorhiza (Marsh orchids), Bee orchids etc.
Catalogue; Mail order; Toilets

The Daily Telegraph *Green Fingers* — **Garden Centres & Nurseries**

MacPenny Nurseries
154 Burley Rd, Bransgore,
Christchurch, Dorset BH23 8DB
Contact: T M Lowndes
Tel/fax: 01425 672348
Hours: *9am–5pm Mon–Sat, 2–5pm Sun. Closed Xmas & New Year*

Traditional nursery, 17 acres, including 4 acre woodland gardens (open in aid of National Gardens Scheme) which have been converted from gravel pits.
Catalogue; Mail order

Milton Garden Plants
Milton on Stour, Gillingham,
Dorset SP8 5PX
Tel/fax: 01747 822484
Hours: *8.30am–5.30pm Tues–Sat & Bank Hols, 10am–5pm Sun*
Catalogue

Naked Cross Nurseries
Waterloo Rd, Corfe Mullen,
Wimborne, Dorset BH21 3SP
Tel/fax: 01202 693256
Hours: *9am–5pm daily*

Dorset's leading heather specialists plus large selection of shrubs and trees. Personal advice and service freely given. Catalogue 2 x 1st class stamps.
Catalogue; Mail order

Three Counties Nurseries
Marshwood, Bridport, Dorset
DT6 5QJ
Tel/fax: 01297 678257
Hours: *Mail order only*
Catalogue; Mail order

Trehane Nurseries
Stapehill Road, Hampreston,
Wimborne, Dorset BH21 7NE
Tel/fax: 01202 873490
Hours: *9.30am–4.30pm Mon–Fri. 10am–4.30pm weekends Spring & Autumn*

Camellia and blueberry specialists, plus pieris, azaleas and other ericaceous plants. Visit our peaceful woodland nursery, or send for our mail order catalogue £1.50.
Catalogue; Mail order; Toilets

Wimbourne Road Nurseries
393 Wimbourne Road East,
Ferndown, Dorset BH22 9NR
Tel/fax: 01202 813998

Wyevale Garden Centre
24 Wareham Rd, Owermoigne,
Dorchester, Dorset DT2 8BY
Tel: 01305 852324
Fax: 01305 854027

Wyevale offers a huge selection of plants, shrubs, gift ideas, furniture, BBQs and tools. Most centres have pet and aquatic departments and a restaurant. 0800 413213 for nearest stockist.

Wyevale Garden Centre
Van Dukes Garden Centre,
229-247 Wimbourne Rd West,
Stapehill, Wimborne, Dorset
BH21 2DN
Tel: 01202 874208
Fax: 01305 854027

See Dorchester centre above.

Essex

B & H M Baker
Bourne Brook Nurseries,
Greenstead Green, Halstead,
Essex CO9 1RJ
Tel/fax: 01787 476369
Hours: *9am–4.30pm Mon–Fri, 9am–12pm 2–4.30pm Sat & Sun*

Young plants, fuchsia, geraniums, patio plants, house plants, bedding plants, herb and hanging baskets available.
Catalogue

Beeches Nursery
Ashdon, Saffron Walden, Essex
Tel/fax: 01799 584362

Beth Chatto Gardens Ltd
Elmstead Market, Colchester,
Essex CO7 7DB
Tel/fax: 01206 825933
Hours: *Phone for opening times*

6 acres of gardens of differing character. Admission £2.50. Specialist perennial nursery. Mail order available, catalogue £2.50.
Catalogue; Mail order; Toilets

Bramleys Nurseries
331 Benfleet Rd, South Benfleet,
Essex SS7 1PU
Hours: *10am–4pm seasonally*

Send for free catalogue of fruit trees, bedding plants and more.
Catalogue; Mail order

Bushukan Bonsai
Ricbra, Lower Rd, Hockley,
Essex SS5 5NL
Tel: 01702 201029
Fax: 01702 200103

Bypass Nurseries
72 Ipswich Rd, Colchester,
CO1 2YF
Tel: 01206 865500
Fax: 01206 865810
Hours: *9am–5.30pm Summer, 9am–5pm in Winter, 10.30am–4.30pm Suns*

Bypass Nurseries make a special effort to offer the best quality plants and advice. If you require help on gardening matters, we'll be pleased to help.

Cants of Colchester
Nayland Rd, Mile End,
Colchester, Essex CO4 5EB
Tel: 01206 844008
Fax: 01206 855371
Hours: *Times vary. Phone first*
Catalogue; Mail order

Copford Bulbs
Dorsetts, Birch Rd, Copford,
Colchester, Essex CO6 1DR
Tel/fax: 01206 330008
Catalogue; Mail order

Cottage Garden
Langham Rd, Boxted,
Colchester, Essex CO4 5HU
Tel/fax: 01206 272269
Hours: *8am–5.30pm Mon–Sat. 9.30am–5.30pm Sun. Cosed Tues/Wed in Winter*

Plant nursery offering wide range of traditional cottage garden perennials, also shrubs, trees and garden artefacts, antique and new. Leaflet available, but no catalogue.

County Park Nursery
384 Wingletye Lane,
Hornchurch, Essex RM11 3BU
Tel/fax: 01206 262811
Hours: *9am–6pm Mon–Sat, 10am–5pm Sun Mar–Oct. Closed Wed*
Catalogue; Mail order

Flora Exotica
Pasadena, South Green,
Fingringhoe, Colchester, Essex
CO5 7DR
Tel/fax: 01206 729414
Hours: *Mail order only*
Catalogue; Mail order

Frances Mount Perennial Plants
1 Steps Farm, Rectory Hill,
Polstead, Colchester, Essex
CO6 5AE
Contact: Frances Mount
Tel/fax: 01206 262811
Hours: *10am–5pm Tues/Wed/Sat, 2–6pm Fri. Check weekends & Bank Hols*

Small retail nursery in beautiful Suffolk countryside specialising in hardy geraniums/cranesbills. Entrance free. Mail order catalogue 3 x 1st class stamps.
Catalogue; Mail order

Gardening Direct (DPA Direct Ltd)
PO Box 225, South Woodham
Ferrers, Chelmsford, Essex
CM3 5XT
Tel/fax: 01245 323301
Mail order

Hull Farm Conifer Centre
John Fryer & Sons, Spring Valley
Lane, Ardleigh, Colchester, Essex
CO7 7SA
Tel: 01206 230045
Fax: 01206 230820
Hours: *10am–4.30pm daily*

Specialist growers of over 300 varieties of garden conifers from hedging to miniatures.

Kemlawns Nursery
Warley Gap, Warley, Brentwood,
Essex CM13 3LG
Tel/fax: 01277 210116
Hours: *10am–3pm Fri–Mon*

Small family nursery specialising in fuchsias. Catalogue available for 3 x 1st class stamps. A wide variety of other shrubs and plants to choose from.
Catalogue; Mail order

Ken Muir Nurseries
Honeypot Farm, Rectory Road,
Weeley Heath, Clacton on Sea,
Essex CO16 9BJ
Tel: 01255 830181
Fax: 01255 831534
Hours: *9am–5pm daily*

Fruit growers and distributors of ministry-certified stocks of tree, cane and bush fruits for gardeners.
Catalogue; Mail order; Toilets

Langthorns Plantery
Little Canfield, Dunmow, Essex
CM6 1TD
Tel/fax: 01371 872611
Hours: *10am–5pm daily. Closed Xmas fortnight*

Plantery specialises in huge range of hardy herbaceous, shrubs, trees and alpines. Lovely demonstration beds and superb range of conservatory plants in Summer.
Catalogue

Mill Race Nursery
New Rd, Aldham, Colchester,
Essex CO6 3QT
Tel: 01206 242324
Fax: 01206 241616
Hours: *9am–5.30pm daily*
Catalogue

Notcutts Garden Centre
Station Rd, Ardleigh, Colchester,
Essex CO7 7RT
Tel/fax: 01206 230271
Hours: *8.30am–5.30pm Mon–Sat, 10am–5.30pm Sun*
Catalogue

Ornamental Grasses
Thorpe Park Cottage,
Thorpe-le-Soken, Essex CO16
0HN
Contact: Trevor Scott
Tel/fax: 01255 861308
Hours: *By prior appointment March–Nov*

Ornamental grasses specialist, over 300 grasses available. Garden open by appointment. 5 x 1st class stamps for instructive, descriptive catalogue.
Catalogue

Plantworld
Burnam Rd, South Woodham Ferrers, Chelmsford, Essex CM3 5QP
Tel/fax: 01245 320482
Hours: *10am–4pm Tues–Sun. Closed Mon*
Catalogue; Mail order

Rhodes & Rockliffe
2 Nursery Rd, Nazeing, Essex EN9 2JE
Contact: David Rhodes
Tel: 01992 463693
Fax: 01992 440673
Hours: *By appointment only*

Specialists in begonia species and hybrids. Many unusual varieties. Visitors welcome by appointment. Catalogue cost 2 x 1st class stamps. Largest private collection in UK.
Catalogue; Mail order; Toilets

South Ockendon Garden Centre
South Rd, South Ockendon, Essex RM15 6DU
Tel: 01708 851991
Fax: 01708 859138
Hours: *9am–6pm Mon–Sat, 10am–6pm Sun*
Refreshments

Whitehouse Ivies
Brookhill, Halstead Rd, Fordham, Colchester, Essex CO6 3LW
Tel/fax: 01206 240077
Hours: *By appointment only*
Catalogue; Mail order

Wyevale Garden Centre
Cressing Rd, Braintree, Essex CM7 8DL
Tel: 01376 553043
Fax: 01376 553004
Hours: *9am–6pm Mon–Sat, 11am–5pm Sun*

Wyevale offers a huge selection of plants, shrubs, gift ideas, furniture, BBQs and tools. Most centres have pet and aquatic departments and a restaurant. 0800 413213 for nearest stockist.
Toilets; Refreshments

Wyevale Garden Centre
Homelands Retail Park, Cuton Hall Lane, Springfield, Chelmsford, Essex CM2 5PX
Tel: 01245 466466
Fax: 01245 451263
See Braintree centre above.

Wyevale Garden Centre
Cowdray Avenue, Colchester, Essex CO1 1DP
Tel: 01206 575300
Fax: 01206 48986
See Braintree centre above.

Wyevale Garden Centre
Eastwood Rd, Rayleigh, Essex SS6 7QA
Tel: 01702 527331
Fax: 01702 421203
See Braintree centre above.

Wyevale Shop
10/12 Market Place, Braintree, Essex CM7 6HG
Tel/fax: 01376 321344
Hours: *9am–6pm Mon–Sat, 11am–5pm Sun*

Wyevale Shop
91/92 High Street, Brentwood, Essex CM14 4AP
Tel/fax: 01277 222089
Hours: *9am–6pm Mon–Sat, 11am–5pm Sun*

Gloucestershire

Barnsley Park Box Hedging
2 Garden Cottage, Barnsley Park Estate, Barnsley, Cirencester, Gloucestershire GL7 5EG
Contact: Paul Rich
Tel: 01283 740302
Fax: 01285 740675

Dwarf and common box for edging and hedging. Send SAE for information leaflet and order form. Laurel and yew also available.
Catalogue; Mail order

Bedding Plant Centre - Churt Nurseries
Uckinton, Cheltenham, Gloucestershire GL51 9SL
Tel/fax: 01242 860366
Catalogue; Mail order

Chris Pattison (Nurseryman)
Brookend, Pendock, Gloucestershire GL19 3PL
Tel/fax: 01531 650480
Hours: *9am–5pm Mon–Fri or by appt*

Wide range of shrubs and alpines concentrating on the more unusual varieties; specialising in grafted stock, especially Japanese maples. 3 x 1st class stamps for catalogue.
Catalogue; Toilets

Cowcombe Farm Herbs
Gipsy Lane, Chalford, Stroud, Gloucestershire GL6 8HP
Tel/fax: 01285 760544
Hours: *10am–5pm Wed–Sat. 2–5pm Sun Easter–Sept*
Catalogue; Mail order

Four Counties Nursery
Todenham, Moreton-in-Marsh, Gloucestershire GL56 9PN
Tel: 01608 650522
Fax: 01608 650591
Hours: *9am–6pm Mon–Sat in Summer, 9am–5pm in Winter, 11am–5pm Suns*

Specialists in the rare and unusual. Huge variety of plants. Specimen trees. Specialists in conservatory plants including citrus. Café in summer. Mail order on request.
Catalogue; Mail order; Toilets; Refreshments

Highfield Nurseries
Whitminster, Gloucestershire GL2 7PL
Tel/fax: 01452 740094

Hoo House Nursery
Hoo House, Gloucester Rd, Tewkesbury, Gloucestershire GL20 7DA
Contact: Julie Ritchie
Tel/fax: 01684 293389
Hours: *2–5pm Mon–Sat*

Alpine and herbaceous perennials. Over 800 varieties. Reasonable prices. Retail and mail order (Oct to March). Catalogues 3 x 1st class stamps and specify.
Catalogue; Mail order

Hunts Court Garden & Nursery
Hunts Court, North Nibley, Dursley, Gloucestershire GL11 6DZ
Contact: T K Marshall
Tel/fax: 01453 547440
Hours: *9am–5pm Tues–Sat. Closed Aug*

Specialities - old roses, unusual shrubs, penstemons, geraniums, potentillas. Catalogue 3 x 2nd class stamps. Admission to garden £1.50. 400 roses, 70 potentillas and much more in 2 acre garden.
Catalogue; Toilets

Hurrans Garden Centre Ltd
Cheltanham Rd East, Churchdown, Gloucestershire GL3 1AB
Tel: 01452 712232
Fax: 01452 857369
Hours: *9am–6pm Mon–Sat, 10am–6pm Sun*

Lechlade Garden Centre
Fairford Rd, Lechlade, Gloucestershire GL7 3DP
Tel: 01367 252372
Fax: 01367 252782
Hours: *9am–6pm Summer, 9am–5pm Winter*
Refreshments

Mount Pleasant Trees
Rockhampton, Berkeley, Gloucestershire GL13 9DU
Tel/fax: 01454 260348
Hours: *By appointment only*

Grower of native trees and hedging. Young Christmas trees and forestry trees; trees for arboreta and larger gardens. £1 coin or stamps for catalogue.
Catalogue

Norfields
Lower Meend, St Briavels, Gloucestershire GL15 6RW
Contact: Andrew Norfield
Tel: 01594 530134
Fax: 01594 530113
Hours: *Mail order only*

Young trees sent by mail. Small trees for garden and bonsai. Maples, magnolia, betula, stewartia, carpinus, nothofagus plus other rare and difficult to obtain species.
Catalogue; Mail order

Old Manor Nursery
Twyning, Gloucestershire GL20 6DB
Tel/fax: 01684 293516
Hours: *2–5pm Mon Mar–Oct*
Catalogue

Priory Garden Nursery
The Priory, Kemerton, Tewkesbury, Gloucestershire GL20 7JN
Tel/fax: 01386 725258
Hours: *2–7pm Thur only*

Westonbirt Plant Centre
Forest Enterprise, Westonbirt Arboretum, Tetbury, Gloucester, Gloucestershire GL8 8QS
Contact: Glyn Toplis
Tel: 01666 880544
Fax: 01666 880559
Hours: *10am–5pm Winter, 10am–6pm Summer*

Retail stockist of trees and shrubs, many unusual. Situated adjacent to the world famous arboretum. (See our full colour advertisement on page 150).
Mail order; Toilets; Refreshments; Disabled access

Wyevale Garden Centre
Shurdington Rd, Brockworth, Gloucestershire GL3 4PU
Tel: 01452 862334
Fax: 01452 864839

Wyevale offers a huge selection of plants, shrubs, gift ideas, furniture, BBQs and tools. Most centres have pet and aquatic departments and a restaurant. 0800 413213 for nearest stockist.

Wyevale Garden Centre
Milbury Heath, Wotton under Edge, Gloucestershire GL12 8QH
Tel: 01454 412247
Fax: 01454 281502

See Brockworth centre above.

Hampshire

Agars Nursery
Agars Lane, Hordle, Lymington, Hampshire SO41 0FL
Contact: Mrs Diana Tombs
Tel/fax: 01590 683703
Hours: 10am–4pm daily except Thurs. Closed 20 Dec–Feb 1. Phone first
Wide selection of herbaceous shrubs, climbers with quality advice.

Apple Court
Hordle Lane, Hordle, Lymington, Hampshire SO41 0HU
Contact: Diana Grenfell & Roger Grounds
Tel/fax: 01590 642130
Hours: Daily July & Aug. Thurs–Mon Feb 1–Oct 31
Specialising in hostas, daylilies, ferns, grasses, white garden plants, foliage plants for flower arrangers. Display garden has hosta walk, spectacular daylily and grass plantings, fern path. Mail order catalogue 4 x 1st class stamps.
Catalogue; Mail order

Blackthorn Nursery
Kilmeston, Alresford, Hampshire SO24 0NL
Tel: 01962 771796
Fax: 01962 771071
Hours: 9am–5pm Fri/Sat Mar–June
Wide range of alpines and perennials, including rarities. Specialities daphnes, epimediums and hellebores.
Catalogue; Toilets

Christopher Fairweather Ltd
The Garden Centre, High Steet, Beaulieu, Hampshire SO42 7YR
Tel: 01590 612307
Fax: 01590 612615
Hours: 8.45am–5.30pm daily
Catalogue; Refreshments

Denmead Geranium Nurseries
Hambledon Rd, Denmead, Waterlooville, Hampshire PO7 6PS
Tel/fax: 01705 240081
Hours: 9am–5pm Mon–Fri, 9am–12.30pm Sat
Catalogue; Mail order

Drysdale Garden Exotics
Bowerwood Rd, Fordingbridge, Hampshire SP6 1BN
Contact: David Crampton
Tel/fax: 01425 653010
Hours: 9.30am–5.30pm Wed–Fri, 10am–5.30pm Sun
Plants for exotic and foliage effect. National Collection of Bamboos. Garden open during nursery hours. For catalogue please send 3 x 1st class stamps.
Catalogue; Mail order

Exbury Enterprises Ltd
Exbury, Southampton, Hampshire SO4 1AZ
Tel/fax: 01703 898625
Hours: 10am–5.30pm daily
Catalogue; Mail order; Refreshments

Family Trees
PO Box 3, Botley, Hampshire SO3 2EA
Tel/fax: 01329 834812
Hours: 9.30am–12.30pm Wed & Sat Oct 15–Apr 15
Fruit for the connoisseur in a wide variety. Specialists in trained trees. Ornamental trees and old roses. Send for free catalogue.
Catalogue; Mail order

Hardys Cottage Garden Plants
The Walled Garden, Laverstoke Park, Laverstoke, Whitchurch, Hampshire RG28 7NT
Tel/fax: 01256 896533
Hours: 9am–5.30pm Mon–Sat Mar–Oct
Catalogue

Hazel Cottage Nursey
Land of Nod, Headley Down, Bordon, Hampshire GU35 8SJ
Tel: 01428 713269
Fax: 01428 717020
Hours: By appointment only

Higher End Nursery - D J Case
Hale, Fordingbridge, Hampshire SP6 2RA
Tel/fax: 01725 22243
Hours: 10am–5pm Tues–Sat, 2–5pm Sun Apr–Aug
Catalogue; Mail order

Highfield Hollies
Highfield Farm, Hatch Lane, Liss, Hampshire GU33 7NH
Contact: Louise Bendall
Tel/fax: 01730 892372
Hours: By appointment
Ilex. Over 50 species and cultivars including many specimen trees. Please phone for appointment and free catalogue.
Catalogue; Mail order

Hillier Garden Centre
Botley Rd, Romsey, Hampshire SO51 8ZL
Tel/fax: 01794 513459
Hours: 9am–5.30pm Mon–Sat, 10.30am–4.30pm Sun
Good plant oriented garden centre.

Hillier Garden Centre
Farnham Rd, Liss, Hampshire GU33 6LJ
Tel/fax: 01730 892196
Hours: 9am–5.30pm Mon–Sat, 10.30am–4.30pm Sun
Good plant oriented garden centre.
Toilets; Refreshments

Hillier Garden Centre
Romsey Rd, Winchester, Hampshire SO22 5DN
Tel: 01962 842288
Fax: 01962 842299
Hours: 9am–5.30pm Mon–Sat, 10.30am–4.30pm Sun
Good plant oriented garden centre.

Hillier Garden Centre
Woodhouse Lane, Botley, Southampton, Hampshire SO3 2EZ
Tel/fax: 01489 782306
Hours: 9am–5.30pm Mon–Sat, 10.30am–4.30pm Sun
Good plant oriented garden centre.
Toilets; Refreshments

Hillier Garden Centre
Jermyns Lane, Brashfield, Romsey, Hampshire SO51 9PA
Tel/fax: 01794 368407
Hours: 9am–5.30pm Mon–Sat, 10.30am–4.30pm Sun
Good plant oriented garden centre.

Langley Boxwood Nursery
Rake, Nr Liss, Hampshire GU33 7JL
Tel: 01730 894467
Fax: 01730 894703
Hours: 9am–5pm Mon–Fri. Check for Sats
A boxwood and topiary nursery in a beautiful setting. Langley Boxwood Nursery grows and shows a National Collection of the widest range of species, cultivars, hedging and shapes in box and yew. Cultivation advice given. Catalogue and mags 4 x 1st class stamps.
Catalogue; Mail order; Toilets

Little Brook Fuchsias
Ash Green Lane West, Ash Green, Aldershot, Hampshire GU12 6HL
Contact: Carol Gubler
Tel/fax: 01252 29731
Hours: Jan 1–Jul 2. Closed Mon/Tues
Specialist fuchsia nursery stocking both old and new cultivars, species, etc. Catalogue 30p plus SAE.
Catalogue; Toilets; Disabled access

Longstock Park Nursery
Longstock, Stockbridge, Hampshire SO20 6EH
Tel: 01264 810894
Fax: 01264 810439
Hours: 8.30am–4.30pm Mon–Sat, 2–5pm Sun
Catalogue

Nine Springs Nursery
24 Winchester Street, Whitchurch, Hampshire RG28 7AL
Tel/fax: 01256 892837
Hours: By appointment
Catalogue; Mail order

Oakleigh Nurseries
Petersfield Rd, Monkwood, Alresford, Hampshire SO24 0HB
Tel: 01962 773344
Fax: 01962 772622
Email: compuserve 100270.176
Hours: March–June only 7 days a week
Specialities fuchsias and pelargoniums (zonal, regal and ivy leafed etc). Colour catalogue available for 3 x 1st class stamps.
Catalogue; Mail order

Peter Trenear Nurseries
Chequers Lane, Eversley Cross, Hampshire RG27 0NX
Contact: Peter Trenear
Tel/fax: 01734 732300
Hours: 9am–4.30pm. Closed Sun
Young trees, shrubs and conifers, especially unusual and interesting species for garden and bonsai. Stamp for list please. 3 miles north of M3, Junction 4A.
Catalogue; Mail order; Toilets

Pound Lane Nurseries
Ampfield, Romsey, Hampshire SO5 9BL
Tel: 01703 739685
Fax: 01703 740300
Hours: 8.30am–5.30pm Mon–Fri, 9.30am–5.30pm Sun

Ratcliffe Orchids Ltd
Pitcot Lane, Owslebury, Winchester, Hampshire SO21 1LR
Tel: 01962 777372
Fax: 01962 777664
Email: ratcliffe@zoo.co.uk
Hours: Set open days. Phone for listings
Growers and breeders of papmopedilum (Slipper Orchids). Mail order and export only. Suppliers of compost and sundries.
Catalogue; Mail order

Southview Nurseries
Chequers Lane, Eversley Cross, Basingstoke, Hampshire RG27 0NT

Tel/fax: 01734 732206

Hours: *9am–4.30pm Thurs–Sat. Closed Nov–Jan*
Catalogue; Mail order

Spinners
Boldre, Lymington, Hampshire SO41 5QE

Tel/fax: 01590 673347

Hours: *10am–5pm Tues–Sat, or by appt*

Woodland garden. Azaleas, rhododendrons, magnolias, camellias, Japanese maples, hydrangeas etc. interplanted with choice woodland plants. Adjoining internationally known nursery offers as wide a range of less common plants as you will find in the country.
Catalogue; Toilets

Steven Bailey Ltd
Silver Street, Sway, Lymington, Hampshire SO41 8ZA

Tel: 01590 682227
Fax: 01590 683765

Hours: *Weekdays all year. Sat/Sun Mar–June only*

Pinks, carnations and alstroemeria are avaialable by mail order and in our nursery shop. Also a good selection of seasonal plants. Send SAE for catalogue.
Catalogue; Mail order; Toilets

Water Meadow Nursery & Herb Farm
Cheriton, Alresford, Hampshire SO24 0JT

Contact: Mrs Sandy Worth
Tel/fax: 01962 771895

Hours: *9am–5pm Fri/Sat & Bank Hols, 2–5pm Sun Mar–Nov*

Extensive collection of water garden plants, hardy shrubs, fragrant climbers, herbs, 500+ herbaceous perennials, many unusual. All in a garden setting. Mail order catalogue 75p. Landscape and design service available.
Catalogue; Mail order; Toilets

Whitewater Nursery
Hound Green, Mattingley, Heckfield, Basingstoke, Hampshire RG27 8LQ

Tel/fax: 01734 326487

Hours: *Daily*

Wreford Landscapes
Pucknall Farm, Dores Lane, Braishfield, Romsey, Hampshire SO51 0QJ

Contact: Simon Wreford
Tel: 01794 368155
Fax: 01794 368218

Hours: *7.30am–6pm Mon–Fri*

Landscape design and construction for town houses to country manors. Commercial and business developments throughout southern England.

Hereford & Worcester

Abbey Dore Court Garden
Abbey Dore, Hereford, Hereford & Worcester HR2 0AD

Contact: Chris Ward
Tel: 01981 240419
Fax: 01981 240279

Hours: *11am–6pm daily except Weds Mar–Oct*

Five acre rambling and semi-formal garden intersected by the river Dore. Unusual shrubs and perennials. Small nursery, mainly herbaceous perennials. Gift gallery. Licensed restaurant.
Toilets; Refreshments; Disabled access

B R Edwards
Sunnybank Farm, Llanveynoe, Hereford & Worcester HR2 0NL

Tel/fax: 01873 860698

We are a specialist mail order vine supplier, with the largest collection in the UK. Dessert and wine varieties, predominantly outdoors. SAE for catalogue.
Catalogue; Mail order

Baker Straw Partnership
Perhill Nurseries, Worcester Rd, Great Witley, Hereford & Worcester WR6 6JT

Contact: Duncan & Sarah Straw
Tel: 01299 896329
Fax: 01299 896990

Hours: *9am–5pm daily Feb 1–Oct 31*

Large range of herbaceous perennials, alpines and herbs. Over 2,500 species and cultivars grown. Mostly rare and unusual.
Catalogue; Mail order; Toilets

Birlingham Nurseries & Garden Centre
Birlingham, Pershore, Hereford & Worcester WR10 3AB

Tel/fax: 01386 750668

Bouts Cottage Nurseries
Bouts Lane, Inkberrow, Hereford & Worcester WR7 4HP

Tel/fax: 01386 792923

Hours: *Not open to the public*

Old fashioned violas. Send SAE for catalogue.
Catalogue; Mail order

Caves Folly Nurseries
Evendine Lane, Colwall, Malvern, Hereford & Worcester WR13 6DU

Tel/fax: 01684 540631

Hours: *10am–5pm Thurs–Sat*

Nursery situated near the beautiful Malvern Hills selling perennial alpines. Run organically. Display borders etc. Garden Design service.

Cook's Garden Centre
26 Worcester Rd, Stourport-on-Severn, Hereford & Worcester DY13 5PQ

Contact: Paul Cook
Tel: 01299 826169
Fax: 01299 824441

Hours: *9am–6pm 7 days a week*

Full selection of garden plants at keen prices. Specialist in hanging baskets. RHS Gold Medal Winners 1996. Young plants available.

Cotswold Garden Flowers
Sands Lane, Badsey, Evesham, Hereford & Worcester WR11 5EZ

Contact: Bob Brown or Vicky Parkhouse
Tel: 01386 833849
Fax: 01386 47337

Hours: *Daily Mar–Sept. Mon–Fri Oct–Feb*

Display gardens of easy and unusual hardy perennials, probably the widest selection available to buy. Situated half a mile after tarmac ends, Sands Lane.
Catalogue; Mail order; Toilets

Cranesbill Nursery
White Cottage, Earls Common Rd, Stock Green, Redditch, Hereford & Worcester B96 6SZ

Contact: Mrs J Bates
Tel/fax: 01386 792414

Hours: *10am–5pm Easter–October. Closed Wed & Thurs*

Two acre garden, entrance £1. Unusual herbaceous and shrubs. Large collection of hardy geraniums. Plants available on adjacent nursery. Catalogue 4 x 1st class stamps.
Catalogue; Mail order

Fuchsiavale Nurseries
Worcester Rd, Torton, Kidderminster, Hereford & Worcester DY11 7SB

Tel/fax: 01299 251162

Grange Farm Nursery
Guarlford, Malvern, Hereford & Worcester WR13 6NY

Tel/fax: 01684 562544

Hours: *9am–5.30pm Summer, 9am–Dusk Winter. Closed Xmas/NY*

Greenacres Nursery – D & M Everett
Bringsty, Worcester, Hereford & Worcester WR6 5TA

Tel: 01885 482206
Fax: 01885 488160

Hours: *By appointment*
Catalogue

Hayloft Plants
Little Court, Rous Lench, Evesham, Hereford & Worcester WR11 4UR

Contact: Yvonne Walker
Tel/fax: 01386 793361

Our mail order catalogue contains many new and unusual plants for your hanging baskets and patio pots. Catalogues are free of charge and give the address of our nursery in Badsey, open 10am-4pm.
Catalogue; Mail order

International Acers
Acer Place, Coalash Lane, Hanbury, Bromsgrove, Hereford & Worcester B60 4EY

Tel/fax: 01527 821774

Hours: *9am–5.30pm weekends. Other times by appt*
Catalogue

Kingfisher Nurseries
Stourbridge Rd, Catshill, Bromsgrove, Hereford & Worcester B61 0BW

Tel/fax: 01527 835084

Marley Bank Nursery
Whitbourne, Hereford & Worcester WR6 5RU

Tel/fax: 01886 21576

Hours: *By appointment only*
Catalogue

Marston Exotics
Brampton Lane, Madley, Hereford, Hereford & Worcester HR2 9LX

Tel: 01981 251140
Fax: 01432 274023

Hours: *8am–4.30pm Mon–Fri all year, 1–5pm Sat/Sun Mar–Oct*
Catalogue; Mail order; Refreshments

Paul Jasper Trees
The Lighthouse, Bridge Street, Leominster, Hereford & Worcester HR6 8DU

Tel: 01568 611540
Fax: 01568 616499

Hours: *By appointment only*
Catalogue; Mail order

Proculture Plant Centre
Knowle Hill, Badsey, Evesham, Hereford & Worcester WR11 5EN

Contact: Peter & Debbie Taylor
Tel: 01386 831527
Fax: 01386 833913
Hours: *10am–5pm daily*

The Proculture Centre stocks a complete range of plants and is in an ideal location on the edge of the Cotswolds and near Stratford-on-Avon.
Catalogue; Toilets; Refreshments; Disabled access

Rickards Hardy Ferns Ltd
Kyre Park, Tenbury Wells, Hereford & Worcester WR15 8RP

Tel/fax: 01885 410282
Hours: *By appointment only. Phone first*
Catalogue; Mail order

Rushfields of Ledbury
Ross Rd, Ledbury, Hereford & Worcester HR8 2LP

Contact: Mr B Homewood
Tel/fax: 01531 632004
Hours: *11am–5pm Wed–Sat*

Specialist herbaceous plants, including penstemons, hostas, hardy geraniums, euphorbias. Gold Medal at Hampton Court 1996. Catalogue £1 plus 31p A5 SAE.
Catalogue; Toilets

Stone House Cottage Garden & Nursery
Stone House Cottage, Kidderminster, Hereford & Worcester DY10 4BG

Contact: J F Arbuthnott
Tel/fax: 01562 69902
Hours: *10am–5.30pm Wed–Sat Mar–Oct*

Fascinating walled garden with towers. Large amount of unusual wall shrubs and climbers. Many available for sale in adjacent nursery.
Catalogue; Toilets; Disabled access

Toad Hall Produce
Frogmore, Weston under Penyard, Hereford & Worcester HR9 5TQ

Tel/fax: 01989 750214
Hours: *10am–6pm Mon Apr–Sept*
Catalogue; Mail order

Treasures of Tenbury Ltd
Burford House Gardens, Tenbury Wells, Hereford & Worcester WR15 8QH

Contact: Charles Chesshire
Tel: 01584 810777
Fax: 01584 810673
Hours: *10am–5pm daily*

Four acre gardens in beautiful riverside setting. Home to National Clematis Collection - with 250 varieties and 2,000+ other unusual plants, many for sale at the plant centre.
Catalogue; Mail order; Toilets; Refreshments; Disabled access

Webbs of Wychbold
Wychbold, Droitwich, Hereford & Worcester WR9 0DG

Tel: 01527 861777
Fax: 01527 861284
Hours: *Phone for details*

Everything is here at the award winning garden centre. There's coffee or lunch in the "Thatch Restaurant" and play area for children.
Catalogue; Toilets; Refreshments; Disabled access

Wintergreen Nurseries
Bringsty, Worcester, Hereford & Worcester WR6 5UJ

Tel/fax: 01886 821858
Hours: *Wed–Sun March–Oct & by appt*

Small retail nursery specialising in unusual herbaceous and alpine plants, the majority of which can be seen growing in display gardens.
Catalogue

Woolman's Plants Ltd
Knowle Hill, Badsey, Evesham, Hereford & Worcester WR11 5EN

Contact: John Woolman
Tel: 01786 877022
Fax: 01868 72915
Hours: *10am–4pm daily*

Ring John Woolman for your free 32 page colour mail order catalogue of chrysanthemums, dahlias, patio and hanging basket plants.
Catalogue; Mail order; Toilets; Refreshments; Disabled access

Worcester Garden Centre
Droitwich Rd, Worcester, Hereford & Worcester WR3 7SW

Contact: Neil Gow
Tel: 01905 451231
Fax: 01905 755371
Hours: *9am–6pm Mon–Sat, 10am–4pm Sun. Late night Thurs till 9pm*

A modern up-to-date centre, yet with the traditional values of service and advice. High emphasis on plants and everything to do with the garden.
Toilets; Refreshments; Disabled access

Wyevale Garden Centre
Kings Acre Rd, Hereford, Hereford & Worcester HR4 0SE

Tel: 01432 266261
Fax: 01432 341863

AYLETT NURSERIES LTD
AN INDEPENDENT FAMILY OWNED GARDEN CENTRE ESTABLISHED 1955

The Nursery that is proud to grow and sell plants of quality with fully trained staff always at your service.
- Visit our Plant Area for a vast selection of trees, shrubs, herbaceous plants, summer bedding
- Hanging Baskets for both summer and winter
- Garden Furniture and barbeques
- Garden Sundries
- House plants
- Flowershop and floral sundries
- Coffee Shop

Opening hours: Mon–Fri 8.30am–5.50pm
Sat 8.30–5pm. Sun 10.30am–4.00pm
North Orbital Road, St Albans, Herts. AL2 1DH Tel: 01727 822255

Wyevale offers a huge selection of plants, shrubs, gift ideas, furniture, BBQs and tools. Most centres have pet and aquatic departments and a restaurant. 0800 413213 for nearest stockist.

Wyevale Garden Centres plc
Kings Acre Rd, Hereford, Hereford & Worcester HR4 0SE

Tel: 01432 276568
Fax: 01432 341863
Head office.
Catalogue

Hertfordshire

Abbots House Garden, The
10 High Street, Abbots Langley, Hertfordshire WD5 0AR

Tel/fax: 01923 264946/443563
Hours: *9am–1pm 2–4pm Sats Mar–Oct or by appt*

Many unusual shrubs, herbaceous, conservatory plants and primulas. Garden open under National Gardens Scheme.
Catalogue; Mail order; Toilets

Aylett Nurseries Ltd
North Orbital Rd, London Colney, St Albans, Hertfordshire AL2 1DH

Tel: 01727 822255
Fax: 01727 823024
Hours: *9am–5.30pm Mon–Fri, 9am–5pm Sat, 10am–4pm Sun*

Famous for our Gold Medal dahlias, probably one of the best garden centres in the South East - visit us for all your plants and sundries.

Chandlers Cross Garden Centre
Great Gardens of England Ltd, Fir Tree Hill, Chandlers Cross, Hertfordshire WD3 4LZ

Tel: 01923 260488
Fax: 01923 261010
Hours: *9am–5.30pm daily*

Chenies Garden Centre
Chenies, Rickmansworth, Hertfordshire WD3 6ER

Tel: 01494 764545
Fax: 01494 762216
Hours: *9am–5.30pm daily*

Chipperfield Home & Gdn Ctr
Great Gardens of England Ltd, Tower Hill, Chipperfield, Hertfordshire WD4 9LH

Tel: 01442 834364
Fax: 01442 834259
Hours: *9am–5.30pm*

Gannock Growers
Gannock Thatch, Sandon, Buntingford, Hertfordshire SG9 0RH

Tel/fax: 01763 87386
Hours: *10am–4pm Tues–Sun/Bank Hols Mar–Oct & by appt*
Catalogue; Mail order

Godly's Roses
Redbourn by Pass, Redbourn, St Albans, Hertfordshire AL3 7PS

Tel: 01582 792255
Fax: 01582 794267
Hours: *9am–6pm daily. Closed Xmas*

Family owned garden centre and rose nursery. Many thousands of roses can be seen in bloom July to September.
Catalogue; Mail order

Growing Carpets
Christmas Tree House, 16 High Street, Guilden Morden, Royston, Hertfordshire SG8 0JP

Contact: Mrs Eileen Moore
Tel/fax: 01763 852705
Hours: *11am–5pm Mon–Sat March 17 – Oct 31*

We are a small nursery specialising in ground cover plants. Advice regarding planting will willingly be given.
Catalogue; Mail order; Disabled access

Hillier Garden Centre
Leighton Buzzard Road, Piccotts End, Hemel Hempstead, Hertfordshire HP1 3BA
Tel/fax: 01442 242637
Hours: 9am–5.30pm Mon–Sat. 10.30am–4.30pm Sun

Good plant oreinted garden centre.
Toilets; Refreshments

Hopleys Plants Ltd
High Street, Much Hadham, Hertfordshire SG10
Tel: 01279 842509
Fax: 01279 843784
Hours: 9am–5pm daily, 2–5pm Sun. Closed Tues & Jan & Aug
Catalogue; Mail order

Notcutts Garden Centre
Hatfield Rd, Smallford, St Albans, Hertfordshire AL4 0BR
Tel/fax: 01727 53224
Hours: 8.30am–5.30pm Mon–Sat, 10am–5pm Sun. Closes 5pm Winter
Catalogue

Priorswood Clematis
Priorswood, Widbury Hill, Ware, Hertfordshire SG12 7QH
Contact: Gerald or Pauline Greenway
Tel/fax: 01920 461543
Hours: 9am–5pm Tues–Sun. Open Bank Hols

Propagators and growers of clematis, honeysuckle, vines and other climbing plants and wall shrubs. Location B1004, 1 mile out of Ware towards Much Hadham. Catalogue 4 x 1st class stamps.
Catalogue; Mail order

R Harkness & Co Ltd
The Rose Gardens, Cambridge Rd, Hitchin, Hertfordshire SG4 0JT
Tel: 01462 420402
Fax: 01462 422170
Hours: 9am–5.30pm Mon–Fri, 10.30am–5.30pm Sat/Sun

The qualities of roses created by Harkness are known the world over. Comprehensive colour rose catalogue available. For roses come to Harkness first.
Catalogue; Mail order; Toilets; Refreshments

Van Hage Garden Company
Great Amwell, Ware, Hertfordshire SG12 9RP
Contact: Sandra Cronin
Tel: 01920 870811
Fax: 01920 871861
Hours: 9am–6pm Mon–Sat. 10.30am–4.30pm Sun

One of Europe's top gardening emporia offering visitors an outstanding selection of products to meet all gardening requirements.
Catalogue; Mail order; Toilets; Refreshments; Disabled access

Wards Nurseries (Sarrat) Ltd
Dawes Lane, Sarrat, Rickmansworth, Hertfordshire WD3 6BQ
Tel: 01923 263237
Fax: 01923 270930
Hours: 8am–5pm Mon–Sat. 10.30am–4pm Sun

Garden centre offering a very comprehensive range of plants, many grown on our own nursery. Includes a good selection of aromatic and scented plants.
Toilets

Wyevale Garden Centre
Broadwater Garden Centre, Great Gaddesden, Hemel Hempstead, Hertfordshire HP2 3BW
Tel: 01442 231284
Fax: 01442 68987

Wyevale offers a huge selection of plants, shrubs, gift ideas, furniture, BBQs and tools. Most centres have pet and aquatic departments and a restaurant. 0800 413213 for nearest stockist.

Humberside

California Gardens
Boothferry Road, Howden, Nr Goole, Humberside DN14 7TF
Tel: 01430 430824
Fax: 01430 432023
Hours: 9am–6pm weekdays, 5pm Winter & Sats. 10.30am–4.30pm Suns

Owned by the Hall family since 1879. A genuine centre for gardeners with extensive range of plants. Take Exit 37, M62 on Howden Bypass.
Toilets; Refreshments; Disabled access

Devine Nurseries
Withernsea Rd, Hollym, Humberside HU19 2QH
Tel/fax: 01964 613840

Palm Farm
Thornton Hall Gardens, Thornton Curtis, Nr Ulceby, Humberside DN39 6XF
Tel/fax: 01469 531232
Hours: 2–5pm daily except Sats Nov–Mar

Hardy and half hardy palms and hardy exotics a speciality. Conservatory plants, unusual trees and shrubs, herbaceous plants, shrub roses. Demonstration plantings including palm garden.
Catalogue; Mail order

Pennell & Sons Ltd
Garden Centre, Humberston Rd, Grimsby, Humberside DN36 4RW
Tel/fax: 01472 694272
Hours: 8.30am–5.30pm Mon–Sat, 10am–5.30pm Sun & Bank Hols

Isle of Wight

Cranmore Vine Nurseries
Yarmouth, Isle of Wight PO41 0XS
Contact: Nick Poulter
Tel/fax: 01983 760080
Hours: Mail order only

Grapevines. 30 hardy, fully ripening outdoor and indoor varieties. From £2. SAE for catalogue.
Catalogue; Mail order

Deacons Nursery
Moor View, Godshill, Isle of Wight PO38 3HW
Tel: 01983 840750
Fax: 01983 523575
Hours: 8am–4pm Mon–Fri (Oct–Apr Mon–Sat)

Apples, pears, plums, greengages, cherries, peaches, nectarines, apricots, medlars, kiwis, raspberries, strawberries, blackcurrants, loganberries, gooseberries, family trees, hops, grapes, Asian pears, Canadian pears, locquat etc!
Catalogue; Mail order

Kent

Alan C Smith
127 Green Leaves Rd, Keston, Kent BR2 6DG
Contact: Alan C Smith
Tel/fax: 01595 72531
Hours: By appointment only

Speciality sempervivums. Also supply alpine and rock plants. Catalogue price 50p.
Catalogue; Mail order

Ashenden Nursery
Cranbrook Rd, Benenden, Cranbrook, Kent TN17 4ET
Contact: Kevin McGarry
Tel/fax: 01580 241792
Hours: By appointment only, please phone

We are a small family nursery specialising in alpines and perennials, which we exhibit and sell at many specialist events throughout the South East.
Catalogue

Busheyfields Nursery - J Bradshaw & Son
Herne, Herne Bay, Kent CT6 7LJ
Contact: Denis or Martin Bradshaw
Tel/fax: 01227 375415
Hours: 10am–5pm Tues–Sat Mar–Oct & Bank Hol Mon

Climbing and wall plant specialist. Large display field. Catalogue SAE (A5) + 2 x 1st class stamps.
Catalogue

Bybrook Barn Garden & Produce Centre
Canterbury Rd, Kennington, Ashford, Kent TN24 9JZ
Tel: 01233 631959
Fax: 01233 635642
Hours: 9am–5.30pm Mon–Sat, 9.30am–5pm Sun
Refreshments

Church Hill Cottage Gardens
Charing Heath, Ashford, Kent TN27 0BU
Tel/fax: 01233 712522
Hours: 10am–5pm Tues–Sun & Bank Hols. Closed Mon/beg Sept
Catalogue

Connoisseurs' Cacti
51 Chelsfield Lane, Orpington, Kent BR5 4HG
Contact: John Pilbeam
Tel/fax: 01689 837781
Hours: 10am–2.30pm daily

Wide range of cacti and succulents for the discerning enthusiast. SAE for list. Nursery at Woodlands Farm, Shire Lane, Farnborough, Kent. Advisable to phone before visiting.
Catalogue; Mail order; Toilets; Refreshments

Cotton Ash Garden
105 Ashford Road, Faversham, Kent ME13 8XW
Contact: Tim Ingram
Tel/fax: 01795 535919
Hours: 2–6pm. Closed Mon & Fri

Specialist in unusual perennials and plants for dry situations. Fascinating garden attached to nursery. For catalogues of plants or fruit trees please send 4 x 1st class stamps.
Catalogue

Downderry Nursery
649 London Rd, Ditton, Aylesford, Kent ME20 6DJ
Contact: Dr S J Charlesworth
Tel/fax: 01732 840710
Hours: By appointment only

Lavender specialist. 50+ species / varieties. Plugs & liners. Mail order catalogue. Send 2 x 1st class stamps.
Catalogue; Mail order

Forward Nurseries
Borough Green Rd, Ightham,
Kent TN15 9JA
Tel: 01732 884726
Fax: 01732 886626
Hours: 8am–5pm daily

We offer trees, shrubs, conifers, climbers, roses and a wide range of hedging plants. Specialist grower of variegated pot ivies. Hedging catalogue available.
Catalogue; Mail order

Four Elms Cottage Garden Nursery
Bough Beech Rd, Four Elms, Edenbridge, Kent

Catalogue

Friends of Brogdale
Brogdale Horticultural Trust, Brogdale Farm, Faversham, Kent ME9 0PL
Tel: 01795 535286
Fax: 01795 531710
Hours: 9.30am–5pm daily. Weekends only between Xmas & Easter

Home of the National Collections of fruit including over 4000 varieties. Guided orchard walks, historical gardens under construction, plant centre, shop, restaurant. Groups welcome.
Toilets; Refreshments; Disabled access

Fruit Garden
Mulberry Farm, Woodnesborough, Sandwich, Kent CT13 0PT
Tel/fax: 01304 813454
Hours: By appointment only for collection
Catalogue; Mail order

Hazeldene Nursery
Dean Street, East Farleigh, Maidstone, Kent ME15 0PS
Contact: Mrs Jean Adams
Tel/fax: 01622 726248
Hours: 10am–3pm Tues–Sat Mar–Sept

Specialists in pansies, violas and violets. SAE and 1 x 1st class stamp for catalogue.
Catalogue; Mail order

Herbary
89 Station Rd, Herne Bay, Kent CT6 5QQ
Tel/fax: 01227 362409
Hours: 10am–5pm Tues/Wed/Fri/Sat/Sun Mar–Oct
Catalogue

High Banks Nurseries
Slip Mill Rd, Hawkhurst, Kent TN18 5AD
Contact: Jeremy R Homewood
Tel/fax: 01580 753031
Hours: 8.30am–5.30pm Mon–Fri, 9am–5pm Sat, 10am–5pm Sun

Very wide range of interesting and unusual shrubs, perennials, conifers, trees, roses, alpines, climbers. Many large and specimen plants available.
Catalogue

High Winds Nursery
Pike Fish Lane, Laddingford, Maidstone, Kent ME18 6BH
Tel/fax: 01892 730554

Iden Croft Herbs
Frittenden Rd, Staplehurst, Kent TN12 0DH
Contact: Rosemary Titterington
Tel: 01580 891432
Fax: 01580 892416
Hours: 9am–5pm Mon–Sat all year. 11am–5pm Summer Suns/Bnk Hols

Enormous range of herbs, wild flowers. National Collections Mentha, Origanum. Gardens. Refreshments. Access. Open all year. Mail order. SAE for information.
Catalogue; Mail order; Toilets; Refreshments; Disabled access

Keepers Nursery
Gallants Court, East Farleigh, Maidstone, Kent ME15 0LE
Tel/fax: 01622 726465

Fruit tree specialists. Over 600 varieties of apple, pear, plum, cherry etc. Visitors by appointment only. Please send 2 x 1st class stamps for catalogue.
Catalogue; Mail order

Layham Garden Centre
Lower Rd, Staple, Canterbury, Kent CT3 1LH
Tel: 01304 813267
Fax: 01304 615349
Hours: 9am–5pm Mon–Sat, 10am–5pm Sun
Catalogue; Mail order; Refreshments

Longacre Nursery
Longacre, Perry Wood, Selling, Faversham, Kent ME13 9SE
Tel/fax: 01227 752254
Hours: 2–5pm daily Apr–Oct

Small specialist nursery. Hardy herbaceous plants. Garden open under National Gardens Scheme (see Yellow Book for open days), also by appointment - donation please.

Madrona Nursery
Pluckley Road, Bethersden, Kent TN26 3DD
Contact: Liam Mackenzie
Tel/fax: 01233 820100
Hours: 10am–5pm Sat–Tues Mar–Oct

A wide range of unusual, new and rare hardy plants displayed on a uniquely laid out site with Gothic Folly. Comprehensive descriptive catalogue £1.
Catalogue; Mail order; Toilets

Marle Place Gardens & Nursery
Marle Place Rd, Brenchley, Tonbridge, Kent TN12 7HS
Hours: 10am–5.30pm
Catalogue; Mail order

Norton Ash Garden Centre
Norton Crossroads, Norton, Sittingbourne, Kent
Tel/fax: 01795 521549
Refreshments

Notcutts Garden Centre
Newnham Court, Bearstead Rd, Maidstone, Kent ME14 5LH
Tel/fax: 01622 39944
Hours: 9am–5.45pm Mon–Sat, 10am–5.30pm Sun
Catalogue; Refreshments

Notcutts Garden Centre
Tonbridge Rd, Pembury, Tunbridge Wells, Kent TN2 4QN
Tel/fax: 01892 822636
Hours: 8.30am–5.30pm Mon–Sat, 10am–5pm Sun. Closes 5pm Winter
Catalogue

Oldbury Nurseries
Brissenden Green, Bethersden, Nr Ashford, Kent TN26 3BJ
Tel/fax: 01233 820416
Hours: 9.30am–5pm daily Feb–Jun

350 varieties of fuchsias. 120 varieties of pelargoniums. Fuchsia cuttings available February-April. Small plants, hanging pots & baskets available February-June. Catalogue 50p.
Catalogue; Mail order

P H Kellett
The Laurels Nursery, Benenden, Cranbrook, Kent TN17 4JU
Tel/fax: 01580 240463
Hours: 8am–5pm Mon–Thur (4pm Fri) 9–12pm Sat. Other by appt

Growers of wide range of hardy ornamental trees, shrubs, conifers, roses and climbers. Free local delivery. Free catalogue. Garden advice and planning service. Personal attention.
Catalogue

Pete & Ken Cactus Nursery
Saunders Lane, Ash, Nr Canterbury, Kent CT3 2BX
Tel/fax: 01304 812170
Hours: 9am–6pm daily

Come and see our large selection of well gorwn cacti and succulents for the beginner or expert. Mail order list of seedlings available, send SAE.
Mail order; Toilets

Plaxtol Nurseries
The Spoute, Plaxtol, Sevenoaks, Kent TN15 0QR
Tel/fax: 01732 810550
Hours: 10am–5pm daily

Hardy ornamentals, especially foliage and flowering plants for the flower arranger, and Japanese garden plans. Garden open under NGS 29 June 1997, or by appointment for customers.
Catalogue; Toilets

Rosie's Garden Plants
239 Barnsole Road, Gillingham, Kent ME7 4JQ
Contact: Jacqueline Heptinstall
Tel/fax: 01634 575418
Hours: By appointment

Hardy geranium specialist. Species and cultivars, over 75 varieties. Send 2 x 1st class stamps for descriptive mail order catalogue. Liners and plugs available all year.
Catalogue; Mail order

Rumwood Nurseries
Langley (A274), Maidstone, Kent ME17 3ND
Tel: 01622 861477
Fax: 01622 863123

Nurseries and garden centre, established over 30 years, rose specialists with extensive fields open July-September. Garden centre is large, well stocked and interesting.
Catalogue; Mail order; Toilets; Refreshments

Ruxley Manor Garden Centre
Maidstone Rd, Sidcup, Kent DA14 5BQ
Tel: 0181 300 0084
Fax: 0181 302 3879

Starborough Nursery
Starborough Rd, Marsh Green, Edenbridge, Kent TN8 5RB
Tel/fax: 01732 865614
Hours: 10am–4.30pm Thur–Mon. Closed Tues/Wed & Jan & Jul
Catalogue; Mail order

Tile Barn Nursery
Standen Street, Iden Green, Benenden, Kent TN17 4LB
Contact: Peter Moore
Hours: 9am–5pm Wed–Sat

Cyclamen species specialist, catalogue S.A.E. Retail, mail order - home & overseas.
Catalogue; Mail order

Westwood Nursery
65 Yorkland Avenue, Welling, Kent DA16 2LE
Tel/fax: 0181 301 0886
Hours: Mail order only
Catalogue; Mail order

Wyevale Garden Centre
Romney Marsh Garden Centre, Hamstreet, Ashford, Kent TN26 2Q
Tel: 01233 732988
Fax: 01233 733703

Wyevale offers a huge selection of plants, shrubs, gift ideas, furniture, BBQs and tools. Most centres have pet and aquatic departments and a restaurant. 0800 413213 for nearest stockist.

Wyevale Garden Centre
Oakley Rd, Keston Mark, Bromley, Kent BR2 6BY
Tel: 01689 859419
Fax: 01689 862359

See Romney Marsh centre above.

Wyevale Shop
8 Longmarket, Canterbury, Kent CT1 2JS
Tel/fax: 01227 462355
Hours: 9am–6pm Mon–Sat, 11am–5pm Sun

Lancashire

Auldene Garden Centre
Southport Rd, Leyland, Lancashire PR5 3LQ
Tel: 01772 600271
Fax: 01772 601483
Hours: 9am–8pm weekdays. 10am–5.30pm weekends

Award winning garden centre with local delivery service, gardening club, machinery, aquatics, conservatories, coffee shops and everything else you need for the garden.
Toilets; Refreshments; Disabled access

Barkers Primrose Nurseries
Whalley Rd, Clitheroe, Lancashire BB7 1HT
Tel: 01200 23521
Fax: 01200 28160
Hours: 9am–5.30pm Mon–Sat, 10am–5pm Sun & Bank Hols
Catalogue

Barton Grange Garden Centre
Wigan Rd, Deane, Bolton, Lancashire BL3 4RD
Tel: 01204 660660
Fax: 01204 62525
Hours: 9am–5.30pm Mon–Sat, 10.30am–4.30pm Sun

A large garden centre offering top quality plants for the home and garden. Product range includes furniture, barbecues, gifts, books, cards, pet and aquatics.
Toilets; Refreshments; Disabled access

Barton Grange Garden Centre
Garstang Rd, Barton, Preston, Lancashire PR3 5AA
Tel: 01772 864242
Fax: 01772 862863
Hours: 9am–5.30pm Mon–Sat, 10.30am–4.30pm Sun

A large garden centre offering top quality plants for the home and garden. Product range includes furniture, barbecues, gifts, books, cards and pet and aquatics.
Toilets; Refreshments; Disabled access

Brownthwaite Hardy Plants
Casterton, Carnforth, Lancashire LA6 2JW
Tel/fax: 015242 71340
Hours: 10am–5pm Mar 28–Sept 30

Retail nursery producing hardy herbaceous and alpines. Mail order catalogue 3 x 1st class stamps.
Catalogue; Mail order

Burnside Fuchsias
Burnside, Parsonage Road, Blackburn, Lancashire BB1 4AG
Contact: David Johnson
Hours: Mail order only

Specialist fuchsia growers for showbench, house and garden. Cuttings and young plants. Mail order only. Send 2 x 1st class stamps for catalogue.
Catalogue; Mail order

Catforth Gardens
Roots Lane, Catforth, Preston, Lancashire PR4 0JB
Contact: Judith Bradshaw or Chris Moore
Tel/fax: 01772 690561
Hours: 10.30am–5pm daily mid Mar–mid Sept

Nursery specialising in hardy geraniums (National Collection) and herbaceous plants, over 1,500 varieties. Catalogue 5 x 1st class stamps. No mail order. Three glorious gardens covering 2½ acres, giving interest and colour from Spring to Autumn. Admission to gardens £2, children 50p.
Catalogue; Toilets

Craig House Cacti
94 King Street, Southport, Lancashire PR8 1LG
Tel/fax: 01704 545077
Hours: Mail order only

RHS Gold Medal cacti and succulents available by mail order and leading shows. Send 2 x 1st class stamps for catalogue and seed list.
Catalogue; Mail order

Croston Cactus
43 Southport Rd, Eccleston, Chorley, Lancashire PR7 6ET
Contact: John Henshaw
Tel/fax: 01257 452555
Hours: 9am–5.30pm Wed–Sun & Bank Hols. Other times by appt

Retail cacti, succulent and tillandsia nursery. Mail order list produced April/May, 2 x 1st class stamps. Minimum order value £5.
Catalogue; Mail order

Eversley Nurseris
10 Granville Avenue, Hesketh bank, Preston, Lancashire PR4 6AH
Tel/fax: 01772 812538
Hours: By appointment any time
Catalogue; Mail order

Greenacre Nursery
81 Gorsey Lane, Banks, Southport, Lancashire PR9 8ED
Tel/fax: 01704 26791

Holden Clough Nursery
Holden, Bolton by Bowland, Clitheroe, Lancashire BB7 4PF
Contact: Peter Foley
Tel/fax: 01200 447615
Hours: 2–5pm Mon–Sat Suns in Apr/May only. Times vary seasonally

Nursery established 1927 and growing a comprehensive range of alpines, hardy plants, heathers, ornamental grasses, hardy ferns, shrubs, climbers, dwarf conifers. Descriptive catalogue £1 please.
Catalogue; Mail order; Toilets; Disabled access

Marquis Flowers & Plants
PO Box 79, Burnley, Lancashire BB11 5FT
Tel: 01282 453556
Fax: 01282 452106
Catalogue; Mail order

Sellet Hall Gardens
Sellet Hall, Kirkby Lonsdale, Carnforth, Lancashire LA6 2QF
Tel: 015242 71865
Fax: 015242 72208
Hours: 10am–5pm daily
Catalogue; Mail order; Refreshments

Waithman Nurseries
Reginald Kaye Ltd, Silverdale, Carnforth, Lancashire LA5 0TY
Tel/fax: 01524 701252
Hours: 9am–5pm Mon–Sat, 2.30pm–5pm Sun
Catalogue

Wyevale Garden Centre
Preston New Rd, Westby, Kirkham, Lancashire PR4 3PE
Tel: 01772 684129
Fax: 01772 671770

Wyevale offers a huge selection of plants, shrubs, gift ideas, furniture, BBQs and tools. Most centres have pet and aquatic departments and a restaurant. 0800 413213 for nearest stockist.

Leicestershire

A & A Thorp
Bungalow No 5, Main Street, Theddingworth, Lutterworth, Leicestershire LE17 6QZ
Contact: Anita Thorp
Tel/fax: 01858 880496

A range of the more unusual alpines, perennial and woodland plants. A visit is worthwhile. Catalogue SAE + 50p.
Catalogue

Barnsdale Plants & Gardens
The Avenue, Exton, Oakham, Leicestershire LE15 8AH
Contact: Nick Hamilton
Tel: 01572 813200
Fax: 01572 813346
Hours: 10am–5pm Mar–Oct, 10am–4pm Nov–Feb

The Barnsdale TV garden will be open every day from Spring 1997. Also for viewing will be the two gardens built for the Geoff Hamilton's Paradise Gardens series and many other individual gardens. Our small nursery grows a wide range of choice and unusual garden plants. Admission to TV and nursery garden £4.50. Admission to nursery garden only £1.50. Children free. Turn off A606 (Oakham to Stamford road) at the Barnsdale Lodge Hotel, then one mile.
Catalogue; Mail order; Toilets

Fosse Alpines
33 Leicester Rd, Countesthorpe, Leicestershire LE8 5QU
Contact: Tim West
Tel/fax: 0116 2778237
Hours: By appointment – phone first

Alpines, including specilist species in small quantities. Minimum mail order UK £8 + p&p. Catalogue cost 2 x 1st class stamps. Retail.
Catalogue; Mail order

Gandy's Roses Ltd
North Kilworth, Lutterworth, Leicestershire LE17 6HZ
Contact: Rosemary D Gandy
Tel: 01858 880398
Fax: 01858 880433
Hours: 9am–5pm Mon–Sat, 2–5pm Sun

Over 600 varieties of roses. Rose field open to visit July-September. Orders supplied October-April bare root, mail order or for collection.
Catalogue; Mail order

Goscote Nurseries Ltd
Syston Rd, Cossington,
Leicestershire LE7 4UZ

Tel/fax: 01509 812121

Hours: 8am–5pm (4.30pm Winter) Mon–Fri 9am–5pm Sat 10–5pm Sun

Over 1600 varieties of hardy plants including trees, conifers, shrubs, rhododendrons, maples, magnolias, climbing plants, heathers, pieris, fruit trees.
Catalogue; Mail order; Toilets

Hilltop Nurseries
John Smith & Son, Thornton, Coalville, Leicestershire LE67 1AN

Tel/fax: 01530 230331

Hours: 8.30am–5.30pm Suns mid Mar–mid May 10am–4pm.

Fuchsia specialists. Also a wide range of trees and shrubs. Bedding plants and hanging baskets in season.
Catalogue; Mail order

Laburnum Nurseries
6 Manor House Gardens, Main Street, Humberstone Village, Leicestershire LE5 1AF

Contact: William Johnson
Tel/fax: 0116 2766522

Hours: 10am–4pm Spring and Summer only

Internationally renowned fuchsia breeder and grower, including latest varieties from America. Stamp for mail order catalogue. Nursery open free spring/summer only.
Catalogue

Linda Gascoigne Wild Flowers
17 Imperial Rd, Kibworth Beauchamp, Leicestershire LE8 0HR

Tel/fax: 0116 2793959

Hours: By appointment

Wide range of wild flower and wildlife attractive plants grown in an environmentally friendly manner with no peat. 3 x 1st class stamps for plant list.
Catalogue; Mail order

S & S Perennials
24 Main Street, Normanton le Heath, Leicestershire LE67 2TB

Contact: S Pierce
Tel/fax: 01530 262250

Hours: Afternoons

Plant sales - erythronium, fritillaria, hardy cyclamen, iris, hepatica, anemone, ranunculus.
Catalogue; Mail order

Ullesthorpe Garden & Aquatic Centre
Lutterworth Rd, Ullesthorpe, Leicestershire LE17 5DR

Tel: 01455 202144
Fax: 01455 202585

Hours: 9am–6pm Mon–Sat, 10.30am–4.30pm Sun

One of the finest centres for all gardening and aquatic needs, with pet centre and tea room. Well worth a visit. Open 7 days.
Toilets; Refreshments; Disabled access

Ulverscroft Unusual Plants
Ulverscroft Grange Nursery, Priory Lane, Ulverscroft Markfield, Leicester, Leicestershire LE67 9PB

Contact: Ted Brown
Tel/fax: 01530 243635

Hours: 10am–5.30pm Wed–Sun & Bank Hol Mon/Tues

Small specialist nursery with wide range of herbaceous perennials. Also grasses, bamboos and shrubs. Close by Junction 22 M1.

Wyevale Garden Centre
1665 Melton Rd, East Goscote, Leicester, Leicestershire LE7 8YQ

Tel: 0116 2605515
Fax: 0116 2695122

Wyevale offers a huge selection of plants, shrubs, gift ideas, furniture, BBQs and tools. Most centres have pet and aquatic departments and a restaurant. 0800 413213 for nearest stockist.

Lincolnshire

Baytree Nurseries
High Rd, Weston, Spalding, Lincolnshire PE12 6JU

Tel: 01406 370242
Fax: 01406 371665

Hours: 9am–6pm Summer, 9am–5.30pm Winter
Refreshments

C E & D M Nurseries
The Walnuts, 36 Main Street, Baston, Peterborough, Lincolnshire PE6 9PB

Hours: 10am–5pm Fri–Tues. Closed Xmas & Boxing Day
Catalogue; Mail order

Clive Simms
Woodhurst, Essendine, Stamford, Lincolnshire PE9 4LQ

Tel/fax: 01780 55615

Hours: Mail order only

Specialist grower of nut trees and uncommon fruits for the edible garden. 2 x 1st class stamps for catalogue.
Catalogue; Mail order

Cottage Nurseries
Thoresthorpe, Alford, Lincolnshire LN13 0HX

Tel/fax: 01507 466968

Hours: 9am–5pm daily March–Oct. Closed Wed/Thurs Nov–Feb

Large selection of plants, many unusual varieties. Display garden open March-October. Mail order catalogue 3 x 1st class stamps.
Catalogue; Mail order

Donington Plants
Main Rd, Wrangle, Boston, Lincolnshire PE22 9AT

Tel/fax: 01205 870015

Hours: By appointment only

Foliage & Unusual Plants
Dingle Nursery & Gardens, Pilsgate, Stamford, Lincolnshire PE9 3HW

Contact: Margaret Handley
Tel: 01780 740775
Fax: 01780 740838

Hours: 10am–6pm 1 Mar–15 Nov

Large selection of unusual perennials, alpines, shrubs, grasses and conifers including many variegated and coloured foliage plants. Nursery set in quiet and pretty four acre gardens with natural stream. Picnics welcome. Located on B1443, ½ mile east Burghley House. Catalogue 3 x 1st class stamps.
Catalogue; Mail order; Toilets

Glenhirst Cactus Nursery
Station Rd, Swineshead, Nr Boston, Lincolnshire PE20 3NX

Contact: N C & S A Bell
Tel/fax: 01205 820314

Hours: 10am–5pm Thur/Fri/Sun Apr 1–Sept 30

Mail order catalogue all year (2 x 1st class stamps). 3,000 sqare feet of glass housing cacti, succulents, Christmas and orchid cacti, living stones, books, seeds and sundries.
Catalogue; Mail order

Hall Farm Nursery
Hall Farm, Harpswell, Gainsborough, Lincolnshire DN21 5UU

Contact: Pamela Tatam
Tel: 01427 668412
Fax: 01427 688412

Hours: 8am–5.30pm daily. Phone first in winter

Wide range of interesting shrubs, perennials and old roses, most also growing in our garden. Catalogue 80p. Visits from garden clubs etc welcomed.
Catalogue; Toilets

J Walkers Bulbs
Washway House Farm, Holbeach, Spalding, Lincolnshire PE12 7PP

Tel: 01406 26216
Fax: 01406 25468

Hours: Mail order only
Catalogue; Mail order

Judy's Country Garden
The Villa, Louth Rd, South Somercotes, Louth, Lincolnshire LN11 7BW

Contact: Judy Harry
Tel/fax: 01507 358487

Hours: 9am–6pm most days mid Mar–end Sept

Personally run small nursery surrounded by display gardens in the cottage tradition. Herbs, perennials, many hard to obtain elsewhere. 3 x 1st class stamps for list.
Catalogue; Toilets

Kathleen Muncaster Fuchsias
18 Field Lane, Morton, Gainsborough, Lincolnshire DN21 3BY

Tel/fax: 01427 612329

Hours: 10am–dusk Feb–mid July. Phone for other times

Specialist fuchsia nursery. Catalogue 2 x 1st class stamps. Stock plant display and garden of hardy cultivars and species in Summer. Coach parties welcome by appointment.
Catalogue; Mail order; Toilets; Disabled access

Martin Nest Nurseries
Grange Cottage, Hemswell, Gainsborough, Lincolnshire DN21 5UP

Contact: Mrs M A Robinson
Tel: 01427 668369
Fax: 01427 668080

Hours: 9am–4pm Mon–Fri, 10am–5pm Sat & Sun

Wide range of rock plants, primulas and auriculas, saxifrages. No admission charge. Visitors welcome. Mail order.
Catalogue; Mail order; Toilets

Orchard Nurseries
Tow Lane, Foston, Grantham, Lincolnshire NG32 2LE

Contact: Richard or Janet Blenkinship
Tel/fax: 01400 281354

Hours: Daily from 1 Feb–30 Sept

A plantsman's nursery offering a wide range, small flowered clematis, hardy geraniums, plus much more. New introductions: lavatera 'Lisanne', phygelius 'Sunshine' & nemesia 'Fragrant Cloud'.
Toilets

Plant Lovers
Candlesby House, Candlesby, Spilsby, Lincolnshire PE23 5RU

Tel/fax: 01754 890256

Hours: Daily when not at shows

We are specialist growers of cacti/succulent plants supplying wholesale and retail. No lists. Visitors welcome - prior phone call desirable. Exhibitor at Chelsea and other shows.

The Daily Telegraph *Green Fingers* — Garden Centres & Nurseries

Potterton & Martin
The Cottage Nursery,
Moortown Rd, Nettleton, Nr
Caistor, Lincolnshire LN7 6HX

Contact: Mr or Mrs Potterton
Tel: 01472 815792
Fax: 01472 851792

Hours: *9am–5pm daily*

Alpines and dwarf bulbs. Mail order or at nursery. Seven Chelsea Golds and eight consecutive RHS Farrer Trophy awards 1988 to 1995. Catalogue 50p.
Catalogue; Mail order; Toilets

Southfield Nurseries
Bourne Rd, Morton, Bourne,
Lincolnshire PE10 0RH

Tel/fax: 01778 570168

Hours: *10am–4pm daily except Xmas & New Year*

One of the country's largest specialist nurseries growing cacti and succulents. Plants for beginners and connoisseurs. SAE for mail order list.
Catalogue; Mail order; Toilets

Stephen H Smith's Garden & Leisure
Trent Valley, Doncaster Road,
Scunthorpe, Lincolnshire DN15 8TE

Tel: 01724 848950
Fax: 01724 271912

Hours: *9am–5.30pm*

Large garden centre with own production nurseries. Hillier and Blooms premier stockist. Massive range of everything for the garden - plants, garden furniture, giftware and aquatics.
Toilets; Refreshments; Disabled access

Valley Clematis Nursery
Hainton, Lincoln, Lincolnshire LN3 6LN

Tel/fax: 01507 313398

Catalogue; Mail order

London

Alexander Palace Garden Centre - Capital Gardens
Alexandra Palace, Muswell Hill,
London N22 4BB

Contact: David Wylie
Tel: 0181 444 2555
Fax: 0181 883 7937

Hours: *9am–6pm Mon–Sat.
10am–4pm Sun*

Garden centre located in historic Alexandra Park, next to Alexandra Palace. Specialises in plants for London's gardens with seasonal promotions, especially bedding plants for pots and window boxes.
Toilets; Refreshments

Fulham Palace Garden Centre
Fulham Palace Rd, London SW6 6EE

Tel/fax: 0171 736 2640/9820

Highgate Garden Centre - Capital Gardens
1 Townsend Yard, Highgate High Street, London N6 5JF

Contact: Paula Calam
Tel: 0181 340 1041
Fax: 0181 340 8578

Hours: *9am–6pm Mon–Sat.
10am–5pm Sun*

Garden centre specialising in climbing plants with seasonal promotions especially roses and clematis. Car parking, delivery and mail order service available.
Mail order; Toilets

Palm Centre
563 Upper Richmond Rd West, London SW14 7ED

Contact: Martin Gibbons
Tel: 0181 876 3223
Fax: 0181 876 6888

Hours: *10am–6pm daily*

Palms and cycads, exotic and sub-tropical, hardy, half-hardy and tropical. Seedlings to mature trees. Colour catalogue for palms and cycads £2.95.
Catalogue; Mail order

Temple Fortune Garden Centre - Capital Gardens
788a Finchley Road, London NW11 7TF

Contact: Sue Borenius
Tel: 0181 455 5363
Fax: 0181 455 1102

Hours: *9am–6pm Mon–Sat.
9.30am–5pm Sun*

A smaller centre that specialises in houseplants and plants for London's gardens with seasonal promotions on 'starter plants'. The shop caters for one-stop gardeners in a hurry for that particular fertiliser, compost or garden tool.
Toilets

Wyevale Garden Centre
Lower Morden Lane, Morden,
London SM4 4SJ

Tel/fax: 0181 337 7781

Wyevale offers a huge selection of plants, shrubs, gift ideas, furniture, BBQs and tools. Most centres have pet and aquatic departments and a restaurant. 0800 413213 for nearest stockist.

Manchester, Greater

Daisy Nook Garden Centre
Failsworth, Manchester,
Manchester, Gt M35 9WJ

Tel: 0161 681 4245
Fax: 0161 688 0822

Refreshments

Primrose Cottage Nursery & Garden Centre
Ringway Rd, Moss Nook,
Wythenshawe, Manchester, Gt M22 5WF

Contact: Caroline Dumville
Tel: 0161 437 1557
Fax: 0161 499 9932

Hours: *8.30am–6pm Mon–Sat.
9.30am–5.30pm Sun*

Growers of a large range of herbaceous perennials, alpines, herbs, patio and basket plants. 2 x 1st class stamps for catalogue. Coffee shop.
Catalogue; Toilets; Refreshments; Disabled access

Vicarage Gardens
Carrington, Urmston,
Manchester, Gt M31 4AG

Tel: 0161 775 2750
Fax: 0161 775 3679

Hours: *10am–5.30pm Fri–Wed Apr–Sept. 10am–5pm Oct–Mar*
Catalogue; Mail order; Refreshments

Worsley Hall Nurseries & Garden Centre
Leigh Rd, Boothstown, Worsley,
Manchester, Gt M28 4LJ

Tel/fax: 0161 790 8792

Hours: *Summer 8am–5.30pm Mon–Sat/10.30am–4.30pm Suns*

Large Victorian walled plant area. Facilities include: shop, café, picnic area, children's playground, toilets, free parking. dogs welcome. Coach parties welcome by appointment. Member of HTA and GCA.
Refreshments

Merseyside

Porters Fuchsias
12 Hazel Grove, Southport,
Merseyside PR8 6AX

Tel: 01704 533902
Fax: 01704 832196

Hours: *10.30am–4pm Thur–Sun Jan–May 2*
Catalogue; Mail order

Middlesex

Airport Aquaria
Heathrow Garden Centre,
Sipson Rd, West Drayton,
Middlesex UB7 0HR

Tel/fax: 0181 897 2563

Hours: *7 days a week*

Bypass Nurseries
Country World, Cattlegate Rd,
Crews Hill, Enfield, Middlesex EN2 9DP

Contact: John Wild
Tel: 0181 367 3377
Fax: 0181 364 5315

Hours: *9am–6pm Mon–Sat.
10.30am–4.30pm Sun*

Bypass Nurseries make a special effort to offer the best quality plants and advice. If you require help on gardening matters, we'll be pleased to help.

Chelsea Gardener, The
c/o Country World, Cattlegate Road, Crews Hill, Enfield, Middlesex EN2 9DP

Tel: 0181 367 3377
Fax: 0181 364 5315

Hours: *9am–6pm Mon–Sat.
10.30am–4.30pm Sun*

Where gardens come to life all year round. Indoors and out, from the ordinary to the extraordinary. Everything you need for the perfect garden and more.
Toilets; Refreshments; Disabled access

Derek Lloyd Dean
8 Lynwood Close, South Harrow, Middlesex HA2 9PR

Hours: *Mail order only*

Wide range of pelargoniums by mail order only. UK and export sales. Send 2 x 1st class stamps for catalogue.
Catalogue; Mail order

CAPITAL GARDEN CENTRES

Alexandra Palace	Morden Hall Park	Temple Fortune	Highgate Village
London N22	Morden Hall Road	788A Finchley Road	Highgate N6
0181-444 2555	Morden SM4	London NW11	0181-340 1041
	0181-646 3002	0181-455 5363	

'Best of all is the enthusiasm of the staff – THE TIMES
Winners of the Best Courtyard Display in
the City of London 1994
Open 7 days a week. Car Parking available at all centres.
Delivery service throughout London.

Garden Centre at Hounslow Heath
Staines Rd, Hounslow, Middlesex TW4 5DS

Tel: 0181 572 3211
Fax: 0181 572 5623

Hours: 9am–6pm daily
Refreshments

Great Gardens of England (Syon)
The Garden Centre, Syon Park, Brentford, Middlesex TW8 8JG

Tel: 0181 568 3908
Fax: 0181 847 3865

Hours: 9am–5.30pm Mon–Fri(8pm Wed), 9.30am–6pm Sat/Sun

Jacques Amand Ltd
The Nurseries, Clamp Hill, Stanmore, Middlesex HA7 3JS

Tel: 0181 954 8138
Fax: 0181 954 6784

Hours: 8.30am–5pm Mon–Fri, 8am–1pm Sat, 9am–1pm Sun
Catalogue; Mail order

Plantation Garden Plant Centre
Kenton Rd, Harrow, Middlesex

Tel/fax: 0181 423 2073

Hours: 8.30am–6pm seven days a week

Tendercare Nurseries Ltd
Southlands Rd, Denham, Uxbridge, Middlesex UB9 4HD

Tel/fax: 01895 835544

Wyevale Garden Centre
Cattlegate Rd, Crews Hill, Enfield, Middlesex EN2 9DX

Tel: 0181 367 0422
Fax: 0181 366 3810

Wyevale offers a huge selection of plants, shrubs, gift ideas, furniture, BBQs and tools. Most centres have pet and aquatic departments and a restaurant. 0800 413213 for nearest stockist.

Wyevale Garden Centre
Headstone Lane, Harrow, Middlesex HA2 6NB

Tel: 0181 428 3408
Fax: 0181 420 1833

See Enfield centre above.

Wyevale Garden Centre
Holloway Lane, Harmondsworth, West Drayton, Middlesex UB7 0AD

Tel: 0181 897 6075
Fax: 0181 759 5739

See Enfield centre above.

Norfolk

African Violet Centre
Station Rd, Terrington St Clement, Kings Lynn, Norfolk PE34 4PL

Tel: 01553 828374
Fax: 01553 827520

Hours: 10am–5pm Mar–Oct
Catalogue; Mail order; Refreshments

Bawdeswell Garden Centre
Bawdeswell, Dereham, Norfolk NR20 4SJ

Tel: 01362 88387
Fax: 01362 88504

Hours: 8am–5.30pm Summer, 8am–5pm Winter
Catalogue; Refreshments

Bressingham Plant Centre
Bressingham, Diss, Norfolk IP22 3XL

Tel: 01379 687464
Fax: 01379 688061

Hours: 9am–5.30pm daily. Closed Xmas & Boxing Day

Thousands of hardy plants, including the new, classic and unusual from traditional Norfolk nurserymen Blooms of Bressingham, plus the friendly advice of skilled plantsmen.
Toilets; Refreshments; Disabled access

Croftacre Hardy Plants
Croftacre, Ellingham Rd, Scoulton, Norfolk NR9 4NT

Tel: 01953 850599
Fax: 01953 851399

Hours: By appointment only
Catalogue; Mail order

Daphne ffiske Herbs
Rosemary Cottage, The Street, Bramerton, Norwich, Norfolk NR13 7DW

Contact: Daphne ffiske
Tel/fax: 01508 538187

Hours: 10am–4pm Thur–Sun Mar–Sept

Comprehensive selection of herb plants. Retail only. Home grown in cottage garden. Available March to September. Situated S.E. Norwich off A146 Lowestoft road. SAE for list.
Catalogue; Mail order

Five Acres Fuchsia Nursery
Marsh Rd, Potter Heigham, Great Yarmouth, Norfolk NR29 5LN

Tel/fax: 01692 670647
Catalogue

Four Seasons
Forncett St Mary, Norwich, Norfolk NR16 1JT

Tel: 01508 488344
Fax: 01508 488478

Hours: Mail order only

A wide selection of hardy herbaceous perennials. Catalogue £1 or 4 x 1st class stamps. Mail order only.
Catalogue; Mail order

Hoecroft Plants
Severals Grange, Holt Rd, Wood Norton, Dereham, Norfolk NR20 5BL

Tel/fax: 01362 684206

Hours: 10am–4pm Wed/Fri/Sat/Sun Apr 1–Sept 30

Specialists in ornamental grasses, variegated and foliage plants. Descriptive mail order catalogue £1 or 5 x 2nd class stamps.
Catalogue; Mail order; Toilets

Jenny Burgess Alpines
Alpines Nursery, Sisland, Norwich, Norfolk NR14 6EF

Contact: Jenny Burgess
Tel/fax: 01508 520724

Hours: Any time by appt

Wifde variety of alpine plants. Mail order only for sisyrinchium, of which we hold National Collection. Catalogue 3 x 1st class stamps.
Catalogue; Mail order; Toilets

Norfolk Lavender Ltd
Caley Mill, Heacham, Kings Lynn, Norfolk PE31 7JE

Tel: 01485 570384
Fax: 01485 571176

Open all year (except 2 weeks after Christmas). Free admission. Fragrant garden, herb garden, National Collection of Lavenders. Guided tour of fields/gardens. Gift/plant shop. Tearoom - home-made cakes, scones, lunches. Play area.
Catalogue; Mail order; Toilets; Refreshments; Disabled access

Norwich Heather & Conifer Centre
54a Yarmouth Rd, Thorpe St Andrew, Norwich, Norfolk NR7 0HE

Tel/fax: 01603 39434

Hours: 9am–5pm Mon–Sat, 2–5pm Sun. Closed Thurs
Catalogue; Mail order

Notcutts Garden Centre
Daniels Rd, Norwich, Norfolk NR4 6QP

Tel/fax: 01603 53155

Hours: 8.30am–5.30pm Mon–Sat, 10am–5.30pm Sun
Catalogue; Refreshments

P W Plants
Sunnyside, Heath Rd, Kenninghall, Norwich, Norfolk NR16 2DS

Contact: Paul Whittaker
Hours: Every Friday and last Saturday in month.

Catalogue: 5 first class stamps. We specialise in foliage plants, bamboos, grasses, shrubs and climbers.
Catalogue; Mail order; Toilets

Peter Beales Roses
London Rd, Attleborough, Norfolk NR17 1AY

Tel: 01953 454707
Fax: 01953 456845

Hours: 9am–4.30pm Mon–Sat, 10am–4.30pm Sun

Specialists in old-fashioned and classic roses by mail order. Container roses (collection only) during the summer. 2½ acre rose garden.
Catalogue; Mail order; Toilets

Raveningham Gardens
Estate Office, Raveningham Hall, Raveningham, Norwich, Norfolk NR14 6NS

Tel: 01508 46222
Fax: 01508 468958

Catalogue; Mail order

Reads Nursery
Hales Hall, Loddon, Norfolk NR14 6QW

Tel: 01508 548395
Fax: 01508 548040

Hours: 10am–5pm Tues–Sat. Closed Xmas/New Year

Wide variety of fruit trees, conservatory plants, citrus, vines, figs, topiary and hedging in box and yew. Catalogue 4 x 1st class stamps.
Catalogue; Mail order

Romantic Garden Nursery
Swannington, Norwich, Norfolk NR9 5NW

Contact: John Powles
Tel: 01603 261488
Fax: 01603 871668

Hours: 10am–5pm Wed/Fri/Sat

A specialist nursery with one of the largest selections of topiary in the country, all available by mail order. Send 4 x 1st class stamps for catalogue.
Catalogue; Mail order

Simpsons Nursery/ Landscaping & Tree Surgery
The Plant Nursery, High Street, Marsham, Norwich, Norfolk NR10 5QA

Contact: Gillian Simpson
Tel/fax: 01263 733432

Hours: 10am–5.30pm or dusk daily

A qualified horticultural family business growing unusual, interesting, good quality, reasonably priced plants. Sympathetic garden designs and landscaping service to suit customers' requirements. Professional advice.

Thorncroft Clematis Nursery
The Lings, Reymerston,
Norwich, Norfolk NR9 4QG
Tel/fax: 01953 850407
Hours: 10am–4.30pm daily
Mar–Oct. Closed Wed

Specialist clematis grower with large display garden. Send 4 x 2nd class stamps for catalogue.
Catalogue; Mail order; Toilets; Disabled access

Trevor White Old Fashioned Roses
Chelt Hurst, Sewell Rd,
Norwich, Norfolk NR3 4BP
Tel: 01603 418240
Fax: 01603 482967
Hours: Mail order only
Catalogue; Mail order

Whispering Trees Nursery
Chris Bowers & Son,
Wimbotsham, Norfolk PE34 8QB
Tel/fax: 01366 388752
Hours: 9am–5pm
Catalogue; Mail order

Wyevale Garden Centre
Blue Boar Lane, Sprowston,
Norwich, Norfolk NR7 8RJ
Tel: 01603 412239
Fax: 01603 402949

Wyevale offers a huge selection of plants, shrubs, gift ideas, furniture, BBQs and tools. Most centres have pet and aquatic departments and a restaurant. 0800 413213 for nearest stockist.

Northamptonshire

Coton Manor Garden
Nr Guilsborough, Northampton,
Northamptonshire NN6 8RQ
Contact: Ian Pasley-Tyler
Tel: 01604 740219
Fax: 01604 740838
Hours: 12noon–5.30pm Wed–Sun
Easter–Sept

Extensively planted old English garden laid out on different levels covering ten acres with herbaceous borders, rose, herb and water gardens. Nursery selling unusual plants.
Catalogue; Toilets; Refreshments; Disabled access

E L F Plants
Harborough Rd Nth,
Northampton,
Northamptonshire NN2 8LU
Tel/fax: 01604 846246
Hours: 10am–5pm Thurs–Sat.
Closed Nov–Jan

Specialist growers of dwarf and unusual shrubs and conifers. Catalogue 50p. Nursery along track by Kingsthorpe Cemetary, off A508, north side of Northampton.
Catalogue

Hill Farm Herbs
Park Walk, Brigstock,
Northamptonshire NN14 3HH
Tel: 01536 373694
Fax: 01536 373246
Hours: 10.30am–5.30pm daily
(May vary in Winter)

Specialist nursery with display gardens and barn shops. Herbs, cottage garden plants and scented conservatory plants, dried flowers, seeds, books, herb products, preserves and gifts.
Toilets; Refreshments

Mears Ashby Nurseries Ltd
Glebe House, Glebe Rd, Mears Ashby, Northamptonshire
NN6 0DL
Tel/fax: 01604 811811/812371
Hours: 9.30am–5.30pm daily

Podington Garden Centre
High Street, Podington,
Wellingborough,
Northamptonshire NN29 7HS
Contact: Colin Read
Tel: 01933 53656
Fax: 01933 410332
Hours: 9am–6.30pm Summer,
9am–5.30pm Winter,
10.30am–4.30pm Sun

A plant person's paradise with thousands of plants all year round. Also a wide range of garden sundries, furniture, aquatics, garden ornaments, fencing and paving.
Toilets; Refreshments; Disabled access

Ravensthorpe Nursery
6 East Haddon Rd,
Ravensthorpe,
Northamptonshire NN6 8ES
Contact: Richard & Jean Wiseman
Tel/fax: 01604 770548
Hours: 10am–6pm or dusk if earlier Tues–Sun & Bank Hol Mons

Wide range of shrubs, herbaceous and bedding plants with many unusual varieties. Expert advice from professional gardener. Search/delivery service for lists. Display garden.
Catalogue; Mail order

Wyevale Garden Centre
Newport Pagnell Rd,
Hardlingstone, Northampton,
Northamptonshire NN4 0BN
Tel: 01604 765725
Fax: 01604 700492

Wyevale offers a huge selection of plants, shrubs, gift ideas, furniture, BBQs and tools. Most centres have pet and aquatic departments and a restaurant. 0800 413213 for nearest stockist.

Northumberland

Glantlees Trees & Hedging
Newton-on-the-Moor, Felton,
Northumberland NE65 9LR
Tel: 01665 570304
Fax: 01665 570035

Halls of Heddon
West Heddon Nurseries,
Heddon on the Wall, Newcastle upon Tyne, Northumberland
NE15 0JS
Tel/fax: 01661 852445
Hours: 9am–5pm Mon–Sat,
10am–5pm Sun

Chrysanthemum and dahlia specialists. Mail order catalogues: 2 x 2nd class stamps. Visitors welcome to view flower fields September/October. Garden centre open all year round.
Catalogue; Mail order

Heighley Gate Garden Centre
Morpeth, Northumberland NE61 3DA
Tel: 01670 513416
Fax: 01670 510013
Hours: 9am–5pm Mon–Fri
9.30am–5pm Sat/Sun
Refreshments

Hexham Herbs
Chesters Walled Garden,
Chollerford, Hexham,
Northumberland NE46 4BQ
Contact: Kevin White
Tel/fax: 01434 681483
Hours: 10am–5pm daily
March–end Oct. Phone for Winter opening times

Beautiful walled garden, extensive herb collection. Many unusual herbaceous perennials, old roses, Roman herbs, famous Thyme Bank. Award-winning nursery. Herbal gift shop. Woodland walk.
Catalogue

Northumbria Nurseries
Castle Gardens, Ford, Berwick upon Tweed, Northumberland
TD15 2PZ
Tel: 01890 820379
Fax: 01890 820594
Hours: 9am–6pm Mon–Fri all year, 10am–6pm Sat/Sun Mar–Oct
Catalogue; Mail order

Ryal Nursery
East Farm Cottage, Ryal,
Northumberland NE20 0SA
Contact: Ruth Hadden
Tel/fax: 01661 886562
Hours: 1–5pm Tues, 10am–5pm Suns Mar–July. Also by appt

Alpine and woodland plants a speciality. Please send SAE for catalogue.
Catalogue; Mail order

Nottinghamshire

Brinkley Nurseries
Fiskerton Rd, Southwell,
Nottinghamshire NG25 0TP
Contact: Celia Steven
Tel/fax: 01636 814501
Hours: Daily – hours on enquiry

Specialists in an exciting range of shrubs, trees and conifers. Catalogue £2.
Catalogue; Toilets

Field House Alpines
Leake Rd, Gotham, Nottingham,
Nottinghamshire NG11 0JN
Contact: Doug & Val
Tel/fax: 0115 9830278
Hours: 9am–5pm daily except Thurs

Specialist growers of auriculas, primulas and alpine plants and suppliers of a wide range of quality seeds. Catalogues 4 x 1st class stamps please.
Catalogue; Mail order; Toilets

Hewthorn Herbs & Wild Flowers
82 Julian Road, West Bridgford,
Nottinghamshire NG2 5AN
Contact: Julie Scott
Tel/fax: 0115 9812861
Hours: Strictly by appointment

Medicinal herbs, wild flowers and native pond plants by mail order. All organically grown. Please send 4 x 2nd class stamps for list.
Mail order

Mill Hill Plants
Mill Hill House, Elston Lane, East Stoke, Newark, Nottinghamshire NG23 5QJ
Tel/fax: 01636 525460
Hours: 10am–6pm Wed–Sun & Bank Hol Mon Mar–Oct
Catalogue; Mail order

Norwell Nurseries
5 Marston Cottages, Woodhouse Rd, Norwell, Nr Newark,
Nottinghamshire NG23 6JX
Contact: Dr Andrew Ward
Tel/fax: 01636 636337
Hours: 10am–5pm Sun–Thurs
March 1–Oct 30 & by appt

Specialising in choice and unusual herbaceous perennials and alpines, especially penstemon, hardy geraniums, primulas, grasses and potentillas. Display gardens. Catalogue 2 x 1st class stamps.
Catalogue; Mail order

Richard Stockwell – Rare Plants (GF)
64 Weardale Rd, Sherwood, Nottingham, Nottinghamshire NG5 1DD

Contact: Richard Stockwell
Tel/fax: 0115 9691063

Hours: Mail order only

Rarest climbers and dwarf species, many unavailable elsewhere. Seed exported world wide. Send 4 x 2nd class stamps or two International Reply Coupons for latest seed catalogue.
Catalogue; Mail order

Salley Gardens
32 Lansdowne Drive, West Bridgford, Nottingham, Nottinghamshire NG2 7FJ

Contact: Richard Lewin
Tel/fax: 0115 9233878

Hours: Not open to the public

Medicinal plants and wildflowers, herbs and seeds by mail order only. List free.
Catalogue; Mail order

Wheatcroft Ltd
Landmere Lane, Edwalton, Nottingham, Nottinghamshire NG12 4DE

Tel: 0115 9216060
Fax: 0115 9841247

Hours: 9am–6pm

Visit our garden centre with a vast range of roses and shrubs or send for mail order list of roses.
Refreshments; Disabled access

Oxfordshire

Burford Garden Company
Shilton Rd, Burford, Oxfordshire OX18 4PA

Tel: 01993 823117
Fax: 01993 823529

Hours: 9am–5.30pm Mon–Sat, 9.30am–5.30pm Sun

Situated in the Costwolds, an independent garden centre offering a comprehensive range of both essential and luxury items for the gardener. With play area and restaurant on site.
Toilets; Refreshments; Disabled access

Mattock Roses
Nuneham Courtenay, Oxford, Oxfordshire OX44 9PY

Tel: 01865 343265
Fax: 01865 343267

Hours: 9am–5.30pm Mon–Sat, 10.30am–5.30pm Sun
Catalogue; Mail order; Refreshments

Newington Nurseries
Newington, Wallingford, Oxfordshire OX10 7AW

Tel: 01865 400533
Fax: 01865 891766
Email: newnurse@btinternet.com

Hours: 10am–5pm Tues–Sun
Refreshments

Wildlife Gardening Centre
Witney Rd, Kingston Bagpuize, Abingdon, Oxfordshire OX13 5AN

Contact: Jenny Steel
Tel/fax: 01865 821660

Hours: 10am–4pm Tues–Sat

Growers of wildflowers, cottage garden plants, herbs, native trees and shrubs. Send 3 x 1st class stamps for informative catalogue.
Catalogue; Mail order

Wyevale Garden Centre
Old London Rd, Wheatley, Oxfordshire OX9 1YJ

Tel: 01865 873057
Fax: 01865 875321

Wyevale offers a huge selection of plants, shrubs, gift ideas, furniture, BBQs and tools. Most centres have pet and aquatic departments and a restaurant. 0800 413213 for nearest stockist.

Shropshire

Barbara Molesworth
Byeways, Daisy Lane, Whittington, Oswestry, Shropshire SY11 4EA

Tel/fax: 01691 659539

Old fashioned species, rare and unusual herbaceous perennials. Plant list 15p. Open by appointment and at Newtown Market on Tuesday and Oswestry Market on Wednesday.
Catalogue; Toilets

Hall Farm Nursery
Kinnerley, Oswestry, Shropshire SY10 8DH

Contact: Christine Ffoukes-Jones
Tel/fax: 01691 682135

Hours: 10am–5pm Wed–Sat Mar 1–Sept 27

Attractive nursery specialising in unusual herbaceous plants. Spring, Summer and Autumn flowering plants, ornamental grasses and foliage plants. For catalogue send 4 x 1st class stamps.
Catalogue

Hillview Hardy Plants
Worfield, Nr Bridgnorth, Shropshire WV15 5NT

Contact: Ingrid Millington
Tel/fax: 01746 716454

Hours: 9am–5pm Mon–Sat, Mar–Oct. Other times by appt

Auriculas and unusual / old fashioned hardy herbaceous perennials are our speciality. Send 5 x 2nd class stamps for our mail order catalogue or pay us a visit.
Catalogue; Mail order; Toilets

Lingen Nursery & Garden
Lingen, Nr Bucknell, Shropshire SY7 0DY

Contact: Kim W Davis
Tel/fax: 01544 267720

Hours: 10am–6pm Feb–Oct

Alpine, rock garden and herbaceous plants displayed in extensive gardens and for sale. Descriptive catalogue 3 x 1st class stamps.
Catalogue; Mail order; Toilets

Llanbrook Alpine & Wildflower Nursery
3 Llanbrook, Hopton Castle, Clunton, Shropshire SY7 0QG

Contact: John Clayfield
Tel/fax: 015474 298

Hours: By appointment only. Phone first

I grow an interesting range of alpines, native wildflowers and other hardy and cottage plants in a peat-free compost. Open by appointment.

Merton Nurseries
Bicton, Shrewsbury, Shropshire SY3 8EF

Contact: J M Pannett
Tel/fax: 01743 850773

Hours: 9am–5pm daily

A small family business growing and supplying a wide variety of plants (many unusual). Extensive show garden as featured in Practical Gardening.
Toilets

Nordybank Nurseries
Clee St Margaret, Craven Arms, Shropshire SY7 9EF

Tel/fax: 01584 823322

Hours: 12noon–6pm Mon/Wed/Sun Easter–mid Oct

One acre plantsman's cottage garden with small nursery, specialising in unusual herbaceous plants, all organically grown. Plant list 2 x 1st class stamps. Garden admission £1.50.
Catalogue; Toilets; Refreshments

Oak Cottage Herb Garden
Nesscliffe, (Opp Nesscliffe Hotel), Shrewsbury, Shropshire SY4 1DB

Contact: Edward or Jane Bygott
Tel/fax: 01743 741262

Hours: 11am–5.30pm March–Sept

Mainly herbs. Also cottage garden plants, wild flowers. Catalogue 3 x 1st class stamps. Also visit by appointment Oak Cottage one acre walled garden, Atcham, Shrewsbury (near Attingham).
Catalogue; Mail order

Perrybrook Nursery
Brook Cottage, Wykey, Ruyton XI Towns, Shrewsbury, Shropshire SY4 1JA

Contact: Gayle Williams
Tel/fax: 01939 261120

Hours: 1–6pm Tues–Fri. Other times by appt

An extensive range of unusual and choice perennials for the discerning. Displays of tricyrtris tiarellas, epimediums and centaureas. Catalogue 4 x 1st class stamps.
Catalogue

Somerset

Avon Bulbs
Burnt House Farm, Mid-Lambrook, South Petherton, Somerset TA13 5HE

Tel/fax: 01460 242177

Hours: 9am–4.30pm Thurs–Sat mid Feb–end Mar & mid Sep/Oct
Catalogue; Mail order

BURFORD GARDEN COMPANY

"One of the country's leading Garden Centres"

Every plant for the English Country Garden
- Pets & Water Gardening • Floristry Department
- Gifts & Interior Furnishings
- Coffee Shop/Restaurant • Summerhouses & Gazebos
- Bookshop • Speciality Foods
- Conservatory Furniture
- Statuary & Stoneware • Children's Playground

Open 7 days a week
Shilton Road, Burford, Oxfordshire – 01993 823117

The Daily Telegraph *Green Fingers* **Garden Centres & Nurseries**

Bradley Batch Cactus Nursery
64 Bath Rd, Ashcott, Bridgwater, Somerset TA7 9QJ
Tel/fax: 01458 210256
Hours: 10am–6pm Tues–Sat. Closed Mon

Broadleigh Gardens
Bishops Tull, Taunton, Somerset TA4 1AE
Tel: 01823 286231
Fax: 01823 323464
Hours: 9am–4pm Mon–Fri. Viewing only – collection by appt
Specialists: small and unusual bulbs - narcissus, tulips, crocuses, colchicums (June catalogue); cyclamen, snowdrops in growth, woodland, herbaceous plants (January catalogue). Catalogue 2 x 1st class stamps.
Catalogue; Mail order

Elworthy Cottage Plants
Elworthy Cottage, Elworthy, Nr Lydeard St Lawrence, Taunton, Somerset TA4 3PX
Contact: Jenny Spiller
Tel/fax: 01984 656427
Hours: 11am–6pm Tues/Thurs/Fri. Also by appt
Large range of herbaceous perennials, especially hardy geraniums, origanums, pulmonarias, violas and grasses. 3 x 1st class stamps for list. Garden also open. Admission £1.
Catalogue; Toilets

Hadspen Garden
Hadspen Garden, Castle Cary, Somerset BA7 7NG
Tel/fax: 01963 350939
Hours: 9am–6pm Thurs–Sun & Bank Hols
Catalogue; Refreshments

Kelways Ltd
Barrymore Farm, Langport, Somerset TA10 9EZ
Contact: Susan Farrell
Tel: 01458 250521
Fax: 01458 253351
Hours: 9am–5pm Mon–Fri, 10am–4pm Sat/Sun
Famous peony and iris specialists offer a wide range of plants from our shop. Orchid house. Ample parking. Mail order catalogue free.
Catalogue; Mail order; Toilets

Littleton Nursery
Littleton, Somerton, Somerset TA11 6NT
Tel/fax: 01458 272356

Lower Severalls Garden & Nursery
Crewkerne, Somerset TA18 7NX
Contact: Mary R Cooper
Tel: 01460 73234
Fax: 01460 76105
Hours: 10am–5pm Mon–Sat, 2–5pm Sun. Closed Thurs
Nursery specialises in herbs, herbaceous perennials and conservatory plants. For catalogue send 4 x 1st class stamps.
Catalogue

Mallet Court Nursery
Curry Mallet, Taunton, Somerset TA3 6SY
Tel: 01823 480748
Fax: 01823 481009
Hours: 9am–5pm Mon–Fri. Weekends by appt
Trees and woody plants both rare and unusual. Catalogue - send large SAE stamped 31p.
Catalogue; Mail order

Margery Fish Plant Nursery
East Lambrook Manor, East Lambrook, South Petherton, Somerset TA13 5HL
Contact: Mark Stainer
Tel: 01460 240328
Fax: 01460 242344
Hours: 10am–5pm Mon–Sat Mar–Oct (Closed Sat Nov–Feb)
Specialist plant nursery offering wide range of herbaceous and perennial plants. National Geranium Collection. Most propagated from East Lambrook Manor Garden.
Catalogue; Mail order; Toilets

Mill Cottage Plants
The Mill, Henley Lane, Wookey, Somerset BA5 1AP
Contact: Mrs Sally Gregson
Tel/fax: 01749 676966
Hours: Wed only Mar–Sept or by appt
Small nursery specialising in unusual and traditional cottage garden perennials, ferns and grasses. Visitors please ring for directions. Catalogue 3 x 1st class stamps.
Catalogue; Mail order

Miniature Garden Company
Ilminster, Somerset TA19 9QZ
Catalogue

Monkton Elm Garden Centre
Monkton Heathfield, Taunton, Somerset TA2 8QN
Tel: 01823 412381
Fax: 01823 413910
Hours: 9.30am–5.30pm Mon–Sat, 11am–5pm Sun

Knowledgeable and helpful staff always available. Pet and aquatic department. Licenced restaurant. Shrubs, trees, bedding, patio, garden sheds, greenhouses, composts, pots, seeds, chemicals, gifts, furniture.
Toilets; Refreshments; Disabled access

Otters Court Heathers
Back Street, West Camel, Yeovil, Somerset BA22 7QF
Contact: Mrs D H Jones
Tel/fax: 01935 850285
Hours: 9am–5.30pm Wed–Sun. Closed Mon & Tues
We specialise in a wide range of species for all soils and offer a design service. Send 3 x 1st class stamps for catalogue.
Catalogue; Mail order

P M A Plant Specialities
Lower Mead, West Hatch, Taunton, Somerset TA3 5RN
Contact: Karan Junker
Tel: 01823 480774
Fax: 01823 481046
Hours: Strictly by appointment only
Specialist mail order grower of choice woody plants, many grafted including daphne, acer, magnolia, cornus, wisteria. Catalogue 5 x 2nd class stamps. Quality plants and personal service.
Catalogue; Mail order

Patricia Marrow
Kingsdon, Somerton, Somerset TA11 7LE
Tel/fax: 01935 840232
Hours: Dawn–dusk daily. Phone first

Scotts Nurseries (Merriott)
Merriot, Somerset TA16 5PL
Tel/fax: 01460 72306
Hours: 9am–5pm Mon–Sat, 10.30am–4.30pm Sun
Comprehensive garden centre and nursery with large acreage of ornamental & fruit trees and roses.
Catalogue; Mail order; Toilets

Shepton Nursery Garden
Old Wells Rd, Shepton Mallet, Somerset BA4 5XN
Tel/fax: 01749 343630
Hours: 9.30am–5pm Tues–Sat
Chaenomales and a good collection of herbaceous and alpines.
Catalogue

Somerset Wildlife Trust
Fyne Court, Broomfield, Bridgwater, Somerset TA5 2EQ
Tel: 01823 451587
Fax: 01823 451671
Email: soment@cix.compulink.co.uk
Hours: 9am–6pm Mon–Fri, 2–6pm Sat/Sun

Full range of native trees, shrubs, plants, wild flowers, herbs. Tree price list available. Bark chippings, peat-free compost, logs, gardening books.
Toilets; Refreshments; Disabled access

Triscombe Nurseries
West Bagborough, Taunton, Somerset
Tel/fax: 01984 618267
Hours: 9am–1pm 2–5.30pm Mon–Sat, 2–5.30pm Sun
Traditional nursery within a Victorian walled garden. Fantastic selection of plants grown at Triscombe by enthusiastic plantsmen. Specialities - herbaceous, rock plants and shrubs. Also a large range of climbers, ornamental trees and fruit. No catalogue or mail order. Turning off A358 to Triscombe.

West Someret Garden Centre
Mart Rd, Minehead, Somerset TA24 5BJ
Tel: 01643 703612
Fax: 01643 706470
Excellent selection of a wide range of trees and shrubs grown in our own nursery. Wheelchair available.
Catalogue; Toilets; Refreshments; Disabled access

Wyevale Garden Centre
Pen Elm, Norton Fitzwarren, Taunton, Somerset TA2 6PE
Tel: 01823 323777
Fax: 01823 323773
Wyevale offers a huge selection of plants, shrubs, gift ideas, furniture, BBQs and tools. Most centres have pet and aquatic departments and a restaurant. 0800 413213 for nearest stockist.

Y S J Seeds
Kingsfield Cons Nursery, Broadenham Lane, Winsham, Chard, Somerset TA20 4JF
Tel/fax: 01460 30070
Hours: Phone first
Catalogue; Mail order

Staffordshire

Barncroft Nurseries
Dunwood Lane, Longsdon, Nr Leek, Stoke on Trent, Staffordshire ST9 9QW
Contact: Mr S Warner
Tel/fax: 01538 384310
Hours: 9am–7pm or dusk if earlier Fri–Sun
Very large range of heathers, conifers, trees and shrubs, climbers and alpines. Display garden containing 400 heather varieties open to the public at weekends.
Toilets

Bretby Nurseries
Bretby Lane, Burton on Trent, Staffordshire DE15 0QS

Tel: 01283 703355
Fax: 01283 704035

Hours: *9am–5pm Mon–Sat, 10.30am–4.30pm Sun*

A wide range of plants, shrubs and trees available. The Bothy Tea Rooms have an excellent choice of snacks/meals. Well stocked gift shop also on site.
Toilets; Refreshments; Disabled access

Byrkley Park Centre
Rangemore, Burton on Trent, Staffordshire DE13 9RN

Tel: 01283 716467
Fax: 01283 716594

Hours: *9am–5pm Mon–Sat (9pm Fri), 10.30–4.30pm Sun*

Large garden centre set in the former Bass estate. Kitchen gardens with tea room and carvery, play area, farm animals, aquatics department, conservatories, craft shops.
Toilets; Refreshments; Disabled access

Cedarwood Lily Farm
134 Newpool Rd, Brownlees, Biddulph, Stoke on Trent, Staffordshire ST8 6NZ

Tel/fax: 01782 519154

Cottage Garden Roses
Woodland House, Stretton, Stafford, Staffordshire ST19 9LG

Tel/fax: 01785 840217

Hours: *9am–6pm daily*
Catalogue; Mail order

Fuchsia World
521 Pye Greed Rd, Hednesford, Cannock, Staffordshire WS12 4LP

Tel/fax: 01543 424564

Hours: *9am–5pm Mon–Sat. Closed Sun*

Jackson's Nurseries
Main Street, Clifton Campville, Nr Tamworth, Staffordshire B79 0AP

Tel/fax: 01827 373307

Hours: *10am–5pm Mon/Wed–Sat, Sun. Closed Tues*

Young fuchsia plants available March to June. SAE for list. Nursery 3 miles from Junction 11 M42/A42.

Planters Garden Centre
Woodlands Farm, Trinity Road, Whateley, Tamworth, Staffordshire B78 2EY

Tel: 01827 251511
Fax: 01827 262440

Hours: *9am–6pm Mon–Sat; 11am–5pm Sun*

80,000 sq ft of garden plants, sundries, seeds & bulbs and giftware. Large aquatic and bonsai shops. Coffee shop. Conservatories and greenhouses. Come and join us.
Toilets; Refreshments; Disabled access

Wyevale Garden Centre
Wolseley Bridge, Stafford, Staffordshire ST17 0YA

Tel: 01889 574884
Fax: 01889 574881

Wyevale offers a huge selection of plants, shrubs, gift ideas, furniture, BBQs and tools. Most centres have pet and aquatic departments and a restaurant. 0800 413213 for nearest stockist.

Suffolk

Brian Sulman Pelargoniums
54 Kingsway, Mildenhall, Bury St Edmunds, Suffolk IP28 7HR

Tel/fax: 01638 712297
Hours: *Phone first*
Catalogue; Mail order

Bypass Nurseries
Old London Rd, Capel St Mary, Suffolk IP9 2JR

Contact: Tessa Reeves
Tel: 01473 310604
Fax: 01473 311110

Hours: *9am–5.30pm Mon–Sat summer (5pm in winter), 10.30am–4.30pm Sun*

Bypass Nurseries make a special effort to offer the best quality plants and advice. If you require help on gardening matters, we'll be pleased to help.

Crown Asparagus
Marward House, Stock Corner Farm, Beck Row, Bury St Edmunds, Suffolk IP28 8DW

Contact: Trevor Sore
Tel: 01638 712779
Fax: 01638 712244

Asparagus crowns first year F1 varieties. Boonlim, Geynlim, Franklim, Venlim. Open pollenated connovers colossal.
Mail order

Denbeigh Heathers
All Saints Rd, Creeting St Mary, Ipswich, Suffolk IP6 8PJ

Tel/fax: 01449 711220
Hours: *Phone first*
Catalogue; Mail order

Fisks Clematis Nursery
Westleton, Saxmundham, Suffolk IP17

Tel/fax: 01728 648263

Leading clematis specialists. Call in and see us if you're in the area or for more information or advice please phone.
Catalogue; Mail order

Goldbrook Plants
Hoxne, Eye, Suffolk IP21 5AN

Contact: Sandra Bond
Tel/fax: 01379 668770

Hours: *10.30am–6pm Thur–Sun. Closed Jan, Chelsea & Hampton Court*

Specialist nursery. Over 400 hostas; over 100 hemerocallis. Shade perennials. Chelsea Gold Medal for hostas and perennials 1988-1996. Catalogue 4 x 1st class stamps.
Catalogue; Mail order

Gouldings Fuchsias
Link Lane, Bentley, Ipswich, Suffolk IP9 2DP

Contact: Mr E J Goulding
Tel/fax: 01473 310058

Hours: *10am–5pm Sat–Thurs 7 Jan–2 July 1995*

Fuchsia specialist. New and unusual introductions, Tryphylla, species, Encliandra, hardy, basket and bedding. Catalogue 3 x 1st class stamps.
Catalogue; Mail order

Home Meadows Nursery Ltd
Top Street, Martlesham, Woodbridge, Suffolk IP12 4RD

Tel/fax: 01394 382419

Hours: *8am–5pm Mon–Sat Closed Sun*
Catalogue; Mail order

Mickfield Fish & Watergarden Centre
Debenham Rd, Mickfield, Stowmarket, Suffolk IP14 5LP

Contact: Mick C Burch
Tel: 01449 711336
Fax: 01449 711018

Hours: *9am–5pm daily. Closed Xmas/Boxing Day & New Year*

Two acres ornamental watergardens and nursery. Specialists in established water and pondside plants. Pond and water feature design and construction and maintenance. Large retail section. Catalogue 50p.
Catalogue; Mail order; Refreshments; Disabled access

Mickfield Market Garden
The Poplars, Mickfield, Stowmarket, Suffolk IP14 5LH

Tel/fax: 01449 711576
Catalogue; Mail order

Mills Farm Plants
Norwich Rd, Mendlesham, Suffolk IP14 5NQ

Contact: Susan Russell
Tel/fax: 01449 76625

Hours: *9am–5.30pm daily except Tuesdays. Closed January*

Specialists in pinks, old roses and herbaceous perennials. Mail order for pinks and roses only. Send 5 x 2nd class stamps for catalogue.
Catalogue; Mail order

Nareys Garden Centre
Bury Rd, Stowmarket, Suffolk IP14 3QD

Tel/fax: 01449 612559

Hours: *8.30am–5.30pm Summer, 8.30am–5pm Winter*

Notcutts Nurseries
Woodbridge, Suffolk IP12 4AF

Tel: 01394 383344
Fax: 01394 385460

Hours: *9am–5.30pm Mon–Sat, 10am–5.30pm Sun*
Catalogue; Mail order

Paradise Centre
Twinstead Rd, Lamarsh, Nr Bures, Suffolk CO8 5EX

Tel/fax: 01787 269449

Hours: *10am–5pm Sat/Sun*

Growers of unusual plants. Open to the public admission £1.50 adults, £1 children. Landscaped gardens, pet paddock. Mail order catalogue 4 x 1st class stamps.
Catalogue; Mail order; Toilets; Refreshments

Park Green Nurseries
Wetheringsett, Stowmarket, Suffolk IP14 5QH

Contact: Richard T G Ford
Tel: 01728 860139
Fax: 01728 861277

Hours: *10am–5.30pm daily Mar–Sept*

A nursery specialising in hostas, ornamental grasses and a wide range of other hardy perennial plants.
Catalogue; Mail order; Toilets

Parkhouse Plants
Chantry Farm, Campsea Ashe, Woodbridge, Suffolk IP13 0PZ

Contact: Caroline Shove
Tel: 01728 747113
Fax: 01728 747725
Email: 101626.3273@compuserve.com

A specialist nursery offering an excellent range of rare and unusual hardy plants. For a mail order catalogue please send 3 x 1st class stamps.
Catalogue; Mail order; Toilets

Grow with us...

- Medal-winning market leaders in the South East • Comprehensive range of quality plants, products and gifts for all seasons • Gift Vouchers • Personal attention • Home delivery service • Refreshments at Woldingham, Chelsham and Godstone • Easy access and parking

Nag's Hall Nursey
Oxted Road, Godstone
01883 74 2275

Ivy Mill Nursery
Bletchingly Road, Godstone
01883 74 2665

Rosedene Nursery
Woldingham Road, Woldingham,
01883 65 3142

Chelsham Place
Limpsfield Road, Chelsham
01883 62 2340

Potash Nursery
Cow Green, Bacton,
Stowmarket, Suffolk IP14 4HJ
Tel/fax: 01449 781671

Rougham Hall Nurseries
A14, Rougham, Bury St Edmunds, Suffolk IP30 9LZ
Tel: 01359 270577
Fax: 01359 271149
Hours: 10am–4pm March–Oct

Please send 5 x 1st class stamps for our colour catalogue or send S.A.E. for a leaflet about us. Coach parties welcome.
Catalogue; Mail order

Siskin Plants
Davey Lane, Charsfield,
Woodbridge, Suffolk IP13 7QG
Contact: C J Wheeler
Tel/fax: 01473 37567
Hours: 10am–5pm Tues–Sat & Bank Hols. Closed Nov–Jan

Specialist growers of alpines and dwarf hebes (National Collection holders). Full mail order service.
Catalogue; Mail order

Smallscapes Nursery
3 Hendon Close, Stradishall, Newmarket, Suffolk CB8 9YF
Tel/fax: 01440 820336
Hours: By appointment only
Catalogue; Mail order

Walled Garden, The
Park Rd, Benhall, Saxmundham, Suffolk IP17 1JB
Tel/fax: 01728 602510
Hours: 9.30am–5pm Tues–Sun. Reduced Winter hours

Interesting perennials, shrubs and climbers for sale in a beautiful old walled garden. For price list send 1st class stamp.
Catalogue; Toilets; Disabled access

Woottens of Wenhaston
Blackheath, Wenhston, Halesworth, Suffolk IP19 9HD
Tel/fax: 01502 478258
Hours: 9.30am–5pm daily

Renowned nursery specialising in herbaceous plants. No mail order. Send 3 x 50p stamps for 130 page illustated catalogue.
Catalogue

Wyevale Garden Centre
Rougham Rd, Bury St Edmunds, Suffolk IP33 2RN
Tel: 01284 755818
Fax: 01284 706184

Wyevale offers a huge selection of plants, shrubs, gift ideas, furniture, BBQs and tools. Most centres have pet and aquatic departments and a restaurant. 0800 413213 for nearest stockist.

Wyevale Garden Centre
Newton Rd, Chilton, Sudbury, Suffolk CO10 0PZ
Tel: 01787 373628
Fax: 01787 373714

See Bury St Edmunds centre above.

Wyevale Garden Centre
Grundisburgh Rd, Woodbridge, Suffolk IP12 4UT
Tel: 01394 380022
Fax: 01394 380740

See Bury St Edmunds centre above.

Wyevale Shop
39 Westgate Street, Ipswich, Suffolk IP1 3DX
Tel/fax: 01473 288198
Hours: 9am–6pm Mon–Sat, 11am–5pm Sun

Wyevale Shop
4 Ipswich Street, Stowmarket, Suffolk IP14 1AQ
Tel/fax: 01449 613121
Hours: 9am–6pm Mon–Sat, 11am–5pm Sun

Surrey

Beechcroft Nursery
127 Reigate Rd, Ewell, Surrey KT17 3DE
Tel/fax: 0181 393 4265
Hours: 10am–5pm Summer, 10am–4pm Winter/Sun

Wholesale and retail nursery. Conifers, alpines, perennials, fuchsias and general bedding plant lines in season. Catalogue and specialist lists free with SAE. Conifer display garden.
Catalogue

Brian Hiley
25 Little Woodcote Estate, Wallington, Surrey SM5 4AU
Tel/fax: 0181 647 9679
Hours: 9am–5pm Wed–Sat
Catalogue; Mail order

Bromage & Young
St Marys Gardens, Worplesdon, Surrey GU3 3RS
Tel/fax: 01483 232893

Chelsham Place - Knights Garden Centre
Limpsfield Rd, Chelsham, Surrey CR6 9DZ
Tel: 01883 622340
Fax: 01883 627252
Hours: 8.30am–5.30pm Mon–Sat, 10.30am–4.30pm Sun

Knights' centres are easily accessible from Junction 6 of the M25, and all offer one-stop shopping for all gardening needs.
Toilets; Refreshments; Disabled access

Clay Lane Nursery
3 Clay Lane, South Nutfield, Redhill, Surrey RH1 4EG
Contact: K W Belton
Tel/fax: 01737 823307
Hours: 9am–5pm Tues–Sun Feb 1–Aug 31

Fuchsias - from the usual to the unusual including a large collection of fuchsia species. 2 x 1st class stamps for catalogue.
Catalogue

Constable Daffodils
45 Weydon Hill Rd, Farnham, Surrey GU9 8NX
Tel/fax: 01252 721062
Hours: Mail order only
Catalogue; Mail order

D N Bromage & Co Ltd
St Marys Gardens, Worplesdon, Guildford, Surrey GU3 3RS
Tel/fax: 01483 232893
Hours: 10am–4pm. Closed Wed

Bonsai trees from Japan and China. Pots, books and all accessories. Situated on the A322 next to the White Lion.
Catalogue; Mail order

Foliage Scented & Herb Plants
Walton Poor Cottage, Ranmore Common, Dorking, Surrey RH5 6SX
Tel/fax: 01483 282273
Hours: Wed–Sun & Bank Hols Mar–Sept

Garson Farm Garden Centre
Garson Farm, Winterdown Rd, Esher, Surrey KT10 8LS
Tel: 01372 460181
Fax: 01372 468757
Hours: 9am–5pm Mon–Sat, 11am–5pm Sun

One of the largest garden centres in North East Surrey, Garson Farm also has a charming farm shop and over 30 pick-your-own crops.
Toilets; Refreshments; Disabled access

Green Farm Plants
Bentley, Farnham, Surrey GU10 5JX
Tel/fax: 01420 23202
Hours: 10am–6pm Wed–Sat mid Mar–mid Oct
Catalogue

Herons Bonsai Ltd
Herons Bonsai Nursery, Wire Mill Lane, Newchapel, Lingfield, Surrey RH7 6HJ
Tel: 01342 832657
Fax: 01342 832025
Hours: 9am–6pm daily

Britain's premier bonsai nursery. Set in 7 acres with beautiful Japanese gardens and display areas. Besides bonsai we sell garden ornaments and rare Japanese plants.
Catalogue; Mail order

Hillier Garden Centre
London Rd, Windlesham, Surrey GU20 6LN
Tel/fax: 01344 23166
Hours: 9am–5.30pm Mon–Sat. 10.30am–4.30pm Sun

Good plant oriented garden centre.
Toilets

Hydon Nurseries
Clock Barn Lane, Hydon Heath, Nr Godalming, Surrey GU8 4AZ
Contact: Arthur George
Tel: 01483 860252
Fax: 01483 419937
Hours: 8am–5pm Mon–Sat flowering season. Closed for lunch

Specialist growers of rhododendrons and azaleas including Yakushimanum hybrids and large specimens in 25 acres. Open weekends throughout May. Illustrated catalogue £2 including postage inland.
Catalogue; Mail order

Ivy Mill Nursery - Knights Garden Centre
Bletchingly Road, Godstone, Surrey RH9 8DB

Tel/fax: 01883 742275

Knights' centres are easily accessible from Junction 6 of the M25, and all offer one-stop shopping for all gardening needs.

Knap Hill Nursery Ltd
Barrs Lane, Knaphill, Woking, Surrey GU21 2JW

Contact: Joy West
Tel: 01483 481214
Fax: 01483 797261

Hours: 9am–5pm Mon–Fri

Specialises in rhododendrons and azaleas. Established 1795. Catalogue 50p.
Catalogue; Mail order; Toilets; Refreshments

Lincluden Nursery
Bisley Green, Bisley, Woking, Surrey GU24 9EN

Tel: 01483 797005
Fax: 01483 474015

Merrist Wood College Plant Centre
Merrist Wood College, Worplesdon, Guildford, Surrey GU3 3PE

Tel: 01483 232424
Fax: 01483 236518

Hours: 9am–5pm Mon–Fri, 10.30am–5.30pm weekends in Spring and Summer

The plant centre on the college campus stocks a wide range of trees, shrubs, conifers, perennials, alpines, bedding and houseplants, mainly grown by our students. All are available at very reasonable prices. The college is situated opposite the White Lion public house in Worplesdon village, or off the A323 in Holly Lane. Please follow the signs to the plant centre when on the campus.
Catalogue; Toilets

Millais Nurseries
Crosswater Lane, Churt, Farnham, Surrey GU10 2JN

Contact: David Millais
Tel: 01252 792698
Fax: 01252 792526

Hours: Tues–Fri, Sats in March/April/May/Oct/Nov

650 different varieties of rhododendrons and azaleas. Choice new and old hybrids, rare species. 10 acre display garden open May. Mail order catalogue 5 x 2nd class stamps.
Catalogue; Mail order

Morden Hall Garden Centre - Capital Gardens
Morden Hall Road, Morden, Surrey SN4 5JD

Contact: Richard Dimmock
Tel: 0181 646 3002
Fax: 0181 687 0640

Hours: 9am–6pm Mon–Sat. 10am–4pm Sun

A picturesque setting in an old kitchen garden with tributary of River Wandle flowing through garden centre. Large car park and delivery service available.
Toilets; Refreshments; Disabled access

Nags Hall Nursery - Knights Garden Centre
Godstone Rd, Godstone, Surrey RH9 8DB

Tel: 01883 742275
Fax: 01883 744429

Hours: 8.30am–4.30pm Mon–Sat, 10.30am–4.30pm Sun

Knights' centres are easily accessible from Junction 6 of the M25, and all offer one-stop shopping for all gardening needs.
Toilets; Refreshments

Nettletons Nursery
Ivy Mill Lane, Godstone, Surrey RH9 8NF

Tel/fax: 01883 742426

Hours: 8.30am–1pm 2–5.30pm Mon–Sat, Suns Mar–Jun. Clsd Weds
Catalogue

Notcutts Garden Centre
Waterers Nurseries, 150 London Rd, Bagshot, Surrey GU19 5DG

Tel: 01276 72288
Fax: 01276 453570

Hours: 9am–5.30pm Mon–Sat, 10am–5.30pm Sun. Closes 5pm Winter

Our products are attractively displayed in comfortable surroundings to stimulate new ideas for home and garden. Restaurant and easy parking. Catalogue £4.50 inc. postage.
Catalogue; Toilets; Refreshments; Disabled access

Notcutts Garden Centre
Guildford Rd, Cranleigh, Surrey GU6 8LT

Tel/fax: 01483 274222

Hours: 9am–5.30pm Mon–Sat, 10am–5.30pm Sun. Closes 5pm Winter
Catalogue

Pantiles Nurseries Ltd
Almners Rd, Lyne Chertsey, Surrey KT16 0BJ

Tel/fax: 01932 872195/873313

Peters Plants & Garden Centre
Stoke Road, Stoke d'Abernon, Cobham, Surrey KT11 3PU

Tel: 01932 862530
Fax: 01932 866865

Hours: Daily. Sun 11am–5pm

High quality garden company providing comprehensive retail and contracting services. Excellent plants, aquatics, garden and conservatory furniture, gifts and coffee shop. Well worth a visit.
Toilets; Refreshments; Disabled access

Planta Vera
Farm Close, Lyne Crossing Road, Chertsey, Surrey KT16 0AT

Contact: Morris May
Tel/fax: 01932 563011

Hours: Last w/e in Summer, Bank Hols, or by appt

The world's largest viola collection (section Melanium) offering over 400 species and cultivars, many planted in display beds. Full colour mail order catalogue 4 x 1st class stamps. Five minutes from junction 11 on M25, 15 miles from Wisley.
Catalogue; Mail order; Toilets

R H S Garden Wisley Plant Centre
Woking, Surrey GU23 6QB

Tel/fax: 01483 211113

Hours: Mon–Sat. Sun RHS members only

One of the UK's most comprehensive plant centres with over 9,000 varieties for sale.

Rosedene Nursery - Knights Garden Centre
Woldingham Rd, Woldingham, Surrey CR3 7LA

Tel: 01883 653142
Fax: 01883 652221

Hours: 8am–5.30pm Mon–Sat, 10.30am–4.30pm Sun

Knights' centres are easily accessible from Junction 6 of the M25, and all offer one-stop shopping for all gardening needs.
Toilets; Refreshments; Disabled access

Rupert Bowlby
Rocky Lane, Gatton, Reigate, Surrey RH2 0TA

Tel/fax: 01737 642221

Hours: Sat & Sun afternoons Mar/Sept/Oct

Retail mail order flower bulbs, especially alliums. Catalogue 3 x 2nd class stamps.
Catalogue; Mail order

Secretts Garden Centre
Old Portsmouth Rd, Milford, Godalming, Surrey GU8 5HL

Tel: 01483 426633
Fax: 01483 426855

Hours: 9am–5.30pm Mon–Sat, 10am–5pm Sun & Bank Hols

Seymours Garden & Leisure Group
The Pit House, Ewell By-Pass, Surrey KT17 1PS

Contact: James Seymour
Tel: 0181 393 0111
Fax: 0181 393 0237

Hours: Open daily. Sun 10am–4pm

Landscape and leisure centre with aquatics, landscape supplies, garden leisure departments and coffee shop under same ownership as Peters Plants and Garden Centre at Cobham (01932 862530).
Toilets; Refreshments

Surrey Primroses
Merriewood, Sandy Lane, Milford, Godalming, Surrey GU8 5BJ

Tel/fax: 01483 416747

Primroses - older named cultivars. Send SAE for mail order descriptive catalogue.
Catalogue; Mail order

V H Humphrey - Iris Specialist
Westlees Farm, Logmore Lane, Westcott, Dorking, Surrey RH4 3JN

Contact: Mrs P J Brown
Tel: 01306 889827
Fax: 01306 889371

Hours: By appointment in bloom season

Large selection of irises - Bearded, Siberian, Pacific Coast, Japanese, species. Send A5 SAE or 3 x 1st class stamps for mail order catalogue.
Catalogue; Mail order

Vernon Geranium Nursery
Cuddington Way, Cheam, Sutton, Surrey SM2 7JB

Tel: 0181 393 7616
Fax: 0181 786 7437

Hours: 9.30am–5.30pm Mon–Sat, 10am–4pm Sun Feb–July

Europe's largest specialist mail order grower offering mail order rooted cuttings with larger pot grown plants available from the nursery.
Catalogue; Mail order; Toilets

Wisley Plant Centre
R H S Garden, Wisley, Woking, Surrey GU23 6QB

Tel/fax: 01483 211113
Hours: 10am–6.30pm Summer, 10am–5.30pm Winter
Refreshments

Sussex, East

Bond Garden Care Agencies
Royal Mires Nursery, London Rd, Lye Green, Crowborough, Sussex (E.) TN6 1UU
Tel: 01892 66850
Fax: 01892 863540
Hours: 9am–5pm daily

Specialists in summer and winter hanging baskets and bedding plants. Large range of shrubs, herbs, houseplants and cut flowers, seeds, birdtables, terracotta pots and stoneware.

Coghurst Nursery
Ivy House Lane, Near Three Oaks, Hastings, Sussex (E.) TN35 4NP
Tel/fax: 01424 756228
Hours: 12–4.30pm weekdays, 10am–4.30pm Sun. Closed Sats

Camellia specialists. Azaleas, rhododendrons, eucryphias, hydrangea. Over 300 varieties of camellia, including autumn flowering, many fragrant. Quality plants at reasonable prices. Catalogue 2 x 2nd class stamps.
Catalogue; Mail order

Glyndley Garden Centre
Hailsham Rd, Stone Cross, Sussex (E.) BN24 5BS
Tel: 01323 763240
Fax: 01323 760900
Hours: 8.30am–5pm Mon–Sat, 10am–4pm Sun

A busy garden centre with a comprehensive range of products, including trees, shrubs, garden furniture, stoneware, an aquatic section and a garden buildings showsite.
Toilets; Refreshments; Disabled access

Great Dixter Nurseries
Dixter Rd, Northiam, Sussex (E.) TN31 6PH
Tel: 01797 253160
Fax: 01797 252879
Hours: 9am–12.30pm & 1.30–5pm Mon–Fri, 9am–12am Sat all year

Christopher Lloyd's internationally renowned garden and nursery. Clematis specialist, unusual and rare shrubs, perennials. Mail order available. Catalogue: 3 x 1st class stamps. Expert advice.
Catalogue; Mail order; Toilets

Harvest Nurseries
Harvest Cottage, Boonshill Farm, Iden, Nr Rye, Sussex (E.) TN31 7QA
Contact: Mr D A Smith
Tel/fax: 0181 325 5420
Hours: Mail order only

Epiphyllums, plus a good, general range of cacti and succulents. Catalogue 2 x 1st class stamps.
Catalogue; Mail order

Just Roses
Beales Lane, Northiam, Nr Rye, Sussex (E.) TN31 6QY
Tel/fax: 01797 252355
Hours: 9am–5pm Tues–Fri, 10am–4pm Sat/Sun

Small family business specialist in all types of roses, carefully selected to offer the best of old and new varieties. Catalogue sent free on request.
Catalogue; Mail order

Kent Street Nurseries
Kent Street (A21), Sedlescombe, Sussex (E.) TN33 0SF
Contact: P Stapeley & D Downey
Tel/fax: 01424 751134
Hours: 9am–6pm daily

Very wide range of fuchsia & pelargoniums with bedding, shrubs, conifers etc all grown on site on our family run nursery.
Catalogue

Lime Cross Nursery
Herstmonceux, Hailsham, Sussex (E.) BN27 4RS
Tel: 01323 833229
Fax: 01323 833944
Hours: 8.30am–5pm daily

Specialist growers of over 300 varieties of ornamental conifers plus extensive range of shrubs, trees, herbaceous, alpines, ericas, roses etc.
Catalogue

Long Man Gardens
Lewes Rd, Wilmington, Polegate, Sussex (E.) BN26 5RS
Tel/fax: 01323 870816
Hours: 9am–12pm 2.30–5pm Tues–Sun. Phone first
Catalogue; Mail order

McBeans Orchids
Cooksbridge, Lewes, Sussex (E.) BN8 4PR
Tel: 01273 400228
Fax: 01273 401181
Hours: 10am–4pm daily

McBeans, world famous orchid growers, offer a wide range of orchids from our shop and by mail order. Catalogue free. Parking available. Conducted tours in season.
Catalogue; Mail order; Toilets

Merriments Gardens
Hawkhurst Rd, Hurst Green, Sussex (E.) TN19 4JP
Tel: 01580 860666
Fax: 01580 860324
Hours: 10am–5.30pm daily
Catalogue

Norman Bonsai
3 Westdene Drive, Brighton, Sussex (E.) BN1 5HE
Tel/fax: 01273 506476
Hours: 10.30am–6pm Mid Apr–Oct

Perryhill Nurseries
Hartfield, Sussex (E.) TN7 4JP
Tel: 01892 770377
Fax: 01892 770929
Hours: 9am–5pm Summer, 9am–4.30pm Winter

Wide range of perennials, roses, shrubs, trees, rhododendrons and azaleas. Catalogue £1.65 inc postage.
Catalogue

Stone Cross Nurseries
Rattle Rd, Stonecross, Pevensey, Sussex (E.) BN24 5EB
Tel: 01323 763250
Fax: 01323 460406
Hours: 8.30am–5.30pm weekdays, 10am–4pm Suns

Shrubs, trees, conifers, climbers, fruit, alpines, herbaceous, bedding plants. Garden sundries, stoneware, terracotta, fencing, aquatics. Nursery stock trade enquiries please phone 01323 763355.
Toilets

Usual & Unusual Plants
Onslow House, Magham Down, Hailsham, Sussex (E.) BN27 1PL
Contact: Jennie Maillard
Tel/fax: 01323 840967

Specialities herbaceous perennials especially less usual, choice varieties. Developing garden. Catalogue SAE + 30p. Erysimums, euphorbias, hardy geraniums, penstemons, salvia, grasses and lots more.
Catalogue

Wyevale Garden Centre
Newhaven Rd, Kingston, Lewes, Sussex (E.) BN7 3NE
Tel: 01273 473510
Fax: 01273 477135

Wyevale offers a huge selection of plants, shrubs, gift ideas, furniture, BBQs and tools. Most centres have pet and aquatic departments and a restaurant. 0800 413213 for nearest stockist.

Sussex, West

Allwood Bros
Mill Nursery, Hassocks, Sussex (W.) BN6 9NB
Contact: Mrs Susan James
Tel/fax: 01273 844229
Hours: 9am–4pm Mon–Fri (closed weekends)

Specialist growers of Alwoodii border pinks, perpetual and border carnation plants. Mail order catalogue available, please enclose two first class stamps. Plants delivered spring and autumn.
Catalogue; Mail order

Apuldram Roses
Apuldram Lane, Dell Quay, Chichester, Sussex (W.) PO20 7EF
Contact: Mrs D R Sawday
Tel: 01243 785769
Fax: 01243 536973
Hours: 9am–5pm Mon–Sat/10.30am–4.30pm Suns & Bank Hols

Specialist rose nursery with over 300 varieties. Rose garden and field to view. Catalogue sent on request. Garden centre stocking everything for growing perfect roses.
Catalogue; Mail order; Toilets; Refreshments; Disabled access

Architectural Plants
Cooks Farm, Nuthurst, Horsham, Sussex (W.) RH13 6LH
Tel: 01403 891772
Fax: 01403 891056
Hours: 9am–5pm Mon–Sat

Hardy but exotic looking evergreen trees and shrubs including palms, yuccas and bamboos. Please send 4 x 1st class stamps for catalogue.
Catalogue; Mail order; Toilets

Cheals Garden Centre
Horsham Rd, Crawley, Sussex (W.) RH11 8LY
Tel: 01293 522101
Fax: 01293 524255
Hours: 9am–5.30pm Mon–Sat, 10am–5.30pm Sun

Coombland Gardens
Coneyhurst, Billingshurst, Sussex (W.)
Tel/fax: 01403 741549
Hours: 2–4pm Weekdays or by appt

Cottage Garden Plants
Mytten Twitten, High Street, Cuckfield, Sussex (W.) RH17 5EN
Tel/fax: 01444 456067
Hours: Phone for details
Catalogue; Mail order

Croftway Nursery
Yapton Rd, Barnham, Bognor Regis, Sussex (W.) PO22 0BH
Tel/fax: 01243 552121
Hours: 9am–5.30pm daily. Closed Xmas & Weds from Nov–Feb
Catalogue; Mail order

Denmans Garden Plant Centre
Clock House, Denmans, Fontwell, Arundel, Sussex (W.) BN18 0SU
Contact: John Brookes
Tel: 01243 542808
Fax: 01243 544064
Hours: 9am–5pm daily inc Bank Hols

Plant centre stocking a wide range of unusual plants including shrubs and perennials, a fair proportion of which are propagated from the garden.
Refreshments

Fleur de Lys Conservatory Plants
The Lodge, Upperton Farm, Petworth, Sussex (W.) GU28 9BE
Contact: Lisa Rawley
Tel/fax: 01798 343742

Fleur de Lys grows, sells, advises upon and maintains collections of conservatory plants. Contact Lisa Rawley for the best advice before you plant. Visits by appointment only.
Catalogue

Geranium Nursery
Chapel Lane, West Wittering, Sussex (W.) PO20 8QG
Tel/fax: 0860 586256
Hours: 10am–5pm Good Fri–Mid June. Closed Mon ex Bank Hols

Hillier Garden Centre
Brighton Rd, Horsham, Sussex (W.) RH13 6QA
Tel/fax: 01403 210113
Hours: 9am–5.30pm Mon–Sat. 10.30am–4.30pm Sun

Good plant oriented garden centre.
Toilets; Refreshments

Holly Gate Cactus Nursery
Billingshurst Rd, Ashington, Sussex (W.) RH20 3BA
Contact: Mr T M Hewitt
Tel/fax: 01903 892930
Hours: 9am–5pm daily. Closed 25–26 Dec

Leading cactus and succulent grower. Thousands of tropical and desert plants for sale, very reasonable prices. Visit our nursery or send 4 x 2nd class stamps for catalogue.
Catalogue; Mail order; Toilets; Refreshments

Houghton Farm Plants
Houghton Farm, Arundel, Sussex (W.) BN18 9LW
Tel: 01798 831100
Fax: 01798 831138
Hours: 10am–5pm Mon–Fri, 2–5.30pm Sun Mar–Oct. Closed Sat
Catalogue; Mail order

Leonardslee Plants
Market Garden Cottage, Lower Beeding, Sussex (W.) RH13 6PP
Contact: Chris Loder
Tel: 01403 891412
Fax: 01403 891336
Hours: By appointment only

Rhododendrons for connoisseurs, expert staff to cater for your individual requirements. Availability list 2 x 1st class stamps. Mail order, collection preferred, export.
Catalogue; Mail order

Old Barn Nurseries
Dial Post (A24), Horsham, Sussex (W.) RH13 8NR
Tel: 01403 710000
Fax: 01403 710010
Hours: 9am–6pm Mon–Sat, 10.30am–4.30pm Sun. Old Barn Pantry daily 9am–6pm

Top quality trees, plants, shrubs. Beautiful silk plants and flowers. Garden sundries. Unusual gift ideas. Plus breakfast, lunch or tea in The Old Barn Pantry.
Toilets; Refreshments; Disabled access

Plants 'n' Gardens
at World of Water, Turners Hill Road, Worth, Crawley, Sussex (W.) RH10 4PE
Contact: Paul Grimmer
Tel/fax: 01293 882992
Hours: 9am–6pm Mon–Sat. 10.30am–4.30pm Sun

We stock both the usual and the unusual. Specimens of herbaceous plants and ornamental grasses. Wide range of sundries, composts, terracotta and statues.
Toilets

Principally Plants
37 Glebelands, Pulborough, Sussex (W.) RH20 2BZ
Tel: 01798 873454
Fax: 01789 874422

Roundstone Garden Centre
Roundstone Bypass, Angmering, Sussex (W.) BN16 4BD
Tel: 01903 776481
Fax: 01903 785433
Hours: 8.30am–5.30pm Summer & Weekends, 9am–5pm Winter
Catalogue; Refreshments

Vesutor Ltd
Marringdean Rd, Billingshurst, Sussex (W.) RH14 9EH
Tel: 01403 784028
Fax: 01403 785373
Hours: By appointment only

Specialist in airplants and bromeliads. Catalogue £1. Plant/price list 20p stamp. Mail order only.
Catalogue; Mail order

W E Th Ingwersen Ltd
Birch Farm Nursery, Gravetye, East Grinstead, Sussex (W.) RH19 4LE
Tel/fax: 01342 810236
Hours: 9am–4pm daily Mar–Sept. Closed Sat/Sun Oct–Feb

Alpines and hardy plants for all types of rock garden. Our nursery is just off the B2110. Send 2 x 1st class stamps for 1997 list.
Catalogue; Toilets

Wyevale Garden Centre
Copthorne Rd, Felbridge, Sussex (W.) RH19 2PD
Tel: 01342 328881
Fax: 01342 317184

Wyevale offers a huge selection of plants, shrubs, gift ideas, furniture, BBQs and tools. Most centres have pet and aquatic departments and a restaurant. 0800 413213 for nearest stockist.

Tyne & Wear

Birkheads Cottage Garden & Nursery
Birkheads Cottages, Nr Sunniside, Newcastle upon Tyne, Tyne & Wear NE16 5EL
Tel/fax: 01207 232262
Hours: 10am–5pm Sat/Sun & Bank Hols Apr–Sept

Plantswoman/garden designer's cottage garden (1½ acres) with hardy, uncommon plants. Nursery attached.
Toilets

Cowells Garden Centre
Main Rd, Woolsington, Newcastle upon Tyne, Tyne & Wear NE13 8BW
Tel: 0191 286 3403
Fax: 0191 271 2597
Hours: 9am–6pm Summer, 9am–5pm Winter

Peter Barratt's Garden Centre
Gosforth Park, Newcastle upon Tyne, Tyne & Wear NE3 5EN
Tel: 0191 236 7111
Fax: 0191 236 5496
Hours: 9am–5.30pm Mon–Sat (7pm Thurs), 10.30am–4.30pm Sun

Excellent range of quality plants, gifts, gardening sundries and garden furniture. Large pet and aquatic centre, bird of prey centre, plus 120 seater restaurant.
Toilets; Refreshments; Disabled access

Wyevale Garden Centre
The Peel Centre, District 10 (A1231), Washington, Tyne & Wear NE37 2PA
Tel: 0191 417 7777
Fax: 0191 415 4787

Wyevale offers a huge selection of plants, shrubs, gift ideas, furniture, BBQs and tools. Most centres have pet and aquatic departments and a restaurant. 0800 413213 for nearest stockist.

Warwickshire

Bernhards Rugby Garden & Leisure Centre
Bilton Rd, Rugby, Warwickshire CV22 7DT
Tel: 01788 811500
Fax: 01788 816803
Hours: 9.30am–6pm daily
Refreshments

Diana Hull – Species Pelargonium Specialist
Fog Cottages, 178 Lower Street, Hillmorton, Rugby, Warwickshire CV21 4NX
Tel/fax: 01788 536574
Hours: By appointment only – phone after 4pm

A collection of pelargonium species and primary hybrids, propagated to order. SAE for free listing. Cultural advice freely given.
Catalogue; Mail order

Fibrex Nurseries Ltd
Honeybourne Rd, Pebworth, Stratford upon Avon, Warwickshire CV37 8XT
Tel/fax: 01789 721162
Hours: 12–5pm Mon–Fri Jan–Mar/Sept–Nov. Clsd Mon/Fri Apr/Aug
Catalogue

Hillier Garden Centre
Henley Road, Mappleborough Green, Studley, Redditch, Warwickshire B80 7DR
Tel/fax: 01527 852266
Hours: 9am–5.30pm Mon–Sat. 10.30am–4.30pm Sun

Good plant oriented garden centre.
Toilets; Refreshments

John Beach (Nursery) Ltd
9 Grange Gardens, Wellesbourne, Warwickshire CV35 9RL
Contact: John Beach
Tel: 01789 840529
Fax: 01789 841520
Hours: 10am–5pm

Postal address only - nursery at Tanworth Lane, Henley-in-Arden. Clematis, climbers, fruit trees and plants, ornamental trees, bedding plants, organic young vegetable plants in season.
Catalogue; Mail order; Toilets

Millbern Geraniums
Pye Court, Willoughby, Nr Rugby, Warwickshire CV23 8BZ

Preston-Mafham Collection
2 Willoughby Close, Kings
Coughton, Alcester,
Warwickshire B49 5QJ
Tel/fax: 01789 762938
Hours: *10am–5.30pm Mon–Fri
Apr–Oct. Other times by appt*

Tollgate Cottage Nursery
Ladbrooke, Leamington Spa,
Warwickshire CV33 0BY
Tel/fax: 01926 814020
Hours: *11am–5pm Fri–Sun &
Bank Hols Easter–mid Oct*
Catalogue; Mail order

Woodfield Brothers
71 Townsend Rd, Tiddington,
Stratford upon Avon,
Warwickshire CV37 7DF
Tel/fax: 01789 205618

West Midlands

Ashwood Nurseries
Greensforge, Kingswinford,
Midlands (W.) DY6 0AE
Tel: 01384 401996
Fax: 01384 401108
Hours: *9am–6pm Mon–Sat,
9.30am–6pm Sun*
Catalogue; Mail order; Refreshments

David Austin Roses Ltd
Bowling Green Lane, Albrighton,
Wolverhampton, Midlands (W.)
WV7 3HB
Tel: 01902 373931
Fax: 01902 372142
Hours: *9am–5pm Mon–Fri,
10am–dusk Sat–Sun March,
9am–6pm Mar–Oct & Weekends*
Rose grower and hybridiser. Mail
order and plant centre selling
roses and other plants. Rose
gardens open to the public.
Catalogue; Mail order

H Woolman (Dorridge) Ltd
Grange Rd, Dorridge, Solihull,
Midlands (W.) B93 8QB
Contact: John Woolman
Tel: 01564 776283
Fax: 01564 770830
Hours: *8am–4pm Mon–Fri*
Chrysanthemums by mail order.
Send for free catalogue.
Catalogue; Mail order

Harefield Herbs
131 Harefield Rd, Coventry,
Midlands (W.) CV2 4BT
Tel/fax: 01203 450172
400 varieties of herbs and wild
flowers. Seeds and plants
available. Lavender hedging and
chamomile lawns are specialities.
Send 50p stamp for catalogue.
Mail order and trade only.
Catalogue; Mail order

Notcutts Garden Centre
Stratford Rd, Shirley, Solihull,
Midlands (W.) B90 4EN
Tel/fax: 0121 744 4501
Hours: *9am–6pm Mon–Sat,
10am–6pm Sun*
Catalogue; Refreshments

Plantables
The Old Orchard, Hall Lane,
Hurst Hill, Coseley, Midlands
(W.) WV14 9RJ
Tel/fax: 01902 662647
Hours: *Mail order only. Collection
by appt*
Catalogue; Mail order

R P P Alpines
6 Bentley Rd, Bushbury,
Wolverhampton, Midlands (W.)
WV10 8DZ
Tel/fax: 01902 784508
Catalogue

Roses & Shrubs Garden Centre
Newport Rd, Albrighton,
Midlands (W.) WV7 3EE
Tel: 01902 373233
Fax: 01902 372443
Hours: *9am–6pm Mon–Sat.
11am–5pm Sun (Winter
9am–5pm Mon–Fri)*
We are a gardener's garden centre
offering a wide range of plants
and garden sundries, including
some leisure products, floristry,
gift and aquatics.
Toilets; Refreshments

Wyevale Garden Centre
Hampton Rd, Eastcote, Hampton
in Arden, Solihull, Midlands (W.)
B92 0JJ
Tel: 01675 442031
Fax: 01675 443859
Wyevale offers a huge selection of
plants, shrubs, gift ideas,
furniture, BBQs and tools. Most
centres have pet and aquatic
departments and a restaurant.
0800 413213 for nearest stockist.

Wiltshire

Barters Plant Centre
High Street, Chapmanslade, Nr
Westbury, Wiltshire BA13 4AL
*Contact: Duncan Travers or Paul
Kempster*
Tel: 01373 832694
Fax: 01373 832677
Hours: *9am–5pm Mon–Sat,
10am–5pm Sun*
Barters grow their plants on a 15
acre nursery, specialising in
shrubs, trees, ferns, ground
covers, half hardy perennials.
Also carry roses, fruit, heathers etc.
Catalogue; Toilets

Botanic Nursery
Cottles Lane, Atworth,
Melksham, Wiltshire SN12 8NU
Tel/fax: 01225 706597
Hours: *10am–5pm daily. Closed
for lunch & all Jan*
Catalogue; Mail order

Bowood Garden Centre
Bowood Estate, Calne, Wiltshire
SN11 0LZ
Tel/fax: 01249 816828
Hours: *10am–6pm Apr–Oct,
10am–5pm Nov–Mar*
Catalogue

**Broadleas Gardens
Charitable Trust Ltd**
Devizes, Wiltshire SN10 5JQ
Contact: Lady Anne Cowdray
Tel/fax: 01380 722035
Hours: *2–6pm Wed/Thur/Sun
Apr–Oct*
A fascinating garden on
greensand where magnolias,
camellias, rhododendrons
flourish. Underplanted with
erythroniums, trilliums and
sanguinarias. Also roses and rare
perennials. Plants for sale. Adults
£2.50, children £1, groups £2.20.
Toilets; Refreshments

**Corsley Mill (Brigid
Quest-Ritson)**
Highfield House, Shrewton,
Salisbury, Wiltshire SP3 4BU
Hours: *By appointment only for
collection*
Catalogue; Mail order

Landford Trees
Landford Lodge, Landford,
Salisbury, Wiltshire SP5 2EH
Contact: C D Pilkington
Tel: 01794 390808
Fax: 01794 390037
Hours: *8am–5pm Mon–Fri*
Landford Trees is growing 600
varieties of quality trees,
ornamental fruit and forestry.
Specialities include acer, malus,
prunus, sorbus. Delivery at cost.
Free catalogue.
Catalogue; Toilets

Longhall Nursery
Stockton, Warminster, Wiltshire
BA12 0SE
Contact: Mr & Mrs Dooky
Tel/fax: 01985 850914
Hours: *9.30am–6pm Wed–Sun
Mar 22–Oct 1 or by appt*
A nursery specialising in beautiful
garden-worthy plants. A large
selection of chalk tolerant species
including eryngium, digitalis,
euphorbia and campanula.
Catalogue 3 x 1st class stamps.
Catalogue; Mail order

Mead Nursery
Brokerswood, Westbury,
Wiltshire BA13 4EG
Tel/fax: 01373 859990
Hours: *9am–5pm Wed–Sat &
Bank Hols, Noon–5pm Sun*
Growers of herbaceous
perennials, alpines and pot grown
bulbs for the retail market.
Colourful display gardens for
ideas. Descriptive catalogue 5 x
1st class stamps.
Catalogue

Parham Nursery
W & L Harley, The Sands,
Market Lavington, Devizes,
Wiltshire SN10 4QA
Tel/fax: 01380 813712
Hours: *9.30am–5pm Sat
Mar–Nov (Closed Aug) or by appt*
Catalogue; Mail order

Sherston Parva Nursery
Malmesbury Road, Sherston,
Wiltshire SN16 0NX
Contact: Martin Rea
Tel: 01666 841066
Fax: 01666 841132
Hours: *10am–5pm Mon–Sat,
12–5pm Sun Mar 1–Oct 31*
Specialist in clematis, climbers
and wall shrubs.
Catalogue; Mail order

Special Plants
Hill Farm Barn, Greenways Lane,
Cold Ashton, Chippenham,
Wiltshire SN14 8LA
Contact: Derry Watkins
Tel/fax: 01225 891686
Hours: *11am–5pm daily
Apr–Sept, Oct–Mar please ring.*
Unusual plants for conservatory,
terrace and garden. Many new
introductions from South Africa.
Catalogue 4 x 2nd class stamps.
Catalogue; Mail order; Toilets

Walter T Ware
Woodborough Garden Centre,
Nursery Farm, Woodborough,
Pewsey, Wiltshire SN9 5PF
Tel/fax: 01672 851249
Unusual plant centre in rural
surroundings offering year-round
interest, extensive patio range,
uncommon shrubs and
perennials, PYO daffodils, fruit,
vegetables and much more.
Toilets; Refreshments; Disabled access

West Kington Nurseries Ltd
West Kington, Chippenham,
Wiltshire SN14 7JG
Tel: 01249 782822
Fax: 01249 782953
Hours: *10am–5pm Wed–Sun*
Catalogue

Whitehall Garden Centre
Lacock, Chippenham, Wiltshire
SN15 2LZ
Tel: 01249 730204
Fax: 01249 730755
Hours: 9am–5.30pm daily (Summer 6pm). Sun 10.30am–4.30pm

A completely plant orientated garden centre offering a full range of garden sundries, expert help available.
Toilets; Refreshments; Disabled access

Yorkshire, East

Hardy Northern Trees
Ivy House, Church Lane, Hollym, Yorkshire (E.) HU19 2SQ
Tel/fax: 01964 612929

Swanland Nurseries
Beech Hill Rd, Swanland, Hull, Yorkshire (E.) HU14 3QY
Tel: 01482 633670
Fax: 01482 634064

White Cottage Alpines
Sunnyside Nurseries, Hornsea Road, Sigglesthorne, Yorkshire (E.) HU11 5QL
Contact: Mrs Sally Cummins
Tel/fax: 01964 542692
Hours: 10am–5pm Thurs–Sun. Closed Dec/Jan

Specialist nursery offering alpines and rockery plants for beginners or enthusiasts. Mail order by next day carrier. Send 4 x 1st class stamps for descriptive catalogue.
Catalogue; Mail order

Yorkshire, North

Ashfield Hellebores - Rarer Plants
Ashfield House, Austfield Lane, Monk Fryston, Leeds, Yorkshire (N.) LS25 5EH
Contact: Anne Watson
Tel/fax: 01977 682263
Hours: 10am–4pm Sun/Mon Feb 1 – June 1

Open Sundays, Mondays 1st February to 1st June for sales of helleboreus orientalis Ballard strain. 650 flowering plants available Spring 1997. SAE for list. No mail order.
Catalogue

Battersby Roses
1, Peartree Cottages, Battersby, Great Ayton, Yorkshire (N.) TS9 6LU
Tel/fax: 01642 723402

Specialist rose nursery on edge of North Yorkshire moors. Hardy plants at reasonable prices. Many exhibition and patio varieties. List free for SAE.
Catalogue; Mail order

Cruck Cottage Cacti
Cruck Cottage, Cliff Rd, Wrelton, Pickering, Yorkshire (N.) YO18 8PJ
Contact: Ronald Wood
Tel/fax: 01751 472042
Hours: 10am–5pm most days & weekends

Specialist nursery in a garden setting, selling small and mature specimens. Display area shows a large variety of plants. Sempervivums and a few choice houseplants. Phone first if coming from a distance.
Toilets

Daleside Nurseries
Ripon Rd, Killinghall, Harrogate, Yorkshire (N.) HG3 2AY
Tel: 01423 506450
Fax: 01423 527872
Hours: 9am–5pm Mon–Sat, 10am–12pm 1.30–4.30pm Sun

Gardenscape
Fairview, Smelthouses, Summerbridge, Harrogate, Yorkshire (N.) HG3 4DH
Contact: Michael D Myers
Tel/fax: 01423 780291
Hours: By appointment only

Horticultural advisory and design service. Hard and soft landscaping - free quotes. Small nursery specialising in rare and unusual woodland plants. Hand-carved stone ornaments.
Catalogue; Mail order

Hippopottering Nursery
Orchard House, Brackenhill Rd, East Lound Haxey, Doncaster, Yorkshire (N.) DN9 2LR
Tel/fax: 01427 752185
Hours: By appointment only
Catalogue; Mail order

Hutton Nurseries
The Estate Office, Hutton Wandersley, York, Yorkshire (N.) YO5 8LL
Hours: Not open to the public
Catalogue

J & D Marston
Cullag, Green Lane, Nafferton, Yorkshire (N.) YO25 0LF
Hours: 1.30–4.30pm Sat/Sun Apr–Sept. Other times by appt

Ferns for garden and greenhouse, a wide range of pot-grown plants. Catalogue £1.25.
Catalogue; Mail order

Kingswood Pelargoniums
113 Kingsway North, Clifton, York, Yorkshire (N.) YO3 6JH
Tel/fax: 01904 636785
Hours: By appointment only
Catalogue; Mail order

Norden Alpine Nursery
Hirst Rd, Carlton, Selby, Yorkshire (N.) DN14 9PX
Tel/fax: 01405 861348
Hours: Weekends & Bank Hols Mar–Sept

Nunnington Hall
Nunnington, York, Yorkshire (N.) YO6 5UY
Tel: 01439 748283
Fax: 01439 748284
Hours: 1.30–4.30pm Wed–Sun Apr–Oct

A riverside walled garden with its peacocks, orchard and clematis collection complements this mellow 17th century manor house, steeped in history.
Toilets; Refreshments; Disabled access

Orchard House Nursery
Orchard House, Wormald Green, Harrogate, Yorkshire (N.) HG3 3PX
Tel/fax: 01765 677541
Hours: 9am–5pm Mon–Sat, 2–5pm Sun

A specialist nursery growing hardy herbaceous perennials and ferns serving the retail and wholesale trade. SAE for catalogue A5 envelope please.
Catalogue; Toilets

Perry's Plants
River Gardens, Sleights, Whitby, Yorkshire (N.) YO21 1RR
Contact: Pat Perry
Tel/fax: 01947 810329
Hours: 10am–5pm late Mar – end Oct

Small family nursery specialising in uncommon hardy and container plants. Landscaped riverside gardens, licensed Victorian tearoom (home baking), putting. Free admission. Large S.A.E. for plant list.
Catalogue; Toilets; Refreshments

R V Roger Ltd
The Nurseries, Pickering, Yorkshire (N.) YO18 7HG
Contact: I M Roger
Tel: 01751 472226
Fax: 01751 476749
Hours: 9am–5pm Mon–Sat, 1–5pm Sun. Closed Dec 25–Jan 2

Growers of roses, fruit trees, bulbs, shrubs, heathers, conifers, ornamental trees and perennial plants on our 250 acre farm.
Catalogue; Mail order; Toilets

Rivendell Nursery
Menagerie Farm, Skipwith Rd, Escrick, York, Yorkshire (N.) YO4 6EH
Contact: Dave Fryer
Tel/fax: 01904 728690
Hours: 10am–5pm Suns. Other times by appt

One of the few completely organic nurseries. Over 15 years experience. 300 varieties shrubs, alpines, conifers, heathers. catalogue 2 x 1st class stamps. Landscaping and design.
Catalogue; Toilets

Rolawn (Turf Growers Ltd)
Elvington, York, Yorkshire (N.) YO4 5AR
Tel: 01904 608661
Fax: 01904 608272
Hours: 8.30am–5pm Mon–Fri in Spring & Autumn

Insist on Britain's finest turf - grown from the world's top cultivars to give a classic British lawn. Don't compromise. Buy genuine Rolawn turf.

Stillingfleet Lodge Nurseries
Stillingfleet, York, Yorkshire (N.) YO4 6HW
Contact: Vanessa Cook
Tel/fax: 01904 728506
Hours: 10am–4pm Tues/Wed Fri/Sat 1 Apr–18 Oct

Catalogue 5 x 1st class stamps. Hardy geraniums, grasses, silver foliage, clematis. Garden open Wednesday afternoons May, June.
Catalogue; Mail order

Strikes Garden Centre
York Rd, Knaresborough, Yorkshire (N.) HG5 0SP
Tel/fax: 01423 865351
Hours: 9am–7pm Mon–Sat, 10am–6pm Sun Summer(1hr less Winter)

Strikes Garden Centre
Boroughbridge Rd, Northallerton, Yorkshire (N.) DL7 8BN
Tel/fax: 01609 773694
Hours: As Strikes Knareborough

Strikes Garden Centre
Meadowfields, Stokesley, Yorkshire (N.) TS9 5HJ
Tel/fax: 01642 710419
Hours: As Strikes Knaresborough

Whitestone Gardens Ltd
Sutton, Thirsk, Yorkshire (N.) YO7 2PZ
Tel/fax: 01845 597467
Hours: Dawn–dusk daily. Fri by appt

Cacti and other succulent plants and associated books and sundries. 50 page illustrated catalogue 4 x 2nd class stamps.
Catalogue; Mail order; Toilets

Wyevale Garden Centre
Boroughbridge Rd, Poppleton, York, Yorkshire (N.) YO2 6QE
Tel: 01904 795920
Fax: 01904 794987

Wyevale offers a huge selection of plants, shrubs, gift ideas, furniture, BBQs and tools. Most centres have pet and aquatic departments and a restaurant. 0800 413213 for nearest stockist.

Wytherstone Nurseries
The Estate Office, Pockley, York, Yorkshire (N.) YO6 5TE
Tel/fax: 01439 70012
Hours: *10am–5pm Wed–Sun Apr–Oct*
Catalogue; Mail order

Yorkshire Garden World
Main Road, West Haddlesey, Nr Selby, Yorkshire (N.) YO8 8QA
Tel/fax: 01757 228279

Six acres of beautiful display and nursery gardens, everything grown organically. Small admission for gardens only. Gift shop & pets corner. Over 1,000 different varieties of plants for sale. Specialist growers of herbs, heathers and conifers. Garden design and landscaping service.
Catalogue; Mail order; Toilets; Refreshments; Disabled access

Yorkshire, South

Beeches Nursery
Prospect Farm, Misson Springs, Doncaster, Yorkshire (S.) DN10 6ET
Tel: 01302 772139
Fax: 01302 772823

Specialist geranium/pelargonium nursery supplying Zonal, Regal Fancy Leaf, Ivy Trailing, Scented Dwarf/Miniature, Angel, Stellar types. Mail order or collection. Catalogue available, send 2 x 1st class stamps.
Catalogue; Mail order; Toilets

Ferndale Nursery & Garden Centre
Dyche Lane, Coal Aston, Sheffield, Yorkshire (S.) S18 6AB
Tel/fax: 01246 412763
Hours: *9am–6pm Mon–Sat, 11am–5pm Sun*

We specialise in flowers, plants and gardens, with a wide range of stock. Coffee shop, Interflora florist, Blooms of Bressingham key stockist.
Toilets; Refreshments; Disabled access

Oscrofts Dahlias
Sprotborough Rd, Doncaster, Yorkshire (S.) DN5 8BE
Tel/fax: 01302 785026
Hours: *Dawn–dusk daily*
Catalogue; Mail order

Yorkshire, West

Armitages Garden Centre
Pennine Garden Centre, Huddersfield Rd, Shelley, Huddersfield, Yorkshire (W.) HD8 8LG
Tel: 01484 607248
Fax: 01484 608673
Hours: *9am–5.30pm daily. Closes 8pm in Summer*

Parking for over 200 cars. Coffee shop. Pet and aquatic centre. Teleflorist. Huge houseplant department. Trees and shrubs. HTA gift tokens. Access/Visa.
Toilets; Refreshments; Disabled access

Cravens Nursery
1 Foulds Terrace, Bingley, Yorkshire (W.) BD16 4LZ
Contact: Mr or Mrs Craven
Tel/fax: 01274 561412
Hours: *Thurs–Sun by appt*

The world's leading auricula specialists, also stocking a wide range of primula species, diathus and alpines. Specialist seeds.
Catalogue; Mail order

Greenslacks Nurseries
Ocot Lane, Scammonden, Huddersfield, Yorkshire (W.) HD3 3FR
Tel/fax: 01484 842584
Hours: *10am–4pm Mar–Oct. Closed Mon & Tues*

A huge range of alpine and rockery plants from the very rare to the common-place. Mail order our forte. Catalogue £1 in stamps please.
Catalogue; Mail order; Toilets

Mansell & Hatcher Ltd
Woodlands Drive, Rawdon, Leeds, Yorkshire (W.) LS19 6LQ
Tel/fax: 0113 2502016
Hours: *9am–5pm Mon–Fri*

We supply all types of orchid plants. Send 3 x 1st class stamps for our catalogue.
Catalogue; Mail order

Newton Hill Alpines
335 Leeds Rd, Wakefield, Yorkshire (W.) WF1 2JH
Contact: Mrs Sheena Vigors
Tel/fax: 01924 377056
Hours: *9am–5pm daily. Closed Thurs*

A small retail/wholesale nursery specialising in alpines, especially saxifrages. Catalogue 2 x 1st class stamps.
Catalogue

Springwood Pleiones
35 Heathfield, Leeds, Yorkshire (W.) LS16 7AB
Contact: Mr K Redshaw
Tel/fax: 0113 2611781
Hours: *By appointment only*

Mail order service supplying bulbs of the near-hardy orchid, pleione. Catalogue free on receipt of S.A.E.
Catalogue; Mail order

Stephen H Smith's Garden & Leisure
The Garden Centre, Pool Rd, Otley, Yorkshire (W.) LS21 1DY
Contact: Peter Scott
Tel: 01943 462195
Fax: 01943 850074
Hours: *9am–5.30pm Mon–Sat, 10am–4pm Suns*

Comprehensive range of outdoor plants, houseplants, garden furniture, BBQ, garden sundries, giftware and water garden. Key stockists for Blooms of Bressingham, Austin Roses, Hilliers Premier Plants.
Toilets; Refreshments; Disabled access

Stephen H Smith's Garden & Leisure
Aire Valley, Wilsden Road, Harden, Bingley, Yorkshire (W.) BD16 1BL
Tel: 01535 274653
Fax: 01535 274691
Hours: *9am–5.30pm*

Large garden centre with own production nurseries. Hillier and Blooms premier stockist. Massive range of everything for the garden - plants, garden furniture, giftware and aquatics.
Toilets; Refreshments

Stephen H Smith's Garden Centres
Wharfe Valley, Pool Road, Otley, Yorkshire (W.) LS21 1DY
Tel: 01943 462195
Fax: 01943 850074
Hours: *9am–5.30pm*

As Bingley centre above.
Toilets; Refreshments; Disabled access

Strikes Garden Centre
Red Hall Lane, Wellington Hill, Leeds, Yorkshire (W.) LS17 8NA
Tel/fax: 0113 2657839
Hours: *9am–7pm (10am–6pm Suns) Closes 1hr earlier in Winter*

Strikes Garden Centre
Selby Rd, Swillington Common, Leeds, Yorkshire (W.) LS15 4LQ
Tel/fax: 0113 2862981
Hours: *As Strikes above*
Refreshments

Totties Nursery
Greenhill Bank Rd, Totties, Holmfirth, Huddersfield, Yorkshire (W.) HD7 1UN
Tel: 01484 683363
Fax: 01484 688129
Hours: *9am–5pm daily*

Tropical Rain Forest
66 Castle Grove Avenue, Leeds, Yorkshire (W.) LS6 4BS
Tel/fax: 0113 2789810

N Ireland

Co Antrim

Carncairn Daffodils
Carncairn Grange, Broughshane, Ballymena, Co Antrim BT43 7HF
Contact: Mrs Kate Reade
Tel/fax: 01266 861216
Hours: *Phone for appointment*

Gold medal daffodil business breeding and supplying bulbs worldwide to exhibition and garden enthusiasts. Send 1st class stamp for free catalogue available from March 95.
Catalogue; Mail order

Colemans Nurseries
6 Old Ballyclare Rd, Templepatrick, Ballyclare, Co Antrim BT39 0BJ
Tel: 01849 432513
Fax: 01849 432151
Hours: *9am–8pm Mon–Sat, 12–5.30pm Sun Spring–less in Summer*
Catalogue; Mail order

Landscape Centre
24 Donegore Hill, Dunandry, Co Antrim BT41 2QU
Tel: 01849 432175
Fax: 01849 432051
Hours: *9am–5pm Mon–Sat, 2–5pm Sun (8pm Wed/Thur) Apr–Aug*
Refreshments

Co Down

Ballydorn Bulb Farm
Ballydorn Hill, Killinchy, Newtownards, Co Down BT23 6QB
Tel/fax: 01238 541250
Catalogue; Mail order

Ballyrogan Nurseries
The Grange, Ballyrogan, Newtownards, Co Down BT23 4SD
Contact: Gary Dunlop
Tel/fax: 01247 810451 eves
Hours: *By appointment for collection only*

Primarily a postal nursery supplying a range of unusual plants, mostly herbaceous, by division from open ground grown plants. Catalogue 2 x 1st class stamps.
Catalogue; Mail order

Daisy Hill Nurseries Ltd
Hospital Rd, Newry, Co Down
BT35 8PN
Tel/fax: 01693 62474
Hours: 9am–5pm Mon–Fri
Catalogue; Mail order

Dickson Nurseries Ltd
Milecross Rd, Newtownards,
Co Down BT23 4SS
Tel: 01247 812206
Fax: 01247 813366
Hours: 8am–5pm Mon–Thur
8am–1pm Fri. Closed for lunch
Catalogue; Mail order

Donaghadee Garden Centre
Stockbridge Rd, Donaghadee,
Co Down BT21 0PN
Tel: 01247 883603
Fax: 01247 883030
Hours: 9.30am–5.30pm
Mon–Sat, 12.30–5.30pm Sun

Quality garden centre specialising in plants. Cafe-restaurant. Children's play area. Large shop with gift area. Many plants on sale are produced at our own nursery.
Toilets; Refreshments; Disabled access

Lisdoonan Herbs
98 Belfast Rd, Saintfield,
Co Down BT24 7HF
Contact: Barbara Pilcher
Tel/fax: 01232 813624
Hours: Wed & Sat mornings, or by appt

Environmentally friendly nursery offering herbs, aromatics, unusual vegetables, salads. Occasional workshops and demonstrations on growing and using herbs, organic techniques. Catalogue 2 x 1st class stamps.
Catalogue

Seaforde Nursery
Seaforde, Downpatrick,
Co Down BT30 8PG
Contact: Patrick Forde
Tel: 01396 811225
Fax: 01396 811370
Hours: 10am–5pm Mon–Sat,
1–6pm Sun

A nursery containing a large selection of trees and shrubs. Also open - beautiful gardens, maze and tropical butterfly house.
Catalogue; Mail order; Toilets; Refreshments; Disabled access

Timpany Nurseries
77 Magheratimpany Rd,
Ballynahinch, Co Down BT24 8PA
Tel/fax: 01238 562812
Hours: 10am–6pm Mon–Sat.
Closed every Sun and Mon in Winter
Catalogue; Mail order

Co Tyrone

Baronscourt Nurseries
Abercorn Estates,
Newtownstewart, Co Tyrone
BT78 4EZ
Tel: 016626 61683
Fax: 016626 62059
Hours: 10am–5pm Mon–Sat,
2–5pm Sun
Refreshments

Scotland

Borders

Pringle Plants
Grooms Cottage, Kirklands,
Ancrum, Jedburgh, Borders
TD8 6UJ
Tel/fax: 01835 3354
Hours: By appointment only
Catalogue; Mail order

Central

Blairhoyle Nursery
East Lodge, Blairhoyle, Port of Menteith, Stirling, Central
FK8 3LF
Tel/fax: 01877 385669
Hours: 10am–5.30pm
Mon/Thurs/Fri/Sat, 12–5pm
Wed/Sun
Catalogue

Dumfries & Galloway

British Wild Plants
Stockerton Nursery,
Kirkudbright, Galloway, Dumfries
& Galloway DG6 4XS
Tel/fax: 01557 31226
Catalogue; Mail order

Cally Gardens
Gatehouse of Fleet, Castle
Douglas, Dumfries & Galloway
DG7 2DJ
Tel: 01557 814361
Fax: 01557 815029
Hours: 10am–5.30pm Sat/Sun
only Easter–Oct

We specialise in new and rare perennials; about 3,500 varieties growing in an 18th century walled garden. Please send 3 x 1st class stamps for the mail order catalogue.
Catalogue; Mail order; Toilets

Charter House Hardy Plant Nursery
2 Nunwood, Dumfries, Dumfries
& Galloway DG2 0HX
Tel/fax: 01387 720363
Hours: 10am–5pm Sat/Sun &
Scottish School Hols & by appt
Catalogue; Mail order

Craigieburn Garden
Graigieburn House, Moffat,
Dumfries & Galloway DG10 9LF
Contact: Bill Chudziak & Janet Wheatcroft
Tel/fax: 01683 221250
Hours: 10.30am–6pm Tues–Sun
& Bank Hols Good Friday–end Oct

Plantsman's garden in an idyllic setting. Formal borders, Autumn garden, woodland glade, rare and Himalayan plants. 2½ miles east of Moffat on A708 Selkirk road. Specialist plant nursery. Featured on C4 'Bloom'.
Catalogue; Toilets; Refreshments

J Tweedie Fruit Trees
Maryfield Road Nursery, Nr
Terregles, Dumfries, Dumfries &
Galloway DG2 9TH
Contact: John Tweedie
Tel/fax: 01387 720880
Hours: 9.30am–2pm Sats 21
Oct–Mar

A wide range of old and new varieties of top and soft fruit. Specialities rhubarb and gooseberries. SAE for mail order list.
Catalogue; Mail order

Whitehills Nurseries
Minnigaff, Newton Stewart,
Dumfries & Galloway DG8 6SL
Tel: 01671 402049
Fax: 01671 403106
Hours: 8.30am–4.30pm Mon–Fri.
Other times by appt
Catalogue; Mail order

Fife

Dalgety Bay Garden Centre
Western Approach Rd, Dalgety
Bay, Fife KY11 5XP
Tel/fax: 01383 823841

Hill of Tarvit House
Cupar, Fife KY15 5PD
Tel/fax: 01334 53127
Hours: 10am–sunset daily

Pennyacre Nurseries
Station Rd, Springfield, Fife KY15 5RU
Tel/fax: 01334 55852
Catalogue

Roots Garden Centre Ltd
1 Caskieberran Rd, Glenrothes,
Fife KY6 2NR
Contact: Jim McGregor
Tel: 01592 756407
Fax: 01592 758973
Hours: 8am–6pm Mon–Fri
(9am–5pm Winter), 9am–5.30pm
Sat, 10am–5.30pm Sun

Get your shoots from Roots. Trees, shrubs, houseplants, paving & fencing. Interflora. Landscaping. Open 7 days.
Catalogue; Mail order; Toilets; Refreshments

Grampian

Ben Reid & Co
Pinewood Park Nurseries,
Countesswells Rd, Aberdeen,
Grampian AB9 2QL
Tel: 01224 318744
Fax: 01224 310104
Hours: 9am–5pm Mon–Sat,
10am–5pm Sun
Catalogue; Mail order

Christie - Elite Nurseries Ltd
Freepost, Forres, Grampian
IV36 0TW
Contact: Richard Ogilvy
Tel: 01309 672633
Fax: 01309 676846
Hours: 8am–5pm Mon–Sat.
10am–5pm Sun

Growers and distributors via mail order from a free catalogue of woodland and ornamental trees, shrubs and plants. For service call Free 0500 626070.
Catalogue; Mail order

Findlay Clark (Aberdeen)
Hazeldene Rd, Hazlehead,
Aberdeen, Grampian AB9 8QU
Tel: 01224 318658
Fax: 01224 325029
Hours: 9am–5.30pm daily

Extensive ranges of shrubs, trees, climbers, herbaceous, alpines, heather, conifers and rhododendrons. Flowering and foliage plants, all types of gardening sundries, pet centre.

James Cocker & Sons
Whitemyres, Lang Stracht,
Aberdeen, Grampian AB9 2XH
Tel: 01224 313261
Fax: 01224 312531
Hours: 9am–5pm daily
Catalogue; Mail order; Refreshments

T & W Christie (Forres) Ltd
The Nurseries & Garden Centre, Forres, Moray, Grampian IV36 0EA
Tel: 01309 672633
Fax: 01309 676846
Hours: 8am–5pm Mon–Fri 8am–12pm Sat Closed Sun
Catalogue; Mail order

Tough Alpine Nursery
Westhaybogs, Tough, Alford, Grampian AB33 8DU
Contact: Fred or Monika Carrie
Tel: 019755 62783
Fax: 019755 63561
Hours: 10am–4pm Mon–Fri Feb–Oct
Alpine plant specialists offering a wide range of quality plants including many rare and unusual varieties. Send 3 x 2nd class stamps for descriptive catalogue.
Catalogue; Mail order

Highland

Abriachan Gardens & Nursery
Loch Ness Side, Inverness, Highland IV3 6LA
Tel/fax: 01463 861232
Hours: 9am–7pm or dusk daily Feb–Nov.
Outstanding garden and nursery. Over 2 acres. Garden walk. (Entry £1). Adjacent nursery. Hardy perennials a speciality. Mail order catalogue - 3 x 1st class stamps.
Catalogue; Mail order

Ardfearn Nursery
Bunchrew, Inverness, Highland IV3 6RH
Tel/fax: 01463 243250
Catalogue; Mail order

Arivegaig Nursery
Acharacle, Argyll, Highland PH36 4LE
Tel/fax: 01967 85331
Hours: 9am–5pm or dusk daily Easter–October
Catalogue; Mail order

Evelix Daffodils
Aird Asaig, Evelix, Dornoch, Sutherland, Highland IV25 3NG
Contact: D C Macarthur
Tel/fax: 01862 810715
Hours: By appointment only
New varieties of narcissi for garden display and exhibition. Catalogue 3 x 1st class stamps for mail order customers.
Catalogue; Mail order

Garden Cottage Nursery
Tournaig, Poolewe, Achnasheen, Ross-shire, Highland IV22 2LH
Tel/fax: 01445 86339
Hours: 12–7pm Mon–Sat Mar–Oct
Catalogue; Mail order

Highland Liliums
Kiltarlity, Beauly, Inverness, Highland IV4 7JQ
Tel/fax: 01463 74272
Hours: 9am–5pm Mon–Sat
Catalogue; Mail order

Jack Drake
Inshriach Alpine Nursery, Aviemore, Inverness-shire, Highland PH22 1QS
Tel: 01540 651287
Fax: 01540 651656
Hours: 9am–5pm Mon–Fri, 9am–4pm Sat. Closed Sun
Catalogue; Mail order

Lochside Alpine Nursery
Ulbster, Wick, Highland KW2 6AA
Tel/fax: 01955 85320
Hours: 10am–6pm daily Mar–Oct & by appt
Catalogue; Mail order

Poyntzfield Herb Nursery
Black Isle, Dingwall, Ross & Cromarty, Highland IV7 8LX
Contact: Duncan Ross
Tel/fax: 01381 610352
Hours: 1–5pm Mon–Sat March 1–Sept 30
Culinary, aromatic and especially medicinal herb plant and seed specialists, including native species and organic/biodynamic cultivations. Informative mail order catalogue 3 x 1st class stamps and SAE.
Catalogue; Mail order

Speyside Heather Garden & Visitor Centre
Skye of Curr, Dulnain Bridge, Inverness-shire, Highland PH26 3PA
Contact: David & Betty Lambie
Tel: 0147 9851359
Fax: 0147 9851396
Hours: 7 days except restricted hours in Winter – please enquire
Show garden, exhibition, gift shop, Clootie Dumpling restaurant. Plant sales, area with approx 300 varieties of heathers & conifers, shrubs, alpines etc.
Mail order; Toilets; Refreshments; Disabled access

Uzumara Orchids
9 Port Henderson, Gairloch, Highland IV21 2AS
Contact: Mrs Isobyl La Croix
Tel/fax: 01445 741228
Hours: By appointment only
African and Madagascar orchids, many rare, in cultivation. Young plants grown from seed. SAE for list. Mail order. We will export, with required documents.
Catalogue; Mail order

Lothian

Dobbie & Co Ltd - Melville Garden Centre
Melville Nursery, Lasswade, Midlothian, Lothian EH18 1AZ
Tel: 0131 663 1941
Fax: 0131 654 2548
Hours: 8.30am–5pm Mon–Fri, 9am–5pm Sat, 10am–5pm Sun
Refreshments

Plants from the Past
The Old House, 1 North Street, Belhaven, Dunbar, Lothian EH42 1NU
Tel/fax: 01368 63223
Hours: 1–5pm daily except Tues Mar–Sept
Catalogue; Mail order

Strathclyde

Ardencaple Garden Centre
Rhu Road Higher, Helensburgh, Strathclyde G84 8JT
Tel/fax: 01436 71202
Hours: 8.30am–5pm Mon–Fri, 9am–5pm Sat, 10am–5pm Sun

Ballagan Nursery & Garden Centre
Gartocharn Rd, Alexandria, Dumbartonshire, Strathclyde G83 8NB
Tel: 01389 752947
Fax: 01389 711288
Hours: 9am–6pm daily
A family run garden centre and nursery growing on site a wide range of shrubs, trees, alpines, heathers, herbaceous and bedding plants.

Barwinnock Herbs
Barrhill, Girvan, Ayrshire, Strathclyde KA26 0RB
Contact: Mon & Dave Holtom
Tel/fax: 01465 821338
Hours: 10am–9pm daily Apr–Oct
Culinary, medicinal and fragrant leafed plants. Many unusual varieties. Unique garden and nursery in remote exposed moorland. A collector's haven. Informative mail order catalogue 3 x 1st class stamps please.
Catalogue; Mail order

Chatelherault Garden Centre
Chatelherault Country Park, Ferniegair, Hamilton, Strathclyde ML3 7UE
Tel/fax: 01698 457700
Hours: 8.30am–5pm Mon–Fri, 9am–5pm Sat, 10am–5pm Sun

Duncans of Milngavie
Flower & Garden Centre, 101 Main Street, Milngavie, Glasgow, Strathclyde G62 6JJ
Tel: 0141 956 2377
Fax: 0141 956 6649
Hours: 8.30am–5.30pm Mon–Sat, 10am–5pm Sun
Refreshments

Findlay Clark (Dykebar)
Barrhead Road, Paisley, Strathclyde PA2 7AD
Tel: 0141 887 5422
Fax: 0141 887 5512
Hours: 9am–5.30pm daily
Extensive ranges of shrubs, trees, climbers, herbaceous, alpines, heathers, conifers and rhododendrons. Flowering and foliage plants, all types of gardening sundries. Gift area.
Toilets; Refreshments; Disabled access

Findlay Clark Garden Centre
Boclair Rd, Milngavie, Glasgow, Strathclyde G62 6EP
Tel: 01360 620712
Fax: 01360 622833
Hours: 9am–8pm Summer, 9am–6pm Winter
Extensive range of shrubs, trees, climbers, herbaceous, alpines, heathers, conifers and rhododendrons. Flowering and foliage house plants, all types of gardening sundries, pet centre.

Kinlochlaich House Gardens
Appin, Argyll, Strathclyde PA38 4BD
Contact: D E Hutchison MI Hort
Tel: 01631 730342
Fax: 01631 730482
Hours: 9.30am–5.30pm Mon–Sat, 10.30am–5.30pm Suns. Closed Suns Oct–Mar
Nursery garden centre specialising in garden plants in amazing variety. Probably the largest selection in Scotland! On A828 midway between Oban and Fort William.
Toilets

Westerwood Garden Centre
Eastfield Rd, Westerwood, Cumbernauld, Strathclyde G68 0EB
Tel/fax: 01236 736100

Tayside

Angus Heathers
10 Guthrie Street, Letham, Tayside DD8 2PS
Tel/fax: 01307 818504
Hours: 9am–5pm daily

Belwood Nurseries Ltd
Brigton of Ruthven, Meigle, Perthshire, Tayside PH12 8RQ

Tel: 01968 673621
Fax: 01968 678354

Hours: By appointment only (01828 640219)

Specialists in semi-mature trees and specimen shrubs. 300 acres field-grown and container grown. Availability list (unpriced) free. Delivery/planting can be arranged.

Bonhard Nursery
Scone, Perth, Tayside PH2 7PQ

Tel/fax: 01738 552791

An enchanting nursery set within a Victorian walled garden, with original glasshouses and vines. Large selection of plants and trees and an inviting tea room.
Toilets; Refreshments; Disabled access

Christie's Nursery
Downfield, Main Rd, Westmuir, Tayside DD8 5LP

Tel/fax: 01575 572977

Hours: 10am–5pm daily Mar–Oct

Findlay Clark (Kinross)
Turfhills, Kinross, Tayside KY13 7NQ

Tel: 01577 863327
Fax: 01577 863442

Hours: 9am–5.30pm daily

Extensive ranges of shrubs, trees, climbers, herbaceous, alpines, heathers, conifers and rhododendrons. Flowering and foliage plants, all types of gardening sundries. Gift area.
Toilets; Refreshments; Disabled access

Glendoick Gardens Ltd
Glendoick, Perth, Tayside PH2 7NS

Tel: 01738 86205/0738862
Fax: 01738 86735

Hours: 9am–5pm Winter, 9am–6pm Summer
Catalogue; Mail order

Perth Garden Centre
Crieff Rd, Perth, Tayside PH1 2NR

Tel/fax: 01738 38555

Western Isles

Island Plants
The Old Manse, Knock, Isle of Lewis, Western Isles PA86 0BW

Catalogue

Wales

Clwyd

Aberconwy Nursery
Graig, Glan Conwy, Colwyn Bay, Clwyd LL28 5TL

Hours: 10am–5pm Tues–Sun. Closed Mon except Bank Hols

Large range of choice and staple alpines, gentians, dwarf rhododendrons, shrubs, hellebores, penstemons etc, grown on a spectacular hillside site with views of the mountains.
Catalogue; Toilets

Dibleys Nurseries
Llanelidan, Ruthin, Clwyd LL15 2LG

Tel: 01978 790677
Fax: 01978 790668

Hours: 9am–5pm Apr–Oct

A very wide range of streptocarpus, begonias, coleus and gesneriads; available mail order, on nursery, at all major flower shows and through good garden centres.
Catalogue; Mail order

Eucalyptus Trees Ltd
Allt-y-Celyn, Carrog, Corwen, Clwyd LL21 9LD

Contact: Andrew McConnell
Tel/fax: 01490 430671

Hours: 9am–5pm Mon–Fri Mar–Oct

Specialist growers of proven cold hardy eucalyptus. 3000 trees growing on exposed hillside at 800ft. Mail order. Colour brochure 1st class stamp.
Catalogue; Mail order; Toilets

Halghton Nursery
C & K Jones, Whitchurch Rd, Halghton, Bangor on Dee, Clwyd SY14 7LX

Tel/fax: 01948 74685

Hours: 9am–5pm daily
Catalogue; Mail order

Paul Christian Rare Plants
PO Box 468, Wrexham, Clwyd LL13 9XR

Tel/fax: 01978 366399

Hours: Mail order only
Catalogue; Mail order

Dyfed

Cae Hir Gardens
Cae Hir, Cribyn, Lampeter, Dyfed SA48 7NG

Contact: Mr Wil Akkermans
Tel/fax: 01570 470839

Hours: Daily except Mon, but open Bank Hol Mons

Beautiful, peaceful 6 acre garden. Many unusual features. Red, yellow, blue and white subgardens. Bonsai room, stonework, ponds, views, bog-garden. Plants for sale. Featured on C4 television and on radio. Admission £2, OAP £1.50, children 50p.
Toilets; Refreshments

Cilwern Plants
Cilwern, Talley, LLandeilo, Dyfed SA19 7YH

Contact: Anne Knatchbull-Hugessen
Tel/fax: 01558 685526

Hours: 11am–6pm daily Mar–Oct. 11am–4pm Nov–Feb

In a beautiful Welsh valley this small nursery adjoins a large garden started 17 years ago on unpromising marshy scrubland. Garden open to visitors. Nursery offers wide variety of plants including many interesting perennials especially hardy geraniums and grasses.

Exotic Fuchsias
Pen-y-Banc Nurseries, Crwbin, Nr Pontyberem, Kidwelly, Dyfed SA17 5DP

Contact: Terry or Sue Evans
Tel/fax: 01269 870729

Hours: 9am–5pm Mon–Fri. 10am–5pm Sat/Sun Mar–Sept

Fuchsia specialists. 800 varieties, many new Dutch imports. Free colour catalogue on request. Wide range of species. Top grade mail order packaging.
Catalogue; Mail order

Llainwen Nursery
Llainwen Nebo, Bronwydd, Camarthen, Dyfed SA33 6HN

Tel/fax: 01267 253329

Catalogue

Wyevale Garden Centre
Myrtle Hill, Pensarn, Camarthen, Dyfed SA31 2NG

Tel: 01267 221363
Fax: 01267 221316

Wyevale offers a huge selection of plants, shrubs, gift ideas, furniture, BBQs and tools. Most centres have pet and aquatic departments and a restaurant. 0800 413213 for nearest stockist.

Wyevale Garden Centre
Bynea, Llanelli, Dyfed SA14 9SR

Tel: 01554 772189
Fax: 01554 777938

See Camarthen centre above.

Glamorgan, Mid

Wyevale Garden Centre
Village Farm Industrial Estate, Pyle, Glamorgan, Mid CF33 6NU

Tel: 01656 741443
Fax: 01656 744693

See Camarthen centre above.

Glamorgan, South

Wyevale Garden Centre
Newport Rd, Castleton, Cardiff, Glamorgan (S.) CF3 8UQ

Tel: 01633 680002
Fax: 01633 680769

See Camarthen centre above.

Glamorgan, West

Afan College Nursery
Twyn-yr-Hydd, Margham Park, Port Talbot, Glamorgan (W.) SA13 2TJ

Contact: Richard Coleman
Tel/fax: 01639 883712

Hours: 9am–4pm Mon–Fri March–Nov

Horticultural courses: NVQs in Amenity and Commercial Horticulture. Nursery specialising in herbaceous perennials plus shrub, bedding and pot plants, house plants and free advice.

Flower Kabin Nursery
192 Craig Rd, Godrergraig, Swansea, Glamorgan (W.) SA9 2NX

Contact: Mrs I Murdoch
Tel/fax: 01639 845030

Hours: By appointment. Mail order all year

Container-grown cottage garden plants by post. Bargain colllections our speciality. "How to create a Cottage Garden" booklet with advice and plans £2.
Catalogue

Wyevale Garden Centre
Valley Way, Swansea Enterprise Park, Morriston, Swansea, Glamorgan (W.) SA6 8QP

Tel: 01792 310052
Fax: 01792 310608

See Camarthen centre above.

Gwent

Penpergwm Plants
Penpergwm Lodge, Abergavenny, Gwent NP7 9AS

Contact: Mrs C Boyle
Tel/fax: 01873 840208

Hours: 2–6pm Thur/Fri/Sat Apr–Sept

Nursery selling unusual herbaceous perennials, some climbers and shrubs, all propagated on site. Open in conjunction with spacious garden of colour co-ordinated terraces and borders.
Catalogue; Toilets

Waterwheel Nursery
Bully Hole Bottom, Usk Rd, Shirenewton, Chepstow, Gwent NP6 6SA
Contact: Des & Charlotte Evans
Tel/fax: 01291 641577
Hours: 9am–6pm or dusk if earlier Mon–Sat
Interesting nursery with wide range of garden-worthy plants - trees to ground cover. Many unusual species and varieties. List and map for two stamps. Mail order in winter.
Catalogue; Mail order; Toilets

Wye Valley Herbs
The Nurtons, Tintern, Chepstow, Gwent NP6 7NX
Contact: Elsa or Adrian Wood
Tel/fax: 01291 689253
Hours: 10.30am–5pm daily Mar–Oct

On A466, 6 miles north of Old Severn Bridge. Garden of considerable botanical interest and nursery with wide range of herbaceous perennials, including comprehensive herb collection.
Catalogue

Gwynedd

Crug Farm Plants
Griffiths Crossing, Caernarfon, Gwynedd LL55 1TU
Tel/fax: 01248 670232
Hours: Feb 22–Sept 28 1997
Plantsman's garden, 2-3 acres grounds to country house. Featured on BBC TV Gardener's World.
Catalogue; Toilets

Fron Nursery
Fron Issa, Rhiwlas, Gwynedd SY10 7JH
Contact: Thoby Miller
Tel/fax: 01691 600605
Hours: By appointment – please phone
Specialising in hardy trees, shrubs and perennials grown from seed at high altitude.
Catalogue; Mail order

Gwydir Plants
Plas Muriau, Betws-y-coed, Gwynedd LL24 0HD
Contact: Mrs L Scharer
Tel: 01690 710201
Fax: 01690 750379
Hours: 10am–5.30pm Tues–Sat, 2pm–5.30pm Sun March–Oct
A small nursery growing a wide range of perennials, herbs, wild flowers and native trees in an old garden setting. List 2 x 1st class stamps.
Catalogue

Henllys Lodge Plants
Henllys Lodge, Beaumaris, Anglesey, Gwynedd LL58 8HU
Contact: Mrs E Lane
Tel/fax: 01248 810106
Hours: 11am–5pm daily except Tues & Thurs April–Oct
We specialise in hardy geraniums and herbaceous perennials. Garden open by appointment and on National Garden Days.
Catalogue; Toilets; Refreshments

Holland Arms Garden Centre
Gaerwen, Anglesey, Gwynedd LL60 6LA
Tel/fax: 01248 421655
Hours: 9am–5.30pm Mon–Sat, 10am–5.30pm Suns & Bank Hols
Refreshments

Ty'n Garreg Nurseries
Rhyd-y-Clafdy, Pwllheli, Gwynedd LL53 8PL
Contact: Nigel Pittard
Tel/fax: 01766 720868 (24hrs)
Hours: 1–5pm Thurs–Sun Apr–Aug inc.
We specialise in hardy herbaceous perennials, including an expanding range of agapanthus, aquilegia and campanula. SAE and 2 x 1st class stamps for catalogue and leaflet.
Catalogue; Mail order

Ty'r Orsaf Nursery
Maentrog Road Station, Ty Nant, Gellilydan, Gwynedd LL41 4RB
Tel/fax: 01768 590233
Hours: 10am–6pm Summer, 10am–dusk Winter
A small organic nursery, set in the Snowdonia National Park. Specialities: hardy herbaceous, shrubs and alpines including sidalceas, potentillas, astilbes, scabiosa, geraniums, campanulas etc.
Catalogue; Mail order

GARDENS TO VISIT

Channel Islands

Jersey

Jersey Lavender Ltd
Rue du Pont Marquet, St Brelade, Jersey JE3 8DS
Contact: David Christie
Tel: 01534 42933
Fax: 01534 45613
Hours: 10am–5pm Mon–Sat May 19–Sept 20

This is a working lavender farm with distillery, bottling room, shop and tea room. Beautiful garden with collections of lavenders, herbs, conifers and bamboos.
Catalogue; Mail order; Toilets; Refreshments; Disabled access

England

Avon

American Museum in Britain
Claverton Manor, Bath, Avon BA2 7BD
Contact: Susan Carter
Tel: 01225 460503
Fax: 01225 480726
Hours: Gardens 1–6pm, Museum 2–5pm (Closed Mondays)

Gardens include replica of George Washington's garden and an arboretum of North American trees and shrubs. Garden £2, museum £3.
Toilets; Refreshments

Badminton
Chipping Sodbury, Avon GL9 1DB
Tel/fax: 01454 218346
Hours: Phone for open days
Toilets; Refreshments; Disabled access

Bath Botanic Gardens
Royal Victoria Park, Bath, Avon
Tel: 01225 448433
Fax: 01225 480072
Hours: Dawn–dusk daily all year
Toilets; Disabled access

Claverton Manor
Bath, Avon BA2 7BD
Tel/fax: 01225 460503
Hours: 2–5pm daily except Mon Apr–Oct

National Collection of Passiflora
Lampley Rd, Kingston Seymour, Clevedon, Avon BS21 6XS
Tel: 01934 833350
Fax: 01934 877255
Hours: 9am–1pm 2pm–5pm Mon–Sat

Living plant collection of 220 species, exhibition of drawings, paintings, photographs. Selection of passiflora cards, books and products for sale.
Catalogue; Mail order

University of Bristol Botanic Garden
Bracken Hill, North Rd, Leigh Woods, Bristol, Avon BS8 3PF
Tel/fax: 0117 733682
Hours: 9am–5pm Mon–Fri all year
Toilets

Bedfordshire

Luton Hoo
The Mansion House, Luton, Bedfordshire LU1 3TQ
Tel: 01582 22955
Fax: 01582 34437
Hours: Easter–mid Oct Fri/Sat/Sun

Stately home - art collection open to the public plus gardens, herbaceous borders enclosed by yew hedged oblong, fountain in box edged area. Shurbs, trees and a secluded rock garden with a pet cemetery.
Toilets; Refreshments; Disabled access

Swiss Garden
Old Warden, Biggleswade, Bedfordshire
Contact: Sally Wileman
Tel/fax: 01234 228330
Hours: Ring for up to date information

A charming 19th century garden with plants from all over the world. Small admission charge, plants for sale. Refreshments available nearby. Ring for details.
Toilets; Disabled access

Woburn Abbey
Woburn, Bedfordshire MK43 0TP
Tel: 01525 290666
Fax: 01525 290271
Hours: Apr 20, May 24/25, Aug 17 (1997)

The private gardens and maze are open on certain days of the year under the National Gardens Scheme. Please ring for details.
Toilets; Refreshments; Disabled access

Wrest Park & Gardens
Silsoe, Luton, Bedfordshire MK45 4HS
Tel/fax: 01525 860152
Hours: 10am–6pm Sat/Sun & Bank Hols beg Apr–end Sept

18th century Great Garden, containing Orangery, Bath House, Pavilion and other monuments. Also west flower garden and kitchen garden with parterre in front of house.

Berkshire

Hollington Herb Garden
The Walled Garden, Hollington, Woolton Hill, Newbury, Berkshire RG20 9XT
Tel: 01635 253903
Fax: 01635 254990
Hours: Daily March–Sept. Winter – please phone.

One acre walled herb garden, with a series of fragrant rooms, with herbs, roses, climbers and box. Admission £1. Plants for sale in nursery.
Toilets; Refreshments

Old Rectory Garden
Burghfield, Berkshire RG3 3TH
Tel/fax: 01734 833200
Hours: 11am–4pm 2nd & last Wed in mth Feb–Oct

4½ acre plantsman's garden. 5 miles south-west of Reading. Spring bulbs, old fashioned roses, late flowering herbaceous borders. Plants for sale. Admission £2.
Toilets; Refreshments; Disabled access

Wyld Court Rainforest
Conservation Centre of the, World Land Trust, Hampstead Norreys, Nr Newbury, Berkshire RG16 0TN
Tel: 01635 200221
Fax: 01635 202440
Hours: 10am–5.30pm March–Oct. 10am–4.30pm Nov–Feb

Experience the sheer beauty of this unique conservation project. A collection of dramatic and endangered rare plant species and rainforest creatures thrive in tropical temperatures under 20,000 feet of glass. Visit the Vinery full of plants for sale, and the crafts and book shop. All profits go to the World Land Trust, a registered charity helping to preserve rainforests and other biologically important habitats from destruction. Every visitor to Wyld Court is helping to save a rainforest!
Toilets; Refreshments; Disabled access

Buckinghamshire

Chenies Manor
Chenies, Rickmansworth, Buckinghamshire WD3 6ER
Contact: Elizabeth Matthews
Tel/fax: 01494 762888
Hours: 2–5pm Wed/Thurs & Bank Hols Apr–Sept

Beautiful gardens and historic Tudor Manor house. Between Rickmansworth and Amersham (A404). Also charming and unusual topiary birds for sale. Varying sizes from £45.
Toilets; Refreshments; Disabled access

Chicheley Hall
Newport Pagnell, Buckinghamshire MK16 9JJ
Tel: 01234 391252
Fax: 01234 391388
Hours: 2.30–5pm Suns Apr/May/August
Toilets; Refreshments

Cliveden
Taplow, Maidenhead, Buckinghamshire SL6 0JA
Tel: 01628 605069
Fax: 01628 669461
Hours: 11am–6pm Mar–Oct, 11am–4pm Nov–Dec
Toilets; Refreshments; Disabled access

Stowe Landscape Gardens
Stowe, Buckingham, Buckinghamshire MK18 5EH
Tel/fax: 01280 822850
Hours: 10am–6pm Open intermittently. Phone first
Toilets; Refreshments

Waddesdon Manor
Aylesbury, Buckinghamshire HP18 0JH

The Daily Telegraph *Green Fingers* — **Gardens to Visit**

Waddesdon Manor Gardens contain a magnificent parterre, large parklands with mature trees, pleasant walks with splendid views, and a rococco-style aviary housing over 300 birds.
Toilets; Refreshments; Disabled access

West Wycombe Park
West Wycombe,
Buckinghamshire HP14 3AJ
Tel/fax: 01494 524411
Hours: *2–6pm Tues–Thurs Jun–Aug(Sun/Wed/Bnk Hls Apr/May)*

Cambridgeshire

Abbots Ripton Hall
Abbots Ripton, Cambridgeshire
Tel: 01487 3555
Fax: 01487 3545
Hours: *2–6pm Several days in May/June. Phone for details*
Toilets; Refreshments

Anglesey Abbey & Gardens
Lode, Cambridge,
Cambridgeshire CB5 9EJ
Tel/fax: 01223 811200
Hours: *11am–5.30pm Wed–Sun Apr–Oct*

National Trust. Historic garden and house with plant centre. Featuring the Fairhaven Collection of statuary within the 40 hectare landscape garden.
Toilets; Refreshments; Disabled access

Bury Farm
Meldreth, Roston,
Cambridgeshire SG8 6NT
Tel/fax: 01763 260475
Hours: *1st Sunday in the month April–July*
Toilets; Disabled access

Crossing House Garden
78 Meldreth Rd, Shepreth,
Royston, Cambridgeshire
SG8 6PS
Tel/fax: 01763 261071
Hours: *Dawn–dusk daily*

Railwayside quarter acre garden crammed with a multitude of plants in box edged beds. Pools of wildlife and three greenhouses add year round interest. Admission free.
Disabled access

Docwras Manor
Shepreth, Royston,
Cambridgeshire SG8 6PS
Tel/fax: 01763 261557
Hours: *10am–4pm Mon/Wed/Fri, 2–5pm 1st Sun in month Apr/Oct*

Admission to garden £1.50. Extra charge for special openings. Unusual plants with all year interest. Designed in enclosed areas of varying character.
Toilets; Disabled access

Hardwicke House
High Ditch Rd, Fen Ditton,
Cambridge, Cambridgeshire
CB5 8TF
Tel/fax: 01223 292246
Hours: *For NGS & by appt*

Original Terracotta Shop
8 Moorfield Road, Duxford Village, Cambridgeshire CB2 4PS
Tel/fax: 01223 832700
Hours: *Summer 9am–5.30pm 7 days/Winter (Jan–1 Mar) weekends 10am–5pm APT during week*

Secret gardens lie behind the Terracotta Shop. Around every corner new aspects and scents make you welcome. Lectures available to groups.
Catalogue; Disabled access

Padlock Croft
Padlock Rd, West Wratting,
Cambridgeshire CB1 5LS
Contact: Peter Lewis
Tel/fax: 01223 290383
Hours: *10am–6pm Wed–Sat mid Apr–mid Oct & by appt*

Plantsman's garden with National Collections of campanula, symphyandra, adenophora & platycodon; also other campanulaceae and rare, interesting plants. Donation box. List: 4 x 2nd class stamps.
Catalogue; Disabled access

Peckover House
North Brink, Wisbech,
Cambridgeshire PE13 1JR
Tel/fax: 01945 583463
Hours: *House & Garden Sun/Wed. Garden Sat/Mon/Tues 1 Apr–31 Oct*
Toilets; Refreshments; Disabled access

University Botanic Gardens
Cory Lodge, Bateman Street,
Cambridge, Cambridgeshire
CB2 1JF
Tel: 01223 336265
Fax: 01223 336278

Forty acres of fine gardens, with glasshouses, winter garden and lake, near the centre of Cambridge, incorporating nine National Collections, including geranium and fritillaria. Open daily 10am-4pm (winter) 10am-6pm (summer). Entrance in Bateman Street. Admission: £1.50/adult, £1.00/OAP/child. Tea room and Gift Shop in the Gilmour Building. Guided tours by the Friends of the Garden available by arrangement. Parties must pre-book. Enquiries (Monday-Friday) tel: 01223 336265
Toilets; Refreshments; Disabled access

Wimpole Hall
Arrington, Cambridgeshire
SG8 0BW
Contact: Philip Waites
Tel: 01223 207257
Fax: 01223 207838
Hours: *10.30am–5pm Tues/Wed/Thurs/Sat/Sun*

National Trust. Gardens charge £2. Recently restored Victorian parterre, formal Dutch garden with spring bulbs, hardy fuchsias and topiary. Pleasure grounds with specimen conifers, informal rose garden.
Toilets; Refreshments; Disabled access

Cheshire

Adlington Hall
Macclesfield, Cheshire SK10 4LF
Tel: 01625 829206
Fax: 01625 828756
Hours: *2–5.30pm Sun & Bank Hols 1 April–2 October*
Toilets; Refreshments

Arley Hall & Gardens
Great Budworth, Nr Northwich,
Cheshire CW9 6NA
Contact: Eric Ransome
Tel: 01565 777353
Fax: 01565 777465
Hours: *Mar 28–Sept 29 1997. Closed Mons*

Early Victorian hall set in 12 acres of magnificent gardens, containing rare and unusual plants and shrubs. Double herbaceous border, specialist plantsman's gardens. The Arley Garden Festival, 26-27 July 1997, offers unusual plants from specialist nurseries and individual garden accessory stalls. Restaurant, gift shop, disabled facilities, plant nursery, dogs on leash welcome.
Toilets; Refreshments; Disabled access

Bridgemere Garden World
Bridgemere, Nantwich, Cheshire
CW5 7QB
Hours: *10am–6pm (4pm in Winter) daily*
Toilets; Refreshments; Disabled access

Capesthorne Hall
Siddington, Macclesfield,
Cheshire SK11 9JY
Tel: 01625 861221
Fax: 01625 861619
Hours: *12–6pm Sun (Apr–Sept) & Wed (May/Aug/Sept)*
Toilets; Refreshments; Disabled access

Cholmondeley Castle Gardens
Malpas, Cheshire SY14 8AH
Tel: 01829 720383
Fax: 01829 720519
Hours: *12.30–5pm Wed/Thur Apr–beg Oct, 12–5.30pm Sun/Bk Hl*
Toilets; Refreshments; Disabled access

Dorfold Hall
Nantwich, Cheshire CW5 8LD
Tel: 01270 625245
Fax: 01270 628723
Hours: *2–5pm Tues & Bank Hols 1 Apr–31 Oct*
Toilets

Gawsworth Hall
Macclesfield, Cheshire SK11 9RN
Tel/fax: 01260 223456
Hours: *2–5pm daily Apr–Oct*

Granada Arboretum
Jodrell Bank, Lower Withington,
Macclesfield, Cheshire WA16 8QH
Tel: 01477 571339
Fax: 01477 511695
Hours: *10am–5.30pm Mid Mar–end Oct. Shorter hours in Winter*

Unique position beside the world famous Lovell radio telescope. Beautiful in any season. National Collections of Malus and Sorbus. Arborist's guided walks on set days.
Toilets; Refreshments; Disabled access

EXPERIENCE MAGIC IN OUR ARBORETUM

Tree species from all over the world. National Sorbus and Malus collections, endless interest and timeless tranquillity at Britain's gateway to the universe.

Jodrell Bank Arboretum
NR. MACCLESFIELD, CHESHIRE (OFF A535)
TEL: 01477 571339

Hare Hill Garden
Garden Lodge, Over Alderly, Macclesfield, Cheshire SK10 4QB

Tel/fax: 01625 828981

Hours: 10am–5pm Wed/Thur/Sat/Sun & Bank Hols Apr 1–Oct 31
Toilets

Jodrell Bank Arboretum
Lower Withington, Nr Macclesfield, Cheshire SK11 9DL

Tel: 01477 571339
Fax: 01477 571695

Hours: 10.30am–5.30pm daily March–Oct. 11am–4.30pm Sat/Sun Nov–Feb

This 35 acre arboretum is beautiful in any season with its National Collections of Malus and Sorbus and over 2,500 species of trees and shrubs.
Toilets; Refreshments; Disabled access

Little Moreton Hall
Congleton, Cheshire CW12 4SD

Contact: Stephen Adams
Tel/fax: 01260 272018

Hours: Wed–Sun Easter – Nov 2

National Trust. One acre garden surrounding best known timber framed moated house in Britain. Yew tunnel, herbaceous borders, 17th century vegetables and knot garden.
Toilets; Refreshments; Disabled access

Lyme Park
Disley, Cheshire SK12 2NX

Tel: 01663 762100
Fax: 01663 765035

Hours: 11am–4.45pm Mar–Oct (Otherwise 4pm). Closed Xmas
Toilets; Refreshments; Disabled access

Ness Botanic Gardens
Neston, South Wirral, Cheshire L64 4AY

Contact: Dr Joanna Sharples
Tel: 0151 353 0123
Fax: 0151 353 1004
Email: ejs@liverpool.ac.uk

Hours: 9.30am–dusk March–Oct, 9.30am–4pm Nov–Feb

64 acre garden with all year beauty and interest. Visitor centre, shop with plant sales and cosy tea rooms.
Catalogue; Toilets; Refreshments; Disabled access

Norton Priory Museum & Gardens
Tudor Rd, Manor Park, Runcorn, Cheshire WA7 1SX

Contact: John Budworth
Tel/fax: 01928 569895

30 acres of peaceful woodland gardens contain award-winning walled garden, museum, priory remains, sculpture, events and exhibitions, plants and produce. Adults £2.90, concessions £1.60.
Toilets; Refreshments; Disabled access

Penn
Macclesfield Rd, Alderley Edge, Cheshire SK9 2BT

Tel/fax: 01625 583334

Hours: 2–5pm Mid Apr–May
Toilets; Refreshments

Peover Hall
Over Peover, Knutsford, Cheshire

Hours: 2–4.30pm Mons & Thurs 1 May–30 Sept
Toilets; Disabled access

Stapeley Water Gardens Ltd
London Rd, Stapeley, Nantwich, Cheshire CW5 7LH

Tel: 01270 623868
Fax: 01270 624919

Hours: From 10am daily except Xmas Day

The world's largest water garden centre - for all your water garden needs, with The Palms Tropical Oasis, a huge tropical house and Yesteryear Museum.
Catalogue; Mail order; Toilets; Refreshments; Disabled access

Tatton Park Gardens
Tatton Park, Knutsford, Cheshire WA16 6QN

Tel: 01565 750780
Fax: 01565 650179

Hours: 10.30am–6pm Tues–Sun (Winter 11am–4pm)

Japanese, Italian, rose gardens and rhododendrons. Owner National Trust, managed by Chesire CC. Located off M6-J19 and M56-J7. Adults £2.50, children £1.50, family £7.50.
Toilets; Refreshments; Disabled access

Cleveland

Town Farm Nursery
Whitton Village, Stockton on Tees, Cleveland TS21 1LQ

Contact: David Baker
Tel/fax: 01740 631079

Hours: 10am–6pm Fri–Mon. Closed in Winter

Specialist nursery within easy reach of A1(M). Sheltered 3/4 acre garden with many unusual alpines, perennials and shrubs. Catalogue 3 x 1st class stamps. Open Friday to Monday. Closed mid-week except by previous appointment.
Catalogue; Mail order; Toilets

Co Durham

Barningham Park
Richmond, Co Durham DL11 7DW

Tel: 01833 21202
Fax: 01833 21298

Hours: 2–6pm Open days in May/June/Sept. Phone for details
Toilets; Refreshments

Eggleston Hall Gardens
Eggleston Hall, Barnard Castle, Co Durham DL12 0AG

Tel: 01833 650403
Fax: 01833 650378

Hours: 10am–5pm daily

An interesting walled garden with nurseries, specialising in the unusual. A stream and winding paths add interest. Organic produce in season.
Catalogue; Toilets; Disabled access

Elly Hill Herbs
Elly Hill house, Barmpton, Darlington, Co Durham DL1 3JF

Contact: Mrs Nina Pagan
Tel/fax: 01325 464682

Hours: 9.30am–12.30pm 4–5.30pm daily Mar–Oct. Phone first

Elly Hill Herbs has a herb display garden. Herb parties with talk or tour. Individuals welcome too. Herb products and plants for sale. Brochure available.
Catalogue

Houghall College
Durham City, Co Durham DH1 3SG

Tel: 0191 386 1351
Fax: 0191 386 0419

Hours: Gardens open 12.30–4.30pm daily except Xmas Day

Services provided - extensive gardens, special open days, gardening advice, soil testing, wide range of short and full-time courses. For further details telephone 0191 3861351.
Disabled access

Raby Castle
Staindrop, Barnard Castle, Co Durham

Tel/fax: 01833 660202

Hours: 1–5.30pm Sun–Fri Jul–Sept. Open other times – phone
Toilets; Refreshments

Rookhope Nurseries
Rookhope, Weardale, Co Durham DL13 2DD

Tel/fax: 01388 517272

Hours: 9am–4pm daily mid Mar–end Sept

The highest nursery in Northumbria (1100ft). Spectacular scenery. Mature garden with wide use of coloured foliage (free). We specialise in growing only the very best quality alpines and perennials, with many unusual varieties. Catalogue 3 x 1st class stamps.
Catalogue; Mail order

University of Durham Botanic Garden
Hollingside Lane, Durham City, Co Durham DH1 3TN

Tel: 0191 374 2671
Fax: 0191 374 7478

Hours: 10am–5pm 1 Apr–31 Oct
Toilets; Refreshments; Disabled access

Westholme Hall
Winston, Darlington, Co Durham DL2 3QL

Tel/fax: 01325 730442

Hours: 2–6pm Open days in May/July/Aug. Phone for details
Toilets; Refreshments; Disabled access

Cornwall

Antony Woodland Garden
Antony House, Torpoint, Cornwall PL11 2QA

Tel/fax: 01752 812364

Hours: 11am–5.30pm daily mid Mar–end Oct
Toilets; Refreshments

Bosvigo
Bosvigo House, Bosvigo Lane, Truro, Cornwall TR1 3NH

Tel/fax: 01872 275774

Hours: 11am–6pm Wed–Sat Mar–Sept

A series of colour-themed enclosed and walled gardens surrounding Georgian house. Planted mostly with herbaceous material and has most colour in the Summer months.
Catalogue; Toilets

Caerhays Castle
Gorran, St Austell, Cornwall PL26 6LY

Tel: 01872 501310
Fax: 01872 501870

Hours: 11am–4pm Mon–Fri end Mar–June & charity open days
Toilets; Refreshments

Carwinion
Mawnan Smith, Falmouth, Cornwall TR11 5JA

Tel/fax: 01326 250258

Hours: 10am–5.30pm daily or by appt
Toilets; Refreshments

Chyverton
Zelah, Truro, Cornwall TR4 9HD

Tel/fax: 01872 540324

Hours: By appointment Mar–June

The Daily Telegraph *Green Fingers* — **Gardens to Visit**

Cotehele
St Dominick, Saltash, Cornwall PL12 6TA

Tel/fax: 01579 50434

Hours: *Garden open dawn–dusk all year*

National Trust. Sheltered valley with medieval pond and dovecote. Victorian garden. Herbaceous borders, cutting garden. Many tender wall plants, trees and shrubs. Daffodil meadow, orchards, plant sales.
Toilets; Refreshments; Disabled access

Ken Caro
Bicton, Pensilva, Liskeard, Cornwall PL14 5RF

Tel/fax: 01579 62446

Hours: *2–6pm Mon–Wed & Sun Apr–June Tues/Wed in June*

Lanhydrock Gardens
Lanhydrock House, Bodmin, Cornwall PL30 5AD

Contact: Mrs A Marchington
Tel: 01208 73320
Fax: 01208 74084

Hours: *11am–6pm Apr 1–Oct 31*

National Trust. The 22 acre garden is set on a hillside overlooking the Fowey Valley. There is a formal area near the house and a higher garden planted with rare shrubs and trees. Magnolias and rhododendrons are particular features. In addition there are almost 1,000 acres of park and woodland with many lovely walks. Admission £3 adults, £1.50 children.
Toilets; Refreshments

Lost Gardens of Heligan
Pentewan, St Austell, Cornwall PL26 6EN

Contact: Colin Howlett
Tel: 01726 844157
Fax: 01726 843023

Hours: *10am–6pm daily (except Xmas Day)*

Europe's largest garden restoration - 57 acres of working Victorian gardens including: five walled gardens, kitchen garden, Italian garden, grotto and twenty-two acre jungle garden.
Mail order; Toilets; Refreshments; Disabled access

Mount Edgcumbe Gardens
Cremyll, Torpoint, Cornwall PL10 1HZ

Tel: 01752 822236
Fax: 01752 822199

Hours: *Dawn–dusk all year*
Toilets; Refreshments; Disabled access

Old Mill Herbary
Helland Bridge, Bodmin, Cornwall PL30 4QR

Contact: Mrs Brenda Whurr
Tel/fax: 01208 841206

Hours: *10am–5pm Mon–Sun. Closed Wed. Apr–Oct 19th*

5 acres semi-wild organic garden. Culinary, medicinal, aromatic herbs, arboretum, climbers, water garden around Greek fertility theme, in Camel Valley. Adults £2.50, children £1.

Pencarrow
Washaway, Bodmin, Cornwall PL30 3AG

Tel/fax: 01208 84369

Hours: *1.30–5pm Sun–Thurs Apr–Oct, 11am–5pm Jun–Sept*
Toilets; Refreshments; Disabled access

Porthpean House Gardens
Porthpean, St Austell, Cornwall PL26 6AX

Tel/fax: 01726 72888

Hours: *Nursery open 9am–5pm Mon–Fri*

Seaside garden with over 200 varieties of camellia. 2 miles south east of St Austell. View by appointment. Nursery open daily.
Catalogue

St Michaels Mount
Marazion, Cornwall TR17 0HT

Tel: 01736 710507
Fax: 01736 711544

Hours: *10.30am–5.30pm Mon–Fri Apr 1–May 31 & some Weekends*
Toilets; Refreshments

Trebah Garden
Mawnan Smith, Nr Falmouth, Cornwall TR11 5JZ

Contact: Barbara Pascoe
Tel: 01326 250448
Fax: 01326 250781

Hours: *10.30am–5pm (last admission) all year*

Magnificent 25 acre sub-tropical ravine garden running down to private beach on Helford River. Plant sales, gift shop, restaurant. Admission: adults £3, children/disabled £1.
Toilets; Refreshments; Disabled access

Tregrehan Garden
Tregrehan House, Par, Cornwall PL24 2SJ

Tel: 01726 812438
Fax: 01726 814389

Hours: *Mid–March – end June (Exc. Easter Sun) by appt*

Large garden on A390 1 mile west of St Blazey. Also nursery (speciality camellia cuttings) open all year by appointment.
Toilets; Refreshments; Disabled access

Trelissick (Feock)
Feock, Truro, Cornwall TR3 6QL

Contact: R C Taylor
Tel/fax: 01827 862090

Hours: *10.30am–5.30pm Mon–Sat, 12.30–5.30pm Sun Mar–Oct*

25 acre garden in parkland setting. Rhododendrons, hydrangeas and azaleas, as well as exotic flora make the garden an all-season attraction.
Toilets; Refreshments; Disabled access

Trengwainton Gardens
Madron, Penzance, Cornwall TR20 8RZ

Tel/fax: 01736 63148

Hours: *10.30am–5.30pm Wed–Sat & Bank Hols Mar–Oct*
Toilets; Refreshments; Disabled access

Trerice
Kestle Mill, Newquay, Cornwall TR8 4PG

Contact: Brian Kirby
Tel: 01637 875404
Fax: 01637 879300

Hours: *11am–5.30pm (5pm in Oct) March 30–Oct 31*

A delightful summer garden with unusual plants. Situated 3 miles S.E. of Newquay via A392 and A3058. Admission: Adult £3.60. Tearoom. Shop.
Toilets; Refreshments; Disabled access

Tresco Abbey
Isles of Scilly, Cornwall TR24 0QQ

Tel: 01720 22849
Fax: 01720 22807

Hours: *10am–4pm daily*
Toilets; Refreshments; Disabled access

Trewithen
Grampound Rd, Truro, Cornwall TR2 4DD

Tel: 01726 882763
Fax: 01726 882301

Hours: *10am–4.30pm Mon–Sat Mar–Sept*
Toilets; Refreshments; Disabled access

Cumbria

Acorn Bank Garden
Acorn Bank, Temple Sowerby, Penrith, Cumbria CA10 1SP

Tel/fax: 017683 61893/61281

Hours: *10am–5.30pm Apr–Oct*
Toilets; Refreshments; Disabled access

Brantwood Trust
Coniston, Cumbria LA21 8AD

Tel: 015394 41396
Fax: 015394 41263

Hours: *Open throughout the year*

John Ruskin's home 1872-1900. The Lakeland landscape garden. Active and imaginative renovation of this unique garden of ideas. Lakeside and woodland gardens and walks. Fern and European alpine collections. Museum, restaurant and fine craft gallery. Plants for sale. House and gardens £3.50. Gardens only £1. Access by road or by ferry from Coniston.
Toilets; Refreshments; Disabled access

Dalemain Historic House & Gardens
Daleman, Penrith, Cumbria CA11 0HB

Contact: Mr B McDonald
Tel: 017684 86450
Fax: 017684 86223

Hours: *11.15am–5pm Sun–Thurs Easter–early Oct*

Medieval, Tudor and early Georgian house. Historic gardens with many rare plants and old fashioned roses. Licensed reataurant and tea room. Plant sales.
Toilets; Refreshments; Disabled access

Graythwaite Hall
Ulverston, Hawkshead, Cumbria LA12 8BA

Tel: 015395 31248
Fax: 015395 30060

Hours: *10am–6pm daily Apr 1–June 30*
Toilets

Holehird Gardens
Patterdale Rd, Windermere, Cumbria LA23 1NP

Tel/fax: 015394 46008

Hours: *Dawn–dusk all year*

The gardens contain many fine and unusual plants, also the National Collections of astilbes, hydrangeas and polystichum ferns. Entry is free. Guide books etc. available.
Toilets

Holker Hall
Cark-in-Cartmel, Grange over Sands, Cumbria LA11 7PL

Tel: 015395 58328
Fax: 015395 58776

Hours: *10am–6pm Fri–Sun 2 Apr–31 Oct. Last admission 4.30pm*

Inspirational and magical 25 acre formal and woodland gardens with water features. "Amongst the best in the world..."(GGG '96). Many rare shrubs and trees.
Toilets; Refreshments; Disabled access

Levens Hall
Kendal, Cumbria LA8 0PD
Tel/fax: 015395 60321
Hours: 11am–5pm Sun–Thurs Apr–Sept

World famous topiary gardens circa 1694 beautifully maintained in original design. Admission (gardens only) Adults £2.90 Over 65 £2.70 Children £1.80.
Toilets; Refreshments; Disabled access

Lingholm Gardens
Lingholm, Keswick, Cumbria CA12 5UA
Tel/fax: 017687 72003
Hours: 10am–5pm daily 1 Apr–31 Oct

Impressive formal and woodland gardens. Rhododendrons, azaleas, Himalayan blue poppies, primulas, gentians. Magnificent trees and shrubs, spring daffodils, autumn colours. Plant centre. Tearoom.
Refreshments

Rydal Mount
Ambleside, Cumbria LA22 9LU
Tel/fax: 015394 33002
Hours: 9.30am–5pm Mar–Oct, 10am–4pm Nov–Feb
Toilets

Derbyshire

Calke Abbey
Ticknall, Derbyshire DE7 1LE
Tel/fax: 01332 863822
Hours: 11am–5pm Wed–Sat
Toilets; Refreshments; Disabled access

Chatsworth
Bakewell, Derbyshire DE4 1PP
Tel: 01246 582204
Fax: 01246 583536
Hours: 11am–5pm End Mar–end Oct
Toilets; Refreshments; Disabled access

Derbyshire Wildlife Trust
Elvaston Castle, Derby, Derbyshire DE72 3EP
Tel/fax: 01332 756610

A series of wildlife and other gardens open between May and August 1995 in aid of the trust. Send large SAE for details.

Haddon Hall
Bakewell, Derbyshire DE45 1LA
Tel: 01629 812855
Fax: 01629 814379
Hours: 11am–5pm daily Mar 27–Sept 30. Closed Suns in August

One of the chief glories of this magnificent Medieval and Tudor manor house are the terraced rose gardens, added in the 16th century.
Toilets; Refreshments

Hardwick Hall
Doe Lea, Chesterfield, Derbyshire S44 5QJ
Hours: 12–5.30pm daily Apr–Oct
Toilets; Refreshments; Disabled access

Lea Gardens
Lea, Matlock, Derbyshire DE4 5GH
Contact: Jon Tye
Tel: 01629 534380
Fax: 01629 534260
Hours: 10am–7pm Mar 20–July 6 or by appt

A rare collection of rhododendrons, azaleas, alpines and conifers in a lovely woodland setting. Refreshments with home baking and specialist plant sales.
Catalogue; Mail order; Toilets; Refreshments

Melbourne Hall Gardens
Melbourne, Derbyshire D73 1EN
Tel: 01332 862502
Fax: 01332 862263
Hours: 2–6pm Wed/Sat/Sun/Bank hol Mon April–Sept

Historic garden, as planned by Rt. Hon. Thomas Coke in 18th century. Robert Bakewell's wrought iron "birdcage". Amazing yew tunnel. Adults £3 OAPs £1.50.
Toilets; Refreshments

Renishaw Hall Gardens
Renishaw Hall, Nr Sheffield, Derbyshire S31 9WB
Contact: William Town
Tel: 01777 860755
Fax: 01777 860707
Hours: Fri/Sat/Sun & Bank Hol Mon Easter–mid-Sept

Italian style gardens with terraces, yew hedges, fountains and statues. Also museum and galleries in Georgian stables. Admission: adults £3, OAP £2.
Toilets; Refreshments

Devon

Ann & Roger Bowden (Hostas)
Sticklepath, Okehampton, Devon EX20 2NN
Tel: 01837 840481
Fax: 01837 840482
Hours: By phoned arrangement & under NGS

Gardens of about one acre incorporating National Collection of Hostas and nursery. Admission £1. Mail order catalogue of 184 varieties 4 x 2nd class stamps.
Catalogue; Mail order; Toilets

Arlington Court
Arlington, Barnstaple, Devon EX31 4LP
Tel/fax: 01271 850296
Hours: 11am–5.30pm Apr–Oct. Closed Sats
Toilets; Refreshments; Disabled access

Bicton Park Gardens
East Budleigh, Budleigh Salterton, Devon EX9 7DP
Tel/fax: 01395 68465
Hours: 10am–6pm daily Apr–Sept
Toilets; Refreshments; Disabled access

Burrow Farm Gardens
Dalwood, Axminster, Devon EX13 7ET
Contact: Mary Benger
Tel/fax: 01404831285
Hours: 2–7pm Apr–Sept

Beautiful 5 acre gardens appealing to plantsmen and those seeking tranquility. Shrubs, herbaceous borders, courtyard garden, ponds and woodland garden. Many unusual plants for sale.
Toilets; Refreshments

Castle Drogo
Drewsteignton, Devon EX6 6PB
Tel: 01647 433306
Fax: 01647 433186
Hours: 10.30am–5pm daily Apr–Oct

National Trust. Terraced formal garden with colourful herbaceous borders, rose beds, spring shrubs and rhododendrons. Croquet lawn with hired equipment. Admission £2.30 adult. Plant sales.
Toilets; Refreshments; Disabled access

Coleton Fishacre Garden
Coleton, Kingswear, Dartmouth, Devon TQ6 0EQ
Tel/fax: 01803 752466
Hours: 10.30am–5.30pm Wed–Fri & Sun Apr–Oct (Sun pms Mar)
Toilets; Refreshments

Dartington Hall
Dartington, Totnes, Devon TQ9 6EL
Tel/fax: 01803 862271
Hours: Dawn–dusk daily
Toilets

Docton Mill
Lymebridge, Spekes Valley, Hartland, Devon EX39 6EA
Contact: Martin Bourcier
Tel/fax: 01237 441369
Hours: 10am–5pm daily 1 Mar–31 Oct

8 acres of gardens internationally renowned, having been featured on both BBC and ITV. "An ancient mill and waterways restored near the sea".
Toilets; Refreshments

Exeter University Gardens
Exeter, Devon EX4 4PX
Tel: 01392 263059
Fax: 01392 264547
Hours: All year

Fortescue Garden Trust
The Garden House, Buckland Monachorum, Yelverton, Devon PL20 7LQ
Tel/fax: 01822 854769
Hours: 10.30am–5pm daily Mar 1–Oct 31

An 8 acre garden including a romantic, terraced, walled garden around 16th century ruins. A well-stocked plant centre and tea rooms. Admission £3 adult, £2.50 senior citizen, £1 child.

Hill House Nursery & Gardens
Landscove, Nr Ashburton, Newton Abbot, Devon TQ13 7LY
Contact: R Hubbard
Tel/fax: 01803 762273

We have a great nursery and marvellous tea room. Geoff Hamilton introduced us in March 1996 as "That fabulous garden in Devon" and finished by saying "The owner is a man after my own heart". And that's good enough by me.
Toilets; Refreshments

Killerton House
Killerton, Broadclyst, Exeter, Devon EX5 3LE
Tel/fax: 01392 881345
Hours: 10.30am–dusk daily

National Trust. 18 acre garden, open throughout the year. Landscaped in the 18th century, the garden contains a wealth of rare trees, herbaceous borders. Plant centre sells plants raised from the garden.
Toilets; Refreshments; Disabled access

Knightshayes Court
Tiverton, Devon EX16 7RH
Tel/fax: 01884 253264
Hours: 10.30am–5.30pm Apr–Oct
Toilets; Refreshments; Disabled access

Marwood Hill Gardens
Marwood, Barnstaple, Devon EX31 4EB
Contact: Dr J Smart
Tel/fax: 01271 42528
Hours: Dawn–dusk daily. Plant sales 11am–5pm

20 acre gardens. Many rare trees and shrubs. Camellias, alpines. Three lakes and streamside plantings. Plants for sale. Three National Collections.
Catalogue; Toilets; Refreshments

Overbecks Garden
Sharpitor, Salcombe, Devon TQ8 8LW
Tel/fax: 01548 842893/843238
Hours: 10am–8pm daily or sunset if earlier
Toilets; Refreshments

The Daily Telegraph *Green Fingers* **Gardens to Visit**

Paignton Zoo & Botanical Gardens
Totnes Rd, Paignton, Devon TQ4 7EU
Tel: 01803 557479
Fax: 01803 523457
Hours: 10am–6pm (5pm in Winter) daily. Closed Xmas Day
One of England's biggest zoos in the beautiful setting of 75 acre gardens. Registered educational and scientific charity owned by the Whitley Wildlife Conservation Trust.
Toilets; Refreshments; Disabled access

Pleasant View Garden
Two Mile Oak, Newton Abbot, Devon TQ12 6DG
Contact: Mrs C Yeo
Tel/fax: 01803 813388
Hours: 2–5pm Wed & Fri May–Sept
Plantsman's 2 acre garden with many rare and unusual shrubs plus field planted as an arboretum. National Collections of Abelia and Salvia. No dogs. Admission £1.50.
Toilets

Pounsley Plants
Pounsley Combe, Spriddlestone, Brixton, Plymouth, Devon PL9 0DW
Contact: Mrs Jane Hollow
Tel/fax: 01752 402873
Hours: 10am–5pm Mon–Sat but please phone first
Unusual herbaceous perennials and cottage plants. Selection of clematis and old fashioned roses.
Catalogue; Mail order

R H S Garden Rosemoor
Rosemoor, Great Torrington, Devon EX38 8PH
Tel/fax: 01805 624067
Hours: 10am–6pm Apr–Sept, 5pm Mar–Oct, 4pm Nov–Feb
A stunning garden of national significance, set in a beautiful Devon valley. Adults £3.20, children £1 (under 6 free of charge). Attendant for disabled visitors free. Groups of more than 20 £2.75.
Toilets; Refreshments; Disabled access

Rowden Gardens
Brentor, Tavistock, Devon PL19 0NG
Contact: John Carter
Tel/fax: 01822 810275
Hours: 10am–5pm Sat/Sun & Bank Hol Mon Apr 1–Sept 30 or by appt
One of the leading specialists in aquatic and damp-loving plants. Also famous for its many rare and unusual varieties. Gardens admission £1. Catalogue £1.50.
Catalogue; Mail order; Toilets

Saltram
Plympton, Plymouth, Devon PL7 3UH
Contact: Brian Ludford
Tel: 01752 336546
Fax: 01752 336474
Hours: 11am–4pm Sun–Thurs
National Trust plantsman's garden laid out late 18th century. Rare and unusual trees and shrubs. 18th century Orangery and summerhouse (The Castle). Orange grove with pond.
Toilets; Refreshments; Disabled access

Tapeley Park Gardens
Instow, Biddeford, Devon EX39 4NT
Contact: Kirsty Christie
Tel/fax: 01271 860528
Hours: 10am–6pm Good Fri–1st Oct. Closed Sat.
Tapeley Park Gardens are stunning Italianate gardens overlooking the sea, undergoing an exciting restoration. Open Good Friday to 1st October every day except Saturday 10am–6pm. On the North Devon coast off the A39 between Bideford and Barnstaple.
Toilets; Refreshments; Disabled access

Dorset

Abbotsbury Sub-Tropical Gardens
Abbotsbury, Weymouth, Dorset DT3 4LA
Tel/fax: 01305 871344/412
Hours: 10am–5pm daily. Closed Mon Nov–Feb
Catalogue; Mail order; Toilets; Refreshments

Athelhampton
Puddletown, Dorchester, Dorset DT2 7LG
Tel: 01305 848363
Fax: 01305 848135
Hours: 12–5pm Wed/Thur/Sun/Bank Hols Apr–Oct. Also Mon & Fri in July & Aug
Athelhampton Gardens are some of the finest in England with unique topiary pyramids, fountains, pavilions, many rare plants and trees, encircled by the River Piddle.
Toilets; Refreshments; Disabled access

Chiffchaffs
Chaffeymoor, Bourton, Gillingham, Dorset SP8 5BY
Contact: Mr K R Potts
Tel/fax: 01747 840841
Hours: 2–5.30pm Wed/Thurs & 1st/3rd Sun each month
The garden surrounds a typical old Dorset Stone cottage and contains a very wide range of bulbs, herbaceous, trees and shrubs. It is divided into small gardens and surprise views. The planting is planned to give an extremely long period of interest. A half acre woodland garden contains very many unusual trees, shrubs and moisture-loving plants and spring bulbs. We open from 30th March to end of Septemebr. Admission £2. Groups by appointment. Plants for sale.

Cranbourne Manor
Cranbourne, Dorset BH21 5PP
Tel/fax: 01725 512248
Hours: 9am–5pm Weds 1 Mar–30 Sept
Toilets

Forde Abbey Gardens
Chard, Dorset TA20 4LU
Tel: 01460 220231
Fax: 01460 220296
Hours: 10am–4.30pm daily all year
30 acres of outstanding gardens, surrounding 12th century monastery. Herbaceous borders, bog garden, rockery, kitchen garden. Christies gardens award winner. 4m S. of Chard.
Toilets; Refreshments; Disabled access

Ivy Cottage
Aller Lane, Ansty, Dorchester, Dorset DT2 7PX
Tel/fax: 01258 880053
Hours: 10am–5pm Thurs Apr–Oct. Also for NGS

Kingston Lacy
Wimbourne Minster, Dorset BH21 4EA
Hours: 11.30am–6pm Sat–Wed 1 Apr–31 Oct
Toilets; Refreshments; Disabled access

Kingston Maurward Gardens
Dorchester, Dorset DT2 8PY
Contact: Mike Hancock
Tel: 01305 264738
Fax: 01305 250059
Email: kmc.ac.uk
35 acres of fine Edwardian gardens set in rolling parkland. Lakeside nature trail. Animal park. Walled demonstration garden. Visitor's centre. Plant sales. National Collections of Penstemon cultivars and Salvias.
Catalogue; Toilets; Refreshments; Disabled access

Mapperton House Garden
Beaminster, Dorset DT8 3NR
Tel/fax: 01308 862645
Hours: 2–6pm daily Mar–Oct

Minterne
Minterne Magna, Dorchester, Dorset DT7 7AU
Tel: 01300 341370
Fax: 01300 341747
Hours: 10am–7pm daily 1 Apr–31 Oct
Toilets

Parnham House
Beaminster, Dorset DT8 3NA
Tel: 01308 862204
Fax: 01308 863494
Hours: 10am–5pm Sun/Wed/Bank Hols Apr–Oct
Toilets; Refreshments; Disabled access

Sticky Wicket Garden
Buckland Newton, Dorchester, Dorset DT2 7BY
Contact: Paul Lewis
Tel/fax: 01300 345476
Hours: 10.30am–8pm Thurs mid June–mid Sept
2 acre colourist and conservationists' garden created by the owners in the last 10 years and in its final year of opening to the public.
Toilets; Refreshments

Essex

Audley End House & Gardens
Saffron Walden, Essex CB11 4JF
Tel/fax: 01799 522842
Hours: 9am–6pm Wed–Sun & Bank Hols April–Sept
English Heritage Historic Property. Magnificent 18th century landscape park with temple, transformed in 1762 by Capability Brown. Newly restored flower garden to original early 19th century design to east of house.
Toilets; Refreshments

Fens
Old Mill Rd, Langham, Colchester, Essex CO4 5NU
Contact: Mrs Ann Lunn
Tel/fax: 01206 272259
Hours: For NGS – see Yellow Book
16th century cottage with 2 acre garden. Open for National Gardens Scheme. Pond, ditch with masses of moisture and shade loving plants.
Toilets; Refreshments

Olivers
Olivers Lane, Colchester, Essex CO2 0HJ
Tel: 01206 330575
Fax: 01206 330336
Hours: 2–6pm Open days in May & 2–5pm Weds Apr–June
Toilets; Refreshments; Disabled access

Ornamental Grasses - Trevor Scott
Thorpe Park Cottage, Thorpe-le-Soken, Essex CO16 0HN

Contact: Trevor Scott
Tel/fax: 01255 861308

Hours: By prior appointment March–Nov

Ornamental grasses specialist, over 300 grasses available. Garden open by appointment. 5 x 1st class stamps for instructive, descriptive catalogue.
Catalogue

R H S Garden Hyde Hall
Royal Horticultural Soc Gdns, Rettendon, Chelmsford, Essex CM3 8ET

Tel/fax: 01245 400256

Hours: 11am–6pm Wed–Sun/Bank Hols end Mar–Oct

An attractive hilltop garden and plantsman's paradise. Open Wednesday to Sunday and Bank Holiday Mondays from 26 March to 26 October. Adults £3, children 70p, under 6 free.
Toilets; Refreshments; Disabled access

Saling Hall
Great Saling, Braintree, Essex CM7 5DT

Tel: 01371 850243
Fax: 01371 850274

Hours: 2–5pm Wed May/June/July. Groups by appt
Toilets; Refreshments; Disabled access

Volpaia
54 Woodlands Rd, Hockley, Essex SS5 4PY

Tel/fax: 01702 203761

Hours: 2.30–6pm Thurs & Suns beg Apr–end June or by appt

Gloucestershire

Abbotswood
Stow-in-the-Wold, Cheltenham, Gloucestershire GL54 1LE

Tel/fax: 01451 830173

Hours: 2–6pm Open days in Apr/May/June. Phone for details
Toilets; Refreshments

Batsford Arboretum
Batsford, Moreton-in-Marsh, Gloucestershire GL56 9QF

Tel/fax: 01608 650772

Hours: 10am–5pm Mar 1–1st week Nov. Last admission 4.30pm

A private arboretum of about 50 acres with collections of oaks, maples, mountain ash, birch, magnolias, flowering cherries, conifers and bamboos. Particularly attractive in the Spring with magnolia, cherry blossom and carpets of spring bulbs. In the Autumn the trees bear a spectrum of colour from yellow through to scarlet for which the arboretum is renowned. There are many other rarities of interest for the visitor to seek out. All specimens are labeled. Other attractions: Batsford Garden Centre and The Apple Store Tea Rooms, tel: 01386 700409. Costwold Falconry Centre, tel: 01386 701043 open daily 10.30am-5pm 1 March-5 Nov. The Aquatic Centre, tel: 01386 701213. Batsford Garden Machinery Centre, tel: 01386 700520.
Toilets; Refreshments; Disabled access

Berkeley Castle
Berkeley, Gloucestershire GL13 9BQ

Tel/fax: 01453 810332

Hours: Apr–Sept Opening times vary. Phone for details
Toilets; Refreshments

Bourton House
Bourton-on-the-Hill, Moreton-in-Marsh, Gloucestershire GL56 9AE

Tel: 01386 700121
Fax: 01386 701081

Hours: 12–5pm Thurs/Fri end May–end Sept
Toilets; Refreshments

Cowley Manor
Cowley, Cheltenham, Gloucestershire GL53 9NL

Contact: Noel Kingsbury
Tel/fax: 01242 870526

Hours: 10am–6pm Tues–Sun March–Oct

New style perennial planting in classic English landscape garden. Unique Victorian cascade. Plant sales.
Toilets; Refreshments

Ernest Wilson Memorial Garden
High Street, Chipping Campden, Gloucestershire GL55 6AF

Tel/fax: 01386 840764

Hours: Dawn–dusk daily
Disabled access

Frampton Court
Frampton-on-Severn, Gloucestershire GL2 7EU

Tel/fax: 01452 740698

Hours: By appointment
Toilets

Hidcote Manor
Hidcote Bartrim, Chipping Campden, Gloucestershire GL55 6LR

Tel/fax: 01386 438333

Hours: 11am–7pm daily except Tues/Fri Apr–Oct
Toilets; Refreshments; Disabled access

Hodges Barn
Shipton Moyne, Tetbury, Gloucestershire GL8 8PR

Contact: Charles Hornby
Tel: 01666 880202
Fax: 01367 718096

Hours: 2–5pm Mon/Tues/Fri Apr–Sept

8 acres of intensive herbaceous, shrubs and roses, water and woodland gardens. Parties by appointment.
Catalogue; Toilets; Refreshments

Hunts Court Garden & Nursery
Hunts Court, North Nibley, Dursley, Gloucestershire GL11 6DZ

Contact: T K Marshall
Tel/fax: 01453 547440

Hours: 9am–5pm Tues–Sat. Closed Aug

Specialities - old roses, unusual shrubs, penstemons, geraniums, potentillas. Catalogue 3 x 2nd class stamps. Admission to garden £1.50. 400 roses, 70 potentillas and much more in 2 acre garden.
Catalogue; Toilets

Kiftsgate Court Gardens
Kiftsgate Court, Chipping Campden, Gloucestershire GL55 6LW

Contact: Mr & Mrs J Chambers
Tel/fax: 01386 438777

Hours: 2–6pm Wed/Thur/Sun Apr–Sept

Kiftsgate Court Gardens are perched on the edge of the Costwolds with views towards the Malvern Hills. The garden is stocked with many rare plants.
Toilets; Refreshments

Lydney Park Gardens
The Estate Office, Old Park, Lydney, Gloucestershire GL15 6BU

Contact: Mrs Beryl Butcher
Tel: 01594 842844
Fax: 01594 842027

Hours: Easter–8 June. Suns, Bank Hols, Wed 11am–6pm

Rhododendron, azalea and shrubs in a lakeland valley. Magnolias, daffodils, bluebells. Roman temple site and museum. Picnic and deer park. Teas. Admission £2.20, children free.
Toilets; Refreshments

Miserden Park
Miserden, Stroud, Gloucestershire GL6 7JA

Tel: 01285 821303
Fax: 01285 821530

Hours: 9.30am–4.30pm Tues/Wed/Thurs Apr–Sept

Spring bulbs, large double herbaceous border, specimen trees, fine topiary, traditional roses. Spectacular situation overlooking "Golden Valley".

Painswick Rococo Garden Trust
The Stables, Painswick House, Painswick, Gloucestershire GL6 6TH

Contact: P R Moir
Tel/fax: 01452 813204

Hours: 11am–5pm Wed–Sun Jan 8–Nov 30

Unique 18th century garden set in hidden Cotswold valley. Charming garden buildings, woodland walks, kitchen garden and herbaceous borders. Lovely snowdrop display in spring.
Toilets; Refreshments; Disabled access

Priory
Kemerton, Gloucestershire GL20 7JN

Contact: Mrs E Healing
Tel/fax: 01386 725258

Hours: 2–7pm Thurs End May–end Sept also some Suns

Interesting 4 acre garden and nursery. Parties over 25 by appointment.
Toilets; Refreshments; Disabled access

Rodmarton Manor
Rodmarton, Cirencester, Gloucestershire GL7 6PF

Tel/fax: 01285 841253

Hours: Sat mid May–end Aug or by appt
Toilets; Disabled access

Sudeley Castle
Winchcombe, Gloucestershire GL54 5JD

Tel: 01242 602308
Fax: 01242 602959

Hours: 11am–5.30pm daily
Toilets; Refreshments; Disabled access

Westbury Court
Westbury-on-Severn, Gloucestershire GL14 1PD

Tel/fax: 01452 760461

Hours: 11am–6pm Wed–Sun & Bank Hols Apr–Oct. Closed Good Fri
Toilets; Disabled access

Westonbirt Arboretum
Westonbirt, Tetbury, Gloucestershire GL8 8QS

Tel: 01666 880220
Fax: 01666 880559

Hours: 10am–8pm or dusk all year
Toilets; Refreshments; Disabled access

Hampshire

Apple Court
Hordle Lane, Hordle, Lymington, Hampshire SO41 0HU
Contact: Diana Grenfell & Roger Grounds
Tel/fax: 01590 642130
Hours: Daily July & Aug. Thurs–Mon Feb 1–Oct 31

Specialising in hostas, daylilies, ferns, grasses, white garden plants, foliage plants for flower arrangers. Display garden has hosta walk, spectacular daylily and grass plantings, fern path. Mail order catalogue 4 x 1st class stamps.
Catalogue; Mail order

Bramdean House
Bramdean, Alresford, Hampshire SO24 0JU
Tel: 01962 771214
Fax: 01962 771095
Hours: 2–5pm Various open days. Phone for details
Toilets; Refreshments

Broadlands
Romsey, Hampshire
Tel/fax: 01794 516878
Hours: 12–4pm daily (Fris in Aug only) Easter–Sept
Toilets; Refreshments

Exbury Gardens
Exbury, Southampton, Hampshire SO45 1AZ
Contact: Sheila Wise
Tel: 01703 891203
Fax: 01703 243380
Hours: 10am–5.30pm or dusk daily mid Feb–end Oct

Woodland garden containing the famous Rothschild rhododendrons and azaleas near Beaulieu. New "trails" help visitors appreciate many other aspects of this beautiful 200 acre garden.
Catalogue; Toilets; Refreshments; Disabled access

Fairfield House
Hambledon, Waterlooville, Hampshire PO7 4RY
Tel/fax: 01705 632431
Hours: Open for NGS & by appt
Refreshments; Disabled access

Furzey Gardens
Minstead, Nr Lyndhurst, Hampshire SO43 7GL
Contact: Stephen Cole
Tel: 01703 812464
Fax: 01703 812297
Hours: 10am–5pm daily except Xmas/Boxing Day

Eight acres of tranquil, informal garden with exceptional views of the New Forest. Extensive collections of azaleas and rhododendrons with summer and winter flowering shrubs and trees. Lake, fernery, nursery shop, craft gallery and restored 16th century forest cottage. All proceeds after maintenance to charity.
Toilets

Gilbert White's House & Garden
The Wakes, High Street, Selborne, Nr Alton, Hampshire GU34 3JH
Contact: Mrs Anna Jackson
Tel/fax: 01420 511275
Hours: 11am–5pm daily end Mar–Christmas. Weekends in Winter

Charming 18th century house and garden, home of Rev. Gilbert White. Many old varieties of plants, herb garden, topiary. Plant sales. Excellent shop. Tea parlour. Unusual Plants Fair 22/23 June. Mulled Wine Day 24 November.
Toilets; Refreshments; Disabled access

Greatham Mill
Liss, Hampshire GU33 6HH
Tel/fax: 01420 7219
Hours: 2–6pm Suns/Bank Hols mid Apr–Sept

Hawthorns Urban Wildlife Centre
The Common, Southampton, Hampshire
Tel/fax: 01703 671921
Hours: 10am–5pm Mon–Fri, 12–4pm Sat & Sun

Highclere Castle
Highclere, Newbury, Hampshire RG15 9RN
Tel: 01635 255317
Fax: 01635 254051
Hours: 2–6pm Wed–Sun & Bank Hols July–Sept
Toilets; Refreshments; Disabled access

Hinton Ampner
Bramdean, Alresford, Hampshire SO24 0LA
Tel/fax: 01962 771305
Hours: 1.30–5pm Mon–Wed/Sat/Sun/Bank Hols Apr–Sept
Toilets; Refreshments; Disabled access

Houghton Lodge Garden & Hydroponicum
Houghton, Stockbridge, Hampshire SO20 6QL
Contact: Mr & Mrs Martin Busk
Tel: 01264 810502
Fax: 01794 388072
Hours: 10am–5pm Sat/Sun/Bank Hols. Weekdays 2pm–5pm except Wed

Late 18th century landscaped pleasure grounds overlook the tranquil beauty of the River Test. Traditional walled garden with greenhouses (fuchsia collection) and hydroponicum. Exhibition of soilless horticulture.

Jenkyn Place
Bentley, Farnham, Hampshire GU10 5LU
Tel/fax: 01420 23118
Hours: 2–6pm Thur–Sun Apr–Sept
Toilets

Langley Boxwood Nursery
Rake, Nr Liss, Hampshire GU33 7JL
Tel: 01730 894467
Fax: 01730 894703
Hours: 9am–5pm Mon–Fri. Check for Sats

A boxwood and topiary nursery in a beautiful setting. Langley Boxwood Nursery grows and shows a National Collection of the widest range of species, cultivars, hedging and shapes in box and yew. Cultivation advice given. Catalogue and mags 4 x 1st class stamps.
Catalogue; Mail order; Toilets

Longstock Water Gardens
Longstock, Stockbridge, Hampshire SO20 6EH
Tel: 01264 810894
Fax: 01264 810430
Hours: 2–5pm 3rd Sunday in the month Apr–Sept
Toilets; Disabled access

Manor House Upton Grey
Upton Grey, Basingstoke, Hampshire RG25 2RD
Contact: Wallinger
Tel/fax: 01256 862827
Hours: 2–4pm Weekdays May–July

A meticulously restored 1908 Gertrude Jekyll garden with copies of her original plans on display. An arts and crafts gem in 5 acres.
Toilets

Mottisfont Abbey
Romsey, Hampshire SO51 0LJ
Tel/fax: 01794 41220
Hours: 12–6pm (8.30pm in June) Sat–Wed Apr–Oct
Toilets; Refreshments; Disabled access

Queen Eleanors Garden
Winchester Castle, Winchester, Hampshire
Tel/fax: 01962 840222
Hours: 10am–5pm daily

Sir Harold Hillier Gardens & Arboretum
Jermyns Lane, Ampfield, Nr Romsey, Hampshire SO51 0QA
Contact: Mrs W Pidduck
Tel: 01794 368787
Fax: 01794 368027
Hours: 10.30am–6pm (Apr–Oct), 10.30am–5pm or dusk (Nov–Mar) all year

One of the finest collections of trees and shrubs in the country set in 166 acres. A garden for all seasons. Admission charge. No dogs. Closed over Xmas holidays.
Toilets; Refreshments; Disabled access

Spinners
Boldre, Lymington, Hampshire SO41 5QE
Tel/fax: 01590 673347
Hours: 10am–5pm Tues–Sat, or by appt

Woodland garden. Azaleas, rhododendrons, magnolias, camellias, Japanese maples, hydrangeas etc. interplanted with choice woodland plants. Adjoining internationally known nursery offers as wide a range of less common plants as you will find in the country.
Catalogue; Toilets

Tudor House Garden
Tudor House, Bugle Street, Southampton, Hampshire SO1 0AB
Tel: 01703 635904
Fax: 01703 339601
Hours: 10am–12am 1–5pm Tues–Fri, 10–12am 1–4pm Sat, 2–5pm Sun. Closed Mons

Tudor House Garden is a unique reconstruction of a 16th century garden with a central knot, bee skeps, period plants and over 100 other features.
Toilets; Disabled access

Water Meadow Nursery & Herb Farm
Cheriton, Alresford, Hampshire SO24 0JT
Contact: Mrs Sandy Worth
Tel/fax: 01962 771895
Hours: 9am–5pm Fri/Sat & Bank Hols, 2–5pm Sun Mar–Nov

Extensive collection of water garden plants, hardy shrubs, fragrant climbers, herbs, 500+ herbaceous perennials, many unusual. All in a garden setting. Mail order catalogue 75p. Landscape and design service available.
Catalogue; Mail order; Toilets

White Windows
Longparish, Nr Andover, Hampshire SP11 6PB
Contact: Jane Sterndale-Bennett
Tel/fax: 01264 720222
Hours: 2–6pm Wed April–Sept by appt only

A wide selection of herbaceous plants displayed in a country garden of 2/3 acre with emphasis on flower colour and attractive foliage for all seasons.

Hereford & Worcester

Abbey Dore Court Garden
Abbey Dore, Hereford, Hereford & Worcester HR2 0AD

Contact: Chris Ward
Tel: 01981 240419
Fax: 01981 240279

Hours: *11am–6pm daily except Weds Mar–Oct*

Five acre rambling and semi-formal garden intersected by the river Dore. Unusual shrubs and perennials. Small nursery, mainly herbaceous perennials. Gift gallery. Licensed restaurant.
Toilets; Refreshments; Disabled access

Berrington Hall
Leominster, Hereford & Worcester HR6 0DW

Tel/fax: 01568 615721

Hours: *1.30–5.30pm Wed–Sun Apr–Sept, 1.30–4pm Sat/Sun Oct*

Burford House Gardens
Treasures of Tenbury, Tenbury Wells, Hereford & Worcester WR15 8HQ

Tel: 01584 810777
Fax: 01584 810673

Hours: *10am–5pm (dusk in winter) all year*
Toilets; Refreshments; Disabled access

Cottage Herbery
Mill House, Boraston, Tenbury Wells, Hereford & Worcester WR15 8LZ

Tel: 01584 7821575
Fax: 01584 781483

Hours: *Suns only May to July. Weekdays by appt*

Beautiful tranquil setting, a true cottage garden with herbs, scented plants, old roses and vegetables. Totally organic. Good range of plants for sale. 4 x 1st class stamps for informative catalogue and seed list.
Catalogue; Mail order; Toilets; Refreshments

Eastgrove Cottage Garden Nursery
Sankyns Green, Nr Shrawley, Little Witley, Worcester, Hereford & Worcester WR6 6LQ

Contact: Malcolm & Carol Skinner
Tel/fax: 01299 896389

Hours: *2–5pm March 27–Oct 18 & for NGS*

Unique old world country flower garden. Fine collection of hardy and tender perennials. Wide range of well grown less usual plants. Owners give help and advice.
Catalogue; Toilets

Eastnor Castle
Eastnor, Ledbury, Hereford & Worcester HR8 1RL

Tel: 01531 633160
Fax: 01531 631776

Hours: *Easter–Sept Sun & Bank Hols. July/Aug Sun–Fri*

Magnificent Georgian castle set in Malvern Hills with famous arboretum, deer park and lake. New garden centre and maze. Adult grounds tickets only £2.
Toilets; Refreshments

Hergest Croft Gardens
Kington, Hereford & Worcester HR5 3EG

Tel/fax: 01544 230160

Hours: *1.30–6.30pm daily Mar 28–Oct 26*

From Spring bulbs to Autumn colour, this is a garden for al seasons. Plants for sale.
Toilets; Refreshments; Disabled access

Hill Court Gardens & Garden Centre
Hom Green, Ross-on-Wye, Hereford & Worcester HR9 5QN

Tel/fax: 01989 763123

Hours: *9.30am–5.30pm daily*

How Caple Court Gardens
How Caple, Hereford, Hereford & Worcester HR1 4SX

Tel: 01989 86626
Fax: 01989 86611

Hours: *9am–5pm Mon–Sat, 10am–5pm Suns (May–Oct 29)*

11 acres Edwardian gardens overlooking River Wye. Italian water garden undergoing restoration. Nursery specialising in old rose varieties, apples, herbaceous plants. Admission £2.50, child £1.25.
Catalogue; Toilets; Refreshments

Lakeside
Gaines Rd, Whitbourne, Worcester, Hereford & Worcester WR6 5RD

Hours: *Various days in Summer Check NGS*
Toilets; Refreshments

Picton Garden
Walwyn Rd, Colwall, Malvern, Hereford & Worcester WR13 6QE

Contact: Paul Picton
Tel/fax: 01684 540416

Hours: *10am–1pm 2.15–5.30pm Apr–Oct*

National Collection of Michaelmas Daisies and wide range of perennials in attractive garden and nursery seen on BBC TV's "Gardeners World". Booked group visits welcome.
Catalogue; Mail order

Snowshill Manor
Snowshill Broadway, Hereford & Worcester WR12 7JU

Tel/fax: 01386 852410

Hours: *Daily except Tues Apr–Oct. Also open Tues July/Aug*

National Trust. Charming terraced Cotswold garden, organically run. Borders and water features. Adjacent to Manor House containing collection of craftsmanship.
Toilets; Refreshments

Spetchley Park Garden
Spetchley Park, Nr Worcester, Hereford & Worcester WR5 1RS

Contact: R J Berkeley
Tel/fax: 01905 345213

Hours: *11am–5pm Tues–Fri, 2pm–5pm Sun Mar 28–Sept 30*

39 acre private garden containing large collection of trees, shrubs and plants, many rare or unusual. Deer park close by, with Red and Fallow deer.
Toilets; Refreshments; Disabled access

Treasures of Tenbury Ltd
Burford House Gardens, Tenbury Wells, Hereford & Worcester WR15 8QH

Contact: Charles Chesshire
Tel: 01584 810777
Fax: 01584 810673

Hours: *10am–5pm daily*

Four acre gardens in beautiful riverside setting. Home to National Clematis Collection - with 250 varieties and 2,000+ other unusual plants, many for sale at the plant centre.
Catalogue; Mail order; Toilets; Refreshments; Disabled access

Hertfordshire

Beale Arboretum
West Lodge Park, Cockfosters Rd, Hadley Wood, Barnet, Hertfordshire EN4 0PY

Tel: 0181 440 8311
Fax: 0181 449 3698

Hours: *2–5pm Wed Apr–Oct*
Toilets; Refreshments; Disabled access

Benington Lordship
Benington, Stevenage, Hertfordshire SG2 7BS

Tel/fax: 01438 869228

Hours: *12–5pm Wed, 2–5pm Sun Apr–Aug*
Toilets; Refreshments

Hatfield House
Hatfield, Hertfordshire AL9 5NQ

Tel: 01707 262823
Fax: 01707 275719

Hours: *11am–6pm daily except Suns & Good Fri Mar–July*
Toilets; Refreshments; Disabled access

Knebworth House & Gardens
Knebworth, Stevenage, Hertfordshire SG3 6PY

Contact: Jacky Wilson
Tel: 01438 812661
Fax: 01438 811908

Hours: *12–5pm (not daily – check open days) Apr 1–Oct 1*

The formal gardens adjoin the house and contain many beautiful features including the Gertrude Jekyll Herb Garden, a Victorian wilderness area and pleached lime trees.
Toilets; Refreshments

Royal National Rose Society
Chiswell Green, St Albans, Hertfordshire AL2 3NR

Contact: Lt Col K V Grapes
Tel: 01727 850461
Fax: 01727 850360
Email: rnrs.org.uk

Hours: *9am–5pm Mon–Sat, 10am–6pm Sun & Bank Hols mid June–mid Oct*

The RNRS is the world's oldest and largest specialist plant society. It maintains the world famous Gardens of the Rose.

Humberside

Burnby Hall Gardens
c/o August Cottage, Burnby Lane, Pocklington, Humberside YO4 2QE

Contact: Mrs D Hughes
Tel/fax: 01759 302068

Hours: *10am–6pm daily Apr 1–Oct 9*

Home of the National Collection of Waterlilies, with over 85 hardy varieties grown to perfection in beautifully landscaped 7-acre gardens. Also historic collection of Stewart artifacts.
Toilets; Refreshments; Disabled access

Burton Constable Hall
Burton Constable, Nr Hull, Humberside HU11 4LN

Tel: 01964 562400
Fax: 01964 563229

Hours: *Sun–Thurs Easter Sun–Sept 30. Sat July & Aug*

The parkland and grounds of Burton Constable have received the attention of many great landscape architects since the building of the hall commenced in mid-16th century.
Toilets; Refreshments; Disabled access

Sledmere House
Sledmere, Driffield, Humberside YO25 0XG

Tel: 01377 236637
Fax: 01377 236560

Hours: *12–5pm daily except Mon & Fri Easter–30 Sept*
Toilets; Refreshments; Disabled access

Isle of Wight

Barton Manor Gardens & Vineyards Ltd
Whippingham, East Cowes, Isle of Wight PO32 6LB
Tel: 01983 292835
Fax: 01983 293923
Hours: 10.30am–5.30pm daily Apr 1–2nd Sun in Oct

Award-winning attraction with beautiful, historic gardens, indoor attractions, café, woodland walks and the island's largest rose hedge maze. Surprisingly good value for money.
Mail order; Toilets; Refreshments; Disabled access

Mottistone Manor
Newport, Isle of Wight
Hours: 2–5pm Wed & Bank Hol Mons Mar–Sept

Owl Cottage
Hoxall Lane, Mottistone, Newport, Isle of Wight PO30 4EE
Tel/fax: 01983 740433
Hours: 2.30–5.30pm by appt for groups only
Disabled access

Ventnor Botanic Garden
Undercliff Drive, Ventnor, Isle of Wight PO38 1UL
Tel/fax: 01983 855397
Hours: All day every day
Toilets; Refreshments; Disabled access

Kent

Bedgebury National Pinetum
Weald Forest District, Nr Goudhurst, Cranbrook, Kent TN17 2SL
Contact: Colin Morgan
Tel: 01580 211044
Fax: 01580 212423
Hours: 10am–5pm Easter–Dec. Visitor Centre all year

Bedgebury Pinetum is the National Conifer Collection, 300 acres providing the most complete collection of trees in Europe. Adults £2, OAPs £1.50, children £1.20.
Toilets; Refreshments

Belmont
Belmont Park, Throwley, Faversham, Kent ME13 0HH
Contact: Lt Col F E Grant
Tel/fax: 01795 890202
Hours: 2–5pm Sat/Sun & Bank Hol Mons Easter–Sept

Charming 18th century manor by Samuel Wyatt in extensive grounds. Walled garden and pinetum. Pets' cemetery. House and garden £4.75. Garden only £2.75. Tea room. Gifts.
Toilets; Refreshments; Disabled access

Brogdale Horticultural Trust
Brogdale Road, Faversham, Kent ME13 8XZ
Contact: Paul Smith
Tel/fax: 01795 535286
Hours: 9.30am–5.30pm all year.

Over 4,000 varieties of fruit, the home of the National Fruit Collection. Guided tours, gift shop, special events, licensed restaurant, group discounts available, coaches welcome.
Mail order; Toilets; Refreshments; Disabled access

Chartwell
Westerham, Kent TN16 1PS
Tel/fax: 01732 866368
Hours: 12–5.30pm Tues–Thur, 11am–5.30pm Sat/Sun Apr–Oct
Toilets; Refreshments; Disabled access

Chilham Castle Gardens
Chilham, Canterbury, Kent CT4 8DB
Tel/fax: 01227 730319
Hours: 11am–5pm daily end Mar–mid Oct
Toilets; Refreshments

Crittenden House
Crittenden Rd, Matfield, Tonbridge, Kent TN12 7EN
Tel/fax: 01892 832554
Hours: 2–6pm open several days in Mar–Jun
Toilets

Emmetts Garden
Ide Hill, Sevenoaks, Kent TN14 6AY
Tel/fax: 01732 750367/750429
Hours: 11am–1pm Wed/Thur/Sun/Bank Hls Apr–Oct
(See our full colour advertisement on page 150).
Toilets; Refreshments

Friends of Brogdale
Brogdale Horticultural Trust, Brogdale Farm, Faversham, Kent ME9 0PL
Tel: 01795 535286
Fax: 01795 531710
Hours: 9.30am–5pm daily. Weekends only between Xmas & Easter

Home of the National Collections of fruit including over 4000 varieties. Guided orchard walks, historical gardens under construction, plant centre, shop, restaurant. Groups welcome.
Toilets; Refreshments; Disabled access

Godington Park
Ashford, Kent TN23 3BW
Tel/fax: 01233 620773
Hours: 2–5pm or by appt Easter Weekend/Bank Hols Jun–Sept
Toilets

Goodnestone Park Gardens
Nr Wingham, Canterbury, Kent CT3 1PL
Tel/fax: 01304 840107
Hours: Wed–Fri & Sun March–Oct

14 acre garden. Fine trees, woodland area and large walled garden. Roses, herbaceous and climbing plants. Jane Austen visited frequently.
Toilets; Refreshments; Disabled access

Hever Castle & Gardens
Edenbridge, Kent TN8 7NG
Tel: 01732 865224
Fax: 01732 866796

Spectacular, award-winning gardens created by W W Astor from 1903. Includes Italian, Tudor and rose gardens, maze and lake. Adults £4.40, OAPs £3.90, child £2.60.
Toilets; Refreshments; Disabled access

Jan Martinez Garden Designs
Everden Farmhouse, Alkham, Dover, Kent CT15 7EH
Contact: Jan Martinez
Tel/fax: 01303 893462
Hours: Sun Oct 6 & by appt any time.

Designer's own garden open for National Gardens Scheme (Yellow Book). Selling plants, teas, American samplers, quilts to order. Current schemes include private projects and on-going development of planting for Eastern Docks, Dover Harbour.

Leeds Castle
Maidstone, Kent ME17 1PL
Tel: 01622 765400
Fax: 01622 735616
Hours: Daily except Xmas and prior to evening events

Visit the gardens of the "loveliest castle in the world". Highlights include the Wood Garden, the Russell Page designed Culpepper Garden, greenhouses, aviary, maze and grotto.
Toilets; Refreshments; Disabled access

Long Barn
Long Barn Rd, Weald, Sevenoaks, Kent TN14 6NH
Tel/fax: 01732 463714
Hours: 2–5pm One day in May/Jun/Jul. Phone for details
Toilets

Longacre Nursery
Longacre, Perry Wood, Selling, Faversham, Kent ME13 9SE
Tel/fax: 01227 752254
Hours: 2–5pm daily Apr–Oct

Small specialist nursery. Hardy herbaceous plants. Garden open under National Gardens Scheme (see Yellow Book for open days), also by appointment - donation please.

Penshurst Place & Gardens
Penshurst, Nr Tonbridge, Kent TN11 8DG
Tel: 01892 870307
Fax: 01892 870866
Hours: Grounds 11am–6pm daily Apr–Sept. Weekends Mar/Oct

Magnificent Medieval manor house with 10 acres of Tudor walled gardens, divided by one mile of yew hedges into garden compartments. Colour all year round.
Toilets; Refreshments; Disabled access

Pickards Magnolia Gardens
Stodmarsh Rd, Canterbury, Kent CT3 4AG
Tel/fax: 01227 463951
Hours: 12–dusk daily except Mon Feb–Xmas Eve

Port Lympne Wild Animal Park
Mansion and Gardens, Port Lympne, Nr Hythe, Kent CT21 4PD
Contact: Dr Cheryl Butler
Tel: 01303 264647
Fax: 01303 264944
Hours: 10am onwards daily

The gardens of Port Lympne were originally designed by Sir Philip Sassoon. Cut out of the old sea cliffs overlooking Romney Marsh and the English Channel, they have a beauty and atmosphere not found in other gardens. Hydrangea walk, rose terrace. Historic mansion and many rare and endangered animal species. Admission £6.99, children/OAPs £4.99.
Toilets; Refreshments; Disabled access

Scotney Castle
Lamberhurst, Tunbridge Wells, Kent TN3 8JN
Tel: 01892 890651
Fax: 01892 890110
Hours: 11am–6pm Wed–Fri, 2–6pm weekends Apr–Oct

National Trust. One of England's most romantic gardens surrounding the ruins of a moated 14th century castle. Rhododendrons, azaleas and wisteria. Autumn colours. Admission fees.
Toilets

Sissinghurst Castle
Sissinghurst, Cranbrook, Kent TN17 2AB
Tel: 01580 715330
Fax: 01580 713911
Hours: 11am–6pm Wed–Fri Apr–Oct, 2–6pm Sat/Sun & Bank Hls
Toilets; Refreshments; Disabled access

Lancashire

Catforth Gardens
Roots Lane, Catforth, Preston, Lancashire PR4 0JB
Contact: Judith Bradshaw or Chris Moore
Tel/fax: 01772 690561
Hours: 10.30am–5pm daily mid Mar–mid Sept

Nursery specialising in hardy geraniums (National Collection) and herbaceous plants, over 1,500 varieties. Catalogue 5 x 1st class stamps. No mail order. Three glorious gardens covering 2½ acres, giving interest and colour from Spring to Autumn. Admission to gardens £2, children 50p.
Catalogue; Toilets

Leighton Hall
Carnforth, Lancashire LA5 9ST
Tel: 01524 734474
Fax: 01524 702375
Hours: 2–5pm daily except Sat & Mon May–Sept
Toilets; Refreshments; Disabled access

Leicestershire

Barnsdale Plants & Gardens
The Avenue, Exton, Oakham, Leicestershire LE15 8AH
Contact: Nick Hamilton
Tel: 01572 813200
Fax: 01572 813346
Hours: 10am–5pm Mar–Oct, 10am–4pm Nov–Feb

The Barnsdale TV garden will be open every day from Spring 1997. Also for viewing will be the two gardens built for the Geoff Hamilton's Paradise Gardens series and many other individual gardens. Our small nursery grows a wide range of choice and unusual garden plants. Admission to TV and nursery garden £4.50. Admission to nursery garden only £1.50. Children free. Turn off A606 (Oakham to Stamford road) at the Barnsdale Lodge Hotel, then one mile.
Catalogue; Mail order; Toilets

Belvoir Castle
Belvoir, Grantham, Leicestershire
Tel/fax: 01476 870262
Hours: 11am–5pm Tues–Thurs/Sat/Sun Apr–Sept. Open Bank Hls
Toilets; Refreshments

Burrough House Gardens
Burrough on the Hill, Melton Mowbray, Leicestershire LE14 2JQ
Tel: 01664 454226
Fax: 01664 454854
Hours: 1–6pm Bank Hol Suns & Mons May & Aug

Historic hunting box set in superb 5 acre garden with many unique features including the Bower House where Edward VII and Mrs Simpson met. Also open Tulip Sunday 11th May, Wisteria Sunday 8th June, Delphinium/Peony Sunday 13th July. Admission £2. Guide dogs only.
Toilets; Refreshments; Disabled access

Rockingham Castle
Market Harborough, Leicestershire LE16 8TH
Contact: Miss K Barton
Tel: 01586 770240
Fax: 01586 771692
Hours: 1.30–5.30pm Sun/Thur/Bnk Hl Mon/Tues Easter–Sept

Elizabethan house with fortifications of Norman Castle. Stunning views. 19 acre gardens, wild and formal, dating from 17th century.
Toilets; Refreshments

University of Leicester Botanic Gardens
Beaumont Hall, Stoughton Drive, Oadby, Leicestershire LE2 2NA
Tel/fax: 0116 2717725
Hours: 10am–4.30pm (3.30pm on Fri) Mon–Fri all year
Toilets

Whatton House
Long Whatton, Loughborough, Leicestershire LE12 5BG
Tel: 01509 842302
Fax: 01509 842268
Hours: 2–6pm Wed/Sun/Bank Hols Easter–30 Aug. Also for NGS
Toilets; Refreshments; Disabled access

Lincolnshire

Belton House
Grantham, Lincolnshire NG32 2LS
Tel/fax: 01476 61541
Hours: 11am–5.30pm Wed–Sun Apr–Oct
Toilets; Refreshments; Disabled access

Doddington Hall
Doddington, Lincoln, Lincolnshire LN6 4RU
Tel/fax: 01522 694308
Hours: 2–6pm Wed/Sun/Bank Hols May–Sept. Mar–Apr Sun 2–6pm

Superb walled Elizabethan gardens. Wild gardens with beautiful spring bulbs and shrubs. House also open May–September. Refreshments, shop, nature trail and garden trail.
Toilets; Refreshments; Disabled access

Foliage & Unusual Plants
Dingle Nursery & Gardens, Pilsgate, Stamford, Lincolnshire PE9 3HW
Contact: Margaret Handley
Tel: 01780 740775
Fax: 01780 740838
Hours: 10am–6pm 1 Mar–15 Nov

Large selection of unusual perennials, alpines, shrubs, grasses and conifers including many variegated and coloured foliage plants. Nursery set in quiet and pretty four acre gardens with natural stream. Picnics welcome. Located on B1443, ½ mile east Burghley House. Catalogue 3 x 1st class stamps.
Catalogue; Mail order; Toilets

Grimsthorpe Castle
Grimsthorpe Estate Office, Bourne, Lincolnshire PE10 0NB
Contact: Michael Tebbutt
Tel: 01778 591205
Fax: 01778 591259
Hours: Thurs/Sun/Bank Hols Mar–Sept. Sun–Thurs Aug

Grimsthorpe Castle - large formal and ornamental vegetable gardens surrounding Tudor house with Vanbrugh additions. Licensed tea room, Red Deer herd, nature trail, Capability Brown parklands.
Toilets; Refreshments; Disabled access

Hall Farm Nursery
Hall Farm, Harpswell, Gainsborough, Lincolnshire DN21 5UU
Contact: Pamela Tatam
Tel: 01427 668412
Fax: 01427 688412
Hours: 8am–5.30pm daily. Phone first in winter

Wide range of interesting shrubs, perennials and old roses, most also growing in our garden. Catalogue 80p. Visits from garden clubs etc welcomed.
Catalogue; Toilets

Riseholme Hall
Lincs College of Agr & Hort, Riseholme, Lincolnshire LN2 2LG
Tel: 01522 522252
Fax: 01522 545436
Hours: Groups by appt
Toilets; Disabled access

Springfields (World of Flowers)
Camelgate, Spalding, Lincolnshire PE12 6ET
Contact: Brian R Willoughby
Tel: 01775 724843
Fax: 01775 711209
Hours: 10am–6pm March 22 – May 11 1997

25 acre show garden dedicated to displaying tulips, daffodils, hyacinths, etc. Admission £3. Don't miss the Spalding Flower Festival 3-5 May 1997.
Catalogue; Toilets; Refreshments; Disabled access

London

17 Fulham Park Gardens
Fulham, London SW6 4JX
Tel/fax: 0171 736 4890
Hours: Open for NGS

Cannizaro Park
West Side Common, Wimbledon, London SW19
Tel/fax: 0181 946 7349
Hours: 8am–sunset Mon–Fri 9am–sunset Sat/Sun All year
Toilets

Chelsea Physic Garden
Swan Walk, Royal Hospital Road, London SW3 4HS
Tel: 0171 352 5646
Fax: 0171 376 3910
Hours: 2–5pm Wed, 2–6pm Sun Apr–Oct

London's 4 acre "secret garden" of medicinal plants, rare, tender and historic species. Founded 1673. With glasshouses and summer exhibitions. Admission £3.50, £1.80 limited concessions.
Toilets; Refreshments; Disabled access

Chiswick House
Burlington Lane, Chiswick, London W4 2RP
Tel/fax: 0181 742 1225
Hours: 10am–dusk daily
Toilets; Refreshments

Fenton House - National Trust
Hampstead Grove, London NW3 6RT
Tel/fax: 0171 435 3471
Hours: 2–5pm Sat/Sun Mar, 11–5.30pm Sat/Sun/Bk Hls Apr–Oct, 2–5.30pm Wed/Thurs/Fri

A William and Mary merchant's house set in the winding streets of Old Hampstead. The panelled rooms contain an outstanding collection of Oriental and European porcelain. Fenton is also home to the Benton Fletcher Collection of early keyboard and other instruments. Charming walled garden.

Hampton Court Palace
East Molesey, London KT8 9AU
Tel/fax: 0181 781 9500
Hours: Dawn–dusk daily
Toilets; Refreshments; Disabled access

Kenwood Park
Hampstead Lane, London NW3
Hours: Dawn–dusk daily all year
Toilets; Refreshments; Disabled access

Osterley Park
Isleworth, London TW7 4RB
Tel/fax: 0181 560 3918
Hours: 9am–7.30pm daily
Toilets; Refreshments; Disabled access

Queen Marys Garden
Inner Circle, Regents Park,
London NW1
Tel/fax: 0171 486 7905
Hours: Dawn–dusk daily

Roof Gardens
99 Kensington High Street,
London W8 5ED
Tel/fax: 0171 937 7994
Hours: 9am–5pm daily. Phone first–may be closed for function

Walpole House
Chiuswick Mall, London W4 2PS
Hours: Open for NGS

Manchester, Greater

Dunham Massey
Altrincham, Manchester, Gt
WA14 4SJ
Contact: Janet Edwards
Tel/fax: 0161 9411025/9269291
Hours: 11am–5.30pm daily
Apr–Oct
National Trust 25 acre Victorian plantsman's garden with moat, lake, orangery and fine lawns, extensively planted with herbaceous and shrubs in a woodland and waterside setting.
Toilets; Refreshments; Disabled access

Fletcher Moss Botanical Gardens
Mill Gate Lane, Didsbury,
Manchester, Gt M20 2SW
Contact: Nigel Joynson
Tel/fax: 0161 434 1877
Hours: 8am–dusk daily. Orchid House closed evgs/weekends
Interesting and colourful in every season. Rock garden, herbaceous borders, heathers, orchid house in parsonage gardens, rare trees, shrubs and alpines. Tennis and bowls.
Toilets; Refreshments; Disabled access

Merseyside

Croxteth Hall & Country Park
Croxteth Hall Lane, Liverpool,
Merseyside L12 0HB
Contact: Irene Vickers
Tel: 0151 228 5311
Fax: 0151 228 2817
Hours: 11am–5pm daily
Easter–Sept
Five hundred acres of woodland and parkland. Victorian walled garden. Rare breeds farm. Historic mansion special events throughout the year. Entrance to parkland/car park FREE.
Toilets; Refreshments; Disabled access

Middlesex

Myddelton House
Bulls Cross, Enfield, Middlesex
Tel/fax: 01992 717711
Hours: 10am–3.30pm weekdays
Feb–Oct
Toilets; Disabled access

Syon Park
Brentford, Middlesex TW8 8JF
Tel/fax: 0181 560 0881
Hours: 10am–6pm daily
Mar–Oct. 10am–sunset Nov–Feb
Toilets; Refreshments; Disabled access

Norfolk

Blickling Hall & Gardens
Blickling, Norwich, Norfolk
NR11 6NF
Contact: Property Manager
Tel: 01263 733084
Fax: 01263 734924
Hours: 12–5pm daily except Mon & Thurs Mar–Oct
Extensive colourful garden (admission £2.50). Picnic area and plant centre (admission free). Guided garden tours available, please ask for dates. Fine Jacobean mansion. B1354, Aylsham.
Toilets; Refreshments; Disabled access

Euston Hall - Suffolk
Euston, Thetford, Norfolk IP24 2QP
Contact: Mrs L H Campbell
Tel: 01842 766366
Fax: 01842 766764
Hours: 2.30–5pm Thurs June–Sept
12m N. of Bury St Edmunds, Suffolk. Terraced lawns, herbaceous borders, rose garden, 17th century pleasure grounds designed by John Evelyn, park and temple by William Kent.
Toilets; Refreshments

Fairhaven Garden Trust
2 The Woodlands, Wymers Lane,
South Walsham, Norwich,
Norfolk NR13 6EA
Contact: George Debbage
Tel/fax: 01603 270449
Hours: 11am–5.30pm Tues–Fri & Sun. 2–5.30pm Sat
Delightful natural woodland and water gardens with private inner broad. Boat trips available. Light refreshments. Plant sales area. Gift shop.
Catalogue; Mail order; Toilets; Refreshments; Disabled access

Felbrigg Hall
Roughton, Norwich, Norfolk
NR11 8PR
Tel: 01263 837444
Fax: 01263 838297
Hours: 11am–5.30m Sat–Mon
Wed–Thur Apr–Oct
Toilets; Refreshments; Disabled access

Holkham Hall
Holkham, Wells-next-the-Sea,
Norfolk
Hours: 1.30–5pm Sun–Thurs 31
May–29 Sept
Toilets; Refreshments; Disabled access

Mannington Gardens
Mannington Hall, Norwich,
Norfolk NR11 7BB
Tel: 01263 584175
Fax: 01263 761214
Hours: 12noon–5pm Suns
May–Sept. 11am–5pm
Wed/Thurs/Fri June–Aug
Beautiful gardens around medieval moated manor house. Heritage rose gardens. Lake, trees and shrubs. Rose sales and advice. Country walks. Refreshments.
Toilets; Refreshments; Disabled access

Norfolk Lavender Ltd
Caley Mill, Heacham, Kings Lynn,
Norfolk PE31 7JE
Tel: 01485 570384
Fax: 01485 571176
Open all year (except 2 weeks after Christmas). Free admission. Fragrant garden, herb garden, National Collection of Lavenders. Guided tour of fields/gardens. Gift/plant shop. Tearoom - home-made cakes, scones, lunches. Play area.
Catalogue; Mail order; Toilets; Refreshments; Disabled access

Oxburgh Hall
Oxborough, Kings Lynn, Norfolk
PE33 9PS
Tel/fax: 01366 328258
Hours: 12–5pm Sat–Wed end
Mar–Oct
Toilets; Refreshments; Disabled access

P W Plants
Sunnyside, Heath Rd,
Kenninghall, Norwich, Norfolk
NR16 2DS
Contact: Paul Whittaker
Hours: Every Friday and last Saturday in month.
Catalogue: 5 first class stamps. We specialise in foliage plants, bamboos, grasses, shrubs and climbers.
Catalogue; Mail order; Toilets

Rainthorpe Hall Gardens
Tasburgh, Norwich, Norfolk
NR15 1RQ
Tel: 01508 490191
Fax: 01508 470618
Hours: 10am–5pm Wed/Sat/Sun
Bank Hols Easter–Oct
Toilets; Refreshments; Disabled access

Sandringham House & Grounds
Sandringham, Kings Lynn,
Norfolk PE35 6EN
Contact: Mrs Gill Pattinson
Tel: 01553 772675
Fax: 01485 541571
Hours: 10.30am–5pm Easter–mid
July, early Aug–Oct
Sixty acres of glorious grounds surround H.M. the Queen's country home. Admission £4.50 inc. house and museum. Plants from the royal gardens on sale.
Toilets; Refreshments; Disabled access

Sheringham Park
Gardeners Cottage, Sheringham
Park, Sheringham, Norfolk NR26 8TB
Tel/fax: 01263 823778
Hours: Dawn–dusk daily all year
Toilets; Disabled access

Northamptonshire

Canons Ashby House
Canons Ashby, Daventry,
Northamptonshire NN11 6SD
Tel/fax: 01327 860044
Hours: 1–5.30pm or dusk
Wed–Sun & Bank Hls Apr–Oct

Castle Ashby Gardens
Castle Ashby, Northampton,
Northamptonshire NN7 1LQ
Tel: 01604 696696
Fax: 01604 696516
Hours: 10am–dusk all year
Toilets; Refreshments; Disabled access

Coton Manor Garden
Nr Guilsborough, Northampton,
Northamptonshire NN6 8RQ
Contact: Ian Pasley-Tyler
Tel: 01604 740219
Fax: 01604 740838
Hours: 12noon–5.30pm Wed–Sun
Easter–Sept
Extensively planted old English garden laid out on different levels covering ten acres with herbaceous borders, rose, herb and water gardens. Nursery selling unusual plants.
Catalogue; Toilets; Refreshments; Disabled access

Cottesbrooke Hall
Northampton,
Northamptonshire NN6 8PF

Contact: Administrator
Tel: 0604 505808
Fax: 0604 505619

Cottesbrooke Hall: 10m N of Northampton. Close to A14-A1/M1 Link Road. Nr Creaton on A50, near Brixworth on A508. Architecturally magnificent Queen Anne house reputed to be the pattern for Jane Austen's 'Mansfield Park'. The gardens are both celebrated and of great distinction. They include fine old cedars and specimen trees with formal parterres and magnificent double herbaceous borders, as well as small individually planted courtyards. All this is set in a remarkable eighteenth century landscaped park with vistas and lakes, focusing on the renowned c675 AD Saxon church at Brixworth. In addition there are water and wild gardens including rhododendrons, bamboos, gunneras and fine foliage plants. Home grown plants as seen in the gardens can be purchased. Admission to gardens only £2.50; house and garden £4.00. Private bookings for group visits by prior arrangement. House & gardens open Easter to end September. Gardens: Wed/Thurs/Fri/Bk Hol Mons, plus Suns in Sept - 2-5.30pm. House: Thurs/ Bk Hol Mons, plus Suns in Sept - 2-5.30pm.
Toilets; Refreshments

Holdenby House Gardens
Holdenby, Northampton,
Northamptonshire NN6 8DJ

Tel/fax: 01604 770074
Hours: 1–6pm Weekdays, 2–6pm Sun, 1–6pm Bank Hols Apr–Sept
Toilets; Refreshments; Disabled access

Old Rectory Sudborough
Sudborough, Northamptonshire
NN14 3BX

Tel: 01832 73324
Fax: 01832 733832
Hours: By appointment only
Toilets

Sulgrave Manor
Manor Rd, Sulgrave, Banbury,
Northamptonshire OX17 2SD

Contact: Martin Sirot-Smith
Tel/fax: 01295 760205
Hours: 2–5pm Mon–Fri except Weds Apr–Oct. 10.30am–5.30pm Sat/Sun

Sulgrave Manor presents a typical wealthy man's home of the Tudor period. Gardens designed by Sir Reginald Blomfield in 1921 to create a setting for the house.
Toilets; Refreshments

Northumberland

Bide-a-Wee Cottage Garden
Stanton, Netherwitton, Morpeth,
Northumberland NE65 8PR

Contact: Mark Robson
Tel/fax: 01670 772262
Hours: 1.30–5pm Sats May 3–Aug 30

Quarry garden 7 miles north west of Morpeth with small nursery specialising in herbaceous plants. Admission £1.75.
Catalogue

Chillingham Castle
Chillingham, Alnwick,
Northumberland NE66 5NJ

Contact: The Administrator
Tel: 01668 215359
Fax: 01668 215463
Hours: 1–5pm Easter and May–Sept

Wyatville garden, 1828. Topiary and herbaceous borders, rhododendrons, fine trees, lake, 100 acre woodland walks. Apartments to let in castle. Tearoom, shop, group catering by arrangement.
Toilets; Refreshments

Cragside
Rothbury, Morpeth,
Northumberland NE65 7PX

Tel/fax: 01669 20333/20266
Hours: 10.30am–5.30pm Tues–Sun Apr–Oct
Toilets; Refreshments

English Heritage
Belsay Hall, Belsay,
Northumberland NE20 0DX

Contact: The Custodian
Tel: 01661 881636
Fax: 01661 881043
Hours: 10am–6pm Apr–Oct. 10am–4pm Nov–March

Unfurnished 19th century hall, 14th century castle, ruins of 17th century manor house, 30 acres of gardens. Adults £3.50, concessions £2.60, children £1.80. Shop, tea room, coach & car parking.
Catalogue

Herterton House Gardens & Nursery
Hartington, Cambo, Morpeth,
Northumberland NE61 4BN

Contact: Frank Lawley
Tel/fax: 01670 774278
Hours: 1.30pm–5.30pm daily Apr–Sept. Closed Tues & Thurs

Small formal country garden around 16th century farmhouse. Topiary, physic and flower gardens. Nursery selling herbaceous plants. Admission £1.40, children free. Pre-booked parties only.
Toilets

Hexham Herbs
Chesters Walled Garden,
Chollerford, Hexham,
Northumberland NE46 4BQ

Contact: Kevin White
Tel/fax: 01434 681483
Hours: 10am–5pm daily March–end Oct. Phone for Winter opening times

Beautiful walled garden, extensive herb collection. Many unusual herbaceous perennials, old roses, Roman herbs, famous Thyme Bank. Award-winning nursery. Herbal gift shop. Woodland walk.
Catalogue

Howick Hall
Alnwick, Northumberland
NE66 3LB

Tel/fax: 01665 577285
Hours: 1–6pm daily early Apr–late October

Fine woodland garden established in 1930. Many rare species. Good summer borders surrounding Georgian house. Good spring bulbs and autumn colour.
Toilets

Wallington Hall
Cambo, Morpeth,
Northumberland NE61 4AR

Tel/fax: 01670 74283
Hours: 10.30am–7pm Apr–Sept, 10.30–6pm Oct. Closes dusk in Winter
Toilets; Refreshments; Disabled access

Nottinghamshire

Clumber Park
The Estate Office, Worksop,
Nottinghamshire S80 3AZ

Tel: 01909 476592
Fax: 01909 500721
Hours: 10.30am–5pm (6pm in Summer) daily all year
Toilets; Refreshments; Disabled access

Felley Priory Garden
Underwood, Jacksdale,
Nottinghamshire NG16 5FL

Contact: Hon Mrs Chaworth-Musters
Tel/fax: 01773 810230

Old fashioned garden round Elizabethan house. Orchard of daffodils, herbaceous borders, pond, topiary, rose garden of old roses, nursery of unusual plants and shrubs. Admission £1.50, children free. Gardens and nursery open Tuesday, Wednesday, Friday 9am-12.30pm all year; every 2nd and 4th Wednesday 9am-4pm February-October. Refreshments always available. Also for parties by appointment. Garden ½ mile West from M1 junction 27 or A608.
Toilets; Refreshments; Disabled access

Hodsock Priory
Blyth, Worksop,
Nottinghamshire S81 0TY

Tel/fax: 01909 591204
Hours: 2–5pm Sun Easter–mid Jul. By appt in Feb
Toilets; Refreshments; Disabled access

Morton Hall
Ranby, Retford, Nottinghamshire
DH22 7HW

Tel/fax: 01777 701142
Hours: Open days in Apr/May & Oct. Phone for details
Toilets; Refreshments; Disabled access

Newstead Abbey
Newstead Abbey Park,
Nottinghamshire NG15 8GE

Tel/fax: 01623 793557
Hours: 10am–7pm Summer, 10am–5pm Winter
Toilets; Refreshments; Disabled access

St Helens Croft
Halam, Nottinghamshire

Tel/fax: 01636 813219
Hours: Irregular opening. Phone for details & appts

Oxfordshire

Blenheim Palace
Woodstock, Oxford,
Oxfordshire OX20 1PX

Tel: 01993 811091
Fax: 01993 813527
Hours: 10.30am–4.45pm daily mid Mar–Oct
Toilets; Refreshments

Brook Cottage
Well Lane, Alkerton, Banbury,
Oxfordshire OX15 6NL

Tel/fax: 01295 87303
Hours: 9am–6pm Mon–Fri Apr–Oct
Toilets; Refreshments

Broughton Castle
Broughton, Banbury,
Oxfordshire OX15 5EB

Contact: Gill Cozens
Tel/fax: 01295 262624
Hours: 2–5pm Wed/Sun & Bank Hols May 18 –14 Sept. Thurs in Jul/Aug

Moated 14th & 16th century house, formal walled garden. Mixed herbaceous borders. Old roses. Parkland. Plants on sale.
Toilets; Refreshments; Disabled access

Buscot Park
Faringdon, Oxfordshire SN7 8BU

Tel/fax: 01367 240786-weekday
Hours: 2–6pm Wed-Fri & 2nd/4th Sat/Sun in month Apr–Sept
Toilets; Refreshments

The Daily Telegraph *Green Fingers* — **Gardens to Visit**

Clock House
Coleshill, Faringdon, Oxfordshire
Contact: Mrs Denny Wickham
Tel: 01793 762476
Fax: 01793 861615
Hours: May 14, June 18, July 2, Sept 10 and Thurs afternoons or by appt

Overlooking parkland and vale of the White Horse with plan of old house laid out as a garden, unusual plants, walled flower garden, vegetables, etc. 19th century estate village.
Toilets; Refreshments

Greys Court
Rotherfield Greys,
Henley-on-Thames, Oxfordshire
RG9 4PG
Tel/fax: 01491 628529
Hours: 2–6pm daily except Thur/Sun Apr–Sept. Closed Good Fri
Refreshments

Greystone Cottage
Colmore Lane, Kingwood Common, Henley-on-Thames, Oxfordshire RG9 5NA
Tel: 01491 628559
Fax: 01491 628839
Hours: For NGS & by appt. Phone for details
Toilets; Refreshments

Kingston Bagpuize House
Kingston Bagpuize, Abingdon, Oxfordshire OX13 5AX
Tel/fax: 01865 820259
Hours: 2.30–5.30pm Sun/Bank Hol Mons Apr–Sept. Also for NGS

Charles II manor house with large garden (A415/A420). Groups by appointment. Rates on request.
Toilets; Refreshments

Mount Skippet
Ramsden, Witney, Oxfordshire
GX7 3AP
Tel/fax: 01993 868253
Hours: By appointment only
Toilets

Nuneham Courtenay Arboretum
Nuneham Courtenay,
Oxfordshire
Hours: 9am–5pm Mon–Sat, 2–5pm Sun May–Oct

Old Rectory Farnborough
Farnborough, Wantage,
Oxfordshire OX12 8NX
Tel/fax: 01488 638298
Hours: Phone for details

Oxford Botanic Gardens
High Street, Oxford, Oxfordshire
OX1 4AX
Tel/fax: 01865 26920
Hours: 9am–5pm daily all year except Good Fri & Xmas Day
Disabled access

Rousham House
Steeple Aston, Oxford,
Oxfordshire OX5 3QX
Tel/fax: 01869 47110
Hours: 10am–4pm daily all year
Toilets

Stanton Harcourt Manor House & Gardens
Stanton Harcourt, Witney,
Oxfordshire OX8 1RJ
Contact: The Hon Mrs Gascoigne
Tel/fax: 01865 881928
Hours: 2–6pm April–Sept. Stated dates only – ring for details

Unique mediaeval buildings - old kitchen, (Alexander) Pope's tower and domestic chapel in 12 acres of garden with great fish pond. Admission: adults £4, children & OAPs £2.
Toilets; Refreshments; Disabled access

Waterperry Gardens Ltd
Waterperry, Nr Wheatley,
Oxfordshire OX33 1JZ
Tel: 01844 339226
Fax: 01844 339883
Hours: 10am–5.30pm daily. Closed Xmas/New Year hols & July 17–20 1997

Beautiful gardens, river walk, Saxon church. Garden shop and plant centre. Pear Tree Teashop - delicious home-made food. Art in Action gallery - fine arts, crafts.
Toilets; Refreshments; Disabled access

Shropshire

Benthall Hall
Broseley, Shropshire TF12 5RX
Tel/fax: 01952 884028
Hours: 1.30–5.30pm Suns/Weds/Bank Hols Apr–Sept
Toilets; Disabled access

Dolwen
Cefn Coch,
Llanrhaedr-ym-Mochnant,
Oswestry, Shropshire SY10 0BLL
Tel/fax: 01691 780411
Hours: 2–4.30pm every Fri & last Sun in month May–mid Sept

4 acre woodland and water garden in the Berwyn mountains. Plants for sale. Entrance £1.
Toilets; Refreshments

Erway Farm House
Pentre Coed, Ellesmere,
Shropshire SY12 9ED
Contact: B N Palmer
Tel/fax: 01691 690479
Hours: 2–6pm Last Sun in every month Feb–Sept. Also Easter Sat–Mon

Sophisticated cottage garden with extensive collections of early bulbs and hellebores. Rare plants from garden for sale when open for National Gardens Scheme. Entry £1.
Toilets

Hodnet Hall Gardens
Hodnet, Market Drayton,
Shropshire TF9 3NN
Contact: Mrs M Taylor
Tel: 01630 685202
Fax: 01630 685853
Hours: 2–5pm Tues–Sat, 12–5.30pm Sun/Bank Hols Apr–Sept

Beautiful woodland walks through trees and shrubs in 60 acres of flowering lakeside gardens. Tearooms. Gift shop. Kitchen garden. Sales area. Dogs allowed on leads.
Toilets; Refreshments; Disabled access

Lingen Nursery & Garden
Lingen, Nr Bucknell, Shropshire
SY7 0DY
Contact: Kim W Davis
Tel/fax: 01544 267720
Hours: 10am–6pm Feb–Oct

Alpine, rock garden and herbaceous plants displayed in extensive gardens and for sale. Descriptive catalogue 3 x 1st class stamps.
Catalogue; Mail order; Toilets

Lower Hall
Worfield, Bridgnorth, Shropshire
WV15 5LH
Tel/fax: 01746 4607
Hours: By appointment only
Toilets; Refreshments; Disabled access

Nordybank Nurseries
Clee St Margaret, Craven Arms,
Shropshire SY7 9EF
Tel/fax: 01584 823322
Hours: 12noon–6pm Mon/Wed/Sun Easter–mid Oct

One acre plantsman's cottage garden with small nursery, specialising in unusual herbaceous plants, all organically grown. Plant list 2 x 1st class stamps. Garden admission £1.50.
Catalogue; Toilets; Refreshments

Preen Manor
Church Preen, Church Stretton,
Shropshire SY6 7LQ
Tel/fax: 01694 771207
Hours: For NGS & by appt
Toilets; Refreshments

Ruthall Manor
Ditton Priors, Bridgnorth,
Shropshire WV16 6TN
Tel/fax: 01764 34608
Hours: 2–6pm Spring Bank Hol Wkend. Open for NGS & by appt
Toilets

Swallow Hayes
Rectory Rd, Albrighton,
Wolverhampton, Shropshire
WV7 3EP
Tel/fax: 01902 372624
Hours: Open for NGS or by appt

Two acre garden planned for easy maintenance and all year interest. National Collections of Hamamelis and Russell Lupins.
Toilets; Refreshments

Weston Park
Weston under Lizard, Nr Shifnal,
Shropshire TF11 8LE
Contact: Alison Kaye
Tel: 01952 850207
Fax: 01952 850430
Hours: Easter–Sept. Please phone for details

17th century stately home set in 1,000 acres Capability Brown parkland. Beautifully restored formal gardens surrounding the house. Wide variety of trees and shrubs provide colour throughout the season.
Toilets; Refreshments; Disabled access

Somerset

Ammerdown Park
Kilmersdown, Radstock, Bath,
Somerset BA3 5SH
Tel/fax: 01761 437382
Hours: 11am–5pm Bank Hol Mons Apr–Oct

Barrington Court
Barrington, Nr Ilminster,
Somerset TA19 0NQ
Contact: David Smith
Tel/fax: 01460 241938
Hours: Daily except Fri Mar 22–Oct 30

National Trust. Elizabethan house and garden influenced by Gertrude Jekyll. Admission £4, children £2. Parties (pre-booking required) £3.50, children £1.80.
Toilets; Refreshments; Disabled access

Cannington College
Cannington, Bridgwater,
Somerset TA5 2LS
Contact: Mr S J Rudhal
Tel: 01278 652226
Fax: 01278 652479
Hours: 2–5pm daily Easter–Oct

Heritage gardens and plant centre containing one of the largest plant collections in the south-west, including eight National Collections. Large tropical glasshouse complex.
Catalogue; Mail order; Toilets

Clapton Court Gardens
Garden Cottage, Clapton Court,
Crewkerne, Somerset TA18 8PT
Tel/fax: 01460 73220

No tea rooms. No plant centre. No playground. Simply 10 acres of beautiful gardens and woodland walk, plus the largest ash tree in Great Britain.
Toilets

Dunster Castle
Minehead, Somerset TA24 6SL
Tel/fax: 01643 821314
Hours: 11am–4pm daily Feb/Mar/Oct–mid Dec, 11–5pm Apr–Sept
Toilets; Refreshments; Disabled access

East Lambrook Manor Garden
East Lambrook, South Petherton, Somerset TA13 5HL
Tel: 01460 240328
Fax: 01460 242344
Hours: 10am–5pm Mon–Sat Mar–Oct
Created by the late Margery Fish, this Grade I garden with its abundant planting provides old world peace and tranquility throughout the seasons.
Catalogue; Mail order; Toilets; Refreshments

Elworthy Cottage Plants
Elworthy Cottage, Elworthy, Nr Lydeard St Lawrence, Taunton, Somerset TA4 3PX
Contact: Jenny Spiller
Tel/fax: 01984 656427
Hours: 11am–6pm Tues/Thurs/Fri. Also by appt
Large range of herbaceous perennials, especially hardy geraniums, origanums, pulmonarias, violas and grasses. 3 x 1st class stamps for list. Garden also open. Admission £1.
Catalogue; Toilets

Gaulden Manor
Tolland, Lydeard St Lawrence, Somerset TA4 3PN
Tel/fax: 01984 7213
Hours: 2–5.30 Sun/Thur 1st Sun in May–1st Sun in Sept
Toilets; Refreshments

Greencombe Garden Trust
Porlock, Somerset TA24 8NU
Tel/fax: 01643 862363
Hours: 2–6pm Sat–Tues Apr–Jul
Toilets

Hadspen House
Castle Cary, Somerset BA7 7NG
Tel/fax: 01963 50939
Hours: 9am–6pm Thurs–Sun & Bank Hol Mons Mar–Sept
Toilets; Refreshments; Disabled access

Hestercombe House
Somerset County Council, Cheddon Fitzpaine, Taunton, Somerset TA2 8LQ
Tel: 01823 337222
Fax: 01823 413030
Hours: 9am–5pm Mon–Fri, 2–5pm Sat/Sun May–Sept
Toilets

Lower Severalls Garden & Nursery
Crewkerne, Somerset TA18 7NX
Contact: Mary R Cooper
Tel: 01460 73234
Fax: 01460 76105
Hours: 10am–5pm. 2pm–5pm Sun. Closed Thurs March–Oct
2½ acre plantsman's garden. Mixed borders around early Hamstone farmhouse includes features such as wadi, woven willow baskets.

Lytes Cary Manor
Charlton Mackrell, Somerton, Somerset TA11 7HU
Tel/fax: 01458 223297
Hours: 2–6pm Mon/Wed/Sat Apr–Oct
Toilets

Milton Lodge
Old Bristol Rd, Wells, Somerset BA5 3AQ
Tel/fax: 01749 672168
Hours: 2–6pm Sun–Fri Easter–end Oct
Toilets; Refreshments

Montacute House
Montacute, Yeovil, Somerset TA15 6XP
Tel/fax: 01935 823289
Hours: 11am–5.30pm daily except Tues
Formal garden with Elizabethan framework overlaid by Victorian design. Some 20th century planting features include fine stonework, famous old yew hedges, mixed borders and old roses.
Toilets; Refreshments; Disabled access

Ston Easton Park
Ston Easton, Bath, Somerset BA3 4DF
Tel/fax: 01761 241631
Hours: By appointment unless visiting restaurant
Toilets; Refreshments

Tintinhull House
Tintinhull, Yeovil, Somerset BA22 8PZ
Tel/fax: 01985 847777
Hours: 2–6pm Wed/Thurs/Sat/Bank Hol Mons Apr–Sept
Toilets; Refreshments; Disabled access

Wayford Manor
Crewkerne, Somerset TA18 8QG
Contact: Mr & Mrs R L Goffe
Tel/fax: 01460 73253
Hours: For NGS or by appt for parties

A fine Elizabethan manor house with 3 acre terraced garden redesigned by Harold Pets in 1902. Noted for magnolias and acers. Always interesting, best in Spring.
Toilets; Refreshments

Staffordshire

Alton Towers
Alton, Stoke on Trent, Staffordshire ST10 4DB
Tel: 01538 702200
Fax: 01538 704097
Hours: March–Nov
200 acres of stunning 19th century landscaped gardens forming part of the UK's largest theme park. Park admission including gardens £17.50 adult, £13.50 child.
Toilets; Refreshments

Biddulph Grange
Biddulph, Stoke on Trent, Staffordshire ST8 7SD
Tel/fax: 01782 517999
Hours: 12–6pm Wed–Fri, 11–6pm Sat & Sun April 1–end Oct
National Trust. A rare and remarkable survival of a high-Victorian garden, divided into many settings - willow pattern "China" garden, Egypt, pinetum, dahlia walk.
Toilets; Refreshments

Dorothy Clive Garden
Willoughbridge, Market Drayton, Staffordshire TF9 4EU
Tel/fax: 01630 647237
Hours: 10am–5.30pm daily Apr–Oct
Rhododendrons predominate in a woodland garden created in an old gravel quarry: spectacular waterfall. A hillside garden has splendid views and colourful features throughout the season. Delightful tea room serving home baking.
Toilets; Refreshments; Disabled access

Moseley Old Hall
Fordhouses, Staffordshire WV10 7HY
Contact: David Lee
Tel/fax: 01902 782808
Hours: 15 March–21 Dec. Check days & times before visit
National Trust. Reconstructed 17th century style with formal box parterre, 17th century plants only are grown. House, tea-room and shop open as garden opening times.
Toilets; Refreshments; Disabled access

Oulton House
Oulton, Stone, Staffordshire ST15 8UR
Tel/fax: 01785 813556
Hours: June 24– July 7 by appt

Three acre garden with fine views. Herbaceous borders, old shrub roses, conservatory, large rock garden. Plants for sale.
Toilets; Refreshments

Rode Hall
Church Lane, Scholar Green, Stoke on Trent, Staffordshire ST7 3QP
Tel: 01270 882961
Fax: 01270 882962
Hours: 2–5pm Wed & Bank Hols Apr–Sept
Toilets

Shugborough Estate
Great Haywood, Milford, Staffordshire ST17 0XB
Tel: 01889 881388
Fax: 01889 881323
Hours: 11am–5pm March 29–Sept 28. Sundays only Oct
Lord Lichfield's ancestral home. 900 acres of magnificent gardens and parkland. Neo-classical monuments, Edwardian rose garden, formal terraces and herbaceous border. Glorious Spring rhododendrons, azaleas and wisteria.
Toilets; Refreshments; Disabled access

Trentham Park Gardens
Trentham, Stoke on Trent, Staffordshire
Hours: 10am–6pm daily beg Apr–beg Oct
Toilets; Refreshments

Wolseley Garden Park
Wolseley Bridge, Stafford, Staffordshire ST17 0YT
Contact: David Harper
Tel/fax: 01889 574888
Hours: 11am–4pm daily all year including Suns & Bank Hols
Toilets; Refreshments; Disabled access

Suffolk

Bucklesham Hall
Bucklesham, Ipswich, Suffolk IP10 0AY
Tel/fax: 01473 659263
Hours: By appointment only

Haughley Park
Stowmarket, Suffolk IP14 3JY
Tel: 01359 240205
Fax: 01359 240546
Hours: 3–5.30pm Tues May–Sept & 1st two Suns in May
Toilets; Disabled access

Helmingham Hall Gardens
Stowmarket, Suffolk IP14 6EF
Tel: 01473 890363
Fax: 01473 890776
Hours: 2–6pm Suns Apr 27–Sept 7. Wed 2–5pm by appt

Grade I listed garden comprising ancient walled garden, brilliant herbaceous borders, rose collection, parterre, herb and knot garden, gift shop, plant sale, delicious cream teas.
Toilets; Refreshments

Ickworth House - Park & Gardens
Horringer, Bury St Edmunds, Suffolk IP29 5QE

Contact: Property Secretary
Tel/fax: 01284 735270

Hours: *Gardens 10am–5pm Mar 23–Nov 3, 10am–4pm 4 Nov–April 1996*

Stylized Italian landscape garden to reflect the extraordinary design of the house. The Albana Wood, recently restored, incorporates a fine circular walk. Recently planted vineyard next to elegant summerhouse by the canal in walled garden.
Toilets; Refreshments; Disabled access

Somerleyton Hall & Gardens
Somerleyton, Lowestoft, Suffolk NR32 5QQ

Tel: 01502 730224
Fax: 01502 732143

Hours: *Easter–Sept Sun/Thurs. July–Aug Tues/Wed/Thurs/Sun*

Anglo-Italian style Victorian stately home with five architectural features, state rooms and superb 12 acre gardens including famous maze, Paxton glasshouses, pergola and original Victorian ornamentation.
Toilets; Refreshments; Disabled access

Wyken Emporium
Wyken Hall, Stanton, Bury St Edmunds, Suffolk IP31 2DW

Contact: Carla Carlisle
Tel: 01359 502240
Fax: 01359 250240

Hours: *10am–6pm Thurs–Sun & Bank Hol Mon*

A garden lover's paradise, including herb, knot and rose gardens featuring old roses, traditional English kitchen garden, wildflower meadows, nuttery and newly planted area.
Toilets; Refreshments; Disabled access

Wyken Hall
Stanton, Bury St Edmunds, Suffolk IP31 2DW

Tel: 01359 50287
Fax: 01359 50240

Hours: *10am–6pm Thurs/Suns/Bank Hols May–Sept*
Toilets; Refreshments; Disabled access

Surrey

Brook Lodge Farm Cottage
Blackbrook, Dorking, Surrey RH5 4DT

Tel/fax: 01306 888368

Hours: *Irregular opening. Phone for details*
Toilets; Refreshments; Disabled access

Clandon Park
West Clandon, Guildford, Surrey GU4 7RQ

Tel/fax: 01483 222482

Hours: *1.30–5.30pm Sat–Wed & Good Fri Apr–Oct*
Toilets; Refreshments; Disabled access

Claremont Gardens
Portsmouth Rd, Esher, Surrey KT10 9JG

Tel/fax: 01372 469421

Hours: *10am–6pm (5pm Nov–Mar & 7pm Sat/Sun Apr–Oct) all year*
Toilets; Refreshments; Disabled access

Ham House
Ham Street, Richmond, Surrey TW10 7RS

Tel: 0181 940 1950
Fax: 0181 332 6903

Hours: *10.30am–6pm or dusk if earlier daily except Friday all year*

National Trust. Formal 17th century garden, east parterre of box-edged beds filled with lavender and santolina, south garden with eight lawns and formal wilderness, also a rose garden.
Toilets; Refreshments; Disabled access

Isabella Plantation
Richmond Park, Richmond, Surrey TW10 5HS

Tel: 0181 948 3209
Fax: 0181 332 2730

Hours: *Dawn–dusk daily*

Mature woodland garden with pools and streams containing fine collections of rhododendrons, azaleas, camellias and magnolias. Main flowering: April/May. Good autumn colour. Entrance free.
Toilets; Disabled access

National Gardens Scheme Charitable Trust
Hatchlands Park, East Clandon, Guildford, Surrey GU4 7RT

Tel: 01483 211535
Fax: 01483 211537

Publishes the Yellow Book, a guide to 3,500 private gardens open for six nursing and gardening charities.

Painshill
Portsmouth Rd, Cobham, Surrey KT11 1JE

Contact: Mrs E Fox
Tel: 01932 868113
Fax: 01932 868001

Walk through this restored 158 acre 18th century garden. Huge lake, giant water wheel, crystal grotto, Gothic temple, Turkish tent, replanted vineyard and shrubberies, surprising vistas. Open April-October & Bank Holidays 10.30am-4.30pm (last ticket). Gates close 6pm. November-February every day except Mondays & Fridays, Xmas Day & Boxing Day 11am-4pm or dusk if earlier.
Toilets; Refreshments; Disabled access

Pinewood House
Heath House Rd, Worplesdon Hill, Woking, Surrey GU22 0QU

Tel/fax: 01483 473241

Hours: *Parties by appt Apr–Oct*
Toilets

Polesden Lacey
Great Bookham, Dorking, Surrey RH5 6BD

Tel/fax: 01372 458203

Hours: *11am–6pm daily all year*
Toilets; Refreshments; Disabled access

R H S Garden Wisley
Woking, Surrey GU23 6QB

Tel: 01483 224234
Fax: 01483 211750

Hours: *Mon–Sat. Sun RHS members only*

One of the world's largest and justifiably famed gardens. Centre for the RHS research and education projects. Adults £5, children up to 16 £1.75, under 6 free.
Toilets; Refreshments; Disabled access

Ramster
Chiddingfold, Surrey GU8 4SN

Tel/fax: 01428 64422

Hours: *2–6pm daily end Apr–beg June. Also Sat/Sun in June*
Toilets; Refreshments; Disabled access

Savill Garden
Wick Lane, Englefield Green, Egham, Surrey TW20 0UU

Contact: Mr J D Bond
Tel: 01753 860222
Fax: 01753 859617

Hours: *10am–6pm daily Mar–Oct. 10am–4pm Nov–Feb. Closed 25 & 26 Dec*

World renowned woodland garden containing a fine range of trees and shrubs and associated woodland plants. Adjoining rose gardens, herbaceous borders and large new temperate house. Truly a garden for all seasons. Gift shop, plant centre and restaurant. Admission adults £3.50, senior citizens £3.
Toilets; Refreshments; Disabled access

Valley Gardens Windsor
Windsor Great Park, Wick Rd, Englefield Green, Surrey

Contact: Mr J D Bond
Tel: 01753 860222
Fax: 01753 859617

Hours: *8am–7pm or sunset if earlier all year*

Woodland garden on north bank of Virginia Water lake. Car park via Wick Rd, Englefield Green, or one mile walk from car park on A30.
Toilets

Vann
Hambledon, Godalming, Surrey GU8 4EF

Tel: 01428 683413
Fax: 017267 9344

Hours: *Open Apr–June (for details see NGS Yellow book) and by appt*

"Best preserved Jekyll water-garden". Jane Brown. 5 acre garden surrounding listed Surrey farmhouse. Godalming 6 miles. £2.50 admission. Catalogue 50p
Toilets

Water Gardens
Warren Rd, Kingston-upon-Thames, Surrey

Tel/fax: 01932 864532

Hours: *For NGS*

Winkworth Arboretum
Hascombe Rd, Godalming, Surrey GU8 4AD

Tel/fax: 0148 632477

Hours: *All year dawn–dusk*
Toilets; Refreshments

Sussex, East

Batemans
Burwash, Etchingham, Sussex (E.) TN19 7DS

Tel/fax: 01435 882302

Hours: *11am–5pm Sat–Wed Apr–Oct*
Toilets; Refreshments

Bates Green
Arlington, Polegate, Sussex (E.) BN26 6SH

Contact: Carolyn McCutchan
Tel/fax: 01323 482039

Hours: *10.30am–6pm Thursdays April–Oct*

Plantsman's tranquil 1½ acre garden. Colour themed herbaceous borders, pond, shaded foliage areas. Admission £2. Farmhouse accommodation available all year.
Toilets

Cabbages & Kings
Wilderness Farm, Wilderness Lane, Hadlow Down, Sussex (E.) TN22 4HU

Contact: Ryl Nowell
Tel: 01825 830552
Fax: 01825 830736

Hours: 11am–6pm Fri–Sun & Bank Hols Easter–end Sept

Imaginative garden developed by designer Ryl Nowell to help people realise the full potential of their own gardens. Adults £2.50, senior citizens & children £2. Plants for sale. Teas.
Toilets; Refreshments; Disabled access

Frewen College
Brickwall House, Northiam, Nr Rye, Sussex (E.) TN31 6NL

Contact: Mrs M Parsons
Tel: 01797 223329
Fax: 01797 252567

Hours: 2–5pm Sats & Bank Hols Apr–Oct

Home of the Frewen family since 1666, now boys' school. Chess garden, arboretum, knot garden with unusual plants. Admission £2.50.
Toilets; Disabled access

Michelham Priory
Upper Dicker, Hailsham, Sussex (E.) BN27 3QS

Tel: 01323 844224
Fax: 01323 844030

Hours: From 11am Wed–Sun Mar–Oct, daily in Aug

7 acres of gardens and lawns surrounding Medieval priory and Tudor house, surrounded by Medieval moat with waterside margins, physic herb garden, cloister garden.
Toilets; Refreshments; Disabled access

Pashley Manor Gardens
Ticehurst, Wadhurst, Sussex (E.) TN5 7HE

Contact: Mr James Sellick
Tel/fax: 01580 200102

Hours: 11am–5pm Tues–Thurs, Sat & Bank Hol Mons Apr 12 – Sept 27

Admission £3.50, OAPs/children aged 6-12 £3. Coach parties welcome. Special garden events. Home-made refreshments. Wine licence. Situated on the B2099, off the A21.
Catalogue; Toilets; Refreshments

Sheffield Park
Uckfield, Sussex (E.) TN22 3QX

Tel/fax: 01825 790655

Hours: 11am–6pm Tues–Sat/Sun/Bnk Hls Apr–Nov (4pm Nov–Dec)
Toilets; Refreshments; Disabled access

Sussex, West

Apuldram Roses
Apuldram Lane, Dell Quay, Chichester, Sussex (W.) PO20 7EF

Contact: Mrs D R Sawday
Tel: 01243 785769
Fax: 01243 536973

Hours: 9am–5pm Mon–Sat/10.30am–4.30pm Suns & Bank Hols

Specialist rose nursery with over 300 varieties. Rose garden and field to view. Catalogue sent on request. Garden centre stocking everything for growing perfect roses.
Catalogue; Mail order; Toilets; Refreshments; Disabled access

Berri Court
Yapton, Arundel, Sussex (W.) BN18 0ED

Tel/fax: 01243 551663

Hours: Vary – phone for opening dates
Toilets; Disabled access

Borde Hill Garden
Balcombe Road, Haywards Heath, Sussex (W.) RH16 1XP

Tel: 01444 450326
Fax: 01444 440427
Email: www.bordehill.co.uk

Hours: 10am–6pm daily

Borde Hill is Britain's best private collection of champion trees. Tranquil gardens with rich variety of all season colour set in 200 acres of parkland and bluebell woods. A rose and herbaceous garden was designed in 1995 by Robin Williams. Planted from 1893 with trees and shrubs from China, Asia, Tasmania, the Andes and Europe, Borde Hill is known for an award winning collection of azaleas, rhododendrons, magnolias and for creating the camellias Donation and Salutation. Attractions include coarse fishing, children's trout fishing, Pirates adventure playground, tea room, restaurant, gift shop and plant centre. There are also extensive woodland walks and lakes with picnic area. Wheelchairs can access most areas and dogs are welcome on leads. Admission: adults £2.50, children £1, family day ticket £6.
Toilets; Refreshments; Disabled access

Coates Manor
Fittleworth, Pulborough, Sussex (W.) RH20 1ES

Contact: Mrs G H Thorpe
Hours: 11am–5pm Oct 19 & 20 & by appt

1 acre, mainly shrubs and foliage of special interest. Small walled garden with tender and scented plants. Featured in foreign and UK magazines.
Toilets; Refreshments

Denmans Garden
Clock House, Denmans, Fontwell, Arundel, Sussex (W.) BN18 0SU

Contact: John Brookes
Tel: 01243 542808
Fax: 01243 544064

Hours: 9am–5pm daily Mar–Dec inc Bank Hols

World famous garden planned with an emphasis on shape, colour, texture and form, something to see throughout the year. Also School of Garden Design.
Toilets; Refreshments

Garden In Mind
Stansted Park, Rowlands Castle, Sussex (W.)

Hours: Sun/Mon/Tues May–Sept
Refreshments

High Beeches
Handcross, Sussex (W.) RH17 6HQ

Tel/fax: 01444 400589

Hours: 1–5pm daily beg Apr–end Jun & beg Sept–end Oct
Toilets

Highdown
Littlehampton Rd, Goring by Sea, Sussex (W.) BN12 6NY

Tel/fax: 01903 248067

Hours: 10am–4.30pm daily all year (8pm Weekends Apr–Sept)
Toilets; Refreshments; Disabled access

Holly Gate Cactus Garden
Billingshurst Rd, Ashington, Sussex (W.) RH20 3BA

Contact: Mr T M Hewitt
Tel/fax: 01903 892930

Hours: 9am–5pm daily except Xmas

Visit the world famous cactus garden. Wander at leisure amongst thousands of fascinating, exotic plants. The largest collection in the UK. Admission only £1.50.
Toilets; Refreshments

Leonardslee Gardens
Brighton Road, Lower Beeding, Horsham, Sussex (W.) RH13 6PP

Tel: 01403 891212
Fax: 01403 891305

Hours: 10am–6pm daily Apr–Oct

Peaceful 240-acre valley with seven beautiful lakes, famous for magnificent rhododendrons and azaleas in Spring, charming rock garden, Summer wildflowers and mellow Autumn tints. Enjoy the fascinating bonsai exhibition, alpine house and the collection of Victorian motorcars (new for 1997). Watch the wallabies, deer and wildfowl on the lakes. Restaurant, gift shop and lots of plants for sale. Admission £3.50 (£4.50 in May), children £2,.
Toilets; Refreshments

Nymans
Handcross, Haywards Heath, Sussex (W.) RH17 6EB

Tel/fax: 01444 400321

Hours: 11am–7pm daily Apr–Oct
Toilets; Refreshments; Disabled access

Parham House & Gardens
Parham Park, Pulborough, Sussex (W.) RH20 4HS

Contact: Patricia Kennedy
Tel: 01903 742021
Fax: 01903 746557

Hours: Afternoons Wed/Thurs/Sun/Bank Hol Mons Apr–Oct

The beautiful Elizabethan house with its eleven acres of fine gardens is idyllically sited in the heart of an ancient Sussex deer park.
Toilets; Refreshments; Disabled access

Petworth House
Petworth, Sussex (W.) GU28 0AE

Tel/fax: 01798 42207

Hours: 8am–dusk daily (not Mon/Fri) Apr–Oct Open Bank Hols
Toilets; Refreshments; Disabled access

Royal Botanic Gardens Kew
Wakehurst Place, Selsfield Road, Ardingly, Sussex (W.) RH17 6TN

Tel: 01444 8940661
Fax: 01444 894069

Hours: From 10am daily. Closing times vary

National botanic garden noted for one of the finest collections of rare trees and flowering shrubs amidst exceptional natural beauty. Displays 4 National Plant Collections.
Toilets; Refreshments; Disabled access

Standen
East Grinstead, Sussex (W.) RH19 4NE

Contact: Jonathan Ingram
Tel: 01342 323029
Fax: 01342 316424

Hours: 12.30pm–6pm Wed–Sun & Bank Hol Mons Mar 26–Nov 2, 1–4pm Fri–Sun Nov 7–Dec 21

National Trust. Beautiful hillside garden; fine views over Medway & Ashdown Forrest. Features include quarry and bamboo gardens, a rhododendron dell and three summer houses. Entrance £3.
Toilets; Refreshments; Disabled access

West Dean Gardens (Edward James Foundation)
College Office, West Dean College, West Dean, Chichester, Sussex (W.) PO18 0QZ

Contact: Diana Lemmon
Tel: 01243 811301
Fax: 01243 811342
Email: westdean@pavilion.co.uk

Offers unrivalled facilities for garden courses. These are available for all levels from beginner to experienced gardener. For full details contact Diana Lemmon.
Catalogue; Refreshments; Disabled access

Tyne & Wear

Birkheads Cottage Garden & Nursery
Birkheads Cottages, Nr Sunniside, Newcastle upon Tyne, Tyne & Wear NE16 5EL

Tel/fax: 01207 232262
Hours: *10am–5pm Sat/Sun & Bank Hols Apr–Sept*

Plantswoman/garden designer's cottage garden (1½ acres) with hardy, uncommon plants. Nursery attached.
Toilets

Warwickshire

Arbury Hall
Nuneaton, Warwickshire CV10 7PT

Tel: 01203 382804
Fax: 01203 641147
Hours: *Easter–Sept Sundays. May, June, July Wed*

Spring flowers, daffodils and bluebells together with native wild flowers. Substantial rhododendron walk providing blaze of colour in Summer. Rose garden. Shrub borders etc.
Toilets; Refreshments

Charlecote Park
Wellesbourne, Warwick, Warwickshire CV35 9ER

Tel/fax: 01789 740277
Hours: *11am–6pm Fri–Tues (Closed Good Fri) Apr–Oct*
Toilets; Refreshments; Disabled access

Farnborough Hall
Banbury, Warwickshire OX17 1DU

Tel/fax: 01295 89202
Hours: *2–6pm Wed–Sat Apr–Sept*
Toilets

Packwood House
Lapworth, Solihull, Warwickshire B94 6AT

Tel/fax: 01564 782024
Hours: *2–6pm Wed–Sun/Bnk Hls Apr–Sept, 12–4pm Wed–Sun Oct*

Sherbourne Park
Sherbourne, Warwick, Warwickshire CV35 8AP

Tel/fax: 01926 624255
Hours: *By appointment only*
Toilets

Upton House
Banbury, Warwickshire OX15 6HT

Tel/fax: 01295 87266
Hours: *2–6pm Sat–Wed May–Oct & Sat/Sun/Bnk Hls in April*
Toilets; Refreshments; Disabled access

Warwick Castle
Warwick, Warwickshire CV34 4QU

Tel/fax: 01926 495421
Hours: *10am–5.30pm (4.30pm in Winter) daily except Xmas Day*
Toilets; Refreshments

West Midlands

Birmingham Botanical Gardens & Glasshouses
Westbourne Rd, Edgbaston, Birmingham, Midlands (W.) B15 3TR

Tel: 0121 454 1860
Fax: 0121 454 7835
Hours: *9am (Sun 10am)–dusk*

A 15 acre oasis of delight. Tropical to arid glasshouses and the finest collection of plants in the Midlands. Aviaries. Playground. Restaurant. Shop. Open daily.
Toilets; Refreshments; Disabled access

Castle Bromwich Hall
Chester Rd, Castle Bromwich, Midlands (W.) B36 9BT

Tel/fax: 0121 749 4100
Hours: *1.30–4.30pm Mon–Thur, 2–6pm Weekends/Bank Hol Mon*
Toilets; Refreshments

Henry Doubleday Research Association (HDRA)
Ryton Organic Gardens, Ryton-on-Dunsmore, Coventry, Midlands (W.) CV8 3LG

Tel: 01203 303517
Fax: 01203 639229

Britain's premier organic gardening organisation, with demonstration gardens at Coventry and Maidstone. Members get free advice, quarterly magazines, discounts from extensive mail order catalogue plus free entry to RHS and other gardens. Runs Heritage Seed Library for endangered vegetables. SAE for details.
Catalogue; Mail order; Toilets; Refreshments; Disabled access

Wightwick Manor
Wightwick, Wolverhampton, Midlands (W.) WV6 8EE

Tel: 01902 761108
Fax: 01902 764663
Hours: *2–6pm Thurs & Sat May–Sept*
Toilets; Refreshments

Wiltshire

Avebury Manor
Avebury, Marlborough, Wiltshire

Tel/fax: 01985 847777
Hours: *11am–5.30pm daily except Mon/Thur end Mar–Oct*

Bowood House
Calne, Wiltshire SN11 0LZ

Tel: 01249 812102
Fax: 01249 821757
Hours: *11am–6pm daily end Mar–Oct*
Toilets; Refreshments; Disabled access

Broadleas Gardens Charitable Trust Ltd
Devizes, Wiltshire SN10 5JQ

Contact: Lady Anne Cowdray
Tel/fax: 01380 722035
Hours: *2–6pm Wed/Thur/Sun Apr–Oct*

A fascinating garden on greensand where magnolias, camellias, rhododendrons flourish. Underplanted with erythroniums, trilliums and sanguinarias. Also roses and rare perennials. Plants for sale. Adults £2.50, children £1, groups £2.20.
Toilets; Refreshments

Corsham Court
Corsham, Wiltshire SN13 0BZ

Tel/fax: 01249 712214
Hours: *2–6pm Aug–Sept*
Toilets

Courts
Holt, Trowbridge, Wiltshire BA14 6RR

Tel/fax: 01225 782340
Hours: *2–5pm Sun–Fri Apr–Oct*
Toilets

Heale House
Middle Woodford, Salisbury, Wiltshire SP4 6NT

Tel/fax: 01722 72504
Hours: *10am–5pm all year*
Toilets

Iford Manor Gardens
Iford Manor, Bradford-on-Avon, Wiltshire BA15 2BA

Tel: 01225 863146
Fax: 01225 862364
Hours: *2–5pm Sun Apr/Oct, 2–5pm May–Sept. Closed Mon & Fri*

South of Bradford-on-Avon, 7 miles from Bath, Peto's enchanting garden by the River Frome is not to be missed. Entrance £2.20, OAP £1.60.
Toilets; Refreshments

Lackham Gardens
Lacock, Chippenham, Wiltshire SN15 2NY

Contact: Oliver Menhinick
Tel: 01249 443111
Fax: 01249 444474
Hours: *11am–5pm daily Mar–Nov*

Attached to Lackham College.
Catalogue; Toilets; Refreshments

Lacock Abbey
Lacock, Chippenham, Wiltshire SN15 2LG

Contact: Simon Taylor
Tel/fax: 01249 730227
Hours: *NGS Suns Feb 16/23 & Mar 2 12–5pm (1997)*

Early 19th century wooded garden, early Spring interest. Crocus, drifts of snowdrops, aconites. 13th century abbey with cloisters.

Longleat House
Warminster, Wiltshire BA12 7NW

Tel: 01985 844400
Fax: 01985 844885
Hours: *All year*
Toilets; Refreshments

Sheldon Manor
Chippenham, Wiltshire SN14 0RG

Tel/fax: 01259 853120
Hours: *12.30–6pm Thur/Sun/Bank Hols Easter–1st Sun in Oct*
Toilets; Refreshments

Stourhead Landscape Garden
Stourton, Warminster, Wiltshire BA12 6QD

Contact: Mr John Turner
Tel/fax: 01747 841152
Hours: *9am–dusk daily all year*

National Trust. World famous English landscape garden with lakes, temples, trees and shrubs. A garden for all seasons. Plant centre and refreshments available.
Toilets; Refreshments; Disabled access

Stourton House
Stourton, Zeals, Warminster,
Wiltshire BA12 6QF
Tel/fax: 01747 840417
Hours: 11am–6pm
Wed/Thurs/Sun Apr–Nov

Televised plantsman's flower garden with all season colour and interest from unusual plants, daffodils, azaleas, delphiniums, roses. 250 different hydrangeas. Dried flowers and plants sold.
Toilets; Refreshments; Disabled access

Wilton House
Wilton, Salisbury, Wiltshire
SP2 0BJ
Tel: 01722 743115
Fax: 01722 744447
Hours: 11am–6pm daily end Mar–end Oct
Toilets; Refreshments

Yorkshire, North

Beningbrough Hall
Shipton by Beningbrough, York, Yorkshire (N.) YO6 1DD
Tel: 01904 470666
Fax: 01904 470002
Hours: 11am–5pm Sat–Wed Apr–Oct. Open Fri July/Aug

Exciting new walled garden, ornamental gardens, formal gardens, parkland and wilderness surrounding an impressive 18th century mansion. Restaurant and shop. Walled garden produce for sale.
Toilets; Refreshments; Disabled access

Castle Howard
York, Yorkshire (N.) YO6 7DA
Tel: 01653 648333
Fax: 01653 648462
Hours: 10am–4.30pm daily Mar–Oct
Toilets; Refreshments

Constable Burton Hall Gardens
Constable Burton, Leyburn, Yorkshire (N.) DL8 5LJ
Contact: Mr Phil Robinson
Tel/fax: 01677 450428
Hours: 9am–6pm Mar 25–Oct 31

Large romantic terraced garden surrounded by 18th century parkland. Superb John Carr house (not open), woodland walks, garden trails, extensive borders, set in beautiful Wenslydale.
Toilets

Duncombe Park
Helmsley, York, Yorkshire (N.) YO6 5EB
Contact: Sally Potter
Tel: 01439 770213
Fax: 01439 771114
Hours: Good Friday–Nov 2 Sat–Wed. May–Sept daily

This unique early 18th century green garden has been described as "The supreme masterpiece of the art of the landscape gardener". Admission £2.95, child £1.50.
Toilets; Refreshments; Disabled access

Gilling Castle
Gilling East, Yorkshire (N.)
Tel/fax: 0143 93 238
Hours: For NGS 10am–4.30pm daily Jul–Aug

Harlow Carr Botanical Gardens
Beckwithshaw, Harrogate, Yorkshire (N.) HG3 1QB
Tel/fax: 01423 565418
Hours: 9.30am–6pm or dusk if earlier daily

Ornamental gardens, trial grounds, streamside, woodland and arboretum, covering 68 acres. Shop. Restaurant.
Toilets; Refreshments; Disabled access

Newby Hall & Gardens
Ripon, Yorkshire (N.) HG4 5AE
Contact: Robin Alexander
Tel: 01423 322583
Fax: 01423 324452
Email:
www.yorkshire.co.uk/newbyhall
Hours: Tues–Sun & Bank Hol Mons Easter–end Sept

25 acres of award-winning gardens; stunning double herbaceous borders with seasonal compartmented gardens. One of England's renowned Adam houses; miniature railway and children's adventure garden.
Toilets; Refreshments; Disabled access

Norton Conyers
Wath, Ripon, Yorkshire (N.) HG4 5EH
Contact: Lady Graham
Tel/fax: 01765 640 333

18th century walled garden near main house. Herbaceous borders flanked by large yew hedges leading to late 18th century orangery. Unusual hardy plants. Pick your own fruit. Entrance free; donations are welcome. Open: 2-5pm Bank Holiday Sundays and Mondays. Every Sunday from 23 June to 1 September, Mondays in July, and daily from 23 to 27 July.

Parcevall Hall Gardens
Skyreholme, Skipton, Yorkshire (N.) BD23 6DE
Tel/fax: 01756 720311
Hours: 10am–6pm Good Fri–31 Oct (Winter by appt)

This beautiful woodland garden with terraces, rock gardens, streams and pools grows many flowering plants, trees and shrubs: the orchard is delightful for picnics.
Toilets

Perry's Plants
River Gardens, Sleights, Whitby, Yorkshire (N.) YO21 1RR
Contact: Pat Perry
Tel/fax: 01947 810329
Hours: 10am–5pm late Mar – end Oct

Small family nursery specialising in uncommon hardy and container plants. Landscaped riverside gardens, licensed Victorian tearoom (home baking), putting. Free admission. Large S.A.E. for plant list.
Catalogue; Toilets; Refreshments

Rievaulx Terrace
Helmsley, Yorkshire (N.)
Tel/fax: 0143 96 340
Hours: 10.30am–6pm daily end Apr–Oct

Ripley Castle
Ripley, Harrogate, Yorkshire (N.) HG3 3AY
Contact: William Myles
Tel: 01423 770152
Fax: 01423 771745
Hours: 11am–5pm (4pm Mar/3.30pm Nov–Dec) daily Mar–Dec

Beautiful Victorian walled gardens with massive herbaceous beds and home to the National Hyacinth Collection. The hothouses provide a plethora of tropical plant selections.
Toilets; Refreshments; Disabled access

Stillingfleet Lodge Nurseries
Stillingfleet, York, Yorkshire (N.) YO4 6HW
Contact: Vanessa Cook
Tel/fax: 01904 728506
Hours: 10am–4pm Tues/Wed Fri/Sat 1 Apr–18 Oct

Catalogue 5 x 1st class stamps. Hardy geraniums, grasses, silver foliage, clematis. Garden open Wednesday afternoons May, June.
Catalogue; Mail order

Sutton Park Stately Home
Sutton-on-the-Forest, York, Yorkshire (N.) YO6 1DP
Tel: 01347 810249
Fax: 01347 811251
Hours: 11am–5pm daily Easter–Oct

Wonderful award-winning gardens visited by enthusiasts from both home and abroad. A haven of beauty and tranquility set around this beautiful Georgian stately home.
Toilets; Refreshments

Thorp Perrow Arboretum
Bedale, Yorkshire (N.) DL8 2PR
Contact: Louise McNeill
Tel/fax: 01677 425323
Hours: Dawn–dusk all year

85 acres, one of the largest collections of trees in the north of England, including a 16th century medieval spring wood and 19th century pinetum.
Toilets; Refreshments; Disabled access

Valley Gardens Harrogate
Harrogate Borough Council, Dept of Leisure/Amenity, St Lukes Avenue, Harrogate, Yorkshire (N.) HG1 2AA
Tel/fax: 01423 500600 Ex 3211
Hours: At all times

Valley Gardens is Grade 2 listed and is recognised for its formal and informal excellence. Varied attractive landscape features lead to rhododendron and woodland walks.
Toilets; Refreshments

Yorkshire, South

Sheffield Botanical Gardens
Clarkehouse Rd, Sheffield, Yorkshire (S.) S10 2LN
Tel/fax: 0114 2671115
Hours: 8am–8pm Summer/8am–4pm Winter
Toilets; Disabled access

Wentworth Castle Gardens
Northern College, Wentworth Castle, Stainborough, Barnsley, Yorkshire (S.) S75 3ET
Tel: 01226 285426
Fax: 01226 284308
Hours: 10am–5pm Spring Bank Hol & by appt May/June
Toilets

Yorkshire, West

Bramham Park
Bramham Park, Wetherby, Yorkshire (W.) LS23 6ND
Tel: 01937 844265
Fax: 01937 845923
Hours: Easter, May Day, Spring Bank Hol weekends. Phone for details

66 acres of formal gardens inspired by André Le Notre with ornamental ponds, cascades, beech hedges and loggias. Gardens noted for display of daffodils.
Toilets; Disabled access

Canal Gardens
Roundhay Park, Street Lane, Leeds, Yorkshire (W.)
Tel/fax: 0113 2661850
Hours: All year (Tropical World closes at dusk)
Toilets; Refreshments

Golden Acre Park
Otley Rd, Bramhope, Leeds, Yorkshire (W.) LS16 5NZ
Tel/fax: 0113 2782030
Hours: All year
Toilets; Refreshments

The Daily Telegraph *Green Fingers* **Gardens to Visit**

Harewood House & Gardens
Harewood, Leeds, Yorkshire (W.) LS17 9LQ
Tel: 0113 2886331
Fax: 0113 2886467

Magnificent award-winning garden in 1,000 acres of Capability Brown parkland. Spectacular rhododendrons, hostas and Victorian terrace. Adult £4, child £2. On A61 between Leeds and Harrogate.

Hollies Park
Weetwood Lane, Leeds, Yorkshire (W.) LS16 5NZ
Tel/fax: 0113 2782030
Hours: All year
Toilets

Lotherton Hall
Aberford, Leeds, Yorkshire (W.)
Tel/fax: 0113 2813259
Hours: Dawn–dusk daily
Toilets; Refreshments; Disabled access

Temple Newsam Park
Managers Office, Temple Newsam Park, Leeds, Yorkshire (W.) LS15
Tel/fax: 0113 645535
Hours: All year
Toilets; Refreshments

N Ireland

Co Down

Castlewellan National Arboretum
Castlewellan Forest Park, Castlewellan, Co Down BT31 9BU
Contact: Sam Harrison
Tel: 01396 778664
Fax: 01396 771762
Hours: 10am–1 hour before sunset all year

The National Arboretum contains a magnificent collection of trees and shrubs. The Annesley Garden is particularly notable for its collection of southern hemisphere species.
Toilets; Refreshments; Disabled access

Mount Stewart
The National Trust, Mount Stewart Estate, Grey Abbey, Newtownards, Co Down BT22 2AD
Tel/fax: 01247 788387
Hours: 10.30am–6pm daily Apr–Sept. Weekends only in Oct
Toilets; Refreshments; Disabled access

Rowallane Gardens
Saintfield, Co Down BT24 7LH
Tel: 01238 510131
Fax: 01238 511242
Hours: 10am–6pm Mon–Fri, 2–6pm Sat/Sun Apr–Oct

National Trust. 52 acre garden famous for its rhododendrons and azaleas. Holds the National Collection of Penstemon.
Toilets; Refreshments; Disabled access

Co Fermanagh

Florence Court
The National Trust, Enniskillen, Co Fermanagh BT92 1BD
Tel: 01365 348249
Fax: 01365 348873
Hours: Estate open all year

Pleasure grounds with ice house, water powered saw mill and rebuilt summer house. Walled garden. Outstanding views over surrounding mountains.
Toilets; Refreshments; Disabled access

Co Londonderry

Guy Wilson Daffodil Garden
University of Ulster, Coleraine, Co Londonderry BT52 1SA
Tel: 01265 44141
Fax: 01265 40912
Hours: All year
Toilets; Disabled access

Scotland

Borders

Dawyck Botanic Garden
Stobo, Peebles, Borders EH45 9JV
Tel: 01721 760254
Fax: 01721 760214
Hours: 10am–6pm daily mid Mar–end Oct

Historic landscaped arboretum, impressive collection of trees and shrubs provide backdrop to herbaceous plants. Landscaped walks through plant collection rich in wildlife.
Toilets; Refreshments

Manderston
Duns, Berwickshire, Borders TD11 3PP
Contact: The Lord & Lady Palmer
Tel/fax: 01361 883450
Hours: 2–5.30pm Sun/Thur Mid–May–end Sept

Manderston: stately home standing in 56 acres of formal gardens. A must for those visiting the Scottish Borders. Tea room, gift shop. Telephone for details.
Catalogue; Toilets; Refreshments

Mellerstain
Gordon, Borders TD3 6LG
Tel: 01573 410225
Fax: 01573 410388
Hours: 12.30–5pm daily except Sats May–Sept & by appt

Laid out by Sir Reginald Blomfield in 1909, the terraced gardens command a glorious view over lawns and lake to Cheviot Hills.
Toilets; Refreshments

Central

Blairhoyle
Port of Menteith, Stirling, Central FK8 3LF
Tel/fax: 01877 385210
Hours: 1–5pm Wed Apr–Oct or by appt
Toilets

Dumfries & Galloway

Arbigland Gardens
Kirkbean, Dumfries, Dumfries & Galloway DG2 8BQ
Contact: Capt J B Blackett
Tel/fax: 01387 880283
Hours: 2–6pm Tues–Sun & Bank Hols May 1–Sept 30

The ideal family visit, as these gardens give access to a sheltered, sandy bay where youngsters (and dogs) can play.
Toilets; Refreshments

Castle Kennedy
Rephad, Stranraer, Dumfries & Galloway DG9 8BX
Tel: 01776 702024
Fax: 01776 706248
Hours: 10am–5pm daily 1 Apr–30 Sept

Beautiful landscaped gardens set between two large lochs, extending to 75 acres. Famous for rhododendrons, azaleas and embothriums. Located 5 miles east of Stranraer on A75.
Toilets; Refreshments

Craigieburn Garden
Graigieburn House, Moffat, Dumfries & Galloway DG10 9LF
Contact: Bill Chudziak & Janet Wheatcroft
Tel/fax: 01683 221250
Hours: 10.30am–6pm Tues–Sun & Bank Hols Good Friday–end Oct

Plantsman's garden in an idyllic setting. Formal borders, Autumn garden, woodland glade, rare and Himalayan plants. 2½ miles east of Moffat on A708 Selkirk road. Specialist plant nursery. Featured on C4 'Bloom'.
Catalogue; Toilets; Refreshments

Glenwhan Garden
Dunragit, By Stranraer, Dumfries & Galloway DG9 8PH
Tel/fax: 015814 400222
Hours: 10am–5pm daily 1 Apr–30 Sept

Unique young garden with spectacular sea views in South West Scotland. Nursery, tea-room.
Toilets; Refreshments

Logan Botanic Gardens
Port Logan, Stranraer, Dumfries & Galloway DG9 9ND
Tel: 01776 860231
Fax: 01776 860333
Hours: 10am–6pm daily mid Mar–Oct
Toilets; Refreshments; Disabled access

Threave School of Horticulture
Threave Garden, Castle Douglas, Dumfries & Galloway DG7 1RX
Tel: 01556 502575
Fax: 01556 502683
Hours: 9.30am–sunset

A 65 acre garden for all seasons. Walled garden, glasshouses, rock garden, formal peat and heather gardens. 1 mile west of Castle Douglas.
Refreshments; Disabled access

Fife

Balcaskie
Pittenweem, Fife KY10 2RD
Hours: 2–6pm Sat–Wed June–Aug
Toilets; Refreshments

Earlshall Castle
Leuchars, St Andrews, Fife KY16 0DP
Tel/fax: 01334 839205
Hours: 2–6pm Easter & Suns in Apr. Daily May–Sept

Falkland Palace
Falkland, Cupar, Fife KY7 7BU
Contact: Mrs Veronica Woodman
Tel/fax: 01337 857397
Hours: 11am–5.30pm Mon–Sat, 1.30–5.30pm Sun Apr 1–Oct 22

The 16th century palace of the Scottish kings shelters this magnificent garden. Heavily scented, herbaceous, shrubs, orchard and Real Tennis court. Garden admission £2 Concession £1.
Toilets

Kellie Castle
Pittenweem, Fife KY10 2RF
Tel/fax: 01333 8337
Hours: 10am–dusk daily May–Oct & weekends in April
Toilets; Refreshments

Murrel Gardens
The Murrel, Aberdour, Fife
KY3 0RN

Hours: 10am–5pm Mon–Fri
Apr–Sept
Toilets; Refreshments

St Andrews Botanic Garden
The Canongate, St Andrews, Fife
KY16 8RT

Tel/fax: 01334 76452

Hours: 10am–7pm daily
May–Sept, 10–4pm Apr/Oct,
Mon–Fri Wntr
Toilets

Grampian

Crathes Castle
Banchory, Grampian AB31 3QJ

Tel: 0133 044 525
Fax: 0133 044 797

Hours: 9.30am–sunset daily all year
Toilets; Refreshments; Disabled access

Cruickshank Botanic Garden
University of Aberdeen, Dept of Plant & Soil Science, St Machar Drive, Aberdeen, Grampian
AB9 2UD

Tel/fax: 01224 272704

Hours: 9am–4.30pm Mon–Fri
Oct–Apr, 2–5pm Sat/Sun May–Sept

Admission to the 11 acre garden free. Main features include the rock terrace and rose gardens, the arboretum, sunken garden and the herbaceous border.

Kildrummy Castle
Kildrummy, Alford, Grampian
AB33 8RA

Tel/fax: 019755 71264/71277

Hours: 10am–5pm daily Apr–Oct
Toilets; Refreshments

Leith Hall & Gardens
Kennethmont, Huntly, Aberdeen, Grampian AB54 4QQ

Tel/fax: 01464 3269

Hours: 9.30am–sunset daily all year

National Trust for Scotland. 7 miles south of Huntly, Aberdeenshire. Interesting house, 6 acres of gardens, alpines and herbaceous.
Toilets; Refreshments; Disabled access

Pitmedden
Ellon, Grampian AB4 0PD

Tel/fax: 01651 842352

Hours: 10am–5.30pm daily
May–Sept
Toilets; Refreshments; Disabled access

Highland

Allangrange
Munlochy, Black Isle, Highland
IV8 8NZ

Tel: 01463 81249
Fax: 01463 81407

Hours: 2–5.30pm 3 days only or by appt. Phone for details
Toilets; Refreshments; Disabled access

Cawdor Castle
Cawdor Castle, Nairn, Highland
IV12 5RD

Contact: Secretary
Tel: 01667 404615
Fax: 01667 404674

Hours: 10am–5pm daily May–Sept

The most romantic castle in the Highlands, with a maze and paradise garden. Open every day from May 1st to the first Sunday in October.
Toilets; Refreshments; Disabled access

Dochfour Gardens
Inverness, Highland IV3 6JY

Tel: 01463 86218
Fax: 01463 86336

Hours: 10am–5pm Mon–Fri,
2–5pm Sat/Sun Apr–Oct

Dunrobin Castle & Gardens
Golspie, Sutherland, Highland
KW10 6RR

Contact: Keith Jones
Tel: 01408 633177
Fax: 01408 634081

Hours: Apr–Oct 15. Closed Sun

Superb historic garden lying between fairytale castle and the sea. Original parterres and fountains plus herbaceous borders and magnificent trees.
Toilets; Refreshments

Inverewe
Poolewe, Ross & Cromarty, Highland IV22 2LQ

Tel: 01445 86441
Fax: 01445 86497

Hours: 9.30am–dusk all year
Toilets; Refreshments; Disabled access

Lochalsh Woodland Garden
Balmacara, Kyle of Lochalsh, Highland IV40 8DN

Hours: 9am–dusk daily

Woodland garden on shore of Loch Alsh featuring rhododendrons, bamboos, ferns, hydrangeas, fuchsias. Leaflet available. Adult admission £1, child 50p. 3 miles from Skye Bridge.
Toilets

Kittoch Mill Hosta Garden
Kittoch Mill, Carmunnock, Glasgow G76 9BJ

Contact: Mrs Pat Jordan
Tel/fax: 0141 644 4712

Hours: Sun June 22 & July 6 1997 or by appt

National Collection of Hostas. Waterfall, woodland walk, Japanese-style garden, many unusual plants. £1 entry to gardening charities. Groups and conducted tours by appointment.

Lothian

Dalmeny House
Rosebery Estates, South Queensferry, Lothian EH30 9TQ

Hours: 12–5.30pm Mon/Tues,
1–5.30pm Sun May–Sept
Refreshments

Edinburgh Butterfly & Insect World
Dobies Gardening World, Lasswade, Lothian

Tel/fax: 0131 663 4932
Refreshments

Inveresk Lodge Garden
24 Inveresk Village, Musselburgh, Lothian EH21 7TE

Hours: 10am–4.30pm Mon–Fri,
2–5pm Sun all year
Toilets

Malleny House
Balerno, Lothian EH14 7AF

Tel/fax: 0131 449 2283

Hours: 10am–dusk daily all year
Toilets

National Trust for Scotland
5 Charlotte Square, Edinburgh, Lothian EH2 4DU

Tel: 0131 226 5922
Fax: 0131 243 9302

The National Trust for Scotland manages 30 major Scottish gardens for you to visit and enjoy. Send now for our free leaflet, "Visit Scotland's Best".

Royal Botanic Garden Edinburgh
Inverleith Row, Edinburgh, Lothian EH3 5LR

Tel: 0131 552 7171
Fax: 0131 552 0382

Hours: 10am–6pm Mar–Apr
Sept–Oct(8pm May–Aug/4pm
Nov–Feb)
Toilets; Refreshments; Disabled access

Strathclyde

Achamore Gardens
Isle of Gigha, Argyll, Strathclyde
PA41 7AD

Tel: 01583 505254
Fax: 01583 505244

Hours: Dawn–dusk daily all year

20 minutes' ferry crossing from Tayinloan - 1 3/4 miles walk to gardens full of rhododendrons, azaleas, camellias and semi-exotic plants. Meals, snacks and accomodation from hotel.
Toilets

Ardtornish Garden
Lochaline, Morvern by Oban, Strathclyde PA34 5XA

Tel/fax: 01967 421288

Hours: 10am–5pm daily Apr–Oct
Toilets

Arduaine Gardens
Loch Melfort Hotel, Oban, Strathclyde PA34 4XQ

Tel/fax: 01852 2366

Hours: 9.30am–sunset daily
Toilets

Barwinnock Herbs
Barrhill, Girvan, Ayrshire, Strathclyde KA26 0RB

Contact: Mon & Dave Holtom
Tel/fax: 01465 821338

Hours: 10am–9pm daily Apr–Oct

Culinary, medicinal and fragrant leafed plants. Many unusual varieties. Unique garden and nursery in remote exposed moorland. A collector's haven. Informative mail order catalogue 3 x 1st class stamps please.
Catalogue; Mail order

Biggar Park Gardens
Biggar, Lanarkshire, Strathclyde
ML12 6JS

Contact: Mrs Susan Barnes
Tel/fax: 01899 20185

Hours: Apr–July by appt

Seasonal ten acre private garden. Daffodils, meconopsis, azaleas, rhododendrons, fritillaries, roses, pools, traditional walled garden with fruit, vegetables and herbaceous borders. Starred in Good Gardens Guide.

Brodick Castle
Isle of Arran, Strathclyde
KA27 8HY

Tel/fax: 01770 302202

Hours: 9.30am–dusk daily all year
Toilets; Refreshments; Disabled access

Crarae Gardens
Crarae, Inverary, Strathclyde
PA32 8YA

Tel/fax: 01546 86614

Hours: 9am–6pm daily
Easter–Oct. Daylight hours
Nov–Easter
Toilets; Refreshments; Disabled access

Culzean Country Park
Maybole, Ayrshire, Strathclyde
KA19 8LE

Tel: 01655 6269
Fax: 01655 6615

Hours: 9.30am–dusk daily all year
Toilets; Refreshments; Disabled access

Glasgow Botanic Gardens
730 Great Western Rd, Glasgow, Strathclyde G12 0UE

Contact: Louise Bustard
Tel: 0141 334 2422
Fax: 0141 339 6964

Hours: *Gardens 7am–dusk daily. Glasshouses 10am–4.15pm*

Free entry, open 365 days. Famous tropical plant collections including orchids and tree ferns. Kibble Palace, herb garden, herbaceous borders and arboretum.
Toilets; Disabled access

Glenarn
Rhu, Helensburgh, Strathclyde G84 8LL

Contact: Sue Thornley
Tel/fax: 01436 820493

Hours: *Dawn–dusk daily Mar 21–June 21*

Spectacular woodland garden with world famous collection of species rhododendrons and many other interesting plants including magnolias, embothriums and wild daffodils. Plants sometimes for sale.

Greenbank Garden
Flenders Rd, Clarkston, Glasgow, Strathclyde G76 8RB

Tel/fax: 0141 639 3281

Hours: *9.30am–sunset daily all year*
Toilets; Refreshments; Disabled access

Tayside

Branklyn Garden
Dundee Rd, Perth, Tayside PH2 7BB

Tel/fax: 01738 33199

Hours: *9.30am–sunset daily Mar–Oct*
Toilets

Cluny House Gardens
Aberfeldy, Tayside PH15 2JT

Contact: Wendy Mattingley
Tel/fax: 01887 820795

Hours: *10am–6pm daily Mar 1–Oct 31*

Beautiful 6 acre Himalayan woodland garden set on a hillside in central Pertshire. Magnificent collections of primulas, lilies, trilliums, meconopsis and specimen trees grown.

Drummond Castle Gardens
Muthill, Perthshire, Tayside PH5 2AA

Tel: 01764 681257
Fax: 01764 681550

Hours: *Eastertime, then 2–6pm daily May–Oct*

Scotland's largest Italianate formal gardens. Among the finest in Europe. Magnificent parterre and vistas. Adults £3, OAPs £2, children £1.50. Coach parties please contact.
Toilets

Edzell Castle
Edzell, Angus, Tayside DD9 7TG

Tel/fax: 01365 648631

Hours: *9.30am–6pm Mon–Sat, 2–6pm Sun Apr–Sept (4pm Oct–Mar)*
Toilets; Disabled access

Pitmuies Gardens
House of Pitmuies, By Forfar, Angus, Tayside DD8 2SN

Contact: Mrs Farquhar Ogilvie
Tel/fax: 01241 828245

Hours: *10am–5pm daily Apr–Oct*

Renowned gardens adjacent to 18th century mansion house. Massed Spring bulbs, Summer roses and herbaceous. Woodland and riverside walks by turreted doocot and Gothick washhouse.
Toilets

University of Dundee Botanic Garden
Riverside Drive, Dundee, Tayside DD2 1QH

Tel: 01382 566939
Fax: 01382 640574

Hours: *10am–4.30pm Mon–Sat, 11–4pm Sun*

Landscaped teaching garden, temperate tropical planthouses, water features, native plants. Small selection of seeds, plants and postcards on sale. Visitors' centre.
Toilets; Disabled access

Wales

Clwyd

Bodnant Gardens
Tal-y-Cafn, Nr Colwyn Bay, Clwyd LL28 5RE

Contact: Ann Harvey
Tel: 01492 650460
Fax: 01492 650448

Hours: *10am–5pm mid Mar–end Oct*

National Trust. Magnificent 80 acre garden, rhododendrons, magnolias, camellias and the famous Laburnum Arch in Spring, glorious Summer colour and stunning Autumn colours in October.
Toilets; Refreshments; Disabled access

Chirk Castle
Chirk, Wrexham, Clwyd LL14 5AF

Tel: 01691 777701
Fax: 01691 774706

Hours: *11am–6pm Wed–Sun Apr 2–Sept 30, Sat/Sun in Oct*

National Trust. 5½ acre gardens, terrace, roses, rockery, rhododendrons, azaleas, flowering trees, shrubs, pool, statuary. Garden: adults £2.20, children £1.10. Guide 50p. Tearoom.
Toilets; Refreshments; Disabled access

Erddig
Wrexham, Clwyd LL13 0YT

Contact: The Property Manager
Tel: 01978 355314
Fax: 01978 313333

Hours: *11am–5pm daily Apr–Oct except Thur/Fri*

National Trust. Large walled garden restored to its 18th century formal design with Victorian parterres and yew walk. Contains National Ivy Collection. Phone 01978 313333, our information line.
Toilets; Refreshments; Disabled access

Eucalyptus Trees Ltd
Allt-y-Celyn, Carrog, Corwen, Clwyd LL21 9LD

Contact: Andrew McConnell
Tel/fax: 01490 430671

Hours: *9am–5pm Mon–Fri Mar–Oct*

Specialist growers of proven cold hardy eucalyptus. 3000 trees growing on exposed hillside at 800ft. Mail order. Colour brochure 1st class stamp.
Catalogue; Mail order; Toilets

Dyfed

Cae Hir Gardens
Cae Hir, Cribyn, Lampeter, Dyfed SA48 7NG

Contact: Mr Wil Akkermans
Tel/fax: 01570 470839

Hours: *Daily except Mon, but open Bank Hol Mons*

Beautiful, peaceful 6 acre garden. Many unusual features. Red, yellow, blue and white subgardens. Bonsai room, stonework, ponds, views, bog-garden. Plants for sale. Featured on C4 television and on radio. Admission £2, OAP £1.50, children 50p.
Toilets; Refreshments

Dingle
Dingle Lane, Crundale, Haverfordwest, Dyfed SA62 4DJ

Contact: Mrs A Jones
Tel/fax: 01437 764370

Hours: *10am–6pm Wed–Sun Mar–Oct*

Three acres of beautifully landscaped gardens in picturesque rural setting. Open under NGS. £1 adults, 50p children over 5.
Catalogue; Mail order; Toilets; Refreshments

Picton Castle
The Rhos, Haverfordwest, Dyfed SA62 4AS

Contact: Roddy Milne
Tel/fax: 01437 751370

Hours: *10.30am–5pm Tues–Sun & Bank Hols Apr–Sept*

Beneath the majestic ancient trees grow beautiful exotic shrubs including a unique rhododendron collection set in enchanted glades. Admission £2. Rare shrubs for sale.
Toilets; Refreshments; Disabled access

Post House Gardens
Cwmbach, Whitland, Dyfed SA34 0DR

Contact: Jo Kenaghan
Tel/fax: 01994 484213

Hours: *9am–sunset Apr 1–June 30. By appt thereafter*

5 acre woodland garden. Large collection of rhododendrons, unusual trees and shrubs, pool, bog garden, riverside walks. Entrance £1.50.
Toilets; Refreshments

Glamorgan, Mid

Dyffryn Gardens
St Nicholas, Cardiff, Glamorgan, Mid CF5 6SU

Contact: Richard Davies
Tel: 01222 593328
Fax: 01222 591966

Hours: *10am–dusk (Free entry Nov–March)*

The finest example of a grand Edwardian garden in Wales. A garden for all seasons which overflows with rare and exotic plants and trees.
Toilets; Refreshments; Disabled access

Glamorgan, West

Clyne Gardens
Mumbles Rd, Blackpill, Swansea, Glamorgan (W.)

Tel: 01792 302420
Fax: 01792 302408

Hours: *Dawn–dusk daily all year*
Toilets; Refreshments

Plantasia
Parc Tawe, Swansea, Glamorgan (W.) SA1 2AL

Tel: 01792 474555/302420
Fax: 01792 652588

Hours: *10.30am–5.30pm Tues–Sun/Bank Hols All year*
Toilets

Gwent

Tredegar House & Park
Newport, Gwent
Tel/fax: 01633 815880
Hours: Easter–end Oct & for NGS. Phone for details
Toilets; Refreshments

Wye Valley Herbs
The Nurtons, Tintern, Chepstow, Gwent NP6 7NX
Contact: Elsa or Adrian Wood
Tel/fax: 01291 689253
Hours: 10.30am–5pm daily Mar–Oct
On A466, 6 miles north of Old Severn Bridge. Garden of considerable botanical interest and nursery with wide range of herbaceous perennials, including comprehensive herb collection.
Catalogue

Gwynedd

Bodysgallen Hall
Llandudno, Gwynedd LL30 1RS
Tel: 01492 584466
Fax: 01492 582519
Hours: All year
Refreshments

Cefyn Bere
Cae Deintur, Dolgellau, Gwynedd LL40 2YS
Tel/fax: 01341 422768
Hours: Spring–early Autumn by appt

Penryn Castle
Bangor, Gwynedd LL57 4HN
Tel: 01248 353084
Fax: 01248 371281
Hours: 12–5pm daily except Tues Apr–Oct, 11am–5pm Jul–Aug
Toilets; Refreshments; Disabled access

Plas Brondanw Gardens
Plas Brondanw, Llanfrothen, Panrhyndeudraeth, Gwynedd LL48 6SW
Tel/fax: 01766 770484
Hours: 9am–5pm daily
Italian inspired gardens, designed by Sir Clough Williams-Ellis, architect of Portmeirion. Interesting topiary, vistas and folly. Adults £1.50, children 25p.

Plas Newydd
Llanfairpwll, Anglesey, Gwynedd LL61 6EQ
Tel/fax: 01248 714795
Hours: 12–5pm Sun–Fri Apr–Sept. Fri/Sun only in Oct
Toilets; Refreshments

Plas Penhelig
Aberdovey, Gwynedd LL35 0NA
Tel: 01654 767676
Fax: 01654 767783
Hours: Mid Mar–end Oct
Toilets; Refreshments

Plas-yn-Rhiw
Rhiw, Pwllheli, Gwynedd LL53 8AB
Tel/fax: 01758 88219
Hours: 12–5pm daily except Sat Apr–Sept. Suns only in Oct
Toilets

Portmeiron
Penrhyndeudraeth, Gwynedd LL48 6ET
Tel/fax: 01766 770228
Hours: 9.30am–6pm daily

Powys

Dingle Welshpool
Welshpool, Powys
Tel/fax: 01938 555145
Hours: 9am–5pm daily except Tues all year
Toilets

Glansevern Hall Gardens
Berriew, Welshpool, Powys SY21 8AH
Contact: Mr & Mrs Thomas
Tel: 01686 640200
Fax: 01686 640829
Hours: 2–6pm May 2 – Sept 27 Fri/Sat/Bank Hols
13 acres incorporating 4 acre lake, lakeside walk, water garden, Victorian grotto, herbaceous beds, borders, rose gardens, large number of unusual trees, tea room and shop. Plants for sale.
Toilets; Refreshments; Disabled access

Powis Castle
Welshpool, Powys SY21 8RF
Tel: 01938 554338
Fax: 01938 554336
Hours: Tues–Sun Jul–Aug Wed–Sun Sept–Oct
Toilets; Refreshments; Disabled access

INFORMATION & EDUCATION

Good gardening is an intellectual, as well as a physical challenge. There is a book or journal for almost every aspect of gardening, and an increasing number of courses are offered for the amateur as well as the professional gardener.

We hope that you will find in this section sources of information on every gardening problem; organisations that can help you to gain more from your hobby or profession; events that will inspire you to greater achievements and, perhaps, a well-earned holiday in the company of other enthusiasts.

BOOKSELLERS SPECIALISING IN GARDENING BOOKS

A & P M Books
37b New Cavendish Street,
London W1M 8JR
Tel: 0171 935 0995
Fax: 0171 486 4591
Hours: Post, phone or fax only
Catalogues: Rare, out-of-print, good secondhand and antiquarian books. Booksearch (fees 5%-15% only if successful).
Catalogue; Mail order

Anna Buxton Books
Redcroft, 23 Murrayfield Rd,
Edinburgh, Lothian EH12 6EP
Tel: 0131 337 1747
Fax: 0131 337 8174
Hours: By appointment only
Mainly mail order business, buying and selling antiquarian, out-of-print and new books on gardening and all related subjects. Two free catalogues a year.
Catalogue; Mail order

B S B I Publications (F & M Perring)
Greenacre, Wood Lane, Oundle,
Peterborough,
Northamptonshire PE8 4JQ
Tel: 01832 273388
Fax: 01832 274568
Hours: By appointment only
Catalogue; Mail order

Berger & Tims
7 Bressenden Place, London
SW1E 5DE
Tel: 0171 834 9827
Fax: 0171 976 5976
Hours: 9am–6pm Mon–Fri
Mail order

Besleys Books
4 Blyburgate, Beccles, Suffolk
NR34 9TA
Contact: P Besley
Tel/fax: 01502 715762
Hours: 9.30am–5pm. Closed
Weds & Suns
Large general secondhand bookshop specialising in gardening and natural history books. One or two catalogues per year.
Catalogue; Mail order

Chantrey Books
24 Cobnar Rd, Sheffield,
Yorkshire (S.) S8 8QB
Tel/fax: 0114 2748958
Hours: By appointment only
Out-of-print and antiquarian books on all aspects of gardening, botany and rural life. Regular catalogues issued. Visitors welcome by appointment.
Catalogue; Mail order

Country Garden
Broad Leys Publishing Company,
Buriton House Station Rd,
Newport, Saffron Walden, Essex
CB11 3PL
Tel: 01799 540922
Fax: 01799 541367

D & D H W Morgan Second-Hand Books
St James Tree, Whitmore,
Umberleigh, Devon EX37 9HB
Gardening books: a wide range of good value second-hand books for sale. Send 2 x 2nd class stamps for list.

Hatchards
187 Piccadilly, London W1V 9DA
Tel/fax: 0171 439 9921

Ivelet Books Ltd
Church Street Bookshop, 26
Church Street, Godalming,
Surrey GU7 1EW
Tel: 01483 418878
Fax: 01483 418656
Hours: 10.30am–5.30pm
Mon–Sat
Catalogue; Mail order

Jill Hedges Bookseller
The Mill, Longtown, Hereford &
Worcester HR2 0LY
Tel: 01873 860236
Fax: 0171 286 4006
Hours: By appointment
Secondhand horticultural books and ephemera bought and sold. Free booksearch service. Mail order, free catalogue or view by appointment in London or Herefordshire.
Catalogue; Mail order

John Henly
Brooklands, Walderton,
Chichester, Sussex (W.)
PO18 9EE
Tel: 01705 631426
Fax: 01705 631544
Secondhand gardening books bought and sold.
Catalogue; Mail order

Kew Shop
Mail Order Section, Royal
Botanic Gardens Kew,
Richmond, Surrey TW9 3AB
Tel/fax: 0181 332 5653
Hours: 9am–5pm (telephone orders). Shop open
9.30am–5.30pm
Catalogue; Mail order

Landsmans Bookshop Ltd
Buckenhill, Bromyard, Hereford
& Worcester HR7 4PH
Tel/fax: 01885 483420
Hours: 9am–4.30pm Mon–Fri.
Weekends by appt
Specialist horticultural bookshop supplying books by post and from a mobile bookshop. 50 years of first class service. Catalogue of over 5,000 titles £1.25 inc p&p.
Catalogue; Mail order

Lloyds of Kew
9 Mortlake Terrace, Mortlake
Road, Kew, Surrey TW9 3DT
Tel/fax: 0181 940 2512
Hours: 10am–6pm Tues–Sat,
2pm–5pm Sun
Specialists in antiquarian and out-of-print books on botany, gardening and horticulture plus large general stock. Books bought, booksearch service.

M R Clark
18 Balmoral Place, Halifax,
Yorkshire (W.) HX1 2BG
Tel/fax: 01422 357475
Hours: Appt only
Secondhand and out-of-print gardening books. S.A.E. for catalogue.
Catalogue; Mail order

Mary Bland
Augop, Evenjobb, Presteigne,
Powys LD8 2PA
Tel/fax: 015476 218
Hours: By appointment only
Catalogue; Mail order

Mike Park
351 Sutton Common Rd, Sutton,
Surrey SM3 9HZ
Contact: Mike Park & Ian Smith
Tel: 0181 641 7796
Fax: 0181 641 3330
Hours: By appointment only
We stock a wide range of gardening and botany books - secondhand, antiquarian and out-of-print. We are also keen to purchase books and collections.
Catalogue; Mail order

Peter M Daly Rare Books
20a Jewry Street, Winchester,
Hampshire SO23 8RZ
Contact: Peter Daly
Tel/fax: 01962 867732
Hours: 10am–4.30pm Wed/Fri/Sat
Small selection of rare and second hand gardening and botanical books always in stock.

R H S - The Robin Herbert Centre
RHS Garden Rosemoor, Great
Torrington, Devon EX38 8PH
Tel/fax: 01805 624067
Hours: 10am–6pm Apr–Oct, 5pm
Oct–Mar, 4pm Nov–Feb
A comprehensive range of gardening books and a wide selection of gifts from stationery to preserves. Free entry.
Toilets; Refreshments; Disabled access

R H S Garden Wisley Shop
Woking, Surrey GU23 6QB
Tel/fax: 01483 211113
Hours: Mon–Sat. Sun RHS
members only
The shop offers the finest stock of horticultural books in the world and a superb selection of gifts including china, glass and pictures.

COLLEGES & HORTICULTURAL EDUCATION

Search Press Ltd
Wellwood, North Farm Rd,
Tunbridge Wells, Kent TN2 3DR
Contact: Ruth Saunders
Tel: 01892 510850
Fax: 01892 515903

Publishers of a colourful series of organic gardening books, produced in conjunction with the Henry Doubleday Research Association, and available from our mail order service.
Catalogue; Mail order

Summerfield Books
Summerfield House, High Street,
Brough, Kirkby Stephen,
Cumbria CA17 4BX
Contact: Jon & Sue Atkins
Tel/fax: 017683 41577
Hours: By appointment – best to ring first

Specialist booksellers: new and secondhand books on botany, forestry and gardening. Callers welcome. Booksearch service. Send for free catalogue (Orders over £40 post free).
Catalogue; Mail order

W C Cousens
The Leat, Lyme Rd, Axminster,
Devon EX13 5BL
Tel/fax: 01297 32921
Hours: By appointment only

Secondhand and antiquarian gardening books bought and sold. Postal business, member PBFA. Sales stand at events in SW England.
Mail order

Wyseby House Books
Kingsclere Old Bookshop, 2A
George Street, Kingsclere,
Newbury, Hampshire RG15 8NQ
Contact: Dr Tim Oldham
Tel/fax: 01635 297995
Email:
wyseby.books@pop3.hiway.co.uk
Hours: 10am–5pm Mon–Sat

Out-of-print gardening books. Catalogues issued. Bookshop.
Catalogue; Mail order

Aberdeen College
Clinterty Centre, Kinellar,
Aberdeen, Grampian AB21 0TZ
Contact: Bruce Gilliland
Tel: 01224 612773
Fax: 01224 612750

Offers a wide range of short horticultural courses both for the amateur and the professional throughout the year.

Afan College Nursery
Twyn-yr-Hydd, Margham Park,
Port Talbot, Glamorgan (W.)
SA13 2TJ
Contact: Richard Coleman
Tel/fax: 01639 883712
Hours: 9am–4pm Mon–Fri March–Nov

Horticultural courses: NVQs in Amenity and Commercial Horticulture. Nursery specialising in herbaceous perennials plus shrub, bedding and pot plants, house plants and free advice.

Angus College
Keptie Rd, Arbroath, Tayside
DD11 3EA
Contact: Mr Scott Anderson
Tel: 01241 432600
Fax: 01241 876169

Angus College offers a range of courses in Amenity Horticulture and Nursery Stock Production at both SCOTVEC National Certificate and Higher National Certificate levels. We also offer Scottish vocational qualifications in horticulture. Courses can be attended on either a part-time or full-time basis.

Architectural Association
34-36 Bedford Square, London
WC1B 3ES
Tel: 0171 636 0974
Fax: 0171 636 0996

Architectural Association school of architecture. Conservation of historic landscapes, parks and gardens Dip 2 years part-time. Contact the Conservation Co-ordinator.

Aylesbury College
Hampden Hall, Stoke Mandeville,
Aylesbury, Buckinghamshire
HP22 5TB
Contact: Mrs J Vyse
Tel/fax: 01296 714366

BTEC 1st Diplomas, NVQ courses, RHS General Examination, amateur gardening certificates, floristry and flower arranging, short courses. Also agriculture and conservation.

Barking College
Dagenham Rd, Romford, Essex
RM7 0XU
Contact: G D Chalk
Tel: 01708 66841
Fax: 01708 731067

Barking College delivers quality courses in horticulture to NVQ Level Two and floristry to NVQ Level Three. Specialist short courses provided on demand.

Barnsley College of Technology
Church Street, Barnsley,
Yorkshire (S.) S70 2AX
Tel: 01226 730191
Fax: 01226 298514

Barony College
Parkgate, Dumfries, Dumfries & Galloway DG1 3NE
Contact: Richard Baines
Tel: 01387 860251
Fax: 01387 860395
Email: admin@barony.ac.uk

Barony College provides quality education and practical training in SVQ Amenity Horticulture (Level II), Nursery and Greenkeeping. We also offer short and part time courses.
Catalogue; Refreshments; Disabled access

Berkshire College of Agriculture
Hall Place, Burchetts Green,
Maidenhead, Berkshire SL6 6QR
Tel: 01628 824444
Fax: 01628 824695

Education and training for amateurs and professionals: horticulture: landscape design: greenkeeping: gardening: conservation: RHS. Easily accessible via M4 and M40; residential accomodation; excellent facilities.
Catalogue; Refreshments; Disabled access

Bicton College of Agriculture
East Budleigh, Budleigh Salterton,
Devon EX9 7BY
Tel: 01395 68353
Fax: 01395 67502

Bourneville College of Further Education
Bristol Road South, Northfield,
Birmingham, Midlands (W.) B31 2AJ
Tel/fax: 0121 411 1414

Brackenhurst College
Southwell, Nottinghamshire
NG25 0QF
Tel: 01636 812252
Fax: 01636 815404

Brinsbury College
Brinsbury, North Heath,
Pulborough, Sussex (W.) RH20 1DL
Tel/fax: 01798 873832

Broomfield College
Morley, Ilkeston, Derbyshire
DE7 6DN
Contact: Phil Bradbury
Tel: 01332 831345
Fax: 01332 830298

Horticulture courses for beginners or more advanced. Qualifications including City & Guilds National Certificate and BTEC National Diploma as well as organic gardening and RHS.
Toilets; Refreshments; Disabled access

Cambridgeshire College of Agriculture & Horticulture
Landbeach Rd, Milton, Cambridge, Cambridgeshire CB4 6DB

Contact: Mrs Kate Ross
Tel: 01223 860701
Fax: 01223 860262

Hours: Evening & daytime courses offered

Further education college providing a range of horticultural courses including Royal Horticultural Society General, Garden Design, Amenity Horticulture and Greenkeeping on a part-time basis.

Capel Manor
Bullsmoor Lane, Enfield, Middlesex EN1 4RQ

Tel: 0181 366 4442
Fax: 01992 717544

Capel Manor is Greater London's specialist college of horticulture and countryside studies with informative richly planted gardens open to the public. Please telephone for details.
Refreshments; Disabled access

Cardiff Institute of Higher Education
Llandaff Centre, Western Avenue, Cardiff, Glamorgan (S.) CF5 2YB

Tel/fax: 01222 551111

Catriona Boyle's Garden School
Penpergwm Lodge, Abergavenny, Gwent NP7 9AS

Contact: Catriona Boyle
Tel/fax: 01873 840208

Hours: As per catalogue

Ten day courses from 22/4/97 to 1/7/97 in large country house and garden, with nationally known garden celebrities plus excellent lunch.
Catalogue; Toilets; Refreshments; Disabled access

Cheltenham & Gloucester College of Higher Education
Francis Close Hall Campus, Swindon Rd, Cheltenham, Gloucestershire GL50 4AZ

Tel: 01242 532922
Fax: 01242 532997

Chisenbury Priory Gardening Courses
Chisenbury Priory, Pewsey, Wiltshire SN9 6AQ

Tel/fax: 01980 70406

College of Garden Design
Administrative Office, Cothelstone, Taunton, Somerset TA4 3DP

Tel: 01823 433215
Fax: 01823 433812

Consumers Association Library
2 Marylebone Rd, London NW1 4DX

Tel: 0171 486 5544
Fax: 0171 935 1606

Hours: 10am–6pm Mon–Fri at Chief Librarian's discretion

Country Courses
Corranmor House, Ardfern, Lochgilphead, Strathclyde PA31 8QN

Tel: 01852 5609/221
Fax: 01852 5627

Craven College of Adult Education
High Street, Skipton, Yorkshire (N.) BD23 1JY

Tel/fax: 01756 791411

Ealing Tertiary College
Norwood Hall Centre, Norwood Green, Southall, London UB2 4LA

Tel: 0181 574 2261
Fax: 0181 571 9479

Easton College
Easton, Norwich, Norfolk NR9 5DX

Tel: 01603 742105
Fax: 01603 741438

Full time, part time and short courses in Horticulture, Landscaping, Arboriculture and Turf Management and supervisory training, COSHH, pesticides, machinery, health and safety, training needs analysis etc.

Edinburgh College of Art - Heriot-Watt University
Sch of Landscape Architecture, Lauriston Place, Edinburgh, Lothian EH3 9DF

Tel: 0131 229 9311
Fax: 0131 228 8825

Elmwood College
Carslogie Rd, Cupar, Fife KY15 4JB

Tel: 01334 52781
Fax: 01334 56795

English Gardening School
Chelsea Physic Garden, 66 Royal Hospital Rd, London SW3 4HS

Tel: 0171 352 4347
Fax: 0171 376 3936

An unrivalled range of professional and amateur courses for all garden lovers. Courses cover garden design, gardening, botanical painting and many other associated topics. See advertisement - write or phone for full details.

Finchale Training College
Durham, Co Durham DH1 5RX

Tel: 0191 386 2634
Fax: 0191 386 4962

Gardeners' Academy
PO Box 262, Guilsborough, Northamptonshire NN6 8RS

Contact: Graham or Chris Pavey
Tel/fax: 01234 826077

Short courses for garden lovers on a variety of horticultural topics. Experienced lecturers, small groups and warm hospitality make all our events both informative and enjoyable.
Catalogue

Gardeners' Breaks
Hill Farm Barn, Greenways Lane, Cold Ashton, Chippenham, Wiltshire SN14 8LA

Contact: Derry Watkins
Tel/fax: 01225 891686

One day practical gardening courses on propagation, conservatories, plants for sale and container planting. Numbers limited to 15. Cost £35 including lunch.
Refreshments

Hadlow College of Agriculture & Horticulture
Hadlow, Tonbridge, Kent TN11 0AL

Tel: 01732 850551
Fax: 01732 851957

Hours: Plant centre Mon–Fri 9am–5pm

Hadlow College is a centre of excellence for horticultural education and training in the south-east of England. Located near the M25 motorway in west Kent.
Catalogue; Refreshments; Disabled access

Hampstead Garden Suburb Adult Education Centre
The Institute, Central Square, London NW11 7BN

Tel/fax: 0181 455 9951

The English Gardening School
AT THE CHELSEA PHYSIC GARDEN

COURSES FOR 1997

ONE YEAR DIPLOMA AND CERTIFICATE COURSES
Garden Design: 2 days/week *Practical Horticulture:* 1 day/week
Plants & Plantsmanship: 1 day/week *Botanical Painting:* 1 day/week

SHORT COURSES
A range of courses covering design, botanical art, gardening & related topics.

GARDEN DESIGN CORRESPONDENCE COURSE
Run in conjunction with KLC School of Interior Design. Plan your own garden by post with the help of our nine comprehensive packs & your own tutor.

for further details please contact

The English Gardening School AT THE CHELSEA PHYSIC GARDEN
66 Royal Hospital Road, London SW3 4HS Tel: 0171-352 4347 Fax: 0171-376 3936

Horticultural Correspondence College
Little Notton Farmhouse, 16 Notton, Lacock, Chippenham, Wiltshire SN15 2NF

Contact: Mrs Janet Elms
Tel/fax: 0800 378 918

Hours: 9am–5pm

Study for your RHS General or Diploma in Horticulture, or other course listed in our free brochure which includes Leisure Gardening, Herbs, Landscape Construction, Garden Design and, separately, Mixed Farming.
Catalogue

Houghall College
Durham City, Co Durham DH1 3SG

Tel: 0191 386 1351
Fax: 0191 386 0419

Hours: Gardens open 12.30–4.30pm daily except Xmas Day

Services provided - extensive gardens, special open days, gardening advice, soil testing, wide range of short and full-time courses. For further details telephone 0191 3861351.
Disabled access

Hugh Baird College
Balliol Rd, Bootle, Merseyside PR8 3JX

Tel: 0151 922 6704
Fax: 0151 934 4469

Ichiyo School of Ikebana
4 Providence Way, Waterbeach, Cambridge, Cambridgeshire CB5 9QJ

Inchbald School of Design
32 Eccleston Square, London SW1V 1PB

Tel/fax: 0171 630 9011

The Daily Telegraph *Green Fingers*   **Colleges & Horticultural Education**

International Correspondence Schools
Clydeway Centre, 8 Elliot Place, Glasgow, Strathclyde G3 8EF
Tel: 0141 221 7373
Fax: 0141 221 8151

Isle of Wight College of Arts & Technology
Medina Way, Newport, Isle of Wight PO30 5TA
Tel: 01983 526 631
Fax: 01983 521707

Kew School of Garden Design
The Adult Education Section, Educ & Marketing Dept, Royal Botanic Gardens Kew, Richmond, Surrey TW9 3AB
Tel: 0181 332 5623/26
Fax: 0181 332 5610

Kew School of Horticulture
Royal Botanic Gardens Kew, Richmond, Surrey TW9 3AB
Contact: Ian Leese
Tel: 0181 940 1171
Fax: 0181 332 5574

The Kew Diploma is a three year course in Amenity Horticulture, combining degree-equivalent theory with practical work experience in the world's finest foremost botanic garden.

Kingston Maurward College
Kingston Maurward, Dorchester, Dorset DT2 8PY
Contact: Mike Hancock
Tel: 01305 264738
Fax: 01305 250059
Email: kmc.ac.uk

Education and training in all aspects of horticulture and land use. Full and part time courses as required.
Catalogue; Refreshments; Disabled access

Knowsley Community College - Landbased Industries
The Kennels, Knowsley Park, Prescot, Merseyside L34 4AQ
Contact: Ruth Brown
Tel/fax: 0151 549 1500

Courses: Horticulture NVQ Levels 2/3, City and Guilds Certificate in Gardening, RHS General Examination, Environmental Conservation Levels 2/3, Floristry NVQ/City and Guilds/NCPF.

Lackham College
Lacock, Chippenham, Wiltshire SN15 2NY
Contact: Oliver Menhinick
Tel: 01249 443111
Fax: 01249 444474

Horticultural courses, full and part time, professional and leisure; turf, landscape, design, plants, machinery, organic, arbor, floristry.

Lambeth College
Clapham Centre, 45 Clapham Common Southside, London SW4 9BL
Contact: Terry Fulham
Tel: 0171 501 5048
Fax: 0171 501 5041

New horticulture centre. Courses available: NVQ Amenity Horticulture Levels 1/2/3. C & G Decorative Horticulture and Urban Wildlife. RHS Exam. Also plant sales.
Disabled access

Langside College
Department of Horticulture, Woodburn House, 27 Buchanan Drive, Rutherglen, Strathclyde G73 3PF
Tel/fax: 0141 647 6300

Leeds Metropolitan University
Landscape Architecture, Brunswick Terrace, Leeds, Yorkshire (W.)
Tel: 0113 2832600
Fax: 0113 2833190

Landscape architecture courses. BA (Hons), Diploma and Masters level also short specialist courses. Research and consultancy services.

Lincolnshire College of Agriculture
Caythorpe Court, Grantham, Lincolnshire NG32 3EP
Tel: 01400 72521
Fax: 01400 72722

Linnean Society of London Library
Burlington House, Piccadilly, London W1V 0LQ
Tel: 0171 434 4479
Fax: 0171 287 9364
Hours: 10am–5pm Mon–Fri by appointment only

Manchester Metropolitan University
Div of Environmental Science, Crewe & Alsager Faculty, Crewe Green Rd, Cheshire CW1 1DU
Tel: 01270 500661
Fax: 01270 251205

Merrist Wood College
Student Services, Worplesdon, Guildford, Surrey GU3 3PE
Tel/fax: 01483 232424

Providing training and education to prepare you for a career in land-based and related leisure industries. See our advertisement - write or phone for full details.

Merton Adult College
Whatley Avenue, London SW20 9NS
Contact: Mrs Brenda Gunter
Tel: 0181 543 9292
Fax: 0181 544 1421
Hours: 9am–10pm

The college offers day and evening examination classes in RHS General Certificate in Horticulture and C & G Certificate in Gardening (Garden Design Modules).
Refreshments; Disabled access

Ministry of Agriculture Fisheries & Food Library
3 Whitehall Place, London SW1A 3HH
Tel/fax: 0171 270 8420/21
Hours: 9.30am–5pm by appt (24 hrs notice)

Moulton College
West Street, Moulton, Northamptonshire NN3 1RR
Tel: 01604 491131
Fax: 01604 491127

A wide range of courses in Amenity Horticulture and Arboriculture including BTEC 1st Diploma and National Diplomas. National Certificates and NVQ Level 1-3.

Myerscough College
Myerscough Hall, Bilsborrow, Preston, Lancashire PR3 0RY
Tel: 01995 640611
Fax: 01995 640842

Newton Rigg College
Cumbria College of Agriculture, Newton Rigg, Penrith, Cumbria CA11
Tel: 01768 63791
Fax: 01768 67249

Norton Radstock Technical College
South Hill Park, Radstock, Bath, Avon BA3 3RW
Contact: Andrew Howson
Tel: 01761 433161
Fax: 01761 436173
Hours: 8am–9pm Mon–Fri & some Sats

Evening classes and short courses for amateurs (some leading to City & Guilds Certificates) in Radstock or Keynsham. Prices from £30 for 12 evenings.
Refreshments; Disabled access

Merrist Wood
— COLLEGE —

Certificate Course in Garden Design

Do you want to know more about garden design — even make a new career of it? Well now you can — at the college that has designed and constructed 11 Gold Medal gardens at the Chelsea Flower Show.

A one year, part time Certificate Course in Garden Design will be starting in September 1996.

For details please contact Student Services at Merrist Wood College, Worplesdon, Guildford, Surrey GU3 3PE, telephone 01483 232424. Please quote ref: DTGF.

Merrist Wood College is an exempt charity providing further and higher education.

Oaklands College
Hatfield Rd, St Albans,
Hertfordshire AL4 0JA
Tel: 01727 850651
Fax: 01727 847987
Offer a wide range of courses to suit the needs of both the professional and amateur gardener. Please write or telephone for full details.

Oatridge Agricultural College
Ecclesmachan, Broxburn, Lothian EH52 6NH
Contact: Mr David Webster
Tel: 01506 854387
Fax: 01506 853373
As Scotland's specialist land-based college, we offer a wide range of full, part-time and short courses in: Horticulture, Greenkeeping and Groundsmanship, Landscaping, Environment and Conservation.
Catalogue; Disabled access

Ohara School of Ikebana
Forresters, Sway Rd, Lymington, Hampshire SO41 8LR
Contact: Mrs H Woodman
Tel: 01590 672418
Fax: 015906 72418
We specialise in the teaching of Japanese flower arranging (Ikebana). Classes are held in London and other parts of the UK. Traditional and modern styles taught.

Otley College of Agriculture & Horticulture
Otley, Ipswich, Suffolk IP6 9EY
Tel: 01473 785543
Fax: 01473 785353

Periwinkle
Freepost, PO Box 25, Sarisbury Green, Southampton, Hampshire SO31 9ZP
Tel/fax: 01489 885645

Pershore College of Horticulture
Avonbank, Pershore, Hereford & Worcester WR10 3JP
Contact: Dr David Hall
Tel: 01386 552443
Fax: 01386 556528
Hours: 9am–4pm Mon–Fri
The extensive working grounds of this centre of training excellence include; model landscape gardens, fruit farm, an arboretum, glasshouses, a nursery and a plant centre.
Catalogue

R H S Garden Wisley
Woking, Surrey GU23 6QB
Tel: 01483 224234
Fax: 01483 211750
Hours: Mon–Sat. Sun RHS members only
One of the world's largest and justifiably famed gardens. Centre for the RHS research and education projects. Adults £5, children up to 16 £1.75, under 6 free.
Toilets; Refreshments; Disabled access

Reaseheath College (Cheshire College of Agriculture)
Reaseheath, Nantwich, Cheshire CW5 6DF
Tel: 01270 625131
Fax: 01270 625 665

Rodbaston College
Rodbaston, Penkridge, Staffordshire ST19 5PH
Tel: 01785 712209
Fax: 01785 715701
An extensive range of full time and part time courses suitable for the keen amateur to the future horticulturist.
Refreshments; Disabled access

Scottish Agricultural College
Auchincruive, Ayr, Strathclyde KA6 5HW
Tel: 01292 520331
Fax: 01292 521119

Shipley College
Exhibition Rd, Saltaire, Shipley, Yorkshire (W.) BD18 3JW
Tel: 01274 757222
Fax: 01274 757201
Hours: 8.30am–7pm Mon–Thurs, 8.30am–4.30pm Fri
Shipley college offers full time and part time courses in Amenity Horticulture and Floristry. Full time programmes include BTEC First and BTEC National. Part time courses include NVQ I, II & III. All our programmes are fully supported by practical work experience in industry. Shipley College has established very strong links with local employers and many students enter employment at craft and supervisory level. We also offer evening classes for the Royal Horticultural Society General Certificate.
Catalogue

Solihull College
Blossomfield Rd, Solihull, Midlands (W.) B91 1SB
Contact: Dorothy Connolly
Tel: 0121 711 2111
Fax: 0121 711 2316
Courses in NVQ Amenity Horticulture, RHS General and General Gardening. Animal Care courses starting 1997. Practical facilities include walled garden with glasshouses, lawns and parkland.

Southend Adult Community College
Ambleside Drive, Southend-on-Sea, Essex SS1 2UP
Tel: 01702 610196
Fax: 01702 601529
Adult education - new prospectus published each June giving details of courses available.

Southport College of Art & Technology
Mornington Rd, Southport, Merseyside PR9 0TT
Tel/fax: 01704 424111

Sparsholt College Hampshire
Sparsholt, Winchester, Hampshire SO21 2NF
Contact: J R Dennis
Tel: 01962 776441
Fax: 01962 776587
For all matters concerning horticultural education including floristry and aquatics contact the college. Complete range of full time, part time and short courses available.

St Helens College
Newton Campus, Crow Lane East, Newton le Willows, Merseyside WA12 9TT
Tel: 01925 24656
Fax: 01925 220437

Stoke-on-Trent College
Burslem Campus, Moorland Rd, Burslem, Staffordshire ST6 1JJ
Tel: 01782 208208
Fax: 01782 828106

Stourbridge College
Hort & Conservation Unit, Leasowes Park Nursery, Leasowes Lane, Halesowen, Midlands (W.) B62 8QF
Contact: Richard Maw
Tel/fax: 0121 550 0007
Hours: 9am–5pm
Courses include: full time National and First Diplomas in Urban and Countryside Conservation, NVQ2 Floristry, part time - Horticulture, Floristry, Environmental Conservation and Leisure classes.
Refreshments

Sue's Garden Design
21 Bederic Close, Bury St Edmunds, Suffolk IP32 7DR
Contact: Mrs S Robinson
Tel/fax: 01284 764310
Royal Horticultural Society Speaker, giving illustrated lectures on gardening topics, including flower arranging, with plants for sale.

Threave School of Horticulture
Threave Garden, Castle Douglas, Dumfries & Galloway DG7 1RX
Tel: 01556 502575
Fax: 01556 502683
Hours: 9.30am–sunset
A 65 acre garden for all seasons. Walled garden, glasshouses, rock garden, formal peat and heather gardens. 1 mile west of Castle Douglas.
Refreshments; Disabled access

University Botanic Gardens
Cory Lodge, Bateman Street, Cambridge, Cambridgeshire CB2 1JF
Tel: 01223 336265
Fax: 01223 336278
Forty acres of fine gardens, with glasshouses, winter garden and lake, near the centre of Cambridge, incorporating nine National Collections, including geranium and fritillaria. Open daily 10am-4pm (winter) 10am-6pm (summer). Entrance in Bateman Street. Admission: £1.50/adult, £1.00/OAP/child. Tea room and Gift Shop in the Gilmour Building. Guided tours by the Friends of the Garden available by arrangement. Parties must pre-book. Enquiries (Monday-Friday) tel: 01223 336265
Toilets; Refreshments; Disabled access

University College London
Dept of Biology (Darwin), Gower Street, London WC1E 6BT
Tel/fax: 0171 387 7050

University College of North Wales
School of Agric/Forest Science, Bangor, Gywnedd LL57 2UW
Tel: 01248 382281
Fax: 01248 354997

University of Aberdeen
Department of Agriculture, 581 King Street, Aberdeen, Grampian AB9 1UD
Tel: 01224 272648
Fax: 01224 273731
Undergraduate (B.Sc) and postgraduate taught (M.Sc) courses and research programmes (M.Phil, Ph.D.) in agriculture, agricultural science, rural environment and rural economics.

University of Derby
Plant Technology Group, Kedleston Rd, Derby, Derbyshire DE22 1GB
Tel/fax: 01332 622222

University of Dundee Botanic Garden
Riverside Drive, Dundee, Tayside DD2 1QH

Tel: 01382 566939
Fax: 01382 640574

Hours: 10am–4.30pm Mon–Sat, 11–4pm Sun

Landscaped teaching garden, temperate tropical planthouses, water features, native plants. Small selection of seeds, plants and postcards on sale. Visitors' centre.
Toilets; Disabled access

University of Edinburgh
Sch of Forestry/Ecol Science, Darwin Building, Mayfield Rd, Edinburgh, Lothian EH9 3JU

Tel: 0131 650 5421
Fax: 0131 662 0478

University of Greenwich
School of Architect/Landscape, Dartford Campus, Oakfield Lane, Dartford, Kent DA1 2SZ

Tel/fax: 0181 316 8000

University of Manchester
School of Landscape, Dept of Planning & Landscape, Manchester, Manchester, Gt M13 9PL

University of Newcastle
Faculty of Agriculture, Dept of Town/Country Planning, Newcastle upon Tyne, Tyne & Wear NE1 7RU

Tel: 0191 222 7802
Fax: 0191 222 8811

University of Nottingham
Dept of Agriculture/Horticult, Sutton Bonington Campus, Loughborough, Leicestershire LE1 5RD

Tel: 0115 9484848
Fax: 0115 9516060

Undergraduate degree courses in: Horticultural Crop Production, Environmental Horticulture, Horticulture with European Studies, Horticulture with Technology. Also postgraduate degree courses. Please write for further information.

University of Reading
Dept of Horticulture, PO Box 221, Whiteknights, Reading, Berkshire RG6 6AS

Contact: Tony Kendle
Tel: 0118 9318071
Fax: 0118 9750630

Hours: 9am–5pm Mon–Fri

Undergraduate and postgraduate degree courses in horticulture and landscape management. Part time Certificate of Garden Design. Short courses in gardening techniques. Consultancy services.
Catalogue; Refreshments; Disabled access

University of Sheffield
Dept of Landscape Architecture, Sheffield, Yorkshire (S.) S10 2TN

Tel/fax: 0114 2768555

Wakefield College
Hemsworth Centre, Station Rd, Hemsworth, Pontefract, Yorkshire (W.) WF9 4JP

Contact: Roger Bennett
Tel: 01924 810610
Fax: 01924 810610

Walford College - Horticulture Dept
Radbrook Centre, Radbrook Rd, Shrewsbury, Shropshire SY2 6QX

Contact: Martin Ford
Tel: 01743 360266
Fax: 01743 357498

Offering a wide range of courses for amateur gardeners and professional horticulturists including RHS General and Diploma, City and Guilds, National Certificate and NVQ.

Welsh College of Horticulture
Northop, Mold, Clwyd CH7 6AA

Tel/fax: 01352 86861

West Dean Gardens (Edward James Foundation)
College Office, West Dean College, West Dean, Chichester, Sussex (W.) PO18 0QZ

Contact: Diana Lemmon
Tel: 01243 811301
Fax: 01243 811342
Email: westdean@pavilion.co.uk

Offers unrivalled facilities for garden courses. These are available for all levels from beginner to experienced gardener. For full details contact Diana Lemmon.
Catalogue; Refreshments; Disabled access

West Oxfordshire College
Warren Farm Centre, Horton-cum-Studley, Oxfordshire OX33 1BY

Contact: Alan Brown
Tel: 01865 351794
Fax: 01865 358931

Warren Farm Centre provides education and training in land based industries in Oxfordshire: agriculture, horticulture, horse care, gamekeeping, floristry, conservation and estate management.

Writtle College
Chelmsford, Essex CM1 3RR

Contact: Student Registrar
Tel/fax: 01245 420705

Wulfran College
Paget Rd, Wolverhampton, Midlands (W.) WV6 0DU

Tel: 01902 312062
Fax: 01902 23070

Wye College
Wye, Ashford, Kent TN25 5AH

Tel: 01233 812401
Fax: 01233 813320

GARDENERS' HOLIDAYS

Abercrombie & Kent Travel
Sloane Square House, Holbein Place, London SW1W 8NS
Tel: 0171 730 9600
Fax: 0171 730 9376

Accompanied Cape Tours
Hill House, Much Marcle, Ledbury, Hereford & Worcester HR8
Tel: 01531 84210
Fax: 01432 351028

Arena Holidays Ltd
Hamilton House, Cambridge Road, Felixstowe, Suffolk IP11 7SW
Tel: 01394 691201
Fax: 01394 271043
Hours: 9am–6pm Mon–Fri. 9am–1pm Sat

Selection of high quality worldwide garden holidays featuring leisurely visits to great gardens as well as adventure-style tours to areas of horticultural importance.
Catalogue

Barfield Travel & Tours
14 Chain Lane, Newark, Nottinghamshire NG24 1AU
Contact: Mrs Jill Lewis
Tel: 01636 640778
Fax: 01636 707600

Tours for individuals with interests in all garden types. Tailor-made itineraries for groups, clubs, societies. Send for free brochures - Jersey, Guernsey, France, Holland, Portugal.

Bates Green
Arlington, Polegate, Sussex (E.) BN26 6SH
Contact: Carolyn McCutchan
Tel/fax: 01323 482039
Hours: 10.30am–6pm Thursdays April–Oct

Plantsman's tranquil 1½ acre garden. Colour themed herbaceous borders, pond, shaded foliage areas. Admission £2. Farmhouse accommodation available all year.
Toilets

Boxwood Tours - Quality Garden Holidays
56 Spring Rd, Abingdon, Oxfordshire OX14 1AN
Tel/fax: 01235 532791

Our 1997 brochure includes garden holidays to California, Italy, Jersey, Flanders, France and England. Tour design and organisation services for groups also available.
Catalogue

Cox & Kings Travel
Gordon House, 10 Greencoat Place, London SW1P 1PH
Contact: Caroline Cotton
Tel: 0171 873 5000
Fax: 0171 630 6038

Botany and wildflower tours led by expert leaders. Destinations include Morocco, Rhodes, Cyprus, Crete, Turkey, Dominica, Andalucia, Romania, Slovenia, Wengen, Rockies, Pyrenees, Obergurgl, Corfu and Malaysia.

Creative Tours Ltd
2nd Floor, 1 Tenterden Street, London W1R 9AH
Tel: 0171 495 1775
Fax: 0171 499 7699

David Sayers Travel
10 Barley Mow Passage, London W4 4PH
Tel: 0181 995 3642
Fax: 0181 742 1066

David Way Associates
Southover, Grove Lane, Hunton, Maidstone, Kent ME15 0SE
Tel: 01622 820876
Fax: 01622 820645

Dormy House Hotel
Willersey Hill, Broadway, Hereford & Worcester WR12 7LF
Tel/fax: 01386 852711

Focus Garden Tours
2 Loose Farm Barns, Battle, Sussex (E.) TN33 0TG
Tel/fax: 01424 773829

Garden Study Tours
Golden Key Building, 15 Market Street, Sandwich, Kent CT13 9DA
Tel/fax: 01304 612248

Gardeners' Breaks
Hill Farm Barn, Greenways Lane, Cold Ashton, Chippenham, Wiltshire SN14 8LA
Contact: Derry Watkins
Tel/fax: 01225 891686

One day practical gardening courses on propagation, conservatories, plants for sale and container planting. Numbers limited to 15. Cost £35 including lunch.
Refreshments

Gardens of Somerset
Hartwood House, Crowcombe Heathfield, Taunton, Somerset TA4 4BS
Contact: David & Rosemary Freemantle
Tel: 01984 667202
Fax: 01984 667508
Email: 101537,2334@compuserve.com

We offer week-long personally guided visits to wonderful private and public gardens. Idyllic tranquil location, small groups, en suite rooms, delicious food. Airport pickup.
Catalogue

Great Yorkshire Gardens Design Tours
Ings Gate, Flaxman Croft, Copmanthorpe, York, Yorkshire (N.) YO2 3TU
Contact: Keith James DipGD LA
Tel/fax: 01904 703833

These are exclusively unique design weekends aimed at the discerning garden lover who wishes to combine a wonderful weekend away visiting large and small country gardens in North Yorkshire, with expert designers and horticulturists offering their advice on your own projects, and the chance to taste the flavour of the area as well. Tour dates 1997: Spring - May; Summer - June/July; Autumn - September. The tours are strictly limited to 50 persons only per tour date. Write for further information.

Himalayan Kingdoms
20 The Mall, Clifton, Bristol, Avon BS8 3BE
Contact: Susie Champion
Tel: 0117 9237163
Fax: 0117 9744993

Pick the best of the bunch for a trip of a lifetime! Sikkim - " the garden kingdom of the Himalayas", Dharmsala - "Valley of the Goddess"...... For further details and a full colour brochure, contact Dept GP
Catalogue

Homesitters Ltd
Buckland Wharf, Buckland, Aylesbury, Buckinghamshire HP22 5LQ
Tel: 01296 630730
Fax: 01296 631555

We provide live-in caretakers to look after your home, pets and garden when you are away. Our clients benefit from reduced insurance premiums.
Catalogue

Irish Tourist Board
150 New Bond Street, London W1Y 0AQ
Tel: 0171 493 3201
Fax: 0171 493 9065

Kenwith Nursery
The Old Rectory, Littleham, Bideford, Devon EX39 5HW
Tel/fax: 01237 473752
Hours: 10am–12pm 2–5pm Wed–Sat. Other times by appt
Catalogue; Mail order

Naturetrek
Chautara, Bighton, Alresford, Hampshire SO24 9RB
Tel: 01962 733051
Fax: 01962 733368
Hours: 9am–5.30pm Mon–Fri

Britain's finest selection of expert-escorted holidays to: Nepal, Sikkim, China, India, Bhutan, Romania, Kazakhstan, Australia, Turkey, Greece, Slovakia, Pyrenees, Corsica, Crete, Cyprus and Morocco.
Catalogue

Penshurst Place & Gardens
Penshurst, Nr Tonbridge, Kent TN11 8DG
Tel: 01892 870307
Fax: 01892 870866
Hours: Grounds 11am–6pm daily Apr–Sept. Weekends Mar/Oct

Magnificent Medieval manor house with 10 acres of Tudor walled gardens, divided by one mile of yew hedges into garden compartments. Colour all year round.
Toilets; Refreshments; Disabled access

Peregrine Holidays
40/41 South Parade, Summertown, Oxford, Oxfordshire OX2 7JP
Tel/fax: 01865 511642

MAGAZINES & JOURNALS

Swan Hellenic Ltd
77 New Oxford Street, London
WC1A 1PP
Tel: 0171 831 1515
Fax: 0171 497 2832

Travel Ideas Ltd
Lyndall House, Plaistow,
Billingshurst, Sussex (W.) RH14 0PX
Tel: 01403 871400
Fax: 01403 871330

Holidays with a gardening theme. All the following destinations are offered: Europe, North America, South Africa, Far East, Australia and New Zealand. The most interesting itineraries at the keenest prices.
Catalogue; Mail order

Trossachs Garden Tours
Orchardlea House, Callander,
Central FK17 8BG
Contact: Hilary Gunkel
Tel: 01877 330798
Fax: 01877 330543
Hours: May–Oct

Small, friendly groups of garden lovers share short breaks in Scotland, England and Ireland, enjoying mainly private gardens where the owners show us round.

Victoria Travel Garden Tours
30 Hewell Road, Barnt Green,
Birmingham, Midlands (W.) B45 8NE
Tel: 0121 445 5656
Fax: 0121 445 6177

We offer quality, inspiring worldwide garden tours hosted by well-known experts, to a wide range of exciting destinations. Call us for our brochure. ABTA no 78024.

Amateur Gardening Magazine
I P C Magazines Ltd, Westover House, West Quay Rd, Poole, Dorset BH15 1JG
Tel: 01202 860586
Fax: 01202 674335

The ONLY full colour weekly magazine for keen gardeners. Covers everything from greenhouses to vegetables, and lawns to houseplants. On sale every Tuesday.

B B C Gardeners World
101 Bayham Street, London NW1 0AG
Tel/fax: 0171 331 8000

Flora International
The Fishing Lodge Studio, 77 Bulbridge Rd, Wilton, Wiltshire SP2 0LE
Tel/fax: 01722 743207

Practical flower arranging and floristry features and related crafts. Also biographical articles of interesting, notable people from the world of flowers and gardens.

Garden
80 Vincent Square, London SW1P 2PE
Tel/fax: 0171 834 4333

Garden Answers Magazine
EPL, Apex House, Oundle Rd, Peterborough, Cambridgeshire PE2 9NP
Tel: 01733 898100
Fax: 01733 898433

Garden News
EPL, Apex House, Oundle Rd, Peterborough, Cambridgeshire PE2 9NP
Contact: John Roach
Tel: 01733 898100
Fax: 01733 898418

Britain's No 1 selling gardening weekly. First for news, views, show reports and an editorial excellence that encourages new innovations. More details call 01733 898100.

Gardener
Westover House, West Quay Rd, Poole, Dorset BH15 1JG
Contact: David Hurrion
Tel: 01202 687418
Fax: 01202 674335

National, monthly consumer magazine for the keen gardener and plantsman. Features detailed plant profiles, practical and creative gardening topics, new products and advice from experts.

Gardening Which?
2 Marylebone Rd, London NW1 4DF
Tel: 0171 830 6000
Fax: 0171 830 6220

From the publishers of Which? - the only gardening magazine you'll ever need. Phone 0800 252 100 for details of a free trial subscription.

Gardens Illustrated
John Brown Publishing, The Boat House, Crabtree Lane, Fulham, London SW6 6LU
Tel: 0171 470 2400
Fax: 0171 381 3930
Email: gardens@johnbrown.co.uk

Voted International Magazine of the Year, Gardens Illustrated brings you the world's finest gardens in a rich mix of stunning photography and sharp writing.
Mail order

Grower
Warwick House, Swanley, Kent BR8 8HY
Tel: 01322 660070
Fax: 01322 667633

Homes & Gardens
Kings Reach Tower, Stamford Street, London SE1 9LS
Tel: 0171 261 5000
Fax: 0171 261 6247

Horticulture Week
38-42 Hampton Rd, Teddington, London TW11 0JE
Tel: 0181 943 5000
Fax: 0181 943 5673

Hortus
Bryan's Ground, Stapleton, Presteigne, Hereford & Worcester LD8 2LP
Tel: 01544 260001
Fax: 01544 260015

A gardening journal. Quarterly by subscription.

House & Garden
Conde Nast Publications Ltd, Vogue House, Hanover Square, London W1R 0AD
Tel: 0171 499 9080
Fax: 0171 493 1345

National Gardens Scheme Charitable Trust
Hatchlands Park, East Clandon, Guildford, Surrey GU4 7RT
Tel: 01483 211535
Fax: 01483 211537

Publishes the Yellow Book, a guide to 3,500 private gardens open for six nursing and gardening charities.

New Plantsman
RHS Subscription Service, PO Box 38, Ashford, Kent TN25 6PR

New Vision Videos
Heron House, Angle Sea Rd, Wivenhoe, Essex CO7 9JR
Tel/fax: 01206 827338
Mail order

Organic Gardening
PO Box 4, Wiveliscombe, Taunton, Somerset TA4 2QY
Contact: Keith Ross
Tel/fax: 01984 623998

Monthly magazine (news-stand and subscription) covering all aspects of gardening - vegetable, fruit, ornamentals, organic fertilisers and pesticides, greenhouse, ponds, tools and equipment. Competitive advertising rates.

Period House & Garden
Times House, Station Approach, Ruislip, Middlesex HA4 8NB
Tel: 01895 677677
Fax: 01895 676027

SHOWS & EVENTS

Practical Gardening Magazine
EPL, Apex House, Oundle Rd,
Peterborough, Cambridgeshire
PE2 9NP

Tel: 01733 898100
Fax: 01733 898433

Search Press Ltd
Wellwood, North Farm Rd,
Tunbridge Wells, Kent TN2 3DR

Contact: Ruth Saunders
Tel: 01892 510850
Fax: 01892 515903

Publishers of a colourful series of organic gardening books, produced in conjunction with the Henry Doubleday Research Association, and available from our mail order service.
Catalogue; Mail order

Water Gardener
9 Tufton Street, Ashford, Kent
TN23 1QN

Contact: Yvonne Rees
Tel/fax: 01584 856560

The specialist consumer magazine for everyone interested in ponds and water features, with top class information on fish, plants, wildlife and design.

Arley Hall & Gardens
Great Budworth, Nr Northwich,
Cheshire CW9 6NA

Contact: Eric Ransome
Tel: 01565 777353
Fax: 01565 777465

Hours: Mar 28–Sept 29 1997. Closed Mons

Early Victorian hall set in 12 acres of magnificent gardens, containing rare and unusual plants and shrubs. Double herbaceous border, specialist plantsman's gardens. The Arley Garden Festival, 26-27 July 1997, offers unusual plants from specialist nurseries and individual garden accessory stalls. Restaurant, gift shop, disabled facilities, plant nursery, dogs on leash welcome.
Toilets; Refreshments; Disabled access

Ayr Flower Show
Kyle & Carrick Dist. Council,
Leisure Sevices, 30 Miller Rd,
Ayr, Strathclyde KA7 2AY

Tel/fax: 01292 282842
Hours: Dates to be confirmed

B B C Gardeners World Live
BBC Haymarket Exhibitions, 60 Waldegrave Rd, Teddington, Middlesex TW11 8LG

Tel/fax: 0181 943 5000

The national flower and garden show features favourite BBC gardening celebrities amidst horticultural exhibits of every description. 1997 show: NEC, Birmingham 11th-15th June.

Chelsea Flower Show
Shows Department, Royal Horticultural Society, 80 Vincent Square, London SW1P 2PE

Tel/fax: 0171 828 1744

The most prestigious event on the horticultural calendar, the Chelsea Flower Show presents an annual combination of breathtaking beauty, horticultural excellence and the latest design ideas. RHS Membership enquiries: 0171 821 300. Shows information (24 hours): 0171 828 1744. 1997 show: 20-23rd May.

Devon NCCPG Autumn Plant Market
Bicton College, East Budleigh, Devon

Contact: Roger Stuckey
Tel/fax: 01395 273636

The Devon Group of the National Council for the Conservation of Plants and Gardens (a registered charity) holds plant markets three times a year to raise money for the Group. Entry £1. Ample parking. Refreshments. Over 30 nurseries represented. 1997: Sunday 14th September 2pm-4.30pm.

Devon NCCPG Summer Plant Market
South Molton Indoor Market, Devon

Contact: Roger Stuckey
Tel/fax: 01395 273636

The Devon group of the National Council for the Conservation of Plants and Gardens (a registered charity) holds plant markets three times a year to raise money for the Group. Entry free. Easy parking. Refreshments. 1997: Sunday 13th July 12 non-4pm.

Felley Priory Garden
Underwood, Jacksdale,
Nottinghamshire NG16 5FL

Contact: Hon Mrs Chaworth-Musters
Tel/fax: 01773 810230

Garden around Elizabethan house. Topiary, rose garden, pergolas, herbaceous borders. Plant Fair in aid of NCCPG in June - phone for details.

Gateshead Summer Flower Show
Metropolitan Borough Council, Leisure Services Dept, Civic Centre, Regent St, Gateshead, Tyne & Wear NE8 1HH

Contact: Graham Scott
Tel: 0191 477 1011
Fax: 0191 478 2345

Gateshead Spring Flower Show Sat 12th April, Sun 13th April 1997. Gateshead Summer Flower Show Sat 26th July, Sun 27th July 1997. The Gateshead shows are a wealth of colour, with the UK's top nurseries taking part. Floral art; horticultural goods and plants; amateur exhibits; trade and society exhibits; entertainment marquee; food hall; craft fair. At Central Nursery, Whickham Highway, Gateshead.

Great Garden & Countryside Festival
Holker Hall, Cark in Cartmel, Grange over Sands, Cumbria LA11 7PL

Contact: Carolyn Johnson
Tel: 015395 58838
Fax: 015395 58776

Hours: 10am–6pm 30/31 May/1 June

Prestigious festival with magnificent horticultural display, plant sales, festival gardens, advice centres, Gardeners' Question Time, countryside displays and much, much more.
Toilets; Refreshments; Disabled access

Hampton Court Palace Flower Show
Shows Department, Royal Horticultural Society, 80 Vincent Square, London SW1P 2PE

Tel/fax: 0171 828 1744

The world's biggest annual gardening event is set in 25 acres of royal parkland and features highlights such as the spectacular Daily Mail Pavilion. 1997 show: Hampton Court Palace, East Molesey, Surrey 8th-13th July.

Houghall College
Durham City, Co Durham
DH1 3SG

Tel: 0191 386 1351
Fax: 0191 386 0419

Hours: Gardens open 12.30–4.30pm daily except Xmas Day

Services provided - extensive gardens, special open days, gardening advice, soil testing, wide range of short and full-time courses. For further details telephone 0191 3861351.
Disabled access

International Spring Gardening Fair
News International Exhibitions, PO Box 495, Virginia Street, London E1 9XY

Tel/fax: 0171 782 6000

Lincolnshire Trust for Nature Conservation
Banovallum House, Manor House St, Horncastle, Lincolnshire LN9 5HF

Contact: Mary Edwards
Tel: 01507 526667
Fax: 01507 525732
Email: lincstrust@cix.compulink.co.uk

Countryside events on nature reserves, including bluebell walks, bat nights, open gardens. Please contact the Trust for free leaflet.

Malvern Autumn Gardening Show
Three Counties Agr Society, The Showground, Malvern, Hereford & Worcester WR13 6NW

Contact: L M Downes
Tel/fax: 01684 892751

Organised by the RHS in conjunction with Three Counties Agricultural Society. A blaze of Autumn flowers, complemented by fruit and vegetable workshops and traditional county show events. 1997 show: 27th-28th September.
Catalogue; Toilets; Refreshments; Disabled access

Malvern Spring Gardening Show
Three Counties Agr Society, The Showground, Malvern, Hereford & Worcester WR13 6NW

Tel/fax: 01684 892751

Organised by the RHS in conjunction with the Three Counties Agricultural Society. Professional nurserymen from around the country and top amateur growers unite to create this now famous springtime spectacular. 1997 show: 9th-11th May.
Catalogue; Toilets; Refreshments; Disabled access

Museum of Garden History
Dept CFS, The Museum of Garden History, Lambeth Palace Rd, London SE1 7LB

Tel: 0171 401 8865
Fax: 0171 401 8869

Hours: 11am–3pm Mon–Fri 6 Mar–11 Dec, 10.30am–5pm Sun
Toilets; Refreshments; Disabled access

North of England Horticultural Society
4a South Park Rd, Harrogate, Yorkshire (N.) HG1 5QU

Contact: Alan Ravenscroft
Tel: 01423 561049
Fax: 01423 536880
Hours: 9.30am–6pm

Harrogate Autumn Flower Show 12/14 Sept 1997 inclusive. Leading nursery displays, twelve specialist amateur horticultural shows, National Onion Championship, gardening accessories, crafts, Yorkshire Food Pantry. Last day closes 5.30pm.
Harrogate Spring Flower Show - April. Britain's finest early horticultural event. Leading nursery displays, gardening sundries. An extravaganza of flower arrangements. Last day closes at 4.30pm.

Primrose Fairs
Hilltop Cottage, Southwell Road, Thurgarton, Nottinghamshire NG14 7GP

Tel/fax: 01636 830756

Rare and unusual plant fairs in and around the Midlands, over 30 exhibitors. For information on dates/venues etc telephone Primrose Fairs 01636 830756.

Rare Plants Fairs
84 Ellenhay Road, Bradley Stoke, Avon BS12 0HB

Contact: Mrs Maureen Willson
Tel/fax: 01179 691570

One day fairs bringing together many of the best specialist nurseries in the country, selling an enormous range of both rare and traditional plants.

Scotland's National Gardening Show
Strathclyde Country Park

The RHS is breaking new ground with the launch of this exciting new flower show featuring the very best exhibitors from north and south of the border. 1997 show: 30th May-1st June.

Scottish Rock Garden Club
PO Box 14063, Edinburgh, Lothian EH10 4YE

Twice yearly journal with articles on rock plants, bulbs etc. Seed list, over 4,000 different. 9 plant shows, 17 local groups in Scotland and England.

Shrewsbury Flower Show
Quarry Lodge, Shrewsbury, Shropshire SY1 1RN

Tel/fax: 01743 364051
Hours: Dates to be confirmed

South East Garden Festival
Historic Dockyard, Chatham, Kent

Hours: 9am–6pm daily

Annual festival held at the end of July, beginning of August. Displays set amongst the Georgian buildings of the Historic Dockyard.

South West Alpine Show
St Thomas High School, Hatherleigh Road, Exeter, Devon

Contact: Roger Stuckey
Tel/fax: 01395 273636

Alpine Garden Society - Exeter Group. 1997 show on Saturday 29th March from 12 noon to 4.30pm. Entry £1. Plant sales start at 10am. On site parking. Refreshments.

Southport Flower Show
42 Hoghton Street, Southport, Lancashire PR9 0PQ

Hours: Dates to be confirmed

Westminster Flower Shows
Shows Department, Royal Horticultural Society, 80 Vincent Square, London SW1P 2PE

Tel/fax: 0171 828 1744

Monthly celebrations of the best plants on offer at every stage of the year, held at the RHS Halls, Westminster. 1997 dates:
21-22 Jan: Ornamental Plant Competition, Botanical Paintings.
18-19 Feb: Ornamental Plant Competition, Botanical Paintings.
8-9 March: London Orchid Show.
18-19 March: Early Spring Flower Show - Early Camellia, Early Rhododendron, Ornamental Plant & Early Daffodil Competitions.
15-16 April: Daffodil Show, Main Camellia & Ornamental Plant Competitions.
29-30 April: Main Rhododendron, Late Daffodil, Tulip & Ornamental Plant Competitions.
24-25 June: Ornamental Plant Competition.
22-23 July: Summer Fruit & Vegetable & Ornamental Plant Competitions.
19-20 August: Gladiolus & Ornamental Plant Competitions, Botanical Photographs.
16-17 Sept: Great Autumn Flower Show.
7-8 Oct: Autumn Fruit & Vegetable, Ornamental Plant Competitions.
4-5 Nov: Ornamental Plant Competition, Botanical Paintings.
25-26 Nov: Ornamental Plant, Late Apple & Pear Competitions, Botanical Paintings.
9-10 Dec: RHS Christmas Show.

Wisley Flower Show
R H S Garden, Wisley, Woking, Surrey GU23 6QB

Tel/fax: 01483 224234

An intimate and exceptionally popular floral celebration held in a marquee on Seven Acres. Free to all visitors to the Garden. 1997 show: 14th-15th August.

Woburn Abbey
Woburn Park, Woburn, Bedfordshire MK43 0TP

Tel: 01525 290666
Fax: 01525 290271

Guided tours during Woburn Abbey Flower and Garden Show - June 8/9.
Toilets; Refreshments; Disabled access

Wrest Park Homes & Gardens Show
Romor Exhibitions Ltd, PO Box 448, Bedford, Bedfordshire MK40 2ZP

Tel/fax: 01234 345725

SOCIETIES & ORGANISATIONS

Alpine Garden Society
AGS Centre, Avon Bank,
Pershore, Hereford & Worcester
WR10 3JP

Tel: 01386 554790
Fax: 01386 554801

Hours: 9am–5.30pm Mon–Thurs,
9am–5pm Fri

The Alpine Garden Society encourages interest in all aspects of alpine and rock garden plants. Publications, shows, seeds, distribution, local groups, tours. 13,500 members. £15 single, £18 family annual subscription.

Alpine Garden Society
59 Whitebridges, Honiton,
Devon EX14 8RZ

Contact: Mrs Liz White
Tel/fax: 01404 41732

Hours: 7pm–9.30pm 3rd Thurs of month, Sept–June

Friendly local group of National Society for anyone, including beginners, who is interested in alpine plants, rockeries etc. Talks, shows, sales, garden visits and parties.

Architectural Association
34-36 Bedford Square, London
WC1B 3ES

Tel: 0171 636 0974
Fax: 0171 636 0996

Architectural Association school of architecture. Conservation of historic landscapes, parks and gardens Dip 2 years part-time. Contact the Conservation Co-ordinator.

Avon Gardens Trust
Station House, Church Lane,
Wickwar, Wotton under Edge,
Gloucestershire GL12 8NB

Berkshire Buckinghamshire & Oxfordshire Naturalists Trust
3 Church Cowley Rd, Rose Hill,
Oxford, Oxfordshire OX4 3JR

Botanical Society of Scotland
c/o Royal Botanic Garden,
Edinburgh, Lothian EH3 5LR

Botanical Society of the British Isles
c/o Dept of Botany, The Natural History Museum, Cromwell Rd, London SW7 5BD

An association of amateur and professional botanists interested in the study of British and Irish flowering plants and ferns.

British & European Geranium Society
Prospect Farm, Misson Springs,
Doncaster, Yorkshire (S.)
DN10 6ET

Tel: 01302 772139
Fax: 01302 772823

Specialist geranium society; local groups, shows, talks, visits etc.

British Bonsai Association
c/o Inglenook, 36 McCarthy Way, Wokingham, Berkshire
RG11 4UA

British Clematis Society
4 Springfield, Lightwater, Surrey
GU18 5XP

Contact: Richard Stothard
Tel/fax: 01276 476387

The Society exists to promote greater knowledge of clematis amongst enthusiasts, gardeners and growers. Features: meetings, plant sales, advice, seed exchange, slide library. Attends shows.

British Fuchsia Society
15 Summerfield Lane,
Summerfield, Kidderminster,
Hereford & Worcester DY11 7SA

Contact: Peter Darnley
Tel/fax: 01562 66688

The Society aims to extend the cultivation and knowledge of fuchsias. Membership £6 single, £9 joint. Benefits include three publications per year, free plants etc.

British Gladiolus Society
24 The Terrace, Mayfield,
Ashbourne, Derbyshire DE6 2JL

Contact: Nigel Coe
Tel/fax: 01335 345443

The promotion of all aspects of gladiolus culture including propagation, cultivation, exhibition and hybridisation.

British Hosta & Hemerocallis Society
Cleave House, Sticklepath,
Okehampton, Devon EX20 2NN

Contact: Roger Bowden
Tel: 01837 840481
Fax: 01837 840482

For annual fee £8 the Society provide library facilities, 3 newsletters, a bulletin, 3 outings/lectures, a plant auction and exchange of information with other members.

British Iris Society
The Old Mill House, Shurton,
Stogursey, Bridgwater, Somerset
TA5 1QG

Contact: C E C Bartlett
Tel/fax: 01278 733485

Growing and showing all irises. Local and specialist groups. Newsletter and year-book published. Seed distribution and plant sales for members.

British Ivy Society
Garden Cottage Westgreen Hse,
Thackham's Lane, Hartley Whitney, Basingstoke,
Hampshire RG27 8JB

British National Carnation Society
23 Chiltern Road, St Albans,
Herts AL4 9SW

Contact: Alex Ketchen

For a modest £9 membership you could exhibit at the RHS Halls in London and help promote the growing of these beautiful flowers.

British Pelargonium & Geranium Society
Maur or Les, 75 Pelham Road,
Bexleyheath, Kent DA7 4LY

Contact: Mr Les Hodgkiss

Membership to the BPGS is £6.50 yearly and entitles members to four quarterly journals full of information, tips and advice plus an annual national show.

British Pteridological Society
16 Kirby Corner Rd, Canley,
Coventry, Midlands (W.) CV4 8GD

TELEFLORIST

Teleflorists offer a worldwide professional service for all your floral requirements.

The dove sign is displayed by all Teleflorists throughout the UK and Southern Ireland.

For further information apply:
Administration Department
British Teleflower Service Limited
Teleflower House, Unit 35
Romsey Industrial Estate
Greatbridge Road, Romsey, Hants SO51 0HR
Telephone: 01794 526460

The Daily Telegraph *Green Fingers*   **Societies & Organisations**

British Rose Growers Association
46 Alexandra Rd, St Albans, Hertfordshire AL1 3AZ
Tel/fax: 01727 833648

British Teleflower Service Ltd
Unit 35, Romsey Industrial Estate, Greatbridge Road, Romsey, Hampshire SO51 0HR
Tel: 01794 511116
Fax: 01794 511199

Worldwide flower relay network. Teleflorists display the name and dove sign and will be pleased to offer you this service on any occasion calling for flowers.

Butterfly Conservation
PO Box 222, Dedham, Colchester, Essex CO7 6EY
Contact: Mrs D Scullion
Tel: 01206 322342
Fax: 01206 322739

Butterfly Conservation, a registered charity dedicated to saving wild butterflies and their habitats, produces a booklet entitled Gardening for Butterflies. Please write for details.

Carnivorous Plant Society
174 Baldwins Lane, Croxley Green, Hertfordshire WD3 3LQ

Cheshire Wildlife Trust
Grebe House, Reseheath, Nantwich, Cheshire CW5 6DA
Tel/fax: 01270 610180

Cleveland Wildlife Trust
Bellamy House Unit 2a, Brighouse Business Village, Riverside Park, Middlesbrough, Cleveland TS2 1RT
Tel/fax: 01642 253716

Conservatory Association
2nd Floor, Godwin House, George Street, Huntingdon, Cambridgeshire PE18 6BU
Contact: Bunny Lane
Tel: 01480 458278
Fax: 01480 411326
Hours: 8.30am–5pm Mon–Fri

The Conservatory Association exists to regulate the industry. Members must satisfy standards of design, manufacture, trading practices and are strictly vetted prior to Association membership.
Catalogue; Mail order

Cornwall Gardens Society
Liskeard Water Gardens, Pengover Rd, Liskeard, Cornwall PL14 3NL
Tel/fax: 01579 342278

Cornwall Gardens Trust
Tredarvah Vean, Penzance, Cornwall TR18 4SU
Contact: Daphne Lawry MBE
Tel/fax: 01736 63473

To record, conserve and enhance garden and parkland in Cornwall.

Cornwall Wildlife Trust
Five Acres, Allet, Truro, Cornwall TR4 9DJ
Contact: Trevor Edwards
Hours: 8.30am–4.30pm Mon–Fri

Advice on gardening for wildlife, including design and management. Selection of appropriate native species available.

Cottage Garden Society
Hurstfield house (CGS), 244 Edleston Rd, Crewe, Cheshire CW2 7EJ
Contact: Clive Lane
Tel: 01270 250776/820258
Fax: 01270 250118

The society aims to keep alive the cottage garden tradition through quarterly newsletters, garden visits, local groups, annual seedlists. UK single membership £5.

Cyclamen Society
Tile Barn House, Standen St, Iden Green, Benenden, Kent TN17 4LB
Contact: Peter Moore

Seed exchange, shows, conference, slide and book library, advisory panel, Registered charity No 280528.

Delphinium Society
Takakkaw, Ice House Wood, Oxted, Surrey RH8 9DW
Contact: Shirley Bassett

Annual membership £5 brings seeds on joining, year book, show ticket, access to hand-pollinated seed. Cultivation guide £2.50. Cheques payable to "Delphinium Society".
Mail order

Devons Gardens Trust
Lucombe House, Devon Country Council, County Hall, Exeter, Devon EX2 4QW
Tel/fax: 01884 253803

Dorset Perennial Group
Ivy Cottage, Aller Lane, Ansty, Dorchester, Dorset DT2 7PX

Dorset Trust for Nature Conservation
39 Christchurch Rd, Bournemouth, Dorset BH1 3NS
Tel/fax: 01202 554241

Dyfed Wildlife Trust
7 Market St, Haverfordwest, Dyfed SA61 1NF
Tel/fax: 01437 765462

East Malling Research Association
Bradbourne House, East Malling, Kent ME19 6DZ
Contact: Dr J Quinlan
Tel/fax: 01732 872064

Research association for those interested in fruit and hop growing. Meetings and workshops held regularly.

Essex Wildlife Trust
Fingringhoe Wick Nat Reserve, South Green Rd, Fingringhoe, Colchester, Essex CO5 7DN
Tel/fax: 01206 729678

Federation of British Bonsai Societies
Rivendale, 14 Somerville Rd, Sutton Coldfield, Midlands (W.) B73 6JA
Contact: K Hughes
Tel: 0121 354 8107
Fax: 0121 321 1131

FoBBS provides a central service and forum for 75 member bonsai societies throughout the UK, seeking to support their aims and co-ordinate their activities.

Federation of Edinburgh & District Allotments & Gardens
2 South House Avenue, Edinburgh, Lothian EH17 8EA

Friends of the Royal Botanic Garden Edinburgh
The Royal Botanic Garden, Inverleith Row, Edinburgh, Lothian EH3 5LR
Tel/fax: 0131 552 5339

Friends of the Royal Botanic Gardens Kew
Cambridge Cottage, Kew Green, Kew, Richmond, Surrey TW9 3AB
Tel: 0181 332 5922
Fax: 0181 332 5901

Garden Centre Association
38 Carey Street, Reading, Berkshire RG1 7JS
Tel: 0118 9393900
Fax: 0118 9500686

Visiting an Approved Member centre of the Garden Centre Association visitors can be assured of high quality in both product and service. All members operate the GCA Plant Guarantee.

Garden History Society
77 Cowcross Street, London EC1M 6BP
Contact: Linda Wigley
Tel: 0171 608 2409
Fax: 0171 490 2974

Members receive two journals and three newsletters a year, keeping them informed of the latest developments in garden history, plus a varied membership programme.

Gardeners' Royal Benevolent Society
Dept MGS, Bridge House, 139 Kingston Rd, Leatherhead, Surrey KT22 7NT
Tel: 01372 373962
Fax: 01372 362575

Assists retired gardeners with beneficiary payments, grants and holidays. The society provides sheltered accommodation in Sussex, Cambridgeshire, Gloucestershire and Berwickshire, also residential and nursing in Sussex.
Catalogue; Mail order

Gardening for the Disabled Trust
Hayes Farm House, Hayes Lane, Peasmarsh, Sussex (E.) TN31 6XR

We raise money to give grants to disabled people in order that they can take an active interest in gardening.

Gladiolus Breeders Association
15 Guildhall Drive, Pinchbeck, Spalding, Lincolnshire PE11 3RE

Glamorgan Wildlife Trust
Fountain Rd, Tondu, Bridgend, Glamorgan, Mid CF32 0EH
Tel/fax: 01656 724100
Hours: 9am–5pm Mon–Fri. Closed 1–2pm for lunch

Protecting Glamorgan's wildlife through education. Management of Nature Reserves (46). Maintaining a biological database, monitoring planning applications and advising land owners.
Disabled access

Gloucestershire Gardens & Landscape Trust
Sunny Crest, Eden's Hill, Upleadon, Newent, Gloucestershire GL18 1EE
Tel/fax: 01531 822433

Preserves, enhances or re-creates for public enjoyment and education garden land that exists or existed in the past. This charity welcomes any cash/voluntary assistance.

The Daily Telegraph *Green Fingers* **Societies & Organisations**

Gwent Wildlife Trust
16 White Swan Court,
Monmouth, Gwent NP5 3NY

Tel/fax: 01600 715501

Hampshire Gardens Trust
Jermyn's House, Jermyn's Lane,
Ampfield, Romsey, Hampshire
SO51 0QA

Contact: Mrs J Hebden
Tel: 01794 367752
Fax: 01794 368520

The Hampshire Gardens Trust helps to provide for the long-term care or renewal of gardens, parks and designed landscapes endangered by neglect and development.

Hardy Plant Society
Little Orchard, Great
Comberton, Pershore, Hereford
& Worcester WR10 3DP

Contact: Mrs Pam Adams
Tel: 01386 710317
Fax: 01386 710117

The Hardy Plant Society explores, encourages and conserves all that is best in gardens. Membership details available from the Administrator.

Heather Society
Denbeigh, All Saints Rd, Creeting
St Mary, Ipswich, Suffolk IP6 8PJ

Contact: Anne or David Small
Tel/fax: 01449 711220

Regional groups, conferences, field trips, informative yearbook and three bulletins keep members aware of this international society's activities in the world of heathers for £10 per annum.

Hebe Society
Rosemergy, Hain Walk, St Ives,
Cornwall TR26 2AF

Contact: Geoffrey Scoble
Tel/fax: 01736 795225

International society (1985) for hebe and New Zealand native plants. Identification, registration of new cultivars, libraries, reference collections, magazine, publications, lectures, shows, visits. Cuttings exchange. Membership £6.

Henry Doubleday Research Association (HDRA)
Ryton Organic Gardens,
Ryton-on-Dunsmore, Coventry,
Midlands (W.) CV8 3LG

Tel: 01203 303517
Fax: 01203 639229

Britain's premier organic gardening organisation, with demonstration gardens at Coventry and Maidstone. Members get free advice, quarterly magazines, discounts from extensive mail order catalogue plus free entry to RHS and other gardens. Runs Heritage Seed Library for endangered vegetables. SAE for details.
Catalogue; Mail order; Toilets; Refreshments; Disabled access

Herb Society
134 Buckingham Palace Rd,
London SW1W 9SA

Tel/fax: 0171 823 5583
Hours: 10am–4pm Tues–Fri

Interested in herbs? Growing, medicinal, culinary, historical uses - The Herb Society is for you. We publish two journals, run workshops, seminars and answer your queries.

Herefordshire Nature Trust
25 Castle St, Hereford, Hereford
& Worcester HR1 2NW

Tel/fax: 01432 356872

Hertfordshire & Middlesex Wildlife Trust
Grebe House, St Michaels St, St
Albans, Hertfordshire AL3 4SN

Tel/fax: 01727 858901

Homesitters Ltd
Buckland Wharf, Buckland,
Aylesbury, Buckinghamshire
HP22 5LQ

Tel: 01296 630730
Fax: 01296 631555

We provide live-in caretakers to look after your home, pets and garden when you are away. Our clients benefit from reduced insurance premiums.
Catalogue

Horticultural Research Association
Wellesbourne, Warwickshire
CV35 9EF

Tel/fax: 01789 470382

Research association for those interested in all aspects of horticultural research. £25 annual fee. Meetings and workshops held regularly.

Horticultural Research International
East Malling, Maidstone, Kent
ME19 6BJ

Tel: 01732 843833
Fax: 01732 849067

Horticultural research, development, consultancy, advice and information for growers. Annual report £10. Fruit, ornamentals, nursery stock. See also Horticultural Research Association.

Horticultural Research International
Wellesbourne, Warwickshire
CV35 9EF

Tel/fax: 01789 470382

Horticultural research, development and consultancy. Advice and information for growers. Annual report £10. Fruit, vegetables, ornamentals, nursery stock and mushrooms. See also Horticultural Research Association.

Horticultural Therapy
Goulds Ground, Vallis Way,
Frome, Somerset BA11 3DW

Tel/fax: 01373 464782

HT helps people enjoy a better quality of life through gardening. We provide printed and taped information, training, day-care services and project advice.
Catalogue

Ichiyo School of Ikebana
4 Providence Way, Waterbeach,
Cambridge, Cambridgeshire
CB5 9QJ

International Camellia Society
41 Galveston Rd, East Putney,
London SW15 2RZ

Contact: Hervert C Short Jnr
Tel: 0181 870 6884
Fax: 0181 874 4633
Email:
101333.2537@compuserve.com

The ICS is a non-profit society devoted to camellias. It sponsors an international congress, regional meetings, newsletters and annual journal. Single membership £8.50, double £11.

International Dendrology Society
School House, Stannington,
Morpeth, Northumberland NE61 6HF

International Violet Association
11 Myddlewood, Myddle,
Shrewsbury, Shropshire SO4 3RY

International Water Lily Society
c/o Hooper, Mill Lane, Bradfield,
Manningtree, Essex CO11 2QP

Contact: Mr Harry Hooper

Join other enthusiastic amateur, professional and academic water gardeners. Quarterly journal, symposium and garden tours, reference library, research projects. Over 950 members worldwide dedicated to the furtherance of all aspects of water gardening.

Isle of Wight Gardens Trust
Cassies, Billingham, Newport,
Isle of Wight PO3 3HD

Japanese Garden Society
Groves Mill, Shakers Lane,
Longitchington, Rugby,
Warwickshire CV23 8QB

Contact: Kira Dalton
Tel/fax: 01926 632746

Specialist society with interest in Japanese Gardens, in both Japan and UK. Informative quarterly journal. Regional groups and meetings in most areas.

Kent Trust for Nature Conservation
Tyland Barn, Sandling,
Maidstone, Kent ME14 3BD

Tel/fax: 01622 662012

Leicestershire & Rutland Trust for Nature Conservation
1 West St, Leicester,
Leicestershire LE1 6UU

Tel/fax: 0116 2553904

Lincolnshire Trust for Nature Conservation
Banovallum House, Manor
House St, Horncastle,
Lincolnshire LN9 5HF

Contact: Mary Edwards
Tel: 01507 526667
Fax: 01507 525732
Email:
lincstrust@cix.compulink.co.uk

Countryside events on nature reserves, including bluebell walks, bat nights, open gardens. Please contact the Trust for free leaflet.

LOFA - The Leisure & Outdoor Furniture Association
PO Box 233, Redhill, Surrey
RH1 4YU

Tel/fax: 01376 518861

Representing the major manufacturers and suppliers of garden furniture, barbecues, barbecue accessories, cushions and parasols in the UK. LOFA can help with information on all these products - expert advice is only a phone call away. (See our full colour advertisement on page iii).

London Historic Parks & Gardens Trust
Duck Island Cottage, The
Storeyard, St James Park, London

Tel: 01953 818137
Fax: 01953 39126

Mammillaria Society
26 Glenfield Rd, Banstead, Surrey
SM7 2DG

Contact: W F Maddams
Tel/fax: 01737 354036

Promotion of interest in the genus mammillaria. A quarterly journal, specialist publications and an annual seed distribution. Annual subscription £6.50.

Mesemb Study Group
Brenfield, Bolney Rd, Ansty, Sussex (W.) RH17 5AW
Contact: Mrs Suzanne Mace
Tel: 01444 459151
Fax: 01444 454061
Email: msg@nacc.demon.co.uk

A specialist study group for plants of the family mesembryan-themaleae. Produces quarterly journal - seed distribution. International membership approx 500.

Montgomeryshire Wildlife Trust
Collot House, 20 Severn St, Welshpool, Powys SY21 7AD
Tel: 01938 555654
Fax: 01938 556161
Hours: 9am–5pm Mon–Fri

The Trust has two shops selling a wide variety of environmentally friendly goods - books, seeds, peat-free compost, nesting boxes, bird feeders. Offers garden conservation advice.

National Association of Flower Arrangement Societies
21 Denbigh St, London SW1V 2HF
Tel: 0171 828 5145
Fax: 0171 821 0587
Hours: 9.30am–4.30pm

NAFAS has 100,000 members of 1,500 UK clubs, - contact via Headquarters. NAFAS encourages the art and practice of flower arranging at all levels by sponsoring qualification courses, staging shows and competitions, The Flower Arranger Magazine, and marketing a wide range of books, pamphlets and related items.
Mail order

National Auricula & Primula Society (Southern)
67 Warnham Court Rd, Carshalton Beeches, Surrey SM5 3ND
Contact: Lawrence Wigley

Formed 1876 to encourage cultivation/exhibition of auriculas, gold laced polyanthus, primroses and other primula species/hybrids. Three Spring shows, yearbook, newsletter. Subscription £7. Associated with custodians of various National Collections of Auriculas and other Primulas.

National Back Pain Association
16 Elmtree Rd, Teddington, Middlesex TW11 8ST
Tel: 0181 977 5474
Fax: 0181 943 9895
Hours: 9am–5pm Mon–Fri

Gardener's backache? Solve the problem with "Better Backs for Gardeners", a short, practical video from the National Back Pain Association. Ring 081 977 5474 for details.
Mail order

National Begonia Society
7 Springwood Close, Thurgoland, Sheffield, Yorkshire (S.) S30 7AB

National Bonsai Society
16 Coudray Road, Southport, Merseyside PR9 9NL

The Society offers members 4 publications per year and monthly meetings in Southport with lectures and demonstrations of the Bonsai art.

National Chrysanthemum Society
George Gray House, 8 Amber Business Village, Amber Close Amington, Tamworth, Staffordshire B77 4RD
Tel/fax: 01827 310331

National Collection of Passiflora
Lampley Rd, Kingston Seymour, Clevedon, Avon BS21 6XS
Tel: 01934 833350
Fax: 01934 877255
Hours: 9am–1pm 2pm–5pm Mon–Sat

Living plant collection of 220 species, exhibition of drawings, paintings, photographs. Selection of passiflora cards, books and products for sale.
Catalogue; Mail order

National Council for the Conservation of Plants & Gardens
The Pines, Wisley Garden, Woking, Surrey GU23 6QB
Contact: David Nichol
Tel: 01483 211465
Fax: 01483 211750

To foster and co-ordinate effective action, through voluntary county based groups and a network of National Collections, towards the conservation of garden plants.

National Dahlia Society
19 Sunnybank, Marlow, Buckinghamshire SL7 3BL
Contact: E H Collins
Tel/fax: 01628 473500

National Dahlia Society, the world's largest, giving an unbroken century of service to gardeners. Two annual publications and shows plus biennial classified dirctory. Write for membership.

National Pot Leek Society
8 Nelson Avenue, Nelson Village, Cramlington, Northumberland NE23 9HG

National Society of Allotment & Leisure Gardeners
O'Dell House, Hunters Rd, Corby, Northamptonshire NN17 1JE
Contact: Geoff Stokes
Tel/fax: 01536 266576

The society provides an advice and information service to its members on all allotment matters. Discounted seeds and allotment insurance are also available.

National Sweet Pea Society
3 Chalk Farm Rd, Stokenchurch, High Wycombe, Buckinghamshire HP14 3TB
Contact: J R F Bishop

A society founded in 1900 to encourage the cultivation and improvement of the sweet pea. A registered charity.

National Trust
36 Queen Annes Gate, London SW1H 9AS
Tel: 0171 222 9251
Fax: 0171 222 5097

National Vegetable Society
56 Waun-y-Groes Avenue, Rhiwbina, Cardiff, Glamorgan (S.) CF4 4SZ
Contact: Ivor Garland
Tel/fax: 01222 627994

To encourage the growth of better quality vegetables for the kitchen and to organise a panel of certified judges, lecturers and advisory officers.

National Viola & Pansy Society
Cleeway, Eardington, Bridgnorth, Shropshire WV16 5JT
Contact: Mr J Snocken
Tel/fax: 01746 766909

Benefits of membership include 3 plants on joining, newsletters, access to rare exhibition varieties, library including videos, advice and annual show. Annual subscription £3.

Norfolk Naturalists Trust
72 Cathedral Close, Norwich, Norfolk NR1 4DF
Tel/fax: 01603 625540

North of England Rose Carnation & Sweet Pea Society
16 Granville Drive, Brunton Park, Gosforth, Newcastle upon Tyne, Tyne & Wear NE5 5PA
Tel/fax: 0191 236 2530
Hours: Meetings first Mon of each month 7–9pm

To promote the cultivation of all garden flowers with special interest in roses, carnations, sweet peas and daffodils. Annual flower shows and horticultural events organised.

North Wales Wildlife Trust
376 High St, Bangor, Gwynedd LL57 1YE
Contact: Chris Wynne
Tel/fax: 01248 351541

NWWT aims to promote nature conservation and campaigns for the better protection of wildlife. We can also offer advice on wildlife gardening.

Northamptonshire Wildlife Trust
Lings House, Billing Lings, Northampton, Northamptonshire NN3 4BE
Tel/fax: 01604 405285

Northern Horticultural Society
Harlow Carr Botanical Gardens, Crag Lane, Harrogate, Yorkshire (N.) HG3 1QB
Tel/fax: 01423 565418
Hours: 9.30am–6pm or dusk if earlier daily

The aim of the society is to assess plants for their suitability to northern conditions.
Toilets; Refreshments; Disabled access

Nottinghamshire Wildlife Trust
310 Sneinton Dale, Nottingham, Nottinghamshire NG3 7DN
Tel/fax: 0115 9588242

Ohara School of Ikebana
Forresters, Sway Rd, Lymington, Hampshire SO41 8LR
Contact: Mrs H Woodman
Tel: 01590 672418
Fax: 015906 72418

We specialise in the teaching of Japanese flower arranging (Ikebana). Classes are held in London and other parts of the UK. Traditional and modern styles taught.

The Daily Telegraph *Green Fingers*   **Societies & Organisations**

Orchid Society of Great Britain
Athelney, 145 Binscombe Village, Godalming, Surrey GU7 3QL

Contact: Mrs B Arnold
Tel/fax: 01483 421423

Monthly meetings in London; quarterly journal; extensive lending library; competitions; cultural advice; plant exchange. Joining fee £5, annual subscription £10, family members £2 extra.
Toilets; Refreshments; Disabled access

Professional Gardeners Guild
North Lodge, Upper Winchendon, Aylesbury, Buckinghamshire HP18 0ES

Contact: Michael Walker - Secretary
Tel/fax: 01296 651957

National society for professional gardeners and other professionals involved with historic or heritage gardens and others run in a similar way.

Radnorshire Wildlife Trust
Warwick House, High St, Llandrindod Wells, Powys LD1 6AG

Tel/fax: 01597 823298

Royal Caledonian Horticultural Society
28 Silverknowes, Southway, Edinburgh, Lothian EH4 5PX

Contact: John MacLennan
Tel: 0131 336 5488
Fax: 0131 336 1847

Scotland's leading horticultural society. Based in Edinburgh, we run lectures, excursions, plant sales and social events. Special insurance packages available for affiliated societies.

Royal Gardeners' Orphan Fund
48 St Albans Road, Codicote, Hitchin, Hertfordshire SG4 8UT

Contact: Mrs K A Wallis
Tel/fax: 01438 820783

Registered charity no. 248746. Offers financial assistance to orphans and children of professional horticulturalists.

Royal Horticultural Society
80 Vincent Square, London SW1P 2PE

Tel: 0171 834 4333
Fax: 0171 630 6060
Hours: 9.30am–5.30pm

The purpose of the Society is the encouragement and improvement of the science, art and practice of horticulture in all its branches. For details of £5 discount membership offer see our full colour advertisement on page vi).

Royal National Rose Society
Chiswell Green, St Albans, Hertfordshire AL2 3NR

Contact: Lt Col K V Grapes
Tel: 01727 850461
Fax: 01727 850360
Email: rnrs.org.uk
Hours: 9am–5pm Mon–Sat, 10am–6pm Sun & Bank Hols mid June–mid Oct

The RNRS is the world's oldest and largest specialist plant society. It maintains the world famous Gardens of the Rose.

Saintpaulia & Houseplant Society
33 Church Rd, Newbury Park, Ilford, Essex IG2 7ET

All those who are keen on growing plants in their homes are welcomed as members. Annual subscription £4 single £5 double. Quarterly bulletin. Annual show.

Scottish Allotments & Gardens Society
14/1 Hoseason Gardens, Edinburgh, Lothian EH4 7HQ

Contact: Mrs Jane E Black
Tel/fax: 0131 539 5888

The objects of the society are: the protection, amelioration of conditions and education of allotment holders and gardeners, obtaining the best prices for seeds etc.

Scottish National Sweet Pea Rose & Carnation Society
72 West George St, Coatbridge, Lanarkshire, Strathclyde ML5 2DD

Scottish Rhododendron Society
Stron Ailne, Colintraive, Argyll, Strathclyde PA22 3AS

Contact: H Andrew
Tel/fax: 0170 084285

The Scottish Rhododendron Society is a chapter of the American Rhododendron Society. For full details of the benefits of membership apply to the secretary.

Scottish Rock Garden Club
PO Box 14063, Edinburgh, Lothian EH10 4YE

Twice yearly journal with articles on rock plants, bulbs etc. Seed list, over 4,000 different. 9 plant shows, 17 local groups in Scotland and England.

Scottish Wildlife Trust
Crammond House, Crammond Glebe Rd, Edinburgh, Lothian EH4 6NS

Tel: 0131 312 7765
Fax: 0131 312 8705

Sempervivum Society
11 Wingle Tye Rd, Burgess Hill, Sussex (W.) RH15 9HR

Contact: Peter Mitchell
Tel/fax: 01444 236848

The society was formed in 1970 for all people interested in the genus. Reference collection and newsletter.

Sino-Himalayan Plant Association
81 Parlaunt Road, Slough, Berkshire SL3 8BE

Contact: Chris Chadwell
Tel/fax: 01753 542823

Send 3 x 1st class stamps for seed catalogue offering unusual species from the Himalayas and world-wide.

Society of Floristry
59 Tree Tops, Portskewett, Gwent NP6 4RT

Contact: Margaret Neighbour

A professional society which, by a series of examinations encourages the florist to reach and demonstrate high standards of proficiency. Appreciating floristry as an art form.

Society of Garden Designers
6 Borough Rd, Kingston-upon-Thames, Surrey KT2 6BD

Contact: Sue Moller
Tel/fax: 0181 974 9483

The Society promotes high standards in garden design, recommending SGD-approved designers, courses and offering nationwide workshops and seminars. Send DL S.A.E. to Society Secretary.

Sogetsu - Greater London Branch
Priory Lake Cottage, Park Lane, Reigate, Surrey RH2 8JX

Tel/fax: 01737 245409

Somerset Gardens Trust
St Peters Vicarage, 62 Eastwick Rd, Taunton, Somerset TA2 7HD

Staffordshire Gardens & Parks Trust
c/o Planning Department, South Staffs District Council, Wolverhampton Rd, Codsall Wolverhampton, Midlands (W.) WV8 1PX

Tel/fax: 01902 846111

Staffordshire Wildlife Trust
Coutts House, Sandon, Stafford, Staffordshire ST18 0DN

Suffolk Wildlife Trust
Brooke House, The Green, Ashbocking, Ipswich, Suffolk IP6 9JY

Tel/fax: 01473 890089

The Wildlife Trusts are the premier protectors of the natural environment. Active in every county, with reserves, events, advice and information. In Suffolk ring 01473 890089 for activities near your home.

Surrey Gardens Trust
c/o Planning Department, Surrey County Council, County Hall, Kingston-upon-Thames, Surrey KT1 2DT

Tel/fax: 0181 541 9419

Surrey Wildlife Trust
School Lane, Pirbright, Woking, Surrey GU24 0JN

Tel/fax: 01483 488055

Sussex Wildlife Trust
Woods Mill, Henfield, Sussex (W.) BN5 9SD

Tel/fax: 01273 492630

Urban Wildlife Trust - West Midlands Wildlife Campaign
Unit 310, Jubilee Trades Centre, 130 Pershore St, Birmingham, Midlands (W.) B5 6ND

Tel/fax: 0121 666 7474

Wakefield & North of England Tulip Society
70 Wrenthorpe Lane, Wrenthorpe, Wakefield, Yorkshire (W.) WF2 0PT

The Society brings together growers of English florist and Dutch tulips with the annual shows and a newsletter. Annual membership £4, family £5.

Warwickshire Wildlife Trust
Brandon Marsh Nature Centre, Brandon Lane, Coventry, Midlands (W.) CV3 3GW

Tel/fax: 01203 302912

Welsh Historic Gardens Trust
Coed-y-Ffynnon, Lampeter Velfrey, Narberth, Dyfed SA43 2JD

Contact: Col R H Gilbertson
Tel/fax: 01834 83396

Ten county branches identify, research, conserve and restore historic gardens throughout Wales. Practical work, visits, training, winter lectures and social functions. Quarterly bulletin. Annual journal.

Wild Flower Society
68 Outwoods Rd, Loughborough, Leicestershire LE11 3LY

Wildlife Shop - BBONT
53 St Mary's Street, Wallingford, Oxfordshire OX10 0ER
Tel/fax: 01491 824944
Hours: *9.30am–5pm Mon–Sat*
Bird feeders, wild bird feeders, nesting boxes, bat boxes, wildflower seeds, bird tables, books, gifts, t-shirts, games, jewellery, aprons, tea towels, tea cosies.

Wildlife Trust Bedfordshire & Cambridgeshire
Enterprise House, Maris Lane, Trumpington, Cambridge, Cambridgeshire CB2 2LE
Tel/fax: 01223 846363

Wildlife Trust for Bristol Bath & Avon
Bristol Wildlife Centre, Jacob Wells Rd, Bristol, Avon BS8 1DR

Wildlife Trusts
The Green, Witham Park, Waterside South, Lincoln, Lincolnshire LN5 7JR
Contact: Vivienne O'Connor
Email: wildlifersnc@cix.compulink.co.uk

Protecting and enhancing species and habitats, common and rare, for a UK richer in wildlife. Send SAE for free leaflet 'Gardening for Wildlife'.

Wiltshire Gardens Trust
Treglisson, Crowe Lane, Freshford, Bath, Avon BA3 6EB
Contact: P R Marrack
Tel/fax: 01225 722267

Throughout Wiltshire: assists the conservation of important gardens, conserves garden plants, provides grants to primary schools, arranges lectures, plant sales and events for members.

Wiltshire Wildlife Trust
18-19 High St, Devizes, Wiltshire SN10 1AT
Tel/fax: 01380 725670

INDEXES

COMPANY INDEX

17 Fulham Park Gardens, 92
A & A Thorp, 63
A & P M Books, 106
A Edwards, 24
A J Palmer & Son, 49
A Wright & Son Ltd, 24
Aanco Conservatories, 7
Abbey Conservatories, 7
Abbey Dore Court Garden, 59, 90
Abbey Plants, 55
Abbots House Garden, The, 60
Abbots Ripton Hall, 83
Abbotsbury Sub-Tropical Gardens, 55, 87
Abbotswood, 88
Aberconwy Nursery, 80
Abercrombie & Kent Travel, 112
Aberdeen College, 107
Abriachan Gardens & Nursery, 79
Access Garden Products, 21
Accompanied Cape Tours, 112
Achamore Gardens, 102
Acorn, 18
Acorn Bank Garden, 85
Acorn Landscapes, 10
Acorn Windows & Conservatories, 7
Acres Wild (Landscape & Garden Design), 10
Addlestone Aquaria Pond & Aquatic Centre, 42
Adlington Hall, 83
Afan College Nursery, 80, 107
African Violet Centre, 66
Agars Nursery, 58
Agralan Ltd, 24
Agriframes, 17
Airport Aquaria, 65
Alan C Smith, 61
Alan Phipps Cacti, 48
Alexander Armstrong, 10
Alexander Palace Garden Centre - Capital Gardens, 65
Algoflash UK Ltd, 24
Alibench, 21
Alison Brett Garden Design, 10
Alispeed, 21
Alitags, 24
Alite Metals, 21
Alitex - The Glasshouse Company, 21
Allan Calder, 17
Allan Hart Associates, 10
Allangrange, 102
AllClear Water Purifiers, 42
Allibert Garden Furniture, 18
Allpets (Stanmore) Ltd, 42
Allseasons Landscapes, 10
Allwood Bros, 73
Alpine Garden Society, 116
Alton Garden Centre, 18
Alton Greenhouses, 21
Alton Towers, 96
Altoona Nurseries, 54
Alvenor Aquatics & Water Gardens, 42
Amateur Gardening Magazine, 113
Amdega Ltd, 7
American Museum in Britain, 82
Ammerdown Park, 95
Anderson Ceramics, 24
Andmore Designs Ltd, 21
Andrew Crace Designs, 18, 35

Andrew Evans - Landscape Designer, 10
Andrew Norfield Seeds, 40
Anglesey Abbey & Gardens, 50, 83
Anglia Bulbs, 50
Anglian Conservatory Co, 7
Angus College, 107
Angus Heathers, 79
Ann & Roger Bowden (Hostas), 54, 86
Anna Buxton Books, 106
Annabel Allhusen, 10
Anthea Sokell Cert.GD, 10
Anthony George & Associates, 10
Anthony Short & Partners, 10
Anthos Design, 10
Antony Woodland Garden, 84
Antony Young, 10
Apcon Garden Products, 18
Apple Court, 58, 89
Apuldram Roses, 73, 98
Aqua Company Ltd, 42
Aqua-Soil Products Ltd, 42
Aquaplancton, 42
Aquapost, 42
Aquatic Habit, 42
Aquavita Centre, 42
Aquazoo, 42
Arbigland Gardens, 101
Arbor Exotica, 50
Arbury Hall, 99
Arcadia Nurseries, 52
Archer Designs, 35
Architectural Association, 107, 116
Architectural Heritage, 35
Architectural Landscape Design Ltd, 10
Architectural Plants, 73
Archwood Greenhouses, 21, 24
Ardencaple Garden Centre, 79
Ardep Ltd, 7
Ardfearn Nursery, 79
Ardtornish Garden, 102
Arduaine Gardens, 102
Arena Holidays Ltd, 112
Arena Landscapes, 10
Ariens (UK) Ltd, 32
Arivegaig Nursery, 79
Arley Hall & Gardens, 83, 114
Arlington Court, 86
Armillatox Ltd, 24
Armitages Garden Centre, 77
Arne Herbs, 48
Artscapes & Theseus Maze Designs, 10
Arunfabs Ltd, 21
Ash Consulting Group, 10
Ashcroft Conservatories, 7
Ashenden Nursery, 61
Ashfield Hellebores - Rarer Plants, 76
Ashley-Morris Garden Furniture, 18
Ashwood Nurseries, 66
Ashworth Leisure Ltd, 18
Astbury Meadow Garden Centre, 50
Aston Agricultural Research, 24
Astra Aquatics, 42
Atco-Qualcast Ltd, 32
Athelhampton, 87
Attwoolls Tents Ltd, 18
Audley End House & Gardens, 87
Auldene Garden Centre, 63
Autocar Equipment Ltd, 32

Avebury Manor, 99
Avenue Fisheries, 10, 42
Avon Aquatics, 42
Avon Bulbs, 68
Avon Gardens Trust, 116
Axminster Power Tool Centre, 32
Aylesbury College, 107
Aylett Nurseries Ltd, 60
Ayr Flower Show, 114

B & H M Baker, 56
B & T World Seeds, 40
B A C Conservatories Ltd, 7
B B C Gardeners World, 113
B B C Gardeners World Live, 114
B C S Tracmaster Ltd, 32
B J Crafts, 24
B R Edwards, 59
B S B I Publications (F & M Perring), 106
Backwoodsman Horticultural Products, 21
Badminton, 82
Baker Straw Partnership, 59
Bakker Holland, 40
Balcaskie, 101
Ballagan Nursery & Garden Centre, 79
Ballerina Trees Ltd, 50
Ballydorn Bulb Farm, 77
Ballyrogan Nurseries, 77
Banbury Cross Conservatories, 7
Barbara Molesworth, 68
Barbary Pots, 35
Barfield Travel & Tours, 112
Barkers Primrose Nurseries, 63
Barking College, 107
Barlow Tyrie Ltd, 18
Barncroft Nurseries, 69
Barningham Park, 84
Barnsdale Plants & Gardens, 10, 63, 92
Barnsley College of Technology, 107
Barnsley House Garden Furniture, 18
Barnsley Park Box Hedging, 57
Baronscourt Nurseries, 78
Barony College, 107
Barrington Court, 95
Barters Plant Centre, 75
Bartholomew Conservatories, 7
Barton Grange Garden Centre, 50, 63
Barton Grange Landscapes, 10
Barton Manor Gardens & Vineyards Ltd, 91
Barwinnock Herbs, 79, 102
Basic Bonsai Supplies, 24
Batemans, 97
Bates Green, 97, 112
Bath Botanic Gardens, 82
Batsford Arboretum, 88
Battersby Roses, 76
Bawdeswell Garden Centre, 66
Baxters Ltd, 21
Baylis Landscape Design & Construction, 10
Bayliss Precision Components Ltd, 21
Baytree Nurseries, 64
Beale Arboretum, 90
Beamish Clematis Nursery, 52
Beau Jardin, 10

Bedding Plant Centre - Churt Nurseries, 57
Bedgebury National Pinetum, 91
Beechcroft Nurseries, 53
Beechcroft Nursery, 71
Beeches Nursery, 56, 77
Bel Mondo Garden Features, 42
Belmont, 91
Belmont Gardens by Design, 10
Belton House, 92
Belvoir Castle, 92
Belwood Nurseries Ltd, 80
Ben Reid & Co, 78
Beningbrough Hall, 100
Benington Lordship, 90
Bennetts Water Gardens, 42
Benthall Hall, 95
Bents Garden Centre & Nurseries, 51
Berger & Tims, 106
Berkeley Castle, 88
Berkshire Buckinghamshire & Oxfordshire Naturalists Trust, 116
Berkshire College of Agriculture, 107
Bernhards Rugby Garden & Leisure Centre, 74
Bernilight, 21
Bernwode Plants, 49
Berri Court, 98
Berrington Hall, 90
Berrys Garden Company Ltd, 10
Besleys Books, 106
Beth Chatto Gardens Ltd, 56
Bickerdikes Garden Centre, 48
Bicton College of Agriculture, 107
Bicton Park Gardens, 86
Biddulph Grange, 96
Bide-a-Wee Cottage Garden, 94
Biggar Park Gardens, 102
Biotal Industrial Products Ltd, 24
Birkheads Cottage Garden & Nursery, 74, 99
Birlingham Nurseries & Garden Centre, 59
Birmingham Botanical Gardens & Glasshouses, 93
Black & Decker Ltd, 32
Black Forge Art, 35
Blackmore & Langdon, 48
Blackthorn Nursery, 58
Blackwall Products, 24
Blagdon Water Garden Products plc, 42
Blairhoyle, 101
Blairhoyle Nursery, 78
Blenheim Palace, 94
Blickling Hall & Gardens, 93
Blue Lagoon Aquatics, 42
Bluebell Nursery, 53
Bob Andrews Ltd, 32
Bodnant Gardens, 103
Bodysgallen Hall, 104
Bolingbroke, 18
Bond Garden Care Agencies, 73
Bonhams Chelsea, 35
Bonhard Nursery, 80
Bonita Bulaitis Landscape & Garden Design, 10
Boonwood Garden Centre, 53
Borde Hill Garden, 98
Bosch Ltd, 32
Bosvigo, 84

The Daily Telegraph Green Fingers — Company Index

Bosvigo Plants, 52
Botanic Nursery, 75
Botanical Society of Scotland, 116
Botanical Society of the British Isles, 116
Boughton Loam Ltd, 24
Boulder Barrows, 24
Bourneville College of Further Education, 107
Bourton House, 88
Bouts Cottage Nurseries, 59
Boward Tree Surgery Ltd, 6
Bowood Garden Centre, 75
Bowood House, 99
Boxwood Tours - Quality Garden Holidays, 112
Brackenhurst College, 107
Brackenwood Garden Centre, 48
Brackenwood Plant Centre, 48
Bradley Batch Cactus Nursery, 69
Bradshaws, 43
Brambling House Alpines, 39
Bramdean House, 89
Bramham Park, 100
Bramley Ltd, 18
Bramleys Nurseries, 56
Brampton Garden Centre, 50
Branklyn Garden, 103
Brantwood Trust, 85
Bregover Plants, 52
Brent Surveys & Designs, 11
Bressingham Plant Centre, 49, 50, 66
Bretby Nurseries, 70
Brian G Crane & Associates, 6
Brian Hiley, 71
Brian Sulman Pelargoniums, 70
Bridgemere Garden World, 83
Bridgemere Nurseries, 51
Bridges Decorative Metalwork, 17
Brinkley Nurseries, 67
Brinsbury College, 107
British & European Geranium Society, 116
British Bonsai Association, 116
British Clematis Society, 116
British Fuchsia Society, 116
British Gladiolus Society, 116
British Hosta & Hemerocallis Society, 116
British Iris Society, 116
British Ivy Society, 116
British Museum Replicas, 35
British National Carnation Society, 116
British Pelargonium & Geranium Society, 116
British Pteridological Society, 116
British Rose Growers Association, 117
British Seed Houses, 40
British Teleflower Service Ltd, 117
British Wild Plants, 78
Broadlands, 89
Broadleas Gardens Charitable Trust Ltd, 75, 99
Broadleigh Gardens, 69
Brockings Exotics, 52
Brodick Castle, 102
Brodie & Hickin Landscapes, 11
Brogdale Horticultural Trust, 91
Bromage & Young, 71
Bronze Collection, 35
Brook Cottage, 94
Brook Lodge Farm Cottage, 97
Broomfield College, 107
Broughton Castle, 94
Brownthwaite Hardy Plants, 63
Buckingham Nurseries & Garden Centre, 49
Bucklesham Hall, 96
Bulbeck Foundry, 35
Bulldog Tools Ltd, 24

Bunny Guinness Landscape Design, 11
Burford Garden Company, 68
Burford House Gardens, 90
Burnby Hall Gardens, 90
Burncoose & South Down Nurseries, 52
Burnham Nurseries, 54
Burnside Fuchsias, 63
Burnt Earth Pottery, 24
Burnwode Plants, 49
Burrough House Gardens, 92
Burrow Farm Gardens, 86
Burrows Roses, 53
Burton Constable Hall, 90
Burton McCall Group, 24
Bury Farm, 83
Buscot Park, 94
Busheyfields Nursery - J Bradshaw & Son, 61
Bushukan Bonsai, 56
Butterfields Nursery, 49
Butterflies Galore, 24
Butterfly Conservation, 117
Butyl Products Ltd, 43
Bybrook Barn Garden & Produce Centre, 61
Bypass Nurseries, 56, 65, 70
Byrkley Park Centre, 70

C & C Trees, 6
C D A/Micron Sprayers, 24
C E & D M Nurseries, 64
C F Hanson Ltd, 24
C J Skilton Aquarist, 43
C N Seeds, 40
C S Lockyer, 48
C T D A, 40
C W Groves & Son, 55
Cabbages & Kings, 11, 98
Caddicks Clematis Nursey, 51
Cae Hir Gardens, 80, 103
Caerhays Castle, 84
California Gardens, 61
Calke Abbey, 86
Cally Gardens, 78
Cambrian Controls, 24
Cambridge Glasshouse Company Ltd, 21
Cambridgeshire College of Agriculture & Horticulture, 108
Canadian Cedarworks UK, 7
Canal Gardens, 100
Canford Magna Nurseries, 55
Cannington College, 95
Cannizaro Park, 92
Cannock Gates Ltd, 17
Canons Ashby House, 93
Cantilever Garden Centre, 51
Cants of Colchester, 56
Capel Manor, 108
Capesthorne Hall, 83
Capital Garden Landscapes, 11
Capital Gardens - Four Garden Centres in London, 18
Capstan Software, 24
Cardiff Institute of Higher Education, 108
Carliles Hardy Plants, 49
Carncairn Daffodils, 77
Carnivorous Plant Society, 117
Carnon Downs Garden Centre, 52
Carol Messham, 11
Carwinion, 84
Cascade Blinds, 7
Castle Ashby Gardens, 93
Castle Bromwich Hall, 93
Castle Drogo, 86
Castle Howard, 100
Castle Kennedy, 101
Castlewellan National Arboretum, 101
Catforth Gardens, 63, 92

Catriona Boyle's Garden School, 108
Caves Folly Nurseries, 59
Cawdor Castle, 102
Cecily Hazell Garden Design, 11
Cedarwood Lily Farm, 70
Cefyn Bere, 104
Ceramica UK, 17
Chadwell Himalayan Plant Seed, 40
Chalfont Conservatory Company, 7
Chandlers Cross Garden Centre, 60
Chantrey Books, 106
Charlecote Park, 99
Charles Hogarth Garden Landscapes, 11
Charter House Hardy Plant Nursery, 78
Chartwell, 91
Chase Organics, 24
Chatelherault Garden Centre, 79
Chatsworth, 86
Chatsworth Carpenters, 18
Chatsworth Garden Centre, 53
Cheals Garden Centre, 73
Chelsea Flower Show, 114
Chelsea Gardener, The, 65
Chelsea Physic Garden, 92
Chelsham Place - Knights Garden Centre, 71
Cheltenham & Gloucester College of Higher Education, 108
Chempak Products, 25
Chenies Garden Centre, 60
Chenies Landscapes Ltd, 11
Chenies Manor, 82
Cheshire Aluminium, 21
Cheshire Herbs, 51
Cheshire Wildlife Trust, 117
Chicheley Hall, 82
Chiffchaffs, 87
Chilham Castle Gardens, 91
Chillingham Castle, 94
Chilstone, 17, 18, 35, 43
Chiltern Seeds, 40
Chipperfield Home & Gdn Ctr, 60
Chirk Castle, 103
Chisenbury Priory Gardening Courses, 108
Chiswick House, 92
Cholmondeley Castle Gardens, 83
Chris Burnett Associates, 11
Chris Pattison (Nurseryman), 57
Christie - Elite Nurseries Ltd, 78
Christie's Nursery, 80
Christopher Bradley-Hole, 11
Christopher Fairweather Ltd, 58
Church Hill Cottage Gardens, 61
Chyverton, 84
Cilwern Plants, 80
Citadel Products, 21
Clandon Park, 97
Clapton Court Gardens, 95
Claremont Gardens, 97
Classic Garden, 35
Classic Gates, 17
Claverton Manor, 82
Clay Lane Nursery, 71
Claymore Grass Machinery, 32
Cleveland Wildlife Trust, 117
Clive Simms, 64
Cliveden, 82
Clock House, 95
Clumber Park, 94
Cluny House Gardens, 103
Clyne Gardens, 103
Coates Manor, 98
Coghurst Nursery, 73
Colemans Nurseries, 77
Coleton Fishacre Garden, 86
College of Garden Design, 108
Collinwood Nurseries, 51
Colvin & Moggridge, 11

Complete Tree Services, 6
Compton Acres Garden Centre, 35, 55
Concept Research, 25
Conifer Garden, 49
Connick Tree Care, 6
Connoisseur Sun Dials, 35
Connoisseurs' Cacti, 61
Conservatory Association, 7, 117
Conservatory Factory, 7
Conservatory Gardens, 7
Constable Burton Hall Gardens, 100
Constable Daffodils, 71
Consumer Direct Ltd, 25
Consumers Association Library, 108
Continental Awnings (UK), 25
Cook's Garden Centre, 59
Cookson Plantpak Ltd, 25
Coombland Gardens, 73
Cope Conservatories, 7
Copford Bulbs, 56
Cornhill Conservatories, 7
Cornish Garden Nurseries, 52
Cornwall Gardens Society, 117
Cornwall Gardens Trust, 117
Cornwall Wildlife Trust, 117
Corsham Court, 99
Corsley Mill (Brigid Quest-Ritson), 75
Cotehele, 85
Coton Manor Garden, 67, 93
Cotswold Garden Flowers, 59
Cotswold Range of Garden Ornamental Ironwork, 11, 35
Cottage Garden, 56
Cottage Garden Ceramics, 25
Cottage Garden Plants, 55, 73
Cottage Garden Roses, 70
Cottage Garden Society, 117
Cottage Herbery, 40, 90
Cottage Nurseries, 64
Cottesbrooke Hall, 94
Cotton Ash Garden, 61
Countax, 32
Country Collections, 36
Country Courses, 108
Country Garden, 106
Country Style, 19
Countryside Wildflowers, 50
County Park Nursery, 56
Courts, 99
Courtyard Designs, 7
Courtyard Garden Design, 11
Courtyard Pottery, 36
Cowcombe Farm Herbs, 57
Cowells Garden Centre, 74
Cowley Manor, 88
Cox & Kings Travel, 112
Cragside, 94
Craig House Cacti, 63
Craigieburn Garden, 78, 101
Cranbourne Manor, 87
Cranbourne Manor Garden Centre, 55
Cranesbill Nursery, 59
Cranmore Vine Nurseries, 61
Crarae Gardens, 102
Crathes Castle, 102
Craven College of Adult Education, 108
Cravens Nursery, 77
Creative Tours Ltd, 112
Crest Garden Products, 25
Crews Hill Aquarium & Water Garden Centre, 43
Crittenden House, 91
Croftacre Hardy Plants, 66
Croftway Nursery, 73
Crossing House Garden, 83
Croston Cactus, 63
Crown Asparagus, 70
Crowther Landscapes, 11

Crowther of Syon Lodge, 8, 36
Croxden Horticultural Products Ltd, 25
Croxteth Hall & Country Park, 93
Cruck Cottage Cacti, 76
Crug Farm Plants, 81
Cruickshank Botanic Garden, 102
Culzean Country Park, 102
Cumbrian Koi Co Ltd, 43
Cyclamen Society, 117
Cyprio Ltd, 43

D & D H W Morgan Second-Hand Books, 106
D H E Plants, 39
D I Y Plastics (UK) Ltd, 25
D N Bromage & Co Ltd, 71
D T Brown & Co Ltd, 40
D W Woodward & Son, 17
D Wells Landscaping, 11
Dagenham Landscapes Ltd, 11
Daisy Hill Nurseries Ltd, 78
Daisy Nook Garden Centre, 65
Dalemain Historic House & Gardens, 85
Dales Stone Company Ltd, 38
Daleside Nurseries, 76
Dalgety Bay Garden Centre, 78
Dalmeny House, 102
Daniel Pearson, 11
Daphne ffiske Herbs, 66
Darlac Products, 25
Dartington Hall, 86
David Austin Roses Ltd, 66
David Bell Ltd, 40
David Brown Landscape Design, 11
David Craig, 19
David Ireland Landscape Architect, 11
David Sayers Travel, 112
David Sharp Studio, 36
David Stevens International Ltd, 11
David Way Associates, 112
Davies Systems (C), 25
Dawyck Botanic Garden, 101
Deacons Nursery, 61
Deans Blinds & Awnings Ltd, 8
Deanswood Plants, 43
Debbie Jolley Garden Design, 11
Decorative Foliage, 54
Defenders Ltd, 25
Delphinium Society, 117
Denbeigh Heathers, 70
Denmans Garden, 98
Denmans Garden Plant Centre, 74
Denmead Aquatic Nursery, 43
Denmead Geranium Nurseries, 58
Dennis, 33
Derbyshire Wildlife Trust, 86
Derek Lloyd Dean, 65
Devine Nurseries, 61
Devon NCCPG Autumn Plant Market, 114
Devon NCCPG Summer Plant Market, 114
Devons Gardens Trust, 117
Devonshire Statuary, 36
Dextroplast Ltd, 17
Diana Eldon - Garden Designer, 11
Diana Hull - Species Pelargonium Specialist, 74
Diane Sewell, 50
Dibco Garden Sundries, 25
Dibleys Nurseries, 80
Dickensons Compost, 25
Dickson Nurseries Ltd, 78
Dingle, 103
Dingle Welshpool, 104
Diplex Ltd, 25
Dobbie & Co Ltd - Melville Garden Centre, 79
Dochfour Gardens, 102

Docton Mill, 86
Docwras Manor, 83
Doddington Hall, 92
Dolwen, 95
Domestic Paraphernalia Co, 25
Donaghadee Garden Centre, 78
Donington Plants, 64
Dorfold Hall, 83
Dormy House Hotel, 112
Dorothy Clive Garden, 96
Dorset Perennial Group, 117
Dorset Trust for Nature Conservation, 117
Douglas Lewis Tree Surgeons, 6
Dovecote Joinery, 25
Downderry Nursery, 61
Doyles Dovecotes, 36
Dream Gardens, 11
Dromana Irrigation (UK), 25
Drummond Castle Gardens, 103
Drummonds of Bramley Architectural Antiques, 36
Drysdale Garden Exotics, 58
Duchy of Cornwall Nursery, 52
Duncan Heather, 11
Duncans of Milngavie, 79
Duncombe Park, 100
Dunham Massey, 93
Dunrobin Castle & Gardens, 102
Dunster Castle, 96
Dupre Vermiculite, 25
Durabuild Conservatories Ltd, 8
Durston Peat Products, 25
Dyfed Wildlife Trust, 117
Dyffryn Gardens, 103

E H Thorne (Beehives) Ltd, 25
E J Godwin (Peat Industries) Ltd, 25
E L F Plants, 67
E P Barrus Ltd, 33
E W King & Co Ltd, 40
Ealing Tertiary College, 108
Earlshall Castle, 101
Easilok, 21
East Lambrook Manor Garden, 96
East Malling Research Association, 117
East Midlands Cactus Nursery, 49
East Neuk Water Garden Centre, 43
Eastgrove Cottage Garden Nursery, 90
Eastnor Castle, 90
Easton College, 108
Easy Pot Staging, 22
Echo GB, 33
Eden Greenhouses, 22
Edinburgh Butterfly & Insect World, 102
Edinburgh College of Art - Heriot-Watt University, 108
Edington Sporting Co, 25
Edward Owen Engineering Ltd, 22
Edwin Tucker & Sons, 40
Edzell Castle, 103
Eggleston Hall Gardens, 52, 84
Egmont Water Garden Centre, 43
Elaine Horne, 11
Elizabeth Banks Associates, 12
Elizabeth Whateley Garden Design, 12
Elly Hill Herbs, 52, 84
Elmwood College, 108
Elsworth Herbs, 50
Elworthy Cottage Plants, 69, 96
Emmetts Garden, 91
Emorsgate Seeds, 40
Endsleigh Garden Centre, 54
English Classics, 19
English Gardening School, 108
English Heritage, 94
English Heritage Driveways, 38
English Hurdle Centre, 17
English Oak Buildings, 8

English Woodlands Biocontrol, 26
Equatorial Plant Co, 52
Erddig, 103
Ernest Wilson Memorial Garden, 88
Erway Farm House, 95
Essentials, 22
Essex Wildlife Trust, 117
Eucalyptus Trees Ltd, 80, 103
Euro Tree Service, 6
Euston Hall - Suffolk, 93
Evelix Daffodils, 79
Everglade Windows Ltd, 8
Eversley Nurseris, 63
Exbury Enterprises Ltd, 58
Exbury Gardens, 89
Excalibur (UK) Ltd, 22
Exeter University Gardens, 86
Exotic Fuchsias, 80

F F C Landscape Architects/The Garden Design Studio, 12
F M G Garden Designs, 12
F Morrey & Son, 51
Fairfield House, 89
Fairhaven Garden Trust, 93
Fairmitre Thames Valley, 8
Fairy Lane Nurseries, 51
Falkland Palace, 101
Family Trees, 58
Farm & Garden Bygones, 36
Farnborough Hall, 99
Fawcetts Liners, 43
Federation of British Bonsai Societies, 117
Federation of Edinburgh & District Allotments & Gardens, 117
Feebers Hardy Plants, 54
Felbrigg Hall, 93
Felley Priory Garden, 94, 114
Fenland Bulbs, 50
Fens, 87
Fenton House - National Trust, 92
Ferndale Nursery & Garden Centre, 77
Ferrum Dried Flowers, 26
Ferryman Polytunnels, 22
Fertile Fibre, 26
Fibrex Nurseries Ltd, 74
Field House Alpines, 67
Fiesta Blinds Ltd, 8
Fillan's Plants, 54
Filterplas, 43
Finch Conservatories Ltd, 8
Finchale Training College, 108
Findlay Clark (Aberdeen), 78
Findlay Clark (Dykebar), 79
Findlay Clark (Kinross), 80
Findlay Clark Garden Centre, 79
Fiona Harrison, 12
Fired Earth, 38
Firs Nursery, 51
First Tunnels, 22
Fisks Clematis Nursery, 70
Five Acres Fuchsia Nursery, 66
Fletcher Moss Botanical Gardens, 93
Fletcher-Green Horticulture, 22
Fleur de Lys Conservatory Plants, 8, 74
Flora & Fauna Europe Ltd, 26
Flora Exotica, 56
Flora International, 113
Florence Court, 101
Flower Arrangers Show Shop, 26
Flower Kabin Nursery, 80
Focus Garden Tours, 112
Foliage & Unusual Plants, 64, 92
Foliage Scented & Herb Plants, 71
Forde Abbey Gardens, 87
Forest Fencing Ltd, 17
Forsham Cottage Arks, 26
Fortescue Garden Trust, 86

Forward Nurseries, 62
Fosse Alpines, 63
Four Counties Nursery, 57
Four Elms Cottage Garden Nursery, 62
Four Seasons, 66
Four Seasons Pottery, 36
Foxgrove Plants, 49
Frampton Court, 88
Frances Mount Perennial Plants, 56
Frances Traylen Martin Dip ISGD, 8, 12
Franklin Mint Limited, 26
Freshfields Water Gardens & Aquarium, 43
Frewen College, 98
Friends of Brogdale, 62, 91
Friends of the Royal Botanic Garden Edinburgh, 117
Friends of the Royal Botanic Gardens Kew, 117
Frolics of Winchester, 17, 19
Fron Nursery, 81
Frost & Co, 8
Fruit Garden, 62
Fryer's Nurseries Ltd, 51
Fuchsia World, 70
Fuchsiavale Nurseries, 59
Fulham Palace Garden Centre, 65
Fulmer Plant Park, 49
Furzey Gardens, 89

G D Landscapes, 12
G Miles & Son Ltd, 12, 43
G W Thornton & Sons Ltd, 33
Gandy's Roses Ltd, 63
Gannock Growers, 60
Garden, 113
Garden & Security Lighting, 12
Garden Answers Magazine, 113
Garden Centre Association, 117
Garden Centre at Hounslow Heath, 66
Garden Cottage Nursery, 79
Garden History Society, 117
Garden In Mind, 98
Garden Machinery Direct, 33
Garden News, 113
Garden Relax Ltd, 22
Garden Rewards, 22
Garden Solutions by Design, 12
Garden Store, 33
Garden Study Tours, 112
Gardena UK Ltd, 26
Gardener, 113
Gardeners' Academy, 108
Gardeners' Breaks, 108, 112
Gardeners' Choice, 26
Gardeners' Pal, 26
Gardeners' Royal Benevolent Society, 117
Gardeners' Seed Exchange, 40
GardenGlow, 19
GardenGlow Direct (TGP1), 26
Gardening Direct (DPA Direct Ltd), 56
Gardening for the Disabled Trust, 117
Gardening Which?, 113
Gardens by Graham Evans, 12
Gardens Illustrated, 113
Gardens in Wood, 36
Gardens of Distinction, 12
Gardens of Somerset, 112
Gardenscape, 12, 36, 38, 76
Garson Farm Garden Centre, 71
Gary Edwards Garden Designs, 12
Gate-A-Mation Ltd, 17
Gatehampton Fuchsias, 49
Gateshead Summer Flower Show, 114
Gaulden Manor, 96
Gawsworth Hall, 83

Company Index

Gayways Lawn Mower Centre, 33
Gaze Burvill Ltd, 19
Geebro Ltd, 26
Geoffrey Coombs, 12
Geranium Nursery, 74
Gilbert White's House & Garden, 89
Gillian Temple Associates, 12
Gilling Castle, 100
Gladiolus Breeders Association, 117
Glamorgan Wildlife Trust, 117
Glansevern Hall Gardens, 104
Glantlees Trees & Hedging, 67
Glasgow Botanic Gardens, 103
Glass Houses, 8
Glazed Additions, 8
Glebe Cottage Plants, 54
Glen Pottery, 36
Glenarn, 103
Glenda Biggs BA Dip ISD, 12
Glendoick Gardens Ltd, 80
Glenhirst Cactus Nursery, 64
Glenwhan Garden, 101
Global Orange Groves UK, 55
Globe Organic Services, 26, 33
Gloster Leisure Furniture, 19
Gloucestershire Gardens & Landscape Trust, 117
Glowcroft Ltd, 26
Glyndley Garden Centre, 73
Godington Park, 91
Godly's Roses, 60
Goldbrook Plants, 70
Goldcrest Conservatories, 8
Golden Acre Park, 100
Goldenfield Nursery, 51
Goodnestone Park Gardens, 91
Gordale Nurseries Garden Centre, 51
Goscote Nurseries Ltd, 64
Gouldings Fuchsias, 70
Goulds Pumps Ltd, 43
Grace Landscapes Ltd, 12
Graham A Pavey & Associates, 12
Granada Arboretum, 83
Grandad's Garden, 19
Grange Farm Nursery, 59
Graythwaite Hall, 85
Great Dixter Nurseries, 73
Great Garden & Countryside Festival, 114
Great Gardens of England (Syon), 66
Great Yorkshire Gardens Design Tours, 112
Greatham Mill, 89
Green Farm Plants, 71
Green Gardener for Bio-Control, 26
Green Stock, 12
Green Way, 12
Greenacre Nursery, 63
Greenacres Horticultural Supplies, 26
Greenacres Nursery - D & M Everett, 59
Greenbank Garden, 103
Greencombe Garden Trust, 96
Greenes Garden Furniture, 19
Greenhouses Direct, 22
Greenleaves Garden Centre, 53
Greenoak Gates, 17
Greenslacks Nurseries, 39, 77
Greenspan Designs Ltd, 26
Greenstone Gardens, 12
Greenvale Farm Ltd, 27
Greenway Gardens, 54
Greys Court, 95
Greystone Cottage, 95
Grimsthorpe Castle, 92
Ground Control Ltd, 12
Grovewood Marketing Ltd, 8
Growell Hydroponics & Plant Lighting, 27
Grower, 113
Growing Carpets, 60

Growing Success Organics Ltd, 27
Growth Technology Ltd, 27
Guy Wilson Daffodil Garden, 101
Gwent Wildlife Trust, 118
Gwydir Plants, 81

H & S Wills, 54
H 2 O, 27
H D R A Consultants, 12
H Woolman (Dorridge) Ltd, 66
Haddon Hall, 86
Haddonstone Ltd, 36
Hadlow College of Agriculture & Horticulture, 108
Hadspen Garden, 69
Hadspen House, 96
Halecat Garden Nurseries, 53
Halghton Nursery, 80
Hall Farm Nursery, 64, 68, 92
Hall Farm Products, 19
Halls of Heddon, 67
Ham House, 97
Hambrook Landscapes Ltd, 12
Hampshire Gardens Trust, 118
Hampstead Garden Suburb Adult Education Centre, 108
Hampton Court Palace, 92
Hampton Court Palace Flower Show, 114
Hamptons Leisure, 19
Hanging Garden Pot Holders, 27
Hannays of Bath, 48
Hardwick Hall, 86
Hardwicke House, 83
Hardy Northern Trees, 76
Hardy Orchids Ltd, 55
Hardy Plant Society, 118
Hardys Cottage Garden Plants, 58
Hare Hatch Nursery, 49
Hare Hill Garden, 84
Hare Lane Pottery, 36
Harefield Herbs, 40, 66
Haresclough Pottery, 36
Harewood House & Gardens, 101
Harlow Carr Botanical Gardens, 100
Harold Walker, 51
Harrow Koi Company, 43
Hartley Botanic Ltd, 22
Hartside Nursery Garden, 53
Harvest Nurseries, 73
Haselden Enterprise UK, 27, 33
Hatchards, 106
Hatfield House, 90
Haughley Park, 96
Haws Watering Cans, 22, 27
Hawthorns Urban Wildlife Centre, 89
Hayes Garden World Ltd, 53
Haygate Engineering Co Ltd, 33
Hayloft Plants, 59
Hayne-West, 27
Hayters plc, 33
Hazel Cottage Nusery, 58
Hazeldene Nursery, 62
Headen Ltd, 8
Heale House, 99
Heath Garden, 12
Heather Goldsmark Partnership, 12
Heather Society, 118
Hebe Society, 118
Heighley Gate Garden Centre, 67
Helen Cahill, 12
Helmingham Hall Gardens, 96
Henllys Lodge Plants, 81
Henry Doubleday Research Association (HDRA), 40, 93, 118
Henry Street, 49
Herb Society, 118
Herbary, 62
Herefordshire Nature Trust, 118
Hergest Croft Gardens, 90
Heritage Woodcraft, 19

Herons Bonsai Ltd, 71
Herterton House Gardens & Nursery, 94
Hertfordshire & Middlesex Wildlife Trust, 118
Hestercombe House, 96
Heveningham Collection, 19
Hever Castle & Gardens, 91
Hewthorn Herbs & Wild Flowers, 43, 67
Hexham Herbs, 67, 94
Hidcote Manor, 88
High Banks Nurseries, 62
High Beeches, 98
High Cross Joinery, 19
High Garden, 54
High Winds Nursery, 62
Highclere Castle, 89
Highdown, 98
Higher End Nursery - D J Case, 58
Highfield Hollies, 58
Highfield Nurseries, 57
Highfield Packaging, 22
Highgate Garden Centre - Capital Gardens, 65
Highgates Nursery, 53
Highland Liliums, 79
Hill Court Gardens & Garden Centre, 90
Hill Farm Herbs, 67
Hill Farm Koi, 43
Hill House Nursery & Gardens, 54, 86
Hill of Tarvit House, 78
Hillier Garden Centre, 48, 49, 58, 61, 71, 74
Hillier Landscapes, 12
Hilltop Nurseries, 64
Hillview Hardy Plants, 68
Himalayan Kingdoms, 112
Hinton Ampner, 89
Hippopottering Nursery, 76
Hobby-Fish Farm, 43
Hodges Barn, 88
Hodnet Hall Gardens, 95
Hodsock Priory, 94
Hoecroft Plants, 66
Holden Clough Nursery, 63
Holdenby House Gardens, 94
Holehird Gardens, 85
Holker Hall, 85
Holkham Hall, 93
Holland Arms Garden Centre, 81
Hollies Park, 101
Hollington Herb Garden, 82
Holloways, 36
Holly Gate Cactus Garden, 98
Holly Gate Cactus Nursery, 74
Home Meadows Nursery Ltd, 70
Homecare Products, 27
Homes & Gardens, 113
Homesitters Ltd, 112, 118
Honda UK, 34
Honeysome Aquatic Nursery, 43
Hoo House Nursery, 57
Hop Shop, 27
Hopleys Plants Ltd, 61
Horticultural Correspondence College, 108
Horticultural Research Association, 118
Horticultural Research International, 118
Horticultural Therapy, 118
Horticulture Week, 113
Hortus, 113
Hotbox Heaters Ltd, 27
Hotterotter Group, 27
Houghall College, 84, 108, 114
Houghton Farm Plants, 74
Houghton Lodge Garden & Hydroponicum, 89

House & Garden, 113
How Caple Court Gardens, 90
Howick Hall, 94
Hozelock Ltd, 27
Hugh Baird College, 108
Hull Farm Conifer Centre, 56
Humus Wyse Ltd, 27
Hunts Court Garden & Nursery, 57, 88
Hurrans Garden Centre Ltd, 57
Hurtwood Landscapes, 12
Husqvarna Forest & Garden, 34
Hutton Nurseries, 76
Hydon Nurseries, 71
Hydrocut Ltd, 27

I C I Garden Products, 27
Ian Roscoe, 12
Ichiyo School of Ikebana, 108, 118
Ickworth House - Park & Gardens, 97
Iden Croft Herbs, 62
Iford Manor Gardens, 99
Image Creations, 8
Inchbald School of Design, 108
Indian Ocean Trading Company, 19
Ingram Topiary Frames Ltd, 27
Inside Out, 8
Insublind, 27
International Acers, 59
International Camellia Society, 118
International Correspondence Schools, 109
International Dendrology Society, 118
International Spring Gardening Fair, 114
International Violet Association, 118
International Water Lily Society, 43, 118
Interpet Ltd, 43
Interploy Trading Co, 34
Inveresk Lodge Garden, 102
Inverewe, 102
Irish Tourist Board, 112
Ironart of Bath, 19
Isabella Plantation, 97
Island Plants, 80
Isle of Wight College of Arts & Technology, 109
Isle of Wight Gardens Trust, 118
Ivelet Books Ltd, 106
Ivy Cottage, 87
Ivy Mill Nursery - Knights Garden Centre, 72

J & C R Wood, 22
J & D Marston, 76
J E Martin, 40
J G S Weathervanes, 36
J H May Ltd (Reproductions), 27
J Tweedie Fruit Trees, 78
J W Boyce (Seedsmen), 40
J Walkers Bulbs, 64
Jack Drake, 79
Jack's Patch Garden Centre, 54
Jackson's Nurseries, 70
Jacksons Fine Fencing, 17
Jacques Amand Ltd, 66
Jacqui Stubbs Associates, 13
Jakobsen Landscape Architects, 13
James Bolton Garden Design, 13
James Cocker & Sons, 78
James Henderson & Sons, 40
Jan Martinez Garden Designs, 91
Janet Bacon Garden Design, 13
Japanese Garden Society, 118
Jardine International Ltd, 19
Jardiniere, 19, 36
Jardinique, 36
Jardino Pumps, 43
Jean Goldberry Garden Design, 13
Jeanne Paisley, 13

Company Index

Jekkas Herb Farm, 48
Jemp Engineering, 22
Jenkyn Place, 89
Jenny Burgess Alpines, 66
Jersey Lavender Ltd, 82
Jiffy Products Ltd, 27
Jill Billington Garden Design, 13
Jill Hedges Bookseller, 106
Jim & Jenny Archibald, 41
Joanna Stay Garden Design, 13
Jodrell Bank Arboretum, 84
John A Davies Landscape Consultants, 13
John A Ford Landscape Architects, 13
John B Rickell, 13
John Beach (Nursery) Ltd, 74
John Brookes - Landscape Designer, 13
John Chambers Wild Flower Seeds, 41
John Deere Ltd, 34
John Drake Aquilegias, 41
John H Lucas, 13
John Henly, 106
John McLauchlan Horticulture, 27
John Medhurst Landscape Consultant, 13
John Moreland, 13
John Sanday (Roses) Ltd, 48
Johnsons Seeds, 41
Jopasco Shade Umbrellas, 19
Josephine Hindle - Designer & Gardener, 13
Joy Jardine Garden Designer, 13
Judith Woodget Garden Design, 13
Judy's Country Garden, 64
Julia Fogg & Susan Santer, 13
Julia Mizen BA Dip ISD, 13
Julian Chichester Designs, 19
Julian Dowle Partnership, 13
Julian Treyer-Evans, 13
Jungle Giants Bamboo Growers, 17
Just Blinds, 8
Just Roses, 73

K & C Cacti, 54
K G Aerators, 34
Karen Saynor, 13
Karobar Koi, 43
Katerina Georgi Landscapes, 13
Kathleen Muncaster Fuchsias, 64
Keepers Nursery, 62
Keith Banyard Tree Surgeons, 6
Keith Pullan Garden Design, 13
Kellie Castle, 101
Kelways Ltd, 69
Kemlawns Nursery, 56
Kemp Compos Tumbler, 27
Kemps Coconut Products, 27
Ken Caro, 85
Ken Higginbotham Garden Landscaping, 13
Ken Muir Nurseries, 56
Kent Street Nurseries, 73
Kent Trust for Nature Conservation, 118
Kenwith Nursery, 54, 112
Kenwood Park, 92
Kew School of Garden Design, 109
Kew School of Horticulture, 109
Kew Shop, 106
Kexby Design, 13, 39
Kiddie Wise, 19
Kiftsgate Court Gardens, 88
Kildrummy Castle, 102
Killerton House, 86
King Easton Ltd, 19
Kingfisher Nurseries, 49, 59
Kingston Bagpuize House, 95
Kingston Lacy, 87
Kingston Maurward College, 109
Kingston Maurward Gardens, 87

Kingswood Pelargoniums, 76
Kinlochlaich House Gardens, 79
Kitchen Garden, 36
Kittoch Mill Hosta Garden, 102
Knap Hill Nursery Ltd, 72
Knebworth House & Gardens, 90
Knight Terrace Pots, 36
Knightshayes Court, 86
Knightshayes Garden Trust, 54
Knowsley Community College - Landbased Industries, 109
Koi Kraft, 43
Kontsmide UK Ltd, 27
Kootensaw Dovecotes, 27
Kubota (UK) Ltd, 34
Kut & Dried, 27

L & P Peat Ltd, 27
L B S Horticulture, 27
Labelplant, 27
Labels Unlimited, 27
Laburnum Nurseries, 64
Lackham College, 109
Lackham Gardens, 99
Lacock Abbey, 99
Lady Muck, 28
Lakeside, 90
Lambeth College, 109
Landford Trees, 6, 75
Landlife Wildflowers Ltd, 41
Landmark Designs, 14
Landscape Centre, 77
Landscape Design Studio, 14
Landscape Irrigation Systems, 28
Landscapes by Tim Brayford, 14
Landskip & Prospect, 14
Landsmans Bookshop Ltd, 106
Langdon (London), 28
Langley Boxwood Nursery, 58, 89
Langside College, 109
Langthorns Plantery, 56
Lanhydrock Gardens, 85
Lannock Pottery, 36
Layham Garden Centre, 62
Lea Gardens, 86
Leaky Pipe Systems Ltd, 28, 34
Lechlade Garden Centre, 57
Leeds Castle, 91
Leeds Metropolitan University, 109
Leicestershire & Rutland Trust for Nature Conservation, 118
Leighton Hall, 92
Leisuredeck Ltd, 28
Leith Hall & Gardens, 102
Lemar Wrought Iron, 17
Lennox-Boyd Landscape Design, 14
Leonardslee Gardens, 98
Leonardslee Plants, 74
Levens Hall, 86
Levington Horticulture, 28
Lewdon Farm Alpine Nursery, 54
Lewes Road Sawmills, 8
Lime Cross Nursery, 73
Lincluden Nursery, 72
Lincolnshire College of Agriculture, 109
Lincolnshire Trust for Nature Conservation, 115, 118
Linda Gascoigne Wild Flowers, 64
Lindum Seeded Turf, 28
Lingard & Styles Landscape, 14
Lingen Nursery & Garden, 68, 95
Lingholm Gardens, 86
Link-Stakes Ltd, 28
Linnean Society of London Library, 109
Lisdoonan Herbs, 78
Lister Teak Garden Furniture, 20
Little Brook Fuchsias, 58
Little Creek Nursery, 48
Little Moreton Hall, 84

Little Treasures Nursery, 52
Littleton Nursery, 69
Llainwen Nursery, 80
Llanbrook Alpine & Wildflower Nursery, 68
Lloyd Christie, 8, 17
Lloyds of Kew, 106
Lochalsh Woodland Garden, 102
Lochside Alpine Nursery, 79
LOFA - The Leisure & Outdoor Furniture Association, 118
Logan Botanic Gardens, 101
London Historic Parks & Gardens Trust, 118
Long Barn, 91
Long Man Gardens, 73
Longacre Nursery, 62, 91
Longhall Nursery, 75
Longleat House, 99
Longstock Park Nursery, 58
Longstock Water Gardens, 89
Lord Roberts Workshops, 28
Lost Gardens of Heligan, 85
Lotherton Hall, 101
Lotus Landscapes, 14
Lotus Water Garden Products Ltd, 43
Louis Vincent Garden Design, 14
Lower Hall, 95
Lower Severalls Garden & Nursery, 69, 96
Luton Hoo, 82
Lydney Park Gardens, 88
Lyme Park, 84
Lynkon Aquatic, 22
Lytes Cary Manor, 96

M C Products, 17
M R Clark, 106
M V Fletcher, 49
M W Horticultural Supplies, 28
Macalda Electronics Ltd, 28
Machine Mart Ltd, 34
MacPenny Nurseries, 56
MacPenny Products, 28
Madrona Nursery, 62
Mailbox UK, 28
Malbrook Conservatories Ltd, 8
Malleny House, 102
Mallet Court Nursery, 69
Malvern Autumn Gardening Show, 115
Malvern Spring Gardening Show, 115
Mammillaria Society, 118
Manchester Metropolitan University, 109
Manderston, 101
Mannington Gardens, 93
Manor House Upton Grey, 89
Mansell & Hatcher Ltd, 77
Mapperton House Garden, 87
Margery Fish Plant Nursery, 69
Marianne Ford Garden Design, 14
Marina Adams Landscape Architects, 14
Mark Ross Landscape Architects, 14
Mark Westcott Landscape Architects, 14
Marks Water Garden, 43
Marle Place Gardens & Nursery, 62
Marley Bank Nursery, 59
Marlow Garden & Leisure Centre, 49
Marquis Flowers & Plants, 63
Marshalls, 41
Marston Exotics, 59
Martels Garden World, 48
Martin Berkley Landscape Architects, 14
Martin Nest Nurseries, 64
Marwood Hill Gardens, 86
Mary Ann Lovegrove, 14
Mary Bland, 106

Master Gardeners, 14
Mastermind Products Ltd, 22
Matlock Garden Centre, 53
Matthew Eden, 20
Mattock Roses, 68
Maxicrop International Ltd, 28
Mayflower Greenhouses (A E Headen Ltd), 22
McBeans Orchids, 73
Mead Nursery, 75
Meadow Herbs, 29
Meadowcroft Fuchsias & Pelargonium, 50
Mears Ashby Nurseries Ltd, 67
Melaleuca Pottery, 36
Melbourne Hall Gardens, 86
Melcourt Industries Ltd, 29, 38
Mellerstain, 101
Mellors Garden Ceramics, 36
Mendle Nursery, 39
Merlin Rooted Cuttings, 52
Merriments Gardens, 73
Merrist Wood College, 109
Merrist Wood College Plant Centre, 72
Merton Adult College, 109
Merton Nurseries, 68
Mesemb Study Group, 119
Metalarts, 36
Metpost Ltd, 17
Michael Ballam Design, 14
Michael Banks/Ascender, 34
Michael Hill Garden Furniture, 20
Michael Littlewood Landscape Designer, 14
Michelham Priory, 98
Mickfield Fish & Watergarden Centre, 14, 70
Mickfield Market Garden, 70
Midland Butyl Liners, 43
Mike Park, 106
Mill Cottage Plants, 69
Mill Hill Plants, 67
Mill Race Nursery, 56
Millais Nurseries, 72
Millbern Geraniums, 74
Mills Farm Plants, 70
Milton Garden Plants, 56
Milton Lodge, 96
Miniature Garden Company, 69
Ministry of Agriculture Fisheries & Food Library, 109
Minterne, 87
Miracle Garden Care Ltd, 29
Miserden Park, 88
Misses I Allen & M J Huish, 48
Molecatcher, 29
Monksilver Nursery, 50
Monkton Elm Garden Centre, 69
Monocot Nursery, 48
Monsanto Garden Care, 29
Montacute House, 96
Montezumas, 20
Montgomeryshire Wildlife Trust, 119
Moongate Designs, 14
Morden Hall Garden Centre - Capital Gardens, 72
Morehavens, 50
Morton Hall, 94
Moseley Old Hall, 96
Mossatburn Watergardens, 44
Mottisfont Abbey, 89
Mottistone Manor, 91
Moulton College, 109
Mount Edgcumbe Gardens, 85
Mount Pleasant Trees, 57
Mount Skippet, 95
Mount Stewart, 101
Mr Fothergills Seeds Ltd, 41
Mulberry Landscapes, 14
Multimesh Products, 29

Company Index

Muncaster Plants, 53
Murrel Gardens, 102
Museum of Garden History, 115
Myddelton House, 93
Myerscough College, 109

Nags Hall Nursery - Knights Garden Centre, 72
Naked Cross Nurseries, 56
Nareys Garden Centre, 70
National Association of Flower Arrangement Societies, 119
National Auricula & Primula Society (Southern), 119
National Back Pain Association, 119
National Begonia Society, 119
National Bonsai Society, 119
National Chrysanthemum Society, 119
National Collection of Passiflora, 82, 119
National Council for the Conservation of Plants & Gardens, 119
National Dahlia Society, 119
National Gardens Scheme Charitable Trust, 97, 113
National Pot Leek Society, 119
National Society of Allotment & Leisure Gardeners, 119
National Sweet Pea Society, 119
National Trust, 119
National Trust for Scotland, 102
National Vegetable Society, 119
National Viola & Pansy Society, 119
Native Australian Seeds, 41
Natural Organic Supplies, 29
Natural Pest Control Ltd, 29
Nature's Corners, 44
Naturetrek, 112
Nautilus Aquatics, 44
Neptune Aquatics, 44
Neptune Supplies & Services, 22
Ness Botanic Gardens, 84
Netlon Ltd, 29
Nettletons Nursery, 72
New England Gardens Ltd, 20
New Plantsman, 113
New Technology, 44
New Vision Videos, 113
Newby Hall & Gardens, 100
Newington Nurseries, 68
Newstead Abbey, 94
Newton Hill Alpines, 77
Newton Rigg College, 109
Nicholas Roeber Landscapes, 14
Nicky's Rock Garden Nursery, 39, 54
Nigel Jeffries Landscapes, 14
Nigel L Philips Landscape & Garden Design, 14
Nine Springs Nursery, 58
Nitritech, 44
Noel Kingsbury, 14
Noma Lites Ltd, 29, 34
Nonington Pottery, 36
Norbark (Northern Bark Ltd), 29
Norden Alpine Nursery, 76
Nordybank Nurseries, 68, 95
Norfields, 57
Norfolk Farm Composts Ltd, 29
Norfolk Garden Supplies, 37
Norfolk Greenhouses Ltd, 22
Norfolk Lavender Ltd, 66, 93
Norfolk Naturalists Trust, 119
Norman Bonsai, 73
North Devon Garden Centre, 54
North of England Horticultural Society, 115
North of England Rose Carnation & Sweet Pea Society, 119
North Surrey Landscapes, 14
North Wales Wildlife Trust, 119

Northampton Water Garden Centre, 44
Northamptonshire Wildlife Trust, 119
Northern Horticultural Society, 119
Northside Seeds, 41
Northumbria Nurseries, 67
Northwold Rockery Stone & Crazy Paving, 38, 39
Norton Ash Garden Centre, 62
Norton Conyers, 100
Norton Priory Museum & Gardens, 84
Norton Radstock Technical College, 109
Norwell Nurseries, 67
Norwich Heather & Conifer Centre, 66
Notcutts Garden Centre, 50, 56, 61, 62, 66, 72
Notcutts Nurseries, 70
Nottinghamshire Wildlife Trust, 119
Nugent Gardens, 22
Numbers & Names, 37
Nuneham Courtenay Arboretum, 95
Nunnington Hall, 76
Nutriculture Ltd, 29
Nymans, 98

Oak Cottage Herb Garden, 68
Oak Leaf Conservatories Ltd, 8
Oaklands College, 110
Oakleigh Conservatories, 8
Oakleigh Nurseries, 58
Oase (UK) Ltd, 44
Oatridge Agricultural College, 110
Offshoots - Englefield Garden Centre, 49
Offshore Conservatory Interiors, 8
Ohara School of Ikebana, 110, 119
Okells Nurseries, 51
Old Barn Nurseries, 74
Old Manor Nursery, 57
Old Mill Herbary, 85
Old Rectory Farnborough, 95
Old Rectory Garden, 82
Old Rectory Sudborough, 94
Oldbury Nurseries, 62
Olive Tree Trading Company Ltd, 37
Olivers, 87
Ollerton Engineering, 20
Orchard House Nursery, 76
Orchard Nurseries, 64
Orchid Society of Great Britain, 120
Organic Concentrates Ltd, 29
Organic Gardening, 113
Original Organics Ltd, 29
Original Terracotta Shop, 14, 37, 83
Ornamental Grasses - Trevor Scott, 56, 88
Ornamental Leadwork, 37
Ornate Products, 37
Oryx Trading Ltd, 20
Oscrofts Dahlias, 77
Osterley Park, 93
Otley College of Agriculture & Horticulture, 110
Otter Nurseries (Torbay), 54
Otter Nurseries Ltd, 54
Otter Nurseries of Plymouth, 54
Otters Court Heathers, 14, 69
Oulton House, 96
Outdoor Power Products Ltd, 34
Overbecks Garden, 86
Owen Brown Tents, 8
Owl Cottage, 91
Oxburgh Hall, 93
Oxford Botanic Gardens, 95
Oxford Garden Design Associates, 14
Oxleys Garden Furniture, 20

P A C Organic Products, 29
P G Biddle, 6

P H Kellett, 62
P J Bridgman & Company Ltd, 20
P L C Products, 22
P L M Power Products, 34
P M A Plant Specialities, 69
P W Milne Atkinson, 15
P W Plants, 66, 93
Packwood House, 99
Padlock Croft, 83
Paignton Zoo & Botanical Gardens, 87
Painshill, 97
Painswick Rococo Garden Trust, 88
Palm Centre, 65
Palm Farm, 61
Pamal, 20, 37
Pan Brittanica Industries Ltd, 29
Pantiles Nurseries Ltd, 72
Papronet, 29
Paradise Centre, 70
Parallax, 22
Parcevall Hall Gardens, 100
Parham House & Gardens, 98
Parham Nursery, 75
Paris Ceramics, 38
Park Forge, 29
Park Garden Centre, 48
Park Green Nurseries, 70
Parkhouse Plants, 70
Parkinson Herbs, 52
Parklines (Buildings) Ltd, 22
Parnham House, 87
Parwin Power Heaters, 22
Pashley Manor Gardens, 98
Pathfinder Gardening, 15
Patricia Marrow, 69
Patrick Butler, 15
Patterson Products, 20
Paul Bromfield Aquatics, 44
Paul Christian Rare Plants, 80
Paul Jasper Trees, 59
Paul Miles, 15
Paul Norton Associates, 15
Paul Temple Associates, 15
Peckover House, 83
Pelham Landscapes, 15
Pencarrow, 85
Penn, 84
Pennell & Sons Ltd, 61
Penny Bennett Landscape Architects, 15
Pennyacre Nurseries, 78
Penpergwm Plants, 80
Penryn Castle, 104
Penshurst Place & Gardens, 91, 112
Pentangle Watergardens, 44
Peover Hall, 84
Pepe Garden Furniture, 20
Peregrine Holidays, 112
Period House & Garden, 113
Periwinkle, 110
Perrie Hale Forest Nursery, 54
Perry's Plants, 76, 100
Perrybrook Nursery, 68
Perryhill Nurseries, 73
Pershore College of Horticulture, 110
Perth Garden Centre, 80
Petal Designs Ltd, 15
Pete & Ken Cactus Nursery, 62
Peter Barratt's Garden Centre, 74
Peter Barratt's Garden Centres, 52
Peter Beales Roses, 66
Peter Grayson - Sweet Pea Seedsman, 41
Peter M Daly Rare Books, 106
Peter Rogers Associates, 15
Peter Trenear Nurseries, 58
Peter Wynn Arboricultural Consultant, 6
Peters Plants & Garden Centre, 44, 72
Petworth House, 98
Peveril Clematis Nursery, 54

Phedar Nursery, 51
Phostrogen, 29
Pick Products, 34
Pickards Magnolia Gardens, 91
Picton Castle, 103
Picton Garden, 90
Pilkington Garden Centre, 51
Pinewood House, 97
Pinks & Carnations, 29, 41
Pitmedden, 102
Pitmuies Gardens, 103
Plant Lovers, 64
Plant World Botanic Gardens & Plant Centre, 54
Plant World Seeds, 41
Planta Vera, 72
Plantables, 66
Plantarama, 52
Plantasia, 103
Plantation Garden Plant Centre, 66
Planters Garden Centre, 70
Plants 'n' Gardens, 74
Plants from the Past, 79
Plantworld, 57
Plas Brondanw Gardens, 104
Plas Newydd, 104
Plas Penhelig, 104
Plas-yn-Rhiw, 104
Plastics-by-Post Ltd, 29
Plaxtol Nurseries, 62
Pleasant View Garden, 87
Pleasant View Nursery, 55
Plowman Trading, 37
Plysu Housewares Ltd, 29
Podington Garden Centre, 17, 20, 22, 29, 37, 38, 39, 44, 67
Polesden Lacey, 97
Porous Pipe, 29
Port Lympne Wild Animal Park, 91
Porters Fuchsias, 65
Porthpean House Gardens, 85
Portland Conservatories, 8
Portmeirion, 104
Porton Aquatic Centre, 44
Posh Pots, 37
Post House Gardens, 103
Pot Village, 37
Potash Nursery, 71
Pots & Pithoi, 37
Potterton & Martin, 39, 65
Pound Lane Nurseries, 58
Pounds of Bewdley, 22
Pounsley Plants, 55, 87
Power Garden Products, 29
Powis Castle, 104
Poyntzfield Herb Nursery, 79
Practical Gardening Magazine, 114
Practicality Brown Ltd, 15, 29
Precise Irrigation (UK) Ltd, 29
Preen Manor, 95
Preston-Mafham Collection, 75
Primrose Cottage Nursery & Garden Centre, 65
Primrose Fairs, 115
Primus Ltd, 23, 34
Principally Plants, 74
Pringle Plants, 78
Priorswood Clematis, 61
Priory, 88
Priory Garden Nursery, 57
Proculture Plant Centre, 60
Professional Gardeners Guild, 120
Pumps 'n' Tubs, 44

Quartet Design, 15
Queen Eleanors Garden, 89
Queen Marys Garden, 93

R D Plants, 55
R H S - The Robin Herbert Centre, 106

Company Index

R H S Garden Hyde Hall, 88
R H S Garden Rosemoor, 87
R H S Garden Rosemoor Plant Centre, 55
R H S Garden Wisley, 97, 110
R H S Garden Wisley Plant Centre, 72
R H S Garden Wisley Shop, 106
R Harkness & Co Ltd, 61
R P P Alpines, 66
R V Roger Ltd, 76
Raby Castle, 84
Radnorshire Wildlife Trust, 120
Raffles - Thatched Garden Buildings, 8
Raindrain Ltd, 29
Rainthorpe Hall Gardens, 93
Ramster, 97
Ransoms Garden Centre, 48
Rare Plants Fairs, 115
Ratcliffe Orchids Ltd, 58
Raven Tree Services, 6
Raveningham Gardens, 66
Ravensthorpe Nursery, 67
Raw Talent Consultancy, 15
Ray Cheeseborough, 39
Ray Pitt Landscape Design, 15
Rayment Wirework, 20
Reads Nursery, 66
Real Stone Company, 37
Realwood Conservatories, 8
Reaseheath College (Cheshire College of Agriculture), 110
Redashe Ltd, 29
Redfields Leisure Buildings, 8
Redwood Stone Ltd, 37
Reef Aquatics, 45
Regal, 23
Regency Driveways Ltd, 38
Remanoid Ltd, 45
Renaissance Bronzes, 37
Renaissance Casting, 37
Renishaw Hall Gardens, 86
Rhodes & Rockliffe, 57
Richard Stockwell - Rare Plants (GF), 41, 68
Rickards Hardy Ferns Ltd, 60
Rievaulx Terrace, 100
Riley's Chrysanthemums, 53
Ripley Castle, 100
Riseholme Hall, 92
Rivendell Nursery, 76
Rob Turner, 17
Robert Southern BA Hons NCH(Arb), 6
Robin Williams & Associates, 15
Robinson Penn Partnership, 15
Robinsons of Whaley Bridge, 51
Robinsons of Winchester Ltd, 23
Robus Pottery & Tiles, 37
Roche Court, 37
Rockingham Castle, 92
Rodbaston College, 110
Rode Hall, 96
Rodmarton Manor, 88
Roger Platts Garden Design, 8, 15, 18
Rolawn (Turf Growers Ltd), 29, 76
Romantic Garden Nursery, 66
Romilt Landscape Design & Construction Ltd, 45
Roof Garden Company Ltd, 15
Roof Gardens, 93
Rookhope Nurseries, 52, 84
Room Outside, 8
Roots Garden Centre Ltd, 78
Rosedene Nursery - Knights Garden Centre, 72
Rosemann Greenhouses, 23
Roses & Shrubs Garden Centre, 66
Rosie's Garden Plants, 62
Rougham Hall Nurseries, 71
Roundstone Garden Centre, 74
Rousham House, 95

Rovergarden, 20
Rowallane Gardens, 101
Rowden Gardens, 45, 87
Roy Finch Tree Care, 6
Roy Young Seeds, 41
Royal Botanic Garden Edinburgh, 102
Royal Botanic Gardens Kew, 98
Royal Caledonian Horticultural Society, 120
Royal Gardeners' Orphan Fund, 120
Royal Horticultural Society, 120
Royal National Rose Society, 90, 120
Ruardean Garden Pottery, 37
Rumwood Nurseries, 62
Rupert Bowlby, 72
Rupert Golby, 15
Rusco, 20
Rushfields of Ledbury, 60
Ruskins Arboricultural Group, 6
Ruthall Manor, 95
Rutland County, 9
Ruxley Manor Garden Centre, 62
Ryal Nursery, 67
Rydal Mount, 86
Ryobi Lawn & Garden (UK), 34

S & N Brackley, 41
S & S Perennials, 64
S M McArd, 41
Saintpaulia & Houseplant Society, 120
Saling Hall, 88
Salley Gardens, 41, 68
Saltram, 87
Sampford Shrubs, 55
Samsons, 18
Samuel Dobie & Son Ltd, 41
Samuel Wernick Garden Buildings, 9
Sandringham House & Grounds, 93
Sandvik Saws & Tools, 30
Sarah Burgoyne Revivals, 20
Sarah Massey - Landscape Designer, 15
Sarah Rycroft Landscape Architects, 15
Savill Garden, 97
Sawyers Seeds, 41
Scarcity of Scarecrows, 37
Scarletts Plantcare, 30
Scotland's National Gardening Show, 115
Scotney Castle, 91
Scotsdale Nursery & Garden Centre, 50
Scottish Agricultural College, 110
Scottish Allotments & Gardens Society, 120
Scottish National Sweet Pea Rose & Carnation Society, 120
Scottish Rhododendron Society, 120
Scottish Rock Garden Club, 115, 120
Scottish Wildlife Trust, 120
Scottlandscape, 15
Scotts Clematis, 55
Scotts Nurseries (Merriott), 69
Seaforde Nursery, 78
Seago, 45
Search Press Ltd, 107, 114
Secret Garden Company of Ware Ltd, 9
Secret Garden Designs, 15
Secretts Garden Centre, 72
Seed House, 41
Seeds-by-Size, 41
Sellet Hall Gardens, 63
Sempervivum Society, 120
Sentinel Garden Products, 18
Seven Counties Garden Design, 15
Seymours Garden & Leisure Group, 18, 20, 23, 37, 38, 39, 45, 72
Seymours Landscape Centre, 15, 38

Shamrock Horticulture Ltd, 30
Sheen Developments Ltd, 30
Sheffield Botanical Gardens, 100
Sheffield Park, 98
Sheldon Manor, 99
Shepton Nursery Garden, 69
Sherbourne Park, 99
Sheringham Park, 93
Sherston Earl Vineyards Ltd, 30
Sherston Parva Nursery, 75
Shipley College, 110
Shrewsbury Flower Show, 115
Shugborough Estate, 96
Simon Richards & Associates, 15
Simply Control, 30
Simply Garlands, 30
Simply Plants, 50
Simpsons Nursery/Landscaping & Tree Surgery, 15, 66
Sino-Himalayan Plant Association, 120
Sir Harold Hillier Gardens & Arboretum, 89
Siskin Plants, 71
Sissinghurst Castle, 91
Skyshades, 20
Skyview Systems Ltd, 30
Slack Top Alpines, 39
Sledmere House, 90
Smallscapes Nursery, 71
Smart Systems Ltd, 9
Smeeden Foreman Partnership, 15
Snapper Lawn Equipment (UK) Ltd, 34
Snowshill Manor, 90
Society of Floristry, 120
Society of Garden Designers, 16, 120
Sogetsu - Greater London Branch, 120
Sol Jordens, 16
Solar Tunnels, 23
Solardome, 23
Solargro Products Ltd, 23
Solaris Laminates Ltd, 9
Solihull College, 110
Solo Sprayers, 34
Somerleyton Hall & Gardens, 97
Somerset Gardens Trust, 120
Somerset Postal Flowers, 30
Somerset Wildlife Trust, 69
Song of the Earth, 16
Sonya Millman Garden Design, 16
Sothebys, 37
South East Garden Festival, 115
South East Water Gardens, 45
South Ockendon Garden Centre, 57
South West Alpine Show, 115
Southend Adult Community College, 110
Southern Tree Surgeons, 6
Southfield Nurseries, 65
Southport College of Art & Technology, 110
Southport Flower Show, 115
Southview Nurseries, 59
Southwick Country Herbs, 55
Sparkford Sawmills Ltd, 18
Sparsholt College Hampshire, 110
Spear & Jackson Garden Products, 30
Special Plants, 75
Spetchley Park Garden, 90
Speyside Heather Garden & Visitor Centre, 79
Spinners, 59, 89
Sportsmark Group Ltd, 30
Springfields (World of Flowers), 92
Springwood Pleiones, 77
St Andrews Botanic Garden, 102
St Helens College, 110
St Helens Croft, 94
St Michaels Mount, 85
St Peters Garden Centre, 48

Staffordshire Gardens & Parks Trust, 120
Staffordshire Wildlife Trust, 120
Standen, 98
Stangwrach Leisure Products, 20
Stanton Harcourt Manor House & Gardens, 95
Stapeley Water Gardens Ltd, 45, 51, 84
Starborough Nursery, 62
Starkie & Starkie Ltd, 30
Stella Caws Associates, 16
Stephen C Markham, 37
Stephen H Smith's Garden & Leisure, 65, 77
Stephen H Smith's Garden Centres, 77
Stephenson Blake, 20
Steven Bailey Ltd, 59
Stewarts (Nottm) Ltd, 41
Sticky Wicket Garden, 87
Stiffkey Lampshop, 37
Stihl Ltd, 34
Stillingfleet Lodge Nurseries, 76, 100
Stoke-on-Trent College, 110
Ston Easton Park, 96
Stone Cross Nurseries, 73
Stone House Cottage Garden & Nursery, 60
Stone Lane Gardens, 55
Store More Garden Buildings, 23
Stourbridge College, 110
Stourhead Landscape Garden, 99
Stourton House, 100
Stowe Landscape Gardens, 82
Strikes Garden Centre, 52, 76, 77
Stuart Garden Architecture, 9, 18, 20
Studio Forge, 20
Sudeley Castle, 88
Sue de Bock Rowles Garden Design, 16
Sue Hedger-Brown Landscape Architect, 16
Sue Pack Garden Design, 16
Sue's Garden Design, 110
Suffolk Herbs, 41
Suffolk Smallholders, 30
Suffolk Wildlife Trust, 120
Sulgrave Manor, 94
Summerfield Books, 107
Sun Building Developments Ltd, 9
Sunlight Systems, 30
Sunshine of Africa (UK) Ltd, 30
Super Natural Ltd, 30
Surbiton Aquaria, 45
Surrey Gardens Trust, 120
Surrey Primroses, 72
Surrey Wildlife Trust, 120
Susan Buckley, 16
Susan Symmonds Sculptures, 37
Sussex Wildlife Trust, 120
Sutton Griffin & Morgan, 16
Sutton Park Stately Home, 100
Suttons Seeds, 41
Swallow Hayes, 95
Swan Hellenic Ltd, 113
Swanland Nurseries, 76
Sweerts de Landas, 37
Swiss Garden, 82
Sycamore Park Garden Centre, 51
Symbionics, 45
Syon Park, 93

T & W Christie (Forres) Ltd, 79
T H Barker & Son, 53
T I C Products Ltd, 38
Tamar Organics, 30
Tamarisk Nurseries, 50
Tank Exchange, 30
Tapeley Park Gardens, 87
Tatton Park Gardens, 84

Company Index

Teak Tiger Trading Company, 20
Teamwork Landscaping, 16
Technical Aquatic Products, 45
Telford Garden Supplies, 30
Temple Fortune Garden Centre - Capital Gardens, 65
Temple Newsam Park, 101
Tendercare Nurseries Ltd, 66
Tensor Ltd, 30
Terrace & Garden, 38
Thai House Company, 9
Thames Valley Wirework Co, 30
Thermoforce Ltd, 23, 30
Thompson & Morgan UK Ltd, 41
Thorncroft Clematis Nursery, 67
Thornhayes Nursery, 55
Thorp Perrow Arboretum, 100
Threave School of Horticulture, 101, 110
Three Counties Nurseries, 56
Tibshelf Garden Products, 23
Tiger Developments Ltd, 30
Tile Barn Nursery, 62
TimberKits, 38
Timpany Nurseries, 78
Tintinhull House, 96
Toad Hall Produce, 60
Tokonoma Bonsai, 30
Tollgate Cottage Nursery, 75
Tomperrow Farm Nurseries, 53
Tony Benger Landscaping, 16
Tool-Craft, 34
Topiarist, 6, 16
Torbay Water Gardens, 45
Toro Wheel Horse UK, 34
Totties Nursery, 77
Tough Alpine Nursery, 39, 79
Town & Country Gardens, 16
Town & Country Paving Ltd, 38
Town & Country Products, 30
Town Farm Nursery, 39, 52, 84
Trade & DIY Products Ltd, 30
Trading Bonsai, 20, 30
Traditional Garden Supply Company Ltd, 23
Trailer Barrow Co, 30, 35
Travel Ideas Ltd, 113
Treasures of Tenbury Ltd, 60, 90
Trebah Garden, 85
Tredegar House & Park, 104
Tree Group, 6
Trees in Miniature, 45
Tregrehan Garden, 85
Trehane Nurseries, 56
Trelissick (Feock), 85
Trelliscope, 18
Trengwainton Gardens, 85
Trentham Park Gardens, 96
Trerice, 85
Tresco Abbey, 85
Trevena Cross Nurseries, 53
Trevor White Old Fashioned Roses, 67
Trewidden Estate Nursery, 53
Trewithen, 85
Trewithen Nurseries, 53
Tricia McPherson, 16
Trident Water Garden Products, 45
Triscombe Nurseries, 69
Tropical Rain Forest, 77
Tropicana Nursery, 55
Trossachs Garden Tours, 113
Truggery, 30
Trugrind, 30
Tudor House Garden, 89
Turk Scythes & Trimflex (UK), 35
Two Wests & Elliott Ltd, 23
Ty'n Garreg Nurseries, 81
Ty'r Orsaf Nursery, 81
Tyrite - Brighton Manufacturing Co, 30

Ullesthorpe Garden & Aquatic Centre, 45, 64
Ulverscroft Unusual Plants, 64
University Botanic Gardens, 83, 110
University College London, 110
University College of North Wales, 110
University of Aberdeen, 110
University of Bristol Botanic Garden, 82
University of Derby, 110
University of Dundee Botanic Garden, 103, 111
University of Durham Botanic Garden, 84
University of Edinburgh, 111
University of Greenwich, 111
University of Leicester Botanic Gardens, 92
University of Manchester, 111
University of Newcastle, 111
University of Nottingham, 111
University of Reading, 111
University of Sheffield, 111
Unwins Seeds Ltd, 42
Upton House, 99
Urban Wildlife Trust - West Midlands Wildlife Campaign, 120
Usual & Unusual Plants, 73
Uzumara Orchids, 79

V H Humphrey - Iris Specialist, 72
Vale Garden Houses, 9
Valley Aquatics, 45
Valley Clematis Nursery, 65
Valley Gardens Harrogate, 100
Valley Gardens Windsor, 97
Van Hage Garden Company, 61
Vann, 97
Ventnor Botanic Garden, 91
Vernon Geranium Nursery, 72
Veronica Adams Garden Design, 16
Veronica Ross Landscape Design, 16
Very Interesting Rock Co, 39
Veryans Plants, 55
Vesutor Ltd, 74
Vicarage Gardens, 65
Victor A Shanley, 16
Victoria Travel Garden Tours, 113
Victoriana Conservatories Ltd, 9
Vigo Vineyard Supplies, 35
Volpaia, 88

W C Cousens, 107
W E Th Ingwersen Ltd, 74
W Robinson & Sons Ltd, 42
Waddesdon Manor, 82
Waddesdon Nursery, 50
Waithman Nurseries, 63
Wakefield & North of England Tulip Society, 120
Wakefield College, 111
Walford College - Horticulture Dept, 111
Wall Cottage Nursery, 53
Walled Garden, The, 71
Wallington Hall, 94
Wallis Seeds & Co, 42
Walpole House, 93
Walter Blom & Sons Ltd, 48
Walter T Ware, 75
Walton Conservatories, 9
Wards Nurseries (Sarrat) Ltd, 61
Warrick Warming Cables Ltd, 23
Wartnaby Garden Labels, 31
Warwick Castle, 99
Warwick Warming Cables Ltd, 31
Warwickshire Wildlife Trust, 120
Washington Aquatic & Garden Supplies Ltd, 45
Water Diverter Ltd, 31

Water Features Ltd, 45
Water Garden Nursery, 45
Water Gardener, 114
Water Gardens, 97
Water Meadow Design & Landscape, 16
Water Meadow Nursery & Herb Farm, 45, 59, 89
Water Works, 31
Waterers Landscape Ltd, 16
Waterlife Centre, 45
Waterlock Studios, 45
Watermeadows, 45
Watermill Company, 31
Waterperry Gardens Ltd, 95
Waters Green Direct, 31
Watershed Systems Ltd, 45
Waterwheel Nursery, 81
Waveney Fish Farm, 45
Wayford Manor, 96
Weasdale Nurseries, 53
Weather Signs, 31
Weaver Vale Garden Centre, 51
Webbs Distribution Ltd, 38
Webbs Garden Centre, 53
Webbs of Wychbold, 60
Wells & Winter, 31
Welsh College of Horticulture, 111
Welsh Historic Gardens Trust, 120
Wendy Wright Landscape & Garden Design, 16
Wentworth Castle Gardens, 100
Wessex Horticultural Products Ltd, 31
West Country Ironcraft, 18
West Country Water Gardens, 46
West Dean Gardens (Edward James Foundation), 99, 111
West Kington Nurseries Ltd, 75
West Meters Ltd, 31
West Oxfordshire College, 111
West Somerset Garden Centre, 69
West Wycombe Park, 83
Westbury Conservatories, 9
Westbury Court, 88
Westcountry Water Garden Centre, 46
Westerwood Garden Centre, 79
Westfield Cacti, 55
Westholme Hall, 84
Westland Horticulture, 31
Westminster Flower Shows, 115
Weston Park, 95
Westonbirt Arboretum, 88
Westonbirt Plant Centre, 57
Westwinds Perennial Plants, 52
Westwood Dials, 38
Westwood Nursery, 63
Wetheriggs Pottery, 38
Wharf Aquatics, 46
Whatton House, 92
Wheatcroft Ltd, 68
Whichford Pottery, 38
Whispering Trees Nursery, 67
White Cottage Alpines, 39, 76
White Windows, 89
Whitehall Garden Centre, 76
Whitehills Nurseries, 78
Whitehouse Ivies, 57
Whitestone Gardens Ltd, 76
Whitewater Nursery, 59
Wiggly Wigglers, 31
Wight Butyl Liners, 46
Wightwick Manor, 93
Wild Flower Society, 120
Wild Seeds, 42
Wildlife Gardening Centre, 68
Wildlife Services Ltd, 46
Wildlife Shop - BBONT, 121
Wildlife Trust Bedfordshire & Cambridgeshire, 121

Wildlife Trust for Bristol Bath & Avon, 121
Wildlife Trusts, 121
Wildwoods Water Garden Centre, 46
Wilkinsons, 16
William Sinclair Horticulture, 31
Willow Pottery, 38
Wilmslow Garden Centre, 52
Wilton House, 100
Wiltshire Gardens Trust, 121
Wiltshire Summerhouses, 9
Wiltshire Wildlife Trust, 121
Wimbourne Road Nurseries, 56
Wimpole Hall, 83
Winkworth Arboretum, 97
Wintergreen Nurseries, 60
Wisley Flower Show, 115
Wisley Plant Centre, 72
Witbourne Ltd, 20
Withleigh Nurseries, 55
Woburn Abbey, 82, 115
Wolf Garden, 31
Wolseley Garden Park, 96
Wolverhampton Tree Service, 6
Woodfield Brothers, 75
Woodgrow Horticulture Ltd, 31
Woodside Water Gardens, 46
Woodstock Orchids & Automations, 50
Woodworks Workshop, 9
Woolman's Plants Ltd, 60
Woottens of Wenhaston, 71
Worcester Garden Centre, 60
World of Water, 46
Worsley Hall Nurseries & Garden Centre, 65
Wreford Landscapes, 16, 38, 39, 46, 59
Wrest Park & Gardens, 82
Wrest Park Homes & Gardens Show, 115
Writtle College, 111
Wulfran College, 111
Wychwood Waterlilies, 46
Wye College, 111
Wye Valley Herbs, 81, 104
Wyevale Garden Centre, 48, 49, 50, 52, 53, 56, 57, 58, 60, 61, 63, 64, 65, 66, 67, 68, 69, 70, 71, 73, 74, 76, 80
Wyevale Garden Centres plc, 60
Wyevale Shop, 57, 63, 71
Wyken Emporium, 97
Wyken Hall, 97
Wyld Court Rainforest, 49, 82
Wyseby House Books, 107
Wytherstone Nurseries, 77

Y S J Seeds, 69
Yamaha Motor (UK) Ltd, 35
Yorkshire Garden World, 77

SPECIALITIES INDEX

Alpines

A & A Thorp, 63
Aberconwy Nursery, 80
Alpine Garden Society, 116
Ashenden Nursery, 61
Baker Straw Partnership, 59
Ballyrogan Nurseries, 77
Beechcroft Nursery, 71
Birmingham Botanical Gardens & Glasshouses, 93
Blackthorn Nursery, 58
Brackenwood Garden Centre, 48
Brackenwood Plant Centre, 48
Bressingham Plant Centre, 49, 50, 66
Brownthwaite Hardy Plants, 63
Chadwell Himalayan Plant Seed, 40
Chris Pattison (Nurseryman), 57
Cotswold Garden Flowers, 59
Cottage Garden, 56
Cotton Ash Garden, 61
Cravens Nursery, 77
Cyclamen Society, 117
E L F Plants, 67
Elsworth Herbs, 50
Ferndale Nursery & Garden Centre, 77
Field House Alpines, 67
Fosse Alpines, 63
Gardenscape, 76
H & S Wills, 54
Hartside Nursery Garden, 53
Highgates Nursery, 53
Jenny Burgess Alpines, 66
Kexby Design, 39
Langthorns Plantery, 56
Lingen Nursery & Garden, 68, 95
Llanbrook Alpine & Wildflower Nursery, 68
Martin Nest Nurseries, 64
Marwood Hill Gardens, 86
Mead Nursery, 75
Mendle Nursery, 39
National Auricula & Primula Society (Southern), 119
Newton Hill Alpines, 77
Nicky's Rock Garden Nursery, 39, 54
Norden Alpine Nursery, 76
Norwell Nurseries, 67
Padlock Croft, 83
Plant World Seeds, 41
Podington Garden Centre, 29, 39, 44, 67
Potterton & Martin, 39, 65
Primrose Cottage Nursery & Garden Centre, 65
Richard Stockwell - Rare Plants (GF), 41, 68
Rookhope Nurseries, 52, 84
Ryal Nursery, 67
Scottish Rock Garden Club, 115, 120
Sino-Himalayan Plant Association, 120
Siskin Plants, 71
Tile Barn Nursery, 62
Triscombe Nurseries, 69
Usual & Unusual Plants, 73
W E Th Ingwersen Ltd, 74
Walter T Ware, 75
White Cottage Alpines, 39, 76
Wintergreen Nurseries, 60

Bulbs

Avon Bulbs, 68
Ballyrogan Nurseries, 77
Broadleigh Gardens, 69
Burrough House Gardens, 92
Chirk Castle, 103
Compton Acres Garden Centre, 55
Constable Daffodils, 71
Cottage Garden, 56
Doddington Hall, 92
Evelix Daffodils, 79
Gardenscape, 76
Mead Nursery, 75
Monksilver Nursery, 50
Newington Nurseries, 68
Otter Nurseries Ltd, 54
Paradise Centre, 70
Potterton & Martin, 39, 65
R H S Garden Hyde Hall, 88
R V Roger Ltd, 76
Rupert Bowlby, 72
S & S Perennials, 64
Scottish Rock Garden Club, 115, 120
Springfields (World of Flowers), 92
Suttons Seeds, 41
Walter T Ware, 75

Clematis

Arbury Hall, 99
Barncroft Nurseries, 69
Beamish Clematis Nursery, 52
Bressingham Plant Centre, 49, 50, 66
British Clematis Society, 116
Busheyfields Nursery - J Bradshaw & Son, 61
Caddicks Clematis Nursey, 51
Chelsea Gardener, The, 65
Compton Acres Garden Centre, 55
Cottage Garden, 56
Crug Farm Plants, 81
Ferndale Nursery & Garden Centre, 77
Goodnestone Park Gardens, 91
Highgate Garden Centre - Capital Gardens, 65
Langthorns Plantery, 56
Marwood Hill Gardens, 86
Orchard Nurseries, 64
Peveril Clematis Nursery, 54
Podington Garden Centre, 29, 39, 44, 67
Pounsley Plants, 55, 87
Priorswood Clematis, 61
Richard Stockwell - Rare Plants (GF), 41, 68
Roots Garden Centre Ltd, 78
Scotts Clematis, 55
Sherston Parva Nursery, 75
Stillingfleet Lodge Nurseries, 76, 100
Thorncroft Clematis Nursery, 67
Treasures of Tenbury Ltd, 60, 90
Valley Clematis Nursery, 65
Walter T Ware, 75

Conifers

Arbury Hall, 99
Barncroft Nurseries, 69
Bedgebury National Pinetum, 91
Beechcroft Nursery, 71
Brackenwood Garden Centre, 48
Brackenwood Plant Centre, 48
Bressingham Plant Centre, 49, 50, 66
Christie - Elite Nurseries Ltd, 78
Conifer Garden, 49
Cottage Garden, 56
Duchy of Cornwall Nursery, 52
E L F Plants, 67
Feebers Hardy Plants, 54
Norwich Heather & Conifer Centre, 66
Otter Nurseries Ltd, 54
P W Plants, 66, 93
Podington Garden Centre, 29, 39, 44, 67
Potterton & Martin, 39, 65
Primrose Cottage Nursery & Garden Centre, 65
Somerleyton Hall & Gardens, 97

Fruit

B R Edwards, 59
Ballerina Trees Ltd, 50
Bernwode Plants, 49
Bonhard Nursery, 80
Brogdale Horticultural Trust, 91
Christie - Elite Nurseries Ltd, 78
Clive Simms, 64
Cornish Garden Nurseries, 52
Cottage Garden, 56
Cotton Ash Garden, 61
Deacons Nursery, 61
East Malling Research Association, 117
Family Trees, 58
Friends of Brogdale, 62, 91
Fruit Garden, 62
Global Orange Groves UK, 55
Horticultural Research International, 118
J Tweedie Fruit Trees, 78
Keepers Nursery, 62
Ken Muir Nurseries, 56
Kexby Design, 39
Marshalls, 41
Parcevall Hall Gardens, 100
R V Roger Ltd, 76
Reads Nursery, 66
S M McArd, 41
Somerleyton Hall & Gardens, 97
Thornhayes Nursery, 55

Fuchsia

B & H M Baker, 56
Beechcroft Nursery, 71
Burnside Fuchsias, 63
Christie - Elite Nurseries Ltd, 78
Clay Lane Nursery, 71
Exotic Fuchsias, 80
Five Acres Fuchsia Nursery, 66
Fuchsia World, 70
Fuchsiavale Nurseries, 59
Gatehampton Fuchsias, 49
Gouldings Fuchsias, 70
Hilltop Nurseries, 64
Houghton Lodge Garden & Hydroponicum, 89
Jackson's Nurseries, 70
Kathleen Muncaster Fuchsias, 64
Kent Street Nurseries, 73
Laburnum Nurseries, 64
Little Brook Fuchsias, 58
Meadowcroft Fuchsias & Pelargonium, 50
Oakleigh Nurseries, 58
Oldbury Nurseries, 62
Podington Garden Centre, 29, 39, 44, 67
Porters Fuchsias, 65
Sandringham House & Grounds, 93
Vernon Geranium Nursery, 72

Geranium and Pelargonium

Baker Straw Partnership, 59
Barbara Molesworth, 68
Beeches Nursery, 77
Birkheads Cottage Garden & Nursery, 74, 99
Brian Sulman Pelargoniums, 70
British Pelargonium & Geranium Society, 116
Catforth Gardens, 63, 92
Cotswold Garden Flowers, 59
Cottage Garden, 56
Crug Farm Plants, 81
Denmans Garden, 98
Derek Lloyd Dean, 65
Diana Hull - Species Pelargonium Specialist, 74
Doddington Hall, 92
Eastgrove Cottage Garden Nursery, 90
Geranium Nursery, 74
Hardy Plant Society, 118
Henllys Lodge Plants, 81
Hexham Herbs, 67, 94
Hunts Court Garden & Nursery, 57, 88
Kent Street Nurseries, 73
Kingswood Pelargoniums, 76
Langthorns Plantery, 56
Margery Fish Plant Nursery, 69
Meadowcroft Fuchsias & Pelargonium, 50
Millbern Geraniums, 74
Norwell Nurseries, 67
Oakleigh Nurseries, 58
Oldbury Nurseries, 62
Podington Garden Centre, 29, 39, 44, 67
Rosie's Garden Plants, 62
Seeds-by-Size, 41
Somerleyton Hall & Gardens, 97
Usual & Unusual Plants, 73
Vernon Geranium Nursery, 72

Herbaceous Perennials

Abbey Dore Court Garden, 59, 90
Aberconwy Nursery, 80
Ashenden Nursery, 61
Ashfield Hellebores - Rarer Plants, 76

Baker Straw Partnership, 59
Ballyrogan Nurseries, 77
Barbara Molesworth, 68
Bernwode Plants, 49
Beth Chatto Gardens Ltd, 56
Bide-a-Wee Cottage Garden, 94
Birkheads Cottage Garden & Nursery, 74, 99
Blackthorn Nursery, 58
Brackenwood Garden Centre, 48
Brackenwood Plant Centre, 48
Bregover Plants, 52
Bressingham Plant Centre, 49, 50, 66
Broadleas Gardens Charitable Trust Ltd, 75, 99
Brownthwaite Hardy Plants, 63
Burford Garden Company, 68
Burrough House Gardens, 92
Cally Gardens, 78
Catforth Gardens, 63, 92
Chadwell Himalayan Plant Seed, 40
Chelsea Gardener, The, 65
Chirk Castle, 103
Christie - Elite Nurseries Ltd, 78
Cilwern Plants, 80
Cotswold Garden Flowers, 59
Cottage Garden, 56
Cottage Nurseries, 64
Cotton Ash Garden, 61
Craigieburn Garden, 78, 101
Doddington Hall, 92
Duchy of Cornwall Nursery, 52
Eastgrove Cottage Garden Nursery, 90
Elsworth Herbs, 50
Elworthy Cottage Plants, 69, 96
Feebers Hardy Plants, 54
Ferndale Nursery & Garden Centre, 77
Gardenscape, 76
Goldbrook Plants, 70
Goodnestone Park Gardens, 91
Gwydir Plants, 81
Hall Farm Nursery, 64, 92
Hardy Orchids Ltd, 55
Hardy Plant Society, 118
Henllys Lodge Plants, 81
Hexham Herbs, 67, 94
Hillview Hardy Plants, 68
Judy's Country Garden, 64
Langthorns Plantery, 56
Lingen Nursery & Garden, 68, 95
Little Creek Nursey, 48
Little Treasures Nursery, 52
Longacre Nursery, 62, 91
Lower Severalls Garden & Nursery, 69
Margery Fish Plant Nursery, 69
Marwood Hill Gardens, 86
Mead Nursery, 75
Mill Cottage Plants, 69
Mills Farm Plants, 70
Monksilver Nursery, 50
Newington Nurseries, 68
Nordybank Nurseries, 68, 95
Norwell Nurseries, 67
Orchard Nurseries, 64
Otter Nurseries Ltd, 54
P W Plants, 66, 93
Padlock Croft, 83
Paradise Centre, 70
Park Green Nurseries, 70
Penpergwm Plants, 80
Perry's Plants, 76, 100
Perrybrook Nursery, 68
Plant World Seeds, 41
Plants 'n' Gardens, 74
Podington Garden Centre, 29, 39, 44, 67
Port Lympne Wild Animal Park, 91
Pounsley Plants, 55, 87

Primrose Cottage Nursery & Garden Centre, 65
R D Plants, 55
R H S Garden Hyde Hall, 88
Richard Stockwell - Rare Plants (GF), 41, 68
Rookhope Nurseries, 52, 84
Roots Garden Centre Ltd, 78
Rougham Hall Nurseries, 71
Rushfields of Ledbury, 60
Somerleyton Hall & Gardens, 97
Stillingfleet Lodge Nurseries, 76, 100
Ulverscroft Unusual Plants, 64
Usual & Unusual Plants, 73
V H Humphrey - Iris Specialist, 72
Veryans Plants, 55
Walled Garden, The, 71
Walter T Ware, 75
White Windows, 89
Wintergreen Nurseries, 60
Wye Valley Herbs, 81, 104

Herbs

Arne Herbs, 48
Baker Straw Partnership, 59
Barbara Molesworth, 68
Barwinnock Herbs, 79, 102
Bernwode Plants, 49
Birkheads Cottage Garden & Nursery, 74, 99
Bressingham Plant Centre, 50
Chelsea Physic Garden, 92
Cheshire Herbs, 51
Compton Acres Garden Centre, 55
Cottage Garden, 56
Cottage Herbery, 40, 90
Countryside Wildflowers, 50
Daphne ffiske Herbs, 66
E W King & Co Ltd, 40
Elly Hill Herbs, 52, 84
Elsworth Herbs, 50
Gwydir Plants, 81
Harefield Herbs, 40, 66
Helmingham Hall Gardens, 96
Herb Society, 118
Hexham Herbs, 67, 94
Hill Farm Herbs, 67
Hollington Herb Garden, 82
Iden Croft Herbs, 62
Jekkas Herb Farm, 48
Judy's Country Garden, 64
Langthorns Plantery, 56
Lisdoonan Herbs, 78
Lower Severalls Garden & Nursery, 69
Morehavens, 50
Newington Nurseries, 68
Norfolk Lavender Ltd, 66, 93
Oak Cottage Herb Garden, 68
Old Mill Herbary, 85
Plant World Seeds, 41
Podington Garden Centre, 29, 39, 44, 67
Poyntzfield Herb Nursery, 79
Primrose Cottage Nursery & Garden Centre, 65
Roots Garden Centre Ltd, 78
S M McArd, 41
Salley Gardens, 41, 68
Southwick Country Herbs, 55
Suffolk Herbs, 41
Suttons Seeds, 41
Walter T Ware, 75
Wells & Winter, 31
Wildlife Gardening Centre, 68
Wye Valley Herbs, 81, 104

Organic Gardening

Barwinnock Herbs, 79, 102
Broomfield College, 107
Caves Folly Nurseries, 59
Cottage Herbery, 40, 90
E W King & Co Ltd, 40
English Woodlands Biocontrol, 26
Fertile Fibre, 26
Globe Organic Services, 26
Helmingham Hall Gardens, 96
Henry Doubleday Research Association (HDRA), 40, 93, 118
Hewthorn Herbs & Wild Flowers, 43, 67
Lisdoonan Herbs, 78
Natural Organic Supplies, 29
Nordybank Nurseries, 68, 95
Old Mill Herbary, 85
Port Lympne Wild Animal Park, 91
Poyntzfield Herb Nursery, 79
Rivendell Nursery, 76
Salley Gardens, 41, 68
Seeds-by-Size, 41
Super Natural Ltd, 30
Tamar Organics, 30
Ty'n Garreg Nurseries, 81
Wychwood Waterlilies, 46
Yorkshire Garden World, 77

Rhododendrons and Azaleas

Aberconwy Nursery, 80
Arbury Hall, 99
Barncroft Nurseries, 69
Brackenwood Garden Centre, 48
Brackenwood Plant Centre, 48
Broadleas Gardens Charitable Trust Ltd, 75, 99
Chirk Castle, 103
Christie - Elite Nurseries Ltd, 78
Coghurst Nursery, 73
Dorothy Clive Garden, 96
Duchy of Cornwall Nursery, 52
F Morrey & Son, 51
Furzey Gardens, 89
Greenway Gardens, 54
Harewood House & Gardens, 101
High Garden, 54
Highgates Nursery, 53
Hydon Nurseries, 71
Knap Hill Nursery Ltd, 72
Lanhydrock Gardens, 85
Lea Gardens, 86
Leonardslee Plants, 74
Lost Gardens of Heligan, 85
Lydney Park Gardens, 88
Millais Nurseries, 72
Ness Botanic Gardens, 84
Otter Nurseries Ltd, 54
Podington Garden Centre, 29, 39, 44, 67
Port Lympne Wild Animal Park, 91
Post House Gardens, 103
Potterton & Martin, 39, 65
Sandringham House & Grounds, 93
Seaforde Nursery, 78
Somerleyton Hall & Gardens, 97
Stourhead Landscape Garden, 99
Swiss Garden, 82
Wall Cottage Nursery, 53
Weston Park, 95

Roses

A J Palmer & Son, 49
Apuldram Roses, 73, 98
Arbury Hall, 99

Battersby Roses, 76
Bonhard Nursery, 80
Bramham Park, 100
Bressingham Plant Centre, 49, 50, 66
Broadleas Gardens Charitable Trust Ltd, 75, 99
Broomfield College, 107
Burford Garden Company, 68
Burrows Roses, 53
Chirk Castle, 103
Christie - Elite Nurseries Ltd, 78
Craigieburn Garden, 78, 101
David Austin Roses Ltd, 66
Fryer's Nurseries Ltd, 51
Gandy's Roses Ltd, 63
Godly's Roses, 60
Goodnestone Park Gardens, 91
Helmingham Hall Gardens, 96
Henry Street, 49
Hexham Herbs, 67, 94
Highgate Garden Centre - Capital Gardens, 65
Hunts Court Garden & Nursery, 57, 88
John Sanday (Roses) Ltd, 48
Just Roses, 73
Langthorns Plantery, 56
Margery Fish Plant Nursery, 69
Mattock Roses, 68
Mills Farm Plants, 70
Newington Nurseries, 68
Peter Beales Roses, 66
Port Lympne Wild Animal Park, 91
Pounsley Plants, 55, 87
Primrose Cottage Nursery & Garden Centre, 65
R H S Garden Hyde Hall, 88
R Harkness & Co Ltd, 61
R V Roger Ltd, 76
Roses & Shrubs Garden Centre, 66
Royal National Rose Society, 90, 120
Rumwood Nurseries, 62
Somerleyton Hall & Gardens, 97
Stanton Harcourt Manor House & Gardens, 95
Swiss Garden, 82
Trevor White Old Fashioned Roses, 67
Wheatcroft Ltd, 68

Vegetables

Chelsea Physic Garden, 92
Crown Asparagus, 70
E W King & Co Ltd, 40
Edwin Tucker & Sons, 40
Grimsthorpe Castle, 92
Helmingham Hall Gardens, 96
Henry Doubleday Research Association (HDRA), 40, 93, 118
Horticultural Research International, 118
Johnsons Seeds, 41
Lisdoonan Herbs, 78
Lost Gardens of Heligan, 85
Marshalls, 41
National Vegetable Society, 119
S M McArd, 41
Seeds-by-Size, 41
Somerleyton Hall & Gardens, 97
Suffolk Herbs, 41
Suttons Seeds, 41
Thompson & Morgan UK Ltd, 41

Wild Flowers

Arbury Hall, 99
Arne Herbs, 48
Bramham Park, 100

The Daily Telegraph *Green Fingers* **Specialities Index**

Cornwall Wildlife Trust, 117
Countryside Wildflowers, 50
Doddington Hall, 92
Elsworth Herbs, 50
Glamorgan Wildlife Trust, 117
Gwydir Plants, 81
Harefield Herbs, 40, 66
Hewthorn Herbs & Wild Flowers, 43, 67
Hexham Herbs, 67, 94
John Chambers Wild Flower Seeds, 41
Landlife Wildflowers Ltd, 41
Linda Gascoigne Wild Flowers, 64
Llanbrook Alpine & Wildflower Nursery, 68
Mannington Gardens, 93
Newington Nurseries, 68
Nordybank Nurseries, 68, 95
Old Mill Herbary, 85
Port Lympne Wild Animal Park, 91
Post House Gardens, 103
Rowallane Gardens, 101
Salley Gardens, 41, 68
Scottish Rock Garden Club, 115, 120
Somerset Wildlife Trust, 69
Suffolk Herbs, 41
Suttons Seeds, 41
Wells & Winter, 31
Wild Flower Society, 120
Wild Seeds, 42
Wildlife Gardening Centre, 68

NATIONAL COLLECTIONS

Abelia
Pleasant View Garden, 87
Pleasant View Nursery, 55

Adenophora
Padlock Croft, 83

Alchemillia
University Botanic Gardens, 83, 110

Alder
Stone Lane Gardens, 55

Alnus
Ness Botanic Gardens, 84

Anemone Nemorosa
Gardenscape, 12, 36, 38, 76

Artemisia
Elsworth Herbs, 50

Ash
Thorp Perrow Arboretum, 100

Astilbe
Marwood Hill Gardens, 86

Auriculas - Show & Alpine
Martin Nest Nurseries, 64

Bamboos - all genera
Drysdale Garden Exotics, 58

Begonias - Non-tuberous
Glasgow Botanic Gardens, 103

Bergenia
University Botanic Gardens, 83, 110

Betula
Ness Botanic Gardens, 84
Royal Botanic Gardens Kew, 98

Birch
Stone Lane Gardens, 55

Bonsai
Birmingham Botanical Gardens & Glasshouses, 93

Buxus
Langley Boxwood Nursery, 58, 89

Cactaceae - subtribe Borzicactinae
Whitestone Gardens Ltd, 76

Calluna Vulgaris
R H S Garden Wisley, 97, 110

Campanula
Padlock Croft, 83

Campanula - Herbaceous
Lingen Nursery & Garden, 68, 95

Canna
Brockings Exotics, 52

Celmisia
Ballyrogan Nurseries, 77

Cistus
Chelsea Physic Garden, 92

Citrus
Reads Nursery, 66

Clematis
Treasures of Tenbury Ltd, 60, 90

Clematis Montana & Chrysocoma
Busheyfields Nursery - J Bradshaw & Son, 61

Coleus
Birmingham Botanical Gardens & Glasshouses, 93
Brockings Exotics, 52

Conifers
Bedgebury National Pinetum, 91

Coriaria
Crug Farm Plants, 81

Cornus
R H S Garden Rosemoor, 87

Cornus - Dogwoods
Newby Hall & Gardens, 100

Cotoneaster
Ness Botanic Gardens, 84

Crocosmin
Ballyrogan Nurseries, 77

Crocus
R H S Garden Wisley, 97, 110

Cydonia oblonga - Tree quince
Norton Priory Museum & Gardens, 84

Dabolxia
R H S Garden Wisley, 97, 110

Delphiniums
Rougham Hall Nurseries, 71

Dendrobiums
Glasgow Botanic Gardens, 103

Epinedium
R H S Garden Wisley, 97, 110

Erica, 97, 110

Erodiums
R V Roger Ltd, 76

Eucryphia
Seaforde Nursery, 78

Euphorbia
Ballyrogan Nurseries, 77

Figs
Reads Nursery, 66

Fritillaria
University Botanic Gardens, 83, 110

Gacanthus
R H S Garden Wisley, 97, 110

Gentians (Christies Nursery, Angus)
Scottish Rock Garden Club, 115, 120

Geranium
East Lambrook Manor Garden, 96
Margery Fish Plant Nursery, 69
University Botanic Gardens, 83, 110

Geranium - hardy
Catforth Gardens, 63, 92

Gooseberries
Rougham Hall Nurseries, 71

Grapes
Reads Nursery, 66

Hamamelis
Roses & Shrubs Garden Centre, 66

Hebe
Hebe Society, 118

Hedera
Ness Botanic Gardens, 84

Hepatica
Gardenscape, 12, 36, 38, 76

Hostas
Apple Court, 58, 89
Harewood House & Gardens, 101
Kittoch Mill Hosta Garden, 102

Hostas - hybrid
Ann & Roger Bowden (Hostas), 54, 86

Hypericum
Royal Botanic Gardens Kew, 98

Ilex
R H S Garden Rosemoor, 87

Iris Ensata
Marwood Hill Gardens, 86

Iris Sibirica
Lingen Nursery & Garden, 68, 95

Iris Spuria
English Heritage, 94

Ivy
Erddig, 103

Juglans - Walnuts
Wimpole Hall, 83

Lathyrus
National Sweet Pea Society, 119

Lavandula
Jersey Lavender Ltd, 82
Norfolk Lavender Ltd, 66, 93

Lavender
Downderry Nursery, 61

Ligularia
Brownthwaite Hardy Plants, 63

Lime
Thorp Perrow Arboretum, 100

Lonicera
University Botanic Gardens, 83, 110

Lonicera - climbing
Busheyfields Nursery - J Bradshaw & Son, 61

Malus
Jodrell Bank Arboretum, 84
R H S Garden Hyde Hall, 88

Menoconopsis
Craigieburn Garden, 78, 101

Mentha
Iden Croft Herbs, 62

Monarda
Leeds Castle, 91

Nepeta, 91

Nerium Oleander
Elsworth Herbs, 50

Nothofagus
Royal Botanic Gardens Kew, 98

Nymphaea - Waterlilies
Stapeley Water Gardens Ltd, 45, 51, 84

Nymphaea - hardy
Bennetts Water Gardens, 42

Origanum
Hexham Herbs, 67, 94
Iden Croft Herbs, 62

Paris
Crug Farm Plants, 81

Passiflora
National Collection of Passiflora, 82, 119

Penstemon
Rowallane Gardens, 101

Penstemon cultivars
Kingston Maurward Gardens, 87

Platycodon
Padlock Croft, 83

Platycodon & Gentiana Asclepiadea cvs
Hoo House Nursery, 57

Porophyllum
Waterperry Gardens Ltd, 95

Primula - sections Capitatae, Cortusoides, Farinosae
Plant World Seeds, 41

Primula Marginatta
Gardenscape, 12, 36, 38, 76

Pulmonaria
R H S Garden Wisley, 97, 110
Stillingfleet Lodge Nurseries, 76, 100

Rheum
R H S Garden Wisley, 97, 110

Rhododendrons
Harewood House & Gardens, 101

Ribes
University Botanic Gardens, 83, 110

Rohdea Japonica
Apple Court, 58, 89

Roses
Royal National Rose Society, 90, 120

Rubus
Aberdeen College, 107

Ruscus
University Botanic Gardens, 83, 110

Salix
Ness Botanic Gardens, 84

Salvia
Pleasant View Garden, 87
Pleasant View Nursery, 55

Salvias
Kingston Maurward Gardens, 87

Santolina - Cotton Lavender
Yorkshire Garden World, 77

Saxifraga
University Botanic Gardens, 83, 110

Saxifrages
Waterperry Gardens Ltd, 95

Sisyrinchium
Jenny Burgess Alpines, 66

Skimmia
Royal Botanic Gardens Kew, 98

Sorbus
Jodrell Bank Arboretum, 84
Ness Botanic Gardens, 84

Streptocarpus
Dibleys Nurseries, 80

Styracacae
Holker Hall, 85

Symphyandra
Padlock Croft, 83

Thymus
Hexham Herbs, 67, 94

Tree Ferns
Glasgow Botanic Gardens, 103

Tulbaghia
Marwood Hill Gardens, 86

Tulipa
University Botanic Gardens, 83, 110

Verbascums
Birmingham Botanical Gardens & Glasshouses, 93

Viburnum
R H S Garden Hyde Hall, 88

Violas
Planta Vera, 72

Walnuts
Thorp Perrow Arboretum, 100

Waterlily - Odiham Collection
Wychwood Waterlilies, 46

Woodwardia
Apple Court, 58, 89

GEOGRAPHICAL INDEX

Channel Islands

Guernsey
Martels Garden World, 48

Jersey
Jersey Lavender Ltd, 82
Ransoms Garden Centre, 48
St Peters Garden Centre, 48

England

Avon
Alan Phipps Cacti, 48
Alite Metals, 21
American Museum in Britain, 82
Arne Herbs, 48
Badminton, 82
Bath Botanic Gardens, 82
Blackmore & Langdon, 48
Brackenwood Garden Centre, 48
Brackenwood Plant Centre, 48
C S Lockyer, 48
Claverton Manor, 82
Gloster Leisure Furniture, 19
Hannays of Bath, 48
Hillier Garden Centre, 48
Himalayan Kingdoms, 112
Ironart of Bath, 19
Jekkas Herb Farm, 48
John Sanday (Roses) Ltd, 48
Little Creek Nursey, 48
Misses I Allen & M J Huish, 48
Monocot Nursery, 48
National Collection of Passiflora, 82, 119
Nitritech, 44
Noel Kingsbury, 14
Norton Radstock Technical College, 109
Park Garden Centre, 48
Rare Plants Fairs, 115
Real Stone Company, 37
Shamrock Horticulture Ltd, 30
Smart Systems Ltd, 9
Technical Aquatic Products, 45
Tool-Craft, 34
University of Bristol Botanic Garden, 82
Wildlife Trust for Bristol Bath & Avon, 121
Willow Pottery, 38
Wiltshire Gardens Trust, 121
Wyevale Garden Centre, 48

Bedfordshire
Ashcroft Conservatories, 7
Avenue Fisheries, 10, 42
Bickerdikes Garden Centre, 48
Frost & Co, 8
Garden Relax Ltd, 22
Graham A Pavey & Associates, 12
J G S Weathervanes, 36
Luton Hoo, 82
Plysu Housewares Ltd, 29
Simply Garlands, 30
Swiss Garden, 82
Tree Group, 6
Walter Blom & Sons Ltd, 48
Woburn Abbey, 82, 115
Wrest Park & Gardens, 82
Wrest Park Homes & Gardens Show, 115
Wyevale Garden Centre, 48

Berkshire
Anthony George & Associates, 10
Arena Landscapes, 10
Berkshire College of Agriculture, 107
Black & Decker Ltd, 32
Bob Andrews Ltd, 32
Bressingham Plant Centre, 49
British Bonsai Association, 116
Carliles Hardy Plants, 49
Chadwell Himalayan Plant Seed, 40
Darlac Products, 25
Dromana Irrigation (UK), 25
Fiona Harrison, 12
Foxgrove Plants, 49
Garden Centre Association, 117
Gatehampton Fuchsias, 49
Hare Hatch Nursery, 49
Henry Street, 49
Hillier Garden Centre, 49
Hollington Herb Garden, 82
Jemp Engineering, 22
Jopasco Shade Umbrellas, 19
Kingfisher Nurseries, 49
M V Fletcher, 49
Molecatcher, 29
Offshoots - Englefield Garden Centre, 49
Old Rectory Garden, 82
Pathfinder Gardening, 15
Robin Williams & Associates, 15
Sino-Himalayan Plant Association, 120
Sutton Griffin & Morgan, 16
Thai House Company, 9
Thames Valley Wirework Co, 30
University of Reading, 111
World of Water, 46
Wyevale Garden Centre, 49, 49
Wyld Court Rainforest, 49, 82

Buckinghamshire
A J Palmer & Son, 49
Aylesbury College, 107
Bernwode Plants, 49
Buckingham Nurseries & Garden Centre, 49
Burnwode Plants, 49
Butterfields Nursery, 49
Chenies Landscapes Ltd, 11
Chenies Manor, 82
Chicheley Hall, 82
Cliveden, 82
Conifer Garden, 49
Consumer Direct Ltd, 25
David Stevens International Ltd, 11
Diana Eldon - Garden Designer, 11
East Midlands Cactus Nursery, 49
Fulmer Plant Park, 49
Greenacres Horticultural Supplies, 26
Hobby-Fish Farm, 43
Homesitters Ltd, 112, 118
Hozelock Ltd, 27
Julia Fogg & Susan Santer, 13
Kemps Coconut Products, 27
Langdon (London), 28
Marianne Ford Garden Design, 14
Marlow Garden & Leisure Centre, 49
Morehavens, 50
National Dahlia Society, 119
National Sweet Pea Society, 119
Organic Concentrates Ltd, 29
Practicality Brown Ltd, 15, 29
Professional Gardeners Guild, 120
Quartet Design, 15
S & N Brackley, 41
Stowe Landscape Gardens, 82
Sue Pack Garden Design, 16
Tamarisk Nurseries, 50
Waddesdon Manor, 82
Waddesdon Nursery, 50
West Wycombe Park, 83
Woodstock Orchids & Automations, 50
Wyevale Garden Centre, 50, 50

Cambridgeshire
Abbots Ripton Hall, 83
Alvenor Aquatics & Water Gardens, 42
Anglesey Abbey & Gardens, 50, 83
Anglia Bulbs, 50
Arbor Exotica, 50
Ariens (UK) Ltd, 32
Ballerina Trees Ltd, 50
Brampton Garden Centre, 50
Bressingham Plant Centre, 50
Bulbeck Foundry, 35
Bunny Guinness Landscape Design, 11
Bury Farm, 83
C N Seeds, 40
Cambridge Glasshouse Company Ltd, 21
Cambridgeshire College of Agriculture & Horticulture, 108
Conservatory Association, 7, 117
Countryside Wildflowers, 50
Crossing House Garden, 83
Cyprio Ltd, 43
David Brown Landscape Design, 11
Diane Sewell, 50
Docwras Manor, 83
Elsworth Herbs, 50
Fenland Bulbs, 50
Garden Answers Magazine, 113
Garden News, 113
Greenhouses Direct, 22
Hardwicke House, 83
Honeysome Aquatic Nursery, 43
Ichiyo School of Ikebana, 108, 118
J W Boyce (Seedsmen), 40
Jiffy Products Ltd, 27
John Drake Aquilegias, 41
Marshalls, 41
Meadowcroft Fuchsias & Pelargonium, 50
Monksilver Nursery, 50
Notcutts Garden Centre, 50
Original Terracotta Shop, 14, 37, 83
Padlock Croft, 83
Parwin Power Heaters, 22
Peckover House, 83
Pick Products, 34
Practical Gardening Magazine, 114
Scotsdale Nursery & Garden Centre, 50
Simply Plants, 50
University Botanic Gardens, 83, 110

Unwins Seeds Ltd, 42
Wight Butyl Liners, 46
Wildlife Trust Bedfordshire & Cambridgeshire, 121
Wimpole Hall, 83

Cheshire
Adlington Hall, 83
Arley Hall & Gardens, 83, 114
Astbury Meadow Garden Centre, 50
Barton Grange Garden Centre, 50
Bents Garden Centre & Nurseries, 51
Bridgemere Garden World, 83
Bridgemere Nurseries, 51
Caddicks Clematis Nursey, 51
Cantilever Garden Centre, 51
Capesthorne Hall, 83
Cheshire Herbs, 51
Cheshire Wildlife Trust, 117
Cholmondeley Castle Gardens, 83
Chris Burnett Associates, 11
Collinwood Nurseries, 51
Cottage Garden Society, 117
Dorfold Hall, 83
English Heritage Driveways, 38
Euro Tree Service, 6
F Morrey & Son, 51
Fairy Lane Nurseries, 51
Firs Nursery, 51
Fryer's Nurseries Ltd, 51
Gawsworth Hall, 83
Goldenfield Nursery, 51
Gordale Nurseries Garden Centre, 51
Granada Arboretum, 83
Hare Hill Garden, 84
Haresclough Pottery, 36
Harold Walker, 51
Jodrell Bank Arboretum, 84
Ken Higginbotham Garden Landscaping, 13
Little Moreton Hall, 84
Lyme Park, 84
Manchester Metropolitan University, 109
Ness Botanic Gardens, 84
Norton Priory Museum & Gardens, 84
Okells Nurseries, 51
Penn, 84
Peover Hall, 84
Phedar Nursery, 51
Pilkington Garden Centre, 51
Reaseheath College (Cheshire College of Agriculture), 110
Robinsons of Whaley Bridge, 51
Stapeley Water Gardens Ltd, 45, 51, 84
Store More Garden Buildings, 23
Susan Buckley, 16
Sycamore Park Garden Centre, 51
Tatton Park Gardens, 84
Waters Green Direct, 31
Weaver Vale Garden Centre, 51
Wilmslow Garden Centre, 52
Wyevale Garden Centre, 52

Cleveland
Aanco Conservatories, 7
Arcadia Nurseries, 52
Cleveland Wildlife Trust, 117
Conservatory Factory, 7
Fiesta Blinds Ltd, 8
Peter Barratt's Garden Centres, 52
Plantarama, 52
Strikes Garden Centre, 52
Town Farm Nursery, 39, 52, 84
Westwinds Perennial Plants, 52
Wilkinsons, 16

Co Durham
Amdega Ltd, 7
Barningham Park, 84
Beamish Clematis Nursery, 52

David Craig, 19
Eggleston Hall Gardens, 52, 84
Elly Hill Herbs, 52, 84
Equatorial Plant Co, 52
Finchale Training College, 108
Hanging Garden Pot Holders, 27
Hill Farm Koi, 43
Houghall College, 84, 108, 114
M C Products, 17
Raby Castle, 84
Remanoid Ltd, 45
Rookhope Nurseries, 52, 84
Strikes Garden Centre, 52
Tensor Ltd, 30
University of Durham Botanic Garden, 84
Westholme Hall, 84

Cornwall
Antony Woodland Garden, 84
Bosvigo, 84
Bosvigo Plants, 52
Bregover Plants, 52
Brockings Exotics, 52
Burncoose & South Down Nurseries, 52
Caerhays Castle, 84
Carnon Downs Garden Centre, 52
Carwinion, 84
Chyverton, 84
Classic Gates, 17
Cornish Garden Nurseries, 52
Cornwall Gardens Society, 117
Cornwall Gardens Trust, 117
Cornwall Wildlife Trust, 117
Cotehele, 85
Duchy of Cornwall Nursery, 52
Farm & Garden Bygones, 36
Hebe Society, 118
John Moreland, 13
Ken Caro, 85
Lanhydrock Gardens, 85
Little Treasures Nursery, 52
Lost Gardens of Heligan, 85
Merlin Rooted Cuttings, 52
Mount Edgcumbe Gardens, 85
Multimesh Products, 29
Old Mill Herbary, 85
Parkinson Herbs, 52
Pencarrow, 85
Porthpean House Gardens, 85
St Michaels Mount, 85
Tomperrow Farm Nurseries, 53
Trebah Garden, 85
Tregrehan Garden, 85
Trelissick (Feock), 85
Trengwainton Gardens, 85
Trerice, 85
Tresco Abbey, 85
Trevena Cross Nurseries, 53
Trewidden Estate Nursery, 53
Trewithen, 85
Trewithen Nurseries, 53
Wall Cottage Nursery, 53
Wyevale Garden Centre, 53

Cumbria
Acorn Bank Garden, 85
Ashley-Morris Garden Furniture, 18
Beechcroft Nurseries, 53
Boonwood Garden Centre, 53
Brantwood Trust, 85
Chiltern Seeds, 40
Cumbrian Koi Co Ltd, 43
Dalemain Historic House & Gardens, 85
Elaine Horne, 11
Graythwaite Hall, 85
Great Garden & Countryside Festival, 114
Halecat Garden Nurseries, 53
Hartside Nursery Garden, 53

Hayes Garden World Ltd, 53
Holehird Gardens, 85
Holker Hall, 85
Kut & Dried, 27
L & P Peat Ltd, 27
Levens Hall, 86
Lingholm Gardens, 86
Muncaster Plants, 53
Newton Rigg College, 109
Rydal Mount, 86
Summerfield Books, 107
T H Barker & Son, 53
Thermoforce Ltd, 23, 30
Weasdale Nurseries, 53
Webbs Garden Centre, 53
West Meters Ltd, 31
Wetheriggs Pottery, 38

Derbyshire
Anthony Short & Partners, 10
Armillatox Ltd, 24
Bayliss Precision Components Ltd, 21
Bluebell Nursery, 53
British Gladiolus Society, 116
Broomfield College, 107
Burrows Roses, 53
Calke Abbey, 86
Chatsworth, 86
Chatsworth Carpenters, 18
Chatsworth Garden Centre, 53
Cheshire Aluminium, 21
D H E Plants, 39
David Sharp Studio, 36
Dennis, 33
Derbyshire Wildlife Trust, 86
Greenleaves Garden Centre, 53
Grovewood Marketing Ltd, 8
Haddon Hall, 86
Hardwick Hall, 86
Highgates Nursery, 53
Kontsmide UK Ltd, 27
Lea Gardens, 86
Mailbox UK, 28
Matlock Garden Centre, 53
Melbourne Hall Gardens, 86
Midland Butyl Liners, 43
Owen Brown Tents, 8
P W Milne Atkinson, 15
Peter Grayson - Sweet Pea Seedsman, 41
Renishaw Hall Gardens, 86
Riley's Chrysanthemums, 53
Tibshelf Garden Products, 23
Trade & DIY Products Ltd, 30
Two Wests & Elliott Ltd, 23
University of Derby, 110
Woodgrow Horticulture Ltd, 31

Devon
Alpine Garden Society, 116
Altoona Nurseries, 54
Ann & Roger Bowden (Hostas), 54, 86
Aqua-Soil Products Ltd, 42
Arlington Court, 86
Axminster Power Tool Centre, 32
Bicton College of Agriculture, 107
Bicton Park Gardens, 86
British Hosta & Hemerocallis Society, 116
Burnham Nurseries, 54
Burrow Farm Gardens, 86
Castle Drogo, 86
Coleton Fishacre Garden, 86
Continental Awnings (UK), 25
Country Style, 19
D & D H W Morgan Second-Hand Books, 106
Dartington Hall, 86
Decorative Foliage, 54
Devon NCCPG Autumn Plant Market, 114

Devon NCCPG Summer Plant Market, 114
Devons Gardens Trust, 117
Devonshire Statuary, 36
Docton Mill, 86
Edwin Tucker & Sons, 40
Endsleigh Garden Centre, 54
Exeter University Gardens, 86
Feebers Hardy Plants, 54
Ferryman Polytunnels, 22
Fillan's Plants, 54
Fortescue Garden Trust, 86
Glebe Cottage Plants, 54
Goulds Pumps Ltd, 43
Green Stock, 12
Greenway Gardens, 54
H & S Wills, 54
High Garden, 54
Hill House Nursery & Gardens, 54, 86
Humus Wyse Ltd, 27
Jack's Patch Garden Centre, 54
Jean Goldberry Garden Design, 13
K & C Cacti, 54
Kenwith Nursery, 54, 112
Killerton House, 86
Knightshayes Court, 86
Knightshayes Garden Trust, 54
Kootensaw Dovecotes, 27
Lewdon Farm Alpine Nursery, 54
Louis Vincent Garden Design, 14
Macalda Electronics Ltd, 28
Marwood Hill Gardens, 86
Metalarts, 36
Nicky's Rock Garden Nursery, 39, 54
North Devon Garden Centre, 54
Original Organics Ltd, 29
Otter Nurseries (Torbay), 54
Otter Nurseries Ltd, 54
Otter Nurseries of Plymouth, 54
Overbecks Garden, 86
Paignton Zoo & Botanical Gardens, 87
Perrie Hale Forest Nursery, 54
Peveril Clematis Nursery, 54
Plant World Botanic Gardens & Plant Centre, 54
Plant World Seeds, 41
Pleasant View Garden, 87
Pleasant View Nursery, 55
Pounsley Plants, 55, 87
R D Plants, 55
R H S - The Robin Herbert Centre, 106
R H S Garden Rosemoor, 87
R H S Garden Rosemoor Plant Centre, 55
Rowden Gardens, 45, 87
Saltram, 87
Sampford Shrubs, 55
Samuel Dobie & Son Ltd, 41
Scotts Clematis, 55
South West Alpine Show, 115
Southwick Country Herbs, 55
Stone Lane Gardens, 55
Suttons Seeds, 41
Tamar Organics, 30
Tapeley Park Gardens, 87
Thornhayes Nursery, 55
Tony Benger Landscaping, 16
Torbay Water Gardens, 45
Trelliscope, 18
Tropicana Nursery, 55
Veryans Plants, 55
Vigo Vineyard Supplies, 35
W C Cousens, 107
Water Garden Nursery, 45
West Country Water Gardens, 46
Westcountry Water Garden Centre, 46
Westfield Cacti, 55
Withleigh Nurseries, 55

Dorset
Abbey Plants, 55
Abbotsbury Sub-Tropical Gardens, 55, 87
Amateur Gardening Magazine, 113
Annabel Allhusen, 10
Athelhampton, 87
Bennetts Water Gardens, 42
C W Groves & Son, 55
Canford Magna Nurseries, 55
Chiffchaffs, 87
Compton Acres Garden Centre, 35, 55
Cottage Garden Plants, 55
Cranbourne Manor, 87
Cranbourne Manor Garden Centre, 55
Dorset Perennial Group, 117
Dorset Trust for Nature Conservation, 117
Forde Abbey Gardens, 87
Gardener, 113
Glen Pottery, 36
Global Orange Groves UK, 55
Hardy Orchids Ltd, 55
Hare Lane Pottery, 36
Ivy Cottage, 87
Keith Banyard Tree Surgeons, 6
Kingston Lacy, 87
Kingston Maurward College, 109
Kingston Maurward Gardens, 87
Knight Terrace Pots, 36
Labelplant, 27
MacPenny Nurseries, 56
MacPenny Products, 28
Mapperton House Garden, 87
Mellors Garden Ceramics, 36
Milton Garden Plants, 56
Minterne, 87
Naked Cross Nurseries, 56
Parnham House, 87
Paul Norton Associates, 15
Solaris Laminates Ltd, 9
Sticky Wicket Garden, 87
Three Counties Nurseries, 56
TimberKits, 38
Trehane Nurseries, 56
Water Works, 31
Weather Signs, 31
Wimbourne Road Nurseries, 56
Wyevale Garden Centre, 56, 56

Essex
Alibench, 21
AllClear Water Purifiers, 42
Alton Garden Centre, 18
Anderson Ceramics, 24
Audley End House & Gardens, 87
B & H M Baker, 56
B A C Conservatories Ltd, 7
Barking College, 107
Barlow Tyrie Ltd, 18
Beeches Nursery, 56
Beth Chatto Gardens Ltd, 56
Blue Lagoon Aquatics, 42
Bramley Ltd, 18
Bramleys Nurseries, 56
Bushukan Bonsai, 56
Butterfly Conservation, 117
Butyl Products Ltd, 43
Bypass Nurseries, 56
C J Skilton Aquarist, 43
Cants of Colchester, 56
Cookson Plantpak Ltd, 25
Copford Bulbs, 56
Cottage Garden, 56
Country Garden, 106
County Park Nursery, 56
Crowther Landscapes, 11
Dagenham Landscapes Ltd, 11
E W King & Co Ltd, 40
Easy Pot Staging, 22
Essex Wildlife Trust, 117
Fens, 87
Flora Exotica, 56
Frances Mount Perennial Plants, 56
Gardeners' Seed Exchange, 40
Gardening Direct (DPA Direct Ltd), 56
Gardens in Wood, 36
Gary Edwards Garden Designs, 12
Ground Control Ltd, 12
Homecare Products, 27
Hull Farm Conifer Centre, 56
International Water Lily Society, 43, 118
Jardino Pumps, 43
K G Aerators, 34
Kemlawns Nursery, 56
Ken Muir Nurseries, 56
Langthorns Plantery, 56
Mill Race Nursery, 56
Moongate Designs, 14
New Vision Videos, 113
Notcutts Garden Centre, 56
Olivers, 87
Ornamental Grasses - Trevor Scott, 56, 88
Plantworld, 57
R H S Garden Hyde Hall, 88
Rhodes & Rockliffe, 57
Ruskins Arboricultural Group, 6
Saintpaulia & Houseplant Society, 120
Saling Hall, 88
Samuel Wernick Garden Buildings, 9
Scarletts Plantcare, 30
Skyview Systems Ltd, 30
Solo Sprayers, 34
South Ockendon Garden Centre, 57
Southend Adult Community College, 110
Suffolk Herbs, 41
Trugrind, 30
Volpaia, 88
Wallis Seeds & Co, 42
Westbury Conservatories, 9
Westwood Dials, 38
Whitehouse Ivies, 57
Writtle College, 111
Wyevale Garden Centre, 57, 57, 57, 57
Wyevale Shop, 57, 57

Gloucestershire
Abbotswood, 88
Andrew Norfield Seeds, 40
Aquatic Habit, 42
Architectural Heritage, 35
Attwoolls Tents Ltd, 18
Avon Gardens Trust, 116
Barnsley House Garden Furniture, 18
Barnsley Park Box Hedging, 57
Batsford Arboretum, 88
Bedding Plant Centre - Churt Nurseries, 57
Berkeley Castle, 88
Bourton House, 88
Bridges Decorative Metalwork, 17
Cheltenham & Gloucester College of Higher Education, 108
Chris Pattison (Nurseryman), 57
Colvin & Moggridge, 11
Cotswold Range of Garden Ornamental Ironwork, 11, 35
Cowcombe Farm Herbs, 57
Cowley Manor, 88
Ernest Wilson Memorial Garden, 88
Four Counties Nursery, 57
Frampton Court, 88
Gloucestershire Gardens & Landscape Trust, 117
Glowcroft Ltd, 26
Hamptons Leisure, 19
Hidcote Manor, 88
Highfield Nurseries, 57
Hodges Barn, 88
Hoo House Nursery, 57
Hunts Court Garden & Nursery, 57, 88
Hurrans Garden Centre Ltd, 57
Husqvarna Forest & Garden, 34
Jakobsen Landscape Architects, 13
James Bolton Garden Design, 13
Julian Dowle Partnership, 13
Kiftsgate Court Gardens, 88
Lechlade Garden Centre, 57
Lydney Park Gardens, 88
Melcourt Industries Ltd, 29, 38
Miserden Park, 88
Mount Pleasant Trees, 57
Norfields, 57
Offshore Conservatory Interiors, 8
Old Manor Nursery, 57
Oxleys Garden Furniture, 20
Painswick Rococo Garden Trust, 88
Posh Pots, 37
Priory, 88
Priory Garden Nursery, 57
Rodmarton Manor, 88
Ruardean Garden Pottery, 37
Rusco, 20
Ryobi Lawn & Garden (UK), 34
Scarcity of Scarecrows, 37
Simon Richards & Associates, 15
Sudeley Castle, 88
Westbury Court, 88
Westonbirt Arboretum, 88
Westonbirt Plant Centre, 57
Wyevale Garden Centre, 57, 58

Hampshire
Agars Nursery, 58
Alitex - The Glasshouse Company, 21
Andmore Designs Ltd, 21
Apple Court, 58, 89
Artscapes & Theseus Maze Designs, 10
Blackthorn Nursery, 58
Bramdean House, 89
British Ivy Society, 116
British Teleflower Service Ltd, 117
Broadlands, 89
Burnt Earth Pottery, 24
Christopher Fairweather Ltd, 58
Cottage Garden Ceramics, 25
Denmead Aquatic Nursery, 43
Denmead Geranium Nurseries, 58
Drysdale Garden Exotics, 58
Exbury Enterprises Ltd, 58
Exbury Gardens, 89
Fairfield House, 89
Family Trees, 58
Finch Conservatories Ltd, 8
Frolics of Winchester, 17, 19
Furzey Gardens, 89
Gaze Burvill Ltd, 19
Geoffrey Coombs, 12
Gilbert White's House & Garden, 89
Greatham Mill, 89
Hambrook Landscapes Ltd, 12
Hampshire Gardens Trust, 118
Hardys Cottage Garden Plants, 58
Hawthorns Urban Wildlife Centre, 89
Haygate Engineering Co Ltd, 33
Hazel Cottage Nursey, 58
Heritage Woodcraft, 19
Heveningham Collection, 19
Highclere Castle, 89
Higher End Nursery - D J Case, 58
Highfield Hollies, 58
Hillier Garden Centre, 58, 58, 58, 58
Hillier Landscapes, 12
Hinton Ampner, 89
Hotbox Heaters Ltd, 27
Houghton Lodge Garden & Hydroponicum, 89
Jardinique, 36
Jenkyn Place, 89
Landscape Irrigation Systems, 28
Langley Boxwood Nursery, 58, 89
Little Brook Fuchsias, 58
Longstock Park Nursery, 58
Longstock Water Gardens, 89
Manor House Upton Grey, 89
Mastermind Products Ltd, 22
Meadow Herbs, 29
Mottisfont Abbey, 89
Naturetrek, 112
Nine Springs Nursery, 58
Oakleigh Nurseries, 58
Oase (UK) Ltd, 44
Ohara School of Ikebana, 110, 119
Olive Tree Trading Company Ltd, 37
Periwinkle, 110
Peter M Daly Rare Books, 106
Peter Trenear Nurseries, 58
Pound Lane Nurseries, 58
Queen Eleanors Garden, 89
Ratcliffe Orchids Ltd, 58
Redfields Leisure Buildings, 8
Robinsons of Winchester Ltd, 23
Seed House, 41
Simply Control, 30
Sir Harold Hillier Gardens & Arboretum, 89
Snapper Lawn Equipment (UK) Ltd, 34
Southview Nurseries, 59
Sparsholt College Hampshire, 110
Spinners, 59, 89
Steven Bailey Ltd, 59
Teamwork Landscaping, 16
Toro Wheel Horse UK, 34
Tudor House Garden, 89
Tyrite - Brighton Manufacturing Co, 30
Water Meadow Design & Landscape, 16
Water Meadow Nursery & Herb Farm, 45, 59, 89
White Windows, 89
Whitewater Nursery, 59
World of Water, 46
Wreford Landscapes, 16, 38, 39, 46, 59
Wychwood Waterlilies, 46
Wyseby House Books, 107

Hereford & Worcester
Abbey Dore Court Garden, 59, 90
Accompanied Cape Tours, 112
Allibert Garden Furniture, 18
Alpine Garden Society, 116
Archwood Greenhouses, 21, 24
B R Edwards, 59
Baker Straw Partnership, 59
Berrington Hall, 90
Birlingham Nurseries & Garden Centre, 59
Bouts Cottage Nurseries, 59
British Fuchsia Society, 116
Burford House Gardens, 90
Butterflies Galore, 24
C D A/Micron Sprayers, 24
Caves Folly Nurseries, 59
Cook's Garden Centre, 59
Cotswold Garden Flowers, 59
Cottage Herbery, 40, 90
Courtyard Designs, 7
Cranesbill Nursery, 59
Dormy House Hotel, 112
Eastgrove Cottage Garden Nursery, 90
Eastnor Castle, 90
Fertile Fibre, 26
Forest Fencing Ltd, 17

Fuchsiavale Nurseries, 59
Garden Machinery Direct, 33
Grange Farm Nursery, 59
Greenacres Nursery - D & M Everett, 59
Hardy Plant Society, 118
Hayloft Plants, 59
Hayne-West, 27
Herefordshire Nature Trust, 118
Hergest Croft Gardens, 90
Hill Court Gardens & Garden Centre, 90
Holloways, 36
Hortus, 113
How Caple Court Gardens, 90
International Acers, 59
Jill Hedges Bookseller, 106
Jungle Giants Bamboo Growers, 17
Kingfisher Nurseries, 59
Lakeside, 90
Landsmans Bookshop Ltd, 106
Malvern Autumn Gardening Show, 115
Malvern Spring Gardening Show, 115
Mark Ross Landscape Architects, 14
Marley Bank Nursery, 59
Marston Exotics, 59
Paul Jasper Trees, 59
Pepe Garden Furniture, 20
Pershore College of Horticulture, 110
Picton Garden, 90
Pounds of Bewdley, 22
Proculture Plant Centre, 60
Rickards Hardy Ferns Ltd, 60
Roy Finch Tree Care, 6
Rushfields of Ledbury, 60
Samsons, 18
Snowshill Manor, 90
Song of the Earth, 16
Spetchley Park Garden, 90
Stone House Cottage Garden & Nursery, 60
Symbionics, 45
Toad Hall Produce, 60
Treasures of Tenbury Ltd, 60, 90
Tricia McPherson, 16
Veronica Adams Garden Design, 16
Webbs of Wychbold, 60
Wiggly Wigglers, 31
Wintergreen Nurseries, 60
Wolf Garden, 31
Woolman's Plants Ltd, 60
Worcester Garden Centre, 60
Wyevale Garden Centre, 60
Wyevale Garden Centres plc, 60

Hertfordshire
Abbots House Garden, The, 60
Alitags, 24
Andrew Crace Designs, 18, 35
Aquavita Centre, 42
Aylett Nurseries Ltd, 60
Beale Arboretum, 90
Benington Lordship, 90
Bonita Bulaitis Landscape & Garden Design, 10
British National Carnation Society, 116
British Rose Growers Association, 117
Bronze Collection, 35
Carnivorous Plant Society, 117
Cascade Blinds, 7
Chalfont Conservatory Company, 7
Chandlers Cross Garden Centre, 60
Charles Hogarth Garden Landscapes, 11
Chempak Products, 25
Chenies Garden Centre, 60
Chipperfield Home & Gdn Ctr, 60
Concept Research, 25
Diplex Ltd, 25
Dupre Vermiculite, 25

Easilok, 21
Flora & Fauna Europe Ltd, 26
Gannock Growers, 60
Gardena UK Ltd, 26
Glazed Additions, 8
Godly's Roses, 60
Goldcrest Conservatories, 8
Growing Carpets, 60
Hatfield House, 90
Hayters plc, 33
Headen Ltd, 8
Hertfordshire & Middlesex Wildlife Trust, 118
High Cross Joinery, 19
Hillier Garden Centre, 61
Hopleys Plants Ltd, 61
Joanna Stay Garden Design, 13
Karobar Koi, 43
Knebworth House & Gardens, 90
Labels Unlimited, 27
Lannock Pottery, 36
Leisuredeck Ltd, 28
Mayflower Greenhouses (A E Headen Ltd), 22
Nature's Corners, 44
Notcutts Garden Centre, 61
Oaklands College, 110
Pan Brittanica Industries Ltd, 29
Paul Bromfield Aquatics, 44
Pot Village, 37
Priorswood Clematis, 61
R Harkness & Co Ltd, 61
Realwood Conservatories, 8
Royal Gardeners' Orphan Fund, 120
Royal National Rose Society, 90, 120
Secret Garden Company of Ware Ltd, 9
Seeds-by-Size, 41
Sun Building Developments Ltd, 9
Terrace & Garden, 38
Tokonoma Bonsai, 30
Van Hage Garden Company, 61
Wards Nurseries (Sarrat) Ltd, 61
Water Features Ltd, 45
Webbs Distribution Ltd, 38
Wyevale Garden Centre, 61

Humberside
Baxters Ltd, 21
Burnby Hall Gardens, 90
Burton Constable Hall, 90
California Gardens, 61
Devine Nurseries, 61
J & C R Wood, 22
Mendle Nursery, 39
Palm Farm, 61
Papronet, 29
Pennell & Sons Ltd, 61
Sledmere House, 90

Isle of Wight
Barton Manor Gardens & Vineyards Ltd, 91
Cranmore Vine Nurseries, 61
Deacons Nursery, 61
Isle of Wight College of Arts & Technology, 109
Isle of Wight Gardens Trust, 118
Landscapes by Tim Brayford, 14
Mottistone Manor, 91
Owl Cottage, 91
Plastics-by-Post Ltd, 29
Sunshine of Africa (UK) Ltd, 30
Ventnor Botanic Garden, 91

Kent
Alan C Smith, 61
Architectural Landscape Design Ltd, 10
Ashenden Nursery, 61
Baylis Landscape Design & Construction, 10

Bedgebury National Pinetum, 91
Belmont, 91
Black Forge Art, 35
British Pelargonium & Geranium Society, 116
Brogdale Horticultural Trust, 91
Busheyfields Nursery - J Bradshaw & Son, 61
Bybrook Barn Garden & Produce Centre, 61
Cambrian Controls, 24
Chartwell, 91
Chilham Castle Gardens, 91
Chilstone, 17, 18, 35, 43
Church Hill Cottage Gardens, 61
Connoisseurs' Cacti, 61
Cotton Ash Garden, 61
Crittenden House, 91
Cyclamen Society, 117
David Way Associates, 112
Debbie Jolley Garden Design, 11
Defenders Ltd, 25
Dibco Garden Sundries, 25
Downderry Nursery, 61
East Malling Research Association, 117
Emmetts Garden, 91
Essentials, 22
Forsham Cottage Arks, 26
Forward Nurseries, 62
Four Elms Cottage Garden Nursery, 62
Frances Traylen Martin Dip ISGD, 8, 12
Friends of Brogdale, 62, 91
Fruit Garden, 62
Garden Rewards, 22
Garden Study Tours, 112
Godington Park, 91
Goodnestone Park Gardens, 91
Grower, 113
Hadlow College of Agriculture & Horticulture, 108
Hazeldene Nursery, 62
Herbary, 62
Hever Castle & Gardens, 91
High Banks Nurseries, 62
High Winds Nursery, 62
Hop Shop, 27
Horticultural Research International, 118
Iden Croft Herbs, 62
Jacksons Fine Fencing, 17
Jan Martinez Garden Designs, 91
Keepers Nursery, 62
Kent Trust for Nature Conservation, 118
Koi Kraft, 43
Layham Garden Centre, 62
Leaky Pipe Systems Ltd, 28, 34
Leeds Castle, 91
Long Barn, 91
Longacre Nursery, 62, 91
M W Horticultural Supplies, 28
Madrona Nursery, 62
Marle Place Gardens & Nursery, 62
Mary Ann Lovegrove, 14
Neptune Supplies & Services, 22
New Plantsman, 113
New Technology, 44
Nonington Pottery, 36
Norton Ash Garden Centre, 62
Notcutts Garden Centre, 62, 62
Oldbury Nurseries, 62
P H Kellett, 62
Patrick Butler, 15
Penshurst Place & Gardens, 91, 112
Pete & Ken Cactus Nursery, 62
Pickards Magnolia Gardens, 91
Plaxtol Nurseries, 62
Port Lympne Wild Animal Park, 91
Rayment Wirework, 20

Robus Pottery & Tiles, 37
Rosie's Garden Plants, 62
Rumwood Nurseries, 62
Ruxley Manor Garden Centre, 62
Scotney Castle, 91
Search Press Ltd, 107, 114
Sissinghurst Castle, 91
South East Garden Festival, 115
South East Water Gardens, 45
Starborough Nursery, 62
Super Natural Ltd, 30
Tile Barn Nursery, 62
University of Greenwich, 111
Victor A Shanley, 16
Water Gardener, 114
Waterlock Studios, 45
Wells & Winter, 31
Westwood Nursery, 63
World of Water, 46
Wye College, 111
Wyevale Garden Centre, 63, 63
Wyevale Shop, 63

Lancashire
Ashworth Leisure Ltd, 18
Auldene Garden Centre, 63
Barkers Primrose Nurseries, 63
Barton Grange Garden Centre, 63, 63
Barton Grange Landscapes, 10
Beau Jardin, 10
Brownthwaite Hardy Plants, 63
Bulldog Tools Ltd, 24
Burnside Fuchsias, 63
C F Hanson Ltd, 24
Catforth Gardens, 63, 92
Ceramica UK, 17
Craig House Cacti, 63
Croston Cactus, 63
D T Brown & Co Ltd, 40
Domestic Paraphernalia Co, 25
Eversley Nurseris, 63
Fawcetts Liners, 43
Filterplas, 43
First Tunnels, 22
Gardeners' Choice, 26
Greenacre Nursery, 63
Hartley Botanic Ltd, 22
Holden Clough Nursery, 63
Insublind, 27
L B S Horticulture, 27
Leighton Hall, 92
Lotus Water Garden Products Ltd, 43
Marquis Flowers & Plants, 63
Myerscough College, 109
Natural Organic Supplies, 29
Netlon Ltd, 29
Nutriculture Ltd, 29
Ollerton Engineering, 20
Penny Bennett Landscape Architects, 15
Pinks & Carnations, 29, 41
Porous Pipe, 29
Sellet Hall Gardens, 63
Southport Flower Show, 115
Valley Aquatics, 45
W Robinson & Sons Ltd, 42
Waithman Nurseries, 63
Wyevale Garden Centre, 63

Leicestershire
A & A Thorp, 63
Barnsdale Plants & Gardens, 10, 63, 92
Belvoir Castle, 92
Burrough House Gardens, 92
Burton McCall Group, 24
D W Woodward & Son, 17
Fosse Alpines, 63
Gandy's Roses Ltd, 63
Gardeners' Pal, 26
Goscote Nurseries Ltd, 64
Hilltop Nurseries, 64

J E Martin, 40
Laburnum Nurseries, 64
Leicestershire & Rutland Trust for Nature Conservation, 118
Lemar Wrought Iron, 17
Linda Gascoigne Wild Flowers, 64
Monsanto Garden Care, 29
Pamal, 20, 37
Raffles - Thatched Garden Buildings, 8
Rockingham Castle, 92
Rutland County, 9
S & S Perennials, 64
Starkie & Starkie Ltd, 30
Sunlight Systems, 30
Town & Country Products, 30
Ullesthorpe Garden & Aquatic Centre, 45, 64
Ulverscroft Unusual Plants, 64
University of Leicester Botanic Gardens, 92
University of Nottingham, 111
Wartnaby Garden Labels, 31
Whatton House, 92
Wild Flower Society, 120
Wyevale Garden Centre, 64

Lincolnshire
Bakker Holland, 40
Baytree Nurseries, 64
Belton House, 92
British Seed Houses, 40
C E & D M Nurseries, 64
Clive Simms, 64
Cottage Nurseries, 64
Doddington Hall, 92
Donington Plants, 64
E H Thorne (Beehives) Ltd, 25
Foliage & Unusual Plants, 64, 92
Gladiolus Breeders Association, 117
Glenhirst Cactus Nursery, 64
Grimsthorpe Castle, 92
Hall Farm Nursery, 64, 92
Hall Farm Products, 19
J Walkers Bulbs, 64
Johnsons Seeds, 41
Judy's Country Garden, 64
Kathleen Muncaster Fuchsias, 64
Lincolnshire College of Agriculture, 109
Lincolnshire Trust for Nature Conservation, 115, 118
Lynkon Aquatic, 22
Martin Nest Nurseries, 64
Michael Hill Garden Furniture, 20
Mulberry Landscapes, 14
Orchard Nurseries, 64
Plant Lovers, 64
Potterton & Martin, 39, 65
Riseholme Hall, 92
S M McArd, 41
Southfield Nurseries, 65
Springfields (World of Flowers), 92
Stephen H Smith's Garden & Leisure, 65
Vale Garden Houses, 9
Valley Clematis Nursery, 65
Wildlife Trusts, 121
William Sinclair Horticulture, 31
Woodside Water Gardens, 46

London
17 Fulham Park Gardens, 92
A & P M Books, 106
Abbey Conservatories, 7
Abercrombie & Kent Travel, 112
Alexander Armstrong, 10
Alexander Palace Garden Centre - Capital Gardens, 65
Allan Hart Associates, 10
Anthos Design, 10
Architectural Association, 107, 116
Autocar Equipment Ltd, 32

B B C Gardeners World, 113
Barbary Pots, 35
Bel Mondo Garden Features, 42
Berger & Tims, 106
Berrys Garden Company Ltd, 10
Blackwall Products, 24
Bonhams Chelsea, 35
Botanical Society of the British Isles, 116
Brian G Crane & Associates, 6
British Museum Replicas, 35
C T D A, 40
Cannizaro Park, 92
Capital Garden Landscapes, 11
Capital Gardens - Four Garden Centres in London, 18
Cecily Hazell Garden Design, 11
Chelsea Flower Show, 114
Chelsea Physic Garden, 92
Chiswick House, 92
Christopher Bradley-Hole, 11
Conservatory Gardens, 7
Consumers Association Library, 108
Cox & Kings Travel, 112
Creative Tours Ltd, 112
Daniel Pearson, 11
David Ireland Landscape Architect, 11
David Sayers Travel, 112
Deans Blinds & Awnings Ltd, 8
Dickensons Compost, 25
Ealing Tertiary College, 108
Elizabeth Banks Associates, 12
English Gardening School, 108
F M G Garden Designs, 12
Fenton House - National Trust, 92
Franklin Mint Limited, 26
Fulham Palace Garden Centre, 65
Garden, 113
Garden & Security Lighting, 12
Garden History Society, 117
Gardening Which?, 113
Gardens Illustrated, 113
Glass Houses, 8
Greenstone Gardens, 12
Hampstead Garden Suburb Adult Education Centre, 108
Hampton Court Palace, 92
Hampton Court Palace Flower Show, 114
Hatchards, 106
Helen Cahill, 12
Herb Society, 118
Highgate Garden Centre - Capital Gardens, 65
Homes & Gardens, 113
Honda UK, 34
Horticulture Week, 113
House & Garden, 113
Inchbald School of Design, 108
Indian Ocean Trading Company, 19
Ingram Topiary Frames Ltd, 27
Inside Out, 8
International Camellia Society, 118
International Spring Gardening Fair, 114
Interploy Trading Co, 34
Irish Tourist Board, 112
J H May Ltd (Reproductions), 27
Jill Billington Garden Design, 13
John Medhurst Landscape Consultant, 13
Julia Mizen BA Dip ISD, 13
Julian Chichester Designs, 19
Katerina Georgi Landscapes, 13
Kenwood Park, 92
King Easton Ltd, 19
Lambeth College, 109
Landmark Designs, 14
Lennox-Boyd Landscape Design, 14
Linnean Society of London Library, 109

Lloyd Christie, 8, 17
London Historic Parks & Gardens Trust, 118
Malbrook Conservatories Ltd, 8
Marina Adams Landscape Architects, 14
Mark Westcott Landscape Architects, 14
Master Gardeners, 14
Merton Adult College, 109
Ministry of Agriculture Fisheries & Food Library, 109
Montezumas, 20
Museum of Garden History, 115
National Association of Flower Arrangement Societies, 119
National Trust, 119
Nicholas Roeber Landscapes, 14
Northside Seeds, 41
Oryx Trading Ltd, 20
Osterley Park, 93
P A C Organic Products, 29
Palm Centre, 65
Paris Ceramics, 38
Paul Miles, 15
Petal Designs Ltd, 15
Queen Marys Garden, 93
Ray Cheeseborough, 39
Renaissance Bronzes, 37
Roof Gardens, 93
Royal Horticultural Society, 120
Seago, 37
Sheen Developments Ltd, 30
Swan Hellenic Ltd, 113
Temple Fortune Garden Centre - Capital Gardens, 65
University College London, 110
Walpole House, 93
Wendy Wright Landscape & Garden Design, 16
Westminster Flower Shows, 115
Wyevale Garden Centre, 65

Manchester, Greater
Daisy Nook Garden Centre, 65
Dunham Massey, 93
Fletcher Moss Botanical Gardens, 93
G W Thornton & Sons Ltd, 33
Outdoor Power Products Ltd, 34
Portland Conservatories, 8
Primrose Cottage Nursery & Garden Centre, 65
Regency Driveways Ltd, 38
Sarah Rycroft Landscape Architects, 15
University of Manchester, 111
Vicarage Gardens, 65
Worsley Hall Nurseries & Garden Centre, 65

Merseyside
Croxteth Hall & Country Park, 93
Freshfields Water Gardens & Aquarium, 43
Hugh Baird College, 108
Knowsley Community College - Landbased Industries, 109
Landlife Wildflowers Ltd, 41
National Bonsai Society, 119
Neptune Aquatics, 44
Park Forge, 29
Porters Fuchsias, 65
Primus Ltd, 23, 34
Southport College of Art & Technology, 110
St Helens College, 110

Middlesex
Airport Aquaria, 65
Allpets (Stanmore) Ltd, 42
Aston Agricultural Research, 24
Astra Aquatics, 42

B B C Gardeners World Live, 114
Banbury Cross Conservatories, 7
Bosch Ltd, 32
Boward Tree Surgery Ltd, 6
Bypass Nurseries, 65
Capel Manor, 108
Chelsea Gardener, The, 65
Cope Conservatories, 7
Courtyard Garden Design, 11
Crest Garden Products, 25
Crews Hill Aquarium & Water Garden Centre, 43
Crowther of Syon Lodge, 8, 36
Derek Lloyd Dean, 65
Everglade Windows Ltd, 8
Fletcher-Green Horticulture, 22
Four Seasons Pottery, 36
G D Landscapes, 12
Garden Centre at Hounslow Heath, 66
Gayways Lawn Mower Centre, 33
Great Gardens of England (Syon), 66
Greenspan Designs Ltd, 26
Harrow Koi Company, 43
Jacques Amand Ltd, 66
Jardiniere, 19, 36
Marks Water Garden, 43
Myddelton House, 93
National Back Pain Association, 119
North Surrey Landscapes, 14
P J Bridgman & Company Ltd, 20
Paul Temple Associates, 15
Period House & Garden, 113
Plantation Garden Plant Centre, 66
Sportsmark Group Ltd, 30
Syon Park, 93
Tendercare Nurseries Ltd, 66
Trees in Miniature, 45
Walton Conservatories, 9
Waterlife Centre, 45
Wildwoods Water Garden Centre, 46
Wyevale Garden Centre, 66, 66, 66

Norfolk
African Violet Centre, 66
Algoflash UK Ltd, 24
Anglian Conservatory Co, 7
Bawdeswell Garden Centre, 66
Blickling Hall & Gardens, 93
Bolingbroke, 18
Bressingham Plant Centre, 66
C & C Trees, 6
Croftacre Hardy Plants, 66
Daphne ffiske Herbs, 66
Easton College, 108
Emorsgate Seeds, 40
Euston Hall - Suffolk, 93
Fairhaven Garden Trust, 93
Felbrigg Hall, 93
Five Acres Fuchsia Nursery, 66
Four Seasons, 66
Green Gardener for Bio-Control, 26
Hoecroft Plants, 66
Holkham Hall, 93
Jenny Burgess Alpines, 66
Mannington Gardens, 93
Norfolk Farm Composts Ltd, 29
Norfolk Garden Supplies, 37
Norfolk Greenhouses Ltd, 22
Norfolk Lavender Ltd, 66, 93
Norfolk Naturalists Trust, 119
Northwold Rockery Stone & Crazy Paving, 38, 39
Norwich Heather & Conifer Centre, 66
Notcutts Garden Centre, 66
Oxburgh Hall, 93
P W Plants, 66, 93
Peter Beales Roses, 66
Rainthorpe Hall Gardens, 93
Raveningham Gardens, 66
Reads Nursery, 66

Rob Turner, 17
Romantic Garden Nursery, 66
Roy Young Seeds, 41
Sandringham House & Grounds, 93
Sheringham Park, 93
Simpsons Nursery/Landscaping & Tree Surgery, 15, 66
Stiffkey Lampshop, 37
Thorncroft Clematis Nursery, 67
Trevor White Old Fashioned Roses, 67
Waveney Fish Farm, 45
Whispering Trees Nursery, 67
Wyevale Garden Centre, 67

Northamptonshire
Access Garden Products, 21
Acorn, 18
B S B I Publications (F & M Perring), 106
Boughton Loam Ltd, 24
Canons Ashby House, 93
Castle Ashby Gardens, 93
Coton Manor Garden, 67, 93
Cottesbrooke Hall, 94
E L F Plants, 67
Gardeners' Academy, 108
H 2 O, 27
Haddonstone Ltd, 36
Hill Farm Herbs, 67
Holdenby House Gardens, 94
John Chambers Wild Flower Seeds, 41
Just Blinds, 8
Link-Stakes Ltd, 28
Maxicrop International Ltd, 28
Mears Ashby Nurseries Ltd, 67
Moulton College, 109
National Society of Allotment & Leisure Gardeners, 119
Northampton Water Garden Centre, 44
Northamptonshire Wildlife Trust, 119
Old Rectory Sudborough, 94
Podington Garden Centre, 17, 20, 22, 29, 37, 38, 39, 44, 67
Ravensthorpe Nursery, 67
Ray Pitt Landscape Design, 15
Solargro Products Ltd, 23
Sulgrave Manor, 94
Wyevale Garden Centre, 67

Northumberland
Bide-a-Wee Cottage Garden, 94
Chillingham Castle, 94
Cragside, 94
English Heritage, 94
Glantlees Trees & Hedging, 67
Halls of Heddon, 67
Heighley Gate Garden Centre, 67
Herterton House Gardens & Nursery, 94
Hexham Herbs, 67, 94
Howick Hall, 94
International Dendrology Society, 118
National Pot Leek Society, 119
Northumbria Nurseries, 67
Ryal Nursery, 67
Wallington Hall, 94

Nottinghamshire
Barfield Travel & Tours, 112
Brackenhurst College, 107
Brinkley Nurseries, 67
Clumber Park, 94
Dextroplast Ltd, 17
Felley Priory Garden, 94, 114
Field House Alpines, 67
Gardens by Graham Evans, 12
Hewthorn Herbs & Wild Flowers, 43, 67
Hodsock Priory, 94
John Deere Ltd, 34

Machine Mart Ltd, 34
Mill Hill Plants, 67
Morton Hall, 94
Newstead Abbey, 94
Norwell Nurseries, 67
Nottinghamshire Wildlife Trust, 119
Parallax, 22
Primrose Fairs, 115
Reef Aquatics, 45
Regal, 23
Richard Stockwell - Rare Plants (GF), 41, 68
Salley Gardens, 41, 68
St Helens Croft, 94
Stewarts (Nottm) Ltd, 41
Town & Country Gardens, 16
Wharf Aquatics, 46
Wheatcroft Ltd, 68

Oxfordshire
Berkshire Buckinghamshire & Oxfordshire Naturalists Trust, 116
Blenheim Palace, 94
Boxwood Tours - Quality Garden Holidays, 112
Brook Cottage, 94
Broughton Castle, 94
Burford Garden Company, 68
Buscot Park, 94
Clock House, 95
Complete Tree Services, 6
Countax, 32
D I Y Plastics (UK) Ltd, 25
Duncan Heather, 11
E P Barrus Ltd, 33
Echo GB, 33
Fairmitre Thames Valley, 8
Fired Earth, 38
Gardens of Distinction, 12
Greenes Garden Furniture, 19
Greys Court, 95
Greystone Cottage, 95
Kingston Bagpuize House, 95
Kubota (UK) Ltd, 34
Lewes Road Sawmills, 8
Mattock Roses, 68
Mount Skippet, 95
Newington Nurseries, 68
Nuneham Courtenay Arboretum, 95
Old Rectory Farnborough, 95
Oxford Botanic Gardens, 95
Oxford Garden Design Associates, 14
P G Biddle, 6
Peregrine Holidays, 112
Precise Irrigation (UK) Ltd, 29
Rousham House, 95
Rupert Golby, 15
Sarah Massey - Landscape Designer, 15
Skyshades, 20
Stanton Harcourt Manor House & Gardens, 95
Waterperry Gardens Ltd, 95
West Oxfordshire College, 111
Wildlife Gardening Centre, 68
Wildlife Shop - BBONT, 121
World of Water, 46
Wyevale Garden Centre, 68

Shropshire
Alispeed, 21
Barbara Molesworth, 68
Benthall Hall, 95
Connoisseur Sun Dials, 35
Country Collections, 36
Dolwen, 95
Erway Farm House, 95
Hall Farm Nursery, 68
Heath Garden, 12
Hillview Hardy Plants, 68
Hodnet Hall Gardens, 95
International Violet Association, 118

John B Rickell, 13
Kexby Design, 13, 39
Lingen Nursery & Garden, 68, 95
Llanbrook Alpine & Wildflower Nursery, 68
Lower Hall, 95
Merton Nurseries, 68
National Viola & Pansy Society, 119
Nordybank Nurseries, 68, 95
Oak Cottage Herb Garden, 68
Perrybrook Nursery, 68
Preen Manor, 95
Ruthall Manor, 95
Shrewsbury Flower Show, 115
Swallow Hayes, 95
Telford Garden Supplies, 30
Walford College - Horticulture Dept, 111
Weston Park, 95
Wildlife Services Ltd, 46

Somerset
Ammerdown Park, 95
Avon Bulbs, 68
B & T World Seeds, 40
Barrington Court, 95
Belmont Gardens by Design, 10
Blagdon Water Garden Products plc, 42
Bradley Batch Cactus Nursery, 69
British Iris Society, 116
Broadleigh Gardens, 69
Cannington College, 95
Clapton Court Gardens, 95
College of Garden Design, 108
Dunster Castle, 96
Durston Peat Products, 25
E J Godwin (Peat Industries) Ltd, 25
East Lambrook Manor Garden, 96
Elworthy Cottage Plants, 69, 96
English Hurdle Centre, 17
Gardens of Somerset, 112
Gaulden Manor, 96
Greencombe Garden Trust, 96
Growth Technology Ltd, 27
Hadspen Garden, 69
Hadspen House, 96
Hestercombe House, 96
Horticultural Therapy, 118
John A Ford Landscape Architects, 13
Kelways Ltd, 69
Lady Muck, 28
Littleton Nursery, 69
Lower Severalls Garden & Nursery, 69, 69, 96
Lytes Cary Manor, 96
Mallet Court Nursery, 69
Margery Fish Plant Nursery, 69
Michael Littlewood Landscape Designer, 14
Mill Cottage Plants, 69
Milton Lodge, 96
Miniature Garden Company, 69
Monkton Elm Garden Centre, 69
Montacute House, 96
New England Gardens Ltd, 20
Organic Gardening, 113
Otters Court Heathers, 14, 69
P M A Plant Specialities, 69
Patricia Marrow, 69
Redwood Stone Ltd, 37
Scotts Nurseries (Merriott), 69
Shepton Nursery Garden, 69
Somerset Gardens Trust, 120
Somerset Postal Flowers, 30
Somerset Wildlife Trust, 69
Sparkford Sawmills Ltd, 18
Ston Easton Park, 96
Stuart Garden Architecture, 9, 18, 20
Tintinhull House, 96
Triscombe Nurseries, 69
Wayford Manor, 96

West Country Ironcraft, 18
West Someret Garden Centre, 69
Wyevale Garden Centre, 69
Y S J Seeds, 69

Staffordshire
Allan Calder, 17
Alton Towers, 96
Aquazoo, 42
Barncroft Nurseries, 69
Biddulph Grange, 96
Bretby Nurseries, 70
Byrkley Park Centre, 70
Cannock Gates Ltd, 17
Cedarwood Lily Farm, 70
Cottage Garden Roses, 70
Croxden Horticultural Products Ltd, 25
Dorothy Clive Garden, 96
F F C Landscape Architects/The Garden Design Studio, 12
Fuchsia World, 70
Jackson's Nurseries, 70
Kiddie Wise, 19
Moseley Old Hall, 96
National Chrysanthemum Society, 119
Oulton House, 96
P L M Power Products, 34
Planters Garden Centre, 70
Raven Tree Services, 6
Rodbaston College, 110
Rode Hall, 96
Shugborough Estate, 96
Staffordshire Wildlife Trust, 120
Stoke-on-Trent College, 110
Trentham Park Gardens, 96
Wolseley Garden Park, 96
Wolverhampton Tree Service, 6
Wyevale Garden Centre, 70

Suffolk
Aquaplancton, 42
Arena Holidays Ltd, 112
Atco-Qualcast Ltd, 32
Besleys Books, 106
Brian Sulman Pelargoniums, 70
Bucklesham Hall, 96
Bypass Nurseries, 70
Crown Asparagus, 70
Denbeigh Heathers, 70
Fisks Clematis Nursery, 70
G Miles & Son Ltd, 12, 43
Goldbrook Plants, 70
Gouldings Fuchsias, 70
Haughley Park, 96
Heather Society, 118
Helmingham Hall Gardens, 96
Home Meadows Nursery Ltd, 70
Hydrocut Ltd, 27
Ickworth House - Park & Gardens, 97
Image Creations, 8
Levington Horticulture, 28
Mickfield Fish & Watergarden Centre, 14, 70
Mickfield Market Garden, 70
Mills Farm Plants, 70
Mr Fothergills Seeds Ltd, 41
Nareys Garden Centre, 70
Notcutts Nurseries, 70
Otley College of Agriculture & Horticulture, 110
P L C Products, 22
Paradise Centre, 70
Park Green Nurseries, 70
Parkhouse Plants, 70
Potash Nursery, 71
Rougham Hall Nurseries, 71
Sawyers Seeds, 41
Siskin Plants, 71
Smallscapes Nursery, 71
Somerleyton Hall & Gardens, 97

Sue Hedger-Brown Landscape Architect, 16
Sue's Garden Design, 110
Suffolk Smallholders, 30
Suffolk Wildlife Trust, 120
Teak Tiger Trading Company, 20
Thompson & Morgan UK Ltd, 41
Walled Garden, The, 71
Watermeadows, 45
Woottens of Wenhaston, 71
Wyevale Garden Centre, 71, 71, 71
Wyevale Shop, 71, 71
Wyken Emporium, 97
Wyken Hall, 97

Surrey
Acorn Windows & Conservatories, 7
Addlestone Aquaria Pond & Aquatic Centre, 42
Alison Brett Garden Design, 10
Anthea Sokell Cert.GD, 10
Aqua Company Ltd, 42
Bartholomew Conservatories, 7
Beechcroft Nursery, 71
Boulder Barrows, 24
Brian Hiley, 71
British Clematis Society, 116
Brodie & Hickin Landscapes, 11
Bromage & Young, 71
Brook Lodge Farm Cottage, 97
Capstan Software, 24
Chase Organics, 24
Chelsham Place - Knights Garden Centre, 71
Clandon Park, 97
Claremont Gardens, 97
Clay Lane Nursery, 71
Connick Tree Care, 6
Constable Daffodils, 71
Cornhill Conservatories, 7
D N Bromage & Co Ltd, 71
Delphinium Society, 117
Drummonds of Bramley Architectural Antiques, 36
Edward Owen Engineering Ltd, 22
Egmont Water Garden Centre, 43
Elizabeth Whateley Garden Design, 12
Foliage Scented & Herb Plants, 71
Friends of the Royal Botanic Gardens Kew, 117
Gardeners' Royal Benevolent Society, 117
GardenGlow, 19
GardenGlow Direct (TGP1), 26
Garson Farm Garden Centre, 71
Gate-A-Mation Ltd, 17
Gillian Temple Associates, 12
Green Farm Plants, 71
Green Way, 12
Greenoak Gates, 17
Ham House, 97
Haselden Enterprise UK, 27, 33
Herons Bonsai Ltd, 71
Hillier Garden Centre, 71
Hurtwood Landscapes, 12
Hydon Nurseries, 71
I C I Garden Products, 27
Ian Roscoe, 12
Interpet Ltd, 43
Isabella Plantation, 97
Ivelet Books Ltd, 106
Ivy Mill Nursery - Knights Garden Centre, 72
Jacqui Stubbs Associates, 13
Janet Bacon Garden Design, 13
Jardine International Ltd, 19
Jeanne Paisley, 13
John H Lucas, 13
Joy Jardine Garden Designer, 13
Karen Saynor, 13
Kew School of Garden Design, 109
Kew School of Horticulture, 109

Kew Shop, 106
Knap Hill Nursery Ltd, 72
Lincluden Nursery, 72
Lloyds of Kew, 106
LOFA - The Leisure & Outdoor Furniture Association, 118
Lotus Landscapes, 14
Mammillaria Society, 118
Melaleuca Pottery, 36
Merrist Wood College, 109
Merrist Wood College Plant Centre, 72
Michael Banks/Ascender, 34
Mike Park, 106
Millais Nurseries, 72
Miracle Garden Care Ltd, 29
Morden Hall Garden Centre - Capital Gardens, 72
Nags Hall Nursery - Knights Garden Centre, 72
National Auricula & Primula Society (Southern), 119
National Council for the Conservation of Plants & Gardens, 119
National Gardens Scheme Charitable Trust, 97, 113
Nettletons Nursery, 72
Nigel Jeffries Landscapes, 14
Noma Lites Ltd, 29, 34
Notcutts Garden Centre, 72, 72
Orchid Society of Great Britain, 120
Ornate Products, 37
Painshill, 97
Pantiles Nurseries Ltd, 72
Patterson Products, 20
Pentangle Watergardens, 44
Peter Rogers Associates, 15
Peters Plants & Garden Centre, 44, 72
Pinewood House, 97
Planta Vera, 72
Polesden Lacey, 97
R H S Garden Wisley, 97, 110
R H S Garden Wisley Plant Centre, 72
R H S Garden Wisley Shop, 106
Ramster, 97
Raw Talent Consultancy, 15
Redashe Ltd, 29
Robert Southern BA Hons NCH(Arb), 6
Romilt Landscape Design & Construction Ltd, 45
Roof Garden Company Ltd, 15
Rosedene Nursery - Knights Garden Centre, 72
Rovergarden, 20
Rupert Bowlby, 72
Savill Garden, 97
Scottlandscape, 15
Secretts Garden Centre, 72
Seven Counties Garden Design, 15
Seymours Garden & Leisure Group, 18, 20, 23, 37, 38, 39, 45, 72
Seymours Landscape Centre, 15, 38
Society of Garden Designers, 16, 120
Sogetsu - Greater London Branch, 120
Stephen C Markham, 37
Stihl Ltd, 34
Sue de Bock Rowles Garden Design, 16
Surbiton Aquaria, 45
Surrey Gardens Trust, 120
Surrey Primroses, 72
Surrey Wildlife Trust, 120
Sweerts de Landas, 37
Topiarist, 6, 16
Turk Scythes & Trimflex (UK), 35
V H Humphrey - Iris Specialist, 72
Valley Gardens Windsor, 97
Vann, 97

Vernon Geranium Nursery, 72
Victoriana Conservatories Ltd, 9
Water Diverter Ltd, 31
Water Gardens, 97
Waterers Landscape Ltd, 16
Winkworth Arboretum, 97
Wisley Flower Show, 115
Wisley Plant Centre, 72
World of Water, 46, 46
Yamaha Motor (UK) Ltd, 35

Sussex, East
Agriframes, 17
B J Crafts, 24
Batemans, 97
Bates Green, 97, 112
Bond Garden Care Agencies, 73
Cabbages & Kings, 11, 98
Coghurst Nursery, 73
D Wells Landscaping, 11
English Classics, 19
English Oak Buildings, 8
Focus Garden Tours, 112
Frewen College, 98
Garden Store, 33
Gardening for the Disabled Trust, 117
Geebro Ltd, 26
Glyndley Garden Centre, 73
Grandad's Garden, 19
Great Dixter Nurseries, 73
Harvest Nurseries, 73
Just Roses, 73
Kent Street Nurseries, 73
Lime Cross Nursery, 73
Lister Teak Garden Furniture, 20
Long Man Gardens, 73
McBeans Orchids, 73
Merriments Gardens, 73
Michelham Priory, 98
Nigel L Philips Landscape & Garden Design, 14
Norman Bonsai, 73
Pashley Manor Gardens, 98
Pelham Landscapes, 15
Perryhill Nurseries, 73
Roger Platts Garden Design, 8, 15, 18
Sarah Burgoyne Revivals, 20
Sheffield Park, 98
Stone Cross Nurseries, 73
Studio Forge, 20
Tiger Developments Ltd, 30
Trailer Barrow Co, 30, 35
Truggery, 30
Usual & Unusual Plants, 73
Warrick Warming Cables Ltd, 23
Warwick Warming Cables Ltd, 31
Witbourne Ltd, 20
World of Water, 46
Wyevale Garden Centre, 73

Sussex, West
Acres Wild (Landscape & Garden Design), 10
Allseasons Landscapes, 10
Allwood Bros, 73
Apcon Garden Products, 18
Apuldram Roses, 73, 98
Aquapost, 42
Architectural Plants, 73
Arunfabs Ltd, 21
B C S Tracmaster Ltd, 32
Berri Court, 98
Borde Hill Garden, 98
Brinsbury College, 107
Cheals Garden Centre, 73
Coates Manor, 98
Coombland Gardens, 73
Cottage Garden Plants, 73
Croftway Nursery, 73
Denmans Garden, 98
Denmans Garden Plant Centre, 74
English Woodlands Biocontrol, 26

Ferrum Dried Flowers, 26
Fleur de Lys Conservatory Plants, 8, 74
Garden In Mind, 98
Geranium Nursery, 74
Glenda Biggs BA Dip ISD, 12
Heather Goldsmark Partnership, 12
High Beeches, 98
Highdown, 98
Hillier Garden Centre, 74
Holly Gate Cactus Garden, 98
Holly Gate Cactus Nursery, 74
Houghton Farm Plants, 74
John Brookes - Landscape Designer, 13
John Henly, 106
Julian Treyer-Evans, 13
Leonardslee Gardens, 98
Leonardslee Nurseries, 74
Mesemb Study Group, 119
Natural Pest Control Ltd, 29
Nymans, 98
Oakleigh Conservatories, 8
Old Barn Nurseries, 74
Parham House & Gardens, 98
Petworth House, 98
Plants 'n' Gardens, 74
Pots & Pithoi, 37
Principally Plants, 74
Room Outside, 8
Roundstone Garden Centre, 74
Royal Botanic Gardens Kew, 98
Sempervivum Society, 120
Solar Tunnels, 23
Sothebys, 37
Southern Tree Surgeons, 6
Standen, 98
Sussex Wildlife Trust, 120
Town & Country Paving Ltd, 38
Travel Ideas Ltd, 113
Vesutor Ltd, 74
W E Th Ingwersen Ltd, 74
Washington Aquatic & Garden Supplies Ltd, 45
West Dean Gardens (Edward James Foundation), 99, 111
World of Water, 46
Wyevale Garden Centre, 74

Tyne & Wear
Bernilight, 21
Birkheads Cottage Garden & Nursery, 74, 99
Cowells Garden Centre, 74
Gateshead Summer Flower Show, 114
North of England Rose Carnation & Sweet Pea Society, 119
Peter Barratt's Garden Centre, 74
Robinson Penn Partnership, 15
University of Newcastle, 111
Wyevale Garden Centre, 74

Warwickshire
Alton Greenhouses, 21
Arbury Hall, 99
Avon Aquatics, 42
Bernhards Rugby Garden & Leisure Centre, 74
Charlecote Park, 99
Citadel Products, 21
Claymore Grass Machinery, 32
Diana Hull - Species Pelargonium Specialist, 74
Douglas Lewis Tree Surgeons, 6
Farnborough Hall, 99
Fibrex Nurseries Ltd, 74
Flower Arrangers Show Shop, 26
H D R A Consultants, 12
Hillier Garden Centre, 74
Horticultural Research Association, 118

Geographical Index

Horticultural Research International, 118
Japanese Garden Society, 118
John Beach (Nursery) Ltd, 74
Millbern Geraniums, 74
Packwood House, 99
Preston-Mafham Collection, 75
Pumps 'n' Tubs, 44
Rosemann Greenhouses, 23
Sherbourne Park, 99
Sonya Millman Garden Design, 16
Tollgate Cottage Nursery, 75
Upton House, 99
Warwick Castle, 99
Whichford Pottery, 38
Woodfield Brothers, 75

West Midlands
Ashwood Nurseries, 66
Basic Bonsai Supplies, 24
Birmingham Botanical Gardens & Glasshouses, 93
Bourneville College of Further Education, 107
British Pteridological Society, 116
Canadian Cedarworks UK, 7
Castle Bromwich Hall, 93
David Austin Roses Ltd, 66
Durabuild Conservatories Ltd, 8
Federation of British Bonsai Societies, 117
Globe Organic Services, 26, 33
Growell Hydroponics & Plant Lighting, 27
H Woolman (Dorridge) Ltd, 66
Harefield Herbs, 40, 66
Haws Watering Cans, 22, 27
Henry Doubleday Research Association (HDRA), 40, 93, 118
Highfield Packaging, 22
Kemp Compos Tumbler, 27
Notcutts Garden Centre, 66
Parklines (Buildings) Ltd, 22
Plantables, 66
Power Garden Products, 29
R P P Alpines, 66
Renaissance Casting, 37
Roses & Shrubs Garden Centre, 66
Sandvik Saws & Tools, 30
Solihull College, 110
Staffordshire Gardens & Parks Trust, 120
Stourbridge College, 110
T I C Products Ltd, 38
Trident Water Garden Products, 45
Urban Wildlife Trust - West Midlands Wildlife Campaign, 120
Very Interesting Rock Co, 39
Victoria Travel Garden Tours, 113
Warwickshire Wildlife Trust, 120
Wightwick Manor, 93
Woodworks Workshop, 9
Wulfran College, 111
Wyevale Garden Centre, 66

Wiltshire
Agralan Ltd, 24
Andrew Evans - Landscape Designer, 10
Antony Young, 10
Avebury Manor, 99
Barters Plant Centre, 75
Botanic Nursery, 75
Bowood Garden Centre, 75
Bowood House, 99
Brent Surveys & Designs, 11
Broadleas Gardens Charitable Trust Ltd, 75, 99
Chisenbury Priory Gardening Courses, 108
Corsham Court, 99
Corsley Mill (Brigid Quest-Ritson), 75
Courts, 99
Courtyard Pottery, 36
Edington Sporting Co, 25
Flora International, 113
Gardeners' Breaks, 108, 112
Growing Success Organics Ltd, 27
Heale House, 99
Horticultural Correspondence College, 108
Iford Manor Gardens, 99
Josephine Hindle - Designer & Gardener, 13
Judith Woodget Garden Design, 13
Lackham College, 109
Lackham Gardens, 99
Lacock Abbey, 99
Landford Trees, 6, 75
Longhall Nursery, 75
Longleat House, 99
Matthew Eden, 20
Mead Nursery, 75
Parham Nursery, 75
Porton Aquatic Centre, 44
Roche Court, 37
Secret Garden Designs, 15
Sheldon Manor, 99
Sherston Earl Vineyards Ltd, 30
Sherston Parva Nursery, 75
Sol Jordens, 16
Special Plants, 75
Stourhead Landscape Garden, 99
Stourton House, 100
Traditional Garden Supply Company Ltd, 23
Walter T Ware, 75
Wessex Horticultural Products Ltd, 31
West Kington Nurseries Ltd, 75
Whitehall Garden Centre, 76
Wilton House, 100
Wiltshire Summerhouses, 9
Wiltshire Wildlife Trust, 121

Yorkshire, East
Hardy Northern Trees, 76
Ornamental Leadwork, 37
Swanland Nurseries, 76
White Cottage Alpines, 39, 76

Yorkshire, North
Acorn Landscapes, 10
Ashfield Hellebores - Rarer Plants, 76
Battersby Roses, 76
Beningbrough Hall, 100
Bradshaws, 43
Carol Messham, 11
Castle Howard, 100
Constable Burton Hall Gardens, 100
Craven College of Adult Education, 108
Cruck Cottage Cacti, 76
Dales Stone Company Ltd, 38
Daleside Nurseries, 76
Davies Systems (C), 25
Deanswood Plants, 43
Dovecote Joinery, 25
Dream Gardens, 11
Duncombe Park, 100
Gardenscape, 12, 36, 38, 76
Gilling Castle, 100
Great Yorkshire Gardens Design Tours, 112
Greenvale Farm Ltd, 27
Harlow Carr Botanical Gardens, 100
Hippopottering Nursery, 76
Hutton Nurseries, 76
J & D Marston, 76
John McLauchlan Horticulture, 27
Keith Pullan Garden Design, 13
Kingswood Pelargoniums, 76
Lindum Seeded Turf, 28
Newby Hall & Gardens, 100
Norden Alpine Nursery, 76
North of England Horticultural Society, 115
Northern Horticultural Society, 119
Norton Conyers, 100
Numbers & Names, 37
Nunnington Hall, 76
Oak Leaf Conservatories Ltd, 8
Orchard House Nursery, 76
Parcevall Hall Gardens, 100
Perry's Plants, 76, 100
Plowman Trading, 37
R V Roger Ltd, 76
Rievaulx Terrace, 100
Ripley Castle, 100
Rivendell Nursery, 76
Rolawn (Turf Growers Ltd), 29, 76
Smeeden Foreman Partnership, 15
Solardome, 23
Stillingfleet Lodge Nurseries, 76, 100
Strikes Garden Centre, 76, 76, 76
Susan Symmonds Sculptures, 37
Sutton Park Stately Home, 100
Thorp Perrow Arboretum, 100
Valley Gardens Harrogate, 100
Whitestone Gardens Ltd, 76
Wyevale Garden Centre, 76
Wytherstone Nurseries, 77
Yorkshire Garden World, 77

Yorkshire, South
A Wright & Son Ltd, 24
Archer Designs, 35
Barnsley College of Technology, 107
Beeches Nursery, 77
Brambling House Alpines, 39
British & European Geranium Society, 116
Chantrey Books, 106
Ferndale Nursery & Garden Centre, 77
National Begonia Society, 119
Nugent Gardens, 22
Oscrofts Dahlias, 77
Sentinel Garden Products, 18
Sheffield Botanical Gardens, 100
Spear & Jackson Garden Products, 30
Stephenson Blake, 20
Tank Exchange, 30
University of Sheffield, 111
Wentworth Castle Gardens, 100

Yorkshire, West
Armitages Garden Centre, 77
Bramham Park, 100
Canal Gardens, 100
Cravens Nursery, 77
Eden Greenhouses, 22
Garden Solutions by Design, 12
Golden Acre Park, 100
Grace Landscapes Ltd, 12
Greenslacks Nurseries, 39, 77
Harewood House & Gardens, 101
Hollies Park, 101
Leeds Metropolitan University, 109
Lotherton Hall, 101
M R Clark, 106
Mansell & Hatcher Ltd, 77
Nautilus Aquatics, 44
Newton Hill Alpines, 77
Peter Wynn Arboricultural Consultant, 6
Raindrain Ltd, 29
Shipley College, 110
Slack Top Alpines, 39
Springwood Pleiones, 77
Stephen H Smith's Garden & Leisure, 77, 77
Stephen H Smith's Garden Centres, 77
Strikes Garden Centre, 77, 77
Temple Newsam Park, 101
Totties Nursery, 77
Tropical Rain Forest, 77
Wakefield & North of England Tulip Society, 120
Wakefield College, 111
Watermill Company, 31

N Ireland

Co Antrim
Carncairn Daffodils, 77
Colemans Nurseries, 77
Landscape Centre, 77
Norbark (Northern Bark Ltd), 29

Co Down
Ballydorn Bulb Farm, 77
Ballyrogan Nurseries, 77
Castlewellan National Arboretum, 101
Daisy Hill Nurseries Ltd, 78
Dickson Nurseries Ltd, 78
Donaghadee Garden Centre, 78
Lisdoonan Herbs, 78
Mount Stewart, 101
Rowallane Gardens, 101
Seaforde Nursery, 78
Timpany Nurseries, 78

Co Fermanagh
Florence Court, 101

Co Londonderry
Guy Wilson Daffodil Garden, 101

Co Tyrone
Baronscourt Nurseries, 78
Westland Horticulture, 31

Scotland

Kittoch Mill Hosta Garden, 102
Scotland's National Gardening Show, 115

Borders
Dawyck Botanic Garden, 101
Manderston, 101
Mellerstain, 101
Pringle Plants, 78

Central
Blairhoyle, 101
Blairhoyle Nursery, 78
Trossachs Garden Tours, 113

Dumfries & Galloway
Arbigland Gardens, 101
Barony College, 107
British Wild Plants, 78
Cally Gardens, 78
Castle Kennedy, 101
Charter House Hardy Plant Nursery, 78
Craigieburn Garden, 78, 101
Glenwhan Garden, 101
J Tweedie Fruit Trees, 78
James Henderson & Sons, 40
Logan Botanic Gardens, 101
Threave School of Horticulture, 101, 110
Whitehills Nurseries, 78

Fife
Balcaskie, 101
Dalgety Bay Garden Centre, 78
Earlshall Castle, 101

East Neuk Water Garden Centre, 43
Elmwood College, 108
Falkland Palace, 101
Hill of Tarvit House, 78
Kellie Castle, 101
Murrel Gardens, 102
Pennyacre Nurseries, 78
Roots Garden Centre Ltd, 78
St Andrews Botanic Garden, 102

Grampian
Aberdeen College, 107
Ben Reid & Co, 78
Christie - Elite Nurseries Ltd, 78
Crathes Castle, 102
Cruickshank Botanic Garden, 102
Findlay Clark (Aberdeen), 78
James Cocker & Sons, 78
Kildrummy Castle, 102
Leith Hall & Gardens, 102
Mossatburn Watergardens, 44
Pitmedden, 102
T & W Christie (Forres) Ltd, 79
Tough Alpine Nursery, 39, 79
University of Aberdeen, 110
Veronica Ross Landscape Design, 16

Highland
A Edwards, 24
Abriachan Gardens & Nursery, 79
Allangrange, 102
Ardfearn Nursery, 79
Arivegaig Nursery, 79
Cawdor Castle, 102
Dochfour Gardens, 102
Dunrobin Castle & Gardens, 102
Evelix Daffodils, 79
Garden Cottage Nursery, 79
Highland Liliums, 79
Inverewe, 102
Jack Drake, 79
Lochalsh Woodland Garden, 102
Lochside Alpine Nursery, 79
Poyntzfield Herb Nursery, 79
Speyside Heather Garden & Visitor Centre, 79
Uzumara Orchids, 79

Lothian
Anna Buxton Books, 106
Botanical Society of Scotland, 116
Dalmeny House, 102
David Bell Ltd, 40
Dobbie & Co Ltd - Melville Garden Centre, 79
Edinburgh Butterfly & Insect World, 102
Edinburgh College of Art - Heriot-Watt University, 108
Federation of Edinburgh & District Allotments & Gardens, 117
Friends of the Royal Botanic Garden Edinburgh, 117
Inveresk Lodge Garden, 102
Landscape Design Studio, 14
Lord Roberts Workshops, 28
Malleny House, 102
Michael Ballam Design, 14
National Trust for Scotland, 102
Oatridge Agricultural College, 110
Plants from the Past, 79
Royal Botanic Garden Edinburgh, 102
Royal Caledonian Horticultural Society, 120
Scottish Allotments & Gardens Society, 120
Scottish Rock Garden Club, 115, 120
Scottish Wildlife Trust, 120
Trading Bonsai, 20, 30
University of Edinburgh, 111
Watershed Systems Ltd, 45

Strathclyde
Achamore Gardens, 102
Ardencaple Garden Centre, 79
Ardtornish Garden, 102
Arduaine Gardens, 102
Ash Consulting Group, 10
Ayr Flower Show, 114
Backwoodsman Horticultural Products, 21
Ballagan Nursery & Garden Centre, 79
Barwinnock Herbs, 79, 102
Biggar Park Gardens, 102
Brodick Castle, 102
Chatelherault Garden Centre, 79
Country Courses, 108
Crarae Gardens, 102
Culzean Country Park, 102
Duncans of Milngavie, 79
Findlay Clark (Dykebar), 79
Findlay Clark Garden Centre, 79
Glasgow Botanic Gardens, 103
Glenarn, 103
Greenbank Garden, 103
International Correspondence Schools, 109
Kinlochlaich House Gardens, 79
Kitchen Garden, 36
Langside College, 109
Martin Berkley Landscape Architects, 14
Scottish Agricultural College, 110
Scottish National Sweet Pea Rose & Carnation Society, 120
Scottish Rhododendron Society, 120
Westerwood Garden Centre, 79

Tayside
Angus College, 107
Angus Heathers, 79
Belwood Nurseries Ltd, 80
Bonhard Nursery, 80
Branklyn Garden, 103
Christie's Nursery, 80
Cluny House Gardens, 103
Drummond Castle Gardens, 103
Edzell Castle, 103
Findlay Clark (Kinross), 80
Glendoick Gardens Ltd, 80
Perth Garden Centre, 80
Pitmuies Gardens, 103
University of Dundee Botanic Garden, 103, 111

Western Isles
Island Plants, 80

Wales

Clwyd
Aberconwy Nursery, 80
Bodnant Gardens, 103
Chirk Castle, 103
Dibleys Nurseries, 80
Erddig, 103
Eucalyptus Trees Ltd, 80, 103
Halghton Nursery, 80
Paul Christian Rare Plants, 80
Phostrogen, 29
Welsh College of Horticulture, 111

Dyfed
Cae Hir Gardens, 80, 103
Cilwern Plants, 80
Classic Garden, 35
Dingle, 103
Doyles Dovecotes, 36
Dyfed Wildlife Trust, 117
Exotic Fuchsias, 80
Jim & Jenny Archibald, 41
John A Davies Landscape Consultants, 13
Landskip & Prospect, 14
Llainwen Nursery, 80
Picton Castle, 103
Post House Gardens, 103
Stangwrach Leisure Products, 20
Welsh Historic Gardens Trust, 120
Wyevale Garden Centre, 80, 80

Glamorgan, Mid
Dyffryn Gardens, 103
Glamorgan Wildlife Trust, 117
Wyevale Garden Centre, 80

Glamorgan, South
Biotal Industrial Products Ltd, 24
Cardiff Institute of Higher Education, 108
Metpost Ltd, 17
National Vegetable Society, 119
Native Australian Seeds, 41
Wyevale Garden Centre, 80

Glamorgan, West
Afan College Nursery, 80, 107
Clyne Gardens, 103
Flower Kabin Nursery, 80
Plantasia, 103
Wyevale Garden Centre, 80

Gwent
Ardep Ltd, 7
Catriona Boyle's Garden School, 108
Gwent Wildlife Trust, 118
Hotterotter Group, 27
Penpergwm Plants, 80
Society of Floristry, 120
Stella Caws Associates, 16
Tredegar House & Park, 104
Waterwheel Nursery, 81
Wye Valley Herbs, 81, 104

Gwynedd
Bodysgallen Hall, 104
Cefyn Bere, 104
Crug Farm Plants, 81
Fron Nursery, 81
Gwydir Plants, 81
Henllys Lodge Plants, 81
Holland Arms Garden Centre, 81
North Wales Wildlife Trust, 119
Penryn Castle, 104
Plas Brondanw Gardens, 104
Plas Newydd, 104
Plas Penhelig, 104
Plas-yn-Rhiw, 104
Portmeiron, 104
Ty'n Garreg Nurseries, 81
Ty'r Orsaf Nursery, 81
Wild Seeds, 42

Gywnedd
University College of North Wales, 110

Powys
Dingle Welshpool, 104
Excalibur (UK) Ltd, 22
Glansevern Hall Gardens, 104
Lingard & Styles Landscape, 14
Mary Bland, 106
Montgomeryshire Wildlife Trust, 119
Powis Castle, 104
Radnorshire Wildlife Trust, 120

ADVERTISERS INDEX

Agrevo . . . . v, 151	Growing Success Organics Ltd 26
Alitex - The Glasshouse Company iv	Haygate Engineering Co Ltd 33
Amdega Ltd 150	Hayters plc iii
Architectural Heritage 147	Jodrell Bank Arboretum 83
Ariens (UK) Ltd 32	Knights Garden Centres 71
Ashworth Leisure Ltd vi	L B S Horticulture 28
Aylett Nurseries Ltd 60	Langdon (London) 28
Barlow Tyrie Ltd i	LOFA - The Leisure & Outdoor Furniture Association . . . iii
Bayliss Precision Components Ltd 21	Melcourt Industries Ltd 28
Biotal Industrial Products Ltd ii	Merrist Wood College 109
Bressingham Plant Centre 49	Noma Lites Ltd i
British Teleflower Service Ltd 116	Oase (UK) Ltd 44
Burford Garden Company 68	Pots & Pithoi i
Capital Gardens - Four Garden Centres in London 65	Primus Ltd 34
Claymore Grass Machinery iv	Royal Horticultural Society vi
Countax 148, 149	Rutland County 9
Courtyard Designs 7	Solargro Products Ltd ii
English Classics 19	Technical Aquatic Products Ltd 45
English Gardening School 108	Thermoforce Ltd 23
English Woodlands Biocontrol 24	Wartnaby Garden Labels 31
Forsham Cottage Arks 25	Wessex Horticultural Products Ltd 31
GardenGlow Direct (TGP1) 26	Westonbirt Plant Centre 150
Globe Organic Services 33	

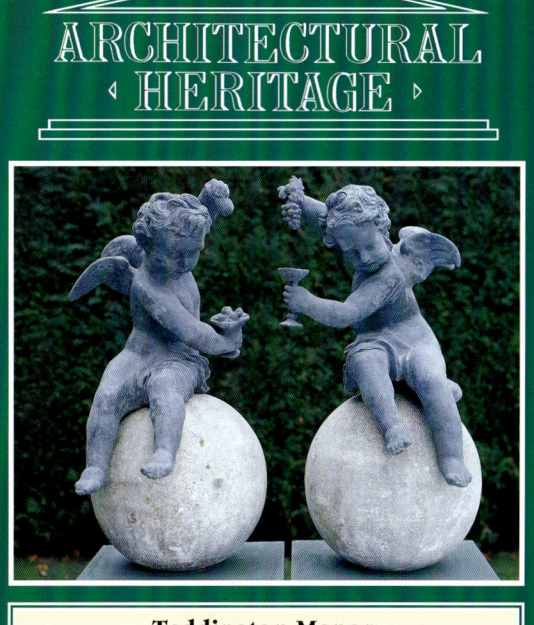

ARCHITECTURAL HERITAGE

**Taddington Manor,
Taddington, Nr Cutsdean, Cheltenham,
Gloucestershire GL54 5RY, England**
Tel: (01386) 584414   Fax: (01386) 584236
e mail: puddy@architectural-heritage.co.uk
web: http://www.architectural-heritage.co.uk

How to get on top of a large lawn

By Jeremy Saise

Grass is both an asset and a tyrant – if you have a garden of half an acre or more, grass probably covers at least 60% of it and accounts for 80% of the work. Look after it, cut it regularly and it will complement your property. Ignore it, even for a few weeks, and it will turn your garden into field.

Until about 15 years ago the owners of large gardens had to accept that they needed two, probably three different mowers to cut their grass: a cylinder mower for the lawn, a rotary for less formal areas and a rough cutter for paddock or woodland.

In the 1960s and 1970s some of these American 'garden tractor' machines were imported but they were too expensive; did not cut close enough, tended to balk at lush wet grass, and to collect poorly.

The big change came in the early 1980s with the first British made garden tractors – they were cheaper and designed to cut and collect the lush wet grass of home. The first British made machines quickly took more than 60% of a rapidly expanding market – by 1985 garden tractors had definitely arrived in Britain, and had come to stay.

Performance ensures that the three British made ranges still account for over 60% of sales and market leader Countax claims to outsell any two of its competitors.

To ride or not to ride?

Most large gardens in Britain are suitable for tractor or rider mowers. But is such a mower right for you? Ask yourself:

1. Do you want to cut mowing time by 50% to 80%?

2. Do you want a single mower to cut both lawn and long grass – a rough-cutter and lawnmower in one?

3. Do you want your mower to do more than just cut grass – to tow trailers and dump trucks and to work with a range of accessories?

4. Would you like your lawnmower to also work as a fast efficient leaf collector – speeding the autumn clear-up?

Riders and tractors with Powered Grass Collectors make fast and efficient leaf sweepers

Choosing a tractor or rider mower

"You gets what you pays for" is an adage that is only partly applicable when choosing a ride-on mower. True – if you pay substantially less than the general asking price of between £1,500 and £3,500 you are very unlikely to get a machine that will cope with British grass – the toughest in the world. Most tractors and rider mowers are made for America where grass is generally robust, broad leafed and dry and will 'vacuum collect' – the cuttings obligingly flying up a tube into the collector. British grass cuttings are usually wet and give a very good imitation of green porridge – they frequently and repeatedly clog a 'vacuum collector'. Tractors and riders with powered (brush) collector or twin-cut (direct) collection are the best for British conditions and only the Powered Brush Collector can be guaranteed never to clog. It also produces those desirable stripes!

'Cut and collect' is generally the best policy in Britain and the Powered Collector works well both in wet and dry conditions. It also does a very good job of lifting thatch and stimulating the turf. But you are left with large piles of collected grass cuttings (a useful mulch and source of compost). However, as an alternative to collecting cuttings, 'mulching' or 'recycling' mowers have recently found a market in Britain. Mulching involves cutting the grass into very small particles and feeding them back to the roots of the grass.

Finally, it's a good idea to ask your dealer for a demonstration, ideally in your own garden – before you buy.

STRIKINGLY BETTER

Britain's Best Selling Garden Tractor

It takes very special quality, performance and value to take the market by storm.

Countax's unrivalled ability to immaculately trim and stripe a fine lawn, quickly tame the roughest paddock and to collect cuttings completely (in any weather) has quickly made these British made tractor mowers the best selling range in the country.

Overseas, where we now sell 50% of our production, Countax succeeds as a premium brand at a premium price. **In quality conscious Germany Countax tractors outsell all German and Japanese produced competitors** and are greatly valued for being quieter and smoother - and for having "greater capability".

In Britain Countax Garden Tractors and Rider Mowers represent extraordinary value - here you can secure the superior specification and performance of a Countax at a very economical price - from £1,395.

Send for 32 page brochure

PHONE FREE 0500 279927

Return to Countax, FREEPOST, Great Haseley, Oxford OX44 7BR
Name _____
Address _____
Postcode _____ Tel _____ G05

Left - the C800HE - Powered by a twin cylinder, 18HP, B&S Vanguard engine, complete with 48" 'IBS' Triple Blade Cutter Deck, electronic cutting height control and the air boosted power collector - £3190 inc. VAT.

COUNTAX

WESTONBIRT PLANT CENTRE

Set adjacent to the world-famous arboretum, the Westonbirt Plant Centre stocks a large range of plants; many of which are rare or unusual.

Mail order November to March.

Advice always available.

Tel. (01666) 880544
Fax. (01666) 880559

Our specialities are:– seedling Acer palmatums, grafted Acer cultivars, Clematis, Viburnums, Hibiscus, trees of all shapes and sizes.

We also stock a good range of herbaceous perennials and garden sundries.

AMDEGA
ESTABLISHED 1874

The Cedar Room

Escape to your easel or simply snooze in the comfort of your Amdega Summerhouse. Made from solid cedar, including the shingle roof, all Amdega Summerhouses have leaded windows and double wall construction for insulation. For a free brochure or visit please

TELEPHONE 0800 591523

AMDEGA LTD, FAVERDALE, DARLINGTON, CO. DURHAM DL3 0PW
CALL NOW FOR AMDEGA'S EXCLUSIVE AIR MILES' OFFERS